THE ROUGH WOOINGS

For
Catherine Ruth Merriman
Elizabeth Hannah Merriman
Nathaniel Paul Merriman

THE ROUGH WOOINGS
Mary Queen of Scots, 1542–1551

Marcus Merriman

TUCKWELL PRESS

First published in Great Britain in 2000 by
Tuckwell Press
The Mill House
Phantassie
East Linton
East Linton EH40 3DG

Copyright © Marcus Merriman, 2000

ISBN 1 86232 090 X

British Library Cataloguing in Publication Data
A catalogue record for this book is available
on request from the British Library

The right of Marcus Merriman to be identified as the
author of this work has been asserted by him in accordance
with the Copyright, Designs and Patents Act 1988

Typeset by Hewer Text Limited, Edinburgh
Printed and bound by The Cromwell Press, Trowbridge, Wiltshire

The illustration on the title page, of a penny of 1547, shows the earliest image of
Mary Queen of Scots. The crown reminds us that she had succeeded her father, James V,
when she was only a week old. Born at Linlithgow on 8 December 1542, she became
Queen six days later.

Contents

Colour Plates

Illustrations, Diagrams, Maps and Family Trees

Acknowledgements

In 1797, John Pinkerton, then a mere thirty-nine years of age, published in London his two-volume masterwork, *The History of Scotland from the Accession of the House of Stuart to that of Mary*. His opening remarks strike a resonant chord in me: 'With a considerable degree of anxiety the author at length delivers to the public candour the greatest labour of his life'. I am sixty and *The Rough Wooings* has been with me a long time. Pinkerton was overly conscious of what he saw as his failings but especially 'the cruel necessity of being his own pioneer, of proceeding as in an American forest, with most cautious steps through the swamps, and earnestly clearing his way amid the brambles and thickets of perplexity and error'. I am sure there will be many errors in this work and there certainly have been perplexities. But it is now done.

This book is dedicated, as well it should be, to my children, with whom *The Rough Wooings* has been for a long time as well. For one thing, the names of both my parents (Ruth and Paul) are enshrined in some of theirs. My researches into this topic began in 1962 and finally bore fruit as a PhD (discussed below) in December 1974, after which my family held a party. Wife, every in-law, the lot: it was a lovely occasion. In September 1975, Kate was born and ever since then has (along with first Hannah and then Nat) nagged me to complete this thing. Our penultimate phone call, before Kate received her Bachelor of Surgery in July 1999, contained the words: 'Dad: the book'. And so this is a work not only about families, but also done by a family. My children's mother actually once just sent the manuscript off to the publisher and told everyone it was done, a plot I aborted. But Pip also gave me one of my best jokes. Seeing on my Amstrad the heading THE ROUEN FETE, she wrote, 'Cheap shoes ruin feet'. It still makes me giggle. And so my thanks to her for that as well for her patience and kindness over the decades.

But all books have many begetters. Mine, having taken this long to appear, has a host. All of the Heads of Department at Lancaster have been uniformly supportive and they should be recognised: Austin Woolrych (who appointed me in 1964), Harold Perkin, Joe Shennan, Martin Blinkhorn, John Gooch (who got me promoted to Senior Lecturer), Michael Heale (he was Best Man at my wedding and I sort of was at his: an honour), Ruth Henig, Eric Evans and Steve Constantine. To all of them my warmest thanks and appreciation: Steve, for example, actually ran me out of town to force me to finish it. But all of my departmental colleagues have been uniformly solicitous: when the word leaked out that it was really at the press, e-mails rained in from Illinois, Missouri and Preston.

When I finally handed the text over to John Tuckwell, his wife Val was there, as were Michael Lynch, Pat Dennison and Norman Macdougall, all of whom had urged me to completion. Michael loaned me his house in Drem during the summer of 1997 and free access to his Departmental Library; John constantly gave me extensions and he and Val did an enormous amount of editing and proof-reading; Norman drove down from St. Andrews to East Linton for the party. I owe them a lot, not least Norman, who had recently linked my name to that of Jamie Cameron, whose book on Mary's father I admire so much. My friend, Irene Lewis, has helped me see the book to its conclusion in ways too numerous to detail.

Speaking of proof-reading, this book should really be dedicated to one of my ex-students from 1974–75 and his mother: Jonathan Bailey and Althea Bailey, who both, and separately, went through every page catching my many errors and suggesting enhancements. Dr. Gordon Glanville also went through my PhD in 1974 with meticulous attention. As extra co-authors, mention should be made of Sandy and Alison Grant, who took away Chapter Three and virtually rewrote it. Ralph Gibson did something similar with the French chapters before his death. Michael Heale and Harry Hanham read through the entirety of the manuscript and gave hearty encouragement. Michael Mullett applied his justly famous generosity and fearsome close eye to going through the page proofs of the entire text and thereby saved me from a host of embarrassments. To him, his wife and his sons I owe great thanks. All of their painstaking efforts have meant that this is a much better work than otherwise it would have been. Dr. Elizabeth Vinestock went through my rather too casual French translations and felicitised them handsomely. Ralph Gibson originally promised to do so, but his illness intervened; one of his last acts was to invite me to speak at his last organised conference: a great honour. Bob Bliss laboured painfully and fruitfully to enhance my chapters on propaganda and the wars.

Gervase Phillips also closely proof-read every page (even to the extent of discovering missing full stops buried deep in the footnotes) and he has saved me from numerous bungles. Even more kindly, he loaned me a copy of the text for his as then not published book, *The Anglo-Scots Wars, 1513–1550: A Military History* (Woodbridge, 1999) which proved a Godsend. As my Head of Department averred, 'That is what one calls superior academic collegiality'. I could not agree more. Speaking of battles, I owe a great deal to the insights of James Bell of Longtown who allowed me access to his work on Solway Moss. David Caldwell has taught me everything a man could wish to know about both Pinkie and Eyemouth. Gordon Ewart and Geoffrey Stell have also been generous with their advice and insights.

Given the money and the time, writing books is not that difficult. Without either, I would have become a railroad station agent. So, I really must thank Sir Charles Carter who appointed me as a Temporary Assistant Lecturer when Lancaster opened in 1964. He then made it a permanent appointment. I owe him and his worthy successors not just a remarkably supportive community, but also that monthly pay cheque. I am also deeply indebted to others who have paid actual funds in support of my researches: The British Academy, The 27 Foundation of the University of

London, The Cassell Trust, The Institute of Historical Research which granted me a year's Fellowship in 1965–66 and Lancaster University's Research Fund. My University's policy on study leave has been both enlightened and generously allowed to me, for which I owe it and my colleagues a great debt.

But pride of place must go to Professor S.T. Bindoff. I first read his classic *Tudor England* as a required part of my First Ordinary course in English Literature at Edinburgh University in an unheated flat (my fingers froze as I went through the night and so I warmed them alternatively in my armpits as I read) in Morningside in 1961. As happened to so many others, I was hooked. Instead of pursuing my first love, eighteenth-century Polish history, which I had gained from Ernst Helmreich at Bowdoin, I turned (with Joel Hurstfield's encouragement) to the Old Alliance and thus to STB. It was an inspired accident, for STB not only got me my job at Lancaster, but also my David Berry Gold Medal from the Royal Historical Society (his secretary, Miss Bignell, typed all of my submission) and my doctorate. He was ever supportive of my efforts and was 'lion-hearted' (Jack Scarisbrick's phrase at his commemorative service) to all of his students. When, in 1976, they saw a photograph of me processing in the Commencement Service at Bowdoin College, both he and his wife commented that I was not wearing a London PhD gown (it was my father-in-law's one as doctor of Birmingham University). They thus gave me hers, originally given to her in 1932 by her first history mistress.

It was a dank December afternoon when he, Joel Hurstfield and Gordon Donaldson viva-ed my thesis in the Scotland Room at the Institute of Historical Research in December 1974. Donaldson, being the expert on this topic (he did Hannay's Special Subject on it at Edinburgh in 1931–32), did most of the work. After our three hours, with the sky steel-slate grey, he looked over his glasses and said, 'Merriman, it has taken twelve years for us to see your thesis; I hope it does not take another twelve years for us to see the book'. We all chuckled. Hurstfield then, ever perky, piped up and said, 'Knowing Merriman as I do, Professor Donaldson, you can probably take that figure and double it'. We all laughed again. I am just sorry none of them lived long enough to see it in print. I may have written Gordon's obituary for the *Scottish Historical Review*, but Joel, dying a month before him, did STB's for *The Times*. All of these men were inspirations for me.

My first foray into this topic was the doing of an essay for the late Dr. Stewart Oakley, in 1960 my tutor at Edinburgh University in the First Ordinary British History course. It was on the battle of Solway Moss and was rubbish, but somehow I ended up mentioned in the University Calendar for 1960–61 for my Second Class performance in that course, in no small measure due to his teaching. I then tackled the wider issue of the Franco-Scottish Alliance in an Honors Thesis at Bowdoin College. My thanks thus go to Professor John Rensenbrink who had the unenviable task of supervising it and to Professor W.B. Whiteside who kindly borrowed books for me from the Widener Library at Harvard during 1961–62. Once again it gained me honourable mention, graduating as I did 'cum laude in History'. The autumn of 1962 then found me being advised by Professors Joel Hurstfield and W. Croft

Dickinson as to my MA at London University. Thus I came to be under the supervision of Professor Bindoff of Queen Mary College and a member of his celebrated seminar (held felicitously and fortuitously in the Scotland Room) at the Institute of Historical Research during 1962–64 and 1965–66. His Early Tudor seminar was a veritable powerhouse and from it flowed many successful PhDs and academic careers.

Lesley Macfarlane not only gave me freely of his vast knowledge of foreign archives, he actually allowed me to spend a night in his house, to take meals with his family and to meet his handsome children. Alf Truckell did something similar and allowed me into his life as well as into his archives. Gladys Dickinson often invited me for tea at her favourite hotel near the BM and helped me enormously with my French problems, as did Nicola Sutherland. Gordon Donaldson, a member of Neale's Tudor seminar along with the Bindoffs in the 1930s, gave me six pages of corrections from my thesis. After that, we became good friends, he ever inviting my students to his house for tea. Iain MacIvor gave me so much of his time and his vast knowledge on the topic of Italianate fortification (and ancient monuments) in general that my debt to him (and his wife) is boundless. Howard Colvin took a very junior scholar and turned him into a contributor to one of the HMSO's more handsome publications. He also often gave me hospitality at College.

Speaking of students, S6 (S2 as it was; 323 as it now is) at Lancaster has given me over 250 of them since 1967 when my special subject was first mounted. They have given me many gifts, not least the annual trips to Scotland which have enabled me to inspect the same sites so many times. To pick out any would be invidious, although I hope none of them will mind me mentioning Van Bell, who actually built a replica section of Scots Dike in his back garden; Conor Davy, whose 46-page dissertation on Pinkie radically altered my views of that battle (he also gave my son a hamster), and Camilla Sweeney whose study of Mary of Guise's French correspondence taught me a great deal. But they all taught me. Moreover, all of them gave me their lives and minds for three hours a week for twenty weeks and to them I am grateful. I have been very lucky over the thirty-two years the course has run.

Custodians of manuscript sources have a special place in the hearts of all academics. Gordon Donaldson once wrote about the arduous labour and near heroism of those who preserved our documents over the centuries, something he felt sharply, being an Air Raid Warden patrolling the rooftop of Register House, Edinburgh during World War II and taking MSS volumes of the Register of the Secret Seal to his bed of a night, along with a cup of cocoa, at Breadalbane Castle where they were stored then. Again, my debts to him are too numerous individually to list. Mme Bailey, the Head of Archives at Bourges, allowed me to inspect Henrisoun's letters in the back room ('and here you can smoke') of her office even though they were too fragile to be photocopied, having been singed in the great fire of 1864 at the Hotel de Ville. She is but one of so many curators who have extended to me kindnesses over the years, especially those in the Salle des Manuscrits at the Bibliothèque Nationale at Paris and Michel du Chêne at the Archives Nationales, as well as the redoubtable M. Plaut of the microfilm room.

Alex Galway at the Scottish Record Office (now the National Archives of Scotland) was always enormously helpful in finding and photocopying for me re-catalogued documents. Longshanks in the Long Room of the Public Record Office (PRO) lured me away from my most favourite of worksites in the world (the Round Room at Chancery Lane) due to his constant solicitousness on my behalf, having documents ready for me the minute I arrived (and once already set up in the infra-red cubicle). During the final stages of this work, Dr. Alison Rosie at the SRO and Anne Crawford at the PRO responded by blitzenreply to requests for help on reproductions. Likewise Stephen Gritt and Melanie Blake of the Courtauld Institute of Art. An especial place in all our hearts must also go to the indefatigable editors of so many of these manuscript sources: Annie Cameron, Marguerite Wood and Gladys Dickinson, to my mind, stand head and shoulders above the rest.

When I first began this study, it was a lonely road down which I travelled: Gordon Donaldson, Ian Rae, Ian Cowan and Athol Murray apart. But how times have changed. There has been Michael Lynch's work along with that of so many of Edinburgh University's PhDs, as well as David Caldwell, Marie-Noëlle Baudouin-Matuszek, Alasdair Hawkyard, Gervase Phillips, Elizabeth Bonner, Stephen Gritt, Simon Pepper, John Childs, Philip Dixon, Geoffrey Stell. Jenny Brown/Wormald and I first met at Lennoxlove, both wanting to see the same document on the same day. All of their publications have enriched mine.

Every academic needs a good Secretary. In my case I would say a Brenda, a Linda and a June (Wright, Persson and Cross; but what about all the others? Ghil, Emma, etc.). But these three have been my mainstays (especially over my disabilities, of which poor hearing is but one) for decades. All of them have, additional to their ever sustaining friendship and listening to my jokes (and *that is friendship*), given me professional competence of the highest order. But that is true not only of myself, but of the entire department at Lancaster. That also goes for porters, and when I mention Donald Smith, Ivor White, David Howarth and Arthur Kirkbride in Furness, I include all of those who have served us all so well since History first moved there. Furness's redoubtable band of cleaners (especially Jackie Lambert) have all too often found me snoozing on my couch and have had to lug tonnes of paper out of my office over the years. The cleaners, porters and secretaries of Pendle where I Vice-Principled for so many happy years have also sustained me in so many ways, as have the College Managers. Let us not forget Librarians (Dr. Lindsay Newman and Winifred Clark spring to mind, but all of ours are towers) and Administrators in University House from the Print Unit to Photography to Student Support (which so often means staff support: Rod Martindale comes immediately to mind) to the Secretaries to the Vice Chancellor and the University Secretary. My thanks to all of them.

Lancaster University is a wonderful institution to work and live in (as I say I often sleep in my office). Lancaster the town has been a wonderful home for myself and my family ever since I first got off the train in 1964. When my brother died in 1983, I could feel the town edge just that bit closer to me and touch my elbow. This list could go on for ever: Arthur and Betty Wild (and many other licensed victuallers: the John O' Gaunt especially), Colin Stockdale and family, Jim Cooper (and many other bank managers, all of whom, it seems, I have shepherded to early retirement), Drs. Frank Rickards, Tony Williams and David Elliott have looked after me brilliantly and attended to my children as well. Without them, I would not be there, so neither would this book. When I pick out Chris and Carole Sales as my newsagents, I thank all of those who have made sure I had something to read in the bath of a morning. If Lancaster has been a thoroughly agreeable home, so has been Holyhedge in Manchester and I must thank my neighbours for making my move there in December 1998 a true joy: John and Myra Brennan, Joe and Jeanette Cullen, Betty especially and Mike Eshrati and his lovely staff. Also Karen Browne, Ludmilla and Revd David Thomas.

And now just a random list: they will all know why they are there, and those whom I have forgotten to include will, I pray, forgive me: Mildred Brown; Kavasier von Erhitz; Dorothy and Neville Borg; Mary Hope and Vic Cockcroft; Jagdish Gundara, Neville Powers, Tony Paul, Henry Martin, Aimee von Huene; Catherine Mattick-Caves; Jay Gordon, Duncan Mathewson; Philippa Glanville, my godson Mathew and his brother James; my niece Nena Ferry and my nephew David and Steve and Kelli; Jean Tallec, Christi Ormsby; Jackie Lambert and Stuart, John Young, Billy Heron, Billy Young; Donovan and Mike Tagg, Tom Lawrenson, John Creed, Wendy Constantine, Loretta Shotter, Francesca Gibson, Gordon Inkster [Lancaster]; Martin Haas, The M&P [Maryland]; Al Levy, Charles Kinard, Paul Carre [McDonogh School]; my stepfather David Yates, Edna, my aunt Max, my sister Tracy [Maine], John Stephens and his most efficient secretary Shirley Winn, Luther Leibensperger, Caroline and Andy Shoemaker, Matt Petrilla, Laurel Oaks who have cared for my father so well [Tennessee]. My thanks also to the family of Ruth Davison, who at Christmas 1993 gave me the print of Linlithgow Palace which graces this book's colour section. I should especially also like to thank her brother, Jonathan.

In 1963, Jack Scarisbrick and I found ourselves seated about a table in a post-lunchtime pub on the Mile End Road as we wrestled with what title my thesis should be given. Finally I dug out both my short version and my full synopsis, thrust it into his hands and asked him to read it afresh while I refreshed our pints. When I returned, Jack looked up at me and said, 'You know, Marcus, this is really rather old-fashioned history that you're doing here'. He was right. My approach was purely narrative and biographical: bang-bang history with a storyline and a string of anecdotes. Not a word about the growth of professions, the gentry, MPs, medicine or technology. Literary rates and political thought figured nowhere. It was utterly innocent of popular social movements, economic theory or sociological analysis. 'What else', I riposted, 'did Thycycides write? Or Bede? Or Gibbon?' Jack gravely responded that none of those men would be viva-ed by an examining board of the University of London. We concocted a title which, however convoluted and prolix, satisfied the committee and allowed me to do what I really wanted to do, which was to ride steam trains between Edinburgh and London and London and Paris. All of Paris's trams had gone before the 1940 occupation (I made do with those in Brussels, Amsterdam and den Haag), but its buses still had balconies and the equipment on its fabled Metro would have made Jules Verne smile. And then life struck: a temporary job, a RHS Gold Medal, a Fellowship, a permanent post, a house, a marriage and children.

This is the result, still rather old-fashioned. But I hope that in the intervening years I have learned something beyond the narrative approach and that the result not only contributes to knowledge about this topic, but also entertains while at the same time teaching. If it does, I shall be well content.

Marcus Merriman
Wythenshawe
Manchester
7th Oct. 2000

Conventions

Footnotes are at the bottom of the page of the item in the text to which the citation refers. This is not crusty ancien-régime academic propriety (scholarly apparatus we used to call it) in operation: it is central to the whole exercise. The facile argument that they just get in the way of the general reader and somehow break up the flow of the prose is nonsense and was so when John Neale, as he was in 1936, first proposed it to Jonathan Cape. One should not be surprised that Neale made the suggestion. That Cape accepted it is, however, food for thought.

Publishing costs for scholarly monographs, during the last phase of hot metal-type printing (c. 1965–1990), then made their employment prohibitively expensive, especially as the convention was that they adhere to the page, but be in a much lower font size. There also emerged the argument (self-serving in reality) that the page as a page looked prettier without all those squiggly bits at the bottom. Also, since printers could no longer cope with squeezing all the references into whatever space could be found at the bottom (as in Donaldson's *James V–VII*), single-line entries gobbled up too much room and left too many gaps. There thus emerged the egregious placing of the authentication of one's scholarship either at the end of each chapter (ever tedious to locate) or at the end of the main body of the text: after the appendices and bibliography, but before the index. This, too, was time-consuming, especially as no one had the sense to number the footnotes by chapter location or to give the chapter numbers in the running titles at the top of every alternative page of text. With the emergence of computer publishing, however, whereby authors can give to their printers a read-only disk with pages fully formatted, the hot-type cost argument no longer applies.

Most manuscript sources (but not those for national repositories) will contain the notation 'MS', location (most of which have accepted abbreviations), then the most recent folio number (indicated by 'fo.' and 'fos.', but 'r' = recto for facing side of the MS is not applied, but 'v' = verso for back of the facing side, will be). Virtually all printed primary source collections have an agreed abbreviation and I shall follow the conventions of the *Scottish Historical Review*. Most references, unless otherwise stated (viz. *LP, CSP Scot., RSS*), will be to page numbers without 'p.' or 'pp.'. In the bibliography for published primary sources, the initial letter of the first principal word, or the initial letter of the abbreviation, will determine its alphabetical location.

As to the form of secondary source citations, again I shall employ a compromise between the older tradition which is difficult for readers to use and the new, ugly, norm: surname of author and date. I believe that a critical element in the appreciation of the historian's craft is when a book was written; I thus always cite the date in a text's first mention. Thereafter, since a full bibliography exists, all secondary sources will be cited by the surname of the author, followed by an obvious short title (italicised for books, enclosed by quotation marks for articles or unpublished theses), then page number. Full scholarly apparatus (place of location, editor, date, etc.) can easily be divined from the bibliography where all sources are listed alphabetically by abbreviation or surname of author.

DATINGS

As is widely appreciated, early modern Europeans operated a variety, sometimes bewildering, of dating conventions, secular, regal, parliamentary-statute and church or, perhaps one should say, ecclesiastical. The bulk of the correspondence for this work was dated by secular convention: day, month, year. However, different conventions applied to when the 'New Year', as what may be called a dating of account (see concept of money of account below), commenced.

Although most European societies accepted 1 January as 'New Year's Day' when celebrations were mounted, presents exchanged and honours bestowed, English and Scottish secretaries only applied the new year's actual numerical date after 25 March, the Feast of the Annunciation. In France, the new year was deemed to begin after Easter, which at least has a certain logic, but makes life even more irksome for the modern researcher. Normally, around Eastertide, French scribes made a notation: 'avant pacques' or 'apres pacques', but so often they got it wrong, just as we do in January when writing our first cheques.

This could lead to the most appalling confusions by editors ignorant of this convention, as happened when the first volume of the *Calendar of State Papers Foreign, Elizabeth* arranged all documents according to the date as written at their bottoms. Thus events which actually happened in January 1559 were placed in the section for January 1558. This led to the scholarly practice of double-date citation: '5 January 1549/50' which recognised that the letter said it was written in 1549, but we know that it refers to events occurring in the month after December 1549. That, too, is somewhat ugly. Thus, in common with most works since the late 1960s, all dates will appear in their modern form: 5 January 1550.

NAME USAGE

Just as there are complexities over datings, so too over proper surnames and placenames. The convention 40 years ago was to anglicise: thus 'Henry II of France'. Recently, it has become fashionable to render surnames in their original language: thus 'Henri II' or 'Marie de Guise-Lorraine', but is he in an English essay 'King of France' or 'roi de France' (should I render in English his title, his name in French?). But should not Charles V thus be cited as Karl V or even Carlos I? This is an acute issue with dukes and seigneurs: Claude duc de Guise or Claude Duke of Guise? I have decided to employ modern English for all the major figures: thus Charles V, Henry II of France and Mary of Guise.

Where the issue becomes more complicated is over the spelling of other surnames.

Whereas d'Oysel has always been known in Scottish and French historiography as Henri Cleutin, sieur d'Oysel, current practice (you spell their name the way they did then) means his most recent biographer transcribes his name as 'Clutin d'Oisel'. I did something similar in 1986 when I stopped referring to James Henderson, but instead spelt him as 'Henrisoun'.

The issue does not end there. For some place-names, there is no trouble: Paris and Orléans are identical in English and French. But is it Lyon or Lyons, Cologne or Köln? And what of James Hamilton, Duke of Châtelherault (and sometimes without the circumflex over the a). No such place-name exists in modern France: it is Châtellerault in my SNCF timetable and Larousse. Consistency is thus almost impossible. I shall adopt the practice of using the style of the country of the personage's principal residence. But I am constrained to call James Hamilton: Duke of Châtelherault. Despite the practice of Marie-Noel Baudouin-Matusek (Henri Clutin, sieur d'Oisel), I will stick with the normal Scottish and English rendering: Cleutin and d'Oysel. I apologise for all of this.

QUOTATION CONVENTIONS

Books should make their wisdoms available to the widest of general, intelligent, interested readerships. To make one's research widely accessible it is now my firm conviction that all quotations should be given in modern spelling and in English. However, in a thoroughly academic history, all quotes from original sources properly should be in the original, i.e. as they were penned (or printed) in, say, 1548. I have thus tried to give the quotations in the original: not just for flavour, but for a more intimate sense of how they thought and spoke then.

This, however, is much easier said than done. Anyone examining the utterly meticulous edition of, say, Gladys Dickinson will immediately see how thorny printing a manuscript can be, given their (and note well: our) propensity to delete passages and to use shorthand abbreviations. Moreover, they often used different letters than we do today. Have a look at one of the nobler attempts to put manuscript sources into print, *The Acts of the Parliaments of Scotland, 1124–1707*, which appeared between 1812 (the original volume had so many errors it had to be suppressed and completely reprinted) and 1875. The editor, Thomas Thomson (1768–1852), a close friend of Sir Walter Scott, replicated every letter, abbreviation and word as it appears in the original register (necessitating the creation of numerous one-off typefaces). The result was something quite remarkable: a book which in effect meant one could destroy the original with no loss to scholarship (expect perhaps the study of palaeography on the one hand and calligraphy on the other). It is beautiful, but also a nightmare: noisome for the modern reader to read and almost impossible for a modern publisher to print. Further problems exist, given how eyewrenching sixteenth-century Scots can be at first (it = ed; and = ing; quh = wh, not to mention a plethora of vocabulary no longer current).

Geoffrey Elton always admonished his research students: 'always go back to the original manuscript' and give all quotes as you find them there. That is to say: do not completely trust those assiduous nineteenth-century editors whose labours are most spectacularly seen in the monumental *Calendar of the Letters and Papers Foreign and Domestic of the Reign of Henry VIII*, which was edited (initially) by the redoubtable J.S. Brewer. Between 1852 and 1910, he and his hard-working colleagues pounded out 21 (many double) volumes which attempted to place in the hands of researchers everything they could find, anywhere, relating to the king's reign. Place-names and surnames were rendered as in the original, so too the more important, colourful or obscure quotations, but the bulk of their renderings were in contemporary English with modern spelling. Professor Elton's advice was and is quite shrewd, but in real-life research it has not been possible to follow such a counsel of perfection. I often simply have not been able to consult the original.

Hence, for English and Scottish quotations, my policy will be somewhat inconsistent: I render as I found it in the source given in the relevant footnote. In situations where the *LP* version with modern spelling is the only one I have been able to consult, the quotation will be in modern spelling.

Yet another consideration is the fact that our story is one-quarter to one-third French. People simply do not read French in 2000 as they did in 1962 when I first began this study. Again, rendering in French all of the letters of Mary to her mother or those of her mother to her brothers would simply result in their not being read, or understood, by the majority of the people for whom this book is intended. Given that situation, I shall give a translation (unless it's blindingly obvious) when I have to quote the original for colour or because its meaning is open to interpretation. I am only too aware that some of my translations are rather loose and even colloquial. I hope purists will not mind too much.

When it comes to rendering documents from the original, I shall modernise 'minims' and extend all abbreviations. To take minims first: sixteenth-century scribes (printers are a slightly different problem) did not make distinctively different writings for ii nor for u, v, n. They simply wrote two undotted 'i's (and they rarely dotted the i): a minim is thus what Hector describes as 'short perpendicular strokes which in varying numbers compose the manuscript letters *i* (often equivalent to *j*)'. So for any of the above, what appears in the manuscript source is 'ii'. Our problem is thus readily apparent: what does one make of three = iii? iv,iu, in, m, ui, vi, ni? Four 'i's could be un, im, nu, mi or (and here hold onto your hat) the number '4'. Although Arabic numbers were becoming fashionable, most writers in the 1540s counted in Roman/Latin numbers: hence vi (or vj) = 6; xx = 20 and xx with iiij superscripted = 20 × 4=80. Six i must be 'ium', a frequently occurring word-ending. But it could be mm, nnn, uun. Thus, for much of the time, one imposes on the calligraphy one's hunch, what one friend called 'knowing what they wrote before you read the document yourself'. In other words, if the minims fit the most likely word, use it. My practice will be always to transcribe the word into its nearest modern equivalent.

As for word contractions or abbreviations, again one must impose one's own hunch as to what the fellow in question 'meant' to write. The most obvious example is our oldest of friends, current still today, the 'y' = 'th'. No one then ever meant for one second to actually say 'yeee' when they wrote 'ye'. They meant 'the'.

I will thus always extend 'y' to read as 'th'. As to 'quh' for 'wh', I am stuck. I like 'quh'.

As for quotations from sixteenth-century printed sources (broadsheets, proclamations, pamphlets, books), again I shall extend abbreviations. For printed works, the problem is not the employment of minims, but the contemporary availability of typefaces on the day when the book was being composed. Printers did not mean to print 'Vnion' when obviously the word is 'Union'. Or 'Iames' for 'James', etc. They simply had run out of Us in their typeface tray that day and used an alternative which they knew their readers would recognise. Modern readers as less tolerant and thus, although I will be guilty of a certain arrogance (telling the then printer what he meant to print), at least readers today will read something very close to what was actually impressed onto the then paper which fortunately has survived for us to consult.

MONEY

England, Scotland and France all employed pounds (livers), shillings (sou) and pence (denier) rendered as £ or 11., then by 's' and then by 'd' with ob = 1/2d. A modern readership should perhaps also be reminded that each pound was composed of 20 shillings and each shilling 12 pence. But other denominations existed.

'Money of account' refers to financial sums rendered by names for which actual coins do not or did not exist. In 1960s Britain I was often charged so many guineas = £1 1 shilling. No such coin was ever given me in normal pub transactions. For this period, there are a bewildering array of such terms (mark or merk being but one common unit), and for the sake of accuracy, I shall employ the term as found within the document. But what does such 'accuracy' accomplish in terms of hard scholarship? In 1558, Henry II stated that his costs for saving Scotland from the English amounted 'a million in gold'. What did that mean in terms of actual specie coin minted and available to be transported in a sack to the Antwerp moneylenders? Or to the Treasurer General of an army in the field? And what does that sum translate into in terms of modern monetary purchasing power?

There was also a bewildering array of different actual coins in circulation: angles, nobles, unicorns, crowns of the sun, not to mention the more humble bawbees. Their value depended largely (although not wholly, as one can see during royal debasements) on their intrinsic worth not as money of account, but as lumps of precious (or in the case of bawbees, base) metal: silver which has been cut to relatively uniform size and then hammered with two dies which impress onto the piece of metal the name and portrait of its monarch and sometimes its date and sometimes its worth.

To repeat, for all three monarchies, the most widely employed actual coinage was £sd. It is almost invariably evident from the text which monarch's coinage is being referred to, but given the possibilities of error or confusion, I deem it best to employ the following conventions:

£ always refers exclusively to English pounds or 'sterling'
£Sc always means the money is Scottish
£t means we are talking about the most common French coin, the *livre tournois*

Thus: £ 1 = £Sc 4 = £t 8. Again, I trust that readers will happily accommodate themselves to this convention.

Different countries' mints produced coinage of different intrinsic worth, and so we have a problem of exchange rates. For the 1540s the exchange rates amongst the principal monies referred to in this work were as follows (although debasement under Henry VIII and Edward VI would alter the English rate toward the end of our period):

> One pound English was worth about four Scottish pounds
> One French livre tournois equalled ten Scottish shillings

When I say that the normal monetary income of the Scottish crown in 1542 was £Sc45,000 whereas the normal annual worth of the English crown was £150,000, what I am saying is that the English crown's income was equivalent to 600,000 Scottish pounds (conversely that James V's income was £11,250 sterling). What these figures actually mean in terms of purchasing power is an entirely different story. When the lumps of metal so embossed were presented to an Antwerp money converter, highly precise measurements of their intrinsic value (although note again: based on a silver/gold market value which could and did fluctuate) could be made (see the wonderful illustrations in C.E. Challis, *Tudor Coinage*), using scales and touchstones. Within their confined domestic environment, specie coins operated in a different world to 'monies of account'. English barrowmen usually received 6d a day; Scottish barrowmen usually received £Sc 0–0s–6d, a much less valuable piece of silver: English (and Italian) commanders of the forts in Scotland were always staggered at how cheaply they could hire Scots labourers. Money is thus, then as now, a problem.

TRANSLATIONS OF FRENCH

Very few non-Francophones read *Le Monde* nowadays, much less *Libération*. Thirty years ago, one could set students French texts in History confident that they would understand them. Those days have passed. It is thus necessary to render French material into English. Otherwise, the majority of readers simply skip those passages. However, translating sixteenth-century French for modern eyes is no mean task. Gladys Dickinson did it brilliantly for her Scottish History Society edition of de la Brosse's two reports of 1543 and 1560. But her punctiliousness still remained trapped by the language in which her source wrote to the point that, even in English, the text remained heavy going.

Antique and specialist vocabulary apart, the nub of the problem lies in the legalese and prolixity of French secretaries of our period. One expects such in, say, an edict for a Cours des Aides (although even some of these can be quite eloquent). In a natural search for precision, resort was made, to the point of dizziness, to one of the most overused words in the language: 'ledit' [var: 'ledict' or just 'led']. I once counted sixteen 'the saids' in one paragraph. To translate into English every exact occurrence makes the passage virtually indigestible: thus readers simply skip it.

Moreover, as anyone who has calendared English or Scots documents knows, all sixteenth-century prose writers were inordinately verbose: their rhetoric (see Wolsey's letters) is quite alien to modern readers. Thus, one simplifies (and hopefully clarifies) as one puts these sentences into modern idiom. Compare any original in the Public Record Office with the version given in *The Letters and Papers of Henry VIII*.

In this work, I have tried to face these problems with French in the following manner. First, I give the original. This is then followed (between square brackets) by an English version. But my translations are not of the Gladys Dickinson sort. Instead, they are rather loose and free and purist scholars may well be offended by them. But what I am seeking to do is to make the text accessible to students and the general public alike. I hope specialists will understand and be indulgent. I want this to be a book which both tells a story, but also teaches. I hope I have succeeded and not made too many overly jazzy renderings or overly egregious mistakes.

CHAPTER ONE

A 'Childe of Prophesy'

The day of 8 December in 1542 was the Feast of the Immaculate Conception of the Virgin Mary.[1] Sometime, probably on this very day, Marie de Guise-Lorraine, Duchesse de Longueville and Queen of Scotland, second wife to her second husband, King James V of Scotland, was delivered of her fifth full-term child, a girl who very shortly was given her Christian name, Mary. Had her father lived to sire yet more children (highly likely given his redoubtable sexual potency and the obvious child-bearing capabilities of his wedded wife), the life of Princess Mary would have been interesting, but probably not very important. Fathers often react to the birth of their children with emotion. James did and died. Birth and death thus is all. James Stewart was the only surviving offspring of the union of his father, James IV, killed at Flodden 9 September 1513, and his mother, Margaret Tudor, elder sister to Henry VIII of England. Had he been possessed of brothers, the eldest would have succeeded as king. But Mary was 'unique' and thus on 14 December 1542 became Queen of Scotland.[2]

Mary's first public act on the stage of history was, of course, the actual moment when she physically emerged from her mother's womb in the Queen's bedroom at Linlithgow Palace. Royal births especially were public occasions.[3] There had to be as many witnesses as possible for the start of such an individual's life on this earth. She would then be under constant gaze (at meals, during walks, whilst taking a bath or during acts of urination and defecation), for she was the most important human being in this political and social unit: the kingdom of Scotland. It must never be possible for anyone to say that this woman was a changeling: not the legitimate offspring of her predecessor, the king.

Mary's second public act would be her almost immediate baptism at the Kirk of

1 The weather was ferocious ('tempestuous' is the word Antonia Fraser employed in 1969): bitter cold and the Tweed deep in ice. Every history of Mary's life begins with the weather, from D. Hay Fleming to the plethora of popular pot-boilers ground out by French hacks once mass literacy and cheap printing emerged in the nineteenth century. For this occasion in history, weather is not important (Linlithgow was quite well provided with fireplaces) and will not be further detailed.
2 The date of her baptism is not clear, but it must have been at this time.
3 One should not forget that when Princess Margaret was born, 21 August 1930, at Glamis Castle to the then Princess Elizabeth of York, the Home Secretary, J.R. Clynes, waited outside the delivery room so as to be the first to see this heir on behalf of Ramsay MacDonald's government. Princess Margaret Rose was the first child in a direct line of succession to the British throne to be born in Scotland since Charles I's birth on 19 November 1600. I am grateful to Mrs. June Cross for telling me of the occasion and to the Lady-in-Waiting to Queen Elizabeth The Queen Mother for supplying me with details from the records.

Fig 1.1.   Childbirth in early modern Europe was a dangerous process for all mothers
and for all children. So often, either one, or the other, or both died in it.
Queen Jane Seymour gave us (and Henry VIII) Prince Edward and thus the
Rough Wooings. She died twelve days later. Mary of Guise's confinement in
December 1542 at Linlithgow (where her husband had been born) was just
such a life-threatening as well as life-creating moment. Both she and her
child Mary survived. Her other four children all died, Francis in the autumn
of 1551, in his mother's arms, at the haunting age of sixteen.

St. Michael, Linlithgow, just by the palace. Baptism in the Europe of our time was
the first (and some argued the most important) sacrament: whereas many failed to
make communion even at Easter or were buried without the final rites, hardly any
Christian was not baptised. The infant had to be taken into the precincts of a church
where, in Peter Ackroyd's felicitous phrasing,[4] 'the child of wrath must be reformed

4 P. Ackroyd, *The Life of Thomas More* (1998), 1–3. I am grateful to I. Lewis for this reference
and for Mary Tudor's being bishoped.

into the image of God, "the servant of the fiend" made into "a son [and daughter] of joy" '. Having crossed the babe at the door to St. Michael's, salt would have been placed in the babe's mouth and the priest would massage her ears and nose with his own saliva: 'let the nose be open to the odour of sweetness'. Mary then was allowed to approach the font where holy water was sprayed and breathed on; wax was made into a cross as oil and chrism were added. Mary would then have been questioned: 'What seekest thou?' 'Dost thou wish to be baptised?' She would then be placed in the priest's hands, and he immersed her three times in the water before she was anointed with chrism and wrapped in a robe:

> Mary, receive a white robe, holy and unstained, which thou must bring before the tribunal of Our Lord Jesus Christ, that thou mayest have eternal life and live for ever and ever.

This potent ritual was a high and public one, both a sacrament and a drama for as large an audience as possible. It was the moment when an infant moved from 'the relative privacy of the birthroom' into the 'public ceremony of incorporation into the community and the church'.[5] Since she was a Princess, that sacrament may well have been accompanied by her also being 'bishoped' (a form of confirmation, although she did not take her first communion until 1552) as happened to Princess Mary Tudor after her birth on 18 February 1516. Was her coming foretold?

Sometime in 1528, Sir David Lindsay of the Mount,[6] then 'Depute' Lyon King of Arms, heard a verbose, highly entertaining, riotously convoluted poem, the 'prophisies of Rymour, Beid and Marlyng'.[7] This sort of prolix demi-epic was the standard fare of touring entertainers who provided a vital element in sixteenth-century popular culture. It was apparently widely popular in Scotland and the North of England and by the 1530s had spread southwards. There numerous Englishmen were tried for repeating it and even listening to it. Prophecies of all sorts flourished in Europe and encompassed the whole range of human experience (the weather, farming life, religion, sex, witchcraft, monstrosities, fables, tall tales and histories) as well as the mythical and the magical, drawing upon and contributing to popular belief and lore. Alexander the Great was a great favourite. So was the History of Helen of Troy, not to mention Jason and the Golden Fleece.

A transcript of this remarkable demi-epic exists due to the Tudor regime's post-

---

5 These phrases come from D. Cressy, *Birth, Marriage, and Death-Ritual, Religion and the Life-Cycle in Tudor and Stuart England* (OUP, 1997), 97.

6 Lindsay and his career are famous. C. Edington, *Court and Culture in Renaissance Scotland: Sir David Lindsay of the Mount* (University of Massachusetts Press, 1994; East Linton, 1995). Reference should also be had to *The Rose and The Thistle: Essays on the Culture of Late Medieval and Renaissance Scotland*, ed. S. Mapstone and J. Wood (East Linton, 1998). See 23–24, 62–71 *passim*, 83–94 *passim*. Also J. Cameron, *James V: The Personal Rule, 1528–1542* (East Linton, 1998), 5, 81, 263–64, 288–89, 331.

7 I first rehearsed this story in my 'Mary Queen of France' article in 1988, 32–34. The prophecy is discussed in J.S.L. Jaech, 'The "prophesies of Rymour, Beid and Marlyng": Henry VIII and a sixteenth-century political prophecy', *Sixteenth Century Journal* (xvi, 1985), 291–99.

Divorce, Reformation-era hysteria.[8] Men uttering such 'foolish sayings' could be held in the Tower, as happened to William Neville for more than a year because of this 'Prophesy'. His tale concerned the rescue of 'a fair lady' by him, as a bear (a future Earl of Warwick), when he mastered 'a darf dragon' in battle. The dragon was obviously Welsh: Henry VIII. The fair lady, of course, was Queen Catherine (aided by an eagle: Charles V).[9] Referring to Henry VIII as 'darf' was treason. Such insults were widespread given his notorious behaviour during the 1530s. The commons were heard to lampoon him as 'a fool' and as 'a tyrant moore cruel than Nero'. All he wanted was 'an apple and a fair wench to dally with'. Sir Edward Neville of Addlington called the king 'a beast and worse than a beast'.[10]

This 'Marlyng' performance should not be made too much of. Such noises swirled about many other claimants to the throne, such as de la Pole, or made other, equally dark forebodings as to the future of the kingdom. But it does demonstrate that James V's nearness in blood to the Tudors was appreciated by quite a considerable audience and that Henry's momentous acts were notorious. What gives this poem particular interest for students of the Rough Wooings is its Preamble. The teller of the tale was a great wanderer ('Over a lande forth I blynte'), which is how he came across the many different and engaging episodes which peppered his entertainment.[11] The stage was set by his espying a beautiful and radiant 'crowned quene in verament':

> her stede was grete & dappyll gray
> her apparell was of silk of Inde
> with peryll and perrye [perle] set full gay
> so R[o]yally in her Arraye
> I stode and mwsyd In my mynde
> all the clerkes a live today
> So fayre a lady colde none ffynd.

She was surrounded by numerous angels and wore a splendid crown. The group moved over field and forest, where 'she halowyd the ground with her owen hand'. Having premonitions of death ('manye a dede corse lye' including 'barnis'), she prayed: 'Jesu, that bowght mankynde so dere, upon the soulles have mercye'. Then suddenly appeared none other than St. George who 'carpyd wordes cruell & kene':

> A goodly men as armyde knyght
> he shoke his spere furyously in hand
> Right cruell and kene
> Styfly & stowre as he wolde stonde.

---

8 G.R. Elton, *Policy and Police* (1972), ch. 2, 'Rumour, Magic and Prophecy'.
9 After the queen's death in 1536, the 'lady' became Princess Mary.
10 For which he was beheaded on Tower Hill, 9 January 1539 (Bindoff, *Parliament*, iii, 7).
11 The full text is reprinted in *The Romance and Prophecies of Thomas of Erceldoune*, ed. J.A.H. Murray (Early English Text Society, 1875), appendix ii. The original is BL, MS Lansdowne 762, fos. 75–88.

Then on the other side of the field appeared another furious knight, whose crest bore 'A red lyon that did rawmpyng be': St. Andrew.[12] He too spoke words 'cruell & kene' and threatened the other. The imagery is obvious: England and Scotland were about to do battle once more. But the queen intervened, her tone severe, her command peremptory:

> This crowned quene rode them between
> Right as fast as she cold hie
> She saith men what do you meane
> stente your Stryff and your follye
> Remember that ye be sayntes in heven
>
> She said Senct Gorge, thow art my kynght
> of wronge heyres have done the tene
> Senct Andrew yet art thow in the right
> of thy men if it be syldom sene
> here shall many a doughty knyght
> And gromes shall grone upon that grene
> here lordly leedes loo shall lyght
> and many a douty knyght bydene.

What an extraordinary tableau. When James V died, leaving his only daughter as queen of Scotland, did Lindsay perhaps recall this prophecy? Could not this child in real politics bring peace at last between two kingdoms which had been warring since 1298, if not since 1068? Was Mary Queen of Scots' birth foretold? And her place in history? In the 'Marylyng' epic, she would 'stent' strife and bring happiness, as this conclusion made clear:

> Here shalbe gladismore that shall glad us all
> Yt shalbe gladyng of oure glee
> Yt shalbe gladmore wher ever yt fall
> But not gladmore by the see.

The village of Gladsmuir is in modern East Lothian, four miles west of Haddington. Knox would preach in its church, some of which stands today. Apart from that and a post office, there is little to it now. Nor was there in 1528. But it was there that one of the largest armies in Scottish history would muster in the late summer of 1547. On 10 September knights of St. George would rout it with over half of its number slaughtered. From that 'Black Saturday' much history would flow and at Pinkie in many respects would begin the epic journey which made Mary Queen of Scots' life so important to European history:

> Brief was her bloom with scarce one sunny day
> 'Twixt Pinkie's field and fatal Fotheringay.[13]

---

12 Ever since Alexander II, the royal shield had contained 'a ruddy lion ramping in his field of tressured gold' (see C.J. Burnett, 'Outward Signs of Majesty, 1535–1540' in Williams, ed., *Stewart Style*, 294).

13 Glasford Bell, quoted in M. Edgar, *Stories from Scottish History* (1906), 185.

THE 'ROUGH WOOINGS': THE DEFINITION OF A TITLE

Princess Mary of Scotland was born on 8 December 1542. A week later, on the 14th, she succeeded to the throne as Queen Mary. Immediately, she became an object of dynastic ambition. 'The Rough Wooing' is a catch-all phrase which describes the English attempt by war (hence the 'rough') to coerce the Scottish government into the betrothal of the queen to the Prince of Wales, in 1547 King Edward VI (thus the 'wooing').[14] The war took place in two stages: first under Henry VIII (from 9 November 1543 to 6 June 1546), then one directed by Edward's Protector, the Duke of Somerset (from 2 September 1547 until 24 March 1550). That actually makes for two rough wooings. If one then includes the vigorous and successful war by the French King Henry II by which he achieved Mary's hand for his four-year-old son (June 1548 to April 1550), there are three wooings. Mary was indeed born into a war, Henry VIII's attack in 1542, which in many senses set the scene for the Tudor attempt to take over the Stewart line, albeit by diplomacy in 1543. Just because they are interconnected does 'not mean encapsulation'.[15]

Actual combatant hostilities were quite time-specific, the first major phase being May 1544 to October 1545. At other periods (and during much of the winter) the warfare was only marginally more severe than the 'normal' raiding along the Border and at sea which characterised 'peacetime'. The second phase had similar intensive spells with very heavy engagements: September 1547 to October 1548 during which the French became actively involved, then June to September 1549, with a final spurt from February to April 1550. In total, these periods of active major warfare probably came to no more than thirty-seven months (except along the Borders).

Contemporaries called it an 'Eight Years' War' because it was felt to have begun in the summer of 1542 and to have continued even after the Scots and English came to peace (Scotland's war with the Emperor Charles V was not concluded until early 1551). That is almost a nine years' war. Scotland and England would again go to war in 1557 (concluded by the Treaty of Cateau-Cambrésis in March-April 1559), the last occasion in history when they did so as independent kingdoms.

Mary had no sisters (and, obviously, no brothers). The Stewart hold on the Scottish crown was so secure that she had no internal rivals for the succession,. In England, Prince Edward was the only male Tudor heir. Should they wed and have children, the eldest (with male preference) would inherit both kingdoms, achieving British union. Men, at the time, were struck with the importance of such a marriage, the like of which had not been seen in the British Isles since the short reign of Queen

14 When I lectured on this topic in Utah in 1978, the University Press Office described it as 'the ill-fated romance between Mary and Edward'. I was also once asked to give a paper on Mary's 'career' in 1548, when she was five years old. Mary's job as a child was to eat regularly, to stay alive and to survive various childhood illnesses, hence the invention of marmalade.

15 A delicious refinement by M.L. Bush in 1975, *Protector Somerset*, 9. Moreover, one must never see the war of 1542 as part of The Rough Wooings: Mary was not even alive or her father dead when it took place, although her betrothal to Edward would end it.

Margaret, 'The Maid of Norway', 1286–90. She had been betrothed to another Edward Prince of Wales (born in 1284), the future Edward II (1307–27). In the circumstances of December 1542, 'For Henry, it was 1286 come yet again'.[16]

When Queen Margaret died at sea in 1290, a major shift occurred in both the internal Scottish political landscape and within the dynamics of Anglo-Scottish relations. The Scottish royal succession now had to be determined since the direct line had utterly expired. Because there were so many close claimants, the Scottish polity was not capable of resolving this issue without recourse to a protracted and bitter civil war in which the kingdom nearly perished. Edward I had come tantalisingly close to attaining control through 'peaceful' means; but when the new Scottish king John Balliol 'revolted' in 1296, Edward resorted to military conquest and the imposition of an English administration. Wallace, then Bruce, resisted him. At Bannockburn Robert the Bruce defeated Edward I's son and established his own family's hold on the monarchy, restoring the kingdom to its ancient liberty. That remarkable achievement had been a very close-run thing. Men, especially in the fifteenth and sixteenth centuries, were all too aware of how the accidents of succession could result in the loss of independence, as examples such as Aragon, Naples and Brittany amply demonstrated.

THE 'ROUGH WOOING': THE MAKING OF A PHRASE

The term 'Rough Wooing' is widely employed, but its currency is very much a twentieth-century phenomenon. We can trace its origin to 10 September 1547, 'Black Saturday': the battle of Pinkie. Two men call for our attention. One was William Patten, a Londoner of Derbyshire origin, who, through his association with William Paget, one of the King's two Secretaries (the future Lord Paget), and John Dudley (the then Earl of Warwick and the future Duke of Northumberland), had been invited to make a record of this invasion of Scotland, what men at the time called a 'voyage' or 'journey'.[17]

To the south-east of the River Esk that morning stood a great English army over fifteen thousand strong. On the other side, camped and entrenched, was one of the largest Scottish hosts in history. They were about to engage in the last great clash of arms[18] between the two as independent monarchies.[19] With the English host went all

16 The phrase was first coined by J.D. Mackie, *The Earlier Tudors* in 1952 and it recurs in R.C. Paterson, *My Wound is Deep – A History of the Later Anglo-Scottish Wars 1380–1560* (Edinburgh, 1997), ch. 10, pp. 169–87.

17 He certainly succeeded in becoming noticed; through his enormously popular account of the campaign he was accepted into Court and eventually became a Customer of the city of London.

18 Something like 40,000 combatants must have fought that day: an enormous number. I do not credit the figures for Towton (1461), where supposedly 100,000 battled: a ridiculous figure for the dead of winter in a civil war engagement when the total population of England could not have been much above 2.5 million.

19 Preston (1648), Dunbar (1650), Worcester (1651), Prestonpans (1745) and Culloden (1746) were 'civil war' battles within a British monarchy or state. Dumbar (and Cromwell's subjugation of Scotland thereafter) is the closest history offers for a purely Anglo-Scottish war after 1559. John D. Grainger agues very forcefully that the Cromwellian War was not 'a civil

the hangers-on of warfare: drovers of the cattle which the army would eat, pioneers to build bridges and fortresses, provisioners of all sorts, cooks, prostitutes and journalists.

Both Patten and Somerset's other Secretary, William Cecil (later to rise to fame under Elizabeth), kept extensive notes on everything they saw during the invasion. Patten later fleshed these out into a long and often highly informative account of the Pinkie campaign which was published in 1548 and was widely read by an eager audience both at the time and afterwards by historians. Thirty years later, Holinshed picked this grim passage to colour his account of the horrors of the English victory:

> Dead corpses lying dispersed abroad. Some with their legs cut off; some but hamstrung and left lying half dead: others, with the arms cut off; divers, their necks half asunder; many, their heads cloven; of sundry, the brains smashed out; some others again, their heads quite off: with a thousand other kinds of killing . . . And thus, with blood and slaughter of the enemy, this chase was continued.[20]

Patten was no soldier; he was also committed to English victory and was biased by his Protestantism. Numerous confusions and mistakes occur in his account, but his *diarie* is intense, detailed and the most vivid we have.

The second man to note was George Gordon, the Earl of Huntly. Unlike the other Scottish leaders, he had equipped himself splendidly with a gilded and highly decorated suit of armour, topped by a splendid helmet. It was he who performed the mandatory pre-battle chivalric ritual of offering to meet Somerset in single-handed combat to decide the issue. Being so conspicuous probably resulted in his capture alive. At the end of the day, he sat on a blasted tree stump, surrounded by the dead and dying, his dented armour caked in mud, his spirits low. One gloating Englishman asked him how he now felt about the joining of the two 'Princes', seeing that God had so amply demonstrated his favour by the outcome of the day. Huntly sighed, 'I wade it sud gea furth, and haud will wyth the marriage, but I lyke not thys wooyng'.[21] Patten was told of the exchange and duly reported it. Gradually the phrase insinuated itself onto the pages of history.

In 1726, both a family historian[22] and G. Crawford[23] reported how Huntly had disliked such a 'rough courtship'. William Robertson (1761) picked up the image.[24]

---

war, but a clear international conflict between sovereign states'. J.D. Grainger, *Cromwell and the Scots – The Last Anglo-Scottish War 1650–1652* (East Linton, 1997). I have my reservations still, but certain it is that Cromwell's most lasting achievement was to re-cement the Stuart composite kingdoms (see his Irish campaigns) which James I created. Why did the English Republic not simply become a single sovereign 'state' in 1649?

20 Holinshed (1578), *English Chronicle*, iv, 384. Oddly, he did not employ this passage in his account of the battle in his *Historie of Scotland* (Ellis edition, 1808, p. 551).

21 Patten, *Expedicion*, 77.

22 W. Gordon, *The History of the Ancient, Noble and Illustrious Family of Gordon* (1726), 173. I am grateful to Mr. A Cherry for this and the subsequent reference.

23 G. Crawford. *The Lives and Characters of the Crown Officers of Scotland* (1726), 85.

24 W. Robertson, *History of Scotland during the reigns of Queen Mary and King James* (Edinburgh, 1761), i, 109. Professor Donaldson supplied this reference.

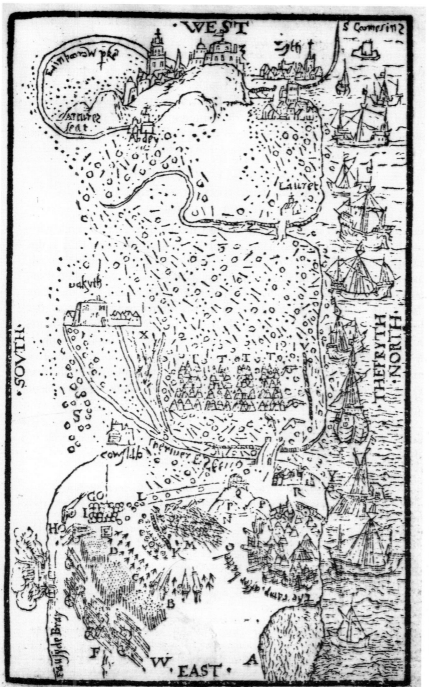

Fig. 1.2. Pinkie (called variously during the sixteenth century: Musselburgh, Fawside, etc.) has left an extraordinary range of representations. The now widely reproduced panels from the Bodleian Roll have great charm. But in some senses, the incredibly crude woodcuts which illustrated Patten's *Expedicion* are the most evocative. Here we see the climactic moment of the engagement when the Scottish host began to disintegrate with men fleeing, shedding their protective clothing, their helmets, their pikes: anything which might impede their flight. What Patten captured in his woodcut was the thicket of discarded pikes: over 20,000 of them. It was in this mêlée that the Earl of Huntly was captured. Edinburgh is to the right.

So did Sir Walter Scott in his highly popular *Tales of a Grandfather Being Stories from the History of Scotland.*[25] It was he who employed the vital word 'wooing', but then muffled the overall effect: 'so rough a mode of wooing'. Not until 1906 did H.E. Marshall's charming *Scotland's Story for Boys and Girls* finally employ the term: 'The fairest lands of Scotland were blackened. It was a rough wooing'.[26] Perhaps because his overall assessment was so germane – 'Too rough to suit the Scotsmen, and not rough enough to conquer them' – his title was adopted. Thereafter historians academic[27] and popular[28] have employed it. It is interesting to note that initially it referred solely to Henry VIII's war. Not until half a millennium after Pinkie was Somerset's war so described.[29] Now it has passed into textbooks and into the mind of the nation.[30]

PROSPECTS FOR ANGLO-SCOTTISH UNION IN THE SIXTEENTH CENTURY

Given James VI's accession in 1603 to the English throne, it is easy to think with hindsight of the sixteenth century as being one of Anglo-Scottish peace. But, as the above description of the field of Pinkie in 1547 should remind us, Anglo-Scottish warfare was quite frequent during this century. On several occasions armed Englishmen either clashed with Scottish soldiers or marched into Scotland:[31] in the years 1513–14 (the Flodden war), 1521–3 (after Scottish aid was offered to France), 1542 (the Solway Moss war), 1544–5 (when Henry VIII tried to force Mary Queen of Scots' marriage to his son Edward), 1547–50 (the duke of Somerset's 'Rough Wooing'), 1557–8 (the Calais war), 1560 (the siege of Leith), 1570 (the earl of Surrey's punitive expeditions), and 1573 (when an English army captured Edinburgh Castle for the first time since 1341). For most Scotsmen, then, England still meant 'our auncient ynemeis'.

25 Sir Walter Scott, *Tales of a Grandfather*, iii, 85; published in 1828 for his grandson, Hugh Littlejohn.

26 H.E. Marshall, *Scotland's Story: A History of Scotland for Boys and Girls* (Edinburgh, 1906), 297.

27 R. Rait, *Mary Queen of Scots* (1899), v. See also his *The Making of Scotland* (Edinburgh, 1911), 140; C.S. Terry, *A History of Scotland* (Cambridge, 1920), 181; J. Glover, *The Story of Scotland* (1960), 130. Croft Dickinson's 1960 textbook, the first of substance since Hume Brown (1908–1909), hovered between Rait's 'English wooing' and Marshall's 'rough wooing', although he had used the term as early as 1949 (Knox, *History of the Reformation in Scotland*, i, pp. xxix-xxx) and favoured 'rough' in his index. *Essays on the Scottish Reformation, 1513–1625*, ed. D. McRoberts (Glasgow, 1962), 10, 71, 421; Donaldson, *Scotland* (1965), 27, 72; T.C. Smout, *A History of the Scottish People* (1969), 57; R. Mitchison, *A History of Scotland* (1970), 106. The term did not find favour with English historians until very recently.

28 A. Fraser, *Mary Queen of Scots* (1969), 43.

29 J. Ferguson, '1547: The Rough Wooing', *Blackwood's Magazine*, ccxii (1947), 183–94.

30 See *Guardian* report, 4 August 1997, on speech by Tony Blair concerning devolution, where the term was widely employed, even though the editor felt it had to be explained.

31 I give the dates of the actual serious campaigning; technically, some of the wars either began earlier or ended later. We must also remember that hostilities were occurring sporadically at sea, and these (like the fighting that continually broke out on the Borders) were often difficult to contain.

Over all these conflicts (save that of 1557–8) there hung the historical and rhetorical framework of overlordship, conquest or partnership – all variants on the theme of union. In 1513 Henry VIII declared himself to be overlord of Scotland, and, as late as 1559, Queen Elizabeth entertained such claims.[32] Alternatively, dynastic union was proposed, as in the 1520s:

And if the Scots would persuade themselves to break the league with the French, and join in amity with the English; they should shortly well understand, that the king of England did not seek after sovereignty, glory, power, or honour; but only studied for a concord amongst themselves, and a league between their nations. For which cause, he would bestow his only daughter Mary upon James the king of Scotland; by which marriage, the Scots should not be subject to the government of England; but contrary, the English under the rule of Scots. For by that means, besides the quenching of great hatred between the nations (and intercourse of merchandise, exchange of mutual courtesies and joinings in affinity) there should be an indissoluble knot made for the honour of the whole Island.[33]

For some Scots, too, union supposedly had its attractions, indicated in this reported declamation by lord Forbes in 1523 against a proposal to invade England:

For the love of France the realm of Scotland suffers great pain as daily appears, for our nobles are slain or taken, our commonalty murdered, our lands overrun, our houses and fortresses burned and razed; we lose the profits of our lands; which mischief we need not have had, but for the love of France, and what helps France . . . If we would keep amity with the realm of England we were out of all these dangers.[34]

Two decades later, unionist propaganda made these points repeatedly: witness James Henrisoun's *Exhortacion* of 1547[35] and Somerset's *Epistle* of 1548.[36] The nub of the

32 J.D. Mackie, 'Henry VIII and Scotland', *Trans. Royal Historical Soc.*, 4th ser., xxix (1947), p. 105 gives the full quote: 'I am the very owner of Scotland and he [James IV] holdest of me by homage'. For Elizabethan examples, see. *Cal. S.P. Scotland*, i, nos. 440, 537 and *Cal. S.P. Foreign 1558–59*, p. 520.
33 *Holinshed* (1808 ed.), v, 497 (writing half a century later, and drawing on Buchanan, lib. 14).
34 G. Donaldson, 'Foundations of Anglo-Scottish Union', in his *Scottish Church History* (Edinburgh, 1985), gives most of the quote which is from E. Hall, *The union of the two noble and illustre famelies of York and Lancaster* (London, 1548), fo. 201v (1809 edition, p. 665).
35 James Henrisoun, *An Exhortacion to the Scottes to conforme themselfes to the honorable, expedient, & godly Union betweene the two realmes of Englande & Scotland* (London, 1547): reprinted in *The Complaynt of Scotlande*, ed. J. A. H. Murray (Early English Text Society, 1872), pp. 207–36. See M.H. Merriman, 'James Henrisoun and "Great Britain": British Union and the Scottish Commonweal', in *Scotland and England 1286–1815*, ed. R. Mason (Edinburgh, 1987), pp. 85–112. It needs to be said that Henrisoun was in English service when he wrote.
36 *An Epistle or exhortacion, to vnitie & peace, sent from the Lorde Protector & others the kynges moste honorable counsaill of England To the Nobilitie, Gentlemen, and Commons, and al others the inhabitauntes of the Realme of Scotlande* (London, 1548), reprinted in *The Complaynte*, pp. 237–46.

message of both these extended tracts was encapsulated in *The proclamation* which preceded the Pinkie invasion of September 1547:

> We mynd nocht by this conjunctioun of marriage to do ony moir prejudice to this realm of Scotland than to the realme of England, bot with the advice of the noble men and gude men of baith realmes to unite thame togidder in any name by the name of Britounis and in such a freindlie kind of leving and suche a libertie and preservatioun of justice to ilk persone equalie as they sall weill find both the glories of God and his worde advance, this bischop of Romes usurpted jurisdiction abolisheit, the honour of baith weil satisfied and contented.[37]

In the even more revealing *prayer*[38] of 1548, God was asked to 'have an eye to this small Isle of Bretaigne' and to complete what he had begun, 'That the Scottish menn and wee might forever and hereafter [live] in love and amitie, knit into one nacion' by the marriage of Edward and Mary. 'Graunt o Lorde that the same might goo forwarde and that our sonnes sonnes and all our posteritie hereafter may fele the benefite and commoditie of thy great gift of unitie graunted in our daies'. Though He was asked to 'putt away frome us all warre and hostilitie', if this was not to be, then He should 'be our sheld and buckle' and 'Lay thy sowrd of punyshement uppoun them' that opposed the marriage. Better still, 'converte their hartes to the better waye'. But these tracts were little more than the song of the aggressor over the centuries: 'We only make war to bring peace' – an early-modern variant on the twentieth-century motif of 'bombing them to the peace table'.

Certainly the horrors of war made the siren calls for peaceful coexistence alluring. The conflicts put severe strains on both countries, especially on their Border communities, and had serious domestic ramifications. It is unsurprising, therefore, that James VI and I made so much of the 'amity and love' brought by his accession to the English throne, and that subsequent historians reacted so positively to the contemporary calls for 'an end to al streife'. In 1966, for example, R.B. Wernham intoned:

> from the marriage of Margaret Tudor to James IV of Scotland there was born the idea of a united realm of Britain, 'with the sea for its frontiers and mutual love for its garrison', that was to haunt statesmen on both sides of the Border until its achievement in 1603.[39]

But three points must be appreciated to understand the historical background to James VI and I's accession. Scotland was not conquerable by war in the sixteenth century. Anglo-Scottish dynastic union would not simply happen automatically.

---

37 The quote is from the *proclamation* which was printed and circulated immediately before the Pinkie invasion of 1547. See *Warrender Papers*, ed. A.I. Cameron (SHS, 1931), i, 17. The only copy of the original is in the Society of Antiquaries of London.

38 *A prayer for victorie and peace* (London, 1548), the only printed copy of which is in the Pepysian Library, Magdalene College, Cambridge. Manuscript of it is in PRO, SP 10/2, fo. 11.

39 R.B. Wernham, *Before the Armada: English Foreign Policy in the Sixteenth Century* (London, 1966), p. 48.

And, in particular, James VI and indeed Scotland had to be Protestant. Each of these issues will be discussed in turn.

THE TUDORS AND SCOTLAND[40]

It has been said that Henry VIII missed a magnificent opportunity after Flodden in 1513; had he invaded, he surely must have conquered.[41] This is mistaken: Surrey's army was severely disorganised by its magnificent victory; it was too late in the season for serious invasion; and Henry had no such intention, having a purely defensive attitude towards Scotland, while sporting on a far more prestigious field of valour in France. Moreover, it is not just that the Flodden war had no unionist intent: most Anglo-Scottish wars in the sixteenth century had no such aim. None of the wars of 1513–14, 1522–3, 1542 and 1557–8 had any serious connection with a possible union, or even the objective of annexing part of Scotland.[42] They were defensive and reactive, consequences of English conflicts with France. As for the last three campaigns of the century (1560, 1570, 1573), these again were not at all unionist, but sought Anglo-Scottish alliance, being English interventions in Scotland's politics in support of a friendly, Protestant, faction.

That leaves the two wars making up what H.E. Marshall later called 'a Rough Wooing' of Mary Queen of Scots (1544–5, 1547–50): these are the only time when the English seriously attempted to bring about Anglo-Scottish union by force of arms. With an infant queen on the Scottish throne (Mary had succeeded in 1542, at the age of one week), and a young prince of Wales waiting to succeed his father in England, the potential for their marriage was immense: in due course, their eldest son (or daughter, failing sons) would inherit both kingdoms. To marry his son and heir to a young queen of Scots was, of course, what Edward I had hoped for in 1286–8.[43] Then, the death of the 'Maid of Norway' had destroyed the chance of a medieval union of the crowns, and led instead to the Scottish Wars of Independence. Now, in 1543, Henry VIII tried to capitalise on the magnificent opportunity of Edward and Mary's co-existence. But his proposal for the marriage was eventually rebuffed by the Scottish political elite, who had no serious desire for union with England. Henry, therefore, turned to war in 1544. But he also invaded France, capturing Boulogne in September 1544, and that took priority over the war in Scotland. Although two massive raids were launched (the seaborne assault on Edinburgh in May 1544 and the

---

40 This section, 'The Tudors and Scotland,' is lifted virtually word for word from my article 'Stewarts and Tudors in the mid-sixteenth century' which appeared in *Uniting the Kingdom? The Making of British History*, ed. A. Grant and K.J. Stringer (1995), 111–18. I will return to its second portion in my final chapter.

41 J.J. Scarisbrick, *Henry VIII* (London, 1968), pp. 37–8. Scarisbrick also suggests that the period after Solway Moss in 1542 was a golden opportunity lost (*ibid.*, p. 436).

42 Though such ideas occasionally surfaced. In 1542, the future duke of Northumberland proposed that Henry should add to his dominions 'that parte of Skotland asmoche as ys thisside of the Frithe on theste side, and asmoche as ys athisside Dunebretayne on the west' (*LP*, xvii, no. 1194). Also, in 1549 it was briefly hoped to keep Berwickshire as an extension of the Border and to make Dunglass a new Berwick.

43 A point nicely captured by J.D. Mackie, *The Earlier Tudors* (Oxford, 1957 ed.), p. 406.

attack on the Merse and Teviotdale in September 1545), they seem simply to have been demonstrations in force, aimed more at forestalling any Scottish invasion of England than at bringing about union.

After Henry's death, however, the Protector, Somerset (who as earl of Hertford had commanded in Scotland in 1544), started the Rough Wooings again. The two-and-a half years following the battle of Pinkie (from September 1547 to March 1550) witnessed the most intense Anglo-Scottish warfare of the sixteenth century. At Pinkie, near Musselburgh, the duke of Somerset, with around 15,000 men, destroyed the Scottish army, and then proceeded to establish garrisons across Lowland Scotland as far north as the Tay. Another invasion by almost as large an army (about 12,000) took place in August 1548. A third was planned for 1549; had not rebellion erupted in England, it probably would have taken place. During this second phase of the Rough Wooings, in fact, Somerset focused as much of England's military might as he could on defeating Scotland. Yet all he achieved was the cementing of the Franco-Scottish alliance. In 1548, Mary Queen of Scots was sent to France, where she married the Dauphin Francis, while a French army of some 6,000 men was sent to Scotland, where it helped to drive Somerset's garrisons out.[44]

The lesson of the Rough Wooings, therefore, was that learned by the three Edwards in the fourteenth century: that, despite crushing victories in the field, Scotland simply could not be made to capitulate through warfare. Anyone who thought otherwise (in particular Somerset) was a fool. The explanation for English failures in Scotland is often found in France, and certainly French help was extremely important to the Scots in 1548–50. That Henry VIII, like Edward III after 1337, was more interested in France is also very significant. But to argue that if Henry had only turned his huge, highly professional, army of 1544 on Scotland instead of wasting it on capturing Boulogne, then conquest would inevitably have followed, is to go too far.

Other considerations should be borne in mind. First, there is Scotland's geography, which the English did not comprehend. In March 1544, for instance, Hertford was instructed to do what damage he could to Edinburgh and as many towns about the city as possible, then to pass over to Fife 'and turne upset downe the Cardinalles town of St. Andrews' – all within three weeks – and to be in France for early June! It simply could not be done.[45] In fact, as in the fourteenth century, the distances involved put most of Scotland beyond the effective reach of the English. An English army as large as that of 1544 could not have lived off the land, but would have needed provisioning from England: an impossible operation, even had there been sufficient cartage capacity to supply it for any length of time.

The second critical consideration is money. The 1540s found the Tudor state as

44 G. Donaldson, *James V-VII*, pp. 63–82; W.K. Jordan, *Edward VI: The Young King* (London, 1968), pp. 230–304; M. Bush, *The Government Policy of Protector Somerset* (London, 1975), pp. 7–39.

45 *A Source Book of Scottish History*, ed. W. Croft Dickinson and others (Edinburgh, 1958), ii, p. 132. The actual damage he did to Edinburgh was minimal and quickly repaired, as the 1560 view makes all too plain.

wealthy as it ever would be, thanks to the Dissolution of the Monasteries. That enabled Henry and Somerset to spend over £3.5 million on sustaining armies in the field for more than six years. But after this once-and-for-all windfall was gone, the Crown was bankrupt, as Northumberland discovered in 1552.[46] Thereafter, the Tudor state never again had the funds to mount a serious major military campaign in the style of the Emperor Charles V, Francis I of France or Philip II of Spain. It was all it could do to reconquer Ireland.

In the third place, there were the castles of Edinburgh and Stirling: two of the most formidable natural defensive strongholds in Europe. In 1544 Hertford failed utterly to take Edinburgh Castle; his attack was repulsed by withering gunfire, and his field engineer found the castle rock impossible to mine. Subsequently, the castle was significantly strengthened with extra guns and then by a vast Italianate bastion. It simply could not be taken with 1540s technology; in 1547, after Pinkie, Somerset did not even bother to try. And behind Edinburgh stood Stirling, which was undergoing similar modernisation; it implacably guarded Stirling Bridge, the key to northern Scotland. One consequence of French entry into Scotland's military establishment in 1547–8 was the erection in the 1550s of yet more modern *trace italienne* fortresses: as Leith, Langholm, Dunbar and Eyemouth were built or re-edified, so Scotland became even less conquerable.[47]

Finally, nothing indicates that the Scottish political elite – beyond a few malcontents – were seriously prepared to agree to union with England during the 1540s. The Governor, the Earl of Arran, did make some unionist utterances in 1543, but these were never genuine, being made merely to gain time to consolidate his own political position. Thereafter, he did everything in his power to enhance his hold on any future succession to the throne, and the very last thing he was prepared to accept was an English marriage for the infant Queen Mary. Instead, when attacked by Somerset, he brought in the French (thus weakening his own chance of power) rather than agree to submit to England.[48]

The Scots simply could not be forced into Anglo-Scottish union by acts of war. The only way that it could come about was through dynastic union.[49] But that would not simply happen of its own accord. Nor, as the Rough Wooings demonstrate, would the Scots permit a Scottish queen or princess simply to be married to an English king. Thus the 'dynastic initiative', so to speak, had to come from Scotland: for Anglo-Scottish union to take place, it was necessary for a Scottish monarch to inherit the English throne. Throughout their adult lives, Mary Queen of Scots and her son James VI both hoped to do so – and James's hopes eventually came true.[50]

46 Bush, *Protector Somerset*, pp. 32–34; F.C. Dietz, *English Public Finance* (London, 1920), i, pp. 144–58, 178–87.
47 M.H. Merriman, 'The Forts of Eyemouth: Anvils of British Union?', *Scottish Historical Review* (lxvii, 1988), pp. 142–55; see esp. p. 151, note 5.
48 See J. Wormald, *Mary Queen of Scots: A Study in Failure* (London, 1988), pp. 43–57.
49 A union of states negotiated by treaty, as happened in 1707, was not an option open to the English and Scottish statesmen of the Tudor century.
50 It should never be forgotten that during most of his life, James V had stood but a few heartbeats away from the English throne.

But to appreciate the 'dynastic accident' of 1603, we must first consider the two countries' succession systems. Since the late eleventh century, succession to the Scottish Crown had (with the major exception of Robert Bruce's seizure of the throne in the crisis of the early fourteenth century) followed the normal rules of primogeniture, with males being preferred but females not being excluded. Admittedly the Scots did remove certain monarchs – James I in 1437, James III in 1488, and Mary in 1567 – but in each case these were replaced by their sons and heirs. Thus, the concept of Scotland's fabled unbroken hereditary line of native-born rulers was established and maintained.[51]

In England, on the other hand, while the same rules of primogeniture applied in theory, in practice during the medieval and early-modern periods they seem only to have operated when the political elite was prepared to let them do so. In a sense, the English political community 'elected' its kings: if not formally, like the Germans, Danes, Poles, Bohemians and Hungarians, in practice the effect was much the same. From 1066 to 1603, fewer than half the instances of English royal succession were simple, with heirs by primogeniture uncomplicatedly succeeding their predecessors. It is not too fanciful to think in terms of the 'Elections' of 1066, 1089, 1100, 1135, 1154, 1199, 1216, 1327, 1399, 1461, 1470, 1471, 1483 and of course 1485; and, for a later period, there were those of 1649, 1660, 1688 and 1714.

In the sixteenth century, Henry VIII may have been returned unopposed in 1509, but he did so on the back of his father's successful 'election campaign' at Bosworth – when the then king, Richard III, was deserted by most of the politically conscious classes, or the 'electorate'. Edward VI likewise seems to have had an easy ride in 1547, but his place in the line of succession had to be guaranteed by an Act of Parliament, his father's will had much to do with what form his government took, and we must remember those two lost days between the death of Henry VIII and the proclamation of his son's kingship.[52] As for Mary Tudor, her accession is the clearest example of a decision being made by the country. Northumberland had an alternative regime in being, Jane Grey as Queen, and 10,000 men to defend it. Mary, however, had more adherents; in effect, she 'won the election'. The point is, it was a contest, and Lady Jane might have won as William III did in 1688, had the wind blown differently in the summer of 1553.[53]

Elizabeth's succession is the most remarkable of all. Her right to succeed depended not on heredity but on a statute of 1544, not to mention *two* Reformations of the English Church. In France, she would have been found a pension, a husband, and a place at court as 'mademoiselle la bâtarde de Bolyn'. In Scotland, something similar would have happened – what did James V's eldest bastard, James Stewart, Earl of Moray, the leader of the faction which removed Queen Mary, think of Elizabeth's

51 But it did take some time for the process to settle down; see G. Donaldson, 'Reflections on the Royal Succession', *Scotland's History: Approaches and Reflections*, ed. James Kirk (Edinburgh, 1995), pp. 103–117.

52 W.K. Jordan, *Edward the Young King*, pp. 51–69.

53 For what Jordan called 'The assault on the succession', see his *Edward VI: The Threshold of Power* (London, 1970), pp. 494–535 and D. Loades, *Mary Tudor* (London, 1989), pp. 171–83.

STEWART

TUDOR

THE ENGLISH ROYAL SUCCESSION

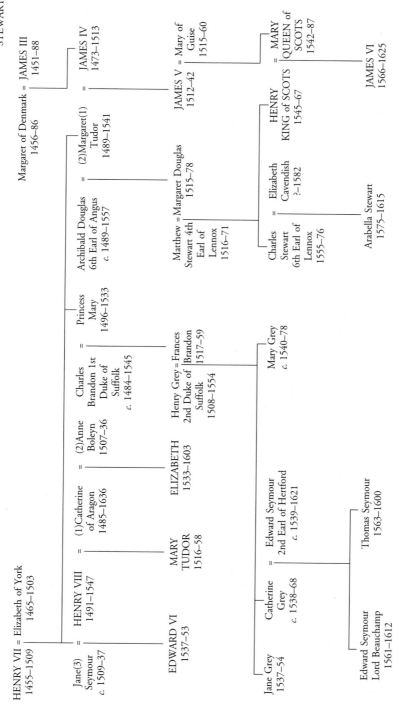

Fig. 1.3. This standard textbook dynastic family tree shows how regal union did come to pass by 1603. But it is too firm: James's accession was indeed 'an accident'. For a while in the 1530s, both Mary Tudor and her sister Elizabeth were officially illegitimate and debarred from any place in the English succession. That changed with the Act of 1544, but one must never forget how fragile was the whole issue of succession.

succession? But in neither Scotland nor France could Elizabeth have come to the throne. And, it could be argued that what actually happened in 1558 was a straightforward *coup d'état*.[54]

Consider, moreover, the extraordinary Bond of Association of 1584. This covenant, drafted by Cecil and Walsingham after the assassination of William of Orange, pledged its adherents to defend the queen with all their power. Thousands signed it. But the English ruling elite also pledged that anyone who tried to kill Elizabeth would be summarily slain – *as would the person in whose name the attempt was made*. So, if Elizabeth were assassinated, Mary Queen of Scots was automatically to be murdered, regardless of her complicity. As John Guy has put it, the Association was 'a political vigilante group' determined to execute 'lynch law'.[55] Even James VI could have been dispatched because of it. That is not normal hereditary dynasticism in operation.

THE MAKING OF GREAT BRITAIN

This study covers a remarkably short period in history.[56] This last attempt by England forcibly to encompass an independent, sovereign Scotland is one of the key episodes in the making of the Kingdom of Great Britain. I believe that certain historical occurrences – like Great Britain – result from men acting in certain ways; that both political and military victories have consequences and that, without them, history would have been different. Without the Rough Wooings there would have been no French troops stationed in Scotland in 1559; without them the Lords of the Congregation would not have been able to gain English support and thereby bring about a Scottish Reformation. Without a Protestant Scotland, James VI could not have succeeded to the English throne in 1603. Without 1603, 1707 would not have happened.

The history of the 'long sixteenth century'[57] is very much one of families and

---

54 The 1536 act which declared her illegitimate was never specifically repealed; parliament in 1559 simply declared her 'lawfully descended and come of the blood royal': M. Levine, *The Early Elizabethan Succession Question, 1558–68* (Stamford, 1966); and see his *Tudor Dynastic Problems* (London, 1973), pp. 66–74. Wallace MacCaffrey, *Elizabeth I* (London, 1993), pp. 12–29. Further, it could be argued that James's accession in 1603 was illegal: see G. Donaldson, 'Succession', p. 177 where he speaks of it being 'in defiance of statute'.

55 J. Guy, *Tudor England* (London, 1990), pp. 331–3, pp. 344–5, 350; J.E. Neale, *Elizabeth and her Parliaments 1584–1601* (London, 1957), pp. 17–18, 33–7, 50–3; MacCaffrey, *Elizabeth I*, pp. 343–54.

56 As ever, the dates can be 'bandied with' (A.J.P. Taylor's phrase) in various ways. Technically the Rough Wooing, defined as English armed aggression to achieve the terms of the Treaty of Greenwich, did not commence until November 1543. But men at the time spoke of 'this Eight Years War' and merged into one the three conflicts commencing with Henry VIII's war with James V in 1542. There was also an Habsburg-Imperial (read the Low Countries under Charles V) dimension to the English attempt to overawe the Scots, but that became virtually an independent bilateral war in September 1544 when Charles V made peace with France. Although the Anglo-French Treaty of Boulogne, 24 March 1550, ended Anglo-Scottish hostilities, disputes such as that over the Debatable Lands were not resolved until the Treaty of Norham in July 1552.

57 Professor Michael Lynch is but the most recent scholar so to see it (M. Lynch, *A History of Scotland* (1992; second edition, 1997)).

inheritance: dynasticism. In this context, the marriage of James IV of Scotland to Henry VIII's elder sister Margaret in 1503 is of singular importance. Anglo-Scottish history prior to 1503 is largely without relevance to the eventual making of union. Only the fruitful marriage of Margaret Tudor and the failure of Henry VIII's children to beget heirs whilst the Scottish line continued to do so matter. But dynasticism does not explain everything. James VI's accession to the throne of Elizabeth was as much a piece of politics as it was a dynastic act. Elizabeth did not name him (as Anne would George I) and no Act of Parliament declared what the succession would be (as the 1544 Act had established Elizabeth's). Since his coming of age in 1585, James was identifiably Protestant (though in 1593 that arch-Puritan Peter Wentworth would rant against his succession) and the most obvious successor. Moreover, the king's entire policy down to 1603 was directed at gaining the English crown and he played his hand with fine skill and with a clear eye to the English political nation.

If James had been provocatively alien, I contend that the English ruling class would have blocked his accession, or aborted it. The Tudors were not totally extinct (nor indeed were the Yorkists). That is why the proposed marriage of Arabella Stuart (also descended from Margaret Tudor as well as a granddaughter of the earl of Lennox who sired Henry Lord Darnley) to Henry IV of France was vetoed by Elizabeth and why her eventual one to William Seymour (a great-great-grandson of Henry VIII's sister Mary) in 1610 was so dangerous that she spent the last five years of her life in the Tower of London. England was not France or Scotland where (with the exception of Robert the Bruce) rules of dynastic succession were strictly adhered to. The English picked and chose as fate, luck and their own inclinations directed.[58] So, too, in 1603.

They would not have picked James had he not been a Protestant and he would not have been a Protestant had it not been for the Rough Wooings. Twenty years ago, received opinion in the British historical cultures (and within Reformation Studies as a discipline) would probably have deprecated such an assertion. Then the Reformation was seen as an inexorable flood which engulfed any dike which might be erected. Noble hesitancy, monarchical resistance, Catholic internal reform: all were overwhelmed. Current opinion is not so clear. The Scottish Reformation was an extraordinarily close-run thing (as indeed was the English). Reform from within might have saved the Catholic church had it been given more time.

There are two aspects of this story for which the Rough Wooings are vitally important. Firstly, the war was a grievous assault on the Catholic church in Scotland. Not only were many of its physical workplaces (parish kirks, monasteries, priories) wrecked by English forces, but the practical intimidation of armies and raiding parties forced many clerics to flee their charges, never to return. Many were slain, as at Pinkie. The financial costs of the war bore more heavily upon the established

---

58 As my colleague Alexander Grant pointed out to me, there are numerous other examples of strict male primogeniture not being adhered to, starting as early as the succession of William Rufus (William II) in 1087. See my 'The High Road from Scotland: British Unionism in the 16th Century', in *Uniting the Kingdoms*, ed. A. Grant and K. Stringer (1995).

church than on any other sector of society, the burgess, perhaps, excepted. But the mercantile elements could recoup; ecclesiastics were forced to liquidate their capital, leaving the kirk further enfeebled. Secondly, without the Rough Wooings, Mary would not have gone to France. It is impossible to conceive of the Scottish reformation happening as and when it did, without those preconditions. They, in turn, were the direct result of English actions in the 1540s. In that deeply ironic sense, Henry VIII and Somerset did achieve their broad policy aims of 1543 and 1547: the creation of a Scotland pro-English, Protestant and then united to England. But they did so despite themselves and certainly did not deserve to do so.[59]

The Rough Wooings had even wider ramifications. If Henry and Somerset had not wasted the treasure of the English crown so prodigiously on warfare in the 1540s (£3,500,000 in less than five years of actual combat, one quarter of which was spent in Scotland), perhaps the monarchy of Charles I might have been better funded and able to ignore parliament. Without Scottish resistance to Charles I, would the Long Parliament ever have been called in the first place? Many historians have endorsed both Henry and Somerset's efforts due to the curious belief that the large nation-state was an inevitable (and beneficial) historical development. 'Countries' absorb localities (Wales), duchies (Brittany), kingdoms (Aragon) to make 'discrete' nations; they in turn are proof against further consolidation into empires: Austria-Hungry, Yugoslavia, the USSR. Henry VIII's 'godly union' becomes a 'right aim' and, by that token, Henry II of France's attempt to incorporate Scotland into a pan-Channel empire was a 'wrong' aim. In the age of the European Community such certitude may well be misplaced.

To understand the Rough Wooings, we need to set a number of scenes, and it can be instructive to start at the end of the story and shift from Mary's cradle at Linlithgow in December 1542 to a parade at Rouen in the early autumn of 1550.

59 I find the concept 'in the long term' fatuous.

CHAPTER TWO

The Anvil of the Centuries

Rouen was one of the great metropolitan centres of Valois France: capital of Normandy, an archiepiscopal seat dominated by one of the most splendid cathedrals of Europe, a vital and prosperous seaport. It contained both a *Quartier Écossais* and a *rue des Écossais*. Scots were no strangers to France. In addition to merchants, they served as soldiers, studied at the universities, visited shrines and took part in diplomatic missions. At the coronation of Catherine d'Medici at Paris, David Paniter, Bishop Elect of Ross, had processed in the train of the King on 18 June 1549 as ambassador to France. The Scots Guard and one of their *Capitaines*, Lorges de Montgomery (who had fought in Scotland in 1545), also marched in the Queen's entrée on the 19th. *Mademoiselle la bastarde d'Escosse* (a daughter of the duke of Albany who had been regent for James V, 1515–24) followed him. Mary of Guise's son, the duke of Longueville, marched alongside his uncle, Francis, then Duke of Aumale.

These numbers were swollen considerably in September 1550. Coming overland from St. Germain en Laye was their queen, Mary, aged seven and a half, and arriving by sea from Scotland was her mother, whose father Claude duc de Guise, had died earlier that year. This was the second major maritime voyage of her life, the first being in 1538 when *Le Petit Michel* and two other galleys had borne her swiftly (and expensively) to the land of James V, her second husband, and the start of her adventure on the European political stage. Her six-ship convoy also conveyed numerous Scots who had just concluded The Rough Wooings in which many had served valiantly.

When Mary of Guise disembarked at Dieppe, so did a large and heterogeneous band of Scottish nobles and lesser folk. Some, such as the Earl of Huntly (who had escaped from England in a daring exploit at Christmas 1548), had proved consistently valiant in the war. Some had been ambivalent, such as William Keith, the Earl Marischal. Although he never actively aided the English, he had been a leading Protestant from the early 1540s and had done much to protect and encourage reformers in the Mearns, Perth and Dundee.[1] Others such as the Earl of Glencairn, the Earl of Cassillis, Lord Maxwell and Sir George Douglas of Pittendriech (brother to the famous Archibald Earl of Angus) had at times notoriously worked for the English. Glencairn's sons were also there; their father had been one of the most

---

1 F.D. Bardgett, *Scotland Reformed: The Reformation in Angus and the Mearns* (Edinburgh, 1989), 15, 26–7, 32–36, 50–53.

LA Royne douairiere d'Escosse

FILLE VNIQVE DE HAVLT ET puissant Prince Monseigneur le Duc de GVYSE, nagueres deffunct desirant saluer le ROY. Et voir sa treschere & bien amée fille seulle heritiere du Royaulme d'Escosse, Affidée à Monseigneur le DAVLPHIN de FRANCE & monseigneur le duc de Longueuille son filz qu'elle n'auoit de long temps veuz, passant la Mer, auec bône & forte escorse de Nauires & Galleres de FRANCE, vint en icelle ville de Rouen, le Ieudy XXV. iour d'icelluy moys & an, faire sô entrée, Ou icelle Dame fut honorablemét & grande magnificence receue de tous les estatz de la ville de Rouen, car tel estoit le bô plaisir du Roy. L'ordre & suptuosité de laquelle entrée ie laisse à cause de briefuete. Et d'abondât le samedy XXVII. iour dudict moys de Septébre. Le ROY & la ROYNE accópaignez des Princes & Princesses de son sâg des seigneurs & dames de sa court, a la suyte d'aultres princes & seigneurs embassadeurs d'estrâges natiôs en grâd nôbre pour paruenir a l'effect de son intétion, qui estoit de faire son entrée en sa ville, ville entre les siennes autant obeissâte q voluntaire à rendre son debuoir, Metropolitaine toutesfoys de son fructueux pays de Normédie, Arriua au Prieuré de Bônes nouuelles, aux faulx bourgs qui font oultre le pont de Rouen. Auquel lieu icelle ROYNE douairiere d'Escosse, accópaignée de plusieurs princes & grans seigneurs d'Escosse, alla pour faire la reueréce au ROY & à la ROYNE, qui d'vne benignité non moindre que d'alaigresse la receurent.

The Queen Dowager of Scotland, only daughter of the high and puissant Prince, Monseigneur the Duke of Guise, recently deceased, desiring to salute the King, and to see her very dear and greatly loved daughter, the only heir to the Kingdom of Scotland, betrothed to Monseigneur the Dauphin of France, and also her half-brother, Monseigneur the Duke of Longueville, the Queen Dowager's son, neither of whom she had seen for a long time, crossed the sea with a good and strong escort of ships and galleys of France and came to this city of Rouen, on Thursday, the 25th [of September 1550] to make her entry. There this Lady was received honourably and with great magnificence by all the estates of the city of Rouen, because such was the good pleasure of the King. The order and sumptuousness of this entry I pass over, for the sake of brevity [etc.].

Fig. 2.1.   That we know so much about the Rouen celebrations is due to the printing press on the one hand and monarchs' need to 'sell themselves' on the other. In 1550, doubtless with crown subsidy, there was published and widely circulated throughout Europe a remarkable quarto booklet recounting every stage in the process. Its greatest impact, however, came through the collection of highly sophisticated and expertly executed engravings of the fête. Colour 'portraits' of the triumph were also made. This figure is merely part of the text, but an important part, for it describes the arrival of Mary of Guise-Lorraine from Scotland, and indeed the occasion was mounted partly in her honour.

prominent nobles captured at Solway Moss in November 1542. Many were out-spokenly Protestant. Their inclusion on this visit was clearly an attempt to impress upon them the power, glory and rewards of France.[2]

In addition, there was a broad band of loyal moderates, men such as Lord Hume and Lord Fleming. Hume had lost his father from a wound received at Pinkie and his castle had been held by the English for over a year. Fleming, too, had proved a patriot and mindful of the wellbeing of his sovereign. Others such as the earls of Sutherland and Menteith had done their duty, as had many lesser folk, such as Sir James Hamilton of Crawfordjohn and William Lauder of Haltoun, or the host of minor ecclesiastics such as the prior of Pittenweem, the vicar of Rossy and the parson of Calder.

Two people call for especial notice. Robert Stewart was still Bishop Elect of Caithness: that is to say, he received the see's revenues and effectively administered it, but no Papal Bull had arrived allowing him to conduct full religious services. He and his brother Matthew, earl of Lennox, had fled their native country to England in 1544, despairing of any advancement in a Scotland dominated by their rival James Hamilton, earl of Arran.[3] Lennox was quickly married to Margaret Douglas, niece of Henry VIII, and from that union had flowed Henry Lord Darnley. Robert wearied of his life in England and in June 1546 returned home, bought off by Arran through the return of his bishopric and other holdings.[4] Another voyager was the nineteen-year-old Lord James Stewart, commendator of the priory of St. Andrews. He, like Darnley, was part Tudor, for his father was James V. During the war, Edward VI had written personally to him and sent him a brooch as a present from 'a kinsman in blood'. Although a bastard, he was a man with a potent future.

Scots abroad usually aroused comment and the English ambassador, the waspish Sir John Mason, sneered that they were 'brawling, chiding and fighting . . . as though they had lately come from some new Conquest'.[5] Indeed they had. Against both Henry VIII and Somerset, the Scots as ever had been victorious.

But the cost had been prodigious in terms of lives, money and material possessions.[6] For example, the once thriving port of Dundee, Scotland's second most important entrepôt before 1542, now lay in ruins. The town's new clock, installed in the burgh kirk with such fanfare in 1546, had been ripped out two years later and taken as war-booty to England. Services in that very building now had to be held under canvas, since it lacked a roof. Haddington in East Lothian had fared somewhat better, but its economy never recovered as fully as Dundee's and its kirk would not be comprehensively repaired until 1978. The war had also been expensive in terms of politics. Somerset's war had seemed sufficiently close to success in 1547 for

---

2 Donaldson (*All the Queen's Men*, 160) termed the exercise 'brain washing'.

3 See my 'Home thoughts from Abroad: Scottish Exiles in the mid-16th Century', in *Social and Political Identities in Western History* (1994).

4 In the fullness of time, he would find himself one of the conforming bishops of the Calvinist church of Scotland. G. Donaldson, *Reformed by Bishops* (Edinburgh, 1987), 53–67.

5 Much of the detail of the Scots' arrival comes from Mason's report in *CSP For., 1547–53*, 56–58.

6 This will be discussed in the final chapter.

the Scottish government to feel it had to surrender the next year its most powerful domestic and international bargaining counter: the betrothal of the Queen. It was the only means by which it could attain sufficient French military assistance to expel the English. Nonetheless, it was a price worth paying, for their Governor had not only bested Henry VIII, but had played no small part in the humiliation of the Duke of Somerset. England now lay impotent and Scots, naturally, were in Rouen to brawl, to celebrate their great triumph, and to watch a victory parade.

Before we attend that marchpast, we should comment on the presence at Rouen of the most important Scot of them all: the Queen, Mary Stewart. Of course, had she dropped dead at any point, they would have found another person to be monarch. But as long as she stayed alive, she was the most important person in the entire Scottish community, be she a mere seven years of age, as she was in October 1550, or eighteen, as when she disembarked at Leith in August 1561. Mary's first five years as Queen of one of the monarchies of Europe had been sedate, domestic, and nearly sedentary. Moved from her birthplace, Linlithgow, in July 1543, outside of a possible trip to Dunblane in May 1544 when the English were firing Edinburgh, she had dwelt, living the life of a growing child, at Stirling Castle under the care of her mother and four Scottish nobles whose probity and patriotism were unquestioned.

However, when the flames of the second Rough Wooing lapped as deep into the country as Lamington in Clydesdale, Saltoun in East Lothian and Dundee in Angus, her life became pretty lively and peripatetic. Given over to the total charge of her mother by a critical meeting of the Scottish Convention in February 1548, she was moved on the 22nd first to Dumbarton to be kept secure in the massive castle there. With her had gone her famous playmates, the four Maries, and two [half] brothers. When a remarkably well-equipped French fleet (containing Henry II's own royal galley) arrived in the Clyde in July, she embarked. Contrary winds delayed the fleet's departure until 7 August when it swept out to sea and transported her magnificently to Roscoff in Brittany on the 13th and thence to Morlaix.

From there she travelled to her grandmother's arms and from Joinville into the household of the children of Henry II and his Queen, Catherine d'Medici. She quickly became close to her future husband, the Dauphin Francis, and his eldest sister, Elizabeth. Mary played with all the children. But in particular, she was made much of by Henry II who called her his 'very own daughter: ma fille propre', and she was celebrated as 'the most perfect child' in all of France. She came not knowing a word of French (indeed she did not learn to speak and write English until 1568 and then did so appallingly), but rapidly was fluent. Thus she and her future father-in-law conversed daily when he was with his brood. They were, after all, the only anointed monarchs around: everyone else had either married into royalty or only had a possible future as a monarch. With the future Francis II, it was said she treated him like a best friend, but also like a mistress. With the King, she was said to converse with the maturity of a twenty-five year mature woman. It had been, thus, a full and active two years in France before she delightedly saw her mother leave ship at the quay. The two of them then watched a spectacular two-day celebration, probably the single most expensive thing Henry II did in 1550.

a   b

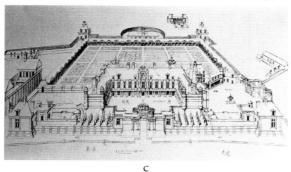

c

Fig. 2.2   (a,b,c). Once Mary moved into the royal household of France, she was
certainly not sedentary any more, for Catherine (and the King) moved
constantly about the kingdom (often, quite independently), as did all French
monarchs as a matter of course: Paris, Fountainebleau, Chambord, Blois,
Amboise, Orléans (where Francis would die), Tours, Lyon. But there were
two chateaux which more than any others were 'home' for this child: St.
Germain en Laye and Anet, both of which can be seen here. The one (a)
and (b), situated on a massive outcrop of cliff over the Seine, had been
begun in 1536, but then became Henry II's favourite residence. It was the
palace on which he imposed his cultural stamp – and a remarkably radical
architectural statement – rather than accepting what his father had done.
Anet (c), on the other hand, was the favourite residence of the king's
celebrated mistress, Diane de Poitiers, who often had the children to stay
and play and who was particularly fond of Mary. By one of those ironies of
history, it was to St. Germain that James VII and II and James VIII and III
lived as guests of Louis XIV before he was forced to expel James VIII and
his son.

THE ROUEN FÊTE

There is in fact a better phrase, now common amongst art historians: 'l'entrée royale'
or the 'solemn entry'. This is described by Sir Roy Strong as

> an essential part of the liturgy of secular apotheosis. It was a vehicle whereby
> public acclamation could be focused on the person of the ruler as the incarnation
> of the State, the anointed of God, the pater patriae, the defender of Holy
> Church and of Religion, the heir of mighty ancestors, the source of all

beneficence whose rule showers peace, plenty and justice on his subjects, and causes the arts to flourish. During the sixteenth century, therefore, the solemn entry became an important part of the cult of the monarch as hero.[7]

Just such a royal entrée was elaborated for Henry II at Rouen in October 1550.[8] As well as the King, it celebrated his whole family, who were present, along with most of the court and the foreign ambassadors. Henry's family in 1550 also included 'ma fille propre', the little queen of Scots.[9]

Fig. 2.3.   Rebuilding Roman triumphal arches became something of a favourite pastime for French kings and emperors: Louis XIV was especially fond of them; so was Napoleon, as any tourist to Paris knows from the Arc de Triomphe de l'Etoile, at the head of the Champs-Elysées. This passion for arches came directly from sixteenth-century Italy and Europeans' fascination with the Roman Empire. This arch at Rouen, called 'The Age of Gold', was only the second such Renaissance edifice to be built in France. The 'Age d'Or' also became a potent lodestone for policy: kings were ordained by God to return Christian life to the time when prosperity and largesse were the norm, and poets sang of it throughout the century.

7 R. Strong, *Art and Power: Renaissance Festivals 1450–1650* (1973, 1984): I have employed the 1995 edition, 46. The earlier version of his work, *Splendour at Court* (1973) can still be used to good effect with its profusion of colour reproductions.
8 The principal source for much that follows is the article by Margaret B. McGowan, 'Forms and themes in Henri II's entry into Rouen', *Renaissance Drama*, I, 199–252. See also her facsimile reproduction of the contemporary publication on the event.
9 Fraser, *Mary Queen of Scots*, 77.

At the centre were the king and his wife, Catherine d'Medici, whom he had married in 1534. For the first ten years their union had been barren; both his father and his father's mistress had mocked them in public. Henry's mistress, Diane de Poitiers, had thus insisted that he should spend more time in his wife's bed so as to establish his royal race.[10] This sage advice worked. Following the birth of Francis, now the Dauphin (and Duke of Brittany), in 1544, ten children would be born. Twins (Victoire and Jeanne in 1556) died shortly after birth, but most lived: Elizabeth in 1546, then her sister Claude the next year, followed by Louis in 1549 and Charles in 1550. Increasingly their names reflected the Imperial pretensions of Henry. Charles's second name was Maximilian; Henry, born in 1551, was given those of Edward (one of his godmothers was Mary of Guise)[11] and Alexander. Margaret, born in 1553, who outlived all of her legitimate family, was followed in 1555 by another Francis, additionally christened Hercules.

This lively household was full of playmates for the young queen of Scots and she clearly was very happy there, becoming particularly close to Elizabeth, future queen to Philip II of Spain, and to her betrothed, Francis. Just recovered from a serious bout of illness, she now saw her mother again. The reunion of Mary the mother and Mary the child (probably on September 25) must have been a delightful occasion, for between them there existed a profound bond of love and warmth.

Henry II had begun his reign with a series of fêtes and entrées:[12] the Rouen celebration was to be the grandest, for it conjoined the twin triumphs of his reconquest of Boulogne and the salvation of Scotland. Entrées were not mere extravagances; they were rooted in political reality. As Henry said in 1547, 'rien qui meintienne un Peuple en obéissance et fidelité, que la vue de son souverain Prince, et naturel Seigneur [nothing maintains a people in their obedience and faithfulness so much as the sight of their sovereign and natural master]'. He was also imitating, and rivalling, the ceremonies of Charles V, such as his coronation as Emperor at Bologna in 1530 or the series of *joyeuses entrées* mounted for his son Philip in the Low Countries in 1548.[13]

Henry was engaged in 'image projection' as 'le plus digne roi' France had seen in two centuries. Various aspects were stressed. Some were mandatory: the king as guardian of the church, as heir to a throne reaching back to Troy and, through his fifty-seven predecessors, as provider of justice and peace. Others were more immediate and personal. One salient ingredient was the popularisation and familiarisation of the new king's *impresa* (his badge or emblem) and his motto:

DONEC TOTUM IMPLEAT ORBEM [THUS GIRDS HE THE GLOBE]

10 R. Marshall, *Mary of Guise*, 132
11 I. Clouas, *Henri II* (Paris, 1985), 303.
12 His progress through his dominions in 1547–48 was replete with them (at Meulan, Nantes, Vernon, Louviers, Troyes) from his coronation at Rheims in April 1547 to his celebrated tour through Piedmont. Then there was his fabulously extravagant entrée into Lyons on 23 September 1548, followed by one into Paris in June 1549, just before which his queen was also led to her coronation.
13 Strong, *Art and Power*, 78–85, 87–91.

The *impresa* of Francis I had been the fabulous salamander (chosen by Francis's ever-intrusive mother), whose mythical properties included a magical ability to endure, consume and extinguish fire. His motto, 'Notrisco al buono et extinguo el reo', linked nicely with the salamander image: 'I nourish myself on good and extinguish evil'. Henry's *impresa* was quite different, deliberately so: the crescent moon (perhaps chosen, as is often alleged, in honour of Diane de Poitiers). It rapidly appeared on the garments of his servants, his banners and his coins. The moon, a symbol mysterious, far distant, yet seen by all, each night circumscribed the world and played its glow over all beneath it. As the Trojan hero Hector proclaimed, Henry II would triumph over death because his blood sprang from a triple crescent, 'qui remplira le monde [which will fill up all the world]'. His motto, *Donec totum impleat orbem*, further emphasised the point. As one reporter of the great Rouen triumph versified:

> Puisque Henry second du nom a pris
> Pour sa devise un celeste croissant
> Sans reins choisir de terrestre pourpris
> C'est bien raison quen bon heur soit croissant
> Tant que tout lorbe ait soubx sa main compris.

> Since Henry the second of that name has taken
> For his device a celestial crescent
> Not choosing anything from the terrestrial realm
> It is natural that he should grow in good fortune
> So much that he will grasp all the world in his hand.[14]

Other ingredients reinforced this theme. In his progress into the town, the king was confronted by two children carrying a coiled snake eating its own tail (a symbol of eternity). Beneath them was inscribed a motto, *Hoc est tempus*: Here is time. The message, although missed by some,[15] was clear enough: Francis had gained lasting renown through his great achievements; Henry should emulate him. But then, dramatically, the tableau became a grand globe, about which lapped the salamander's flames and, even more gripping, out of this orb, which suddenly burst, sprang a Pegasus, the symbol of 'bonne renomme': great fame. As the winged horse pranced, a Triton above it trumpeted and the globe re-emerged, then was transformed into a life image of Henry II himself. 'Donec totum impleat orbem' indeed.

Such a fête was thus a total assault on the senses, involving almost all of the arts: set design, choreography, sculpture, music, poetry, costume and acting. It also employed engineering; the marvel such as the altering globe was but one of the many ingenious mechanical devices whose deliberate intent was to startle. There were exotica: six elephants constructed for the process, with flaming vases mounted on their backs, were accounted 'aprochans si pres du naturel . . . que ceulx mesme qui avoient vue en Affrique de vivantz, les eussent iugez a les veoir elephans non faintz [were so close to nature . . . that those who had seen live ones in Africa pronounced these as 'hardly fantastical'].

14 McGowan, 'Entry', 225.
15 Mason got it quite backwards (*CSP For., 1547–53*, 61).

a

b

Fig. 2.4   (a & b). The elephants (a) are everywhere that day: impressive symbols of power (Hannibal's exploits were the stuff of school textbooks), might and the exotic: Africa. Many historians thought they were real, having been brought up from Paris where they normally lived in the King's famous menagerie of wild and fabulous beasts. But on closer examination it is clear they were 'floats' made out of quite perishable papier maché, mounted on wheels and propelled by men walking inside the 'char'. Some such 'floats', however, had extraordinarily long lives. That of Charles V's great ship of state (b) hauled by sea-elephants was first used for his funeral in 1558, but was still being employed in 1608 in Brussels.

A Renaissance entrée was more than just a parade. Rouen's fell into three main elements for the king on 1 October 1550 (his queen went through a repeat version the next day). The first was something of a marchpast of the notables and functionaries of Rouen before a viewing pavilion erected for the king and his court on the west side of the Seine: members of the guilds, artisans and professions, such as the twenty-four *mesureurs de Grain*, the fifty tax collectors, the fifty crossbowmen, the two mace bearers; then the members of the law. Almost two thousand soldiers of the town were followed by eighteen Roman gladiators, battling amongst themselves with two-handled swords. Stark naked Brazilian natives also appeared.

Then came the second phase, celebrations of the king's recent successes and statements of Henry's aspirations for the future. There were many tableaux here, such as the procession of his fifty-seven ancestors or the chariot (Fig. 2.5) on which townsfolk represented the king in splendid armour, surrounded by palm leaves, his head wreathed like a Roman victor's. Seated at his feet were his four children: Francis, Elizabeth, Claude and then two-year-old Louis. A splendid unicorn-drawn chariot had arrayed on it: a beauteous Vesta – holding a model of the church in her lap – surrounded by 'Royal Majesty', 'Virtue Victorious', 'Reverence' and 'Fear'. They sang of the king's glory, his creation of peace and the upholding of order.

Fig. 2.5.   Happy fortune shows the King surrounded by his family (all of the characters in this fetching tableau were played by actors: citizens of Rouen dressed up for the parade). The king sits robed on a most royal throne as a winged muse holds above his head a closed imperial crown. In his hands are the royal sceptre and a very large palm leaf: symbols of power and peace. Note the crescent moons which adorn both the horses and the king's robe.

The most splendid float was the first. Drawn by four winged horses, it was decorated with friezes of battles, heaped with spoils of war, draped with two dead warriors. At the front was a seated skeleton, but chaining mortality at the other end was the goddess of *Renommée*: Fame, her wings spread and a trumpet to her mouth, who would ever conquer death. Then marched bands of soldiers.

Fig. 2.6. 'Renommée.' Death sits at the feet of an angel, but his fearsome skeleton is bound at the neck. At the other end of that chain sits Fame, who will ensure that the king's great glories during his lifetime will ever be remembered so that his name shall be imperishable despite his eventual end on this earth. Note how much Francis I still lived at Rouen in 1550, over three years after his mortal demise.

Fig. 2.7   One of the greatest *coups d'oeil* of Rouen was the island of naked natives, men and women, totally nude. Everyone at the time remarked upon this display. Again, these were merely local citizens paid to parade about in the all-together and painted pink as well. They demonstrated Henry's outreach to the mysteries and haunting visions of the New World, especially Brazil, to which the French had claims. Henry's moon would one day shine down upon it as a possession of France, and thus would he hold the whole globe in his hand, for beyond Brazil lay even more exciting prospects.

Le Triumphe de la Riuiere.

Fig. 2.8.   Waterfights were a popular ingredient for such triumphs and took place in
the Seine at Paris and in the Rhône at Lyon. Henry II was always fond of
them and became inordinately excited whenever they appeared before his
gaze. Often the ships were loaded with barrels of gunpowder which, when
ignited, made for a spectacular display of fireworks. Unfortunately, this
acting could be hazardous and at Rouen one of the ships prematurely blew
up and most of its crew drowned. A new ship had to be employed the next
day for Queen Catherine.

When Henry left his viewing stand to participate in the third element, his
personal progress into the city, he and his train headed towards the great bridge
over the Seine, on which had been constructed two notable triumphal arches. Just
before the bridge, he paused to view with heightened excitement an elaborate
tableau vivant. On a specially constructed meadow, abundant with trees, shrubs
and wooden native huts and stocked with wildlife, were two tribes of Brazilian
women and men 'sans aucunement couvrir la partie que nature commande [their
private parts uncovered]'. They lazed, hunted, cooked or traded with a French
garrison. A sudden, vicious battle with clubs and arrows then ensued between the
tribes, the victorious Toupinaboux burning to the ground the huts of their
enemies, the Tabagerres.

Then as the king moved through a series of prophetic and instructive scenes on the
bridge, he was arrested by a lively sea-battle or *naumachie* between a French vessel
and a Portuguese one (a reference to the competing claims over parts of Brazil
between the two countries) in which the French triumphed. The actual ship sank
and lives were lost. The king then officially entered the town and participated in a
magnificent *Te Deum* in the cathedral before finally retiring to dine. The next day

almost all of the pageant was repeated for the Queen, with yet another vessel sunk and sailors actually drowned. A fortnight later, the court left the city and proceeded to yet more entrées: Dieppe, Fécamp, Harfleur and Le Havre

This example of art and power in the sixteenth century had significance far beyond that of a mere court masque, revel or *divertissement* (although these delights are not without their importance). As Richard Morison, an English propagandist at the court of Henry VIII, put it almost two decades earlier: 'into the common people things sooner enter by the eyes than the ears, remembering more better that they see than that they hear'.[16] Thus there was great emphasis in these entries on the visual (although music, poetry and inscriptions cannot be ignored).

'VOILA DONDY: SEE HERE DUNDEE'

Let us return to the second phase of the triumph, the marchpast of the soldiers in this Caesarean cavalcade lifted straight from antiquity.[17] The first bands displayed symbols of the king's recapture of Boulogne: models of the forts taken in the campaign of August-September 1549, spoils, victorious laurels, the six elephants, bands of the actual combatants in these great adventurous successes. Chained captives (some naked) were followed by Flora's nymphs strewing flowers before the arrival of the chariot already mentioned which bore a representation of the king. In his hands he grasped the royal sceptre and a palm of peace, while above him sat winged Fortune holding an Imperial crown over his head. About him were clustered his progeny, save Francis[18] who proclaimed from horseback his own homage to his father (Fig. 2.9).

A central element in the occasion was the King's reconquest of Boulogne, which everywhere was elaborated, for thus had Henry reunited a lost part of the kingdom (as he would do with Calais a mere eight years later). Before the audience were paraded, just like Ceasar after his conquest of Gaul, bound captives: prisoners taken in the recent war. Then came another band of Roman-dressed gladiators. On poles they displayed ingeniously crafted models of the various forts which Henry II's army had conquered from the English in August 1549.

16 See Chapter 11 on propaganda.
17 Note that on the king's galley in the great fight with the Portuguese was a banner stating, 'Là pouvoit le triumphe plus grand/que les Romains n'ont fait en leur vivant/Au Scipion l'Affricain, Le vainqueur' [There occurred a triumph even greater than the Romans accomplished during their epoch for Scipio the African Conqueror].
18 Portrayed, as was the king, by a citizen of the town.
19 During the eighteenth century Lille in particular, a city of frontier war, critical to France's security, was massively studied and rendered in bas-relief. See *Plans en Relief: Villes Fortes des Anciens Pays-Bas Français au XVIIIe S.* (Musée des Beaux-Arts de Lille, 1989). I wish to record my thanks to Jonathan Bailey, who took my Special Subject in 1974–75, for giving me a copy of this work.

Fig. 2.9.   Francis the Dauphin, the king's eldest son, was six years of age in 1550, but
            already he was frequently displayed in public religious processions, state
            banquets, court masques and royal progresses. All monarchs did this sort of
            thing with their heirs (James I paraded his son Henry wherever he went
            until the young man died in 1612). There was, thus, a cult not only of
            present kings, but of future kings. Francis was also trumpeted as the future
            husband of an already anointed and crowned Queen, Mary Stewart. Thus,
            he was a future King of Scotland, as well as of France.

A large group, also dressed in Roman costume, carried banners portraying places
defended or captured by French arms in Scotland (Fig. 2.11):[20]

> Voila Dondy, Edimpton, Portugray
> Où Termes prist & Essé le degré
> Pour devenir chevalier de ton ordre
> Tout le pays ou avoit ose mordre
> Sur l'escossois la nation angloise
> Est recouvert par la force francoise
> Apres avoir endure mainctz travaulx
> Sire, voyez ceste Ysle de chevaulx

20 See figure for an illustration of these banners; the poem is rendered by McGowan at pp.
    213–14.

A premiere bande des fix portoit
fur demies picques femées de fleursde lys d'or, les fortz reduitz
au petit pied, q̃ le Roy noftre fouuerain feigneur auoit nagueres
pris au pays de Boullónoys, par fa magnanime vertu & puiffáce,
lefquelz fortz eftoiët fi bien fillez par art de maffonnerie approch͠ie de la chofe

Fig. 2.10. Making and displaying wooden models of 'places forts' was widely done in the sixteenth century: the French ambassador in London had one with him of Turin, and Somerset showed the ambassador his 'dessaing en plateforme' of Haddington. By the seventeenth century, such models became vast and minutely accurate, as can be seen today in the museum at l'Arsenal, for Louis XIV had them done for almost every town or citadel he possessed. They could be 'working models' actually used in the devising of a siege, but often they were trophies to be displayed and admired.

> Voyez aussy le fort chasteau de Fargues
> O quants asssaulx, escarmouches & cargues
> Voila aussy le fort pres de Donglas
> Et plus deca ou est assis ce bourg
> Est le chasteau conquis de Rossebourg
>
> Here are Dundee, Haddington, Broughty Craig
> Where Termes, together with Essé, received the honour
> Of becoming knights of your order.
> All the country where the English nation

Had dared to occupy Scottish territory
Has been recovered by French force
After enduring many labours
Sire, see this Island of Inchkeith,
See also the fortified castle of Fast
O how many assaults, skirmishes and charges
Here also is the fort next to Dunglass
And on this side of where that burgh is situated
Is the captured castle of Roxburgh.

The inelegant translation of this verse does the poetry – in this case – no disservice. But its point is clear enough. France has added fame and renown by her labours far to the north and thus, as at Boulogne and at sea, inflicted exemplary vengeance on England, 'si odeux nation'.

Fig. 2.11. Models for the Scottish conquests of Henry's armies clearly were not to hand, so banners were employed instead, painted on canvas and carried just like modern trade union banners or as used at protest marches.

But these great victories in Scotland were not ends in themselves. They fitted into the king's reign-plan here being so elaborately projected. On 27 September, Henry took time[21] to address a long letter to the Porte, the Sultan at Constantinople. This remarkable missive, a grandiloquent propagandist celebration of the victories of his reign, was intended to impress upon the Grand Turk the prowess and might of France. It rested on one assumption, that the Porte had few independent sources of knowledge about Western Europe on which to rely beyond what his most important ally there told him. It makes extraordinary reading:

> J'ai pacifié le Royaume d'Ecosse que ie tiens et possede avec tel commandement
> et obedissance que i'ai en France, ausquel deux Royaumes, j'en ai joint et uny un
> autre, qui est Angleterre, dont par une perpetuelle union, alliance et
> confederation, ie puis disposer, comme de moy-mesme, du Roy de ses subjects,
> et de ses facultez; de sorte que les dits trois Royaumes ensemble se peuvent
> maintenant estimer une mesme monarchie.

> I have pacified the kingdom of Scotland, which I hold and possess with such
> authority and obedience as I do in France, to which two kingdoms I am joining
> another, namely England, which by a perpetual union, alliance and confederation
> is now under my control, as if it were my own self: the King, his subjects and
> his powers; in such a manner that the said three Kingdoms together can now be
> regarded as one and the same monarchy.[22]

Hence the triple crescents which adorned everything and everybody in the spectacle: Henry thrice king: of France, of Scotland and of England. In the verse version Orpheus, Neptune and Apollo, supported by other deities (Juno, Venus, Pallas and Jupiter whose hatred of the Trojans has been appeased by the late king's patronage of the arts), urged Henry to new triumphs. Neptune especially assured him an easy passage up the Thames; Apollo joins in to entreat 'faire je veulx de deux une courounne [I would you would make of the two one crown]' of England and France, so that 'Henry second' may become 'Henry le neufiesme [Henry IX]'.[23]

Thus the message of this sumptuous triumph was arguably threefold: Henry stands as present King of France. He has inherited the virtues and models of his predecessors, with all their obligations (largesse, justice, religion, peace, prosperity). Secondly, he stands as present saviour of Scotland and immediate controller of England. But beyond this, a third tier beckons: a future encompassing not just exotic Brazil, but all the world. Many of the themes first outlined so clearly in Rouen in 1550 would be repeated over the years, particularly in 1558 when the

---

21 As he was entertained at a convent just outside the town while awaiting the delayed
completion of the preparations for his entrée.

22 *Lettres et memoires d'estate des roys, princes, ambassadeurs et d'autres ministres sous les
regnes de François Premier, Henri II et François II par G. riber*, ed. M. Belot (Paris 1666),
ii, 288–90.

23 *Oeuvres poétiques de Joachim du Bellay*, ed. H. Chamard (Paris, 1912), iii, 77.

Fig. 2.12. Triumphs contained almost all of the arts of the theatre from costume design to mechanics to ballet. They were also intensely musical, as this song sheet demonstrates.

prolific Estienne Perlin nicely captured the mood of French self-esteem with this piece of bombast:

> O bien heureulx te doibs tu estimer Royaulme d'Escosse d'estre favorées, nourry, entretenu, comme l'enfant sus la mamelle du trespuissant & magnanime Roy de France, le plus grand seigneur de tout le monde & monarque futur de toute la machine ronde: car sans luy tu feusses en cendre mis, & le pays gaste, & ruine par les Angloys, du tout de Dieu mauldicts.

> How happy ought you to esteem yourself, kingdom of Scotland, to be favoured, fed and maintained like an infant, on the breast of the most magnanimous King of France, the greatest lord in the whole world, and the future monarch of that round machine. For without him you would have been laid in ashes, your country wasted and ruined by the English, utterly accursed of God.[24]

But Scotland was not just to be suckled; the whole thrust of Henry's policy since late 1547 had been to make her 'une mesme monarchie' with France. How he came to be in such an extraordinary position is the object of this book, but we still need to set the scene more fully by exploring just how pervasive was the Imperial ideology of the sixteenth century.

THE BRUT AND THE USES OF HISTORY

History has its uses, and timing is everything: let us explore these two aphorisms. The beginning of the sixteenth century saw in both of the British cultures a significant widening of opinion concerning the origin myths of each country. The advent of printing had led to a considerable flowering of histories and chronicles being either published for the first time and thus made widely available to an increasingly voracious literate public, or being written for that audience.[25] The nub of English origin myths lay in the immensely popular stories contained in Geoffrey of Monmouth's *History of the Kings of Britain*.[26] It was there, in what has become known as the Galfridian legend, that readers, scholars and kings alike found this evocative prophecy:[27]

> The goddess stood before him and spoke these words to him: 'Brutus (great-grandson of Aeneas), beyond the setting of the sun, past the realms of Gaul, there lies an island in the sea, once occupied by giants. Now it is empty and ready for your folk. Down the years this will prove an abode suited to you and your people: and for your descendants it will become a second Troy. A race of kings will be born there from your stock and the round table of the whole earth will be subject to them'.

24 E. Perlin, *Description des royaulmes d'Angleterre et d'Ecosse* (1558), fo. 30v.
25 The literature on this topic of literature is vast. An easy introduction is still H.S. Bennett, *English Books and Readers, 1457 to 1557* (Cambridge, 1952), *passim.*
26 A topic nicely surveyed by Alan MacColl, 'King Arthur and the Making of an English Britain', *History Today* (March 1999), 7–13.
27 Geoffrey of Monmouth, *The History of the Kings of Britain*, trans. Lewis Thorpe (Penguin, 1966).

Geoffrey, a Welsh cleric (*floruit* 1137), did not create this legend, so much as record and systematise the incoherent, many-faceted and profuse swirl of stories, epics and prophecies which he collected and rendered in a particularly engaging form. Manuscripts of his *History* circulated widely and by the end of the thirteenth century were firmly entrenched in the minds of royal historiographers, witness Edward I's extensive use of Galfridian material in his 1301 justifications to the Pope for his actions in Scotland.[28]

Geoffrey did not just spin tales of how Brutus came to Britain and gave the island its name, or how his eldest son held authority over the two youngest. His net spread much wider. Two key elements were the Roman Emperor Constantine the Great (280–337)[29] and King Arthur (*floruit* sixth century). Constantine was important because he was born in Britain of a British mother and went forth to establish the Christian Roman Empire. He also wore a closed crown Imperial. Arthur not only was directly descended from the great Constantine but also hewed out a vast empire including Scotland, France, Italy and Germany as well as the land of his birth. About his Round Table, a replica of which Henry VIII had constructed,[30] gathered great heroes of European chivalry, and for his heirs Merlin foretold great and wondrous deeds. Britain should be remade whole into an empire which, in time, would gird the world.[31]

Meanwhile, in Scotland, a remarkably similar origins-mythology process had been taking place. Again, the story is complex. But the core of the message was well developed by the time of the Declaration of Arbroath of 1320, when a post-Bannockburn political elite thundered forth on the making of a nation. To the Pope, the 'whole community of the realm of Scotland' declared:

> Most holy Father and Lord, we know and gather from ancient acts and records, that in every famous nation this of Scotland hath been celebrated with many praises: This nation having come from Scythia the greater, through the Tuscan Sea and the Hercules Pillars, and having for many ages taken its residence in Spain in the midst of a most fierce people, could never be brought to subjection by any people, how barbarous soever: And having removed from those parts, above 1,200 years after the coming of the Israelites out of Egypt, did by many victories and much toil obtain these parts in the West which they still possess, having expelled the Britons and entirely rooted out the Picts, notwithstanding of the frequent assaults and invasions they met with from the Norwegians, Danes, and English: And these parts and possessions they have always retained free from all manner of servitude and subjection, as ancient histories do witness.

28 See also the famous 1307 Parliament at Carlisle when English claims to Scotland were further elaborated.

29 Interestingly, there were supposedly three King Constantines of Scotland: 863–79, 900–43, and 995–97.

30 The cult of chivalry made a remarkable resurgence in the sixteenth century, witness Charles V's revival of the Order of the Golden Fleece and Francis I's Order of St. Michel.

31 There are a number of relevant studies: see D. Rees, *Son of Prophecy* (1985), 12–13; T.D. Kendrick, *British Antiquity* (1950), 35.

This kingdom hath been governed by an uninterrupted succession of 113 kings, all of our own native and royal stock, without the intervening of any stranger.[32]

Chroniclers later beavered feverishly to elaborate and authenticate these tales. The most important work was the *Chronica Gentis Scotorum* begun by John of Fordun and continued by abbot Walter Bower. Fordun laboured around 1363–85 and manuscripts of his history were read widely. It was he who invented the figure Gathelus, son of Neolus, a prince of Athens who originated in Scythia. Forced into exile, Gathelus found fame and success as general to the Pharaoh, so much so that he gained the hand of his daughter, Scota. He, his wife, and a mixed band of Greeks and Egyptians then fled at the time of Moses' epic Red Sea departure, and wandered before settling in Spain and Ireland, with the great black Stone of Destiny: wherever it was placed, there the Scots would rule.

From Ireland, Fergus I went to Scotland, bringing with him not only the potent rock but also the royal banner of his people, the red lion rampant. Fergus's heirs had an uneasy time of it for the first 500 years, warring intermittently with the Picts and then the Romans. For a while the tribe had to flee to Norway. But ultimately, a King Fergus II, the 45th in a continuous line of kings, re-established the Scots in Albion. Then, triumphantly, Kenneth, the son of a King Alpin who had been slain by the Picts, completely destroyed that tribe and firmly established the race and kingdom of the descendants of Scota.[33]

There were a number of powerfully compelling elements in this great and complicated epic. One was that the Scots had left Egypt under the leadership of their own Moses. They too were a chosen people. Their heritage mixed the Trojan-defeating Greeks (Brutus was a Trojan) and the mighty, mysterious Egyptians. Secondly, their king-line was native, continuous and unbroken since their first settlement in Scotland. Finally the Scots had always emerged victorious in their wars and had never submitted to slavery. Fordun's confident pride of race even went so far as to remind his audience that since William I of England was a bastard, that crown rightfully belonged to the heirs of St. Margaret. Was she not a granddaughter of King Edmund II (1015–16)? Was not her brother Edgar Atheling recognised as king immediately after Harold's death at Hastings? Had not Edward I foolishly stolen the Stone of Destiny and taken it to London? Surely victorious Scots would be there soon.

Fordun's epic was enormously expanded by Abbot Bower by 1449. His *Scotichronicon* became the standard history for late medieval Scotland and firmly entrenched the Gathelus origin myth. Several decades earlier, Andrew of Wyntoun, prior of St. Serf, had prepared a *Treatise* which regarded most of the current origin myths with scepticism. He certainly did some myth-destroying calculations when

---

32 The literature on the Declaration of Arbroath is staggering. The text is easiest found in *A Source Book of Scottish History*, i, 131–35.
33 These origin myths are traced in Nicolson, *Scotland: The Later Middle Ages*.

subjecting the famous king-list to a mathematical scrutiny. But his reservations had little impact.

An anonymous work, completed most likely around 1460, but revised and still current during the reign of James V, was entitled 'Heir is assignyt the Cause quhy oure natioun was callyt fyrst the Scots'. It finely tuned Fordun's story. Descendants of Scota set foot in their land a good 300 years before the fall of Troy, thus long before Brutus set out on his wanderings:[34]

> saw yat we may say this day in verite that thar
> is na nacioun so fre fra the begynnynge of the
> warld na has standyn sa lang tyme in fredome as
> has the scottis for thae hafe beyne xviii hunder
> zeris and mare unconquest and neuir was subieckit
> to na natioun or king to this day bot euir undir our
> awin blude be rycht line discendand fra our first king
> ferguse befor said to him that now rignis quhome god kepe.

'IUST CAUSES AND CONSIDERACIONS'

Henry VIII, unsurprisingly, believed the Brut story. When Polydore Vergil in 1513, on the completion of the manuscript of his *History of England*, first requested of Henry VIII the honour of dedicating it to him, the king robustly refused.[35] Throughout Vergil was profoundly sceptical of the whole tangle of Galfridian myths. Since Dover was clearly visible from France, it struck him as improbable that Brutus was the first to behold the island of Britain. Moreover, neither Livy nor Dionysius made any reference to a Brutus, descended of Aeneas. He went along with Constantine's British origin, but refuted any Arthurian link with the great Christian Emperor and, worse, deprecated Arthur's accomplishments. When two decades later Vergil was prepared to acknowledge Constantine's contribution as the founder of Britain's greatness and, in particular, celebrated him as the creator of the Imperial closed crown of England, Henry altered his stance, accepted dedication and the work saw publication in 1534.

But the sudden and obvious utility of Vergil to the Reformation did not prevent a gaggle of English historians from assaulting his otherwise stiffly retained reservations. Perhaps most significantly, Edmund Hall, whose influential *Historie of the Unione of the Red Rose and the White* was published in 1548, firmly rejected Vergil's rational approach and resolutely reaffirmed the Brutus myth, Constantine, Arthur and Merlin. John Price in 1553 denounced him roundly for his foreign, Italianate, Romanish corruption;[36] John Leland went for him directly in his *Condrus sine et*

---

34 See also Roger Mason, 'Scotching the Brut: Politics, History and National Myth in Sixteenth-Century Britain', in *England and Scotland 1286–1815*, ed. R.A. Mason (Edinburgh, 1987), 60–84, at 63–66.

35 See *DNB* and D. Hay's introduction to *The anglica historia of Polydore Vergil, 1485–1537* (Camden Society, 3rd ser. (lxxiv, 1950).

36 John Price, *Historiae Brytannicae defensio* (1573 edition).

defensio callofrdi Monumentensis contra Poldorum Vergiium.[37] Brutus had taken the island whole and empty; Constantine was the linear predecessor of Arthur, as was Cadwalader to Henry VII, and Scotland belonged to England. So in 1542, the start of our story, the traditionalists held sway, as can be seen by this scene-setting rehearsal of the Tudor line in Henry VIII's *A Declaration conteynyng the iust causes and consideracions of this presente warre with the Scottes (1542):*[38]

> Concernynge histories, whiche be called witnesses of tymes, the lyght of trueth, and the lyfe of memorye, and fynally the convenient way and meane, whereby thinges of antiquitie may be brought to mens knowledge, they shewe as playnly this matier as could be wyshed or required, with such a consent of writers, as coulde not agree vppon an untruth . . . According wherevnto we rede how Brutus, of whom the realme than callyd Brytayn toke fyrst that name (being before that tyme inhabited with gyaunts, people without order or civilitie), had thre sonnes, Locrine, Albanact, and Camber, and determinyng to haue the whole Isle within the Ocean sea to be gouerned by them thre, appoynted Albanact to rule that nowe is called Scotland, Camber the parties of Wales, and Locrine that nowe is called Englande: vnto whom as being the elder sonne, the other two brothers shuld do homage, recognisinge and knowleagyng hym as theyr superior. Nowe consider if Brutus conquered all this Ilande, as the hystorye sayeth he dyd, and then in his owne tyme made this order of superioritie as of afore: Howe can there be a title diuised of a more playn begynninge, a more iuste begynninge, and more conuenient begynninge for the order of this Ilande, at that tyme specially when the people were rude?

On the other hand, one must not forget that the Scots, too, had their sceptics, their Vergils. In 1521, the eminent theologian, John Major (or Mair), a scholar with a considerable European reputation, published in Paris his great *Historia Maioris Brittanniae tam Angliae.*[39] Major not only argued that the two kingdoms should come together into a Greater Britain, but that both origin myths were untenable. Instead, he was emphatic that 'all men born in Britain are Britons'.[40]

The response was immediate (within the context of sixteenth-century debates): the publication in 1527 (in Paris) of Hector Boece's resounding *Scotorun Historiae a Prima Gentis.* Boece, first Principal at Scotland's new University of Aberdeen (1494) and a considerable scholar himself, developed in an epic history of almost Milton-esque grandeur a resplendent portrayal of Scotland forged on the anvil of the

---

37 And see his *Assertio inclytissimi Arturji Regis Britanniae* (1544), *STC* (2nd ed.), no. 15440. An English edition came out in 1582 (*STC,* no 15441 styling the hero as 'the most noble, valiant, and ernoumed Prince Arthure, King of great Brittaine'. Leyland accepted fully that Arthur was buried at Glastonbury. In Cumbria, they say he was buried at Arthuret Church, the site of the Battle of Solway Moss.

38 *The Declaration,* ed. Murray, 192–206, at 198–99.

39 See Scottish History Society edition.

40 R.A. Mason, 'Kingship, Nobility and Anglo-Scottish Union: John Mair's *History of Greater Britain* (1521)', in his *Kingship and the Commonweal: Political Thought in Renaissance and Reformation Scotland* (East Linton, 1998), 36–77.

centuries. Fordun's master work was improved by an extensive fleshing out of the story. Therein he wove a resplendent version of Scots' triumphs over Picts, Romans, Danes and English alike. Their love of independence was celebrated and enriched by heroes drawn from the powerful images of John Barbour's *The Brus* and Blind Hary's *Wallace*.

This was strong stuff indeed, as can be seen by the fact that James V instituted two royal commissions to effect its translation into Scots,[41] and when the King went to France to claim as his bride the daughter of Francis I, he took a copy with him to present to his future father-in-law, and a French translation was prepared by James Bellenden, then in Paris, for the court and especially for Madeleine, future queen of Scotland.[42] Just how important these alternative versions of the making of the kingdoms were at the time can be seen if we briefly rehearse the stories of three minor Scots who will figure later in this work: John Elder, a cleric from the Highlands, James Henrisoun, an Edinburgh merchant, and William Lamb, rector of Conveth in Fife and a Senator of the College of Justice.

Elder fled from Perth in 1544 because he was known to be a Protestant.[43] Once in London, he prepared for Henry VIII a map of Scotland (one of the first of which we have knowledge), a brief commentary on the geography of his country and a long covering tract in which he violently assaulted the 'fals, flatteringe and jugglinge boxes' of the Romanish clergy, who 'have drunkyne the Frence kynges wynes and taisitide of his cwps' and who 'intendeth to drounde all Scotland in bloude'. He implored the king to effect the marriage of Mary and Edward and wished for Henry the strength and fortitude of Hercules, the manhood and chivalry of Hector and the subtlety and wit of Achilles. Elder then turned quite effortlessly to the origins debate then raging:

> Scotland a part of your Highnes empyre of England, bifor the incummynge of Albanactus, Brutus secound sonne, was inhabitede, as we reide in auncient Yrische storeis, with gyauntes and wylde people . . . But after the incummynge of Albanactus, he reducynge theame to ordour and civilitie, they changed the forsaid name, Eyryn veagg (little Ireland), and called theame Albonyghe, that is to say, Scottische men, be drywyne from Albanactus, our first governour and kynge.

Elder confronted head-on the alternative Gathelus story which was invented, he asserted, by the 'papistical curside spiritualitie':

> They drywithe Scotland and theame selfes, from a certane lady, namede Scota, which (as they alledge) come out of Egipte, a maraculous hote cuntreh, to

41 *Stewart Style 1513–1542*, ed. J.H. Williams (East Linton, 1996), 181–82, 189–90, 216, 232, 292, 295.

42 A.H. Miller, 'Scotland Described for Queen Magdelene', *Scottish Historical Review*, i (London, 1904), 27–38.

43 For all that follows here, see my 'Home Thoughts from Abroad: National Consciousness and Scottish Exiles in the Mid-Sixteenth Century', in *Social and Political Identities in Western History*, ed. C. Bjorn, A. Grant and K. Stringer (Copenhagen, 1994), 90–117 at 93–96.

recreatt hir self emonges theame in the colde ayre of Scotland, which they can not afferme be no probable auncient author.

James Henrisoun fled his native land also in 1544 and likewise offered his services to the English. When Somerset came to power in 1547 he emerged as the chief propagandist for union.[44] Extraordinarily widely read, Henrisoun pasted together a remarkably trenchant, if somewhat diffuse, argument assaulting the myth of Gathelus and getting timing right for the arrival of the Scots in Scotland. He attacked Boece by name on several occasions:

> the fayned alligacions of the contrary part, which convey you from Pharao, the tyraunt of Egipt. And as it is to conjecture, if their willes might take place, thei would bryng you under the servitude of Egypte again.[45]

Portugal ('Port of Gathelus' to Boece) was not known as Lusitania until 1000 years after the supposed arrival of Scota's husband. The only possible time for the Moses-expelling Pharaoh he calculated to be the year of creation 2400, but for a Gathelus, son of a Tyrant of Athens, the date had to be around 3643:

> This beinge true, here were a very unfitted mariage between these twoo personnes, the Bride beinge elder[46] then the Bridegrome, by 1240 yeres. But some wiseman will saye, that folke lived long in those daies, yet can thei not denye, but she was to olde a mayde for so yonge a bachelar, whereby I can worse beleve, that they had any children, she beinge of suche yeares. So that to make this mariage frame, either Gathelos was elder than his father, or she was yonger than her brother by a thousande yeares at the leaste. And syns the tyme of abraham, men by course of nature have not commonlie lyved much above a 100 yeares.

Henrisoun's propaganda will figure prominently later in this study,[47] but for the moment he serves as a vibrant example that myths mattered in the national consciousness of the sixteenth century.

Another Scot to become embroiled in the origins of the kingdoms was William Lamb, who settled down at his leisure during 1548–50 to refute the English claims concerning Brutus's first settlement and subsequent Scottish homages.[48] Lamb's work on the homages – the main, and indeed quite powerful, thrust of his argument – will be discussed later. As to the origins myths, although he devoted scant time to the history behind Henry's 'new-forgit superiorite', he felt they were serious enough to be worthy of attack, if in a roundabout fashion:

44 See my 'James Henrisoun' article in Mason, ed., *Scotland and England* for his career, 85–93.
45 Also see my 'Home thoughts from Abroad' for his time with Elder in London, 99–102.
46 In the printed version, it came out as 'yonger', thus spoiling the joke, somewhat. *The Declaration*, ed. Murray, 222–23, but the original book must be consulted at page E iiii.
47 Chapter 11 on the propaganda war.
48 See the introduction by R.J. Lyall, *William Lamb: Ane Resonyng of ane Scottis and Inglis merchand betuix Rowand and Lionis* (Aberdeen, 1985), x–xix.

It man be said that Brutus monarchie and his thre sonnis is als uncertane except as the origin of all uthir nationis except alanerlie the origin of Isralite peopill be provitioun of God, and also of Inglis origin, quharof the authoris maner is weill knawin to all thame that redis the Inglis historijs.

Lamb was anxious to discredit as best he could the contention that 'Britane was in Brutus and his thre sonnis tyme eftir the Dilugit'. England, he snorted, seemed to think that it had right title to France as well. Well, why stop there: 'Asia, Europia and Aphrica is unit to your kyng be homage and fealtie' since they 'ar continewall in land without separatioun of the sey'. Why not claim them all? From this fancy, he turned with a rhetorical relish redolent of any Oxford Union debate:

Nichtbour, can ony man in Ingland, beand nocht blind in witt, mynd and body (as, alace, ye be now), say that Scotland is or was evir a part of Ingland mair nor France be part of Spanze?[49]

But scholars, lawyers and propagandists were not the only ones drawn into the debate. It was the stuff of ordinary historical awareness. Here is a bond of manrent, drawn up in 1545 between the earl of Arran and Hugh, master of Eglinton:

vnderstanding . . . that our auld Innemy the King of Ingland is movit vpoun the ardent desire that the said king hes consauit to haue oure souerane lady the quenis grace in mariage to his sone Edward prince of Ingland, aganis all law of God and halikirk, and thar throu to mak this realme and liegis tharof thrallis to him and his successouris kingis of Ingland, howbeit the samyn hes bene ane fre realme and pepill sen the begynnyng, broukand the auld name of Scotland the liberteis and thai avne lawis quhilkis thai can nocht failze to tyne gif thai cum vnder the subiection of the said King of Ingland and his successouris . . . and because sen the first king that euir broukit this realme thare wes neuir strangear that rang or had domination tharof bot the kingis of ane blude that hes heddertillis roung be just richt of successioun. Thairfor we willing to haif this realme standing at the auld blude, liberte and lawis of the samin, and to be rewlit be ane prince borne of the realme self declaris for our part that our said souerane lady sall nocht be mareit bot vpoun ane prince borne of the realme self.[50]

These examples illustrate how widely spread and believed were the various origin myths. They were, in a sense, the stuff of history and they were important in the 1540s because Scottish independence was again a matter of debate after James V's death and the succession of Mary Queen of Scots at the age of one week.

BUIKHOWSE AND REGISTER HOUS

So far, we have explored one side of the mentality of sixteenth-century Britons: their addiction to myths and fables, and to literary debate. Sixteenth-century people were

49 Lamb, *Ane Resonyng*.
50 HMC, Hamilton Papers, i, 34.

intensely litigious and they resorted to their various courts of law almost instinctively.[51] This was particularly so over contracts and land tenure. For example, Scottish bonds of manrent were agreements to perform a mutually accepted set of actions: good lordship for good service. They were signed, witnessed (very important) and the parties affixed their seals thereunto. A duplicate copy was held by each party to be presented to a court of law should any variance, dispute or non-performance occur. Men kept these contracts in secure chests or registered them in notarial copybooks: they were important, as were deeds, pardons and royal grants of any sort. Monarchs were no different to ordinary landowners and the security of their contracts was vital. Thus we see almost everywhere the creation of royal archives. During 1538–42, the Scots built a new 'register hous' in Edinburgh Castle itself (arguably the first purpose-built archive in Europe).[52] Charles V in the same period was gathering his papers together into a castle, at Simancas. He had been often embarrassed by their dispersal and some were deliberately torched during the revolt of 1520. When Henry VIII's 'great matter' blew up in 1528, Ferdinand's copy of the papal bull allowing Katherine of Aragon to marry her dead husband's brother could not be found for six months.

A treaty between two monarchs was (and is) in reality little more than a contract between individuals, the terms of which were often known only to the participants. But to whom could an aggrieved regal party turn in the sixteenth century? The Pope no longer wielded effective arbitration. No international court existed. Kings thus all too often turned to war, to the literate public and to the bar of history. In 1532, the English parliament enacted a piece of legislation, the modern short title for which is 'An Act in Restraint of Appeals'. Contained within this actually quite modest measure lay a justification of momentous proportions. It asserted that England was an empire. The rulers thereof were thus accountable to no other earthly power, potentate or authority, but to God alone.

Dr. G.D. Nicholson's work[53] on the uses of historical argument in the Henrician reformation illustrates how the crown's propagandists searched out any proofs which could be found in 'dyvers sundrie olde authentike histories and cronicles', or in what the Act also charmingly termed 'olde authentike storyes', for England's Imperial status. Now there were many sources on which sixteenth-century research students could and did draw for their material. One very interesting compendium was housed in the City of London's Guildhall, felicitously called its 'buikhowse'.

Therein was contained a great manuscript collection compiled at the end of the thirteenth century and then copied for the City's use, known as the *liber custumarum*, which had been consulted as recently as Henry V's time. It would appear that, at

---

51 Thus have I argued for decades in lectures to undergraduates that what they have to do to understand the sixteenth century is to turn *The Times* inside out and first read: the court circular, then the law reports and book reviews. They should only read the parliamentary reports last.

52 Obviously it was not a 'public' record 'office', although the Crown did allow scholars to consult its contents; certainly Henrisoun seems to have seen some documents therein.

53 Much of what follows comes from G.D. Nicholson, 'The nature and function of historical argument in the Henrician Reformation'. Unpublished dissertation for D.Phil. (Cambridge, 1977).

some point in 1532, one of Henry's propagandists went to the City, borrowed the book (the return of which took decades) and then cursored through it hunting for proofs of English Imperial status. Within the book was a section entitled 'Collectanea satis copiosa'. Within it was found a large collection headed 'Regum Angliae in Walliam Hiberniam et Scotiam dicto'.

All of these discoveries served to reinforce a current belief that King Arthur's seal had declared him to be 'Patricius Arcturus Britanniae, Galliae, Germanie, Dacie Imperator'. When the Duke of Norfolk confidently trotted this out for the Imperial ambassador, Eustace Chapuys twitted the gullible Norfolk that it was a shame that no mention was made of 'Asie'.[54] Henry's Imperial inheritance was reinforced by the fact, apparently proved in the copies of 'Regum Angliae in . . . Scotiam', that the kings of England had always enjoyed authority over not just one, but a number of realms, 'sine dubio pertinent corne et dignitati regni Britannie'. As embodied in the Act in Restraint of Appeals, England was an empire because it had and continued to receive tribute from the kings of Scotland, but in return owed none; it had possessed a 'libera prae emenentia' over all of Britain since antiquity.

Thus were the 'auncient stories' of Brutus conjoined to the historical facts of numerous homages by kings of Scotland to kings of England, the originals of which were tenaciously guarded, and full records of which were kept not only by the royal chancery, but with copies also held in various other repositories: York, Durham, Canterbury and the 'buikhowse' of the City of London. But all English renderings of Anglo-Scottish relations deliberately failed to mention either the Quitclaim of Canterbury, 1189 (when Richard I sold to William the Lion of Scotland the overlordship which William had previously surrendered to Henry II) or the Treaty of Edinburgh-Northampton, 1328 (another contract), whereby Edward II and Edward III recognised Robert the Bruce as sovereign of his realm and annulled all instruments 'touching the subjection of the people or of the land of Scotland to the King of England'. Perhaps English 'experts' on Scotland honestly did not know about the pacts of either 1189 or 1328; bishop Tunstall of Durham certainly seemed genuinely astounded in 1548 to run across a copy of the 1328 treaty.[55]

HENRY KING OF SCOTS (1565–67)
AND WILLIAM DUC DE CHÂTELLERAULT (1864)

In 1565, Henry Lord Darnley married Mary Queen of Scots and thus became King of Scotland. His father, Matthew, 4th Earl of Lennox, had earlier been allowed back to the land of his birth and it was there that he died in 1571. Matthew Stewart, born in 1521, had first left Scotland in 1532 to live in France with his kinsmen. His father had been slain in a famous brawl at Linlithgow in 1527 and his family was concerned for his safety. He then returned in March 1543 as both a French citizen and the ambassador of Francis. In May 1544 it became clear through a series of bitter

---

54 See John Guy, 'The Tudor Theory of "Imperial" Kingship, *History Review* (xvii, 1993), 13 who recounts this interview.

55 In a book of homages compiled by the then Chancellor of England 'in henry vii dayes' (BL, MS Calig. B vii, fo. 336).

domestic and military battles that James Hamilton, 2nd Earl of Arran, his rival to be 'second person of the realm', had won. Lennox was forced to flee to England, where Henry VIII received him with heartiness and largesse. But there he was to languish, forfeit of all his lands, for over twenty years.[56]

There is little remarkable in such a story of exile. The Earl of Angus, Archibald Douglas, was banished in 1528 and went into exile the next year. He did not return to his lands, goods and the dramatic castle at Tantallon until 1543, after James V's death. Both men are classic examples of the 'exile phenomenon' which has always been with us in history and is with us today. Other notable sixteenth-century examples include Cardinal Reginald Pole (in Rome from 1534 until 1554), the duke of Bourbon (with Charles V from 1525 until his death in his cause in 1536), not to mention the 'White Rose' Yorkist pretender who had to flee Henry VIII's terror in 1514 and perished at Pavia in 1525.

In 1544, Lennox played what cards he had well and Henry VIII rewarded his defection with the hand of Margaret Douglas, Angus's daughter by Henry VIII's sister, Margaret, widow of James IV. Their son, Darnley, thus had a strong claim to the English crown in his own right, as well as Lennox's claim to that of Scotland. When his son married the queen on 29 July 1565, he had the satisfaction not only of his family attaining regality, but seeing Arran [now Châtelherault] exiled. After the assassination of Moray in 1570, Lennox found himself advanced by Queen Elizabeth I of England to become regent of the kingdom, a post which he at last attained in July, only to be slain in September 1571. Despite his abrupt end, the moral of Lennox's story is clear: wait. Never relinquish a claim.

Lennox must have been particularly pleased that his son's marriage to Queen Mary had been so strenuously opposed by the Hamiltons that the head of the family, his arch-enemy of a score of years, was in 1565 disgraced while his son went mad. James Hamilton then spent three years (largely in France) pleading to be restored to his Dukedom of Châtelherault. How Arran had become Duke of Châtelherault need not detain us here. The point is that he had been granted that title with lands to the value of 12,000 *livres tournois* (approximately £6000 Scots) which was enjoyed by his son James from 1549 until his defection to the Lords of the Congregation in 1559. The French crown of Mary and Francis, however, declared Hamilton forfeit of Châtelherault and in 1563 the lands (much depleted by the 3rd Earl's lavish expenditure) were granted to Diane de France, Henry II's daughter by Diane de Poitiers, who lived until 1617. Hamilton was given a 4000 francs pension and plate worth 1500 crowns by Charles IX.[57] But he never ceased to style himself Duke of Châtelherault. Indeed Hamilton's second son, John, was granted 1000 marks by James VI in 1598 in compensation for his family's loss 'be ressone of his assistance given to the removing of strangeris and foreneris furthe of our realme'. On 17 April 1599, he was created Marquis of Hamilton, a handsome advancement of which his father would have been proud.

---

56 See my 'Home thoughts from Abroad', 108–111 and entry for the *DNB* additional to the standard texts covering Darnley and his marriage to Mary.
57 HMC, Hamilton Papers, i, 49.

The Hamiltons, as so many families did, then fissured and regrouped. Their claims went in many directions, largely between the descendants of the John just mentioned and Claude, his fourth son. The one branch became dukes of Hamilton, the other dukes of Abercorn. The Abercorns rose especially under Charles II, but also William III; indeed James Earl of Abercorn was a Privy Councillor to Queen Anne, George I and George II.[58] During the seventeenth century, the claim to the French duchy remained part of the families' ragbag of pretensions and fantasies. In 1685, James Hamilton, son to William Earl of Selkirk, who was also a favourite of both Charles and James, had printed in Paris *Requeste et pièces pour milord conte d'Aran . . . touchant la restitution du duché de Chastellerault.* Nothing happened. Then, in 1696, William III decided to present Louis XIV with claims to 'any pretensions and franchise that the Scots had in France . . . that we may be restored to them when the general peace is made'.[59]

But again, nothing happened. However, during the prolonged negotiations for the Treaty of Utrecht between England and France in 1713, Louis XIV finally agreed in the 22nd article that the Earl of Abercorn, as the most direct heir of the second Earl of Arran, was entitled to be restored to the duchy. But the issue was dauntingly complex, with other Hamilton contenders involved. Indeed even Jonathan Swift became involved, as he put it, in 'mediating between the Hamilton family'.[60] The now gloriously restored Châtelherault dog kennels, just outside modern Hamilton, are also a vibrant part of this story.

Further printed justifications of the claims were published in Paris in 1713: *Titres et pièces justificatives des légitimes pretentions de la Maison de Hamilton sur le duché de Chastellerault and Requestes pour Milord comte de Selkirk touchant la restitution de Chastellerault.* But the sudden death of the two men specified in the treaty rendered Clause 22 void, doubtless to Louis' relief.

But still the claim was battled over. In the nineteenth century, Hamilton pretensions were not just to a French duchy. Alexander, 10th Duke of Hamilton and 7th Duke of Brandon (he succeeded to these titles in 1819; interestingly, he was MP for Lancaster in 1802 and had grown up in what is now the local golf clubhouse), harked back to the Hanoverian 'usurpation' and to his claims to the crown of Scotland. Duke Alexander was also enraptured with France, with grandeur – witness his stunning Palace at Hamilton – and with Napoleon.[61] His son William, quite addicted to the gaming table (he was forced to sell the family's vast estates in Lancashire in 1852 for £500,000), married the daughter of Stephanie de Beauharnais, Napoleon I's adopted daughter. When he succeeded as 11th Duke in 1852, he kept a close contact with his wife's third cousin, now Napoleon III.

Then on 13 January 1862, James Hamilton 2nd Marquis and later 1st Duke of Abercorn, had his entitlement to be styled Duke of Chatelherault accepted by the

58 See Bishop Gilbert Burnet, *The History of the Dukes of Hamilton.*
59 See HMC 21 (Supplement Hamilton Ms), 107, 110, 137.
60 Reference should also be had to HMC Hamilton Papers, i, 112–114 and *Maitland Miscellany*, iv (1847).
61 For each of these individuals, see relevant entry in *DNB*.

Sheriff of Chancery in Scotland in Edinburgh.[62] This was war, and William immediately contacted the most knowledgeable French archivist of the day on Scottish matters, the celebrated Jean Baptiste Théodore Alexandre Teulet, Conservateur at the Archives de l'Empire. Teulet quickly prepared *Memoire justicatif pour M. le duc d'Hamilton*, which was published in 1863. But William, in Paris to proceed with his claim, died there on 15 July that very year. The Abercorns counter-attacked with *Consultation pour marquis D'Abercorn contre le Duc D'Hamilton*, which did not come out until 1865.

Fig. 2.13. This rather modest piece of paper, a printed form with blank spaces which were then filled in, gave the Hamiltons what they had sought for almost four centuries: recognition of their entitlement to be styled Duc de Châtellerault, as it was now spelt. Alexander, the 10th Duke, had the title boldly chiseled above his casket which was placed in his famous mausoleum at Hamilton. The coffin has since been reburied because it was thought (wrongly) that the structure had become unsafe. The famous Châtelherault Dog Kennels, just down the A74 from where the Palace used to stand, is another such monument to the Hamilton fixation with their lost French grandeur. The town palace, in which James Hamilton, 3rd Earl of Arran, lived, 1548-59, is now the Bibliothèque Municipale.

62 G. Donaldson, *Sir William Fraser: The Man and his Work* (Edinburgh, 1985), 32.

However, in the meantime, letters of nobility were granted by Napoleon III to the 12th Duke of Hamilton on 4 July 1864 and confirmed by an Act of High Court of Session in Edinburgh in 1865.[63] Neither the chateau of Châtellerault (now the municipality's library) nor the lands actually passed into his hands, and by 1882 he had been forced to liquidate virtually all of his grandfather's priceless art collection.[64] Still today at Lennoxlove (to which the Hamiltons moved in 1947 after the nationalisation of their coal mines) can be seen Napoleon III's grant of the courtesy title of Duc de Châtellerault. And to this day Debretts still assigns the title to the Dukes of Hamilton, although the Abercorn claim is also mentioned. That, too, is illustrative of what dynasticism is all about: the fierce, seemingly absurd, clinging to an entitlement until, somehow or other, it might just be realised. In that sense, very little separated the Arran Hamiltons and the Lennox Stewarts in the sixteenth century, or afterwards. Kings, men and policy makers could not in 1542, of course, be aware of the lessons to be gained from keeping a close eye on Napoleon III's court register, but they did not need to. The model of Charles V was there for all to see.

'THE EXAMPILL OF BRYTANNY'

And the vord is heir that he gyffis tham [the earl of Argyll to lords in the Isles and to James McConnell in 1559] the persuasion that the France ar cumin in and sutin down in this realm to occupy it and to put furtht the inhabitantis tharoff, and siclik to occupy all uther menis rowmes pece and pece, and to put away the blud of the nobilitie: and makis the exampill of Brytanny.[65]

It was by all accounts a splendid ceremony, one of those public spectacles which the French monarchy did so well. The king's eldest son the dauphin Francis (his third child to survive) was now fourteen years of age (Note: the 'second age' of man) and had thus entered his majority. Two days previously he and his father had made a magnificent entrée into the city of Rennes; then on 14 August 1532, seated on the throne of the last Duke of Brittany – Francis II who had died in 1488 – he was crowned Duke Francis III. Richly garbed in blue velvet, the ducal coronet on his head, the young proprietor of the duchy was presented with the sword of state by the bishop of Rennes in an elaborate transaction whereby the Duchy of Brittany became definitively annexed to the crown of France. When Francis died two years later, his brother, Henry, now Dauphin, also became 'duc titulaire'; on his becoming king in 1547, his eldest son Francis assumed that title, amongst of course many others, such as Duke of Châtelherault.

Brittany's annexation by France in 1532 is a long story. Independent throughout the Middle Ages, it had been as autonomous and free as any of the Iberian provinces, such as Aragon and Valencia, or any of the great German spur duchies, such as

63 The grant is on display at Lennoxlove.
64 Royal Museum of Scotland, Catalogue.
65 John Hamilton, Archbishop of St. Andrews, to Mary of Guise, 29 September 1559, recorded in *Mary of Lorraine Corresp.*, 427.

Brandenburg and Bavaria.[66] However, its history was inextricably bound up with that of royal France, and indeed its Duke was always in theory a vassal of the King of France. But it was sovereign in matters of finance, law, foreign policy, ecclesiastical appointments, etc. Its *parlement*, known as *les Grands Jours* down to 1554, and its estates were supreme under its own ducal family.[67]

However, in 1488 dynastic tragedy struck when Francis II, the last male duke, died leaving two daughters, Anne who succeeded as Duchesse, and Isobel. Weeks before his death, Francis had signed the Treaty of Sablé, acknowledged himself to be a vassal of France, promised to marry neither of his daughters without the permission of Charles VIII and agreed to send away some English and other foreign troops who had aided him. In the confusion after the Duke's death, assistance came to the Bretons from Henry VII, Ferdinand of Aragon and Maximilian of Habsburg, then King of the Romans (he did not became Holy Roman Emperor until 1493). Anne was then married by proxy, also in Rennes Cathedral, to Maximilian (whose first wife, Mary of Burgundy, had died in a horse-riding accident in 1482). War ensued in Flanders, Roussillon and Brittany. But as Burgundy was being absorbed into the Habsburg domains on the death of its last male ruler in 1477, so Brittany lost its independence. Charles finally marched into Rennes. Exhausted and friendless, the duchesse accepted his suit, celebrated their engagement (again in Rennes Cathedral) and then on 5 December 1491 married the King at the royal chateau of Langeais, thereby becoming Queen of France at the age of fourteen.

On the death of Charles in 1498 without heirs of his body, the throne of France passed to his brother-in-law and cousin, Louis of Orléans. Louis XII was naturally concerned that France should retain control of Brittany, for Anne was now free to return to Rennes (as indeed she did, in theory as independent Duchesse). He thus promptly divorced his first wife, Jeanne de France (Charles VIII's sister), and in 1499 wed Anne. This marriage was fruitful, but Anne's eight pregnancies produced only two girls: the ugly but sweet-tempered Claude (born in 1499) and Renée (born in 1510, to be married to Ercole II Duke of Ferrara). Thus the royal line passed, not without some moments of apprehension (such as when Louis XII married Henry VIII's sister Mary), to the Angoulême line of the Orléans family in 1515.

Amalgamation of Brittany with France was, however, not yet definitely finalised. An agreement of 1499 by the Breton estates was ambiguous as to the succession. After Anne's death in 1513, the duchy became Claude's. In 1506, after one of Louis' severe illnesses, the Estates General of France, meeting at Plessis-lés-Tours, requested of him that his daughter Claude should be married to the heir apparent, 'Monsieur Francoys cy present qui est tout Francoys', a deliberate and nice play on words. The two children were thus formally betrothed by the Cardinal of Amboise on 21 May

66 See the still useful G. Zeller, *Histoire des relations internationales de Chritophe Colomb à Cromwell* (Paris, 1953).

67 R.J. Knecht, *Francis I* (1982), 6–12, 242–43; and his *The Rise and Fall of Renaissance France* (1996), 29–36, 58–59, 65–70, 163–64; R. Doucet, *Les institutions de la France au XVIe siècle* (Paris, 1948); A. Duprey, *Histoire de la réunion de la Bretagne à la France* (Paris, 1921); D.L. Potter, *A History of France 1460–1560* (1995), 111–13, 120.

1506. Anne had hoped that her eldest daughter would marry Charles of Habsburg (such indeed had been agreed in the Treaty of Blois, 1501), but no sensible monarch of France would have allowed such a calamity to come to pass. In 1514, immediately after the death of Anne, Francis and Claude were married and when, on New Year's Day 1515, Louis died, they became King and Queen of France.

Claude, who was to bear her husband seven children, was quickly persuaded to grant to him the administration of her duchy (April 1515); then, failing rapidly in 1524, she willed that her eldest son Francis should inherit upon her death, which came on 26 July. Since he was then only six years old, his father continued to head the administration. Brittany did continue to have a considerable sway over its own affairs; the Concordat of Bologna, for example, was not enforced there. Its estates met regularly; usually only Bretons held office (although Duprat, Chancellor of France, was also Chancellor of the Duchy after 1518). As Francis the Dauphin approached his age of majority, Duprat began negotiations with various members of the Grands Jours, and lavish bribes preceded the King during 1532 before he took up residence with his son at the famous castle of Suscinio on the Presqu'ile de Rhuys at the head of which stands Vannes where the estates met in the summer to discuss the duchy's union with France. A series of conditions were agreed to by the King, and Francis III swore at his installation to uphold the ancient laws, liberties and freedoms of the province.

In some respects, the story is quite unremarkable; this sort of thing was happening all over Europe. As Gaston Zeller put it, 'L'affaire Bretagne présente les mêmes complexe d'intérêts enchevêtrés que les guerres d'Italie, mais non pas les mêmes variétés de combinaisons' [The Breton affair demonstrated the same complex of entangled interests as the Italian Wars, but not the same variety of complications/combinations].[68] The most celebrated examples were the union of the Habsburg heritable lands with those of Burgundy when Mary of Burgundy's marriage with Maximilian took place in 1477 and was followed by the birth of Philip the Fair; and that of Aragon with Castile, where Ferdinand continued to administer the kingdom after his wife's death, thanks to the death of his daughter Joanna's husband Philip (the same Philip the Fair mentioned above) and her subsequent madness. Thus Charles V came, by gradual stages from 1506 to 1519, to inherit by (fairly) normal, accepted, legal, dynastic practices the greatest empire Europe had seen since the time of Charlemagne. But note that in the case of Brittany, the process was not immediate, but spanned three generations (Francis II-Anne-Claude-Francis III) and took some forty-six years. Nonetheless, that case history is most illustrative and, in certain respects, it marked a turning point of sorts. As Zeller remarked, the annexation of Brittany was 'à la fois l'épilogue des guerres anglaises et le prélude des luttes entre la France et la maison d'Autriche' [at the same time the end of the Hundred Years' War and the opening phase of the Habsburg-Valois struggle].

The relatively simple lesson contained in the example of Brittany (and indeed that of Burgundy) was one widely appreciated by all in Europe: avoid if possible a female

68 G. Zeller, *Relations internationales*, 93.

succession. But the statistical possibilities of only girls surviving the traumas of birth and early childhood were quite high, and proof was amply provided in the sixteenth century: Mary Queen of Scots, Mary Tudor and Elizabeth I. And note how rich the century was in famous women regents: Katherine of Aragon administered England while Henry fought in France in 1513; Louise (Francis' mother) was regent while he lay captive in Madrid after his capture at Pavia in 1525; Charles V's sister Mary (Queen Dowager of Hungary: her husband Lewis was killed at the great slaughter of Mohacs when the Turks conquered Hungary) administered the Low Countries, as would one of his illegitimate daughters in the 1560s. And, of course, there are the examples of Mary of Guise, regent of Scotland 1554–60, and Catherine d'Medici, regent of France 1561–74.

The story is also fraught with 'hind-sightism' and can appear too firm, fixed and final. There is nothing more wooden and inflexible than family trees. They tell us what did happen, how the succession did materialise. But at the time, it was uncertain, shimmering, pregnant with potentialities not realisable until births and deaths worked out right. For every example of Brittany which did result in long-term consequences (indeed for every example of Great Britain), there were hosts of 'failures', dynastic possibilities which did not work out: the union of France and Naples; France and Milan; England and the Low Countries; France and Poland; Sweden, Poland and Muscovy. Polish elections apart (and see too the break-up of the Union of Kalmar – Denmark, Sweden and Norway – in 1523), marriage was the tie that created the claim; inheritance was the means by which the union would be achieved. The point to be appreciated most strongly is that once a province or kingdom was thus absorbed into another through marriage, as Zeller again trenchantly remarked about Brittany, 'à partir de ce moment, en tout cas, [il] cesse de se poser sur le terrain de la politique internationale. [From that point in time, it ceases to have any importance in international relations]'. Although that general-isation is just a bit too sweeping (the English would fish in Breton waters whenever they were troubled well into the eighteenth century, just as the French backed Stuart pretenders), it reminds us of a powerful fact of dynastic life and death.

Subjects were vividly aware of how the uncertain fecundity rates of their royal lines could threaten the stability of the realm. The example of Brittany was one every courtier was aware of, as is neatly caught in Mary Queen of Scots' supposed first public participation in a royal fête. It was not the outdoor, public sort described before, but an indoor one performed before a much more select audience. In this court masque, played out at St. Germain en Laye, Henry II's favourite château and the one he created (rather than inherited from his father's monstrous building programme), the twelve-year-old Mary, elaborately costumed as the demi-goddess Sybil, Delphic oracle, addressed her future husband, since 1547 Duc de Bretagne, with this prediction, penned by the distinguished poet, Melin de Saint-Gelais:

> Delphica Delphini si mentem oracula tangunt
> Britanibus junges regna Britana tuis.

> If Delphic oracles move the mind of the Dauphin
> You will join Britain's realms with your Bretons.[69]

That Mary should have found herself uttering such lines is a classic example of what dynasticism, the principal engine of politics in the sixteenth century, was all about. It is also a powerful commentary on one of the most disastrous decades in English foreign affairs. In 1540, Scotland, although allied with France and a refuge for a small number of religious exiles from England, posed little threat to Henry VIII, his dynasty or his kingdom, even though James V was in theory a claimant to the throne should the Tudors die out.

But from 1543, with Mary Queen of Scots' birth, Henry and Somerset embarked on a forward, aggressive policy which sought to amalgamate the two kingdoms into what Henry called Britain and what Somerset termed, increasingly in 1548, 'Great Britain'. This endeavour, coupled with Henry's disastrous capture of Boulogne in 1544, had resulted however in the direct opposite. The 1550s would see Scotland becoming bound to France much more closely than ever she had been and not just as an independent ally, but increasingly as a monarchy under fairly close direction from France, as the English would find to their cost in 1557–58. From an English perspective, the Rough Wooings were a 'monstrous failure of policy' and as clear an example of counter-productivity as the century can offer. From the French point of view, the affair of Mary Queen of Scots is more complex. For Henry II, it was a golden opportunity in the business of empire-building. It was, of course, a great gamble, but it was one he rightly thought worth taking and he almost brought it off. As for the Scots, as our story will show, it was yet another episode in their endeavour to remain independent, and it was one in which, as ever so far, they had been successful.

One should also remember that outright conquest was not 'just'; that was the sort of thing the Ottoman Turk did, forbidden to any Christian prince, bound as he was by the moral constraints and the accepted practices of the Christian republics of which he was a member. The acquisition of a new title could come only if there was a just and right title to the territory in question and this could come (largely) through inheritance. That of course depended very largely on how the normal practices of any land were interpreted, but kings nonetheless had to 'know' that they had a rightful God-given entitlement. The will of God should be carried out and Shakespeare was not totally disingenuous when he had Henry V proclaim, 'No King of England unless King of France'. Just and right title was, of course, undergoing considerable elaboration with the remarkable discovery of new lands beyond the Ocean Seas, as when Hernan Cortés discovered Mexico. 'Right title' there was vested in a blend of papal sanction and first sight of land (previously unclaimed by any other Christian prince), by a servant of the king who could now claim the land as his own. Such exciting competition was not possible in 'Europe'. But excitement and competition there certainly were, of a sort different to that of Cortés and his fellow *conquistadores*.

69 J.E. Phillips, *Images of a Queen* (1964), 4 and see 15.

In this ancient cauldron of momentous chance, great gamble and high ambition, Scotland continued to be hammered on the anvil of the centuries.

This hammer of the Scots was Henry VIII, the first English monarch since Edward III to attempt to master the Kingdom to the North. As with Edward III, the King's commitment to making Scotland the prime focus of his policy must be doubted, for both monarchs would expend much more of their treasure and their time assaulting France which by its very existence (and thus temptation) saved Scotland. To a large extent, there would have been no Rough Wooings without the infant Mary Queen of Scots, although reservations can be held even about that platitude: James V's claim to the throne of England was closer than his daughter's and he was male. Nonetheless, without Henry VIII's decision to seek the marriage of his heir to her, there would have been no Rough Wooings. It is thus critical that we examine the mind of this King.

CHAPTER THREE

Henry VIII and the Road from Solway Moss

HENRY VIII, KING OF ENGLAND, UNCLE TO JAMES V

As of 22 April 1542 Henry VIII, fifty years of age, was in the thirty-fourth year of his reign. He would celebrate his fifty-first birthday that 28th of June. In under five years he would be dead. Just two months before (on 13th February) he had executed his young fifth wife, Catherine Howard.[1] Normally gregarious to a high degree, the King retired from public life, drank heavily, attended to matters of state only fitfully and 'attended to the ladies' not at all. He hunted with a fervour bordering on frenzy, so much so that men of state feared for his health. The King had been subject to a number of humiliations recently. He had sought as his fourth wife Mary of Guise-Lorraine who had wittily (and publicly) declared her neck to be too small and then married the King's nephew James V. Henry's then marriage to Anne of Cleves was an obvious mistake and was never sexually consummated. His closest adviser, Thomas Cromwell, was ennobled as Earl of Essex on 17 April 1540 only to be executed the following 28 July. On 30 June 1541, Henry set forth to York for a meeting with his nephew. After a leisurely progress, the King arrived on 18 September, waited for a little over a week and departed, apparently snubbed, on the 27th. It was on his return that Archbishop Cranmer was compelled to begin to lay before the King the undoubted evidence of his queen's 'adultery'. By 14 November, the Queen was arrested at Syon House and on 10 December, her two alleged lovers (Francis Dereham and Thomas Culpepper) were executed. Henry was old and cuckolded, he stank, he was disgruntled and hungry for some notable exploit with which to regain esteem and honour. How much did Scotland figure in this 'late-life crisis'?

Anglo-Scottish relations had been relatively pacific since 1523, despite incursions along the ragged frontier. Henry VIII interfered in Scottish politics during the period 1524–42 as much as circumstances permitted, not least by offering refuge and pensions to two of James's most fiercely hated men: Archibald Douglas, 5th Earl of Angus, and his brother, George of Pittendriech.[2] Though he was largely ignorant of its cosmology, Scotland did rate a separate category of classification within the crude filing system for state papers which Wolsey initiated in 1524, and the King kept a

---

1 Only two days before, Parliament had to pass an Act making it treason for an 'unchaste woman' to marry a King of England. See Lacey Baldwin Smith, *A Tudor Tragedy* (1961).

2 The most satisfactory account of Anglo-Scottish relations for James V's reign is to be found in Jamie Cameron's *James V* (esp. 286–323 for 1542) which easily supersedes R.C. Eaves, *Henry VIII's Scottish Diplomacy, 1513–1524*, Wernham, Slavin and Scarisbrick, but J.D. Mackie's article can still be read to effect: 'Henry VIII and Scotland', *Trans. Royal Historical Society*, 4th ser., xxix (1947), 93–114.

fairly close watching brief on events north of the border. Few of the King's compatriots shared this interest, which is hardly surprising. For one thing there was hardly any Anglo-Scottish contact similar to that with France. The wardens on the respective marches of course kept in touch and in the 1530s there were several embassies between the two monarchies, but neither seemed anxious to facilitate intercourse.[3] The odd Englishman settled in Edinburgh and Scots were anxious to buy English horses, but contact was not encouraged.[4]

The Scots were, perhaps naturally, the more apprehensive and some forms of normal intercourse were interdicted by act of Parliament, as James Riddell and his brother Andrew, both burgesses of Jedburgh, found in 1537 when they suffered for selling their sheep to the English.[5] In 1541 the Convention of Royal Burghs appointed two searchers of all English ships resorting to any of the country's ports; in 1538 all trade along the borders was temporarily banned 'because of the pestilence now rissin'.[6] In time of war, of course, any 'intercommouning' was punishable by death, as some oyster fishermen in the Forth discovered after selling their cargo to an English fleet in 1542: 'The Kyng causyd hangg tham all'.[7]

Such repressiveness was not unpopular, for most Scots had little need to go to England, always seen as the land of 'our auld inemies'.[8] Trade with that country ranked a very low fourth after that with the Netherlands, France and the Baltic, and even along the border little exchange of goods could have taken place. To pinpoint just one commodity, of some 1300 books which survive from pre-Reformation Scottish libraries, only seven were printed in England. However, some Scots did study in England, such as George Wishart at Cambridge in 1543, learning new doctrines about the scriptures.[9]

Henry VIII, despite the indifference of his countrymen and the dislike of the Scots, remained deeply concerned about relations with his nephew, as can be seen by the brief Anglo-Scottish war of 1542. The year 1542 was one of war over most of Europe. The Franco-Turkish axis launched a remarkably well co-ordinated assault upon the Habsburgs: Suleyman once more besieged Buda; Francis' eldest son

3 For Border contacts, see Rae, *Administration of the Scottish Frontier*, 167–79, where he touches on the period 1534–39. The Scottish embassy of 1535 is detailed in J.A. Inglis, *Sir Adam Otterburn of Redhall King's Advocate, 1524–1538*. R.B. Armstrong, *The History of Liddesdale, Eskdale, Ewesdale, Wauchopedale and the Debateable Land* is also still useful for the period down to 1542. The manuscript for his uncompleted vol. ii is also of note (NLS, MS 6110–20).

4 *RSS*, ii, no. 4338; *CSP Scot.*, i, no. 33. G. Donaldson, 'Foundations of Anglo-Scottish Union', in *Essays Presented to Sir John Neale*, ed. S.T. Bindoff and others, gives examples of contact predating 1542, e.g. 284, 307–10.

5 Pitcairn, *Trials*, i, 181–82, and see 179 for another example.

6 *RSS*, ii, no. 4275; *Records of the Convention of the Royal Burghs of Scotland*, i, 555; *TA*, vii, 430, 432.

7 *TA*, v, 203, 217; *HP*, i, lxx, lxxii.

8 As in 1533 (*RSS*, ii, no. 1514).

9 *The Works of John Knox*, ed. D. Laing (Edinburgh, 1846–64), i, 534–37; vi, 667–70. See also O. Rogers, 'Memoir of George Wishart, the Scottish Martyr', *Trans. Royal Historical Society*, 1st ser., vi (1876), 260–363.

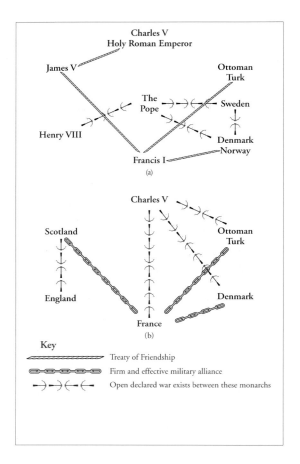

Fig. 3.1.   (a) Europe at peace: 1538-42

(b) European Alliances and War, July to November 1542

Charles V and Francis I became allies by a pact negotiated at Aigues-Mortes in June 1538 (Pope Paul III also came in his barge) and signed at Compiègne on 23 October. Charles actually travelled through France and celebrated Christmas 1539 at Fontainebleau. However, by the summer of 1542, flames of war again lapped all over Europe. Francis I (in league with Suleyman the Magnificent and the Duke of Guelders) launched a multi-pronged attack upon Charles V and his brother Ferdinand (who 'ran' the Austrian-Bohemian-Silesian territories, as well as 'Imperial Hungary'). His ally, the Duke of Guelders, manoeuvred an army to the gates of Brussels in the summer of 1543. Francis' armies invaded the Low Countries, Northern Italy, and Northern Spain. The Danes closed the Sond to all Habsburg shipping. The Great Turk moved up the Doner/Danube to capture Budapest. Scotland was also singed when Henry VIII invaded to Haddon Rigg and James V responded by ordering three attacks on England. Only the third one penetrated into that country, at Longtown (Solway Moss). England only technically called a 'truce' for that war in January 1543.

Charles successfully invaded Luxembourg and his second surviving son, Henry, laid siege to Perpignan. The heterogeneous French European alliance also worked with some stunning effect. Christian II of Denmark closed off the Sound to the vital 'mother trade' of the Netherlands: the transport of the wheat riches of the Polish plain down the Vistula to Western Europe and his navy threatened Groningen. The armies of the Duke of Cleves (married to Francis' sister and claimant to Gelderland) crashed devastatingly into the heartland of the Low Countries and even threatened Brussels itself. Somewhat improbably, these flames of war lapped Scotland as well.

THE ANGLO-SCOTTISH WAR, JULY TO NOVEMBER 1542

It is still difficult to come to any satisfactory explanation for the brief Anglo-Scottish war of 1542. Relations between the two countries had been strained, especially in the later '30s, but they were not hostile. Henry entertained Scottish rebels, James gave sanctuary to refugees from the aftermath of the Pilgrimage of Grace. James made two French marriages. Sadler's two missions to Scotland in 1537, and 1540, proof of Henry's anxiety to induce James to make some sort of reformation, were fruitless. Henry naturally was genuinely angered by his nephew's sudden refusal to meet him at York in September 1541. Flimsy grounds in themselves, yet war did then erupt.

Negotiations which Henry had initiated had completely broken down by the summer of 1542. But negotiations for what? The most generally accepted explanation is that Henry was trying to effect some sort of accommodation with his nephew to secure his dynasty and his reformation. Some lay the root of his impatience at his advanced years, poor health and the fragility of his only male heir (not to mention the 'illegitimacy' of his daughters). James stood too close to the English throne to be ignored.

But the war's origins must also be seen in terms of that wider European context; England had been preparing for war for years. In December 1538, Pope Paul III, enraged at Henry's desecration of the tomb of St. Thomas à Becket (bits of which were blown into the countryside out of the mouths of Henry's cannons), declared him excommunicate (again). That took place within the context of a reconciliation between Charles V and Francis I: the interviews celebrated at Aigues-Mortes. Behind all of these was seen (and with a bit of justice) the hand of Reginald, Cardinal Pole, whose stiff-necked refusal to bend to Henry's reformation and whose family's dynastic proximity to the English Crown made him the man the King most deeply feared. Could not the Franco-Imperial-Papal rapprochement of 1538 herald great peril for England? Certainly that is what Henry and his great minister Thomas Cromwell concluded.

They thus set about the greatest fortification of the realm seen since the reign of Edward I, if not the Normans, if indeed since the Romans. This mighty works programme, which cost almost £290,000 in four years, created massive fortifications from the Scilly Isles to the Fal to the Thames, the Humber, the Tyne to (relevant for our focus) the Tweed and the Solway. A noted government propagandist, Richard Morison, celebrated these mighty constructions in 1539 in his resounding clarion call, *An Exhortation to styrre all Englyshemen to the defence of theyr countreye*: 'his highnesse careth for all and not for some onely; he fortyfyeth Barwycke, bothe towne and castelle, Carliel, towne and castel, setting men a worke for the repayring of Warke castelle'.[10]

Walls make for protection, but they also isolate. What Henry sought in 1542 was to free himself from that isolation, and this he thought he could do thanks to the renewal of Habsburg-Valois hostilities. He thus was beginning to come to terms with the Emperor for another invasion of France, a story to which we return later. Did he not seize this opportunity to chastise the Scots in order to leave his rear relatively unthreatened whilst engaged in recovering the patrimony of Henry V? Was Flodden in fact more of a fright in 1513 than the complacent crowings afterwards would lead us to suppose?[11]

On 24 August 1542, the English border commander, Robert Bowes,[12] was sent into Scotland where his force was clobbered at Hadden Rig, four miles from Kelso; most of those not killed were taken prisoner. Both the Scots and the French exulted and Henry, by all account furious, ordered Norfolk to prepare as formidable an army as possible to invade Scotland. In the end, his invasion in early November was a fiasco.

ROYAL PROPAGANDA

As the orders went out to Norfolk, so did more curious ones, reflecting the printing knee-jerk instinct mentioned above. The Archbishop of York and the Bishop of Durham were told to search their 'old registers and ancient places of keeping such writings' to provide proof of the King's lordship of Scotland so that 'the King's title to the realme of Scotland be more fully playnly and clerely set fourth to all the world, that the justness of our quarell and demaunde may appear'. York was especially important as it previously had had jurisdiction over all the bishops of Scotland and so could produce 'verye olde auncent authentical monuments of the superiority'. There was a curious reference that the Archbishop 'in tymes past hath taken some paynes in the same thyng'. York and Durham were not the only ones involved either; there were also other 'certaigne learned men to travaile in the same'.[13] Thus was antiquarianism harnessed to affairs of state.

The ultimate fruits of their labours was a book, *A Declaration, conteynying the iust cavses and consyderations, of this present warre with the Scottis, wherein alsoo appereth the trewe & right title, that the kings most royall maiesty hath to the soueraynitie of Scotlande.*[14] Henry, 'beyng nowe enforeced to the warre', wished to 'declare to the worlde our just causes'. The *Declaration*, as its title implies, falls into two halves. The

10 Colvin, *King's Works*, iv, 370–71.
11 Dr. Bonner suggests that 1542 represented a 'Flodden in reverse', a concept I have employed, but with a different meaning. Bonner, 'Genesis'.
12 See biography of him by Helen Miller in Bindoff, *Parliament*, I, 471–73.
13 *SP Henry VIII*, v, 212–13; *LP*, xviii (2), no. 898. Six years later, when Tunstall was sent on a similar errand, he remarked having seen a copy, probably made at this time, of a book of homage compiled by the chancellor of England 'in henry vii dayes' (BL, MS Calig, B vii, fo. 336).
14 *STC*, no. 9179; reprinted in *Complaynt*, 192–206. The two following extended quotes are from pp. 196–98.

first made purely contemporary justifications: James's failure to appear at York, his harbouring of rebels, his refusal to surrender disputed land.

Henry had patiently borne with his nephew during his minority, resolutely refusing to destroy Scotland after Flodden because of their nearness of blood and because of his natural affection for the babe. But this time the King of Scots had gone too far. Bowes had been viciously attacked on English soil and the Scots even refused to allow ransom for him and his fellows. No other prince in Christendom had been so used. Yet, Henry declared, we 'vse nowe our force and puisaunce againste hym, no for reuengeaunce of our priuate displeasure (being so often deluded as we haue ben) but for recouerye of our right, preservation of our subjects from iniuries and for obseruation of leagues of peace'.[15]

The second half of the *Declaration* was something quite different, for here was to be found the result of the learned men's labours, Henry's claim to the sovereignty of Scotland and a potent fusion of the two strands discussed above: origin myths and contracts in law. Great care was made that this enunciation would appear to be only an appendix to the main body of the work. Besides the phrase in the title, 'wherein alsoo appereth', it was specifically declared in the text, 'For which cause nevertheless we do not enter this warr, ne mynded to demunde any suche matter'. But over half of the *Declaration* expounds the King's title as fully and as logically as possible.

The evidence came from chronicles, from instruments in the treasury and from registers 'iudicially and autentiquely made'. The compilation was formidable. Beginning, of course, with Brutus, there appears the year of the homage, mention of which Scottish king rendered to which English overlord, the number of years between this and the last homage and the particular circumstances of the event. A detailed recitation of the adjudication of Edward I amongst the Scottish claimants in 1291 was made. Bruce was merely a rebel. Edward II's renunciation of overlordship by the Treaty of Northampton in 1328 was ignored. One hundred and ten of the last one hundred and twenty hundred four years since the last formal homage was rendered were explained away by the exigencies of the civil war, the sedition which plagued the reign of Henry VII and the tender regard of Henry VIII for his young nephew. All this to manifestly demonstrate that

> Ne in any other realme a prince that hath more iuste title, more euident title, more certayn title, to any realme that he can clayme than we haue to Scotland . . . lineally descended from the begynnynge of that astate established by our progenitours, and recognised to successiuely of the Kings of Scotlande by dedes, wordes, actes & writinges continually almost without interuption, or at the leest intermission, til the reigne of our pregenitour Henry the VI.

The London printer Richard Grafton (to replace Berthelet as HMSO in 1547), who would be given Edmond Hall's manuscript in 1547 to print, stated that the *Declaration* was first 'set forth', and only then did Norfolk invade.[16] Lee and

---

15 *The Complaynte*, ed. Murray, 198.
16 *Grafton's Chronicle: or the History of England*, ed. H. Ellis (1809), ii, 477.

Tunstal, however, were not ordered to root around their records until 3 October and Berthelet's delivery of 36 copies of the book to the King was not made until 5 November, by which time Norfolk's army was disbanding. Paget, in Paris, was not sent a copy until 4 December. On 18 December English Protestants studying abroad were corresponding about it, Richard Hilles in Strasbourg writing to Bullinger giving many of its arguments.[17] These bits of timing are not particularly important and, in any case, events were to outstrip its topical relevance and Berthelet's presses more than any one could have imagined in the first fortnight of December.

Most historians have insisted, however, on seeing the *Declaration* in the light of Henry's attempt to conclude the betrothal of Mary and Edward and have criticised him heavily for it. But the *Declaration* was conceived and executed when James was a vigorous thirty and the sex of his unborn heir obviously unknown. The *Declaration* must be judged first not in the light of subsequent events, but as part of the crisis of 1542.

There seem to be three possible explanations for its extraordinary claims. One is that Henry actually believed he was the superior lord of Scotland. Another is that he hoped that such a claim would put James at an initial disadvantage in the negotiations which would follow the war. This is pure speculation and there is no material to support such a contention – not surprising considering the turn of events.

A third possibility is that Henry had got into the habit of public posturing during a crisis. As with his first divorce, the King simply fired off all the literary guns in his arsenal. Certainly the *Declaration* has that same sublime mixture of the absurd and the ridiculous which characterised the early stages of his contest with the Pope. But the point is that Henry was heir to a long tradition which gave him a pan-British pretension; in that sense he had been forged on the anvil of the centuries as much as had the Scots.

THE TEMPER OF THE AGE

But there is a further major issue: why was Henry VIII concerned about Scotland at all?[18] Deducing motives for sixteenth-century statesmen is always problematic:[19] what, really, did Phillip II 'want' in 1588? We can come close, but the process involves us in stitching together from a series of statements and actions our interpretation, now, of what they wanted to accomplish, then. It is highly presumptuous and we are often wrong. Unlike modern politicians who have the leisure to write memoirs (often so highly self-serving as to be useless), monarchs tended to die in post with scant space for mature reflection. Both Charles V and Louis XIV composed remarkably

---

17 *LP*, xviii (2), no. 211; *LP*, xvii, nos. 1166, 1218.
18 Generations of students in my Special Subject at Lancaster University have heard the following in lectures from 1967 until now: all of them have raised engaging questions in their tutorials and their essays and I thank all of them for their useful contributions. Many colleagues have also commented: J.A. Tuck, Sandy Grant, Chris Challis, Jack Scarisbrick to name but a very few. To all of them: my gratitude.
19 We should know? They didn't know.

revealing, sincere and sympathetic fatherly advice in memoranda to their sons. Neither is wholly reliable. Correspondence, diplomatic despatches, Privy Council decisions, Acts of Parliament, internal office memos:[20] all have their limitations and must be treated with extreme caution.[21] It is not just that these men employed different money to us, or different calendars[22] or different units of measurement. They lied[23] or were secretive or were bound by conventions which are alien to us. They often did not really know what they thought, but had to say something.[24]

Other considerations must be borne in mind. These men were often remarkably young and immature: Henry VIII was eighteen when he became King of England and some would say he never really grew up. James V took power at the age of sixteen. Mary Queen of Scots was fifteen when she married, sixteen when she became Queen of France and just over eighteen and a half when she returned to rule Scotland as an adult monarch. In the Scotland of the 1530s, the aristocracy were mostly young because of the wipe-out of a generation at Flodden in 1513. Secondly, a lot of these men and women were 'in drink' much of the time or in genuine physical pain (the two were often related). It was not unusual for those who could afford such a cellar to wake up with a cup of wine, claret or brandy. Beer was regarded as a food. Their diet was appalling. Also, they spoke a different language to modern English, French, Scots, etc. Their diction and rhetoric were fashioned by a community of thought patterns, catch phrases and education quite different to ours, and making their words ours (in effect: translating) is to commit acts of misrepresentation, however unintended.

THE AULD ALLIANCE

In 1558, when the French were triumphant in Scotland, they bragged how God had proven with the fall of Calais to be 'un bon français': an old conceit, not dead even today. Berwick was 'fort faible' and could be taken in a day by a modern army. Newcastle, York, Norwich, Peterborough presented scant obstacles and the walls about London were a joke, effective though they may have been in 1554 against pitchfork-wielding mobs.

Fear of the Auld Alliance was a real consideration. To spell out the obvious: there existed a mutual defence pact between the Scots and the French which became active upon invasion of either by the English. The clearest example remains Flodden in 1513. Louis XII invaded Italy and was defeated at Novara on 6 June 1513; Henry VIII and

---

20 Which were made as part of their working, legal and governmental environments: not for historians.

21 See A.J.P. Taylor's remarkable dissection of the von Scribben memorandum of Hitler's table talk from 1942: *The Causes of the Second World War* (second edition, 1969).

22 All too many nineteenth-century historians did not remember that new years were dated from 25 March in Britain and after Easter in France although, at the time, they sometimes forgot.

23 Contemporary forgeries abounded.

24 See David Starkey's insightful comments about Wolsey's rhetorical style (*The Reign of Henry VIII: Personalities and Politics*, 60–63) and, as he recommends, R.S. Sylvester and D.P. Harding, eds., *Two Early Tudor Lives* on George Cavendish.

the Emperor Maximillan invaded France; James IV invaded England on 22 August. Something similar would occur in 1522 and 1523. English statesmen perforce had to prepare for war on two fronts when attacking France. This necessitated defensive strengths along the Border: Berwick, Wark, Carlisle (Norham technically was the responsibility of the Bishop of Durham). That was why Ferdinand of Aragon had attempted in 1502–1503 to recast Anglo-Scottish relations by the marriage of James IV and Margaret Tudor. As often with his diplomacy, he was too crafty by half, but an intelligent strategy lay behind his stratagem. Henry had variously attempted to neutralise the Scots, going so far as to offer Princess Mary to James V with Berwick as her dowry. But James was received in triumph in Paris in 1536 to marry Francis I's favourite daughter on 1 January 1537. He then married Mary of Guise in 1538.

Scotland was moreover a refugee for pretenders to the English throne. Mention of Berwick should remind us of the last time it was under Scottish jurisdiction, during 1461–82. That was the occasion when Henry VI's wife, Margaret of Anjou (m. 23 April 1445), induced her husband to return the town to the Scots after his defeat at the battle of Towton, 29 March 1461. For the next three years, the king, his wife and Prince Edward (b. 1453) lived in Scotland. Henry then left to participate in an uprising in Lancashire only to be captured at Clitheroe in July 1465.[25] Then Perkin Warbeck arrived in Scotland where he was treated as royalty, Richard IV, by James IV who aided two of his invasions of England, in 1495 and 1496. Few of the many rivals to Henry VIII[26] looked to Scotland; indeed most died in the service of France.[27] But the King was ever fearful, as his concern over William Neville's prophecy illustrates.[28] In April 1541, Sir John Neville carried out a minor revolt against the King; he and his small band achieved refuge across the Border.[29]

So did various refugees from religious persecution in England during the 1530s. The most notable case-history concerns the Pilgrimage of Grace, survivors of which fled North. The most celebrated was Dr Richard Hillyard, about whose defection Henry was particularly hysterical. Beaton gave him sanctuary at St. Salvator's College, St. Andrews, as he did to other English refugees, such as Henry Bretton, Richard Smith and Richard Marshall.[30] Henry badgered James for his extradition; James consistently refused, 'it being contrary to his conscience' as a Catholic.[31] It is worth remembering that James's armies in the autumn of 1542 carried with them a Papal Bull and they sought to enter any church they could find across the Border so as to issue it in Paul's name within the realm of Henry VIII. But it went beyond that.

---

25 Edward would be killed at Tewkesbury, 4 May 1471; Henry was murdered in the Tower of London on the night of 21–22 May. Margaret finally died in 1482.

26 Henry Stafford, Duke of Buckingham, d. 1521; John Dudley, Edmund and Richard de la Pole, Lady Margaret Pole (Countess of Salisbury) or her son, Cardinal Pole.

27 Such as the White Rose, killed at Pavia.

28 D.L. Potter aptly describes Henry's reign of blood against possible pretenders.

29 A kinsman, Sir Edward Neville, had early been a favourite courtier of the King and indeed was something of a look-alike; he was executed (1539) in the campaign against the Boleyn faction. See Starkey, Henry VIII, 25, 54, 83, 118; LP, xvi, no. 763.

30 Sanderson, Cardinal of Scotland, 123.

31 LP, xvi, no 612.

After 1534, England was increasingly alienated within Europe as a whole because of Henry's Reformation, tepid as it may have been. Cardinal Beaton was seen to be inextricably linked to Pope Paul III and thus to Cardinal Reginald Pole.

THE PROBLEM OF THE NORTH

Scotland was a secure bolt-hole for English dissidents. It would not begin to be eradicated until 1570–71 when Scottish governments allowed English armies to invade so as to hunt down rebels: the one in 1571 was truly remarkable, going up the east coast then over to Lanarkshire where it besieged Hamilton Castle, on the Clyde. When James became King of England in 1603, the bolt-hole issue was temporarily solved with the Border-line becoming merely the centre, his 'middle shires'.[32] The Berwick garrison was stood down.[33]

Moreover there was the whole 'problem of the North' during the Tudor period.[34] To begin with, 'the North' was and would remain resistant to the Reformation. This was compounded by the existence there of 'overmighty subjects'. The basis of that problem was the necessity to maintain some sort of military prowess against the Scots. As the government simply did not have the money (or chose not to spend it) to establish permanent garrisons of paid mercenaries along the frontier, it had to rely on the local nobility and gentry. Allowing them the power necessary to resist the Scots meant giving them power which might be (and was) used against the Crown. The great pre-Tudor magnates were powerful: the Cliffords, Nevilles, Dacres, as their roles in the Wars of the Roses demonstrated. They remained powerful. Annexing Lancashire to the Crown was one attempt to tackle this issue. Virtually handing over the rest of the North to a trusted brother, as Edward IV did with Richard Duke of Gloucester, was another. Neither was wholly successful; Henry VII had no brother and neither did his son. Thus various further attempts were essayed, such as the employment of the misnamed 'new men', the establishment of a Council of the North and the appointment of close members of the king's court. But Edward

---

32 I actually do not believe this. See 1640 (when 'English' opponents of Charles I encouraged their more robust Scottish colleagues), not to mention 1650 (when Charles II was crowned at Scone), 1659 (when Monck began his manoeuvres against the Protectorate), 1681 (when the Duke of York was sent to Edinburgh to keep him out of harm's way during the Exclusion Crisis), 1715 (James VIII), 1745 (Bonnie Prince Charlie).

33 The potent symbolism of that act should not blind one to the harsh facts of subsequent history: the first permanent barracks in the British Isles was erected at Berwick in 1727 because England was still seen as under threat from the North. It was, although Bonnie Prince Charlie would invade via Carlisle, thus necessitating the first parliamentary trunk road from Berwick to Carlisle, the present A69 (although in truth the 1757 Military Road mostly parallels it in the hills). The first fifteen miles of that new road were built on top of Hadrian's Wall.

34 This is a complex topic. That the problem was intractable so long as protection against Scotland was necessary can be seen by two articles describing quite different times: J.A. Tuck, 'Richard II and the Border Magnates', *Northern History*, iii (1968), 27–52 and M.L. Bush, 'The Problem of the Far North', *Northern History*, vi (1971), 40–63. The references in these two articles give a fairly full bibliography for the problem, but in particular see M.E. James, *Change and Continuity in the Tudor North*.

Seymour, Earl of Hertford (stationed there 1541–42), and his replacement Viscount Lisle, were virtually useless: they had no local connections, no responsive or trustworthy affinities and no real power except when the Crown sent armies to be commanded by them. Other southerners (Southampton, Surrey and even Norfolk) fared little better during 1540–42.

Norfolk was far too busy to exercise effective dominance. Southampton was grievously ill when he arrived, rapidly sickened and died. Neither Seymour nor Warwick was either cowardly or unintelligent: both were rising Tudor stars, as their subsequent careers in the admiralty and in France would demonstrate, not to mention their careers during the reign of Edward VI. But neither, however industrious and anxious to learn, carried much local clout. Neither stayed for long. Lesser 'new men' were advanced, as the careers of Evers, Carr and Wharton demonstrated, and they could be highly effective in sharply defined, closely targeted missions. But even they would bungle egregiously during the Rough Wooings, and Northumberland was right to supplant them (with himself) in 1550–51, and Queen Mary Tudor likewise turned to others.

Perhaps one of the most striking manifestations of 'the problem' can be seen in the fortresses of the North. The English, unlike the Scots who could rely on their subjects' patriotism, felt they had to fortify on the Border-line. Berwick was always seen as seriously under threat (especially as it was on the wrong side of the Tweed),[35] but as ever with Tudor regimes, they only spent money when they had to, as in 1514 and 1523. Captains and governors of the castle made insistent complaints as to the parlous state of the walls, the heaps of midden and refuse piled against the outside of the walls, the rickety state of the major gatehouses and how the bridge was fit to fall down: ice flows swept it away in 1543. A massive survey was conducted as to the state of the defences in 1522 and 1533, the reparations of the first having decayed into decrepitude by the time of the second. Some towers actually shook in the wind and gunners were terrified that the actual firing of their pieces would bring the towers down about their heads. With the great terror of 1538–40, when England was re-fortified, Berwick benefited. But the only major construction was 'Lord's Mount'. Still, its erection and the re-edification of the walls cost at least £10,000. At Wark, a huge construction gang laboured throughout the summer of 1543; their costs came to over £1800, and even then work had to continue the next year. The year after that, an Italian surveyor sneered that it was a 'marvelouse greate ruyne'.[36] By 1550, a total of just under £3000 had been spent; a decade later it was assessed as virtually useless. A similar story can be told about Carlisle, massively remoulded at considerable cost in 1540–43. Even then, its walls kept falling down when it rained too much.[37] Norham, on which the Bishop of Durham had spent enormous sums after its ignominious

---

35 As, of course, was Newcastle in relation to the Tyne, but that was William I's fault.
36 'It raynethe almost in to everie parte.' See Colvin, *King's Works*, 614–16, 629–39 for Berwick's state.
37 A sardonic report at the end of the century dismissed it as fit only for warfare 'in the Saxsone manner of the Pictys and vandalls against speed and sheld' (Colvin, *King's Works*, iv, 664).

capture by James IV in 1513, was even more of a joke, despite being especially adapted to house artillery.

Behind this Maginot Line stood a degenerate military society, as the massive report on the Borders prepared in 1542 made all too evident. Musters showed declining numbers with every passing year. Tower houses were everywhere in decay. Captains were infirm, aged and inadequate.[38] Sir Ralph Sadler would be sent in 1545 to examine the problems. Some soldiers he found manly enough: John Carr, Captain of Wark, was 'surely a good bordrer', active, able and 'experte in thes frontier warres'. On the other hand, the head of Carlisle was 'lame and impotent' while Carr, for all his virtues, lacked modern expertise: 'yet is he of none experience to the assaulte or defence of a Fortresse'. Both men kept their castles 'more like gentilmennes houses then lyke houses or fortresses of warre'. Little wonder then that the governments of Henry VIII and Somerset would be forced to employ Irish and Spanish mercenaries to man the strongholds during the Rough Wooings.

In its widest geopolitical perspective, Anglo-Scottish relations can be seen as a dialogue between four broad swathes or border-lines: the Tyne-Morecambe Bay one, the Tyne-Solway one, the Tweed-Solway and the Forth-Clyde. The new castle on the Tyne was only built in 1068 as William the Conqueror's northern frontier post. During the twelfth century monarchs of Scotia ruled over Northumberland, Cumberland and Westmorland. The Tweed was only finally recognised as the border in 1236. After the Wars of the Three Edwards (1298–1365), the English still held a large part of Liddesdale in the West[39] and virtually all of the Merse and Teviotdale in the East with major castles at Roxburgh and Berwick. Putting to one side the disputes between the Archbishops of St. Andrews and York, during the fifteenth century, Bishops of Durham appointed clerics to many parishes north of the Tweed, such as Coldstream, and to religious houses such as the priory at Coldingham. Only with the Scottish offensive of 1460, when Roxburgh Castle (bounded by the rivers Teviot and Tweed) was recaptured and Berwick re-occupied, were the English pushed out of Scotland, although in 1482 Richard Duke of Gloucester regained both the Town and the Bounds of Berwick. It was only then that the Anglo-Scottish boundary became (with the exception of the Debatable Land, resolved in 1551–52) what it is now.

Even the crude scrawls which passed for cartography before the age of Mercator squiggled both Hadrian's and Antonine's Walls, and it is worth remembering that should the ocean levels rise by not much more than thirty feet, Scotland north of the Forth would be an island. Henry VIII was certainly aware of the difference between the Solway and the Clyde, as were his commanders in the North. As the paragraph on Border lawlessness above illustrates, wardens along the Marches and members of the Council of the North remained constantly apprehensive about the feuds,

---

38 This was not strictly true, as the war demonstrated: some Border captains were redoubtable, hardy warriors. But within a decade of this period, reports bemoaned: 'the inhabitants there shewth themselves verie disobedient and slacke in service', unable or refusing to guard 'the passages of the waters' or to 'trenche or fortefy' their towns.

39 Bothwell Castle on the Clyde was held by an English garrison in the fourteenth century.

endemic vandalism, gangsterism and local Mafiosi in the North, especially during peacetime.[40]

On 12 December 1542, John Dudley, Viscount Lisle, argued that the King should aim at adding 'that parte of Scotland asmoche as ys athisside the Frithe on theste side, and asmoche as ys athisside Dunebretayne on the west side, to be under your owne obeysance'.[41] Moving the Anglo-Scottish frontier closer to the Antonine Wall may well have been in the back of Henry's mind throughout his reign. Where Dudley,[42] with scant real knowledge of the North, got such an extraordinary (and brilliant) idea is hard to fathom at first. But he may have been present a month before at a conference which discussed the geopolitics of the region (or seen its 'Consultation' drawn up on 5 November):

> if the King's [majesty] entendeth tenlarge his frontyers to the water of Fyeth and there by buylding of fortress and establishing of garrysons to make them till a further opportunitie of conquest the Boundes and Borders of his [majesty's] Realm of England it shall thenn be necessary to use the force of a mayne armye at the begynneng of June next whereby to subdue the countrey.[43]

Viewed in this light, the Forth-Border line idea begins to make more sense. Dudley's suggestion arose from the fact that it was impossible to maintain order along the Marches, especially during time of war. He was, at the time, concerned about the men of Tynedale and Redesdale: 'But sure yt ys, that a perfite reformation wyll not be had their, neyther your lawes executed, ne your highnes ministers duly obeyed' until all southern Scotland was added 'to your domyneons'.[44] Certainly James VI forty years later would perceive the solution of the problem of the Borders in their being transformed into his 'middle shires'; could not Henry have had the same thought in 1543? Certainly, similar proposals would crop up, albeit confusedly, during the Rough Wooings, especially the 1549 idea of retaining Berwickshire and thereby extending the Bounds of Berwick to the Water of Dunglass with a new fortress on its north side.

IRELAND AND THE ISLES

A further aspect of boundaries and sovereignty concerns Ireland on the one hand and the Outer Isles of Scotland (the Lordship of the Isles) on the other. Another issue needlessly exacerbated by Henry's stupid break with Rome (all he had to do was to

40 During wars with Scotland, criminality within England declined markedly: see Wharton's comment in 1547.
41 *Hamilton Papers*, i, 401 (*LP*, xvii, no. 1194).
42 They all were there in 1542: Norfolk, Surrey, Hertford, Warwick. Southampton hated his posting thence so much, he quickly died.
43 LP, xvii, no. 1034: the rendering is from PRO, SP 1/174, fos. 58–63 for which I record my indebtedness to Dr. C.P. Holte (Charles P. Holte, 'Tradition, reform and diplomacy: Anglo-Scottish Relations, c. 1525–42', an unpublished D.Phil. thesis, University of Cambridge, 1992) who kindly allowed me sight of his article 'The Road to Solway Moss: Henry VIII and Scotland 1540–1542'.
44 *Hamilton Papers*, i, 439.

wait until 1536 for Katherine of Aragon to die and none of it would have been necessary) was Ireland. In 1541, fearful that the Pope[45] might effectively exercise his kingship of Ireland, Henry had himself proclaimed King and Ireland made into a Kingdom[46] (Acts of Parliament could do anything, as William Cecil came to believe). Scots also had an interest there, as the campaign by Robert the Bruce's brother in 1315–18 (as King of Ireland) demonstrated. There was in the sixteenth century, of course, a vigorous interchange of goods, people and ideas – and politics[47] – between the Highlands of Scotland and Ulster (particularly with Antrim). Henry had pushed through the Irish Parliament both his overlordship of Church appointments in 1536–37 and his kingship (1541), but was worried by James V's policy towards the country. When a revolt known as the Geraldine League erupted in the summer of 1539, their envoys went to Rome via Scotland. James was reported to be 'a special comforter and abetter' of them. When the King made his celebrated voyage to the Western Isles in 1540, Henry VIII was convinced he aimed at Ireland itself and Lord Robert Maxwell reported to him that James intended to do just that, 'as king'.[48] In 1550, Irish chiefs recognised Henry II of France as King of Ireland,[49] and it is worth remembering that when Mary Queen of Scots became Queen of France in 1559, her seal also styled her as 'R. HIBER'.[50]

A standard reflex action within Anglo-Scottish warfare was what one might call the Ireland-Highlands syndrome: when the Scots fished in the troubled waters of the one, kings of England tried to encourage revolts in the Western Isles. Henry VIII also had one of his geographic fixations (Dumbarton being one) about Shetland and Orkney being the breadbasket of Scotland.[51] How much Henry VIII was interested in the Lordship of the Isles is an engaging question: little before 1542, but he certainly tried to make something of it in 1544–45, as had Edward IV when dealing with James III's brother, the Duke of Albany, in 1479–81, almost as a back door to kingship.[52] The problem had intermittently vexed the Scottish crown ever since James I (1430) and James IV's forfeiture of the Lordship in 1493 and his two expensive naval

---

45 The first Jesuit mission to Ireland was to Ulster in 1542.

46 S.G. Ellis, *Tudor Ireland*, 136 and B. Bradshaw, *The Irish Constitutional Revolution*, 174–80.

47 See two recent publications which vividly demonstrate the vitality of 'British Studies': S.G. Ellis and S. Barber, eds., *Conquest and Union: Fashioning a British State 1485–1725* (1995) and A. Grant and K.J. Stringer, eds., *Uniting the Kingdom? The Making of British History* (1995).

48 *LP*, xiv, no. 1245; xv, nos. 697, 709–10, 720, 736, 983. I am again grateful to Dr. Holte for these references. See also Cameron, *James V*, 236 (and see especially notes 79–81).

49 Manus O'Donnell and Con O'Neill 'avec tous les princes et seigneurs de Hirelande . . . rendrons a vostre Magesté tres-fidelle service . . . a ce qu'il soit accompli que est et sera Roy de France, celluy soit touiours Roy d'Hirlande [along with all the princes and lords of Ireland will render very faithful service to Your Majesty and to whomever is or will be King of France as he will always be King of Ireland]'. D.L. Potter, 'French Intrigue in Ireland', 166.

50 The Pope recognised Ireland becoming a 'kingdom' with the reign of Mary Tudor. For Mary of Scotland's seal, see Merriman, 'Mary, Queen of France', 45–46.

51 Holte again supplies this footnote: *LP*, xvii, no. 799. Philip and Mary would send a naval expedition there in 1557.

52 C. Ross, *Edward IV* (1974).

expeditions in 1494.[53] The incarceration of Donald Dubh, the bastard son of the last pretender to the Lordship, from his birth in 1504 in Edinburgh Castle until 1543, shows how important the issue was considered: his monthly costs came to £40: quite a sum (£18,720) over thirty-nine years.[54] Very few European hostages were kept for so long in prison.

An interesting question is why more was not made by the Scots (and the French) of the Isle of Man, which after all had been part of the realm of Scotland from 1266 to 1341 and for which Scottish kings supposedly paid tribute to the Danish Crown until 1472.[55] Scots did threaten it occasionally and during one celebrated raid in July 1533 stole what became the flagship of the Scottish navy, *The Mary Willoughby*.[56] Island castles at Peel, Castletown and elsewhere were repaired by the Earls of Stanley, to whom Man had been given by the Crown, but not even the Earl of Argyll whose tactical vision stretched from the mouth of the Thames to Carrickfergus mentioned a descent upon the island.

All of these factors are undeniable and were present in however inchoate a form in what may be termed the Tudor decision-making mentality. But there are three further and perhaps paramount considerations: the dynastic-Imperial mindset of all sixteenth-century monarchs, the king as heir to ancient claims to Scotland, and the Tudors not only as usurpers of what was in effect an 'elective' English throne, but as biological failures.

FINEST MATCHES IN CHRISTENDOM

The model of Charles V was there for all to see and it was one men were happy to follow. This lottery aspect of dynasticism – something might turn up – needs always to be borne in mind. Contemporaries knew only too well that the dynastic gamble failed more often than it succeeded, but there were just enough successes (see Charles again) and sudden thunderclaps of fortune (witness Charles's brother Ferdinand being elected King of Hungary and Bohemia after the death of King Lewis at Mohacs) to make the game worth playing. When Charles achieved the marriage of his heir Prince Philip to Mary Tudor, he dubbed it 'the finest match in Christendom', and Mary enjoyed a range of titles by becoming Philip's wife. At the solemn

53   For the essential background to this problem, see R. Andrew McDonald, *The Kingdom of the Isles, c. 1100–c. 1336* (East Linton, 1997); Macdougall, *James IV*, 105–105, 115–16.

54   Cameron, *James V*, 228: see also his Chapter 10, 'Daunting the Isles', *ibid.*, 228–54.

55   Rome continued to bracket it with Scotland: hence the Bishopric of Sodor and the Isles. The 'bishopric' was transferred to York by an Act of Parliament in 1542 (*LP*, xvii, no. 28, cap. 31).

56   A tale delightfully rendered by Cameron, *James V*, 235–37. It was supplanted as flagship by a gift of Francis I, *The Salamander*, in 1537, although James also used another gift from his father-in-law, *The Unicorn*, occasionally called *The Great Unicorn*. *The Salamander* was captured by Hertford in 1544 and sailed in the fleet which attacked Scotland during the Pinkie campaign of 1547, during which *The Mary Willoughby* was retaken. It would see service until sold in 1572. T. Glasgow, 'Naval Administration, 1556–64', 4, 6, 23–25 and Boulind, R., 'Ships of Private Origin in the mid-Tudor Navy: The Lartique, the Salamander, the Mary Willoughby, the Bark Aucher and the Galley Banchard', *The Mariner's Mirror*, lix (London, 1973), 385–408.

rites for her funeral which lasted from 10–13 December 1558 – at which interestingly Margaret the Countess of Lennox was chief mourner – Mary's title-list was intoned as follows:[57]

> The most high, most puissant, and most excellent Princess, Mary the First of that name, late Queen of England, Spain, France, both of the Scillies, Jerusalem and Ireland; Defender of the Faith; Archduchess of Austria; Duchess of Burgundy, Milan and Brabant; Countess of Habsburg, Flanders and Tyrol.

She and Philip were also granted by Charles his interest in the Danish succession. Consider what might have happened had Mary given birth to a son who had lived long enough to bury her and her husband. That she died childless did not mean the gamble had not been worth taking.

Dynasticism, then, provided great opportunities for monarchs to expand their kingdoms and few were able to resist, as this case history of the struggle for the marriage of Mary Queen of Scots will demonstrate. But this expansive aspect, so handsomely underscored by Henry VIII's sweeping phrases in praise of the golden and godly union and Henry II's Scottish touches in his Rouen entry, should not obscure how much dynasticism threatened monarchs and thus forced them to play the game. It wasn't just that one king's success was his adversary's loss. Nor is it simply that claims beget counter-claims, although it is true that as early as the fifteenth century French royal archivists were combing their records to erect a case for French sovereignty over England. Such exercises if anything increased in the sixteenth century, witness the magisterial history of France prepared by Jean du Tillet for Henry II and presented to the king in a magnificent three-volume manuscript edition in 1549[58] which was then widely published. Such studies indeed became something of a cottage industry in the 1570s.

The fecundity and the ingenuity can be seen in French attempts to argue that in truth kings of Scotland were also rightful kings of England, descended as they were from St. Margaret, Malcolm III's second queen, who was sister to Edgar Atheling and granddaughter of King Edmund II Ironside who reigned from 1015 to 1016. A certain factual amnesia was required to make such a claim tenable, but that was the stock-in-trade of genealogists, especially where kingdoms were concerned. Such Scottish claims underscore a most important point. While English policy makers had mythical claims to the overlordship and charters which acknowledged the same, no English monarch had any dynastic claim to Scotland.

One must also remember that claims can work both ways. A female dynastic entity such as the baby Mary Queen of Scots was an opportunity. But she also represented a threat. Were Henry to die heirless, she would have a strong claim, as did her son when Elizabeth passed on in just that condition. Henry thus was threatened by her

---

57 *CSP For.*, 1558–59, introduction.
58 BN, MS fr. 2848, 2856, and see his genealogies: fr. 18,653. It was printed two years later: *La Chronique des Roys de France et des cas memorables aduenuz depuis Phramond iusques au Roy Henry second du nom [etc.]* (Rouen, 1551). For a brief overview of his life, see D.R. Kelley, 'Jean du Tillet, Archivist and Antiquary', 337–354.

birth and had to do something about it. Should she marry a foreign prince, a grave threat to the Tudor family would thereby be created. Had he not addressed that, he would have failed in his obligations to his family: past, present and future.

There is yet a further element of threatening contingency in this breathing babe which one must bear in mind. As long as she remained unwed in this culture, her marriage remained a matter of debate and contest. Even formal betrothal did not settle the issue of her potential, for betrothals could be shelved, delayed, broken to suit circumstances, as indeed marriages could be annulled (witness Louis XII's first wife) when necessary. Only that marriage ceremony, followed by the birth of a child, preferably male, who then lived to adulthood, finalised the issue.

Thus there were a number of stages in the realisation of the dynastic potential of a child: alive, well and unpledged; offered; promised; formally betrothed; married; mother and then beyond further pregnancy. As Mary was to demonstrate most vividly (although Queen Mary of England – once offered to James V as a bride – is equally illuminating, even though she only had one husband to Mary's three), each stage was never quite an end itself, but part of a continuing set of contingencies which only death would resolve. Before we take the story further, we should be aware of recent circumstances which may well have prompted Henry to be even more aware of the dynastic opportunity and threat posed by the existence of an independent monarch of Scotland in 1542.

THE DYNASTIC MENTALITY

We have said that Henry VIII was a dynast, as indeed were all heads of royal and noble families in the sixteenth century. Just what does that term mean? If one had been able to ask Henry himself, he probably would have found the question either incomprehensible (I have yet to see the word[59] appear in a document of the time) or absurd, for dynasticism was an automatic part of the world in which he and his subjects dwelt, as ordinary as the food on their tables. Kings (in truth everyone with land in a society which practised inheritance by primogeniture) never consciously decided to be dynasts at any point in time: they simply were. But it is still necessary to define the term so we can appreciate how it affected monarchs' policies.

It is, actually, not all that easy to articulate in print. One way is to divide the levels of focus into three: family past (during which numerous claims have been accumulated, some of which have been realised, such as one's present holdings, but others of which have not yet been realised); family present (the father and his immediate kin and relatives, who are bound to him and who also in turn bind him to others); and family future (the potential offspring from the marriages of his immediate offspring and those of his relations). Families looked 'backwards', 'sideways' and 'forward'. That is say to parents, grandparents and in-laws (the last generation); then to brothers, sisters and wife (all of the same generation); and then, obviously, to their offspring (the future).

But those widely reproduced, cold, family trees are false in their 'factual finality'.

---

59 The *OED* gives 1487 as the first instance of 'dynastic' in print.

They simply map out what happened, not what might have been. That Henry VII's eldest son, Prince Arthur, died at age 16 or James I's Prince Henry perished at age 18 should not allow us to transform them into non-persons. During their span of years they were the heirs to the throne, full of potential, like Wendell Wilkie in 1944 or Hugh Gaitskell in 1963. But their deadness, potential unrealised, in 1944 and 1964,[60] should not obliterate their earlier importance. The head of a dynasty worked within and was influenced by a number of diffuse considerations. On the one hand he was affected by his previous generation: note how mothers could haunt their sons.[61] So did uncles and aunts and – let us not forget – on both sides: his father's people and his mother's, not to mention his wife's kin.

Then, there were his contemporaries: his brothers, sisters and cousins. At one point Henry VIII had one sister Queen of France while another was Queen Dowager and Regent of Scotland. Something might have been made of this, but Mary's husband Louis XII died in 1515, the same year Margaret was removed as Regent. Charles V was rarely so unfortunate with his sisters, although Isabella's marriage to Christian II of Denmark was one of misery and she died young. That of his sister Mary to Lewis of Hungary was equally wretched, but she was delivered from it by the sword of Suleyman the Magnificent at Mohacs in 1526. She stoutly refused to remarry, a resolve neither of her brothers was able to shake, but she had a long and strikingly successful career as Regent of the Low Countries. Another of Charles's sisters married into the Portuguese royal family, whence flowed Philip II's annexation of that monarchy in 1580. The sister of Henry II of France married into the Savoyard ducal house. The children of sisters mattered: see both Margaret and Mary Tudor and the two daughters of Charles's sister Isabella, whose welfare and potentiality were something the Emperor never abandoned.

The third most important echelon of focus were the children. For a king like Henry II, with eight surviving infancy, the opportunities seemed almost boundless: Scotland, England, Spain, Poland, the Low Countries. His fourth son, Anjou, would be suitor for Elizabeth in 1576. Dynasticism is about one's own family inheritance: keeping what your father passed on to you and passing it on intact to your son. But it is also about trying to seize upon all the opportunities which come along for the enhancement of the family's estate. Charles V inherited Burgundy, the Habsburg lands in Germany, Castile, Aragon and Aragon's Mediterranean possessions, including the Kingdom of Naples. To them he added, either through marriage or physical military conquest, five Netherlandish provinces, Milan, a number of other Italian territories, North African conquests and even more discoveries in the New World. In the aftermath of the great Turkish victory of Mohacs, his brother was elected King of Hungary and Bohemia (including Moravia, Silesia and Lusatia). It

60 Wilkie was a strong contender for the Republican nomination for the Presidential election of November 1944; Hugh Gaitskell very likely would have won the mandatory 1964 General Election for the Labour Party.

61 Catherine d'Medici is perhaps the most notorious, but Francis I always lay under the shadow of his mother as well. See, too, Margaret Beaufort, still alive in 1509, or Louise of Savoy (d. 1531) or Margaret Tudor (d. 1541). I am grateful to Jonathan Bailey for this point.

was the bitterest of disappointments to Charles that he could not pass Austria as well as all of this on to his son Philip, but he was forced by his brother to cede his possessions in Germany. Philip did get the rest and added Portugal in 1580.

THE TUDORS AS FAILURES

The popular vision of Henry VIII as a sexually voracious bluebeard with six wives 'and all that' does little to clarify the realities of 1542 sex-wise. As long ago as 1966, Jack Scarisbrick raised eyebrows by pronouncing the King to be 'sexually timid'. Whatever the facts (randy billygoat or impotent wimp), the plain matter was that the King had three surviving children: Mary (born 18 February 1516), Elizabeth (born 7 September 1533) and Edward (born 12 October 1537). None of these had children and the Tudor line thus utterly expired with the death of Elizabeth (most certainly

Fig. 3.2.   This now widely reproduced engraving of Henry in his last years, in his 50s, shows how corpulent and fleshy he had become over the years as his over-rich diet took its toll. The King's eyes no longer shine, as in the Holbein portraits, but are narrow slits. His once manly hands are now frail, almost timorous. Indeed he was so gross that he could no longer mount a horse without the aid of a hoist. The keen intelligence could still burst forth and his sheer vitality could shine, witness his presence at the siege of Boulogne in 1544 and his taking command at Portsmouth in 1545. But he was now old, his mind wandered and he stank.

conceived out of wedlock and in Catholic eyes a bastard, being born when the King's lawful wife Katherine of Aragon still lived) on 24 March 1603. Indeed, in 1542, only Edward was considered legitimate, the two girls having being declared ineligible to gain the throne by the Act of Succession of July 1536.

That being the case, the Tudor line hung on the life of a frail boy of five, Edward Prince of Wales. James V was thus but two heartbeats away from the English crown. In the Rumour of 'Marlyng' prophesy discussed above, James's nearness was widely appreciated by the English public. In this entertainment, there appeared an appealing figure of a glorious 'Childe' who in one episode gained the Keys to the city of Paris, then received great honour from the Pope before proceeding to Jerusalem both to battle manfully against the Turk and most gloriously to recover the True Cross, which he sent to Rome. On the face it, there would seem to be little that was seditious in such a tall tale, the stock-in-trade of a widely enjoyed legend of the Emperor of the Last Days, a popular apocalyptic tradition. However, the epic of the 'Childe' takes on quite a different complexion when one appreciates that he was often interpreted to be none other than James V of Scotland. Certainly that indeed is what many of the prophesiers and their hearers asserted. Jones told Neville he would become Warwick either under an Edward of Lancastrian-Yorkist descent, or 'the Kyng off Scottes shulde reigne next after the Kynges grace that now is'. A Mistress Armadas, examined in 1533, predicted that England would either be conquered or delivered by James V and Henry banished. John Hill in 1536 trusted to see 'the King of Scottes were the fflower of England'. The next year, a saddler reported being told by numerous Scots 'that their Kyng shulde be Kyng of Englond & crownyd yn London' that year.[62]

We must thus alter our perspective of Henry VIII. Rather than an unfettered tyrant, master of all his Kingdom, the King was actually quite weak and indeed vulnerable. The Tudors had only gained the throne through a battle; might they not lose it similarly? But battle was also a way to glory and renown, and it was to war that Henry returned in the twilight of his life, hoping to regain the pleasures of combat of which he drank so deeply in the summer of 1513. That 'field of glory' clearly lay in France. But first he felt he had to neutralise Scotland, and so erupted the Anglo-Scottish war to which Solway Moss was the capstone.

SOLWAY MOSS: ITS PLACE IN BRITISH HISTORY

During 22 to 28 October, an English army under the Duke of Norfolk made a clumsy and ill-executed raid from Berwick over to Roxburgh and then returned home having done little except to burn Kelso Abbey.[63] Both to meet this force and to retaliate, James V mustered two armies in October. One, under the Earl of Huntly

---

62 The best survey is D.T. Etheridge, 'Political Prophecy in Tudor England' (Thesis).

63 Our understanding of this engagement, and all of the others during the Rough Wooings, has been enormously enhanced by the publication in 1999 of Gervase Phillips's study, *The Anglo-Scots Wars 1513–1550: A Military History* in the Boydell Press series, 'Warfare in History'. The war of 1542 and Solway Moss is treated extensively on pp. 148–53. Cameron, *James V* (1998) nicely chronicles these campaigns in his last chapter.

(the victor of Hadden Rigg), moved from Lauder to Smailholm and then apparently was demobilised, once Norfolk returned to England. The second army under the Earls of Moray and Argyll then also went to Lauder where it, too, dissolved. The figures given by spies for these armies are hard to credit: Huntly with 10,000, Argyll with 12,000. Both of these contingents had to be raised in the Highlands, difficult to do at the best of times, but especially so with constant rain, most rivers in flood and then a foot of snow.

In any case, James clearly was able to reconstitute some sort of force at Lauder on 20 November and then at Peebles on the 21st. It moved off to Hawick the next day and then to Langholm, where much of it apparently encamped on the 23rd. A Scottish spy estimated its size to be 9,000. The next morning, the King staying at Lochmaben, the army invaded the Debatable Lands, crossed the Esk and set about burning the land of the Grahams, a large and troublesome Border family whose towers and lands straddled the Border as it was defined before 1552. Just how large the force was is not clear: Wharton havered between 13,000 and 20,000. William Musgrave said between 17,000 and 18,000. But it clearly included horsemen, numerous nobles and light field artillery.

Before the age of field artillery (and even afterwards), two elements of military activity are particularly germane to an understanding of how a battle happened: the dispositions of the forces before they began to manoeuvre so as to make contact and the 'killing zone': where physical combat actually took place. We can never be totally assured about all of the preliminary dispositions, but the 'killing zone' (a sharp misnomer in this case: 'brawling zone' more like) was clearly by the banks of the river.

Sometime around 8:00 am (one and a half hours after dawn) on 24 November 1542, the Scots having moved from their bases through the Debatable Land, crossed the River Esk and began burning, moving along the south bank of the Esk to 'Akeshawhill' (Oakshawhill). Much of their army must have crossed the river just to the west of what is now Longtown itself. Wharton drew his forces up along the south bank of the River Lyne, probably by Westlinton. At first the Scots moved towards him, but then retired, perhaps to regroup so as to recross the Esk. But it must be clearly borne in mind that this Scottish army was not intending a massive attack upon England or even upon Carlisle. It was simply a massive raiding party which was prevented from raiding or burning further. It is not even clear that this army carried with it the suspected Papal Interdict which was to have been read in an English church, thereby further stigmatising the heretical Henry.

Wharton moved his 1200 horse across the Lyne and to Hopesike Woods and then dismounted to Arthuret 'Howes'. The Scots retired to Arthuret Mill Dam. The English then had to attack from the west, the Scots' left flank (to the east) being protected by what was called a 'grete mosse'.[64] It was probably to the north-west of Arthuret Church, between the banks of the Esk and the mill dam, that the Scottish army disintegrated. The casualties on both sides were remarkably low, with very little

64 The *LP* calendarings are in vol. xvii, nos. 1121, 1128, 1142 (2).

actual physical combat except by Lord Maxwell and some others who, William Musgrave said, 'fought valiantly'. If so, there were few bloodied English heads to show for it and most of the Scots dead appear to have drowned in the Esk. The highest figure for total numbers of dead is between 30 and 40.

How the Scots allowed themselves so to be penned in and why they surrendered so easily is probably not germane. It would seem that four causes emerge. On the one hand, the Scottish army was never all together as a massed force, as it had been at Flodden and would be at Pinkie. This was, after all, a foraging, burning and booty gathering 'raid'. Secondly, there was confusion as to command on the Scots side.[65] Thirdly, the English force was much more compact, disciplined (this is critical) and better (and, being smaller, more easily) led. Furthermore they were local men who knew this piece of geography intimately. The Scots did not. Lastly, as the Scots retired from the church, they found themselves trapped by the rising waters of the tidal Esk. They ended up impacted in a crush, rather as happened to the French at Agincourt in 1415, and had become a tightly packed 'crowd'. The Scottish soldiers simply could not get at the English with their weapons and in that sense defeated themselves.

Oddly enough, perhaps the best short overview account of the engagement is from the Imperial ambassador at London. Writing to Charles V on 15 January 1543, Eustace Chapuys reported that the Scots passed 'a little river which is fordable at low tide'. Being 'ambushed', they then fled to the river 'which they now found deep with the rise of the tide and so were compelled to make a stand'.[66] Very likely that is what happened.

One curious aspect of this engagement is its name: Solway Moss. Wharton, writing in April 1547, did refer to it as 'the solway moss'.[67] The first printed account, Hall's 1548 *History*,[68] clearly discusses the event, but makes no mention of the Solway. Knox, writing in the mid-1560s, however, did locate the retreat as 'Sollen Moss'.[69] 'Solowaie Mosse' was how Bishop Lesley titled it in 1578 in his *History*, and Holinshed took his account and its name from him in 1585.[70] Every nineteenth-

65 Lord Maxwell or Oliver Sinclair of Pitcairn. Almost every writer on the topic has made a great deal of this, but it can be overestimated: all sixteenth-century armies suffered from having only the most rudimentary of communication structures. See G.A. Sinclair, 'The Scots at Solway Moss', *Scottish Historical Review* (ii, 1904), 372–77.
66 *LP*, xviii (1), no. 44.
67 *Cal. State Papers relating to Scotland and Mary Queen of Scots*, i, no. 13.
68 Although it should be noted Hall died in 1547 and his work was only published the next year; hence his account was either written before or added on by another editor.
69 Knox, *History of the Reformation in Scotland*, i, pp. 35–38, and see marginal notation on p. 35. Knox (like Musgrave and Wharton) had an axe to grind and his account is quite untrustworthy, although he captures some colourful elements. But he egregiously plays down the numbers of the English (so as to demonstrate God's hatred of the Catholic king) and describes the English coming together in dribs and drabs, whereas Wharton clearly had gathered forces the day before (*LP*, xvii, no. 1119).
70 *Holinshed's Chronicles of England, Scotland and Ireland* (1808), vol. V (Scotland), pp. 517, 526–28.

century calendaring of the battle refers to it as Solway Moss, and that is how it has consistently appeared in every twentieth-century history either of Scotland or of the reign of Henry VIII.

However, when one examines the original reports executed nearest the time of the event, 'Solway Moss' is not mentioned. The forms of words are thus: Maxwell 'lighted at the waterside', 'the overthrow given to the Scots between Heske and Levyn, by the West Marchers', 'taken prisoners upon Eske and thereabouts', '[The Scots] fled towards the water'. Only in one list of the prisoners taken is mention made of 'Salowe Mosse'.[71] That may be where some of the prisoners were captured (although clearly most were taken on the river bank); certainly a large number of horses were taken there.[72]

The Solway Moss is quite definitely on the north side of the Esk; it appears thus on every map I have ever seen and is noted as the location of a great eruption in the late eighteenth century. The river has very likely shifted its course, as Mr. Bell argues in his paper (to my mind convincingly) and then swept just to the west of the knoll upon which stands Arthuret Church. Wharton, writing in May 1543, clearly refers to the 'overthrow' as having taken place at 'Hartred Church',[73] which must be Arthuret Church, which has not moved since the sixteenth century. We thus have a paradox: whatever happened here, it was not much of a battle and it was not at 'Solway Moss'.

Moreover, it had few far-reaching effects (the way Pinkie would). It was a disintegration with hardly any one killed at all. It was 'an engagement': an affray, a confused brawl, a massive scuffle. Most certainly, as one Scottish contemporary stated, it was 'ane unhappie raid' at which the Scots were 'discomfeist'.[74] A considerable number of men were present: certainly into five figures. The Scots did suffer significant losses: possibly 3000 horses, certainly a large number of carts many of which were armed, at least 24 pieces of minor ordnance (plus many more hand pieces) and quite a large number of notables.

The importance of any battle for a historian depends very much on what he is trying to learn from it. Mostly, Solway Moss has been considered within the context of Scottish, not English, history. The most sweeping interpretation is that is represents a major comment upon the reign of James V. By his relying upon Catholic clerical support (in particular that of David Beaton) for his rule, the king supposedly alienated his nobility to the point where they consistently refused to do their prime duty as subjects and fight for him. By his elevation of 'base born minions' such as Oliver Sinclair, the King (like James III) turned his political elite into a sullen, uncooperative estate, in sharp contrast to his father, James IV, who died at Flodden surrounded by his aristocracy.

The issue goes even further: did the Scottish military caste at Solway Moss refuse to fight because they were deeply infected by Protestantism? Did the King

---

71 *LP*, xviii (1), no. 2 (2).
72 Figures vary between 3000 and 5000.
73 *LP*, xviii (1), no. 592.
74 *A Diurnal of Remarkable Occurrents, that have passed within the country of Scotland, since the death of King James IV, till the year 1575*, ed. T. Thomson (Edinburgh, 1833).

have a secret list (prepared by Beaton) of the most notable proto-heretics and were they especially placed at the front of the Scottish van or 'battle' so as to see them off?

Did the defeat at Solway Moss kill James V? Certainly some thought so at the time: that he fell into a rage and quite simply lost the will to live. Indeed, had the King not died three weeks later (14 December 1542), Solway Moss/Arthuret Church would hardly be mentioned in any history. Three thousand horses are a lot of horses and no monarchy relished losing any of its expensively wrought artillery, especially brass pieces. No monarch, moreover, enjoyed losing face, as Henry VIII knew only too well, having been made the laughing stock of Europe by the notorious adultery of his last wife. James V most certainly did lose public 'face' and English agents abroad happily trumpeted the Scots' discomfiture. But the King was not killed at Solway Moss, nor was he captured. Instead he retired, angry to be sure, to Falkland and died. Did the defeat cause the King's death? James certainly fell into a temper tantrum and became nearly incoherent. He may have been temporarily deranged, but he also clearly was physically sick, vomiting copiously. Howsoever, he died.

The next critical issue is: what effect did the English victory at Solway Moss have on Anglo-Scottish international relations? Did it radically affect Henry VIII's foreign policy? This rests very much on how one views the important prisoners captured on the day. These included some of the great men of the realm: the Earl of Glencairn, the Earl of Cassillis, Lord Robert Maxwell and the Lords Fleming, Gray, Oliphant and Somerville. They were removed to London (arriving by 23 December) and their ransoms were quickly being arranged. One sapient foreigner, Adrien de Croy, writing from Ghent, opined that the Scots would be more astounded by the capture of these men than by the death of their 30-year-old King.[75] Indeed, that is rather the point. The unhappy raid at Arthuret Church was not important because men fought and died, but because shortly thereafter the King of Scots died, leaving a one-week-old daughter as the kingdom's new monarch.

It was the rapid conjunction of these four events: humiliating disintegration of an army, the capture of so many members of the ruling elite, the birth of an infant as his sole heir and the death of the King which made 'Solway Moss' seem significant. For a brief period of months, it appeared as if Henry had an opportunity to bring Scotland to heel. Many historians have been tempted to see Solway Moss as part of Henry VIII's Rough Wooings of Scotland (and by extension Edward VI's) which lasted from November 1543 to March 1550.[76] But in reality, it was the conclusion to quite a different matter, the war of 1542 between Henry VIII and James V. By September 1543, the English king had been decisively outmanoeuvred by the Scottish government in its attempt to gain Mary Queen of Scots for his son. His 'Solway Moss' 'Assured Lords' gained him nothing. The death of James and the birth of Mary are what mattered for Anglo-Scottish relations in 1543. Henry VIII's policy would have

---

75 *LP*, xviii (1), no. 9.
76 To give but one example, see Bernard C. Weber, *The Youth of Mary Queen of Scots* (Philadelphia, 1941), pp. 11–16. R.B. Wernham, *Before the Armada* (1968), pp. 149–50 regards it similarly.

been virtually the same regardless of whether or not he held the Solway Moss prisoners in thrall.

Within the context of European warfare, Solway Moss is a mere flicker of an eyelid, a blip. But even within the parochial confines of Anglo-Scottish relations, its significance is minor, especially when one considers that truces immediately followed it and then a peace in July 1543. When war broke out in earnest again in 1544, Wharton had to start virtually from scratch in his efforts to tame the Scots in the West. Admittedly, he was quite successful, at least until February 1548 when all his efforts came disastrously unstuck at Drumlanrig.

Some actors on our stage had good cause to remember Solway Moss, not least Thomas Wharton himself who found his valour on the day richly rewarded. By February 1544 he was full Warden and had been created a baron. Another beneficiary was Thomas Dacre, a bastard son of the famous Thomas 2nd Lord Dacre of Gilsland, who had commanded the English right wing at Flodden. Thomas was one of the valiant Borderers who performed with such heroism at Arthuret Church and he found himself ennobled and granted the lands of Lanercost Priory, a grant augmented and confirmed in 1553. Others naturally would rue the event, especially those Scots who refused to 'assure' with Henry VIII at Christmas 1542; some of them remained unransomed prisoners-of-war in England until 1551. They certainly were discomfited on the day, but, frankly, history was not.

CHAPTER FOUR

Scotland After James V

THE DEATH OF THE KING OF SCOTS

After the humiliating débâcle at Solway Moss, James V of Scotland wandered disconsolately across his Kingdom.[1] Rumours of royal illness filled the air, and even the weather was more than normally wretched.[2] The King retired from Caerlaverock almost alone; many of his nobility had been captured, including a particular favourite, Oliver Sinclair of Pitcairn, captain of his castle of Tantallon.[3] A brief visit to his Queen in the last stages of her final confinement, at Linlithgow, brought James no comfort; and he then removed himself to Falkland, perhaps the most beloved of palaces for all the sixteenth-century Stewart monarchs.

There he took to his bed and failed rapidly. On 14 December 1542 he died, having lived for only thirty years.[4] Genuine mystery surrounds his last week, and little can be said with certainty about the cause of his death, about his arrangements, if any, for the regency of his daughter Mary (who was born on 8 December), or about his last words. John Knox, ever salacious about those he dismissed as papists, sneered that he had visited a whore and that his final thoughts were of Oliver. Bishop Lesley, more reserved, put prophetic words on his lips: 'Scotland suld be aflicted with the Inglishmen shortlie, and sourlie'.[5]

'Thair wes greit murnyng in Scotland' as messengers were dispatched with the stunning news to Stirling, to the West and the Borders of the Kingdom, and to the Queen.[6] Rothesay Herald, accompanied by Dingwall Pursuivant, took word to Henry VIII of England that 'be the dispositioun of God Omnipotent, quhais will na

---

1 The best account of the King's last days is J. Cameron, *James V*, 320–27.
2 For accounts of the battle, see *ibid.*, 315–320; *LP*, xvii, no. 1249; xviii (1), no. 44; and G.A. Sinclair, 'The Scots at Solway Moss', *SHR*, ii (1905), 357–77.
3 See article above, which tried to exonerate Pitcairn for the mess at Solway Moss, but even more so Cameron, *James V*, 273–74, 270–75, 293–94, 316–21.
4 A.H. Dunbar, *Scottish Kings: A Revised Chronology of Scottish History 1005–1625*, 2nd. ed., 240–43. See also A. Lang, 'A Disputed Date in Knox's History', *SHR*, iii (1906), 230–82 and D. Hay Fleming, *Mary Queen of Scots*, 179–80. For some of the contemporary accounts, see Knox, *History*, i, 38–39; *Diurnal of Occurrents*, 25; *LP*, xvii, no. 1194.
5 Knox, *History* i, 39; Dalrymple, *Historie*, i, 259. See also D. Hay Fleming's attack on Andrew Lang's favourable view of Beaton's role in the business of the King's will: 'Mr Andrew Lang and the murder of Cardinal Beaton', *Contemporary Review*, lxxiv (1898), 375–89. Lang's position is to be found in: *A History of Scotland*, i, 458–68; 'The Truth about the Cardinal's Murder', *Blackwood's Magazine*, clxiii (1898), 344–55; and 'The Cardinal and the King's will', *SHR*, iii (1906), 410–22. See also *LP*, xviii (1), no 395 for Arran's version of the will.
6 *TA*, viii, 143; the phrase is from the *Diurnal of Occurrents*, 25–26.

erdlie creature may resist, oure Soverane and Maister, зour tendir nepho is departit fra yis present life, to our grete desolatioun and as we suppone зour Hienes nocht litill desplesour and treistes'.[7] Similar tidings went to Francis I of France, once James's father-in-law, and to the Holy Father, who had also bestowed honour on him.[8] Meanwhile, the King's body was prepared for his interment, and the new head of government,[9] James Hamilton, second Earl of Arran, granted the King's goods to his late household servants and staff. Michael Durham, 'doctor beand with the kings grace the tyme of his seikness and decess', was given a satin gown; rapiers, crossbows and numerous other personal possessions went to others.[10] Fife nobles and lairds gathered 'for conveying the Kingis grace body fra Falkland to the Ferry'. Thence the procession moved to Edinburgh and the 'Dolours Chapel' in Holyrood Abbey, where extensive preparations were hastened by Sir David Lindsay of the Mount[11] for the funeral service.[12]

'Dule habits' (a French innovation first seen in Scotland on the occasion of the death of James's beloved first wife Madeleine)[13] were readied for Arran and his family, for all the heralds – Lyon, Rothesay, Ross, Albany, Marchmont, Carrick, Bute, Dingwall, Ormond and Unicorn – and for Thomas Marshall, 'maister cuke to our soverane lord'. The chariot, hackney and horse of Mary of Guise, James's second wife, were draped in black. In the chapel, the mattress for the effigy was laid out; banners, the cloth of state, coats of arms were prepared; the crown and sceptre were readied; clubs, spears and chandeliers were coated with black paint. A carver chiselled a lion above a Scottish crown as well as a 'superscriptioun of the tombe in Romane lettres', which was 18 feet long. At the other end of the capital, poor folk and the chaplains made intercession in St Giles' for the soul of the dead monarch.[14] Some time after 3 January, the procession from Fife arrived with the King's body. Lesley, some thirty years later, could still recall the ceremony:

> Heir all was done, fulfillit with al dew ceremonies and all diligence, Torches lychtet, places spred with Tapestrie, qwisselis of dule; Cardinalis al in sadnes, as he held shewe; The erles of Argyle, Arran, Rothesay and Merchal and others in great number of the nobilitie, filthie in dule weid.[15]

---

7   *TA*, viii, 149; *SP Henry VIII*, v, 231 (*LP*, xvii, no. 1227).

8   *LP*, xviii (1), no. 82; *TA*, viii, 149. See also NAS, Capprington MS, fo. 239v.

9   The term 'regent' was never officially applied to Arran: he was Tutor to the Queen's Grace and Governor of her realm.

10   The inventory of the gifts is to be found in BL, MS Royal, 18C, xiv, fos. 209–15. Many of the King's debts were also paid at this time (*TA*, viii, 143; *LP*, xviii 91, no. 13).

11   C. Edington, *Court and Culture in Renaissance Scotland*, 112–13.

12   *TA*, viii, 143; *LP*, xviii (1), no. 13.

13   Buchanan (published in 1582) commented that it was 'then first, I believe, mourning dresses were worn by the Scots' and reflected that 'even now', forty years after the funeral, they 'are not very frequent, although public fashions have greatly increased for the worse': a nice phrase. Buchanan, *History of Scotland*, 315.

14   *TA*, viii, 142–44, 160, 163, 165.

15   Dalrymple, *Historie*, ii, 259–60.

Then, probably on 10 January, the King was laid to rest in the same tomb as 'his sueit wyfe' and his two dead sons.[16]

News, momentous or not, did not travel quickly in sixteenth-century Europe, especially in the dead of winter.[17] It took five days for the word to travel 135 miles from Falkland to Alnwick, where at midnight on 21 December a breathless informant told the startling news to Sir John Dudley, Viscount Lisle, then Warden of the Marches against Scotland; by 23 December it had reached London.[18] The account was, as one would expect, garbled: James had died of poison or of 'regret, sorrow and rage' over Solway Moss; his widow was also like to die; Mary had died; she was 'alyve and good liking'; her name was Elizabeth; she was not of James's loins; she was a son.[19] Lord Lisle's reaction was to halt all hostilities against Scotland, arguing that it was not seemly to war 'open a dedd bodye, or upon a wydowe, or on a yonge suckling', but the snow and frost were so severe (the Tweed had frozen and its wooden bridge would be swept away by the ice flows in the new year) that the wardens could have done little in any event.[20] In London, the news precipitated a frenzy of consultation amongst the King's advisers, and constant meetings of the Privy Council. Scottish prisoners from Solway Moss, recently warded in the city, were suddenly brought before the court and lavishly entertained, while, in King Henry's mind, a plan to marry his only son to the Scottish Queen began to flower.[21]

Across the Channel, Mary, Queen Dowager of Hungary and Regent of the Low Countries, was probably the first to receive anything like an authoritative report of James's death; the Imperial ambassador in London, Eustace Chapuys, sent her word on 23 December. Doubtless she immediately informed her brother, Charles V, who was still in Spain, and he received fuller information from Chapuys three weeks later.[22] Richard Hilles, an English Protestant living in Frankfurt, remembered hearing the news a little after Christmas;[23] William Paget, English ambassador to France, who was with the court of Francis I at Lusignan, received word by 9 January 1543. The French, still digesting the shock of Solway Moss, initially refused to credit the news, but by 17 January a messenger from Cardinal David Beaton, Archbishop of St Andrews, a man implicitly trusted at the French court (he was also bishop of

16 *Nonces en France, 1541–46*, i, 260; LP, xviii (1), no. 26. *Diurnal of Occurrents*, 25, gives 8 January 1543 as the date.
17 Many examples of the time necessary exist: Chapuys received in London on 21 January a letter sent by Granvelle on 3 November from Genoa; the faintest of rumours of Solway Moss did not reach Madrid until 27 January 1543 (*LP*, xviii (1), nos. 63, 56).
18 *LP*, xvii, no. 1221.
19 The various rumours are well catalogued by D. Hay Fleming, *Mary Queen of Scots*, 179. See also Knox, *History*, i, 39. See also *LP*, xvii, nos. 1184, 1193–4, 1196, 1209, 1213–14, 1217, 1221, 1230–31, 1235, 1249.
20 *LP*, xvii, no. 1221, 1249.
21 *Ibid.*, no. 1241. See how Chapuys saw the English court at this hectic time (*LP*, xviii (1), nos. 44, 18, 22, 62).
22 *LP*, xviii (1), nos., 56, 84. The Venetians may also have heard of it very early on, but the evidence is very contradictory (*LP*, xvii, no. 1207, but see also *Calendar of State Papers, Venetian*, ed. R. Brown (1864–), v, 117).
23 *LP*, xviii (1), no. 317.

Mirepoix, a gift of Francis I in 1538), confirmed the death;[24] a frenzy ensued, not unlike that in London less than a month before. When reports arrived in Rome at the end of January, shock and frantic activity occurred there too.[25] A particularly incoherent report reached Madrid via Burgos merchants at the end of February; Denmark did not know until even later.[26]

Thus word of the death of the King of Scots filtered across Europe: slowly and in muddled form. While the sudden demise of any crowned head would presumably have excited European-wide interest, in this case there was an added dimension: James V's Kingdom had been inherited by a one-week-old girl. While Queen Mary's

Fig. 4.1.   As Gordon Donaldson pointed out so long ago, Mary was the only monarch the Scots had in 1542 and they had absolutely no hesitation in accepting her as Queen. All Acts of Parliament, treaties, grants under Great Seal or Privy Seal were done by her authority and in her name. Arran was merely her Tutor and Governor of the realm. Her Majesty can be seen here, in the handsome Great Seal cast upon her father's death.

24 *Nonces en France 1541–46*, 183; *LP*, xviii (1), nos. 35, 63, 84, 93.
25 *LP*, xviii (1), nos. 31, 82, 319, 321.
26 *Ibid.*, nos. 231, 472.

birth meant that Scotland was spared the horrors of a disputed succession,[27] it made another kind of contest inevitable. When she grew up (if she survived infancy, which was by no means a foregone conclusion), she would bring that Kingdom to her husband when – as she was bound to do – she married.

To a Europe whose politics had been transformed by the amazing marital successes of the house of Habsburg, Mary's significance as a dynastic entity was only too obvious. Various matches were to be proposed for her, including a Habsburg prince, the young Earl of Kildare, and the brother and the son of the King of Denmark. But in the years 1543–50 three particularly serious possibilities emerged, all of them boys advanced by their fathers, to whom they were eldest sons: James Hamilton (born in 1536–37); Edward, Prince of Wales (born 12 October 1537); Francis d'Angoulême (born 19 January 1544): a Scotsman, an Englishman and a Frenchman.[28] The three proposed marriages encapsulate the three strands of national interests in the marriage of Mary, Queen of Scots, which were at the heart of the Rough Wooings.

SCOTLAND AND THE EARL OF ARRAN

When James V died, James Hamilton, second Earl of Arran, was probably in his mid- or late twenties.[29] His grandmother was the eldest daughter of James II (d. 1460), and, such had been the depletion of the cadet branches of the royal house of Stewart over the past sixty years, he was Queen Mary's heir presumptive. But there were doubts over his legitimacy, which were to embarrass him continually throughout his career: had his father, the first Earl of Arran, obtained a valid divorce from his first wife before marrying Janet Beaton, the second earl's mother?[30] The question was especially important in 1542–3, for if Arran were illegitimate, then the status of heir presumptive would belong to his kinsman and near-contemporary in age, Matthew, Earl of Lennox; there might have followed a repetition of the bitter struggle to control the government of Scotland during the minority of James V. As it was, Arran's blood position as 'second person of the realm' was accepted, and ensured that on 3 January 1543 (perhaps after a brief power struggle) he emerged as Governor of Scotland during the Queen's minority.[31]

27 Had James V left no legitimate child at all, the senior claimant to the throne would have been the Earl of Arran, but he would have faced resolute opposition from his kinsman Matthew Stewart, Earl of Lennox (about whose legitimacy, unlike Arran's, there was no doubt), and probably from Henry VIII of England, brother to James's mother.

28 One went barking mad, the other two died in their mid-teens, the one a prig, the other a nerd. Mary then married Henry Darnley, who, had Elizabeth and Mary died young, might have become Henry IX of England. The mind reels.

29 The only recent biography is D. Franklin, *The Scottish Regency of the Earl of Arran* (Lampeter, 1996), which is overly reliant on printed sources. Finnie, E., 'The House of Hamilton: Patronage, Politics and the Church in the Reformation Period', *Innes Review* (xxxvi, 1985), 3–28, concentrates on 1554–73.

30 Every history of the period comments on the problem of Arran's legitimacy. Dickinson gives the best précis of the evidence in Knox, *History*, i, 49, no. 1. This was clearly important at the time, as Beaton spelt it out to de la Brosse and Message (Brosse, *Missions*, 26).

31 There is some controversy as to the ease with which Arran gained the regency. *A Source Book of Scottish History*, ed. W.C. Dickinson and others, ii, 125, says that Beaton was 'frustrated in an attempt to seize power'; Donaldson, *Scotland*, 63, suggests that things went smoothly at first. See also the debate between Fleming and Lang mentioned above, n. 5.

THE SCOTTISH ROYAL SUCCESSION

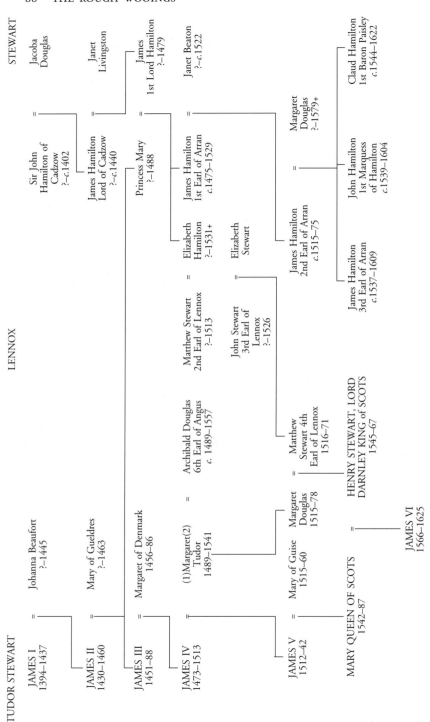

Fig. 4.2.   The Hamilton and Lennox claims to the Scottish succession. As can readily be seen in this interlocked dynastic chart, both the Hamiltons and the Lennox Stewarts had claims to be second person of the realm going back to the children of James II, just as the Yorkists and Lancastrians had claims to the English throne going back to Richard II. The Scots were a more sophisticated political society in any case, but civil wars (at least until 1715) were averted by the uncanny ability of the Royal Stewarts always to produce at least one surviving monarch down to Bonnie Prince Charlie. Vibrant competition did, naturally, ensue. Lennox's father was killed at Linlithgow in 1527 and

Arran was not a conventionally impressive man. Hardly one contemporary had a praiseworthy remark to make of him and historians since have not been kinder.[32] He was said to be foolish, irresolute, easily led, could be bullied and at heart was out solely for the advancement of himself and his family. Under pressure he was known to blubber; in excitement he could weep; when intimidated he would acquiesce; if presented with an opportunity for aggrandisement, his greed always triumphed; in battle he fled; and in the end, in 1554, he was ousted from his post by a woman.

However, if viewed objectively, Arran's achievement during the course of his life was quite impressive. He was, above all else, a great survivor. His implacable rival, the handsome, personable Lennox, spent two decades in exile; he finally achieved his ambition of regent in 1570 only to be killed in 1571. Arran held the post for more than twelve years, longer than any other regent in sixteenth-century Scotland, and when in 1575 he died, he did so in bed. Though an insignificant political figure on the European stage, Arran survived a series of serious domestic revolts in 1544, kept Henry VIII at bay during 1543, then bested him in war during 1544–45. Militarily defeated by Somerset in 1547, he nonetheless was able to hold on until French aid reversed the tide and ousted the English from his country. Though ignominiously removed from the centre of the political stage in 1554, he lived to be a principal agent of the expulsion of the French in 1560. These broad overall considerations must be kept in mind as one examines his career during the period under discussion, even though accusations of greed and irresolution can never be ignored. The same could be said of Henry VIII.

In January 1543, Arran found himself in an extraordinarily precarious position as he assumed the role of Governor of the Kingdom and thus acquired the next best thing to complete monarchical power in Scotland. Firstly, the resources available to whoever directed the Scottish monarchy were, by almost any European standards, feeble. Secondly, the Governorship gave him none of the aura of kingship which surrounded Somerset, for example, in 1547–48.[33] Thirdly, Scotland was essentially an aristocratic polity and the nobility in 1543 were determined to curtail monarchical power. Fourthly, he was confronted by two powerful and resolute personalities, David Beaton, Cardinal Archbishop of St Andrews, a man accustomed to and frighteningly adroit in the exercise of power, and Mary of Guise-Lorraine, mother of the Queen, a member of one of the most powerful and ambitious families of France and seemingly determined to maintain the French alliance and to guard her daughter's inheritance. Lastly he faced the interference of two monarchies, England and France, both of which were determined at different times to control and direct Scottish affairs. If Arran merely survived in the face of such obstacles, surely some credit, if not respect, is his.

32 Fleming gives a catalogue of men's views at the time (*Mary Queen of Scots*, 183, no. 29), but his list is by no means exhaustive.
33 Again, one must be careful. Arran was a better politician than Somerset, not a difficult thing to do. And he did gain access as Governor to all of James V's palaces (save Stirling, the dower house of Mary of Guise) and he lived in their 'Imperial' environment (see recent studies of James V's court and style). He controlled the Great Seal and the Secret Seal and the Crown's money. He was the automatic commander of the nation's military resources.

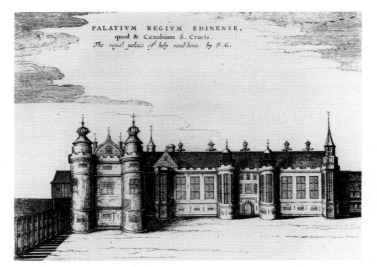

a

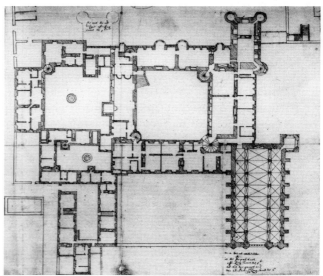

b

Fig. 4.3.   (a), (b). Arran's success in being recognised as Tutor to the Queen and
Governor of the Realm gave him not just enormous political power, but use
of the royal palaces which James IV and V had done so much to enhance
during their reigns. Only Stirling was denied him, being part of Mary of
Guise's dowry. Linlithgow, Falkland, Dunfermline (the Royal Forth) were all
handsome, as were the monarch's apartments in Edinburgh Castle. But the
most splendid of all was Holyrood Palace. (a) An etching of the front of the
palace executed in 1647 shows almost exactly how it appeared in 1542. (b)
Plan of the internal lay-out of the ground floor shows what an enormous
complex of rooms were there for his (and his family's) use: reception rooms,
gallery, chapel, kitchen and numerous store rooms. More accomodation
naturally existed on the first and second floors.

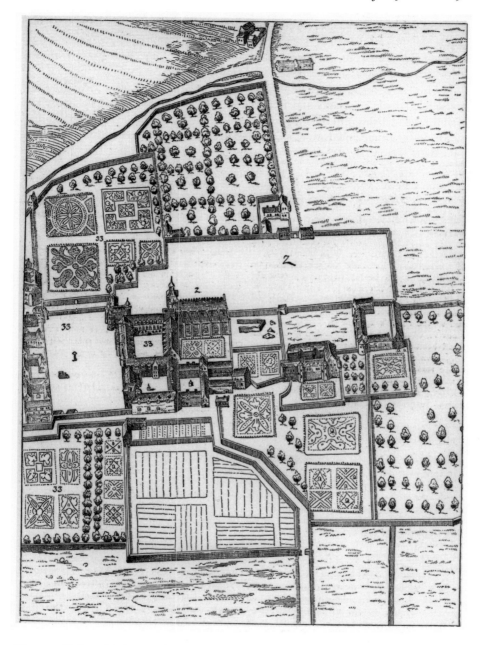

Fig. 4.4. Holyrood Palace was bounded by the Abbey Kirk to its North and by vast gardens to the west. It was in these gardens that the Treaties of Greenwich were ratified by Arran and most of the aristocracy on 25 August 1543.

The King buried, the Governor left Edinburgh for the day to see the Queen and her mother at Linlithgow. He then returned to take up residence in either the King's castle of Edinburgh, or the royal palace of Holyrood House.[34] Either would have made a striking contrast to his own seat of Hamilton, and Arran can be forgiven if he found his elevation a bit breathtaking. He was now in charge of a vastly enhanced household, stock of palaces and financial income. The Queen had no household establishment, being utterly adequately looked after at Linlithgow by her mother, whose dower arrangements were quite generous in any case. Arran (through the royal Treasurer) was to pay for many of her purchases over the next five years, but these were never a major drain.

Arran's power can be seen, if you will, in his signature. A document with his autograph 'JAMES G' on it now had the authority of government. He could issue pardons, call parliaments, raise armies, grant lands and titles with that scrawl on the bottom of a piece of paper.[35] That 'signature' was almost always sufficient authorisation to activate the vital effective instruments of government in a medieval polity: the Great Seal and the Secret Seal. Arran may well have had to share his 'rule' with Cardinal Beaton (September 1543–May 1546) and Mary of Guise (from February 1545), but their signatures had none of the power his did. The main symbols of majesty were in the Governor's hands. Not least of these were the Queen's Officers of Arms: the Lyon King of Arms (since 1542, Sir David Lindsay of the Mount), six Heralds and six Pursuivants. Arran thus had immediate access to the most effective postal system in the kingdom[36] and could have proclamations posted throughout the realm in a matter of days and letters delivered expeditiously to all of the nobility. The Officer of Arms also carried correspondence to England and abroad.[37] One intriguing symbol of majesty not often mentioned was the coinage. Of course his head could not appear thereupon, but he stamped his Governorship into the minds of the Queen's subjects firstly by cinquefoils: a five-pointed star, a Hamilton emblem.[38] He also widely employed on what coinage was struck during this period IG for Jacobus Gubernator.[39]

---

34 It is relatively easy to devise an itinerary for Arran as Governor from the evidence of *APS*, *RPC*, *RSS*, and to a lesser extent from *TA*, not to mention from the datings of royal letters in *Epistolae Jocobi Quarti, Jacobi Quinti et Mariae Regum Scotorum*. However, a much fuller rendering of the Governor's movements can be gained, when those books are missing, from 'Liber Emptorum S.N.D. Regis' (the Crown's household accounts) and from 'Liber Emptorum S.N.D. Regis' (the household's provisionings), NAS, E 31 and E 31 respectively. It was from these sources that the itinerary for Arran during 1542–48 (*RSS*, iii, xxxi–xxxix) was created (a practice regretfully not followed in subsequent volumes). For all mentions of the Governor's movements during July 1550, see NAS, E 32/10.

35 See his signature on the cover of G. Donaldson's popular textbook, *Scottish Historical Documents* (1970).

36 Augmented when necessary by numerous 'boys' and 'messengers' of his household.

37 A topic treated usefully by the Ross Herald of Arms, C.J. Burnett, in 'Outward Signs of Majesty, 1535–1540', in *Stewart Style*, 289–302; and see his other works cited in the footnotes.

38 His brother did something similar by inlaying ciquefoils over the new gateway he built into St. Andrews Castle when he rebuilt it after the French battered it down in 1547.

39 J.K.R. Murray, 'The Scottish Coinage of 1553', *British Numismatic Journal* (xxxvii, 1968), 98–109.

Fig. 4.5. The Crown's business all over Europe was increasingly moving away from authentication by the employment of seals (held usually by the Chancellor) by which commands and grants moved up a hierarchy of validations: signet, secret seal to great seal. By the sixteenth century, we are firmly in the age of the 'sign manual' whereby the monarch's signature (Henry VIII famously had a rubber stamp made for his) was considered sufficient for an order to be acted upon. Arran thus gained with his Governorship a new signature. Before he would simply have written his title ARRAN or Erle ARRANE. Now, however, he became JAMES G, and that on the bottom of a piece of paper, especially if countersigned by his Secretary, could do anything a king could do, such as raise an army or call a Parliament or pardon a murder. That was power.

As one would have expected him to do, the new Governor spent the first six weeks of his regency surrounding himself with men familiar to him, giving them favours and pensions. A feature of Scottish society at this time was the surname affinity. Many men about a lord, regardless of whether they were related to him by blood or not, and regardless of their social station, took his surname and acted in concert with him even though they may not have been tenants on his land, or members of his family, or of his household, or bound to him as a retainer by a contract, in Scotland called a bond of manrent.[40] Thus one should not be surprised to find the royal household changing its personnel almost immediately. James and Andrew Hamilton became porters, Peter became cook, Robert became master of the stable, James Hamilton of Orbiston and other lairds became messengers.[41] Some became keepers or captains of royal castles, such as Matthew of Millburn at Linlithgow (later captain

Fig. 4.6.   The famous 1553 'Da Pacem Domine' testoon, it should be noted, was stamped with cinquefoils, five-pointed stars representing the Earl of Arran's heraldic device. Other coins showed IG for him as Governor. Compared with Francis I's evocative salamander and Henry II's quarter moons, it was rather tame. No high poetry was attached to it. But in an age where communication was highly visual, such an impresa could have an effect. The Hamilton Arms thus became familiar all over the country. When Arran's half-brother John rebuilt St. Andrews Castle, he placed cinquefoils all over the new entrance gateway. Mary of Guise decorated her coinage with the Cross of Lorraine.

40 The affinity created by a bond of manrent has been significantly elaborated by J. Wormald in *Lords and Men in Scotland: Bonds of Manrent, 1442–1603* (Edinburgh, 1985). Some discussion of the topic is to be found in Donaldson, *Scotland*, 14–15 and T.I. Rae, *The Administration of the Scottish Frontier, 1513–1603*, 8, 79. See also Stair Society, *An Introduction to Scottish Legal History*, 285–86. For examples of the practice, which has something in common with English 'indentured retainers', see the following volumes of *HMC*: 10, 10th R., i, 25; 21 *Hamilton*, i, 35–57; 26, 12th R., viii, 94.

41 NAS, E 31/13.

of Blackness) and Robert Hamilton who became captain of Dalkeith Castle, then Dunbar.[42] During the first flush of his Governorship Arran toyed with Protestantism; he had in 1542 been noted as a heretic, and during the excitement to read the scriptures which characterised the period of Beaton's eclipse, from January to July 1543, Arran rather played the role of protector of the new teaching and during this time was munificent to men who later emerged as convinced Protestants, such as the Dr Michael Durham who was with James at his death, his brother Henry, the preacher John Rough and various others.[43]

By Scottish standards Arran had a considerable amount of treasure with which to be generous, for James had both increased royal revenues during his reign and had amassed what many claimed was a large personal fortune.[44] By European standards, however, the Scottish Crown was financially very poor indeed and throughout the country specie was scarce. As one Lord observed in 1548, 'This realme is pwyr'. The aristocracy (the 'greit men in this realme') had 'folkis to sarve them in thair awn boundis but only mone [without any actual coin]'.[45] For the Crown, too, its wealth lay largely in the service it could extract from the extensive lands it held (though even these were small by English and French standards) and from its power of appointment both to Crown and to church offices.

From the start one must remember that by the 1540s the Scottish pound was only worth approximately five shillings sterling.[46] Bearing this exchange rate in mind, the weakness of the Crown is readily apparent when one realises that in 1539/40 ordinary royal revenue was something like £s46,000 or £11,750 Sterling.[47] This at a time when Henry VIII's annual income was exceeding its normal level of the 1530s: £125,000. This ordinary income came from a variety of sources: the income from the royal domain in 1539–40 was £s9325; customs revenue in 1542 was £s5306; profit from the coinage in 1540–41 (admittedly a high year) was £s5187. There was revenue from casualties (wardship, marriage, charters, profits of justice, various compositions); that from escheated goods and the granting of pardons alone in 1541–42 amounted to £s4449.[48] In addition to the ordinary royal revenue which Arran could expect to control, various extraordinary sources existed.

Taxation, of course, could be levied but only with the consent of the three estates, and in the past such parliamentary grants had been rare. Contributions could also be

---

42 *TA*, viii, 223, 299, 367, 261, 222, 347, 444; *RSS*, iii, 610–11.

43 Knox, *History*, i, 42–43; *RSS*, iii, nos. 10, 180.

44 *Brosse Missions*, 19.

45 *Mary of Lorraine Corresp.*, 242. See also Donaldson, *Scotland*, 7–8, 56–68.

46 Note the value of Scots money in terms of the other major European currencies mentioned in this work: one livre Tournois (which was also one franc) was worth 10s. Scots in 1545; one Crown of the sun (écu de soleil) was worth 22s. Scots. I am grateful to Dr. A.L. Murray for this information.

47 All of the figures in the next five paragraphs, unless otherwise stated, are from A.L. Murray, 'The Exchequer and Crown Revenues of Scotland, 1437–1542' (unpublished Ph.D. thesis, University of Edinburgh, 1961), in particular pp. 198, 140, 293, 286, 323–40.

48 The execution of justice was a profitable source of revenue which the Scottish Crown did not ignore; a justice ayre to Dumfries in 1539–40 netted £s1740 (Murray, Thesis, 276).

induced from the Convention of the Royal Burghs of Scotland and from the church as a corporate body. In the next seven years, these extra-ordinary sources of revenue were to be stretched to their limits in the great fight against the English, but in January 1543, Arran could not have expected much from them. A more usual source of extra-ordinary revenue lay in three of James's financial expedients: the income from the abbeys held *in commendam* by his bastard sons, the revenues of which were quickly transferred to Arran's use in his first Parliament, the taxation of the clergy to support the College of Justice, and pensions from France.[49]

The expenses of the royal treasury may have fallen under Arran at first, for he was nothing like the great builder that James had been, but his revenue also fell owing to the fact that he had to conduct his regency in a less authoritarian manner than James had conducted his kingship.[50] A sizeable element of royal income came from the extensive forfeited lands of the Lord of Glamis and the Earl of Angus; both of these forfeitures were reversed in March 1543. Moreover the revenues which Mary of Guise had received as consort now went to her alone as Queen Mother, and these may have amounted to as much as £s10,000 per annum. Nonetheless, Arran spent lavishly and may well have quickly exhausted the £s26,000 which he received early in 1543 of James's accumulated personal treasure. James Wood, the controller in 1543, complained that the regent held 'a greit hous and is at mair sumpteous expensis nor umquhile our said soverane Lord held in his tyme'.[51] Even so, an annual revenue of £s46,000 and a lump sum of £s26,000 was hardly 'sumpteous' by European standards.

The Scottish Crown nonetheless was a potent force within the Scottish political context. In part its power lay in the fact that the Scottish monarchy was the only one the Scots had. Though many Scots obviously held Arran in contempt, no animus existed towards the Queen, Mary Stewart, and the arrangements made for her care and protection in the March 1543 Parliament were both entirely sensible and were generally adhered to until her departure for France in August 1548. Her guardians, appointed by the three estates largely on the basis of their probity, carried out their duties in exemplary fashion, and she was never the pawn that James V had been in his youth.

In some measure this reflected the accepted reverence accorded the monarchy as an institution. Although Arran did not enjoy the aura of majesty, he did come into the Crown's stock of houses, and his elevation must have been startling and awesome.[52] He did gain control of much of the practical power of the Crown:

49 *APS*, ii, 424. Clerical taxation is also a complex topic (Donaldson, *Scotland,* 46–48, 57). One French subsidy is recorded in *TA*, viii, 221.

50 In particular, Lennox aside, he had to be 'gentle' to his fellow aristocrats. See James V's 'fiscal squeezing' of his nobility (something he shared with his father), tellingly discussed by Cameron, *James V,* in his final chapter, but especially 331–34 as well as Chs. Four and Eight.

51 A.L. Murray, Thesis, 270. Beaton was to argue in October 1543 that Arran had 'tres mal et tres Inullement administre les biens du Royaume' (Brosse, *Missions,* 26), a common complaint.

52 For just one example of his temporary inheritance, see H.M. Shire, 'The King in his House: Three Architectural Artefacts belonging to the reign of James V', in *Stewart Style,* ed. J.H. Williams (1996). It is highly doubtful Arran ever viewed the striking ceiling in St. Machar's

its indispensable role in the legal system, its position as the guarantor of land tenure and inheritance and, most importantly, as the dispenser of patronage. In the great battle which lay ahead, both for political survival and for independence from England, Arran was to use all three of these functions adroitly and with success, at least until 1548 when the influx of French pensions eroded his position.

In the first place, the Governor controlled justice. In sixteenth-century Scotland, it was not always blind; its application was usually tempered to the political necessities of any moment. In part this reflected the fact that the enforcement of law depended on the will of the monarch. Regular courts did not always meet; rather justice ayres, at times difficult to distinguish from military expeditions, were led by the Governor and he often sat in judgement.[53] In part, this was due to the Crown's power to grant pardons, be they in the form of remissions or respites, be they free or conditional upon the payment of a composition (in effect a fine for the crime). In the seven years which followed Arran's proclamation as Governor, men were declared guilty of crimes they had not committed, some men guilty of high treason were not proceeded against, whilst others equally culpable suffered severely. The penalty, although not always, fitted the circumstances. Control of justice was important because ultimately most Scots did not wish to leave Scotland. Men like Bothwell and Angus had accepted exile in the 1520s and 1530s; Lennox was to do so in the 1540s; so was Knox. Pensions and livings could be had in England and in France; but ultimately Scotsmen preferred to live in the land in which they were born. This simple fact also gave the government considerable power.

During his regency, Arran was not able greatly to manipulate the power of the Crown to confirm inheritance or to protect tenure (few European monarchies had much discretion in this area) but his control of grants under the Great Seal did give him some power. Patronage, obviously, was the most important weapon in the Governor's arsenal, especially in an economy lacking specie. This power can be exaggerated; the Crown had little leeway, for example, in the choice of sheriffs or even of great officers of state, such as the Admiral. Moreover, given the nature of power in sixteenth-century Scotland, its choices were always limited to those men already powerful by virtue of their own local situation. When it came to granting the post of Warden of the West Marches, for example, Arran could hardly call on the

---

Cathedral in Aberdeen from 1520 (in which Charles of Burgundy – Charles V – figured no less than four times), but he must have seen James V's famous gallery with its statues of antique notables. *Stewart Style* is indispensable reading for anyone engaged by the 'Imperialism' of James V's court, much of which survived his death: architecture, music and poetry being but three examples. And other courtly entertainments such as trumpeters, the hunt and card games. Did Arran use the King's tent at Musselburgh the night before Pinkie? Arran's own 'houses' were quite handsome in themselves, and he added to his stock with the revenues as Governor: see Hamilton Palace, his residence in Edinburgh, and especially Kinneil.

53 Rae, *Administration of the Scottish Frontier*, 132–92. Law is also a complex topic; see in particular: Stair Society, *An Introductory Survey of the Sources and Literature of Scots Law* and *An Introduction to Legal History*; *RSS*, iii, xvi–xvii; Pitcairn, *Trials*; W.K. Dickson, 'The Scots Law of Treason', *Juridical Review* x (1898), 245–55.

Earl of Argyll, in many ways a loyal adherent of his regime, because Argyll lived in the North and had no power around Dumfries. There Arran was faced with a choice of a Maxwell (powerful, but ambitious and invariably disloyal) and a Johnstone (loyal but weak).[54] Though he did try to reward loyalty with position, he never had at his disposal the resources of Henry VIII or Francis I. Those posts which carried with them enough wealth to make them desirable were invariably those for which there were very few possible candidates; those which the government could give to anyone it chose, such as customer of Dundee, were of little value.[55]

If this was the case regarding offices of state and commands within the Kingdom, it was not so true of the most important element in Scottish monarchical patronage: its control of church appointments. Here the Crown had almost complete control over nominations both to 'secular' posts, such as the bishoprics of Dunkeld, Aberdeen or Glasgow (all of which became vacant during the period 1544–47), but also to posts in religious houses. James V had blatantly milked the revenues of the abbeys of Holyrood, Kelso, and Melrose, and the priories of Coldingham and St Andrews, for Crown benefit; Arran was to do so with the abbey of Arbroath and with others.[56] His own brother was abbot of Paisley, not unnaturally near Hamilton itself; he was to become bishop of Dunkeld, then archbishop of St Andrews. The brother of the Earl of Huntly, a noble whose support was vital to Arran's regime, became postulate of Aberdeen, then of Caithness, then Glasgow (and eventually archbishop of Athens). The bastard son of the Earl of Angus became commendator of rich Arbroath at a time when his father was already receiving a pension of £1000 a year from Melrose. James V had exploited this source of power quite effectively during his reign, mostly to advance his own personal wealth; Arran was to do so both to advance his family and to maintain power.

Never in complete control of the apparatus of the Crown, Arran still did exploit it when he could, and his direction of affairs in general was more purposeful than many historians have been prepared to admit. But his room for manoeuvre was further constrained by the royal Stewarts' limited fecundity. As Donaldson remarked, 'The Hamilton proximity to the Crown had been a factor in Scottish history even since the death of James IV [1513], and since the death of Albany in 1536 Arran had been heir presumptive'.[57] Arran certainly appreciated how close he was to the throne; his appointment of Sir James Dundas as 'Master of the King's Stable and Master Sewar' early in 1543 was for the term of his regency and 'endwring our lyftyme giff we happin to come to the Croune of this Realme'.[58] This closeness did not, however, mean that he had to be any less accommodating to his fellow nobles. He was, despite his blood,

54 For a discussion of the appointment of wardens of the marches during the sixteenth century, see Rae, *Administration of the Scottish Frontier*, 74–96.
55 *RSS*, iii, no. 180.
56 This aspect is tellingly, if briefly, treated in *Source Book of Scottish History*, ii, 83–103; M. Mahoney, 'The Scottish Hierarchy, 1513–1565', *Essays on the Scottish Reformation, 1513–1625*, ed. D. McRoberts, 39–84; G. Donaldson, *The Scottish Reformation*, 1–52.
57 See below, pp. 000, 000 and Donaldson, *Scotland*, 66.
58 *HMC* 2, 3rd R., 413.

merely another noble and one who was probably less wealthy than Argyll, Huntly or even Angus. The fact that he held the post of Governor gave him a temporary wealth, but regents had been deposed before; his father, ousted from the regency of James V, lost his life in an attempt to regain power in 1526, a fact Arran never forgot.[59] Thus Arran had to bend to the will of the aristocracy of the Kingdom, or at least he had to ensure that he offended as few of them as possible.

THE NOBILITY OF THE REALM

As a body, the Scottish aristocracy were both powerful and angry in 1542. Their power is evidence of the weakness of the Crown; if the Crown wished to effect its will in the country, it generally had to do so through the active support of the nobility in the localities. Though James did make numerous justice ayres, he would turn to Hume and Maxwell or Huntly and Argyll to do the job, occasionally by granting letters of lieutenancy which gave the recipient virtual viceregal authority.[60] Many nobles, and many lairds, also held their fiefs of the Crown as judicial units either as a 'barony' or as a 'regality' in which they had almost complete judicial competence.[61] This jurisdiction greatly augmented the power a noble could muster from his own household and the tenants on his land.

Most nobles also had an extensive affinity usually created by entering into a bond of manrent, generally with a lesser personage, such as a local laird, which created a mutuality of purpose between the noble, bound to give good lordship, and his man, bound to give good service. The noble thus extended his influence to the lairds and thus throughout society. Nobles also often kept a close watch, Maxwell for example on Dumfries, Huntly on Aberdeen.[62] Despite this power, all nobles and all lairds (in fact, everyone who could do so) sought not only preservation, but the augmentation of their positions. No study of sixteenth-century Scotland which does not appreciate this simple human characteristic will make sense. Love of country there was, and commitment to principle, but most men, be they nobles such as Angus, clergymen such as David Paniter, lairds such as Sir Andrew Kerr of Cessford, or townsmen of Dumfries, had their eyes fixed firmly on the opportunity to advance.

Both English and French observers of Scotland in the 1540s (and since[63]), men who within their own local situations behaved in much the same way, constantly

---

59 Nothing else can explain his constant intimidation by judicial means of those thought to have fought against his father at Linlithgow. For some examples, see *RSS*, iv, nos. 1114, 1211, 1291, 1321, 1504, 2861. Note how Arran's family could benefit from this control of justice (*ibid.*, no. 2581).

60 See *Source Book of Scottish History*, ii, 31–33.

61 See Rae, *Administration of the Scottish Frontier*, 15–18, 77–79 for a short treatment of this aspect. Stair Society, *An Introduction to Scottish Legal History*, also deals with the subject of local jurisdictions. Rae's doctoral thesis ('The Administration of the Scottish Border in the Sixteenth Century', St Andrews, 1961) also includes a map of the jurisdictions in Roxburghshire and Selkirkshire, in many ways a much more accurate manner of describing baronial power than one based on blocks of territorial holdings.

62 Dumfries Burgh Museum, MS. Burgh Records, *passim*; *Abdn. Counc.*, i, 195, 200, 208–09.

63 Joel Hurstfield's characterisation in 1958 of the Scottish aristocracy as 'perhaps the most squalid in Europe' is but one example of such anachronistic ethnocentricity at work.

castigated the Scots for their cupidity, inconstancy and greed. But in reality they were only describing a polity in which desire for advancement was the engine of politics. No one understood this better than Arran who, as Governor, controlled the most powerful weapon of patronage in the country: the Great Seal. Pensions from Henry VIII were welcome but they could be cut off and the paymaster was distant: Arran was at hand and the pensions he could dispense were related to land and offices within the country.

Arran, however, was most anxious to advance his own family; given the similar desires of his peers, this was doubtless a sensible attitude to adopt. But it meant that he constantly faced pressure from his fellow nobles to distribute the gifts within his power more evenly among the aristocracy as a whole. The interference of Henry VIII in Scottish affairs in the 1540s was thus a considerable help to the aristocracy. Arran could not behead or exile every noble who practised treasonably with the English: ultimately there would have been no active adult supporters. He could threaten, but eventually some sort of reconciliation would be a gift within Arran's power.

The Governor was rich in daughters, and these he married almost invariably to families who had at one time or another opposed him. Jonet married the son of Glencairn, Mary the son of Cassillis.[64] Angus found his various revolts and collaboration with Henry VIII rewarded by the revenues of Melrose Abbey. Lennox's brother was bought back by the return of his forfeited bishopric; John Maxwell, merely by allying with the English for a month, gained the hand of the richest ward in the country. Only Lennox, whose closeness in blood to the throne too nearly matched Arran's, had to flee and spend his mature years out of Scotland.

Arran did have one great asset in the early months of his regency; he was not James V. James V had been badly bruised by his treatment by his ex-stepfather Archibald, 5th Earl of Angus, regent during 1525–28, and the first act of the King upon his assumption of effective power in 1528 was to attack Angus and the Douglas family. Subsequently the King was to trust few of his nobles; whereas his father had reigned most effectively through a partnership with the aristocratic ruling elite, James V either shunned their company and their counsel in favour of churchmen and 'base born minions' or harried them.[65] Angus, and his brother, Sir George Douglas of Pittendreich, of course suffered most: they spent a fourteen-year exile in England, and during that time all their lands and castles had reverted to the Crown.[66]

But they were not the only ones; the Earl of Bothwell, warded twice in the 1530s, an experience which led him to wish Henry VIII's coronation in Edinburgh, was also finally banished in 1537. Lady Glamis, perhaps because she was sister to Angus, was burned at the stake in the same year. Sir Walter Scott of Buccleuch and Branxholme spent most of the 1530s imprisoned in Edinburgh Castle under suspicion of treason. Their exclusion

64 *Scots Peerage*, iv, 366–68.
65 The older interpretation of James V's personal reign is best encapsulated in Donaldson's 1965 *Scotland*, 43–62, but must be reconsidered in the light of Jamie Cameron's *James V*, published in 1998.
66 See M.G. Kelley, Angus Thesis, and his article, 'Land Tenure and Forfeiture', *Sixteenth Century Journal* (ix, 1978).

from the most important political arenas, the Council and the Lords of the Articles, during this time and the elevation of men such as David Beaton and Oliver Sinclair greatly angered many of the nobility, even those not actively attacked by the King. No understanding of the crucial year 1543 makes sense which does not incorporate the fact that there was a powerful aristocratic reaction against the politics of James V.[67]

Arran's tenure of the post of Governor, then, was contingent on his being able to satisfy the aspirations to patronage, position and power of the peerage. In addition to managing an aristocracy united only in their desire to reverse the late King's policies, Arran also had to face two formidable personages. One was David Beaton; the other was Mary of Guise, mother to the Queen and now Queen Dowager.

THE CARDINAL AND THE QUEEN DOWAGER

The rise to power of David Beaton, aged 46 in 1543, Cardinal Archbishop of St Andrews and Bishop of Mirepoix, was one of the great success stories of the sixteenth century, and he ranks with Wolsey, Granvelle, Guise, Pole and Farnese as a major European clerical politician.[68] The quite genuine hatred which Knox felt for Beaton coloured almost every subsequent assessment of his career, and even today it is not always easy to view him dispassionately.[69] In many ways, Beaton was more powerful than even Wolsey had been, for Scottish ecclesiastical peers had something of the independence of their lay counterparts.

Like Wolsey, with whom he shares many characteristics, Beaton was something of a late developer. Commendator of Arbroath Abbey (1524) at the age of 30, he did not rise to be Archbishop until 1539. His extraordinary importance in the 1530s was primarily due to the fact that from about 1533 he had almost complete mastery of the King, and all too many of James's policies were seen to be those of the Cardinal. Not unnaturally the death of the King had a profound effect upon the Cardinal's position, and he may well have tried to protect himself by preparing the forged will about which so many of his contemporaries talked.[70] What makes one doubt the truth of the story is that such a mess was made of the business. Arran's claim to the regency was, given Scottish tradition, very strong and he was able to dismiss the attempt to displace him with ease.

Then, as the aristocracy flocked to a Council on which many had not sat for years, Arran was able to remove Beaton altogether at the end of January by placing him in ward, barely a fortnight after making him Chancellor.[71] It must have been an

---

67 That Arran intended to reverse the policies of James can be clearly seen in his judicial prosecution of men such as Duncan May for his 'Giving false information to the late king' which occasioned 'vehement suspicions between him and his earle, barons and lieges' (Pitcairn, *Trials*, i, 329).

68 M. H. B. Sanderson, *Cardinal of Scotland* (1986) is the best study.

69 Something of a rehabilitation was begun in 1915 by J. Herkless and R.K. Hannay in *The Archbishops of St Andrews*, iv, a process carried handsomely forward by Dr. Sanderson in *Cardinal of Scotland*.

70 There is considerable evidence concerning Beaton's exclusion, although several aspects of the event remain hazy. See *RSS*, iii, no. 21; *LP*, xviii (1), no. 88.

71 Sanderson, *Cardinal of Scotland*, 148–59.

enormously popular move, and for the moment Beaton was impotent whilst Arran further courted popularity by welcoming home the exiled lords, freeing those in jail, announcing that he regarded the Pope as merely a bishop and proclaiming an interest in a marriage between Mary and Edward, prince of Wales. Beaton, however, was not to remain powerless for long.

Another individual who was a potential threat and who might prove difficult for Arran was the 28-year-old mother of the Queen, Mary of Guise-Lorraine, Duchess of Longueville, Queen Dowager of Scotland.[72] Mary was 27 when she gave birth to her

Fig. 4.7.   This rather tired portrait of David Beaton has been reproduced in textbooks
for decades; we have virtually nothing else to go by, and this may not have
been done from life. Little of his personality can be divined in it, as one can
do so easily with Holbein's many representations of Henry VIII or Thomas
Cromwell. But in truth, we do not have that many portraits of Cromwell or,
for that matter, Cardinal Wolsey.

72 Until Dr. R. Marshall's 1978 biography, no adequate study existed, except the charming and
rare (if too ardently Catholic and prone to odd mistake) *Mary of Guise-Lorraine Queen of
Scotland* by E. Marianne H. M'Kerlie (Sands & Co, Covent Garden, 1931), the only work I
know of to publish the portrait of her held in Holyroodhouse (frontispiece). This was
despite eight PhDs or studies commenced since 1937 (NAS, card index of research in
progress). M. Wood's introduction to *Balcarres Papers*, i, vii-xxxix is helpful; see also 1–85,
217–27 and her household accounts in NLS, MS Balcarres, vol v. The editing of her Scottish
papers in 1927 by Annie Cameron was, as befits the efforts of the editor of an Ayrshire
newspaper, stunning, placing in the hands of the researcher something formidably useful. E.
Bapst, *Les mariages de Jacques* V, 356–59 discusses her marriage.

last child and had been in Scotland four years. She must have learned much of what politics was like in the household of her father, Claude de Guise, who during the reign of Francis I had brought his family to the forefront of French political life by military service in Italy, by commands within France and by shrewd marriages for his quite numerous brood. Mary had been something of a beauty at court and first married Louis d'Orléans, duc de Longueville, who died in 1537 leaving her a small son and one yet unborn who died.

Fig. 4.8. Mary of Guise is not much more often portrayed than Beaton. This is the 'green' portrait from the Scottish National Portrait Gallery. We do have two double portraits of her and James V: one in the Scottish National Portrait Gallery, the other in Falkland Palace. Both are quite crudely executed and conventional.

During 1537–38 she was one of the most eligible widows in France, and Henry VIII even considered marrying her until Beaton arranged her match to James, also recently widowed. During her time as consort, little can have happened save royal progresses, royal children (two boys, both of whom died early) and perhaps some supervision of the French masons, gardeners and other household servants who came with her from France or followed subsequently. In January 1543, then, Mary's threat to Arran was largely potential. She was closely related to one of the most important families in France and thus indirectly to Beaton, who had been liberally rewarded by

Francis I for protecting French interests. But Queen Mothers in Scotland were never mere cyphers or just mothers.[73]

Illustrative of her passive importance is the fact that Sadler made a point of visiting her early in his embassy.[74] In part this was because, just before James's death, her father had been appointed by Francis to go to Scotland as an ambassador and to administer French military aid to James in his war with Henry. Though he must have been recalled in January from his embassy, wild rumours of his imminent descent upon the country circulated well into March 1543, much to the concern of the English, and doubtless of Arran.[75]

Mary was the embodiment of Scotland's most important international commitment, the Franco-Scottish alliance, which since the revolt of John Balliol from Edward I had been the cornerstone of the country's foreign policy.[76] A treaty of peace and mutual defence with the King of Denmark did exist, as did one of peace and commerce with Burgundy, and both monarchies had provided Scottish consorts in the past. But neither was relevant to the most vital foreign concern of the Scottish Crown: preservation of its independence from England. During the Hundred Years' War, the 1371 statement of the alliance provided a workable framework whereby Frenchmen fought the English at Otterburn in 1388 and Scots fought the English at Verneuil in 1424.[77]

However, during the sixteenth century Valois interests became more complex and contradictory, whereas the Scottish concern remained clear and fixed. There was a brief period, 1502–12, when it seemed that James IV might move towards a different sort of relationship with England, prompted in part by the diplomacy of Ferdinand of Aragon. But Henry VIII's attack on Louis XII in 1512 forced the King to support France. The response fitted an established pattern; the result, however, was the extraordinarily disastrous defeat at Flodden. Though attempts were made by the English to capitalise on their great victory, these were unsustained and unsuccessful.[78] Scotland emerged from the regencies of James V, 1513–28, still bound to France, and nothing came of Henry's efforts to woo his nephew towards a pro-English position.[79]

Nonetheless, the French alliance, perhaps because of the disaster at Flodden, no longer attracted unanimous approval from Scots. One corrosive episode was the regency of John, duke of Albany, 1515–24, during which the inherent ambiguities of

---

73 See the engaging and provocative article by Louise O. Fradenburg, 'Troubled Times: Margaret Tudor and the Historians', in Mapstone, ed., *Rose and Thistle*, 38–58.

74 On 22 March and 2 April (*LP*, xviii (1), nos. 313, 355). See also letters from Suffolk to her in February (*Mary of Lorraine Corresp.*, 5–7).

75 *LP*, xviii (1), nos. 46, 52, 80, 163, 395.

76 E. Bonner, 'Scotland's "Auld Alliance" with France, 1295–1560', *History* (lxxxiv, 1999), 5–30.

77 Henry V's last delirium was that he was surrounded by Scots.

78 See the Scottish threat in 1514, not to mention 1522 and 1523. With the massive refortification of Dunbar by the French (1520?), one might even argue that Scotland emerged from the Flodden episode strengthened, but that probably pushes revisionism too far.

79 See R.L. Mackie, *James IV of Scotland*; M. Wood's introduction to *The Flodden Papers* (SHS, 1933); R.G. Eaves, *Henry VIII's Scottish Diplomacy, 1513–1524*; Donaldson, *Scotland*, 17–42.

the alliance were made apparent. Francis I had eyes fixed on Italy and thus found himself in sustained conflict with Charles V. One of Charles's important alliances was that with England, and had Francis been able either to break the hold of, or at least to neutralise, Henry VIII, his own room for manoeuvre would have been greatly enhanced. However, the price for English neutrality was invariably a free hand in Scotland. So whereas Scottish demands during 1515–24 were clear – aid against England – the French response varied according to the circumstances: in 1517 the Scots were to stay put and not provoke Henry. But in 1523, in company with 2000 French troops, they were to besiege Wark Castle.[80] From this experience, the Master of Forbes learned a lesson which he proclaimed to the Scottish estates in 1523: 'For the love of France the realm of Scotland suffers great pain'; the country should thus 'keep amity with the realm of England'.[81]

Although Albany could not prevent French attempts to reconsider relations with England, he did fashion a revamped Franco-Scottish treaty, that of Rouen in 1517, which in addition to updating the form of mutual assistance, paved the way for considerable commercial advantages to the Scots and embodied a firm commitment that Francis would give James a royal bride.[82] The French were aware of the dilemma (Albany prepared a particularly trenchant memorandum for Francis I at the time of the Field of the Cloth of Gold[83]) but there was little they could do, given the overriding priority of Italy. A French envoy had to admonish the Scottish Estates in June 1525:

> Les gens prudents, sages et discretz ne abandonnent leur anciens amys, esquelz ont trouvé foy, loyaute, secours et amytie, pour en faire d'autre nouveaulx, incogneux [qui] ont esté ennemyz et ont des querelles [Prudent, wise and discreet people do not abandon their old friends, those who have always been found loyal, solid and friendly in order to make new other ones: strangers, who have been enemies and are fractious].[84]

The timing is revealing, for Francis had suffered the most catastrophic defeat of his reign at Pavia that February. For the next eighteen months he was physically a captive in Spain and was forced by Charles V to sign the humiliating Treaty of Madrid in 1526. This was Henry VIII's golden moment when he might have re-conquered part of France. But his previous campaigns (1512–14, 1522, 1523) had exhausted his inheritance and his own hoard of ready money. The English tax-paying class refused outright to pay any more, a lesson from which the King learned much. The moment

---

80 In addition to Eaves, see Teulet, *Relations*, i, 1–42. I am grateful to Gervase Phillips who set me right about this: see his *The Anglo-Scottish Wars, 1513–50* (1999).

81 E. Hall, *The Union of the Two Noble and Illustre famelies of York and Lancaster*, ed. H. Ellis (1809), 665.

82 The treaty is to be found in *Les Ordonnances des Rois de France, règne de Francois Ier* (Paris, 1916), ii, 144–50; also see Teulet, *Relations*, i, 4.

83 Teulet, *Relations*, i, 19–25; J.G. Russell, *The Field of the Cloth of Gold: Men and Manners in 1520*, 187–89; M.W. Stuart, *The Scot who was a Frenchman: Being the Life of John Stewart, Duke of Albany, in Scotland, France and Italy*, 132–36.

84 Teulet, *Relations*, i, 54–55.

passed and never again would France be so vulnerable. The crisis did, however, emphasise to Francis how important Scotland remained. Thus the vague promise of 1517 was eventually honoured when James married Francis' favourite daughter, Madeleine, at Notre Dame on 1 January 1537.[85] She died barely six months later and another French marriage for the Scottish King was expeditiously arranged with Mary of Guise-Lorraine, recently widowed Duchess of Longueville.[86] The wedding occurred by proxy on 9 May 1538 at Châteaudun; Mary then arrived for the celebrations at St. Andrews in June.[87] It showed at least that the French were anxious to continue the alliance and that they correctly anticipated that the then frosty Anglo-Imperial relations would not continue.

James's two marriages emphasise a further point: numerous Scots travelled in France who otherwise might not have done so. David Beaton was an ambassador there as early as 1519. When, on 6 March 1536, the contract for James's first betrothed was negotiated, it was witnessed in France by James Stewart, Earl of Moray (the King's half-brother), the bishop of Aberdeen, John, 5th Lord Erskine, and Sir Thomas Erskine of Brechin. When James then sailed from Scotland on 1 September to acquaint himself with Mary of Bourbon (he found her plain), with him went some five hundred Scots[88] amongst whom were James Hamilton, Earl of Arran and David Beaton (then abbot of Arbroath). Also embarked were Archibald Campbell, 4th Earl of Argyll, George Leslie, 4th Earl of Rothes, Malcolm Lord Fleming, two heads of religious orders and two lairds from the South-West who would see service during the Rough Wooings: James Douglas of Drumlanrig and James Gordon of Lochinvar.[89] Robert, 5th Lord Maxwell was the proxy bridegroom for Mary of Guise in 1538.[90] What did they make of France? Some nobles went for their safety, education and advancement, such as Matthew, 4th Earl of Lennox.[91] David Beaton was not the only clerical visitor;[92] also there were David Paniter, an ambassador to France in 1541–42, and Arran's half-brother John, the abbot of Paisley.[93]

There were also many reminders of the alliance in France. Not least of these were

85 The best account of James's French marriages is D. Bentley-Cranch and R.K. Marshall, 'Iconography and Literature in the Service of Diplomacy: The Franco-Scottish Alliance, James V and Scotland's Two French Queens, Madeleine of France and Mary of Guise', in Williams, ed., *Stewart Style*, 271–88 and accompanying plates. The elaborate ceremony and celebrations mirror strikingly what occurred in 1558 when Mary Queen of Scots married the Dauphin Francis at the same spot.

86 Dr. Bonner nicely reminds us that Francis continued to refer to James as his 'son' even after Madeleine's death; James called him 'père'. E. Bonner, 'The Genesis of the "Rough Wooing" ', *Northern History* (1997), 46–48.

87 D. Bentley-Crouch and R.K. Marshall, 'Scotland's Two French Queens', in *Stewart Style*, 288; Cameron, *James V*, 262–63.

88 Although few of the lists tally very usefully: see Bapst, *Les Mariages de Jacques V*, 286–87; Pitscottie, *Historie*, ii, 361; F.X. Michel, *Les Ecossais en France: Les Français en Ecosse*, i, 338–40.

89 *RSS*, ii, nos. 2173, 2152, 2167, and see 2155.

90 *Ibid.*, no. 2556.

91 *Scots Peerage*, v, 353–54.

92 *RSS*, ii, nos. 1492, 1508, 2166, 4117.

93 *Letters of James V*, 435; Herkless and Hannay, *Archbishops of St Andrews*, v, 2–9.

the numerous French aristocratic families with Scottish blood in their veins and Scottish heraldic devices in their shields: symbols which went back to the 1420s when some 20,000 Scots fought, died and found preferment in France.[94] There was also the 'garde escossais' which protected the King. Though the guard was increasingly staffed by Frenchmen, many Scots, such as George Elphinstone in 1538, still went abroad 'to remane in the King of Francis service' either as one of the 25 'archers du corps' or one of the 77 'archers de la garde'.[95] In 1545 Elphinstone would return to his native land to fight the English, but in a French regiment.[96] Had he served out his time in France, he might have retired to a colony of former Scots guards in the forest of Haute-Drune, near Bourges, where he would have been given land and exemption from taxes and local tolls.[97]

Other colonies of Scots could be found in Normandy and in Guyenne, the two areas which provided most of Scotland's trade with France. From Dieppe came grain, woad, embroidery, lace, delicacies such as sweet peas, and the stuff of war: artillery, iron, powder and munitions.[98] From Bordeaux and the Gironde in general came the great staple of the trade: wine. There too vinegar, olive oil, prunes and fruits in general were purchased. The very holds which carried these goods were often constructed in France; Robert Barton's ship *The Treasurer* was built at Le Conquet in 1506; another was laid down at Dieppe in 1509.[99]

Another commodity which came from France was a great number of books: of the more than 1300 volumes to survive from pre-Reformation Scottish libraries, fully 711 were printed in France.[100] The Crown of course was a major purchaser of French wares. In 1538–39, John Barton, son of the famous Robert and the most important Scottish merchant and privateer of this period, bought large quantities of wine for the King and probably much of his finery: a riding cloak and hat, saddles, two sets of silver spurs, books, gold workmanship, velvet and gowns.[101] Barton

94 A remarkable study of Scots in France, with a considerable amount of heraldic research, is to be found in F.X. Michel, *Les Ecossais en France: les Français en Ecosse.*

95 *RSS*, ii, no. 2790; W. Forbes-Leith, *The Scots Men-at-Arms and Life-Guards in France, 1418–1830*, ii, 131–37. 224. During this period, more Scots went; on 20 March 1544, Mary of Guise wrote her brother Aumale requesting that he aid one gain a place in the 'corps d'archers'. BN, MS, fr. 20457, p. 5.

96 R. Holinshed, *The Chronicles of England, Scotland and Ireland*, ed. H. Ellis (1807–08), v, 338–39.

97 'Archers du corps' who received grants of land include Laurens Henderson, given a plot near Cheninx and Saulmaise (Forbes-Leith, *Scots Men-at-Arm*, ii, 206). There were many other such grants and many such Scots were naturalised, allowed to make wills, succeed to inheritance, hold offices and benefices, 'comme originaire' (J.A.B. Teulet, *Inventaire chronologique des documents relatifs a l'histoire d'Escosse* (Abbotsford Club, 1855), 57–58). These privileges were extended on 2 November 1547 when Henry II granted letters of naturalisation to the entire *garde escossaise* (BL, MS Harl. 1244, fos. 315–18).

98 The best general survey of Scottish trade with France is still S.G.E. Lythe, *The Economy of Scotland in its European Setting, 1550–1625*. See in particular pp. 173–83.

99 W.S. Reid, *Skipper from Leith: The History of Robert Barton of Over Barton*, 64–65, 81.

100 J. Durkan and A. Rose, *Early Scottish Libraries*. The figures are by my own count.

101 The incidentals are too numerous to detail, but for representative examples, see *TA*, vi, 280, 336, 434; vii, 17, 121, 204–205, 339, 400.

performed a similar service for Beaton, who paid him £s245 in 1539 for 110 casks of wine from Bordeaux.[102] Scottish merchants, despite their dependence on the Low Countries, certainly thought the trade important and, for example, paid Beaton £s2000 in 1541 to negotiate the 'doungetting' of a recently imposed customs duty in Normandy.[103]

The third sort of Scots were those who went 'to the shulis to lere thare vertuis and sience'. Most followed the path of Boece, Buchanan and Major to Paris; but Scots, like most scholars, moved about. Gavin Dunbar, archbishop of Glasgow in 1543, had enrolled at Paris and Angers; James Foulis, James V's secretary, went to Paris and Orléans.[104] Dunbar's great rival in the 1540s, David Beaton, studied at Orléans in 1519, and there the Scots were organised as a separate nation and had their own procurators, men with names such as Hepburn, Hamilton and Heriot.[105] Numerous Scots virtually settled and remained. Henry Scrimgeour, son of a Dundee burgess, studied under Budé at Paris in 1534, then went to Bourges and soon found himself tutoring a Fugger, as well as the children of Guillaume Bochetel, a *secrétaire du roy*. George Buchanan entrusted his son to him and he was ever known to be 'learned, eloquent and grave', as well as widely travelled: Padua, Venice and Rome.[106] Perhaps the best example is that of John Lesley, bishop of Ross, whose *Historie* is one of the major literary sources for this period. Lesley went first to Paris after graduating from Aberdeen and then spent four years in Poitiers studying canon and civil law. After a further year at Toulouse, where he obtained a licence in civil law, and another in Paris, where he became a doctor in decreets, he finally returned to King's College, Aberdeen. Scots did go further afield, but the bulk of them found their learning in France. Moreover the fruits of their learning invariably came to light first in France. Although a Scottish printing press existed as early as 1508, Major, Boece, Liddell and Crab had their books printed at Paris, Rouen and Caen.[107] Peripatetic Scots also went 'for doing pilgrimage', or general business, or 'for the cure of a certayne disease'.[108]

Not too many Frenchmen reciprocated. Some came to teach,[109] and some to trade,[110] but they were few. The Crown, however, was a patron of Frenchmen. By

102 *Rentale Sancti Andree*, ed. R.K. Hannay (SHS, 1910), 94.
103 *Edin. Burgh Rec.*, ii, 105, 108; *Records of the Convention of the Royal Burghs of Scotland*, ed. J.D. Marwick (Edinburgh, 1866–90), i, 517–18, 554.
104 The quote is from *RSS*, i, no. 712. For Scottish scholars abroad, see John Durkan, 'The Cultural Background in sixteenth-century Scotland', in *Essays on the Scottish Reformation*, ed. D. McRoberts, 274–331. See also John Plattard, 'Scottish Students and Masters at Poitiers in the second half of the sixteenth century', *SHR*, xxi (1924), 82–86, 168.
105 J. Kirkpatrick, 'The Scottish Nation in the University of Orléans, 1339–1538', *SHS Misc.*, ii (1904), 44–102.
106 John Durkan, 'Henry Scrimgeour, Renaissance Bookman', *Edinburgh Bibliographical Society Transactions* (v, 1971–87), 1–31.
107 Durkan, 'The Cultural Background' 276–80.
108 *RSS*, i, nos. 1425, 1516, 1545, 1588, 1684, 1778, 1840, 2230; ii, nos. 642, 1728, 4352; *The Letters of James V*, ed. R.K. Hannay and D. Hay (Edinburgh, 1954), 228.
109 Durkan, 'The Cultural Background' 280; Lythe, *Scottish Economy*, 169.
110 *RSS*, i, no. 2668; and see *RSS*, ii, xiv–xx.

1538 James V had two French squires, one for 'gathering . . . croce bowis', a tailor, several trumpeters, six pages, a dwarf, Jane, and a gardener, Bertram Galawtre.[111] The King's marriages brought more Frenchmen to the Kingdom, such as Ronsard,[112] a page at the court from the age of 13 until 15, and Mary of Guise's furrier, whose nationality was to cause him some trouble when he tried to return home via England in 1542.[113]

Less trivial tasks were performed by men such as Piers Rowane, Master and Principal maker and melter of the King's guns and artillery; his assistant was Christopher Grandmorceau.[114] Rowane's son, David, took his apprenticeship in the art in France before taking up a post in Scotland in 1541. Arran was to find his skill most useful in the years ahead.[115] Frenchmen also travailed in the arts of peace; Moyse Martin, Nicholas Roy and numerous other masons left a lasting memorial to the alliance in the refashioned Falkland Palace, described by a modern scholar as 'the most uncompromising Renaissance work' in Britain, and in James's brilliant palace at Stirling.[116] Artistic influences can also be seen in the evolution of the portraiture on Scottish coins, where unmistakable Renaissance devices emerged decades in advance of their appearance in England.[117]

Through these means Scotsmen of all ranks knew of France and the benefits of the alliance. The nobility of course were particularly aware, as were the upper clergy. It was they who bought the books and drank the wine which France provided, and it was they who went there on diplomatic missions. The effect of these contacts on ordinary Scotsmen is uncertain. Edinburgh merchants celebrated with bonfires 'the triumph the King of France gat in Lumbardy' in 1515; those of Ayr rang bells to celebrate James's return thence in 1537.[118] But beyond vague memories of Albany's troops in 1522, most Scotsmen would not have been too conscious of France or Frenchmen in 1542. The next eighteen years would change that.

If noble Scots were aware of France, the French did not reciprocate. There were other diplomatic embassies in addition to that of Monseigneur de Sagnes, the conseilleur of the Parlement of Toulouse who admonished the Scottish estates in 1525,[119] but Scotland did not figure prominently in French minds before 1542, if then. When in 1536 it became clear that James would insist upon a royal bride, the court of Francis I confessed itself totally ignorant of the country, and a translation of John

---

111 *TA*, vi, 93, 99, 100, 300, 350, 403, 417; vii, 151. Arran was to continue the use of Frenchmen in many capacities; his 'Franche doctor' in 1546, Godfrey Johan, received a pension of £s34 (*TA*, viii, 457; *RSS*, iii, no. 163).

112 J.H. Williams, ed., *Stewart Style*, 281–2.

113 *TA*, vi, 301; *HP*, i. 217; P. Hume Brown, *Early Travellers in Scotland*, xi.

114 *RSS*, ii, nos. 1213, 3482, 4964.

115 *Letters of James V*, 270, 349, 432; *TA*, vi, 189, 402; vii, 150, 281; *RSS*, ii, no. 4964.

116 S. Cruden, *The Scottish Castle*, 145, 194–96; *Balcarres Papers*, i, 20; *RSS*, ii, no. 3002; *TA*, vii, 331; *Accounts of the Masters of Works.*, ed. H.M. Parton (Edinburgh, 1957), 208, 242, 254–55, 277–78.

117 I. H. Stewart, *The Scottish Coinage*, 91; C.H.V. Sutherland, *Art in Coinage*, 165.

118 *TA*, v. 47; *Ayr Burgh Accounts*, ed. G.S. Pryde (SHS, 1937), 3–4, 15, 20, 22–23, 28.

119 At least 24 can be found from *Letters of James V*, but this figure may well be low.

Bellenden's Scottish version of Boece's *Historia gentis Scotorum* was hastily executed and circulated in manuscript form.[120]

Desmonstiers, who did the translation, published in 1549 *Des Estates et Maisons Plus Illustres de la Chrestiente*. For him the major powers were the Papacy, the Holy Roman Empire and France; Scotland ranked fifth in the second rank, behind Spain, Hungary, England and Denmark, though more important than Poland.[121] Nonetheless, although Estienne Perlin, writing in 1551, might admit that to compare Scotland to France was to put St Morceau beside Paris, he argued that Scotland had always been faithful to France and through it England might easily be conquered, and thus it was vital to the King as a 'buckler' against his enemies.[122]

120 A.H. Miller, 'Scotland Described for Queen Magdalene', *SHS*, i (1904), 27–38. It was published in 1538 in Paris as *Description du Pays Descosse*.
121 P. Desmonstiers, *Des Estates et Maisons Plus Illustres de la Chrestiente*, 3, 39, 68, 77.
122 E. Perlin, *Description des Royaulmes d'Angleterre et d'Escosse* (Paris, 1551), 73–74.

CHAPTER FIVE

The Year 1543

'OUR GREATE AFFAYRE OF SCOTLAND'

F ew years in early Scottish history have received such close attention as 1543,[1] the occasion of Henry VIII's ambitious attempt to put the two countries on the road to union by the betrothal of his son and heir to Mary Queen of Scots. Secondly, it was a year of intense political intrigue about the most fascinating Queen in Scotland's history. Even in her infancy Mary was important. A third reason is the sheer availability of printed documents which put into the hands of historians a wealth of detailed descriptive and quotable material. What did Henry wish to achieve in Scotland? Why did he wish it? How did he fail?

As early as a despatch to Lisle on 8 January 1543, Henry talked of the matter as 'our greate affayre of Scotland'.[2] It is not certain precisely what he meant, for he did not really know. Henry's goals altered with circumstances and there is a distinct difference between what Henry said he wanted and what he actually achieved even at the point of his greatest success, the Treaties of Greenwich of 1 July 1543. The Treaties were of peace, ending the war of 1542, and another for the marriage of Mary and Edward. The peace treaty was largely unremarkable: regulating safe-conducts, rebels, sailors, the Debatable Lands and fishings along the Border; protecting Berwick; specifying exchange of criminals and so forth.[3]

The marriage treaty, on the other hand, was a great diplomatic triumph. Within two months, the Scots would deliver hostages for its eventual performance: two earls

---

1 Every general text places heavy emphasis on the year. It is virtually the only time Scotland is discussed in Scarisbrick's *Henry VIII*, one thing his book has in common with Pollard's. Half of Wernham's chapter on the years 1542–47 is devoted to it; Mackie, Dickinson and Donaldson treat it at some length, something the newer histories have in common with the older (Lang gave 19 pages out of 43 in his rendering of the years 1543–50). For one of the earliest attempts to place it within the context of the 'British problem', see J. Seely, *The Growth of British Policy* (Cambridge, 1897). The most recent general survey is to be found in D.L. Potter, 'Foreign Policy', in *The Reign of Henry VIII: Politics, Policy and Piety*, ed. D.L. MacCulloch (1995). See also Sallie B. Cypher, 'Henry VIII's Foreign Policy, 1538–1547' (unpublished dissertation for Ph.D., University of Wisconsin, 1971).

2 *Hamilton Papers*, i, 362 (*LP*, xviii (1), no. 19).

3 A truce came into effect almost upon the death of James and it was continued until July almost without interruption. See *LP*, xviii (1), nos. 54, 173, 239, 251, 269, 436, but cf. nos. 17, 34, 324. During this time, normal intercourse revived, the Scots put into English hands the murderers of a herald and Arran returned the Order of the Garter which Henry had given James (*ibid.*, no. 591). The striking of a new seal delayed Scottish letters patent accepting the truce (*ibid.*, no. 214) but this did not worry the English. The peace treaty is in *Foedera*, xiv, 786–91 (*LP*, xviii (1), no. 804 (1), but see nos. 3–9, 18, 20).

or their heirs and two 'barons' or their heirs.[4] By January 1553 Mary was to be delivered in person to English commissioners at Berwick, by which time a proxy marriage contract was to have been executed. Once her marriage with Edward was consummated, she would receive £2000 per annum whilst Henry lived, £4000 once he died. If Edward then died without issue, Mary would be free to return to Scotland and that would be the end of the matter. Regardless of what happened, Scotland would keep its name, laws and liberties and Arran would, as Governor, continue to use the revenues of the Crown as he saw fit and would receive an acquittance (an exoneration for any misdeeds while Governor) from Henry and Edward.[5]

The treaty did not specify what would happen should Mary and Edward have surviving issue, but it was clear to all that their heirs were to succeed to a dynastically united England and Scotland. As early as January the phrase that was to echo down through the decade was coined, 'thys godly mariage and union'.[6] That Henry brought off something remarkable by the Treaties was clear; on 15 June the Privy Council sent the proud tidings, 'never prince had so great a conquest of Ireland and Scotland'.[7] But the question remains, what did Henry seek in his 'greate affayre', for the marriage was not only an end, but also a means to others.

The most sensible explanation for the war of 1542 is that Henry was trying to neutralise Scotland before he turned on France, and in the King's reaction to the opportunity provided by James's death and Mary's birth one can see an attempt to end once and for all the Franco-Scottish alliance.[8] But the 1542 war was in some way related to Henry's pretensions to overlordship of Scotland. Initially he seemed to be aiming not at union by marriage, but by conquest. Certainly the impression given to the Imperial ambassador during the frenzy of planning in December 1542 was that Henry aimed at becoming King of Scotland himself. Certainly Henry's Scottish allies agreed in January that should Mary die, he 'should take rule'. The preamble to the subsidy act of 1544 saw the events of December 1542 as creating 'a time apt and prospyse for the recoverye of his said right and tytle to the saide Crown and Realm of Scotland'.[9]

Another possibility is that Henry sought in 1543 not so much the Crown as he did part of the realm. 'The secrete devise' suggested in July 1543 that if the marriage failed, Scots would help Henry 'attenye . . . at leaste the domynion thissyde of the Fethre [Forth]'.[10] On 4 August, when it seemed that Beaton might remove Mary out

---

4 They could be changed every two months if the Scots wished.
5 *Foedera*, xiv, 792–99 (*LP*, xviii (1), no. 804 (2) and see nos. 10–17, 19). But see difference with BL, MS Calig. B. vii, fo. 265v.
6 The idea of the marriage sprang to men's minds the minute James died. For various reactions see *LP*, xvii no. 1233; xviii (1), nos. 26, 29, 62.
7 *LP*, xviii (1), no. 707.
8 See E. Bonner, 'The Genesis of Henry VIII's "Rough Wooing" of the Scots', *Northern History* (xxxiii, 1997), 36–53. I am grateful to Dr. C.P. Hotle for sight of his article on the 1542 conflict, 'The road to Solway Moss: Henry VIII and Scotland, 1540–1542'.
9 *LP*, xvii, no. 1241; xviii (1), no. 22 (4); *The Statutes of the Realm*, ed. A Luders and others (Record Commission, 1810–28), iii, 938.
10 *SP Henry VIII*, v, 319 (*LP*, xviii (1), no. 835).

of Arran's control and marry her elsewhere, Henry promised to make the Governor 'kinge of the reste beionde the Frith', and he doubtless meant to assume sovereignty of southern Scotland himself.[11]

The King then entertained four possible solutions to the Scottish problem: sovereignty itself, union by marriage, control of the area south of the Forth-Clyde line, or at least influence over whatever Scottish government emerged in 1543.[12] It was the latter possibility, which arose from the lucky chance of Solway Moss, which deflected his attention.

'ASSURED LORDS'

Perhaps the greatest triumph of Henry's 1542 war was the capture of a large number of Scottish nobles in the skirmish at Solway Moss, 23 of whom were considered important enough to be warded in the Tower.[13] Word then came of James's death and they were brought before the King, entertained, given gifts and sounded out as to whether or not they would be prepared to collaborate.[14] Ten agreed to become 'Assured Lords': William Cunningham, 3rd Earl of Glencairn; Gilbert Kennedy, 3rd Earl of Cassillis; Robert, 5th lord Maxwell; Malcolm, 3rd lord Fleming; Patrick, 4th lord Gray; Hugh, 4th lord Somerville; and four others.

Of the ten, Glencairn, Cassillis and Maxwell were easily the most important, for they, in conjunction with Angus, controlled an enormous amount of land south of the Forth-Clyde line.[15] Fleming and Somerville, though less wealthy than their colleagues, still were strategically placed in Clydesdale, not far from Arran's extensive lands at Hamilton.[16] Only Gray came from beyond the Forth: his smallish holding at Castle Huntly on the north side of the Tay was not immediately important;[17] and he in any case was quickly to drop from sight in 1543 owing to a bitter dispute for the provostship of Perth.[18]

More important were two of the most interesting Scots of the time: Archibald, 6th Earl of Angus, and his brother, Sir George Douglas of Pittendriech. Angus had married Henry's sister Margaret in 1515 and from that power base rose to direct Scottish affairs during 1525–28. When James V broke loose from his

11 *LP*, xviii (2), nos. 8, 22, 46. The quote is from *Hamilton Papers*, i, 439. See also *LP*, xviii (2), no. 358; xix (1), no. 58.

12 For but one example of the last aspect, see *LP*, xviii (1), no. 835 (2).

13 At the same time, a table was prepared of their wealth (in merks Scots and marks Sterling). See *SP Henry VIII*, v, 232–35 (*LP*, xviii (1), no. 2); *LP*, xvii, nos. 1163 (2), 1143; xviii (1), no. 7.

14 C. Wriothesley, *A Chronicle of England during the reign of the Tudors*, ed. W.D. Hamilton (Camden Society, 1875–77), i, 140; *LP*, xviii (1), no. 436, fo. 87.

15 It would be most instructive to be able to plot exactly how much land each noble owned and where, but this is not possible here; see Cameron, *James V*, p. 248, note 62 for a discussion of their ransoms which give some indication of their relative wealth (*LP*, xviii, (1), no. 805). Biographies of many of these men are to be found in the *Dictionary of National Biography*, but these should be supplemented by *Scots Peerage*; for Angus, see i, 190–93; for Glencairn, iv, 236–38; for Cassillis, ii, 468–71; for Maxwell, vi, 470–80.

16 *Scots Peerage*, viii, 537–42; viii, 15–18.

17 Although it would become so in 1547.

18 *Scots Peerage*, iv, 280–81.

dominance, the Douglases found themselves utterly banished. Both spent their exile in the service of Henry, keeping him abreast of Scottish matters, advising the Wardens of the Marches and constantly sending spies and agent-provocateurs into Scotland.[19]

Angus, by this time probably 53 years of age, was a man born to and used to power and the years of exile must have irked him greatly. His union with Henry's sister was blessed with a daughter, Margaret, who grew up with him in England and was often at court.[20] From the moment word came (interestingly via a Douglas spy)[21] of James's death, both brothers readied themselves to return home where Angus's reputation remained formidable.[22] Extended conferences were held between them and the principal English agents on the Borders, Sir John Dudley, Viscount Lisle, and Sir William Lord Parr.[23] At Darlington, they apparently reaffirmed their oath to serve Henry as their lord and promised to promote the marriage between Edward and Mary.[24] On 10 January 1543, they were joined by the Solway Moss lords.[25]

Before leaving Darlington they signed certain articles binding them to the King.[26] Firstly, if it was true that James was dead and Mary a girl and living, they asked Henry to take her into his keeping, marry her to Edward and thus unite both the realms, a task to which they pledged their support. The next clauses stipulated that they would lay hostages, appear on demand and advertise the King and Wardens of affairs in Scotland. In the fifth, or 'secret article', they pledged that if the Queen died they would help the King 'to take the rule' of Scotland. Later these articles were elaborated to bind them even more to Henry.[27] Patrick Hepburn, 3rd Earl of Bothwell (father of Mary's future husband), had been banished from Scotland in 1540 and now hastened home from Denmark where he had spent some of his exile.[28] He also signed. Bothwell further promised to enlist the support of Hugh Campbell of Loudoun, Sheriff of Ayr, a friend of Glencairn's then in France.[29] Bothwell's extensive holdings in Liddesdale and his massive castle of the Hermitage on the Middle March made him obviously important; he was also Sheriff of Edinburgh and Haddington (Midlothian and East Lothian) and Lord Admiral. But he quickly fell from the English faction, seduced so it was said by the promise of the hand of Mary of Guise.

19 See T.I. Rae, *Administration of the Scottish Frontier*, 167–78, but also *Scots Peerage*, i, 187–88, 190–93; W. Fraser, *The Douglas Book*, ii, 174–78, 189–92.

20 *LP*, xviii (1), nos. 267, 896; xx (1), no. 296.

21 Angus's doctor prepared a map for Henry's use (Scarisbrick, *Henry VIII*).

22 After Solway Moss, James V (it was said) resolved to bring him back to command future armies. If so, it was one of the more intelligent responses by the King to the débâcle.

23 *LP*, xvii, no. 1233; xviii (1), no. 281.

24 *LP*, nos. 1221, 1250; xviii (1), nos. 4, 32, 35–56, 43.

25 *LP*, xviii (1), nos. 22, 37, 43, 60.

26 They had apparently been despatched from London before the articles had been drafted. *LP*, xviii (1), nos. 11, 19, 22 (2, 3), 37.

27 *Ibid.*, no. 835.

28 *Scots Peerage*, ii, 157–61; *LP*, xviii (1), nos. 7 (2), 23, 465.

29 *LP*, xviii (1), nos. 278, 301.

None of these men was all-powerful in his area: Maxwell was opposed by the Johnstone family and in time by Sir James Douglas of Drumlanrig (once married to a sister of Angus's);[30] Angus had rivals in the form of lord Hume and Sir Walter Scott of Buccleuch. Bothwell's positions had been given by James V to Maxwell. But these men also had friends and they made a powerful coalition. Some of them were also bound by similar attitudes towards religion. Glencairn, Cassillis and Maxwell apparently loathed Beaton and were noted as Protestants; later Gray was to emerge also as a most committed reformer. In the end, none was prepared to lose his livings (or income) for the faith, but it did give them a certain unity of purpose during the year which was to follow their return to Scotland in late January 1543.

Thus pledged, the 'assured lords' went North and were greeted with all civility by Arran on 25 January.[31] Although he cannot have welcomed such a powerful bloc of men who might easily intimidate him,[32] they did strengthen his hand enormously at that moment. Ever since his proclamation as Governor on 3 January, he had been forced to work with Beaton and, a week later, had appointed him Chancellor. Immediately upon the arrival of the English lords, however, Arran felt strong enough to put the Cardinal to one side and by the end of the month had warded him in Douglas's castle of Dalkeith, ten miles south of Edinburgh.[33] Arran, in any case, had much in common with the lords, for his name supposedly had headed a notorious list of heretics which, it was widely believed, Beaton had drawn up for James's information.[34] In his third letter written as Governor, Arran declared his intention 'to reform the state of kirk here, set forth God's word and profit the common weal'.[35] If he was dissembling, it was a masterful stroke; but it would appear that Arran at the time was genuinely concerned to promote reform.

Moreover, by the middle of March, when Sir Ralph Sadler[36] reached Edinburgh accredited as Henry VIII's ambassador to Scotland, it seemed that a popular reformation was under way. At the last Parliament, permission had been granted for the reading of the Bible in English and Arran had about him two friars of Glencairn's noted for their reformed views.[37] Beaton's imprisonment moreover meant that the Roman clergy were leaderless, and an interdict against all religious services during the primate's captivity seemed to arouse little concern. Even as late as October it was feared by Catholics that the Protestants sought 'destruyre tous les monasteres et convenz de la ville de lislebourg [Edinburgh]', and the papal legate

30 *Scots Peerage*, vii, 119–28.
31 *Ibid.*, no. 81.
32 Especially as it was mentioned several times by Henry that Arran was merely 'occupying the place of the Governor' (*Ibid.*, nos. 7, 19, 271).
33 *LP*, xviii (1), nos. 88, 157, 174.
34 Knox, *History*, i, 35.
35 *LP*, xviii (1), nos. 56, 174.
36 Sadler's life has been variously treated, not only by the *DNB* and *History of Parliament*: J. Slavin, *Politics and Profit. A Study of Sir Ralph Sadler, 1507–1547* (Cambridge, 1966).
37 *APS*, ii, 415, 425.

who arrived then was most disturbed by the obvious spread of heresy.[38] In Edinburgh, Dundee and Perth minor riots did take place against some of the religious houses, and in Aberdeen Protestant preachers were entertained.[39]

At dinner shortly after Sadler's arrival, Arran confessed disgust at the great abuses within the church, 'the reformation whereof he most earnestly pretendith', and it was then, on 1 April, that Sadler made his famous[40] request to London for the New Testament and Bible in English along with copies of the Acts of Parliament whereby Henry broke his links with Rome.[41] Many others regarded Arran's Governorship as Protestant in direction.[42] Henry for one certainly took his anti-clerical declarations to be true, and in a remarkable 19-page latter, largely prepared by Wriothesley but corrected by the King himself, he instructed the Governor how to proceed.[43]

This turn of events had an obvious effect on what Henry decided to seek in his 'greate affayre of Scotland'. By the Spring of 1543, he can have had no need for an immediate conquest or realisation of overlordship. Both would come by the marriage, by religious reformation (what Sadler had sought in 1537 and 1540) and by support of Arran through the assured lords. In time Scotland and England would be united and England would thus be protected from both France and Rome.

HENRY VIII: 'CAPABLE OR GUILTY OF SUCH HIGH STATESMANSHIP?'

To both Pollard and Wernham, Henry's great affair of Scotland was both rational and statesmanlike.[44] Scarisbrick is surely right to doubt if the King was 'ever either capable or guilty of such high statesmanship'.[45] Why, then, did the King engulf himself in Scottish affairs in 1543? Three answers seem possible.

The first is that the Scottish marriage was there and Henry wished it because he, like his fellow European monarchs, was acquisitive and sought glory. Certainly Habsburg success evoked the wonder and admiration of the Christian Kings of

---

38 Brosse, *Missions*, especially pp. 22, 26. For Grimani's correspondence, which is not to be found either in *LP* or in *Nonces en France, 1541–46*, see R.K. Hannay, 'Letters of the Papal Legate in Scotland, 1543', *SHR*, xi (1911), 1–26. He augmented the French ambassador's view that 'les heresies ont pullule et pullulent en ce Royaume' by stating the Kingdom was divided 'on account of the Lutherans, whose errors had become disseminated throughout almost the whole of the country since the death of the late King' (*ibid.*, 18).

39 At Arran's specific request (*Abdn. Counc.*, i, 189); Knox, *History*, i, 56.

40 Widely reported in subsequent textbooks.

41 *LP*, xviii (1), no. 348. As early as 27 February Scots were requesting the New Testament 'and suche other bokes as be set fourth within [England] in English, as the Prymer and the Psalter'. *Hamilton Papers*, ii, 445 (*LP*, xviii (1), no. 214).

42 Knox, *History*, 1, 41–46; see also Lisle's good opinion (*LP*, xviii (1), no. 157).

43 *LP*, xviii (1), no. 364. Scarisbrick terms the letter one 'few reputations could easily survive' (*Henry VIII*, 437, no. 4). Arran seems to have appreciated its 'cynical worldliness' (*LP*, xviii (1), no. 391).

44 Pollard (*Henry VIII*, 399, 405–08) praised the King for having 'the right aims'; Wernham even argued that Henry's war against France was waged primarily to prevent assistance being given to the Scots (Wernham, *Before the Armada*, 149–59), a curious notion given that Brest was the major port for Scotland.

45 Scarisbrick, *Henry VIII*, 421–26.

Europe, and all, when they could, sought to emulate Charles V.[46] Perhaps for that reason alone the King sought it. Scotland was no Milan, but its union with England would demonstrably enlarge the sheer physical landmass under Henry's governance and thus enhance his Crown.[47] He would emerge more an Emperor and less a King.

This explanation may be somewhat fanciful, but with Henry one never knows. Eustace Chapuys, Charles V's ambassador in London, certainly made an interesting observation towards the end of 1542. In his long memorandum to the Emperor, then in Spain, of 15 January 1543, he outlined all that had happened at court since his last extended despatch on 23 November. Solway Moss and the entire Scottish affair appeared to have greatly lifted the King's heart, for no sooner did the succession of good pieces of news begin to pour in from the North than the King 'rejoiced'. Before that, ever since he had discovered 'the evil conduct of his last Queen', he had been 'disinclined to feasting and ladies'. But now he was directing the whole business, holding constant meetings of the Privy Council (which were so frequent, Chapuys reported on 21 December, 'they had hardly leisure to eat or drink').[48] Perhaps the Scottish opportunity simply gave the ageing King a chance to shine again. Search for glory, for its own sake, must have been there in some form.

Possible manly vanity aside, Henry could have had very sound and obvious reasons for wanting the marriage. The union of the two Kingdoms would have dramatically altered both the security of his dynasty and England's overall European position. Scotland was the back door through which French troops had invaded England in the past. Albany's attacks in 1522–23 had been the last of a series of French feints over the last two-and-a-half centuries. Moreover, the Franco-Scottish alliance meant that England could never engage in a continental war against France without worrying about possible Scottish action on behalf of her ally, as Flodden showed. To marry Edward to the Scottish Queen would go a long way to closing that door.

There is, however, another reason which, although it may not have been clearly expounded in the Council meetings and may not have been uppermost in the King's mind, still inclined him to seek a final solution to the Scottish problem by the marriage. Maintaining some sort of military force along the Scottish frontier was mandatory as long as Scotland was independent. It was also expensive both financially and politically. The cost was high during wars, of course, but even during peacetime, garrisons had to be maintained in addition to the elaborate system of wardens and fortresses along the frontier. The repair, maintenance and some new construction at Berwick came to £7,226 in the period 1539–43 alone.

Yet more vital was the threat posed to the Tudors by this young babe. Royal children-making was a form of controlled animal husbandry, hence the near-

---

46 Scarisbrick's discussion of the relationship between Henry and Charles is most revealing (*Henry VIII*, 426–29, 445–70).

47 Many such remarks were made at the time. In his perhaps fanciful account of a meeting with some Italians in 1547, William Thomas told them that within the cosmology of England 'you must understand Scotland to be comprehended' (BL, MS Harl. 353, fo. 17 v, and see below, pp. 000–00).

48 *LP*, xviii (1), no. 44; xvii, no. 1224.

hysterical accent on purity and legitimacy for royal mothers. Kings might engage in
sexual congress with whomever they wilt, but queens had to be impeccable, their
loins unsullied by any man other than their lawful husband (rather: their wombs
untouched by the sperm of any other man). That is why such play was made of the
wedding night and the breaking of the bride's hymen (and publicly displayed
wedding-night sheets): see Prince Arthur strutting about the morning after, boasting
that he had been 'deep in Flanders'. It also explains why royal births were such public
occasions: to insure that numerous witnesses were present to attest even decades later
as to that adult being from that infant.

The guardianship of a princess's virtue was thus a matter of the utmost
importance, hence the fixation on the dynastic process: courtship, betrothal,
marriage, consummation by penetrative sex, conception and live birth. When
Queen Catherine blurted in 1529 that she came to Henry 'pure' (that is to say
without any carnal knowledge of her first husband), it almost caused an uproar, for
the Papal Bull which had allowed her to marry Henry in the first place was predicated
on her first marriage having been consummated. If she was a virgin still in 1509, then
that Bull was invalid.

One must remember two factors also mentioned earlier: the Tudor line was both
'elected' (and thus could be deselected) and was weak: Stewart monarchs ever since
1513 (that is to say both James V and Mary Queen of Scots) were but heartbeats away
from the throne of England. Henry thus had to insure that Mary slept with no other
man than Edward, his only male heir, both to deny her womb to any other as well as
to reintegrate her bloodline with that of her grandmother. Seen in this light, the
'godly marriage and union' was not just an Imperial opportunity, it was utterly vital
for the security of the Tudor dynasty.

For whatever reasons Henry sought a solution to the problem of Scotland, it
certainly seemed near to success in that spring of 1543. The hope was a false one, as we
know, and by the end of the year Beaton once more directed Scottish affairs, the
marriage was renounced by the Scottish Parliament, and the alliance with France had
been renewed. How did this volte-face happen?

THE TREATIES OF GREENWICH, I JULY 1543

On 18 March 1543, Sadler had arrived in Edinburgh; it was a Sunday and he repaired
to Holyrood Palace where he had his first meeting with Arran. The Governor was
surrounded by a large number of nobles, many of whom were about to leave, having
attended the largest meeting of the Scottish Estates in living memory. It had been an
important six days from 12 to 17 March during which Arran and 67 other Scots
(virtually all the nobility, many of the clergy and burgesses from as far away as
Aberdeen and Ayr) made numerous vital decisions.

Arran had been recognised as Governor of the Kingdom and Tutor to the Queen
(an interesting distinction). Critical elements in his government were appointed: the
Secret Council and the Lords of the Articles. The restoration of Angus, George
Douglas, Glamis and others was passed. Permission to read the scriptures in the
vernacular was passed over the opposition of the clergy. Arrangements for the care and

safekeeping of the Queen were laid down and the terms for her betrothal of marriage to Edward spelt out in detail.[49] Had Sadler arrived a week earlier, he might have been invited to address the body (the Scottish Three Estates were unicameral), and he might have been able to affect some of its decisions, especially regarding the marriage contract. This sort of bad timing was to plague English efforts throughout.[50]

Of first importance were the Scottish terms for the betrothal, for they show that from the outset the government was determined to resist many of Henry's demands. Several were ordinary enough: allowing English tutors for Mary, arranging her dower lands, insisting that should Edward die without issue of the match she return to Scotland. These were accepted. But in the first substantive article, it was made explicit that on no account would the Queen be allowed out of the country until her marriage to Edward and that no hostages or castles within the Kingdom would be given as guarantees. Henry wished to have all three and was also still reluctant to recognise Arran as Governor. But the Scots demanded elaborate protection of his position: Arran was to hold that office for life, or at least until Mary's 'perfect age', the age of her majority. He was to dispose of all the Crown's revenues as he saw fit and would not have to make any account thereof, and his place in the line of succession was to be recognised.

Moreover, the Scottish ambassadors were instructed to ensure that should a dynastic union occur, Scotland's liberties were preserved. The name 'Scotland' should be retained always, its own laws perpetually administered by the College of Justice established by James V, with no appeal outside the Kingdom. Only when a lawful heir of Edward and Mary was born could anyone but a Scottish noble appointed by Arran hold command of any Scottish castle or strength.[51]

Some of these items were obviously negotiable, but they were nothing like what Henry, already angered at what he saw to be unnecessary delay in the despatch of Scottish commissioners, had in mind.[52] When, on 11 April, the Scottish commissioners[53] finally did reach London and had audience with the King and dinner with the Council the next day, they firmly stuck to their charge, refused to declare against France and disparaged Henry's claim to the Kingdom.[54] Little more is heard of the negotiations, but the original Scottish ambassadors were reinforced on 4 May by George Douglas and Glencairn.[55] In the meantime, Henry insisted upon the laying of pledges, renunciation of the French alliance, guarantee that the Scots would make

---

49 *APS*, ii, 409–26 (*LP*, xviii (1), nos. 264, 273, 281, 300).

50 There was, of course, little Sadler could do to rectify this, although it is not clear that he was supposed to address Parliament (*LP*, xviii (1), nos. 271, 290). French ambassadors had done so in the past, as in 1526, and would do so again, in December 1543 and July 1548.

51 These terms for the marriage were the first major item of business and the detail shows that Arran and the Council must have been at work for some time drafting them (*LP*, xviii (1), no. 273).

52 *LP*, xviii (1), nos. 132, 303.

53 Sir James Learmonth of Dairsie, Provost of St. Andrews, and Henry Balnavis of Halhill: both regarded as of the highest probity. Learmonth had been Master of James V's household.

54 *LP*, xviii (1), no. 402.

55 *LP*, xviii (1), no. 501.

Fig. 5.1.   The reception of ambassadors when they first presented their letters of
credence to a monarch was always a high moment of staged Court life.
Something similar occurred when the participants actually penned their
signatures onto the finished top copy of the treaty, and a similar public
audience was held on the envoys' departure. This charcoal drawing of French
envoys being received by Henry VIII at Hampton Court captures nicely
what the scene would have looked like at Greenwich when the Scots saw the
king.

no treaty with any foreign prince without his consent and Arran's Governorship to be contingent upon confirmed 'good devotion and inclynation towardes the Kinges Majestie'.[56] Douglas and Glencairn must have forced the King to climb down, for by 20 May the French issue was being blurred, Mary could remain in Scotland until the age of eight and Arran's position was in part agreed. The Scots did agree eventually to lay hostages; Glencairn and Argyll were two of fifteen to 'giff plegis to ye King of England' for the performance of the marriage.[57]

When Douglas returned to Scotland on 7 June with this draft, Arran's Council tinkered further with the terms, raising the age to ten years, putting in a 'general comprehension' of the French, cutting down the numbers of hostages and so forth. On 8 June, a small meeting of the Estates agreed the final Scottish version, and it was in this form that the eventual treaty was signed in Henry's great palace at Greenwich[58] on 1 July.[59] By and large, the Scottish ambassadors had given very little away, and when Henry commended their 'wisdom and diligence' as he rewarded the five of them with £681.2.11. worth of silver plate on 3 July, he did so without flattery.[60]

'THE STONES IN THE STRETES
WOLDE RYSE AND REBEL AGENST YT'

Scottish insistence on protection of their liberties was not the only difficulty for Henry, for the March estates had also agreed the composition of the two most important advisory Councils about the Governor: the Privy Council and the Lords of the Articles. There was a strong 'English' bloc: Angus, George Douglas, Cassillis, Glencairn and Maxwell (the man who had moved that the scriptures in English be allowed). But, as ever, the Scots 'balanced' and there was also a strong clerical element, headed by Beaton's great rival, Gavin Dunbar, archbishop of Glasgow, and a number of nobles who by no stretch of the imagination could be considered pro-English: George Gordon, 4th Earl of Huntly; Archibald Campbell, 4th Earl of Argyll; and Henry Stewart, 1st lord Methven (another ex-husband of Margaret Tudor and a close confidant of the Queen dowager).[61] Bothwell, soon publicly to renounce Henry, was also a member.[62]

Argyll and Huntly had earlier threatened to hold a rival Parliament at Perth and were publicly known to be opposed to the marriage and to changes in religion.[63] In

56 *LP*, xviii (1), nos. 402 (6), 455, 458.
57 *LP*, xviii (1), nos. 501, 402 (6), 455, 458, 577; NAS, Treaties with England, 35 (now SP 2/55).
58 See *Henry VIII – A European Court in England*, ed. D. Starkey (1991).
59 *LP*, xviii (1), nos. 644, 665, 671, 728.
60 *LP*, xviii (1), no. 812. Payments to them are to be found in *LP*, xviii (2), no. 231, p. 127; xix (1), no. 368, fo. 52. Glencairn also received licence to export 200 tuns of beer from England. *LP*, xviii (1), no. 981 (48).
61 For a brief biography of the careers, see *Scots Peerage*, iv, 534–36; i, 333–39; vi, 166–68.
62 *LP*, xviii (1), nos. 281, 465.
63 *Ibid.*, no. 286. Arran's acceptance of one of their demands, that his Council be representative, obviously helped to gain the attendance at least of Huntly at the March Parliament. Some of these men were in close contact with the Queen Dowager (*Mary of Lorriane Corresp.*, 9, 17–20).

addition, there was a small bloc of 'neutral' lords such as James Stewart, Earl of Moray, a bastard son of James IV; William Keith, 4th Earl Marischal, thought to be pro-English, but never to be active in their support; John 5th Lord Erskine and George 4th Lord Seton, two of the four Guardians appointed to keep the queen safe.[64]

Sadler never appreciated the representativeness of Arran's Council, but what did worry him the minute he arrived was the disturbing news that Beaton had been allowed out of Douglas's custody at Dalkeith and had then been warded by Seton, known to be a confidant of his, before being permitted to return to St Andrews.[65] Arran scoffed at his perturbations on 1 April and joked that he might ward the Cardinal next with Henry, but Sadler was still worried by the reports he received of the Cardinal's movements.[66] This news also annoyed Henry and may have been the germ of his increasing conviction that no Scot could be trusted. In this the King, a bumptious poseur, but no fool, was correct. Arran was the linchpin. If the English were to triumph through 'policy', Arran was the man they had to keep amenable, hence the King's handsome offer of princess Elizabeth's hand for his son. On 1 April 1543, as Sadler fussed and Arran joked over dinner, all seemed well.

Even as the ambassador and the Governor supped, two men sped towards Scotland who were to alter Arran's mind. One was his half-brother, John Hamilton, abbot of Paisley (born in 1512, a natural son of Arran's father). Paisley was probably two or three years older and had spent some time in France. Upon hearing that his family was now at the centre of Scottish politics, he hastened back. Henry, mistakenly thinking he was of a reforming tendency, even assisted his passage.[67] It was yet another blunder, for the minute he arrived home, things began to change. He spent three days closeted with the Cardinal and, shortly after his repairing to Court, Arran's two Protestant preachers, Thomas Guilliaume and John Rough, were removed.[68]

Paisley may also have emphasised that the divorce of Arran's father had certain irregularities and could be re-examined in light of his closeness to the Crown.[69] Although Beaton was still relatively impotent, the government did begin to dampen the more extreme outbreaks of anti-clericalism, and on 2 June the Council forbade 'billis, writtingis, ballatis diffamatouris or schlanderous bukis' and the printing or

---

64 For Moray, Marischal, Erskine and Seton, see *Scots Peerage*, vi, 31–43, 46–48; v, 609–12; viii, 581–83.

65 *LP*, xviii (1), nos. 313, 318, 324, 338; *Rentale Sancti Andree*, ed. R.K. Hannay (SHS, 1913), xlii, 138–48.

66 *LP*, xviii (1), nos. 348, 374 (p. 220), 391, 395.

67 *LP*, xviii (1), nos. 358, 390. For John Hamilton's career, see Herkless and Hannay, *Archbishops of St Andrews*, v, 2–10; R.K. Hannay, 'The Earl of Arran and Queen Mary', *SHR*, xviii (1921), 258–76.

68 Knox, *History*, i, 47–49. Arran had been preparing for his brother's return as early as 15 March (*RSS*, iii, no. 22; *LP*, xviii (1), nos. 281 (p. 160), 395, 425).

69 This is argued by almost every historian of the period. In addition to sources cited in the previous two footnotes, see R.K. Hannay, 'Some Papal Bulls Among the Hamilton Papers', *SHR*, xxii (1924), 23–42, for other inducements made to Arran to alter his religious stance.

possession of 'ony bukis or werkis of condampnit heretikis and of thar appunzeo-nis'.[70] Arran certainly had to reconsider his position in April with the arrival of a second person from France, Matthew Stewart, 4th Earl of Lennox.[71] If the Hamilton claim to the throne could be set aside, the Lennox Stewarts were next in line and Matthew's return dramatically affected Arran's stance. As Henry for one fully appreciated, here was a rival in whose veins also coursed near-royal blood and who could act as a magnet for any of the nobility disaffected with Arran's regency, the marriage or change in religion.[72]

Sent to France by his family in 1532 at the age of 16, Lennox had matured in and about Francis' Court and had received some not inconsiderable honours and lands from the King.[73] Upon hearing of the turn of events in Scotland, he had recalled Claude de Guise and waited for several months to see what developed whilst he solicited papal and Danish assistance to prevent an English triumph.[74] Meanwhile, the King made the obvious move of readying Lennox and sending him with supplies and money. By 5 April, the Earl was with the Queen Dowager at Linlithgow, accredited as Francis' ambassador to Scotland.[75] May and June passed quietly enough with little overt political activity,[76] but Sadler was increasingly apprehensive.

Many Scots had been against the union of the realms from the start. On 5 January, Lisle and Cuthbert Tunstall, bishop of Durham, had an interview with an Archibald Douglas who was passing through Darlington with letters for his masters. As was normally the case, but particularly so at this time, this Scot was closely questioned as to events at home. Asked what he thought of an English marriage, he replied:

> then both the realmes shuld be as one, and Skotland clerely undone . . . albeit the realme of Skotland is but a pore thing to Englond, yet having the state of a

---

70 *ADCP*, 527–28.

71 *LP*, xviii (1), nos. 305, 374; *Scots Peerage*, v, 353–54; Knox, *History*, i, 51.

72 *LP*, xviii (1), nos. 22, 106, 139, 152, 254, 271, 418–19.

73 The French ambassadors certainly made this point most trenchantly to the earl in October: 'Nous . . . Remonstre lhonneur que ses predesseurs luy et les sien ont Receu par cy devant en france et recoivent chascum jour' (*Brosse Missions*, 22). Lennox's uncle, Robert Stewart, was a French noble, sieur d'Aubigny, captain of the 'garde escossois' and a marshal of France. Brother John, also of the 'garde', was sieur Darnley, becoming d'Aubigny upon the death of his uncle that March. There is considerable material for this, but see *LP*, xviii (1), no. 413.

74 Fear of Guise's arrival lasted well into April (*LP*, xviii (1), nos. 106, 113, 140, 395), and Arran in particular was worried (*ibid.*, nos. 261, 313). He had definitely been recalled by 15 February (*ibid.*, nos. 163, 254).

75 Lennox's mission is treated in W.M.A. Bryce, 'A French Mission to Scotland in 1543', *PSAS*, xlii (1908), 243–52. Lennox was certainly seen in April as the ambassador of Francis (*Nonces en France, 1541–46*, 203; *LP*, xviii (1), nos. 391, 462) but de la Brosse argued in October that he had only just made been ambassador: 'a este puys peu de Jours ordonne ambassaduer pour venir en escosse' (*Brosse Missions*, 22). Sadler was clearly concerned about Lennox's role (*LP*, xviii (1), nos. 400, 448); Henry also (*ibid.*, nos. 455, 479).

76 Arran spent the time in the West at his estates, but plans had been made for a trip as far north as Aberdeen, the Council of which was worried that Arran 'is com heir within schort tyme and no provis being made for a triumphe' (*Abdn. Counc.*, i, 189). For Sadler's concern, see *LP*, xviii (1), no. 458.

kynge in yt self, all the revenues therof shuld be spent within the realme, wheras if bothe the realmes were under one, all shuld go to the Kinge of England . . . Skotland nowe being poore alredy, shulde be utterly beggered and undone.[77]

That many other Scots entertained such fears is obvious from the terms demanded by the March Parliament. In another memorable interview, this time between Sadler and Sir Adam Otterburn of Redhill (a past and future ambassador himself), Scottish reservations were trenchantly put. Would the English 'be so ernest in thys matyer', Otterburn asked, 'If your lad was a lass and our lass was a lad?' The Scots would probably prefer that arrangement, but not the present one: 'And thought the hools nobilitie of the realm woulde consent to yt, yet our comen pepul, and the stones in the stretes, wolde ryse and rebel agenst yt'.[78] Popular opinion was not unimportant, but it was the 'nobilitie of the realme' who decided.

During the period April to July the entire political situation altered radically. On the one hand a 'party'[79] emerged, centring on Beaton, Mary of Guise and Lennox, clearly opposed to the marriage: Huntly, Argyll, Eglinton, Moray, Sempill, Seton, Methven, Hume and various others. On the other hand, the assured lords began to wilt. Glencairn, Cassillis, Maxwell and Angus remained relatively firm, but Bothwell was the first to change sides, as early as March. Fleming soon joined him. Even George Douglas was to be in communication with Beaton. Arran knew only too well from the regencies of the 1520s that unpopular Governors could survive only with great difficulty, and it must have been clear that he had to keep the base of his support as wide as possible. In his deliberations, he must have been counselled by two churchmen: Paisley, and David Paniter, prior of St Mary's Isle, increasingly at his side as secretary.[80]

Any doubts Arran may have entertained as to how exposed he now was must have been removed on 26 July. Throughout the month, as he knew only too well, bands had been moving from all over the country towards Linlithgow where the Queen lay. To Sadler, these armed men, a feature of Scottish political life during 1543–44 on which all visitors would comment, were simply another sign of the 'beastly' nature of the country.[81] But Arran knew differently. Scottish Parliaments were rarely the scene

77 *Hamilton Papers*, i, 357 (*LP*, xviii (1), no. 12).

78 As early as 20 March George Douglas warned Sadler that an English attempt to oust Arran would arouse resentment: 'There is not so lytle a boy but he woll hurle stone ayenst it, the wyves woll com out with their distaffes and the comons unyversally woll rather dye'. *Hamilton Papers*, i, 477 (*LP*, xviii (1), no. 305). Otterburn's remark can be found in Slavin, *Politics and Profit*, 131.

79 Such a term is anachronistic, but its alternatives – 'grouping', 'confederation', 'power bloc'– are equally inappropriate.

80 *LP*, xviii (1), 456, 671, 747, 769. Paniter also kept in close touch with Mary of Guise (*Balcarres Papers*, i, 93). Both were with him just before his public 'revolt' against Beaton (*LP*, xviii (2), no. 128).

81 'Non seulement la noblesse est en armes Mays les gens deglise Religeulx et paysans ne marchent par pays que par grandes compaignyes et tous armes de picques espees coucliers et un demye picqu' (*Brosse Missions*, 22). Aberdeen burgesses spoke in July of 'the brokining of this realme, as is daly sene' (*Abdn. Counc.*, i, 191).

of great political debate for a variety of reasons too complex to detail here; in the main they were creatures of faction.[82] If that faction was the King's or represented a large enough proportion of the aristocracy, it was quite significant, as in March 1543 and August 1560. But the June 1543 Parliament[83] which approved the articles of marriage had a very low attendance, and Arran might have guessed even then that the scene of great debate was about to move out of Edinburgh.

When Scottish governments pursued unpopular policies, the normal response was 'rebellion', and Arran was about to face the first of five against him during 1543–44.[84] Rarely enduring mass movements, they generally were aristocratic and clearly aimed at a specific political end. Occasionally these uprisings resulted in actual physical combat in which men died (as happened to Arran's father in 1526, and would happen at Glasgow the following April), but more often than not, the 'side' with the largest number of men on the field won (as happened in January 1544 when Lennox, Glencairn and Angus faced Arran near Leith).

The Governor had rallied as many of his supporters as possible and he also had the military stores of the Crown on which to draw.[85] However, Beaton's force before Linlithgow on 24 July contained the power of four bishops, six abbots or priors, six earls, eight lords and twenty-three lairds. On that day, they pledged to 'remaid' the situation whereby the Queen might be transported to England, 'quharthrow this realm standis in gret danger to be swdewit till our awld enymyis of Ingland'.[86] On the 26th Arran's force gathered before Beaton's; as the Governor's was the lesser, he acquiesced in Beaton's demand that the Queen be removed from Linlithgow to Stirling, where she was to remain for the next five years.[87]

Stirling was a more defensive complex of buildings than the palace of Linlithgow, and Mary of Guise lavishly praised the 'ayre about the house' to Sadler in mid-

82 R.S. Rait, *The Parliaments of Scotland*, may well overstress this aspect. See also his 'Scottish Parliaments before the Union of Crowns', *EHR*, xv (1900), 209–37, 417–44.

83 There is a distinction to be made between a Parliament and a Convention (for which less notice was necessary and for which the membership was smaller), and the June meeting may well have been a Convention, as only thirteen were present, plus ten others in attendance. *APS*, ii, 425 (but see also a contemporary copy of the agreement in BL, MS Add. 32, 651, fo. 7r–v); *LP*, xviii (1), no. 671.

84 Various phrases were used to describe such revolts; that of May 1544 was termed 'thair tressonable coming in with umquhile William, Erle of Glencairn, with displayet baner in plane battell aganis the governour, and lichtland before him on Glasgw mure for suberting of him and his friendis bein gin his cumpany for the tyme' (*RSS*, iv, no. 235).

85 *TA*, viii, 224. Arran sent for help to Glencairn and George Douglas (*LP*, xviii (1), no. 896). Thomas Menzies was sent to Aberdeen to ask 'gif thai vald fortify and menteyne his authorite aganis certane conspiratouris' (*Abdn. Counc.*, i, 191). See also *LP*, xviii (1), nos. 880, 897, 938, 941.

86 *LP*, xviii (1), no. 944.

87 A full account of the events can be gathered from *LP*, xviii (1), nos. 944, 951–52, 966, 974; Henry clearly appreciated what happened (*ibid.*, nos. 971, 979); and see *APS*, ii, 429 (*LP*, xviii (2) no. 474). One of the ironies of the situation was that 26 July was also the day that 'the peax nower taken [with England] was solemnly proclaymed in this towne [Edinburgh] with heraulddes and trompettes'. *Hamilton Papers*, i, 597 (*LP*, xviii (1), no. 952).

August.[88] Stirling was situated atop a steep crag which could be approached from one side only. In many ways, Stirling was stronger than Edinburgh, a castle which would intimidate English armies in 1544 and in 1547. Moreover, whereas Linlithgow was near the sea, Stirling lay on the edge of the Highlands. Should an English army approach, the Queen could easily be spirited into the self-same mountainous fastness which had sheltered Bruce.

What, incidentally, of the Queen's life during this her first year? Mary was treated like any baby of high birth in early modern Europe: swaddled, regularly clean, kept warm and fed regularly by a bevy of nurses and nursemaids. Her mother, having little else in terms of a political or ceremonial life to occupy her in 1543 (something which would change radically in 1544), doubtless attended to her nurture with all due attention. After all she had one of the most redoubtable role models in renaissance France, her mother Marguerite, who raised to adulthood a brood of ten children. As the eldest child of that family, Mary of Guise doubtless had played a large part in the bringing up of the little ones: elder sisters always do. Moreover, she had already given birth to two boys in France and two more boys in Scotland. That only one survived in 1543 was not her doing, but the Lord's.

Mary Queen of Scots responded to this attention the best way a baby can, by eating well and staying alive. That was her job, and it would take two full hacks of the axe by the best executioner in Europe to remove her head in 1587. Prone to illnesses, frail and often hysterically unstable when under stress, Mary Queen of Scots was as tough as old boots. Her queenly roles during her first year after birth and baptism were modest to say the least. Monarchs, as we have seen illustrated above at Greenwich when her betrothal was concluded, often met ambassadors from foreign princes in a massive reception chamber surrounded by their Court. Mary's first ambassadorial reception was at Linlithgow on 22 March 1543, when Sir Ralph Sadler visited her at the invitation of her mother. She was then a possible future Queen of England and Sadler came, in part, to check her out for Henry VIII. The Queen was laid upon a table and fully undressed 'out of her clowtes' before her mother by a nurse. Her mother proudly showed off her utterly naked babe (that 'he might see her in her native loveliness') to this Englishman. Sadler was impressed: 'it is as goodly a child as I have seen of her age, and like to live, with the grace of God'. By early July she was 'breeding of teethe'.[89]

Mary was then removed from Linlithgow Palace to Stirling Castle on 27 July 1543: it took dozens of waggons to transport all of her mother's and her necessities over the rough track between the two residences.[90] The Earl of Lennox made the trip with the queens, along with 2500 horsemen and a thousand heavily armed men on foot. Two weeks after her arrival at what was to be her home for the next five years (to February 1548), Sadler again saw her, pronouncing that she was 'a right fayre and goodlie

88 *LP*, xviii (1), no. 810; (2), no. 22; *Diurnal of Occurrents*, 27–29.
89 Fleming, *Mary Queen of Scots*, 7, 185–6.
90 E.M. Furgol, 'The Scottish itinerary of Mary Queen of Scots, 1542–8 and 1561–8', *PSAS* (cxvii, 1989), 119–231 is concerned almost exclusively with Mary's personal reign.

child'. Mary of Guise again breathed motherly satisfaction: 'her daughter did grow apace, and soon would be a woman, if she took of her mother', as indeed she did.

But, as Sadler was only beginning to comprehend, the Queen's removal marked the end of any hope for the English marriage. Arran was the first to appreciate this, and it is from this time that one must date his renunciation of Henry. However much he may have desired the Queen's hand for his son, Arran gradually came to an understanding with Beaton as to how to see the year out. July was high summer, the middle of the normal campaigning season. If they gave the game away, Henry could still invade. The two obviously agreed to dissemble until such time as Henry's wrath could take little effective form. Throughout August Arran kept his counsel, and on 25 August in the grounds of Holyrood Palace ratified the Treaties of Greenwich in an impressive ceremony which Sadler attended. Only during the first week of September did he become publicly reconciled with Beaton and agreed to the Queen's coronation at Stirling on 9 September.[91] Henry had lost.

To some, this came as no surprise. As early as 6 July Lord Parr seconded the opinion of one of his spies that Arran 'never entendethe, nez is able, to perfourme hys promyses'.[92] In the same despatch he gave his understanding of what Arran had said at a recent meeting of his Council:

> Ye knowe the King of Englande is a mightie prince, and we not able nez of powre to resist his puissance, and for that cause I thinke and take it best by fare wordes and promyses, with the concluding of this peas, to deferre and put over the danger that might otherwise fall upon us.

Why was Parr ignored? Partly it was because the King had too many sources of information;[93] partly it was because Henry (and Sadler) simply did not want to know. Not until 29 August did the King order preparations for a military invasion.[94] By then it was entirely too late.

By then also, Mary had been publicly crowned as Queen. Her reign, of course, began the second her father died, but her coronation was a political act of the first importance (especially coming as did after the public reconciliation of Arran and Beaton): Mary's first big moment on the stage of Scottish, British and European History. In comparison with what she staged for her son at Stirling 22 years later, it was modest, austere and low key.[95] But it was a coronation at which she was crowned, blessed and anointed before her nation. On Sunday, 9 September, in the Chapel Royal within the precincts of the Castle, the child Mary must have been

91 *LP*, xviii (2), nos. 76, 79. See Arran's soothing letter to Henry (*ibid.*, no. 95), clear indication that he was dissembling.

92 *Hamilton Papers*, i, 555 (*LP*, xviii (1), no. 827).

93 What I call in lectures 'the Pearl Harbor clutter syndrome': although the Americans had cracked many Japanese codes and had sapient spies in Tokyo, there was simply too much information available to them.

94 *LP*, xviii (2), no. 93.

95 Sadler's sneer that the ceremony was conducted 'with solempnitie as they doo use in this countrey, whiche is not verie costelie' (*Hamilton Papers*, ii, nos. 26, 30) has been repeated so often that I refuse to dignify it by inclusion in the text of this account.

given the full religious service of becoming an anointed queen by the Cardinal Archbishop of St. Andrews, Primate of all Scotland. In the procession, Arran as Scotland's premier Earl carried the royal crown, only refashioned in 1540 for her mother's coronation; the Earl of Lennox held the sceptre, and Campbell of Argyll bore the sword of state, a gift from Pope Julius II to James IV in 1502. The crown was carried by the current Duke of Hamilton at the opening of the new Scottish Parliament on 1 July 1999, and all of these instruments of majesty can be viewed in Edinburgh Castle today.

The rite completed 'with great solemnity', the day was finished off with celebrations: 'triumph, plays, farces and banqueting and great dancing before the Queen with great lords and French ladies'.[96]

FRANCIS I: 'FRANCOYS/ FRANC/ FRA/ F'

Thus far it would appear that the Scots alone had bested Henry; to a large extent this was the case. But the events of 1543 occurred within a context much wider than Britain. On 10 July 1542 the Habsburg-Valois wars had broken out again. This very much suited Henry, who was anxious to end his isolation from the Continent. As early as December 1541, he had proposed an alliance with Charles. At the time, the Emperor had been cool toward the idea, but as the Turkish threat to Hungary emerged and French intentions became clearer in the early months of 1542, he decided to ally once again with England. On 5 May 1542, Eustace Chapuys was instructed to seek a pact of mutual alliance against France. Now Henry was distant. But, by 5 February 1543 the English suddenly began talking in concrete terms and in less than a week, on the 11th, the pact was agreed. Again, little happened.

Henry's defiance of Francis was not issued until 21 June, and an English contingent of troops, only 5000 strong, arrived in the Low Countries, but not until late summer. By 31 December 1543 a new agreement had to be made for an invasion in 1544, a year later than originally planned.[97] There are various explanations for this considerable delay: the French made attractive counter-proposals; Henry had difficulty raising both money and men; Princess Mary's status vexed negotiations between her father and her mother's nephew; and Henry insisted on being styled Head of the Church. He also was adamant that he take the field in person. All this disrupted the original timetable.

But it is also clear that the King was so 'engulfed' in Scottish affairs that he found it impossible to concentrate on the invasion of France.[98] Certainly Chapuys had seen the possibility of this, and he vainly endeavoured throughout the year to force the King to focus on the larger issue. That he failed is a tribute to the work of Beaton and

---

96 Marshall, *Mary of Guise*, 133. Sanderson, *Cardinal of Scotland*, 170–72, makes no mention of the Cardinal officiating, but he must have done so, having met with Arran in Stirling Greyfriars the day before. D. J. Breeze, *A Queen's Progress* (HMSO, 1987), 21–24.

97 See below, pp. 000–00, for Imperial negotiations during this time.

98 See Wernham, *Before the Armada: The Growth of English Foreign Policy, 1485–1588*, 152–54; Scarisbrick, *Henry VIII*, 434–35, 439, 441.

Arran. Moreover, it is possible that this is just what Francis hoped to achieve. One of the more striking aspects of the events of 1543 is the lack of any serious French involvement in Scotland until October, by which time the English attempt to break the Franco-Scottish alliance had completely failed. One would have thought that the events of March to July would have seriously worried Francis I, now facing a war on two fronts.

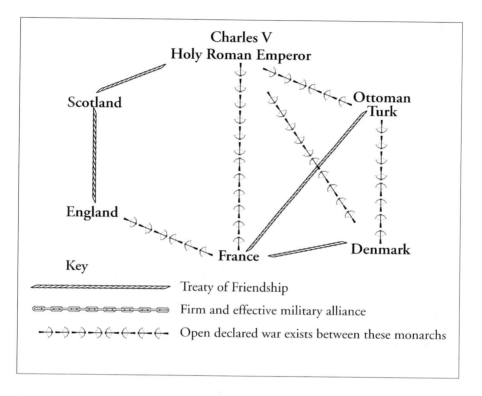

Fig. 5.2. On 11 February 1543, Henry VIII and Charles V signed a formal treaty to effect 'The Enterprise of Paris' and in May/June, Henry VIII formally declared war on Francis I, citing his alliance with the Turk as the cause. On 1 July, the Treaties of Greenwich were signed between England and Scotland, the one being a formal treaty of peace, the other being a contract for the betrothal of Mary Queen of Scots to Prince Edward of Wales.

Certainly at first the King seemed most alarmed by the death of James. Mary of Guise's uncle wrote early in the year:

Il me deplait, Madame, de la fortune qui vous est advenue et a vostre roiaulme, chose qui faire mal au cueur a tous noz parens et amys et croies pour certain ma dame, que le Roy en est deplaisant.

[Madame, the bad luck which has befallen you and your kingdom displeases me; it's something which grieves your parents and friends, and I can assure you that the King is also saddened.][99]

Aid was immediately sought from Denmark and from the Pope; Lennox was despatched in March.[100] Beaton for his part certainly must have outlined the danger of an English marriage and on 20 May he sent James Stewart of Cardonald to France in the ship which had conveyed Lennox.[101] Stewart made a report to the King and had many interviews in June and July with the papal nuncio for Scotland, Marco de Grimani.[102] By 16 July, Stewart had gathered a considerable amount of munitions and money at Dieppe.[103]

In the meanwhile Francis did nothing. Grimani bitterly complained that he was wasting his time in Paris,[104] and it was not until the end of June that a commission was finally prepared,[105] for the direction of Francis' two ambassadors to Scotland, Jacques de la Brosse, closely connected to the Guises and on the first of several embassies to Scotland, and Jules de Mesnage, a counsellor of the Parlement of Rouen.[106] But then almost two months passed before Grimani was finally sent to Brest, and even then the three, plus Stewart of Cardonald, did not sail until 17 September.[107] Why did Francis delay for so long?[108]

---

99 *Balcarres Papers*, i, 87–91.

100 For the request to Denmark, see below, p. 173. For requests to Rome, see *Nonces en France, 1541–46*, 183, 218; *LP*, xvii (1), nos. 319, 387; *Négotiations Diplomatiques de la France avec la Toscane*, ed. A Desjardins (Paris, 1859–86), ii, 54.

101 *LP*, xviii (1), nos. 494, 572, 652, 745.

102 Grimani's mission is discussed by R.K. Hannay, 'Letters to the Papal Legate in Scotland, 1543', *SHR* xi, (1911), 1–26. His letter of credence was given him on 25 March 1543 (*LP*, xviii (1), no. 181), but his instructions of 1 April 1543 (Hannay, *op. cit.*, 8–11 but also see *Nonces en France, 1542–46*, 199–200) had to be sent after him to Paris (*ibid.*, 203). Grimani was to have a thoroughly difficult time in this his last mission (he died in 1544); the English accounted him 'a man of small prudence' and 'more rash than wise' (*LP*, xviii (1) nos. 321, 387); still they feared his master (*ibid.*, nos. 601, 946).

103 *LP*, xviii (1), nos. 753, 880, 900; (2), no. 22.

104 He had hoped to depart for Scotland as soon as he arrived in Paris on 25 April, and was surprised that Francis did not immediately create 'une diversion par l'Escosse'. On 22 July, he hoped to leave in two days, but he was not allowed to go to Brest until 12 August. *Nonces en France, 1541–46*, 201, 205, 208–11. For the reaction of Dandino, the papal nuncio in France at the time, see *ibid.*, 218, 228, 239.

105 Teulet, *Relations*, i, 118–123 (*LP*, xviii (2), no. 499); see also BN, MS fr., 17,890, fo. 7 and BL, MS Harl. 1244, fos. 192–94. The state of an original draft of the credence, prepared at Marolle on 25 June, would indicate that the King decided to delay the mission then; although countersigned by his secretary, Francis doodled over the document. I am grateful to Dr. D.L. Potter for this information.

106 *Brosse Missions*, iii–ix; J. de la Brosse, *Histoire d'un Capitaine Bourbonnais au XVIe siècle: Jacques de la Brosse, 1458–1562*.

107 *Nonces en France, 1541–46*, 211–12; *Brosse Missions*, 15; BN, MS fr. 17,888, fo. 10; 17,890, pp. 18–19; *Mary of Lorraine Corresp.*, 33–34.

108 Henry of course did not see matters in quite that light and his ultimatum laid some stress on French assistance to the Scots. Rumours of aid were very strong in April and July. See *LP* xviii (1), nos. 359, 754; (2), no. 75.

Le feu Roy francois premier

Fig. 5.3. This pen and ink sketch of Francis is both a delightful capturing of the King at his ease, but also getting on in years. By 1543, Francis was three months off his 49th birthday during the summer of 1543. He could still take the field with an army, go on long progresses and maintain a mistress. The great fleet which he assembled to attack England in 1545 was overseen (and dined upon) by him (the royal vessel caught fire and the King barely escaped with his life). He had actually killed men by his own hand on the battlefield. (Did Henry VIII ever do so? Charles V did.) But he was often tired and was clearly ageing. For one thing, most of his favourite children were lost to him (the Dauphin François died in 1536 and Madeleine, James V's first Queen, in 1537). His third son would outlive him by only a year.

Three explanations are possible. Francis himself was busy in 1543 with other concerns, such as fighting a major war. On 25 June, the King was in his army's camp at Marolle, and it was there that these instructions to his ambassadors for Scotland were drafted and clearly discussed at some length. But he knew only too well by then of England's alliance with the Emperor; if he lost Scotland, France would be dangerously exposed. He may well have wished to send more aid, but was prevented by the English fleet, then patrolling the Irish Sea.[109] Communication obviously was difficult,[110] but Lennox had slipped through the English net, and the seven ships which went with Grimani made the voyage from Brest to Dumbarton in nine days.

A third possibility is that Francis deliberately held back overt support of the Scots. No policy document supports such an interpretation, but one (not seen by me) is highly suggestive. The instructions prepared for Mesnage in June at Marolle survive today at Chateau Fort. They apparently were in their final top copy awaiting simply the King's signature and his Secretary's countersign. But Francis never signed them. Instead, Dr. Potter found on their final page doodlings: 'FRANCOYS/ FRANC/ FRA/ F' in the King's characteristic hand. Might not his Council have urged him to hold back until the end of the campaigning season? Thus might Henry be deflected. That is exactly what happened.

It must have taken some courage. To lie dormant in April must have seemed a dangerous gamble; in June, with the marriage agreed and the Treaty of Greenwich about to be signed, it must have been even more worrying. However, Beaton may have confided to the King that little long-term damage to the Franco-Scottish alliance was to be feared. Still the tension must have been considerable. In any event, no English invasion of note occurred in 1543, and by the end of the year the Scottish Parliament had renounced the English marriage and renewed the alliance with France. Already talk of marrying Mary abroad was in the air.[111]

Once French support arrived in Scotland, it was put to as good effect as possible. French policy-makers, however, laboured under considerable handicaps. On the one hand they were convinced that Lennox was trustworthy and were consistently hostile to Arran. Partly this was due to Mary of Guise's and Beaton's stance; partly it was due to their desire to see Lennox replace Arran as Governor.[112] But by October Arran was quickly moving even further into the Cardinal's camp: Beaton was soon reinstated as

109 *Brosse Missions*, 38; *LP*, xviii (1), nos. 652, 900; BN MS fr. 20,510 fo. 279; *Nonces en France, 1541–46*, 212. On 11 September Mary of Guises's mother wrote that up to that time no messengers had been able to get through (*Balcarres Papers*, i, 94–95); and see *Mary of Lorraine Corresp.*, 11.

110 Letters sent on 24 November 1543 did not reach France until 4 January 1544 (*Nonces en France, 1541–46*, 213).

111 BN, MS fr., 17,890, fos. 38–39; Fleming, *Mary Queen of Scots*, 193.

112 They reported on arrival that Lennox 'estoit deliberé mourir pour vostre service' and that Arran supported 'les gens scandaleux qui veulent contemprer les eglises' (BN, MS fr., 17,888, fo. 275). See also *Brosse Missions*, 18–28, *passim*. It was not until November that they appreciated 'que le voiaige faict par ledict de lesnaux comme ambassadeur en ce Royaume a este dommaigeable au Roy et au Royame descosse [that Lennox's trip as ambassador to this Kingdom has been harmful to the King [of France] and to the kingdom of Scotland]' (*ibid.*, 38).

Chancellor and was given custody of Arran's eldest son.[113] Lennox on the other hand was alienated by Beaton's acceptance of Arran as Governor and by November was refusing to part with the money and munitions which de la Brosse and Mesnage deposited in Dumbarton.

Nonetheless, the ambassadors were able to liaise closely with Beaton and large promises of pensions were widely scattered: 1000 Crowns of the Sun[114] apiece for Huntly, Argyll and Moray. English 'Lords', such as Bothwell (1000), Grey (300) and Glencairn (300), were also tempted. Arran was promised 2000 Crowns (the same as Lennox when he was trusted); Beaton and Mary received 6000. Three of the ships still had not yet discharged their cargo of munitions.[115]

Thus, despite the embarrassment of Lennox's volte-face, the French envoys still had clout. They did what they could to make Sadler, already in serious trouble in Edinburgh owing to Henry's seizure in August of 16 ships from the city,[116] even more uncomfortable. They even decided (Mesnage the lawyer at work here) to search the records of Parliament for 'quelque occasion Raisonnable par deffaulte de solemnite et formalite' to annul the betrothal of Mary to Edward.[117] On 3 December 'la seurte et corroboracion de nostredict ancienne amytie et alliance' was achieved; eight days later the same Parliament declared 'violate and brokin' (by reason of Henry's seizure of the ships) 'the artikle proponit tuiching the pece and contractis of mariage laitlie tane and maid'.[118]

French delight at this turn of events was considerable; de la Brosse and Mesnage exulted:

> Nous avons entendu en ce pays Que le Roy dangleterre a este ausse marry de nostre venue avec les finances et municions de Roy comme sil avait perdu une grosse bataille. [We have heard here that the King of England is as furious about our arrival with all this money and munitions as if he had lost a great battle].[119]

The mission was expensive.[120] Still, Francis had good cause to be satisfied with the

---

113 Beaton had Arran's son as pledge by 25 November; he became Chancellor again at the meeting of Parliament on 13 December (*LP*, xviii (2), nos. 425, 491).

114 A French Crown of the Sun was worth approximately 20s 3d Scots (J. Cameron, *James V*, 281, footnote 47).

115 *Brosse Missions*, 33–35. They argued that money was necessary 'pour ce eque en temps de guerre les seigneurs menent leur subiects a la guerre sans leur baller soulde' (*ibid.*, 30). It was even suggested at the time that George Douglas was to receive a French pension (*LP*, xviii (2), no. 424).

116 The curious episode of Henry's (accidental?) seizure of the ships has never been successfully unravelled; he apparently did so as they were bound for France. See *LP*, xviii (2), nos. 47, 83, 111, 154; *Mary of Lorraine Corresp.*, 35–36; *Diurnal of Occurrents*, 29–30.

117 *Brosse Missions*, 42.

118 *APS*, ii, 431 (*LP*, xviii (2), no. 476). Note that the precepts for the December Parliament were sent out in October (*TA*, viii, 231).

119 *Brosse Missions*, 42.

120 41,700 livres was given as pensions alone in addition to all the other costs (BN, MS fr. 17,890, pp. 18–19). See *TA*, viii, 221.

turn of events.[121] In particular, he had reason to praise the work of Mary of Guise, whose contribution to the French triumph has not been sufficiently stressed. Not only did she expend a great deal of her own treasure, but she also built up a party bound to her through obligations, bonds of manrent and, of course, the promise of French pensions.[122] Huntly, Moray and Methven were particularly close to her, but she was vital in detaching Bothwell from the English and did much to cause Glencairn to waver. She even began to build up a close relationship with the merchants of Edinburgh, and it was to her that they turned when the town sustained 'mervalous greit' damage by the loss of the ships.[123] She may have failed to keep Lennox loyal, but this was not for want of trying.

'THE HONOUR OF THIS REALME': SCOTTISH RENUNCIATION OF GREENWICH

Henry certainly had accelerated the deterioration of Anglo-Scottish relations in 1543 by his petulant truculence towards his 'Assured Lords', by his high-handed seizure of the Scottish ships and by his deliberate failure to ratify the Treaties of Greenwich. But on the one hand, Henry was probably correct not to trust men like Angus, and he was not to do so again. On the other, by September the game was clearly lost and he probably did little to ruin chances of the marriage by giving vent to his rage. There was little he could do by then to save the situation. Sadler, too, has been severely criticised and it has been argued that he was simply incompetent.[124] Frankly, he was, but on reflection, neither Henry nor Sadler deserves all that much blame for how the situation was handled. The fault lay in thinking that the situation could be handled in the first place, as happens so often in diplomacy. The English failed to gain the marriage in 1543 because the Scots did not want it; here two men, Beaton and Arran, were crucial.

From the start, Beaton was resolute against the marriage and it was he who, often at some cost to himself and to the church, kept opposition together.[125] In the end, his triumph was complete and it is little wonder that Henry came to hate him. Arran's role should not be minimised. Clearly he did share some reforming tendencies, and initially it was quite profitable for him to seem anti-Beaton, for the marriage, and

121 On 12 February 1544, the King declared his satisfaction with his ambassadors' work: 'si ne les y eust envoyes en la sorte quil a et le bon secours quils ont porte, les Escossois sen alloit entirement perdu et du tout reduct en lobeissance et subjection du Roy dangleterre [Had you not been sent in such sort that you had such good assistance, the Scots would have been entirely lost and completely reduced to the obedience and subjugation of the King of England]' and declared his pleasure that Beaton and Mary worked 'pour estymer les affairs de France et Escosse une mesme chose [in order to consider the affairs of France and Scotland to be the same thing]' (BN, MS fr. 17890; fos. 38–39).
122 *Brosse Missions*, 29. Note Lennox's brother writing to her about his see of Caithness (*Mary of Lorraine Corresp.*, 12–13).
123 Her pension of £1000 to Bothwell on 12 August 1543 was one of several such bonds of manrent (NAS, State Papers, 38a); see also *Mary of Lorraine Corresp.*, 24–52 and especially 35–36, 47–48, 57.
124 As Slavin does, *Politics and Profits*, 113–14.
125 Herkless and Hannay, *Archbishops of St Andrews*, iv, 97–106; appendices xvii–xix.

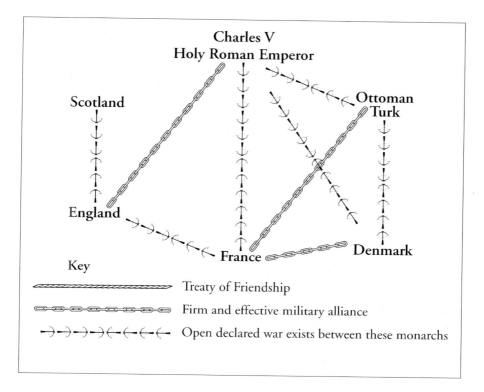

Fig 5.4.   In November 1543, Henry, citing Scottish refusal to enact the Treaties of
           Greenwich (which they had ratified in August), declared open war with
           Scotland. On 15 December, the Scottish parliament renounced the Treaties
           of Greenwich and declared them void at the same time as the French
           defensive alliance was formally renewed in the name of the new monarch of
           Scotland. The first Rough Wooing had begun.

determined to reverse James's policies. However, his family's interests were paramount and it should never be forgotten that Arran very much wanted to see the
Queen married to his son.[126]

There is one final consideration, hitherto not stressed, which I think was highly
important. Arran had a genuine respect for the 'commoun weill and liberte of
Scotland'. In a memorable exchange, Henry accused him on 27 October of
'forgetting your deutye to that realme, your honour and estimation to the worlde,
and your private and secret promesses unto us'.[127] Arran coolly retorted on 10
November that his country's interests were more important, that he worked with 'the
maist and hailest part of the nobilitie of Scotland, faithful subjectis unto the Quenis

---

126 *LP*, xviii (1), nos. 4, 324, 974, and see below for his attempts to build up support for the
    marriage in 1545–46.
127 *Hamilton Papers*, ii, 128, 154–55 (*LP*, xviii (2), nos. 313, 363).

grace' and that he would govern 'to the honour of this realme aganis all thame that wald everte the samin'. Henry's anger was groundless:

> except it greve you that we sufferit nocht sic rigour and extremite of battale to be usit amangis the nobillis and subjectis of this realme, as appaerandlie suld have maid the samyn unhabill eftirwart to have resistit and defendit the invasioun.

These handsome rhetorical phrases may merely have been conceit, but Arran had good reason to be pleased as 1543 ended. He was a patriot.

CHAPTER SIX

The First Rough Wooing

Henry's efforts to achieve the betrothal of Mary and Edward by diplomacy had failed; he now turned to force. Why he did so is unclear. To talk costs little; to make war is expensive. One clear reason why Henry did so is that he had sufficient money to do so. Beaton and Arran had humiliated him and he may have gone to war against Scotland merely out of vexation. More rational considerations did exist. But the war would fail to achieve any of the objectives of 1543. This was because in 1544 Henry's interest turned to France, but it was also because the Scots beat him.

THE OUTBREAK OF WAR

On 20 December 1543, five days after the end of the Scottish Parliament which broke the marriage treaty with England and renewed the alliance with France, Henry Ray, Berwick Pursuivant, appeared before Arran and some of his Council at Edinburgh[1] to 'reade his message uppon the booke'. The nub of his declaration[2] was that Beaton and Arran had broken the peace:[3]

> So . . . by your unfaythefulnesse, ye have given just occasion of the distruction of that which your maistres might have enjoyed, and youe be the cause and occacion wherby the goodes of the poore commens shalbe wasted and spoiled at home, and their entrecourse letted in outward parties.[4]

The Scots, bewitched by 'foyles and perverse fansies' (especially 'promesses of gayn out of Fraunce' and 'maynetenaunce of the Cardinalles appetites') had forgotten that they dealt with 'a Prince of honour that will not suffre your disloyaltye unpunished and unrevenged'.

Various soothing replies were made to Ray's declaration. On 20 December 1543 and 19 January 1544 Arran suggested a meeting to discuss 'the comoun weill of baith thir

---

1 Beaton, Rothes, Moray were there, but the rest of the lords had gone to their estates (*LP*, xviii (2), nos. 521–22); Arran was to pass the Yule at Stirling where he spent £110 'to play at the cartis witht the quenis gracis' (*TA* viii, 242).

2 It was prepared by Paget, but both Wriotheley and Bishop Gardiner (*LP*, xviii (2), nos. 235 (2), (4)) made numerous corrections (17 pages of them). Ray's declaration was intended to be read to the assembled Parliament; he was only sent when it became clear that Sadler could not attend in person. See Sadler's declaration (no. 486), perhaps drafted by Henry (it certainly makes for extraordinary reading).

3 Although Ray declared that the Scots had 'refused peax, foresaken it, trobled it, letted it, broken it', it is worth remembering that Henry never ratified either treaty (*LP*, xviii (2), nos. 78–79, 85, 115–16, 363, 481, 486).

4 *LP*, xix (1), nos. 44, 46 and see 56. Especially Beaton's letter (*ibid.*, no. 91) did not soothe Henry. *TA*, viii, 257.

realmes', and even Beaton wrote to the King of his desire for concord.[5] Both men knew that a difficult period lay ahead. Throughout 1543 Henry had threatened to go to war whenever his will was opposed.[6] As early as 9 September he had thundered that should Sadler continue to be molested over the ships, Edinburgh would suffer 'thextermination of you to the third and fourth generations'. By mid-September plans were being made in great detail (down to the relative advantages of carts as against 'costrells' for transport) for an invasion.[7] His December harangue was the last of a series in which the King's language had become increasingly and childishly truculent.[8]

But Henry had good reason to be enraged, for during the period October 1543 to January 1544 Arran and Beaton effectively consolidated their control over the country. Sadler was forced to flee to Angus's stronghold of Tantallon and then to England.[9] Glencairn made his peace with Mary of Guise.[10] Other 'English Lords' such as Angus and Cassillis retired to their castles and lay low. On 1 November Somerville and Maxwell were arrested in Edinburgh by Paisley's band of guards and were warded in Edinburgh Castle. A week later, George Douglas's castle of Dalkeith was captured.[11] During the well-attended Parliament of 3 to 15 December, Angus, Lennox, Glencairn and Marischal were purged from the Council.[12] Arran declared he would help the church since

> Heretikis mair and mair risis and spredis within this realme sawand dampnable opinionis Incontrar the fayth and lawis of halykirk actis and constitutionis of this realme.[13]

Even before, Arran and Beaton had been moving against heresy. In November they went in person to chastise Dundee where the friaries had been molested.[14] Grimani attributed his tranquil passage through Leith just afterwards to the terror recently visited upon Dundee. On 26 November 'an immense number of New Testaments'

---

5 *Hamilton Papers*, ii, 235–38.

6 As in May when the King's counter-proposals to the Scottish marriage terms were linked with a threat of force (*LP*, xviii (1), no. 479 (2)).

7 *LP*, xviii (2), nos. 195, 196, 198.

8 *LP*, xviii (2), nos. 154–55. See also *ibid.*, no. 319. The King offered to restore the ships if the town would aid his purpose (*ibid.*, nos. 256, 276); the town refused, 'becaus we can nocht condiscend to sic unreasonable desyreis' (*Mary of Lorraine Corresp.*, 35).

9 Sadler was there from 6 November until 11 December (*LP*, xviii (2), nos. 302, 323, 343 and 350–483; *passim*). For the government's hounding of him, see *ibid.*, nos. 397–98, 429; *TA* viii, 236–37.

10 *Mary of Lorraine Corresp.*, 33, 36–37, 42–45.

11 *LP*, xviii (2), nos. 323, 340, 343, 470; *TA*, viii, 235–37, 243.

12 *APS*, ii, 433 *LP*, xviii (2), no. 484; for all the acts of this Parliament, including an amnesty for the Linlithgow gathering by Beaton's supporters, see *APS*, ii, 427–43 (*LP*, xviii (2), nos. 452, 470, 474, 476, 481, 484, 491, 497).

13 *APS*, ii, 443 (*LP*, xviii (2), no. 497).

14 'In this tyme thair was ane greit heresie in Dundie; thair thaj destroyt the kirkis and wald have destroyet Abirbrothok kirk' (*Diurnal of Occurrents*, 29). See also report in *LP*, xviii (2), no. 425. Arran must have gone there on 11 November. The itinerary in *RSS* is inadequate for August 1543 to May 1544; compare datings for letter in *LP*, xviii (2), no. 363 and *RSS*, iii, no. 5170.

and other heretical books were publicly burnt in Edinburgh.[15] The French ambassadors similarly reported a falling off in religious rioting: 'Si tost que notre venue . . . tout cesse et les eglises et estat de Religion demoure comme Il estoit hors de nostre venue. [As soon as we arrived everything stopped and the churches and the state of religion rests as it was before our arrival]'.[16]

The New Year saw no diminution. In early January Angus, Glencairn, Cassillis and Lennox gathered their retainers and moved towards Edinburgh, intent upon forcing Arran to change his policy. However, this time the Governor was admirably well prepared.[17] The lords quickly agreed to make 'trew and manlie resistence of our auld ennemes of Ingland' and either lay pledges (Angus entered his brother George) or enter surety (Lennox's was for £10,000).[18] Immediately, the Governor returned to Fife, Perth, and Dundee. With Beaton he set to 'punising of certane heretiks'.[19]

Open hostilities ensued. By November, when Arran demanded that Angus expel Sadler from Tantallon, he spoke of 'the discharge of ane Inglishmen of yis countrey in tyme of war'.[20] Talk of war had filled the air ever since Arran's 'revolt' in September, and by the end of the year the English wardens were readying themselves: Border raids were almost constant.[21] On 29 January 1544 the King informed Suffolk of the plan of campaign for the Spring.[22]

The war which followed had a number of aims. Clearly Henry sought war to force the Scots to agree to the marriage. Secondly, the war was fought for the reason that the King stated in his letter of 29 January: 'the wynneng . . . and keping of the strong holdes on this side the Frithe' so that 'the Scottes . . . shal have nomaner commonditie of passage to annoye our realm' whilst Henry was in France.[23] A third possible consideration is that Henry sought, as the Berwick Pursuivant had declared in December, simply to 'punish' the Scots for having broken covenants.

Since the time of Edward I, Anglo-Scottish wars had taken on a pattern which had not greatly altered over the years. The English approach had five main ingredients and Henry was to employ all of them during 1544–46: disparagement of Scottish independence, encouragement of domestic aristocratic discontent, devastating the Scottish frontier by raiding parties from the English Marches, major military assaults,

---

15 Hannay, 'Letters of the Papal Legate in Scotland, 1543', *SHR*, xi, 21. Many Protestants began to flee at this time (*LP*, xviii (2), no. 292), and with good reason (Pitcairn, *Trials*, i. 330).

16 *Brosse Missions*, 22. Some religious trouble did continue (*Abdn. Counc.*, i, 206, 208).

17 George Douglas said they were outnumbered ten to one (*LP*, xix (1), no. 33). See also *TA*, vii, 246, 248–54; *Mary of Lorraine Corresp.*, 56–57.

18 *LP*, xix (1), nos. 24, 30; *Mary of Lorraine Corresp.*, 446–47; *RSS*, iii, no. 921; *ADCP*, 536–37.

19 Knox, *History*, i, 52–55; *Diurnal of Occurrents*, 34; *The Chronicle of Perth* (Maitland Club, 1831), 2; *RSS*, iii, nos. 609, 611–14; *TA*, viii, 215, 258–59; *Mary of Lorraine Corresp.*, 58.

20 *LP*, xviii (2), nos. 429, 309, 332, 339, 423, 444.

21 See the plans being drawn up at the end of the year (*ibid.*, no. 523).

22 *LP*, xix (1), nos. 59, 71. The preparations and execution of the invasion of May 1544 have been treated by M.L. Bush, 'The Rise to power of Edward Seymour, Protector Somerset' (unpublished dissertation for DPhil, Cambridge University, 1964), 311–41.

23 *Hamilton Papers*, ii, 265–66 (*LP*, xix (1), no. 71). Suffolk clearly appreciated that Henry's aims were contradictory: to so ravage the South of Scotland would bring him 'no nearer his purpose', as it would only alienate support for the marriage (*LP*, xix (2), no. 136). It did.

and encouragement of rebellion within the Highlands and Isles. Henry added two innovations: encouragement of the reformed faith, and the creation of a body of non-noble Scottish collaborators working for English victory. Let us take these in turn.

HENRY'S 'GOOD JUSTE TYTLE' TO SCOTLAND

The argument that Scotland had no basis as an independent sovereign kingdom[24] has been discussed at length already. The King had been induced during the negotiations of 1543 not to assert his superiority. But such restraint was no longer necessary. Certainly he seemed to think that such a stance would be accepted in England. The preamble to the Subsidy Act of 1544 declared that the Commons were convinced of the King's 'good juste tytle and interest to the Crown and Realme of Scotland':

> It hath pleased Allmightie God by his Divine Providence to call to his mercye the late pretensed King of Scotes [James V], by reason wherof the Kings Majestie . . . hath nowe at the present (by the infinite goodnes of God) a time apt and prospryse for the recoverye of his said right and tytle to the saide Crown and Realme of Scotland.[25]

Throughout the war, the Scots were declared to be rebels.[26] The King's claims were also stressed in his dealings with disaffected nobles. Ever since 1513, Scots who had turned to Henry invariably recognised his claims, as Angus did in 1528. Men anxious for protection or pensions naturally played up to the King's sensibilities on this issue. In 1531, a disgruntled Bothwell professed delight at the thought of Henry crowned King of Scotland in Edinburgh.[27] After the failure of their January attempt against Arran, Lennox and his supporters initially were asked only to be 'perfect friends' with Henry. By 17 May Lennox and Glencairn swore to help make Henry 'King Director and Protector'. In the final Treaty of 26 June, Lennox went further and 'surrendered' to the King his claims to the Crown and acknowledged him as 'supreme sovereign and Governor'.[28] Other Scots who assured with Henry agreed that if Mary was not delivered into his hands, they would advance

> His highness title to the said realme of Scotlande, and eyther by force or pollycie . . . establishe thiese two realmes of England and Scotlande in a perfite unytie, and so knyt theym bothe in one under his majestes rule and domynyon.[29]

24 Henry had made such claims in 1513 and in 1524. J.D. Mackie, 'Henry VIII and Scotland', *Trans. Royal Historical Society*, 4th ser., xxix (1947), 93–114 discusses Henry's pretensions to sovereignty in the early period of his reign.

25 *The Statutes of the Realm*, ii, 938. The Commons declared that they had seen many documents 'openly and manifestly exhibited and maturely read and debated'. To Charles, the King explained that after James's death, he could easily have brought the Scots 'to knowledge their bounden dieiuties of alegeaunce and subjeccion' (*SP Henry VIII*, xi, 534).

26 The proclamation which accompanied the May 1544 invasion clearly mentioned Henry's 'just titulle and interest . . . unto this realme of Skotland' (*Hamilton Papers*, ii, 311–12). See also *LP*, xix (1), nos. 231 (2), (3), 389 (3).

27 *SP Henry VIII*, iv, 5998 (*LP*, v, nos. 595, 609).

28 *LP*, xix (1), nos. 243, 522, 779; and see *SP Henry VIII*, v, 386–87.

29 *Hamilton papers* ii, 376 (*LP*, xix (1), no. 510 (2)).

From April to August 1543, Lennox had worked closely with Beaton and the Queen Dowager and clearly was of the anti-English party. However, Arran's reconciliation with the Cardinal drastically altered matters, and after attending the coronation of Mary, Lennox retired from Stirling to Dumbarton, obviously to the dissatisfaction of Mary of Guise.[30] There he received from de Brosse and Mesnage much of the treasure and munitions which they had brought from France. By 9 October they realised their mistake and there began a complicated set of negotiations in hopes of extracting the supplies from him.[31] Lennox, who had written to Francis I on 10 October for his support,[32] extracted firstly a promise from the Queen Dowager that she would marry him and then on 24 October the agreement of Mary and Beaton that he had sufficient 'integrite de moeurs, vie cappactie . . . dadministrer ledict royaume [integrity of morals, life and capacity to administer the kingdom]'. In return, Lennox agreed to release some of the money.[33] Throughout November, pressure was maintained on the Earl to 'do no thingis till Ingland that ma be prejudiciall and hirt to this realm or liberteis therof' and not to 'ws all mone artalrery and utheris thingis that com out of France to his awn particular efecttis'.[34]

That Lennox would lose all his connections with France should he defect to Henry was obviously put forcibly to him. Francis, in reply to de la Brosse's long report of 24 November on the problem, recommended they be 'les plus gracieux et aymyables . . . qu'on pourra [as gracious and friendly as possible]', and it was in this light on 13 February that the King asked Lennox 'vous en venir par devers moys [come towards me]' to help against the English.[35] By this time Lennox had gathered his friends and allies, in particular Glencairn, and fortified Glasgow and Dumbarton.[36] In March, reacting against the charge that he was 'the principell man the causis division and braik be in this realme', he had one last interview with the Queen Dowager. But by then it was too late,[37] for Arran had resolved to crush him. On 19 March men at Glasgow were forbidden any 'wappin-schawing or rysing or resisting with the Errl of Levinax, under the pane of deid', and the Governor called upon the Queen's lieges to aid him. Men of war, artillery, pioneers and hand guns were all sent west and in the first week of April the Governor's host badly mauled Lennox and Glencairn at Glasgow Moor, then besieged the town which shortly

30 She found his departure 'asses estrange'; he considered 'mes excuses estoient sy resounables' (*Mary of Lorraine Corresp.*, 31).

31 *Brosse Missions*, 15–18; BN, MS fr. 17,888, fo. 275.

32 Expressing the view, 'Toutesfois qu'il y a aucunz personniges qui regardent plus a leur faict particulier que le bien publique [As ever there is no one who prefers public good over their particular desires]' (BN, MS fr. 17,888), no. 10).

33 BN, MS fr. 17,890, fos. 4, 7–12.

34 See the points put by Methven and to Glencairn (*Mary of Lorraine Corresp.*, 38–45).

35 BN, MS fr., 17,890, fos. 37–39. By 15 March 1544, John Campbell wrote to Lennox from Dieppe that Francis considered him 'all the caus of the hayll brek and dewyson that [is] in Scotland quhylk, war nocht ye, all wald be weill'. Campbell saw in his 'daly spendys and waistis the kyng of Francys monye . . . the causer of your awyn distructioun' (*Mary of Lorraine Corresp.*, 68–70).

36 Dalrymple, *Historie*, ii, 272; *LP*, xix (1), no. 143.

37 *Mary of Lorraine Corresp.*, 67; *LP*, xix (1), nos. 181, 253.

capitulated.[38] Lennox was compelled to retreat to Dumbarton where he remained until 18 May when he finally took ship for England and his 21-year exile.[39]

Following his defeat at Glasgow, Lennox turned to Henry. Throughout the winter, tentative negotiations had been taking place between his secretary, Thomas Bishop, and the English Council in London, and by 20 March 1544 the King wrote personally.[40] Lennox clearly wanted assurance that he would receive ample compensation in England for his losses in Scotland and France and proclaimed himself 'far in love' with Margaret Douglas, the King's niece. On 26 March Henry issued preliminary instructions and on 17 May a formal pact was concluded between the King and Lennox and Glencairn.[41]

The indenture is interesting for it shows how much the King still hoped to gain in Scotland. In addition to recognising Henry's position, the Scots pledged to set forth the word of God, to ensure Mary remained in the country and to assist him to capture a string of Border strengths such as Jedburgh, Kelso, Roxburgh, Hume and the Hermitage. By 26 June, Lennox, then in London, pledged to surrender Dumbarton and the Isle of Bute, to work for an English victory, and to govern Scotland at all times at the direction of the King.[42] Three days later, Henry and Queen Catherine attended his marriage with Lady Margaret; in a fortnight he received considerable lands at Temple Newsam, Yorkshire.[43] Just seventeen months later (7 December 1545) the marriage was blessed with a boy, who bore the king's name. Thus Henry VIII gained the only Scottish aristocrat to serve with any effect or faithfulness. With him of course came many of his affinity: Thomas Bishop,[44] Lennox's brother Robert,[45] John Drummond[46] and others.

Henry's success in gaining Lennox was not repeated. Glencairn and Cassillis were useful over the next two years as sources of information and advice, but little else.[47] A similar, though more intricate, story is to be told of the Douglas brothers. By the end of 1544, Angus would become a stalwart of Arran's regime, to which his military abilities were essential and generously given. George continued to intrigue throughout the war with the English, but it was all words, no action. Brothers did that sort of thing during this period: playing both sides of the field just to be on the safe side:

38 TA, viii, 271–76, 282–85, 293–94; RSS, iii, nos. 685–95 (for dates of Arran's presence there); Diurnal of Occurrents, 31; Dalrymple, Historie, i, 271–74; Pitscottie, Historie, ii, 18–28.

39 LP, xix (1), no. 639.

40 LP xix (1), nos. 180–220, 255–57. Previously the King had been most lukewarm towards Lennox (ibid., nos. 39, 60, 103).

41 Ibid., nos. 343, 307. The instructions to Bowes and Wharton were supplemented by a long despatch on 15 April (ibid., no. 337).

42 Ibid., no. 779.

43 Ibid., nos. 799, 900, 1035, 62–63, 95–96.

44 Bishop appears throughout this period too often to mention, but see his memoir of his services drawn up in 1562 when in dispute with his master (CSP Scot., i, no. 1076).

45 Robert, Postulate of Caithness, was only to remain loyal to England until June 1546.

46 For Drummond's activities, see LP, xix (2), nos. 541, 560; xx (1), nos. 40, 48, 522, 725; xx (2), no. 156. He was clearly very useful spying on Scots in the Low Countries.

47 Glencairn was clearly upset by Lennox's flight to England (Mary of Lorraine Corresp., 99–100; LP, xix (1), no. 809).

Arran and Paisley, Archibald and George, George Gordon and his brother Alexander, Edward Seymour (the Protector of Edward VI) and Thomas, Lennox and Robert, the Guises.[48] A spectacular example concerns the Maxwells, which can only be told here in part.

During 1543, the credit of Robert 5th lord Maxwell had fallen considerably with Henry, and when Arran captured him on 1 November, many thought it was a deliberate ploy.[49] Hence when the English released him on 15 May 1544, Hertford took him into custody and sent him to London to be warded in the Tower where he remained until his death in 1546.[50] His son, Robert 6th lord,[51] was also captured, in September 1545, and he too was to remain mostly in the Tower until finally exchanged in 1549.[52] How much the Maxwells were content forcibly to be bound to help the English is unclear; like those of the Douglases, their lands lay close to the Border. Certainly Henry VIII was to have little difficulty in the West and by the end of 1544 was able to place a garrison at one of Maxwell's castles, Langholm.[53] More would follow. While Robert 6th Lord languished in London, as we shall see, his closest brother, John, looked after the family's estates. In February 1548, his defection to Arran's regime would result in a major Scottish military victory, just as Angus had delivered Ancrum Moor in 1545.

ARMIES ROYAL

An army royal was different to a raiding force in that it was commanded by 'the person of the monarch' (with the royal standard unfurled) through a viceroy or Lieutenant, such as Edward Seymour in 1544, 1545 and 1547. For example, such a commander could issue knighthoods in the field, as Somerset did after Pinkie, and the Earl of Essex was to do so egregiously in Ireland in the 1590s. They were vast collections of men and munitions and animals and carts. That of May 1544 probably numbered something like 15,000 men, making it the largest single organisation in the British Isles at that moment. In 1545, Hertford's Border army probably numbered 12,000: still a very considerable number. Their massive raids certainly produced devastation and confusion where they operated, but they did not coerce the Scottish

---

48 And not just during this period. See how Prince Henry had been distanced from his elder brother Arthur during the reign of Henry VII, or Princes Henry and Charles during James VI and I's reign. The example of the Hanoverian brothers (1714–1760) is notorious.

49 *LP*, xviii (2), nos. 328, 343; *Mary of Lorraine Corresp.*, 15–18, 50. The fact that he was freed in April did not help either. See especially *LP*, xix (1), nos. 510, 575, 626 and also 180, 221, 294, 297.

50 *Mary of Lorraine Corresp.*, 146; *LP*, xix (1), nos. 522, 531, 593, 615, 756, 1012–13.

51 For his career, see *Mary of Lorraine Corresp.*, 128–29, 133; *LP*, xx (1), nos. 479, 642; xx (2), nos. 505, 524, 533.

52 His sons also went South and received rewards (PRO, E351/43). For a while they were at Cambridge where they stole a horse from the Master of Peterhouse (*LP*, xxi (1), no. 822). There is abundant material on Maxwell's imprisonment, but see *APC*, ii, 365, 371, 547. The Scottish ambassador in 1547 said he was 'lik to go mad' (*Mary of Lorraine Corresp.*, 180).

53 Langholm had been taken by surprise in October (*LP*, xix (2), nos. 625, 760). Henry also had his eyes on the Maxwell strongholds of Lochmaben, Caerlaverock and Threave (*LP*, xix (1), nos. 338, 449–50).

government into agreeing to the marriage. Desire to do both may have been more than just the stated reason for the assault upon Edinburgh which Hertford carried out in May 1544.[54]

The objectives for the force, issued by Henry VIII on 10 April 1544, have been quoted repeatedly over the centuries as an example of English 'beastliness', most recently by J.D. Mackie in his influential article in 1947, by Gordon Donaldson (p. 69) in 1965, and by Jenny Wormald in 1988. The Privy Council's instructions were:

> Put all to fire and sword, burn Edinburgh town, so razed and defaced when you have sacked and gotten what ye can of it, as there may remain forever a perpetual memory of the vengeance of God lightened upon [them] for their falsehood and disloyalty . . . and as many towns and villages about Edinburgh as ye may conveniently, do your best to beat the castle, sack Holyrood House and sack Leith and burn and subvert it and all the rest, putting man, woman and child to fire and sword, without exception where any resistance shall be made against you; and this done pass over to the Fifeland and extend like extremities and destructions in all towns and villages whereunto ye may reach conveniently, not forgetting among all the rest so to spoil and turn upside down the Cardinal's town of St. Andrews, as the upper stone may be the nether, and not one stick stand by another, sparing no creature alive within the same.[55]

This was utter nonsense. No army could accomplish such a battle plan and be back in Dover for the invasion of France within a month (shortened to three weeks). Unable to devastate Beaton's cathedral city of St Andrews, the army severely looted and burned Edinburgh, and two principal ships of the Scottish navy were captured[56] but it really did very little of any long-term effect. This was due to the power of Edinburgh Castle. Initially, Henry had been thinking of capturing large parts of Scotland, writing to Suffolk in January 1544:

> Nowe for the tyme that the saide armye to be within Scotland – it ys thought that in 12 weeks, the said army should either have battail or else to wynne Edenboro, Sterlinge and all other fortresses and to destroy the country as ys aforesaid.

Another letter written on 29 January to Suffolk makes clears the number of soldiers needed to gain the Castle. If the Castle would not yield, then the orders were to sack

---

54 See Phillips, *Anglo-Scots Wars*, 158–68. The May campaign has been covered in detail by Dr Bush's dissertation, cited above (n.22). The broadsheets and books printed at the time concerning the campaign meant that the older histories also were able to treat it at length; for a short account, see J.B. Paul, 'Edinburgh in 1544 and Hertford's Invasion', *SHR*, viii (1910), 113–31.

55 *Hamilton Papers*, ii, 326 (*LP*, xix (1), no. 314.

56 The two ships were the *Unicorn* and the *Salamander*, the latter a wedding gift of Francis I to James V in 1537 (*LP*, xii (1), no. 1286). They were both used by the English navy during the rest of the war: *LP*, xix (1), nos. 472, 481; xix (2), nos. 167, 502, 580, 674; xxi (1), nos. 489, 762, 874. The *Unicorn* was sold in 1555; the *Salamander* is last noted in 1559. See T. Glasgow, 'List of Ships in the Royal Navy from 1539 to 1588', *The Mariner's Mirror* (1970), 299–308.

the town. As the months passed, preparations were put in hand for the invasion. On 10 April the Privy Council wrote to Hertford, outlining the King's wishes. The twin themes of Scottish treachery and the impending conflict with the French had caused Henry to abandon any pretence of a campaign to encourage assurance and winning Scotsmen over to the English cause. In its place was an invasion designed to wreak major devastation and put on a show of aggression for the Scots. On 12 April, Hertford wrote to Henry VIII arguing for a more permanent incursion. By taking and holding Leith, for example, 'the towne of Edinburgh and the country round to fall to his devotion'. For Hertford himself it would 'grieve him to see the Kings treasure employed only in devastating two or three towns and a little country which would soon recover'.

Calderwood wrote in his history that 'upon the third of May was seen a great navie of shippes in the frith'. It must have been a daunting site for the Scots who, it was said, 'flocked, some to the castle hill, some to the mountains and other places to gaze upon the shippes'. Undaunted, the Cardinal sat down to eat, saying: 'It is the English fleet; they have come to make a showe and putt us in feare; but I sall lodge all the men in myne ey that shall land in Scotland'. By the next day the Cardinal and his forces, on meeting a huge fleet disembarking, turned and fled, their cowardice striking a sour note with the town's citizens after the bravado of the day before. It may have been this which caused the popular outburst of hostility to Beaton, as exemplified in the supposed cries of the women who called out 'woe to the cardinal' as the city burned around them. He had led them to a position where a war was inevitable, but had, along with Arran, deserted them. Indeed Calderwood wrote: 'they approached not after within twenty myles of the action'. With little resistance shown to the fleet and the landing of an army of '10,000 men of warre, with great artillarie and all kinds of munition', the city sent out the Provost, Adam Otterburn of Reidhall, to meet with Hertford and 'remonstrate against such unlooked for hostilities and propose an amicable adjustment of all differences'. Hertford laid out the English terms which were, to say the least, unwelcoming. The only way that an attack on the town could be averted was if the infant Queen was delivered to Henry VIII. The citizens, according to Burton, would have 'rather submitted to their last extremities than purchase safety by so ignominious a course'.

The next day Hertford returned to the walls and issued a last ultimatum. However, 'the inhabitants of one or two houses in the suburbs raised fire and a great smoke and the town prepared to resist'. Hertford had no choice but to continue with the plan that he had discussed with Suffolk three months earlier. The English were not going to be easily accepted into the citadel, for whatever the odds stacked against them were, the soldiers in the Castle put up a resolute defence.

Perhaps more important was the strategic implication of the site of the Castle, situated as it was at the top of a hill, with only one artillery approach and the approach itself covered by the artillery placed on and around the old David's Tower. This gave a comprehensive cover of the street and also the entrance to what is now known the Esplanade. This was the ideal place to set up cannons to further an attempt to take the Castle, but as it was so comprehensively a 'sitting duck area', any

Fig. 6.1.   This representation, executed either by Richard Lee (he was knighted for his services on this journey) or by one of his staff, is the first reliable picture of Edinburgh to come down to us, a rather nice 'fruit of war'. It shows Hertford's force marching over Calton Hill on 5 May 1544 so as to enter the

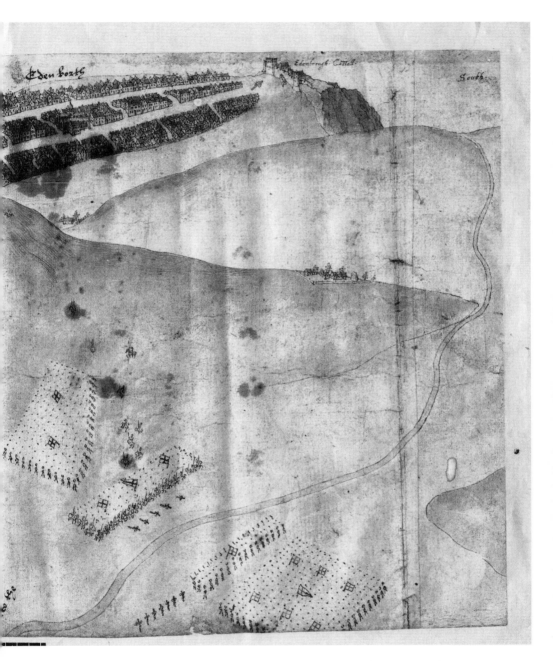

urban area by the Canongate and thence to assault the Nether Port, which they did with some success, although they had to retake it the next day. Getting up the High Street, however, to the Castle proved impossible, for that citadel bristled with artillery and the gunners were remarkably accurate.

attempts to do this would meet, accurate fire permitting, with a large degree of damage. The townspeople had left the city under the cover of night. However, this made the job no easier. Richard Lee, the renowned builder, architect and surveyor, on viewing the approach to the Castle, wrote: 'approach so dangerous as the castle seemed impregnable without a long demour and tarrying about it. It would be but tedious to mine'.

Hertford himself, writing to Henry on May 9th, summed up the problem that faced the direct assault on the Castle: 'their could be as they said no cover designed for the approche'. Again Holinshed caught the essential problem: 'the artillerie of the castle beat so diredctilie alonedst the high street as the Englishmen came up the same'. Thus the English were faced with a problem. The time factor necessitated a speedy campaign, yet the difficulty in getting at the Castle made this seem unlikely. Lindsay of Pitscottie has left a lively account of the retreat of the English in the face of the Castle's significant advantage:

> They shot certain artillaize at the castel but it was so strong they could not win it and certane of the castle men wschit [shot] out and skirmisht them and put thame fre the said castell and wan some of there artillaze and sum they left behind broken quilk remains zeit in Scotland. This being done they seaind they could not be the better of the castle, they past frome it.

Calderwood recorded how 'the whele and the axe tree of one of the English cannons was brokin and some of the men slaine, by a shott of ordinance out of the castell so they left that rash interprise'. There is also evidence that the English forces were not disciplined and prematurely fired at the Castle, thus splitting the fire and rendering it less effective. 'Against orders the gunners attacked the castle, which replied with cannon and slew some and dismounted some of their pieces.'

However disciplined the English forces had been, it is likely that the physical advantage the Scots had would have swung the siege. The position of the gun-loops, in the front wall of the tower, made it impossible for the English to advance up to the base of the Castle walls. The chronicles of Hertford's expedition into Scotland give a clear indication of the problem faced:

> the situation whereof is of such strength that it cannot be approached but by one waye whiche is by the hyghe strete of the towne and the strongest parte of the same lyeth to beate the said streete, which was the loss of dyvers of our men, with the shot of the ordnance out of the sayde castell whiche continually beate alonge the sayde streete.

The judgements of Lee convinced Somerset that he would not be able to take the Castle. 'Consyderenge the strength of the sayde castle with the situation thereof, it was concluded not to lose any tyme nor to waste and consume our munition thereof.' The next day (Holinshed again), 'a certaine number of Englishmen under the leading of Doctor Leigh went againe to Edenburgh and did what they could to destroie the whole towne with fire'. Lord Russell gives a more dramatic account:

next morning we began again so that neither within the walls nor in the suburbs was left any one house unbrent beside the innumerable bodies, pillage and spoils that our soldiers brought from thence . . . also we burnt the abbey called Holyrood House and the abbey adjoining it.

On 15 May, Hertford wrote: 'the enemy shall neither recover this damages while we live, nor assemble any power this year in these parts, whatsoever aid come to them from France or Denmark'. Arran was humiliated.[57] But it was a modest return for such an expensive operation.

In September 1545, another large English army under Hertford invaded, but this was more a massive Border raid and it was aimed not so much at the Scots as at the French.[58] Although considerable destruction was caused, the force did not stray very far from the Tweed; nor did the Scottish government suffer greatly. This was due to a number of factors. It was always difficult to conduct wars at a distance, especially when the geography was unknown: Tudor armies had no maps worth the name. Thus they had to feel their way and blunders inevitably occurred. Edward Seymour had in early 1544 proposed building a fortress at Leith to cut Edinburgh off from the sea, but the Privy Council vetoed his plan in part because they thought such a garrison would be endangered by ordnance placed atop Arthur's Seat. This was plain nonsense. Artillery able to pound Leith accurately from that distance would not exist at any time in the sixteenth century.

In 1545, he returned to his fortress mode, emboldened doubtless by his experiences in France (he was present at a major survey of Guines early in 1545) and with a number of first-rank military engineers, such as Sir Richard Lee and two Italians who had worked in the North at Holy Island and elsewhere: Antonio da Bergamo and Archangelo Arcano. When a retaliatory raid into Scotland was proposed for the autumn of the year, Seymour tried with characteristic zeal to accomplish something more permanent than mere crop destruction and proposed that Kelso be fortified.

A garrison there could 'lye there thys wynter . . . to overrunne dyvast and brenne a gret parte of the countreye thereaboutes . . . also to do some good enterprice upon Hume castell'. The result would be not only the Merse and Teviotdale 'subject to Your Majestie', but the spending of money to better effect. This scheme took clearest shape in Hertford's mind while he was at Newcastle before 11 August, and in a series of ever-insistent memoranda, he pressed it upon the king and council: outlining how the dressed ashlar masonry of the abbey's buildings could be employed, requesting Lee's presence, forwarding blueprints (termed plattes by the Tudors) and readying artillery for the new work.

Henry was impressed, 'lyketh very well your nue platte' and considered that, properly built, the Kelso fort would 'sarve to very good purpose'. But he also passed the idea over to the Council to see what they thought and there, on 8 September, occurred one of those minor classic moments of Tudor drama. Various members (Norfolk, Sir John Gage, Sir Anthony Browne) had been to Kelso years before, and

---

57 For one comment, see *Mary of Lorraine Corresp.*, 83–84.
58 See *LP*, xx (2), nos. 347, 400, 456, 533, 633, and Phillips, *Anglo-Scottish Wars*, 173–75.

their recollection was that the ground was so 'stonye' that the 'pece' could not be completed in time. A half-finished hold would be worse than nothing. More devastating for Hertford's brainstorm was someone's (probably Norfolk, immensely familiar with all of the North) strong impression that the abbey was overlooked: 'subject to one or twoo hylles, from whens thenemyes can easely shote with ther ordnaunce into the said fortress'. Their considered view was that Roxburgh might be a better site.

Seymour might well have thought that the poltergeist of Arthur's Seat had struck again. In a sense it had, for when he arrived actually at the place, it was worse than ever the Council had guessed. Reporting his rejection of the scheme, he threw up a host of inconveniences (brittle soil, rocky ground, lack of time, how rapidly the Tweed could flood), but the nub of his planning fiasco was not just that the abbey was on the wrong side of the river:

> of no lytle importaunce . . . the scituation of the house ys not so good as, before we sawe yt, we thought yt had ben, to set a fortresse on; for on thother side of the water, even hard by, ys a gret hill called Maxwell Hughe, whiche may beate the house, and ys an exceding great enemye to the same.

Thus the army did little (leaving the artillery train behind at Berwick did not help) but demolish the abbey and move on. But come 1547, Seymour would return and, that time, he built at Roxburgh. So men did learn as they went along.

Both armies represented the Tudor state at a high level of military professionalism, as Gervase Phillips argues so convincingly. The May 1544 one was a remarkable affair, involving as it did an ingenious and highly effective demonstration of sea power. Additionally, a large land force invaded and joined up with Hertford's army after it disembarked at Newhaven. But the whole exercise almost came seriously unstuck when the wind turned against the armada at the mouth of the Tyne where it was constrained to tarry for almost a fortnight. The second army royal was, again, most impressive and both emerged covered in superficial glory with numerous knighthoods bestowed, such as on Richard Lee who robbed the Abbey Kirk at Holyrood of its famous Dunblane lectern which he donated to a church near his home near St. Albans. Other notable booty was acquired. But the September 1545 force hardly penetrated deeper into the realm of Scotland than did Norfolk's fiasco of November 1542. This was largely because it was shadowed by a strong Franco-Scottish army which (fortunately) disdained to bring the English to battle. Thus the invasion was largely a Tweed valley raid and little more.

THE HIGHLANDS AND ISLES

The Highlands and Isles were barely administered by the Scottish Crown, which had to rely upon the power of the great nobles, such as Huntly and Argyll, to keep order. Occasionally naval expeditions into the Isles were mounted, as had happened in the reign of James IV and as recently as 1540 and 1541. In 1543 Donald Dubh (Donald McConnell), who had been held by the Scottish crown since 1505 or 1506,[59] either was released (such an action would have been consistent with Arran's renunciation of the policies of James) or escaped from Edinburgh Castle.[60] Dubh had a blood claim to the lordship of the Isles which since 1504 had been judicially and politically united to the Crown, and when he returned to the Highlands, he was greeted as chief and lord by many of the clans.[61] In the words on one chronicler, 'The Scotis that duelt in the mountains and Iles of Jrland now began to schaw taknes of thair inconstancie and gret wildnes'; against them Arran sent Huntly, but this seemed only to make matters worse.[62] By 24 October 1544 Mary of Guise was informed that 'the Lord of the Ilis is broken forth'.

The English also heard that 'a new king' was declared amongst the 'Scottyshe Iyrsshe'[63] and they quickly came to know of Donald Dubh's activities through their agents in Ireland where many of the clan Donald had settled since 1520, especially near Antrim.[64] Henry had all along hoped to use Lennox to gain Dumbarton, and in 1544 an abortive attack took place in the Clyde in which some Islesmen may have been involved.[65] Lennox had held some lands in the south-western Highlands and was related, if distantly, to Donald.[66] The King hoped, by use of Islesmen, to gain Dumbarton cheaply and to annoy both Huntly and Argyll. Commissioners met on 28 July 1545 at Carrickfergus[67] and then at Oatlands on 4 September. An indenture bound Dubh to serve the King if Henry restored him to his lordship.[68]

The plan was for Dubh to muster 6000 men and 180 galleys under command of Lennox, which force, accompanied by an English fleet, would then capture Dumbarton.[69] But the scheme badly misfired. As the Islesmen gathered in Carrickfergus for the expedition, Lennox was foolishly sent to advise Hertford, then at Newcastle about to invade Scotland. By the time Lennox was able to return to Ireland via Chester, the force had dispersed. Only with great difficulty was a much-reduced expedition pieced together at Dublin; by the time it sailed on 17 November, the sea was rough and Dumbarton had been made secure by Arran.[70] Then Donald

59 The last legitimate Lord of the Isles, John Macdonald, died c. 1498, predeceasing his illegitimate son Angus (d. c. 1485). But through his line came Donald Dubh whose pregnant mother was warded in Edinburgh Castle until she was delivered of her son. She was then released; he was kept.
60 He received £54.8s on January 1544 from Arran, but it is not clear if he was free then or not (*TA*, viii, 247).
61 A.M. Mackenzie, *The History of the Macdonalds and Lords of the Isles* gives a clear genealogical account.
62 Dalrymple, *Historie*, ii, 280; *Chronicles of the Frasers*, ed. W. Mackay (SHS, 1904), 133–41; *Abdn. Counc.*, i, 193, 195, 215.
63 *LP*, xix (2), nos. 790, 795, appendix 12.
64 For the connections with Ireland, see W.C. Mackenzie, *The Highlands and Isles of Scotland*, 126–33 and G. Hill, *An Historical Account of the Macdonnells of Antrim*.
65 Dalrymple, *Historie*, ii, 282–85; *LP*, xix (2), no. 813.
66 It was to Lennox that Donald Dubh's first approaches were made, in early 1545 (*LP*, xx (1), nos. 347–48).
67 *Ibid.*, nos. 865, 1298, and see *LP*, xx (2), nos. 40–42, 120, 196, 198, 231, 357.
68 *LP*, xx (2), nos. 291, 294–95, 496 (17).
69 *Ibid.*, nos. 120–21, 290, 293, 306, 792.
70 W.C. Mackenzie, *The Highlands and Isles of Scotland*, 139–40; *LP*, xx (2) nos. 796, 819.

Dubh died suddenly at Drogheda. Henry paid for the funeral, but without any successor to the Lord of the Isles, the rebellion collapsed.[71]

THE BORDERS

There were English armed forces all along the frontier, garrisoned in a string of castles: Berwick-upon-Tweed (and in the town there as well), Norham (properly the responsibility of the Bishop of Durham), Wark and Carlisle. Behind them lay a network of privately owned, but nonetheless quite heavily fortified, towers in which the local families dwelt and which also contained the fighting men who could gather and cross into Scotland to raid, harry and steal. This they did throughout the periods of declared belligerency between the two countries: 1542, 1544–46, 1547–50 and even into 1551.

When Henry expressed a desire to possess Jedburgh, Kelso, Roxburgh, Hume and the Hermitage, he aimed at controlling the Merse, Teviotdale and Liddesdale so completely that no Scottish force would be able to penetrate into England. This was the third tactic. For a while in late 1544, an English force was garrisoned at Coldingham Priory, just inside the East Marches of Scotland.[72] In early 1545 a survey was made of Kelso for a similar purpose.[73] Two major invasions of Scotland by armies royal were made, but these were in the field for a total of only six weeks. For the rest of the time, the war was conducted by traditional raids of armed bands operating under each of the three English wardens.[74]

The amount of material for a study of the Border warfare during 1543–46 is truly prodigious[75] and no detailed study of it can be made here. But it is clear that the warfare was fairly intense.[76] The raiding parties varied in size: they could be as small as 100 men or as large as the 2000 who went with Evers and Sir Cuthbert Ratcliffe to burn Coldingham and district on 18 February 1544, but 4–500 was the average size.[77] The object was to pillage and to burn both crops and houses. Along the East Marches alone, during the two years from June 1544 until the conclusion of the war, 159 different raids were made. During January 1545, for example, seven serious incursions were made into Scotland: on the 1st, 2nd, 4th, 5th, 18th, 26th, and 30th of the month. They took various prisoners, such as Edward Wauchope, laird of Cackmuir, burned various small hamlets, such as Newbigging near Thornton, and killed and robbed. By 4 July 1546, it was calculated that 1654 Scots had been captured and 888 slain;

71 Some of the men who followed Dubh tried to continue their service to Henry, but little was done for them (*LP*, xxi (1), nos. 114, 138, 219, 417, 815).

72 *LP*, xix (2), nos. 335, 360, 439, 526.

73 *LP*, xx (1), nos. 99, 141–42, 146. It was also considered suitable in September (*LP*, xx (2), nos. 19, 169, 308, 347, 494, 533). H.M. Colvin, *The Kings' Works*, iv, 389, 392, 697, 722.

74 R. Robson, *English Highland Clans*, 78–109, 179–202; P. Dixon, 'Fortified Houses on the Anglo-Scottish Border' (unpublished D.Phil. dissertation, Oxford University, 1977).

75 *LP*, xix (2), nos. 33, 625 are just summary lists, behind which lay constant activity.

76 Certainly all of the Scottish commentators remarked on the severity of the English raids. Dalrymple, *Historie*, ii, 285–87; Pitscottie, *Historie*, ii, 28–41; Lord Herries, *Memoirs*, 10–11.

77 They could be even larger, however; the band under Evers and Ratcliff which was defeated at Ancrum Moor probably numbered almost 7,000 including the assured Scots.

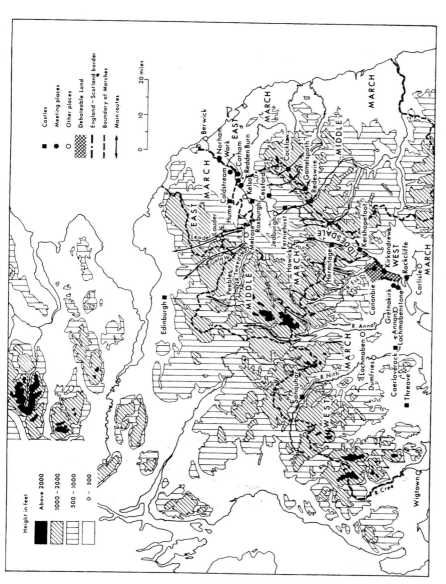

Fig. 6.2. This was the Border battle-zone made famous in legend, song, Sir Walter Scott and Fraser's *The Steel Bonnets*. This is where a broad swathe of Scotland became pockmarked with islands of fortified towers, almost islands of defence. Those unable to retire behind barmkin walls or pull up a wooden ladder to prevent access to the first-floor doorways, or who lacked strong iron yetts (gates), had little choice but to flee. Edinburgh, it was said, was crowded out by such refugees, as were religious houses to the North with priests, rectors and vicars. But the English could be resisted and were never total masters.

moreover 1,813 oxen, 1,384 horse and 13,087 sheep were brought back to England either for sale, mostly in Berwick, or kept by the raiders.[78]

RELIGION

One aspect of the early 1540s only lightly touched upon so far was the spread of Lutheran tracts and ideas within Scotland, something which had been going on since the 1520s. House cells or 'privy kirks' also emerged, such as the notorious one of which James Henrisoun was a member in the 1530s. The King's physician was also known for his reformed views. During the relaxation of heresy persecutions (never severe in any case within Scotland), reformers became more open and the summer of 1543 saw something of an enthusiasm for anti-papal and anti-clerical behaviour. Sadler said that he could see a New Testament in English on every gentleman's table and that he could sell boatloads of Bibles if Henry would but send them. Arran made much of his contempt for the Pope (no more than a bishop and a very bad one at that) and encouraged Henry to advise him how best to proceed. Henry, and Sadler, saw much mileage in this development and tried to encourage it.

Henry clearly saw that identity of religion would promote the union of the realms. The King's consistent attacks on Beaton struck a responsive chord in some Scotsmen, and as early as 1544 plans were discussed for the Cardinal's assassination.[79] Such schemes took more definite form in 1545 when Sadler found himself once again Henry's agent negotiating with disaffected Scots.[80] Knox may have received English money at this time, albeit indirectly as tutor to the son of John Cockburn of Ormiston, who was in English pay.[81] Ormiston's closest confederate was Alexander Crichton of Brunstane, another English pensioner,[82] who proposed Beaton's assassination in 1544 and with whom Sadler parlayed in 1545. Ormiston harboured George Wishart in 1546.[83]

Many Scottish reformers fled to England during this time, such as Dr. Michael Durham, James V's physician, and John Rough, one of the preachers at Arran's court during January to April 1534.[84] John Elder appeared early in London and presented Henry with a Baedeker of his native country[85] and a violently Protestant tract recommending the union of the two realms.[86]

---

78 These figures are taken from *LP*, xxi (1), no. 1279. Tallies of this sort were quite common; see *LP*, xvii, no. 1197; xix (1), no. 533; xx (2), nos. 456, 633.

79 *LP*, xix (1), nos. 350, 404. 'A Skottish man called Wysshert' was involved in these early plots (*ibid.*, 389, 494–94).

80 *LP*, xx (1), nos. 834, 857, 1106, 1177–78.

81 Knox, *History*, i, 70–71; *LP*, xix (1), 472, 510; *RSS*, iii, nos. 1875, 1893; *Mary of Lorraine Corresp.*, 169; *CSP Scot.*, i, no. 41.

82 *LP*, xviii (2), nos. 130, 335, 351, 393; xix (1), nos. 350, 404, 425; xx (1), nos. 5, 359, 340, 706; xx (2), nos. 535, 622.

83 Knox, *History*, i, 61–70.

84 For Durham, see *LP*, xxi (1), no. 1026; *Mary of Lorraine Corresp.*, 184; *TA*, viii, 479. For Rough, see evidence in Knox, *History*, i, 48; *CSP Scot.*, i, nos. 48, 111, 233: *CSP Dom., Add., 1547–65*, 345.

85 BL, Ms Harl., 289, fos. 4–5 He also prepared a map for the English (H.R.C. Inglis and others, *The Early Maps of Scotland*, 12–13). For his subsequent career, see *LP*, xix (1), nos. 278 (71), 1035 (10); xx (2), 533; xxi (1), nos. 650 (85), 970 (7); *APC*, ii, 114.

86 *LP*, xviii (2), no. 539.

THE ASSURED SCOTS[87]

The careers of Rough, Durham, Ormiston, Brunstane and Elder[88] also illustrate the second innovation in English policy towards Scotland during the reign of Henry VIII: the encouragement of a body of collaborators working for English victory. The germ of the idea was Henry's. As early as 9 January 1534 he had written to Lisle:

We have thought that it shuld moch conferre to the advancement of the strength and force of our partie, to have a proclamation made upon all our Marches, that whatsoever Borderure well come in to you . . . and promise to stand with Us in the first article concerning the getting of the child in to our handes, and the government of the realme, subscribing his hande to the same, and also that he shal not attempt any displeasure to our realme and subgiettes, he to be taken as our freedne.[89]

Such a proclamation may have been put out in February 1543. By 6 September 1543, the laird of Mangerton, leader of the Armstrongs, agreed to 'serve faithfully the King of England and all his Officers'. Many of the surnames who inhabited the Border territory (the Eliots, Crosiers, Davidsons, Dells, Pringles) also spent 1543 negotiating to 'be bownd to be the part tayker with England'. By February 1544, virtually all of the small kins had agreed to attack those Scots who did not, such as the Scotts and the Humes.[90]

The English deliberately raided certain Borderers to make them collaborate, as happened to Andrew Kerr of Ferniehirst and Walter Kerr of Cessford.[91] Once they were assured, however, they quickly began to work closely with the English, attacking their principal rival in the area, Sir Walter Scott of Buccleuch, and receiving English payments.[92] The May 1544 invasion and the furious assaults of English captains such as Sir William Lord Evers (Warden of the East March), his son Sir Ralph (Warden of the Middle March) and Brian Laiton forced many other Scots to submit.[93] When Arran besieged Coldingham in December 1544, almost all of the principal men of Teviotdale served with the English.[94] They all came to be regarded as Henry's 'subjectes and requyered . . . to be used in all poyntes as Englishmen'.[95] In the West, the story was much the same; to Buccleuch, Wharton declared on 24 September, waving his hand first east, then west:

87 For a fuller treatment of the topic, see M.H. Merriman, 'The Assured Scots: Scottish Collaborators with England during the Rough Wooing', *SHR*, xlvii (1968), 10–34.
88 For the career of another minor reformer, see I.A. Muirhead, 'M. Robert Lochart', *Innes Review*, xx (1971), 85–100.
89 *SP Henry VIII*, v, 242 (*LP*, xviii (1), no. 23); and see *ibid.*, nos. 37, 43.
90 For lists and oaths, see *SP Henry VIII*, v, 289, 294, 298; *Hamilton Papers*, ii, 376–78, 741–43.
91 *LP*, xix (1), no. 945; xix (2), nos. 128, 262, 274, 302, 448.
92 *LP*, xix (2), nos. 252, 567, 653, 662, 676.
93 For effect of these raids, see comment of *Maitland's Narrative*, fo. 1.
94 *LP*, xix (2), nos. 335, 360, 439, 526.
95 *Ibid.*, nos. 448, 468.

> Sir, look about youe as ye stand . . . These dailles sumtyme did hold of
> Scotland, and now they er all bounde and sworne, with thar hostagies lying at
> Carlisle, to serve the Kinges highnes.[96]

The English efforts did suffer some reverse with the Scottish victory of Ancrum Moor
on 27 February 1545 and the arrival of French aid in June. But Hertford's invasion of
September induced most of the Borderers to assure once again.[97] These assured Scots
were most useful: as spies, guides and troops. They saved Henry money, for they
acted with the English raiding the unassured, but they also remained on good terms
with the Wardens (selling them food, for example), thus further decreasing the
number of troops necessary.[98]

The ingenuity of Henry VIII's tactics, however, cannot hide the fact that he failed
to advance the marriage by these means. He may well have prevented the Scots from
invading England in 1544 and thus disrupting his campaign in France, but his attacks
made it all the more inevitable that a large French force would be welcomed by the
Scots in 1545. If anything, Arran's regime was strengthened and the marriage made
even more unpopular than it had been in 1543. Henry's war failed. Although no
Scottish army invaded in 1544 while he was in France, a Franco-Scottish one almost
did in 1545, requiring a massive allocation of resources to the North in September.
The King only had sufficient finance for one war (or one and a half) and he chose to
concentrate on France during 1544–46.[99] On the other hand, the Scottish government was able to resist effectively.

SCOTTISH RESISTANCE

At first Arran was weakened by the assaults, especially during the second half of 1544,
when he was preoccupied by internal dissensions. The sack of Edinburgh in May had
severely shaken his position. He was directly blamed for the lack of preparedness and
for the ease with which the English accomplished their task.[100] As he was to do in
every crisis, he called a Convention to discuss future strategy; originally it was to meet
at Linlithgow on 28 May but it met instead on 3 June at Stirling. There he obviously
was subjected to plain words of strong criticism, and a committee of lords was
appointed to propose remedies to the situation 'where throughe the commen weale is
hurt'. Those lords, with others, declared three days later:

---

96 *Hamilton Papers*, ii, 468 (*LP*, xix (2), no. 293).
97 *LP*, xx (2), no. 657; *Mary of Lorraine Corresp.*, 128.
98 Even so, Henry was forced to station Spanish mercenaries in the North during 1545.
99 It is not possible in this work to outline the effect of the King's commitment to Boulogne
     other than to say that it existed. A thorough study of the campaign is now available: G.J.
     Miller, *Tudor Mercenaries, 1484–1547*, 49–115. But see also: Scarisbrick, *Henry VIII*, 445–56;
     L.B. Smith, *Masque of Royalty*, 00; F.C. Dietz, *English Public Finance, 1485–1558*, 143–51;
     Shelby *Rogers*, 53–85.
100 Arran certainly was unable to resist the English force and he quickly fled the field: Knox,
     History, i, 56–58; *LP*, xix (1), nos. 518, 533. Arran did try to muster a force, but the earliest
     date for preparations was 21 April 1544, surely too late; he obviously was preoccupied with
     the problem of Lennox: *TA*, viii, 284–97.

oone great part, why inobedience hath ben within this Realme sithens the Kinges Graces decesse, and that other inconveniences which have happened, was and is in my Lorde Governor and his Counsaile that was chosen to have been with him for the time.

Their solution was that Arran should henceforth be much more bound by a Council and that he should work 'adjoyned with' Mary of Guise.[101]

Arran rejected this demand; he was thus declared 'to be suspended and suspending him from the administration of his offices' and the Queen Dowager was declared to be Governor. The 27 lords and prelates who attempted to carry off this coup were a diverse group. On the one hand there were many of the men with whom the Queen had been on close terms throughout 1543: Huntly, Argyll, Moray, Bothwell, St John; others, however, were men previously pro-English: Angus, George Douglas, Cassillis and Maxwell's eldest son. Whether or not they seriously intended ousting Arran or just wished to force him to broaden his Council is not clear; nor is it clear why Mary sought the Governorship at this time.[102] Certainly she wrote to Henry on 21 June proposing that four of her commissioners, including two of her most loyal adherents, Henry lord Methven and Adam Otterburn,[103] should treat with the King for a truce in the war.[104] However, although she endeavoured to give her party some coherence,[105] Arran retained the support of the Cardinal and a number of the lords and nobles.[106]

Summons for treason were issued against Angus, George Douglas and Bothwell at the Parliament which Arran called on 6 November, and this must have had some effect on Mary's rival assembly called for 12 November.[107] In the end, Beaton must have arranged a reconciliation. On 6 March 1545 Mary agreed 'nocht proceed nor consent to na thing at ma be hurt ontill' Arran and to accept him as Governor.[108] Thereafter she was to be present at most meetings of the Council, Conventions and Parliaments.[109] By 1545 the government had some coherence and cohesion.

A general reconciliation had begun even before the Queen Dowager's band with Arran; crucial to this was the meeting of Parliament on 12 December 1544 at

101 *SP Henry VIII*, v, 391–94 (*LP*, xix (1), no. 664).
102 But see George Douglas's very detailed schemes for a course of action for her. *Mary of Lorraine Corresp.*, 88–95. He later received promise of 1000 crowns pension (*ibid.*, 108).
103 Neither was at the Convention, but both were very loyal to her: *Mary of Lorraine Corresp.*, 93–94, Another consistent supporter, Sir Walter Scott of Buccleuch, could not make it because of English activity in his area (*ibid.*, 86–88).
104 *LP*, xix (1), no. 750. Henry's reply was to demand stiff conditions (*ibid.*, no. 841) on which she then hedged (*ibid.*, no. 939).
105 *Mary of Lorraine Corresp.*, 95–116.
106 See the list of attendance for his Parliament in November. *APS*, ii, 446.
107 Note how she was caught out by Arran's calling his Parliament earlier (*Mary of Lorraine Corresp.*, 116–18 and see especially *ibid.*, 106–08).
108 Hamilton Archives (Lennoxlove), MS Chest 53, no. 4.
109 The *RPC* and *APS* lists show marked increase in the Queen's attendance. See also change in the opening phrase of acts of the Privy Council when she was present, e.g. *RPC*, i, 3–5, and 6–9. For Arran writing her, see *Mary of Lorraine Corresp.*, 131–32, 139–40.

which Angus and George Douglas were specifically pardoned both for working
with Henry before 1542 and for all their treasons with the English in 1543–44.
Bothwell was also pardoned.[110] Rewards and pensions for all three shortly sealed
the reconciliation.

For Lennox and his closest family, however, no reconciliation was proposed. Ever
since his revolt of January 1544, Lennox had been judicially prosecuted by the
government, and as early as 3 May his brother Robert was losing his revenues in
Scotland for having acted as his brother's agent in England.[111] This was one point on
which both Arran and Mary of Guise were agreed during their rival administra-
tions.[112] Action at Rome was taken to deprive Robert Stewart of his church
appointments and Matthew was forfeited on 1 October 1545.[113]

Results were felt both politically and on the battlefield. Resistance was stiffened
along the Borders where lairds such as Scott of Buccleuch had raised armed bands
and even the Abbot of Paisley fielded 200 men.[114] Angus was quickly working with
Arran in an attempt to re-establish order there also and on 27 February 1545 the two
men's forces united and destroyed a large English raiding party at Ancrum Moor.
Arran may neither have wept at the slaughter nor kissed Angus twenty times (as
legend has it), but he certainly had cause to be 'moche the meryer', for Angus had
that day at least proved his 'layaltee to his natif country'.[115] This dramatic success
greatly encouraged Borderers to be 'trew Scottis' again.[116]

Meanwhile powers were granted to the nobles in the North to deal with Donald
Dubh and his Islesmen. Huntly was granted wide powers as Lieutenant-General of
the North, and Argyll was made Justiciar.[117] By July a treason summons was executed
in the Isles.[118] Although these measures did little to prevent the September raising of
the force to attack the Clyde, Huntly and Argyll's campaigns obviously did have an

110 *APS*, ii, 449–51; *LP*, xix 2, no. 739.
111 *RSS*, iii, no. 751.
112 On 26 September 1544, she asked Francis to deal 'severely' with Lennox's lands and goods in
France: *LP*, xix (2), 311–12. A distinction was made however between Lennox and his
brother. The French had imprisoned him 'par la faute comisse par Lennox', even though the
Dauphin was against the move: *Maitland Misc.*, i (2), 214). D'Aubigny was then quickly
released: *Balcarres Papers*, i, 128. Some innocent members of Lennox's affinity obviously
suffered; see the lament of James Stewart of Cardonald who had been ambassador in 1543
(*LP*, xxi (2), no. 695).
113 *LP*, xix (2), nos. 737–38; *APS*, ii, 456–58 (*LP*, xx (2), no. 534).
114 *LP*, xx (1), no. 161; *TA*, viii, 318. See also moves made to strengthen the Borders in general
(*LP*, xix (2), no. 636).
115 *Hamilton Papers*, ii, 565 (*LP*, xx (1), no. 301). Angus was clearly dissatisfied with the English
even before the raid on his family tombs at Melrose (*ibid.*, 265). See Phillips, *Anglo-Scots
Wars*, 169–71. Pitscottie, *Historie*, ii, 35–41 gives a Scottish account of the battle. See also *LP*,
xx (1), nos. 280, 311–13.
116 *Diurnal of Occurrents*, 38; *LP*, xx (1), nos. 443.
117 *Abdn. Counc.*, i, 193, 195, 215; Dalrymple, *Historie*, ii, 282; *Diurnal of Occurrents*, 39; *Mary of
Lorraine Corresp.*, 122, 123, 131–33.
118 *TA*, viii, 384, 393, 404, 407. It cost £707. 10s to send the *Lyoun* there with it (*TA*, ix, 23).
For summons against Dubh, see *RPC*, i, 4; *LP*, xx (2), no. 330; xxi (1), nos. 159, 162, 393,
555, 900, 1170.

effect afterwards; by February 1546, groups of Highlanders were requesting pardons of the government.[119]

The French force arrived that summer. Throughout 1544[120] Francis had imprisoned and freed whom the Scots wished[121] and had received and sent ambassadors.[122] The victory at Ancrum gave the French particular delight. They quickly spread the news abroad.[123] 'Never ane prince mar glaid to tel thai thithandis [to hear these tidyings] now he wes'.[124] Even before this good news arrived, he had determined upon some sort of expedition to Scotland as part of a combined attack against England.[125] When his ambassador brought the news at the end of March, a request for immediate aid was promptly granted.[126] By the middle of May enormous preparations were under way at Dieppe and Brest for what John Hay called 'the fairrest support come this 500 year in Scotland':

> large mony tilbe iussit be the consall of Scotland agains our inemys with ane grit quantatie of pouldaris artailzery bollett hakbuttis pykis flour irne, with two thowsand 500 futmen, of the quhilkis ther shalbe 300 hakbuttairis on hors, the Scottis men of arms well monttit and in ordour with 40 archeiris of the gaird.[127]

Before the army came pensions; on 14 April, the sieur de Moullins, second-in-command to Jacques de Lorges, sieur de Montgomery, wrote George Douglas that Angus would receive the Order of St Michel and both brothers a pension 'and certane men allowyt to zow bayth payit by Franz'.[128]

---

119 *RSS*, iii, nos. 1543, 1733. Some had requested pardons as early as April 1545 for participation in the 1544 raid (*ibid.*, no. 1121). The requests soon flooded in (*ibid.*, nos. 1822, 1896, 1970, 2170, 2924).

120 Considerable munitions and artillery were given to Argyll early in 154; Beaton and Mary of Guise received 1500 Crowns [£s1537 10s] on 24 March (BN, MS fr. 17, 890, fo. 27v, 40–41). Merchants were also able to buy considerable military stores in France (*Abdn Counc.*, i, 208–09). See also *Balcarres Papers*, i, 94–109.

121 John Barton had been imprisoned in Dieppe, probably late in 1543. Arran, Beaton and Mary requested that Francis release him as he was 'si bon francoyss' (as his father had been) and would 'vous faire service contre les anglois' (Brussels, Etat et Audience, 402/2 fos. 2–6).

122 *LP*, xix (1), nos., 268, 294; *TA*, viii, 335–36. And see below, p.000.

123 *LP*, xix (1), nos. 311, 332, 334, 602, 797, 1046 (2). *Nonces en France, 1541–46*, 337. The victory was also celebrated in a news pamphlet, *Le deffaict des Anglois par les Ecossois faicte Le Jour de Jeudit Sainct dernier*. It was linked oddly enough with a description of a battle between Barbarossa and Imperial galleys (no. 212 in the list appended to J-P Seguin, *L'Information en France de Louis XII à Henri II*).

124 *Mary of Lorraine Corresp.*, 161 (date should be 1545). Mary's brothers were 'glader nor I can wret to heir of the syndry victoriis' (*ibid.*, 138).

125 When M. de Combas left Scotland in December 1544, he promised aid by April 1545 (*LP*, xix (2), no. 790 (2); *TA*, viii, 335–36); see also *LP*, xx (1), no. 296.

126 *LP*, xx (1), nos. 457, 547; *Nonces en France, 1541–46*, 345.

127 *Mary of Lorraine Corresp.*, 137. Francis apparently personally viewed the preparations at Dieppe (*LP*, xix (1), no. 789). Exactly how much money was sent is not clear (*ibid.*, nos. 457, 1069) and the rumours of the aid were exaggerated (*ibid.*, nos. 590, 630).

128 *LP*, xix (1), no. 508. See also his letter to Beaton (*ibid.*, no. 508). Pensions were also paid to Hume, Bothwell and the Captain of Dumbarton Castle, George Stirling of Gloret (*Balcarres Papers*, 125). Mary received 10,000 francs and a promise of 8,000 more in May (*Mary of Lorraine Corresp.*, 137). Lorges also kindly sent some wine as he had heard 'que vous estiez mal servye de vins' (*Balcarres Papers*, i, 111).

The French force finally arrived at Dumbarton through heavy seas on 4 June 1545.[129] At the convention called on 26 June, Lorges declared his force ready 'to defend or Invaid the commoun Inymy of England'.[130] But little seems to have been accomplished.[131] An invasion of England did take place with an attack on Wark during 9–13 August, but Scottish disunity, other distractions,[132] and perhaps the 'pest', blunted the attack.[133]

No sooner did the army retire from the Borders than an English force invaded; although it ravaged the frontier during 5–23 September, it did not venture deeper into the country, proof of Hertford's concern about the Scots and the aid from France. With the end of the campaigning season, there was little for the French force to do and it made its painful way home during the winter.[134] It had enormously boosted Scottish morale, and when Beaton wrote Francis on 5 October he was not idly boasting when he stated, 'Nous sommes apret pour donner ordre et supporter ceulx de noz frontiers pour Resister a nosdictes enemys qui sont en garnison sur les frontiers dangleterr [We are ready to order and support those troops on our frontier to resist the enemy who are garrisoned on the English Border]'.[135]

Much of the credit for this prompt action must be Beaton's, whose vigour and activity are well attested.[136] He attended all twenty meetings of the Council for which there is record before his death. Although not so regular in attending Parliament, he made the more important sessions. As soon as Hertford left the East, the government quickly reasserted its authority, first tackling the feuds amongst the principal families. On 4 October, Sir Walter Scott of Buccleuch and five of his enemies agreed before Parliament to

ryss concurr togidder without ony fer or dredour for any feild or caus being amangis tham to Resist our auld Inymis of Ingland And defend the Realm And to Resist to all scottis tratouris and thevis.[137]

129 PRC, i, 2–6; TA, viii, 37–83; LP, xx (1), nos. 867, 883, 890–91, 1007, 1074. The ships returned to France by 3 July (BN, MS fr. 20, 510, fo. 11). See also C.G.B. de la Roncière, *Historie de la Marine Française*, iii, 406–13.

130 RPC, i, 6; APS, ii, 594–95 (LP, xx (1), no. 1049).

131 LP, xix (1), nos. 1246, 1288, 1308; xx (2), nos. 7, 54, 87.

132 The *Diurnal* blamed the poor achievement on the 'dissait' of George Douglas and the absence of Argyll's force, busy then in the Highlands against Dubh (*Diurnal of Occurrents*, 39–40). Others agree in part; see Dalrymple, *Historie*, ii, 288–89; Pitscottie, *Historie*, ii, 45–49. For Douglas's behaviour, see LP, xx (1), no. 1106 (2).

133 The 'pest' was 'wonder greit' in Edinburgh and other Scottish towns (*Diurnal of Occurrents*, 39; RPC, i, 5; LP, xx (1), no. 1240; x (2), no. 180), but also in Berwick and throughout Northumberland (*ibid*, no. 524).

134 A muster of 479 footmen was held on 24 December whilst waiting for 'le tempts et le vent bon et propre pour leur en retourner en france' (BL, MS Add, Charters. 13, 302). The French did have a very difficult time returning and some were blown to Denmark (BN, MS fr. nouv. acq. 7306, fo. 33) and the Low Countries (LP, xx (2), no. 985). Lorges finally returned safely on 13 February 1546 (*Mary of Lorraine Corresp.*, 157; LP, xxi (1), nos. 329, 559) and it was clearly an experience he did not wish to repeat (*CSP For.*, 19). Franco-Scottish differences obviously existed (LP, xx (2), nos. 493, 1019–129).

135 BL, MS Egerton, 2805, fo. 6 (LP, xx (2), no. 525).

136 Sanderson, *Cardinal of Scotland*.

137 APS, ii, 461; LP, xx (2), no. 534.

The same day these six men joined with almost twenty other lairds in Teviotdale and the Merse to agree with the son of George Lord Hume, newly appointed Warden of the Marches, to keep the peace and to 'resist and Invaid England'. Hume further entered into a bond of manrent with John, Abbot of Jedburgh, to fight against the English.[138]

This composition of disputes was part of a larger scheme for strengthening the Borders. On 2 October Parliament allowed the levy of a tax for 'support and help of the bordouris' as the area was 'almost distroyit brynt and hereit' by the English. The tax was to pay for locally recruited light cavalry, for three months from 15 October.[139] On 4 October Buccleuch and John Hume of Blackadder were engaged to plant garrisons; Buccleuch was to be paid from the tax of Perth, Hume from that of Renfrew. On 6 October Lord Hume was ordered to supply half of the force, whilst arrangements were put in hand for it to meet under appointed captains at Lauder on 16 October.[140] Later Hume Castle was strengthened (as, interestingly, were Edinburgh and Dunbar).[141]

The government also took action against the 'Assured Scots'. On 2 October an act was passed in Parliament against 'sittin under assurance of the King of Ingland his lieutenentis wardenis uther officiaris and Inglishmen now in tyme of weir'. On 6 October the sheriffs of Roxburgh and Berwick were ordered to indict all such collaborators in Teviotdale and the Merse.[142] In February, March and April 1546 this act was further enforced.[143] One provision also implemented was that the 'landis guids movable and unmovable' of the collaborators were to be 'dispoint to thame that ar leill trew liegis And that dois best service for the defence of the Realme'.[144] The government also tackled the problems of treason and disorder in the West, the Highlands and Isles.[145] Ever since 1544, important Maxwell strongholds had not been under Crown control. Probably in early November, Arran moved against the most important of these, Threave, Caerlaverock and Lochmaben, with men, munitions and artillery. By the end of November all three were once again in government hands; their captains were soon receiving a share of the tax.[146] Whilst there, Arran doubtless bound many of the important lairds to himself and thus to the government.[147]

During this time Arran also sought to strengthen his own political position. His ultimate goal was the marriage of his son James to the Queen, and during 1545 he had some success in gaining consent to such a match. By October, Lord Somerville's son

138 *HMC*, 26, 12th R., viii, 94.
139 *APS*, ii, 460–61; *Edin. Burgh Rec.*, ii, 117–18; *RPC*, i, 16.
140 *RPC*, i, 19, 22; *APS*, ii, 463; *TA*, viii, 338, 340, 352, 408, 483.
141 *TA*, viii, 444; ix, 445. For other examples of preparedness, see *Edin. Burgh Rec.*, ii, 121; *TA*, viii, 399.
142 *APS*, ii, 460–1; *RPC*, i, 16–17.
143 *APS*, ii, 468 and cf. *ibid.*, 465; *RPC*, i, 22–23.
144 *APS*, ii, 463; *RPC*, i, 19, 21.
145 *APS*, ii, 463–5; *RPC*, i, 17.
146 *TA*, viii, 414–5, 427, 430–1; *Mary of Lorraine Corresp.*, 150–1; *LP*, xx (2), 676; *APS*, ii, 465.
147 *HMC*, 21, 11th R., vi, 36.

John wrote to the Queen Dowager that 'maist pert of bayth temporall and spirituall astait of Scotland hes consentit appliit to my lord governeris dissyir and geiffin thair hand vrittis thair apon'.[148] John may have been exaggerating – the only extant bond for the marriage has only one signature on it – or he may simply have been confused: on the one hand he maintained that Angus, George Douglas and James Douglas of Drumlanrig were 'determit formly to ganestand and resist' Arran, but on the other hand all three had signed a bond of manrent with the Governor only two months previously. Other prominent nobles such as Erroll, Glencairn and Bothwell had done likewise earlier in 1545.[149] News of the plan had a wide currency abroad, much to the concern of the French who remained worried about it as late as 1547.[150] Nonetheless, the Governor's schemes had a certain air of unreality about them since his son remained still in St Andrews Castle.[151]

Fig. 6.3. Henry VIII's capture of Boulogne in September 1544 in many senses saved Scotland from serious assault during the rest of his reign. Here we see the siege, during that summer, of Haute Boulogne. It originally was part of a great wall mural at Cowdray House, but has since been lost in a fire. Fortunately a black and white redrawing was made of it and most of its companion pieces, for example the only representation we have of Henry at Portsmouth when the *Mary Rose* keeled over and sank.

148 *Mary of Lorraine Corresp.*, 147.
149 *HMC*, 21, 11th R., vi, 36–37.
150 *LP*, xx (2), no. 926; xxi (1), no. 391.
151 Knox has an interesting rendering of how the Cardinal viewed the situation (Knox, *History*, i, 75).

All of these measures – reconciliation of feuds, military preparedness, prosecution of the assured, collection and disbursement of the tax and the creation of some political cohesion in the kingdom – continued into the new year.[152] In all this, Beaton remained active; his last appearance at the Council in Edinburgh six days before his assassination was the occasion of an order to the Justice Clerk to prepare indictments against collaborators on the Borders.[153] Such vigour worried the English; on 27 May 1546, Sir Robert Bowes, Warden of the English Middle March, described the Scots as boastful and belligerent. They bragged, said he, of sending Angus into England, of placing 2000 permanent troops on the Borders and of receiving aid from France; the Council was to be reorganised and 'grudges' were to be pacified.[154]

The war by this time was virtually over, for the Scots were included in the Treaty of Camp of 6 June 1546, which was to establish a peace of 18 months between the two countries. Credit for their success must go to the ability of the Scottish government to survive and to resist the English assaults. In this the roles of Beaton, Mary of Guise and Arran were most important. Henry was shortly to hear of the assassination of Beaton, but that brought him no nearer to whatever his goal was. Perhaps this was because once 1543 had ended, Henry VIII was not really interested in the Scottish opportunity seriously enough to seek success.

152 *RPC*, i, 20–23.
153 Herkless and Hannay, *Archbishops of St Andrews*, iv, 183–5, 201.
154 *LP*, xxi (1), no. 940.

CHAPTER SEVEN

The World Beyond Britain, 1543–46

D uring the period of Henry VIII's Rough Wooings, Europeans were transfixed by greater issues: the Turkish invasion of Hungary, the renewal of the Habsburg-Valois Wars (1542–44) and the invasion of France by Henry VIII (1544–46). Events in Scotland attracted little notice and even the Venetians made only rare references. An English traveller in Bologna reported some awareness, but it was slight.[1] In Germany, Protestants hoped for Henry's victory, although they and the Pope were almost the only ones to see the war in religious terms. However, four European powers were affected by, and thus interested in, Henry's war for Scotland: France, the Papacy, Christian III of Denmark and Charles V.

The concern of Francis I for his 'oldest ally' has already been discussed. To reiterate: Scotland was important, as the de la Brosse mission, the Lennox episode and Montgomery's army amply demonstrate; see too the lively correspondence maintained with Mary of Guise. But Scotland was – as it had been throughout the fifteenth and sixteenth centuries – subsidiary to France's European aspirations. As had Charles VIII (1483–98) and Louis XII (1498–1515), Francis I focused upon Italy and sought glory and principalities there. This would lock him into a series of wars, principally with the head of the Habsburg dynasty, the Holy Roman Emperor, Charles V (1519–56). Thus Scotland was marginalised. Its importance hinged on Francis' relations with England and Henry VIII's relations with Charles V.

THE HOLY SEE

The Papacy had the most wide-ranging and comprehensive information-gathering apparatus in Europe. Its agents may have been trained in arts other than negotiation and espionage and they were often ill-informed and biased. On occasion their advice was woefully flat-footed. But prelates were politicians, Beaton being a classic example. And they were often at the heart of the councils of princes. Rome also possessed a remarkable postal network. This arose from the massive bureaucracy of ecclesiastical affairs that the Holy See had evolved over a millennium. Messengers (many of them carrying nothing more important than requests for bulls of provision or pension arrangements for a see) carried news in their heads.

It is impossible to calculate how many messages were transmitted between Scotland and the Vatican in any one year, but the Pope had numerous ways by which he could know of the church's Northern daughter, even though distance, the timelag factor and English command of the sea could make contact difficult. Henry's

---

1 *Calendar of State Papers, Venetian*, ed. R. Brown and others (1864–), v, 117–18, 122, 325, 341, 376; *Original Letters*, ii, 37, 412; *LP*, xviii (2), nos. 357; xxi (2), 1354.

agents from Venice to Antwerp also attempted to interdict communication. Nonetheless, information did get through. Minor news flow occurred through what might best be termed 'reflected data' (via nuncios in France) and through the clutch of Scottish agents and factors at Rome transacting business on behalf of clients at home and thus in contact with the bureaucracy and the Curia.

There were two successive nuncios in France during this period: Jeronimo Dandino, Bishop of Caserta and (by 1546) of Imola, and Michael della Torre who replaced him in 1547. They normally corresponded not directly with the Pope, but with Cardinal Farnese. Their detailed reports were relatively frequent and give an accurate reflection of French concern. Throughout 1543 there was a regular flow of information.[2] Marco Grimani also kept Farnese informed during his long wait in France.[3] After 1543 reporting of Scottish events dropped off, only to increase again in 1545 when the French sent an army there[4] and in 1546 when Beaton was assassinated.[5]

Messengers must have given verbal reports on events. Certainly English agents in the Low Countries kept a sharp look-out for clerics bound for Scotland. William Thompson, a chapel clerk in Antwerp and supposedly a servant of Cardinal Pole, was picked up off Hull in 1545 carrying a chest of letters for Beaton. The Governor of the English merchants at Antwerp, Sir Thomas Chamberlain, had heard from a compatriot that a barber he knew had shaved a priest who thought Thompson was 'the Bishop of Rome's collector' in Scotland. He was freed eventually, but apparently never did any collecting.[6]

Another messenger to fall into English hands was Alexander Thedaldinus who first came to Scotland as Grimani's secretary or 'auditor'. Grimani seconded him to Beaton, and at one point it was suggested he might administer the Cardinal's French bishopric at Mirepoix. Sent to France in July 1544, Thedaldinus was captured by the English who held him for three months. He returned to Scotland with Montgomery's force in May 1545 but then was despatched by Beaton to France and Rome. Yet again he was captured when his ship was forced by tempest into Rye on 5 December 1545 where the English extracted from him his message to Francis and the Pope which was that Scotland would have to yield to Henry if aid in money did not come soon. Thedaldinus's own poverty was also vexing; he had to walk to London where some Venetians lent him sufficient funds to pay for the rest of his journey. Reaching Antwerp by 11 January 1546, he went, probably by way of France, to Rome where he and Patrick Liddall, sent by the Governor to promote Scottish interests, jointly reported to the College of Cardinals on the peril of the country.[7]

---

2 For reports from France in 1543, see *Nonces en France, 1541–46*, 186, 188, 190, 228, 237, 249, 300.

3 *Ibid.*, 194, 218, 232; *LP*, xviii (1), nos. 652, 745, 753, 900; (2), nos. 299, 435, 482; xx (1), nos. 138, 298.

4 *Nonces en France, 1541–46*, 337, 345, 365, 368, 395, 426.

5 *Nonces en France, 1546–51*, 337, 345, 365, 368, 395, 426.

6 *LP*, xx (1), nos. 630, 696, 725, 768, 930, 1014; (2), no. 85. He had been to Scotland in 1539 on commercial business for Antwerp (Rooseboom, *Scottish Staple*, 54).

7 *LP*, xx (2), no. 1020; xxi (1), no. 82; (2), nos. 277–9; *Nonces en France, 1541–46*, 337; *Mary of Lorraine Corresp.*, 154–7.

The two most important channels were direct communication from the Scots themselves and occasional papal envoys in the country. Beaton was an obviously important source. Early in 1542 the Cardinal had been called to Rome, but James vetoed the journey: 'His assistance and counsel at present and in the immediate future seem so necessary'.[8] In November that year, the King and Cardinal wrote of their war with Henry. In December, Paul again summoned Beaton to Trent. On 2 May 1543, the Cardinal replied that the brief had not reached him until 13 April and in any case he could not have gone, 'without a great risk to the state'. He also brought Rome up to date as to his freedom from arrest and relations with England.[9]

News also came from Arran and Mary of Guise; the year 1543 was particularly active. The Governor wrote on 14 May, outlining the 'incredible trouble' which threatened from England and from the Scottish nobility.[10] Another spate of letters followed at the end of the year. On 22 November the Queen Dowager warned that

> The realm is marvellously seduced and spoiled by the Lutheran sect, as well by the King of England as by the greater part of the subjects of this realm, so that it is in the way of being lost altogether.[11]

Arran echoed her fears, writing on 8 December to say that Henry was determined on war,

> not only to destroy our liberty, than which nothing can be dearer to men, but also to overthrow our religion and the obedience paid for so many centuries to the Holy See.[12]

By 29 February 1544, the danger from Henry was reported as highly serious.[13] Although the Governor's mood had changed by 20 May 1545 when he was able robustly to announce the remarkable victory at Ancrum Moor, the peril of England still remained firmly emphasised. In September 1546, with the Cardinal slain and his castle withheld, Arran stressed that 'ruin and servitude' would follow English capture of St Andrews.[14] But behind all of these lamentations lay, as ever, a firm political agenda. This can be neatly captured if we examine Grimani's visit in 1543–44 and Rome's reaction to his somewhat hyperbolic report.

Grimani's four-month mission is the only documented case of a papal legateship during Henry's Rough Wooings; Allen's assessment of him (old and bigoted) may well have been apt; certainly he viewed the Protestants he saw in Leith with shock and disgust. His analysis of Henry's motives remained consistently unsophisticated, even naive. On his return to Rome in February 1544, he made what was very much Arran's nub request:

---

8 *LP*, xvii, no. 110.
9 LP, xvii, nos. 1060, 1072; xviii (1), no. 494.
10 *Ibid.*, nos. 542–3.
11 *LP*, xviii (2), no. 416.
12 *Ibid.*, no. 471.
13 *LP*, xix (1), no. 138.
14 *LP*, xx (1), no. 781; *LP*, xxi (2), no. 6. See also *ibid.*, no. 277 (2).

[The Scots] lack all things, especially money, so it must be openly confessed that unless His Holiness and their allies help them, they cannot save their liberty. His Holiness cannot spend money more justly and more gloriously, not even against the Turk, than in the defence of the liberty and religion of the Scots, whose realm is a part of the Holy See.[15]

This was the standard rhetoric. Later that year, one orator (it may have been Grimani) declared to the Pope and curia:

The kingdom of Scotland being catholic and that of England being heretical, why should not the Pope help Catholics against heretics? [As he has helped with men and money against infidels] should he not send help against the heretics, who by the church are held as worse than infidels?[16]

Arran, Beaton, Mary of Guise all enunciated a familiar refrain. Mary of Guise's letter of November 1543 begged for 'succour'; Arran's of a fortnight later made what became the standard plea:

[Against Henry] two things are needed, valour and riches. The first will not be wanting, but against the wealth and power of so great a king, money must be sought elsewhere and for it the common-wealth looks to His Holiness.[17]

Obviously the Pope's views on Scotland turned on his attitudes towards Henry. In his mistimed exhortation to James V of 9 January 1543, he called the English monarch that 'son of perdition and of Satan' who warred on Scotland in his vexation at failing to tempt James 'to perdition'. James was to 'fight bravely in the cause of God'. Certainly in the nervous chatter of English agents abroad (and at home) breathed a real terror of a papal godly crusade. In 1543 Henry became convinced that Cardinal Pole (ever a royal bogey) had taken ship for Scotland with 4000 troops; in 1545 William Thompson said that the Papacy had hired 6000 Germans who would soon aid the country; in December 1547 enough money from the Pope supposedly arrived at Dumbarton to pay 10,000 Scots for a year.[18] But the reality lay in a papal letter to James of early 1543: 'If the power of the Holy See were not so exhausted he would send money'. Better help was promised, but always for the future.[19]

There were, however, two expedients by which the Papacy could and (if reluctantly) did aid the Scots. The first was by granting what in effect was lay taxation of the clergy, thus diverting revenues from Rome. On 9 January 1543 Paul III had granted James V six tenths of the fruits of the church in Scotland for two years to

---

15 *LP*, xix (1), no. 138 (2). Beaton too made pleas in such terms (*LP*, xix (2), no. 774).

16 *LP*, xviii (1), no. 31. *LP*, xix (1), no. 277, gives a slightly different rendering of the oration than the transcript in PRO, 31/9/66, fo. 163. See also *LP* xxi (2), no. 727, for a view from Rome of Henry VIII.

17 *LP*, xviii (2), no. 471.

18 *LP*, xviii (1), no. 601; *CSP Scot.*, i, no. 117.

19 See also *LP*, xxi (2), 277.

fight Henry; Beaton was appointed collector. James had already made considerable inroads on church income; provision of his bastard sons to rich abbeys and annual clerical taxation were just two of his diversions of church revenues to Crown purposes. It was a policy Arran naturally continued.

With James's death and the Cardinal's imprisonment, the task of collection and disbursement was given to Grimani, but it is not clear if he ever made any headway. Upon his departure, the office reverted to Beaton and upon the Cardinal's death there was some discussion of the disposal of the money which had been in his hands. By October 1546 the Papacy had decided 'de retrouver l'argent laisse par Beaton pour que le prelat desinge par S.S. puisse le porter [to recover the money left by Beaton in order that the cleric appointed by the Holy See can carry it]'. Though this emissary's departure for Paris in the New Year was promised in December, it is not clear what transpired.[20]

What is significant is that the French were consulted about these and other moves, for it was only through affecting France that the Papacy could hope to affect events in Scotland. Francis declared himself pleased with the Pope's actions in 1546, as they showed he 'veuille toujours s'occuper de la saufgarde d'Escosse [always wishes to be preoccupied with the safety of Scotland].' In 1548 Henry II was to make repeated requests for two, then three, tenths to be collected in Scotland.[21]

The Scots must have known that appeals for hard Roman cash would have little result. Nonetheless the making of such pleas strengthened their demands for more control over internal church appointments.[22] English hostility thus enhanced the Scottish Crown's already commanding position. Without the diversion of church revenues and benefices, how could one of the poorest monarchies in Western Europe hope to keep its faith? Thus Arran often got his way and not until 1548, when the French increasingly came to manipulate Scottish appointments, was there a serious threat to the Crown's control of ecclesiastical offices.

It is in this light, then, that one must view Scottish-Papal correspondence. Arran's first letter to the Pope of 14 May 1543 (in which he placed the Kingdom under the protection of the Holy See) firmly asked for internal matters to be settled as the government directed. Arran asked that the revenues from the monasteries then held *in commendam*[23] by the sons of James V should be retained by the Crown, the surplus to be converted 'to public use'.[24] The letter of 8 December 1543, after listing Beaton's

20 *Nonces en France, 1546–51*, 92, 99, 102, 116.

21 *Ibid.*, 409; PRO, 31/9/11, fo. 289. Again, the collection or disposal of the monies is obscure. For clear proof of French intervention in Scottish church matters, see *RPC*, i, 89, 91.

22 See D. McRoberts, *Essays on the Scottish Reformation, 1513–1625*, 1–18, 39–77, 32–58; G. Donaldson, *The Scottish Reformation*, 1–52.

23 A commendatorship was a case where someone other than the elected head of the religious house was appointed to receive the revenues of the order even though practical authority remained vested in the abbot or prior or abbess. James V had notoriously appointed many of his bastard sons as commendators to Scottish religious houses as a means of increasing his annual revenues.

24 *LP*, xviii (1), no. 543. Parliament had already determined in March that the revenues be so managed (*APS*, ii, 124). See also *LP*, xviii (1), no. 801.

considerable efforts for rejection of the English marriage, asked for a legateship for him, a demand made more strongly in February 1544. In 1545, the Governor used the occasion of reporting Ancrum Moor to seek papal censure of Gavin Dunbar who had brawled with Beaton at Glasgow.[25] The long report on the Cardinal's death in September 1546 ended with a request for the speedier provision of Arran's secretary, David Paniter, to the Bishopric of Ross.[26]

The government had some grounds for complaint. Until 1543, the papal response rate had been just over three months.[27] Arran would rarely witness such expedition as Dunkeld nicely illustrates. Between December 1543 and January 1544, the see fell vacant, the first to do so in Arran's regency. He chose his half-brother, John Hamilton, Abbot of Paisley, who was nominated on 24 January 1544. Formal provision was not granted until 17 December, but as late as 11 February 1545 Arran was still complaining that Hamilton could not be consecrated, owing to a dispute over the see; it did not happen until 22 August 1546.[28] Another example is David Paniter. When the see of Ross became vacant on 30 November 1545, Paniter, Arran's secretary, was nominated before 23 December, when he received the temporalities, and again on 27 April 1546. Nonetheless, the bull of provision was not issued until 28 November 1547, and then only at French insistence.[29]

Perhaps the most political case concerned the brother of Matthew, Earl of Lennox. In January 1542, Robert Stewart had received the administration of the see of Caithness, but never got round to being consecrated.[30] When his brother defected to Henry VIII in May 1544, Robert accompanied him to England. Although the Scottish government initially attempted to distinguish between the two, on 12 December 1544 it finally asked Paul III to call Stewart to Rome and to redesignate the see to Alexander Gordon, brother of the Earl of Huntly (whose uncle William was Bishop of Aberdeen), a prominent supporter of the regime. On 7 March 1545, the dean and chapter at Dornoch made a similar request to the Pope,[31] one repeated in May and December 1545. Paul III finally declared himself not competent to judge and by 17 March 1546 had handed the case to Beaton as legate. On 13 April, the Cardinal declared that Stewart was guilty of 'lèse majesté', merited removal and that the see should go to Alexander Gordon.[32]

25 The story is a famous one (Knox, *History*, i, 72–74).
26 See below.
27 See *Fasti* for some representative cases such as Moray (1 March–14 June 1538), Orkney (4 April–20 July 1541), Ross (15 December 1538–14 April 1539). Sometimes it could even be quicker, e.g. Galloway (3 July–22 August 1541). *Fasti*, 214, 254, 270, 123.
28 *LP*, xviii (1), nos. 542–3, 801; (2), nos. 477–8; xix (1), no. 723; (2), nos. 428–31, 710–11, 759; xx (1), no. 179n; *Fasti*, 99–100.
29 *LP*, xx (i), no. 472; xxi (1), no. 1465; (2), nos. 6, 277–8; *Fasti*, 270; *RSS*, iii, no. 1446. He called himself Bishop as early as 15 December 1545 (*LP*, xx (2), 986).
30 *Fasti*, 61.
31 *LP*, xix (2), nos. 737–8; NAS, SP 1; Elphinston MS, ii, 130.
32 NAS, Elphinston MS, ii, 125–8, 131–3.

However, two months later, Arran bribed Stewart to return to Scotland with the restoration of his Bishopric of Caithness.[33] The government was then faced with how to content Gordon. Matters were further complicated by the decision to give Arbroath Abbey to Angus's bastard son George,[34] but this meant finding an alternative benefice for the incumbent, James Beaton. Luckily, Glasgow fell vacant on 30 April 1547 and Arran (although initially hoping to pass it over to another natural brother, James) pledged it to Beaton so that Arbroath might be transferred to George Douglas.[35] But Gordon also wanted Glasgow, and for the next four years a complicated struggle ensued which was only solved with papal assistance. Beaton finally gained Glasgow, while the Pope compensated Gordon with the titular title of Archbishop of Athens.[36] It was a long way from Arbroath.

The Papacy, then, could delay the regency's blatant manipulation of ecclesiastical patronage, but in the end the Scots held the upper hand, as can be seen if one returns to John Hamilton. Two days after the assassination of Cardinal Beaton, he was granted the temporalities of St Andrews. In November 1547 he was transferred from Dunkeld, but not until mid-1549 was he exercising full authority as Primate of Scotland.[37] Equally illuminating are the pensions which were provided out of some of the temporalities. In July 1547, when Arran first nominated his natural brother James to Glasgow, he asked that a £1000 pension be granted to his own sons David and Claud. In 1558, the Bishop of Aberdeen was to complain of his poverty since 'my benefice is under grite pension': 1000 marks went annually to Arran and 500 to David Paniter.[38]

Church-state relations are not normally regarded as part of foreign policy analysis, mistakenly as the above discussion demonstrates. Indeed with the Reformation, hardly any issue of international relations over the next two centuries would be devoid of a religious context. Most Scottish intercourse with the Holy See may seem impeccably mundane: provision, pensions and tenths. But they were riveted into a power struggle of high stakes, so it was believed at the time. That is why control of Scottish ecclesiastical appointments would lie in the hands of Arran's government as an essential prop to its maintenance of its war against England.

Much has been made of the fear of a reformation as leading to even worse abuses within Scotland's Catholic church: the rampant milking of the funds of its religious houses, the blatant use of church appointments as a mere extension of state patronage and high taxation for Crown needs. If this led to progressive secularisation of the high offices of the church, it, like the alienation of church

33 See below.
34 The French backed the proposal too (*LP*, xxi (2), nos. 277–9, 544). See also *RSS*, iii, nos. 142, 2074 and 1700. And see Lesley's comment that the proposal caused 'gret cummer' (Dalrymple, *Historie*, ii, 293).
35 *Vetera Monumenta Hibernorum et Scotorum Historiam illustrantia quae ex Vaticani, Neapolis ac Florentae tabulariis deprompsit et ordine chronologico*, ed. A Theiner (Rome, 1864), 1124.
36 *Mary of Lorraine Corresp.*, 329–33. And see *RSS*, iv, no. 513; *TA*, ix, 114, 146, 170, 356; Pitcairn, *Trials*, i, 345.
37 *Fasti*, 149–50, 298.
38 *Mary of Lorraine Corresp.*, 413–14.

lands to pay for the taxation for the war, was ultimately a price Rome was prepared to pay. But one should be careful. All European societies saw their churches exploited by 'the state'; and Scotland in the 1540s was not much more rapacious than Scotland under James IV. David Beaton stands comparison with Bishop Elphinstone. And certainly Arran's Scotland can be compared favourably with Henry VIII's England.[39]

THE KING OF DENMARK

When we turn to Scotland's relations with Denmark, we enter onto somewhat more orthodox grounds: dynasticism and disputed claims, trade and defensive alliances. But there is also the complicating element of marriages. In 1469, James III had married Princess Margaret, daughter of Christian (Christiern) I of Denmark and Norway (1448/50–81). Because of Christian Oldenburg's heavy land purchases in Schleswig and Holstein, he lacked sufficient funds for Margaret's dowry of 58,000 Florins of the Rhine and pledged not only the Orkney and Shetland Islands, but also remitted to the Scottish monarchs the tribute previously paid for the Hebrides and the Isle of Man. The Scottish Parliament declared them to be annexed to the Crown in 1472, a move which brought a number of Danish protests.

The marriage of King Christian II (1513–23)[40] further complicated matters. In 1515 he became the husband to Charles of Burgundy's sister Elizabeth (Isabella), but this did nothing to halt either his sexual affair with his long-term mistress Dyveke or the power of her mother, Sigbrit Villoms. In 1517 Dyveke was poisoned and the King, increasingly erratic, determined to reconquer Sweden. Meanwhile Elizabeth was delivered of two daughters, Dorothy and Isabella, in a marriage of increasing misery. Christian was finally overthrown in 1523 by both his Swedish and his Danish subjects; his uncle Frederick Duke of Holstein-Gottorp was then elected King of Denmark and Norway while Gustav Vasa became Gustav II of an independent Sweden. In that same year, Elizabeth died, her daughters were sent to live with their uncle, now the Holy Roman Emperor, Charles V, and Christian was in effect put under house arrest at Sønderborg. In 1549 he would be removed to Kalunborg, and he remained there in Copenhagen until he died in 1559.

Scotland's foreign relations were affected by this melodramatic tale. Relations were never merely bilateral – the one regime dealing with the other – but were inextricably affected by a much wider context centring principally on Charles V who consistently refused to recognise the 'usurpation' of the Danish Crown by the Holstein line. The two monarchies had concluded treaties of peace and amity throughout the period 1266 to 1426.[41] Scottish trade with Scandinavia was

---

39 Compare Ian Cowan and J. J. Scarisbrick on their different Reformations.
40 He was also briefly King of Sweden, 1520–23.
41 T.L. Christensen, 'Scoto-Danish relations in the sixteenth century: the historiography and some questions', *SHR*, xlviii (1969), 54–63. One can also enter the topic via an early and somewhat simplistic survey by W. Stamford Reid, 'The place of Denmark in Scottish foreign policy, 1470–1540', *Juridical Review*, lviii (1946), 183–200.

throughout the sixteenth century fairly brisk.[42] Contact with Denmark was further maintained by Scots who settled there.[43]

The Danes by no means acceded to definitive Scottish annexation of Shetland and Orkney, but in the last treaty, of 5 May 1492, had accepted the validity of the dowry arrangements of 1468. That treaty also enunciated a pact of mutual defence, but in such vague terms that it meant little more than amity.[44] Certainly when James IV engaged in one of his more bizarre games of international barnstorming – the proposed crusade of 1508 – no Danish fleet joined his, despite a visit to Copenhagen by the *Great Michael*.[45] But history and the present obviously made Arran's government aware of a Danish dimension to his foreign relations. At one point, he would extol Danish might in war and at sea and recalled in lush prose the potent defeats Danes had inflicted upon the English in an earlier millennium.

Moreover, both kingdoms had become further bound through the French Treaty of Fontainebleau of 29 November 1541 (updated in July 1542).[46] This 'triple entente'[47] had arisen as part of Francis I's attempts to weld a 'great league' against Charles V, composed of Scotland, Denmark, Sweden, Russia, Guelders, Cleves and the Ottoman Empire.[48] Christian III of Denmark, who had been elected after the death of his father Frederick I in 1534, still kept Christian II a prisoner in Copenhagen and remained apprehensive of the Emperor's support of the old King's family.[49]

Francis played upon these fears and by 1541 had appointed Christopher Richer to be resident ambassador at the Danish court in his development of a Northern strategy, mirroring that with the Suleyman in the Southeast.[50] By July 1543, Christian had declared war upon the Emperor, and although he took no serious military action,

---

42 Evidence for Scottish trade with Scandinavia is extensive: J. Dow, '*Skotter* in sixteenth-century Scania' (*SHR*, xliv (1965) 34–51; 'Scottish Trade with Sweden 1512–80', *SHR*, xlviii (1969), 64–79). See also S.G.E. Lythe, *The Economy of Scotland in its European Setting, 1550–1625*. For evidence of trade with Denmark, see *TA*, viii, 151–55; *The Exchequer Rolls of Scotland*, ed. J. Stewart and others (Edinburgh, 1878–1908), xviii, 38; *LP*, xviii, no. 476; xviii (1), nos. 326, 682, 771.

43 T.L. Christensen, 'Scots in Denmark in the sixteenth century', *SHR*, xlix (1970), 125–45.

44 For a thorough discussion of this aspect, see B.E. Crawford, 'The Pawning of Orkney, and Shetland: a reconsideration of the events of 1460–9' and K. Horby, 'Christian I and the pawning of Orkney: some reflections on Scandinavian foreign policy 1460–8', *SHR*, xlviii (1969), 18–34, 35–53.

45 An adventure robustly told by N. Macdougall, *James IV*, 254; and see his 'James IV's "Great Michael" ', in his *Scotland and War, AD 79–1918*, 36–60.

46 L. Laursen, *Denmark–Norges Traktater* (Copenhagen, 1916), i, 409–14. I am grateful to the late Dr. S.P. Oakley for this and other references. The treaty with Sweden is calendared in *LP*, xvii, no. 487.

47 This felicitous phrase is rehearsed by Thorkild L. Christensen in his study of the 1540s: 'The Earl of Rothes in Denmark', in *The Renaissance and Reformation in Scotland*, ed. I.B. Cowan and D. Shaw (Edinburgh, 1983), 62.

48 *LP*, xvii, nos. 329, 428, 470, 530, 532, 589, appendix B, 31.

49 For an account of Danish-Imperial relations, see K. Brandi, *The Emperor Charles V, passim* and Scarisbrick, *Henry VIII*, 357–60, 368–70.

50 See C. Richer, *Memoires de sieur Richer, ambassadeur pour les roys . . . François I et Henri II en Suede et en Dannermarch* (Troyes, 1625).

the Low Countries' government was concerned about Danish closure of the Sound (Sønd), piratical attacks and the threat of an invasion.

Henry VIII was of course quite aware of all this and there was always a nagging apprehension that aid to the Scots would suddenly descend from the Sønd. Rumours of great Danish succour during the war of 1542 were constant, lookouts at Holy Island and the Farne Islands frequently espying great fleets in the mists of the North Sea.[51] When negotiations began for the Scottish marriage, Henry (and Chapuys) became nervous as to Franco-Danish counter-moves, especially when French envoys were despatched to Christian immediately after James V's death.[52] When Henry VIII became an ally of Charles V in February 1543, he immediately despatched William Watson to tax Christian about the rumour of Danish aid being sent to Scotland.[53] Watson extracted no categorical denial by the King, but the city councils of Lübeck and Hamburg declared that neither they, nor the Danish monarch, would send any such support.[54] What neither Henry nor the Scots knew was that Christian had no intention of making serious war and would, by the start of 1544, be making overtures to Charles V for a resolution of their dispute.

As far as Arran was concerned, Denmark was an ally and in April 1543 he wrote to Christian of the calamity which had befallen the realm and made use of the pleasing fiction that the dead King's will (there was none) enjoined that his heirs maintain the ancient confederacy with Denmark.[55] In September he went out of his way to assure Christian that, regardless of the Greenwich treaty, the Scots had in no way acted against Denmark.[56] On 18 March 1544, Bothwell, at government prompting, wrote to Christian[57] and by the end of April preparations were completed for the embassy of John Hay, Beaton's nephew, to Denmark.[58] Hay's commission and mandate were sealed in Edinburgh on 30 April 1544, but it is not clear if he took ship before the English attack of 4 May. He probably reached Denmark in June. His instructions were firstly to promise that Arran would 'be attentive to all things touching the Danes and their dominions' and to give the King a long, detailed and relatively accurate account of Anglo-Scottish relations during 1542–44. Since Henry now plotted to seize the kingdom by 'nourishing the dissensions of the Scots' and not by 'matrimonial alliances', Hay was to express the hope that

> The King of Danes will show himself their champion against the inhuman enemy. The Scots are determined under God, not to suffer their ancient

51 *LP*, xvii, nos. 329, 453, 601, 935, 1110 (2), 1199, 1203.
52 *Ibid.*, nos. 532, 786, 746, appendix B, 34. He was also worried the Danes might seize two islands which guarded the approaches to Amsterdam (*ibid.*, appendix B, nos. 24–25, 29, 30–31, 33).
53 *LP*, xviii (1), no. 145.
54 *Ibid.*, nos. 332, 376. Watson did not believe these reports (*ibid.*, nos. 781, 878, 925). See also *LP*, xviii (2), nos. 114, 278.
55 *LP*, xviii (1), nos. 472, 682.
56 *LP*, xviii (2), no. 16.
57 *LP*, xix (1), no. 213. See also *LP*, xviii (1), no. 145.
58 *TA*, viii, 278; *LP*, xix (1), no. 294. The date of Hay's first letter of credence was 15 March (NAS, Elphinstone MS, ii, 77).

kingdom to fall into servitude, provided that the Danish King and other confederate princes will give a measure of support.[59]

Three types of aid were sought: renewal of the treaty between the two kingdoms, assistance in the present war, and licence for Scottish merchants to export 'engines of war', munitions and victuals.

Hay's mission was to be fruitless. Despite a French force being sent to Denmark, by the very time of Hay's despatch Danish ambassadors were at Speyer negotiating with those of Charles and by 7 May a truce had been agreed.[60] Wotton, the English ambassador with Charles at Speyer, was privy to the negotiations. Since by then Henry and Charles were allies, Wotton pressed for Denmark to become a further ally of England and thus to declare war against the Scots. This the Danes refused, being empowered, in a famous phrase, 'to make friends for their master, not enemies'. Whilst they agreed not to aid the Scots, they refused to break the alliance and would not forbid trade.[61] The relevant clause in the Treaty of Speyer of 23 May 1544 read:

> The King of England shall be included in the peace, and as the realm of Scotland has moved war against the King who is in closest alliance with the Emperor, and the Scots have committed hostilities against the Low Countries (so that they are held the Emperor's enemies), Denmark shall show no favour to the Scots to the prejudice of their majesties, but shall not be bound to interdict navigation to the Scots.[62]

Henry was clearly gratified by his inclusion and ratified the treaty fairly quickly. He was also pleased by Christian's agreement not to aid the Scots, and word of this assurance was quickly spread; Wharton in Carlisle knew of it by 10 June.[63] Hay therefore obtained nothing in mid-June when he was received by Christian. The King thanked Arran for a present, declared sorrow at James's death, gladness at Mary's succession. He found Arran's proceedings with Henry 'prudent' and offered to mediate.

The sixteenth century was no stranger to subtle diplomatic falsity. A classic evasion for avoiding a decision a King had no intention of taking in the first place was suddenly to enunciate a doctrine of cabinet collective responsibility or simply to funk by saying that his secretary had gone home early that day. Christian adopted both, firstly telling Hay (with what one assumes was a straight face) that as all of his Councillors were absent from court, no firm response was possible. Smoothly he averred that personally he was willing to renew the defensive alliance of mutual support, but did not have a copy of what he called the 'Norwegian treaty' to hand. Scots could, of course, purchase supplies. Such double-talk would haunt him later, for Arran was no ingénu at pretending to be stupid.

59 *LP*, xix (1), no. 437.
60 BN, MS fr. 15,966, fo. 239; 17, 890, fos. 9–11, 27.
61 *LP*, xix (1), nos. 478–9, 536.
62 *Ibid.*, no. 567. The treaty also included Sweden and Brandenburg, but Sweden did not ratify it until 1551.
63 *LP*, xix (2), nos. 115, 155, 166, 282. Wharton quickly told Glencairn (*LP*, xix (1), no. 662).

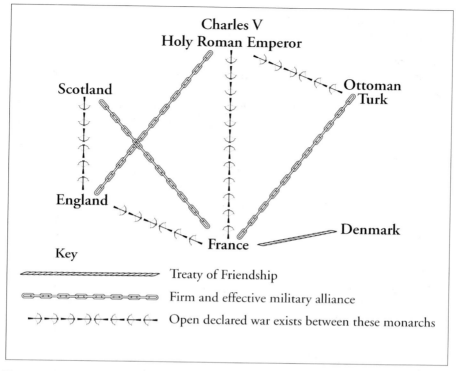

Fig. 7.1. In May 1544, Charles V came to peace (at Speyer) with the King of Denmark, thus concluding that conflict (virtually until the Thirty Years' War). Denmark remained officially ally to both France and Scotland, but did nothing effective in terms of making war against the enemies of either.

Such was the dusty reply Hay brought back when he returned home by way of France, probably in early July.[64] Military aid there was not to be, but relations continued, Arran writing the King on 1 January 1545. A Danish herald was cordially received at Edinburgh that April.[65] Moreover, Christian had no intention of allowing the terms of Speyer to dominate him. Rumours of Danish assistance indeed persisted: the Scots were supposedly raising mercenaries there as early as August 1544.[66] One of Henry VIII's last acts was to send Richard Morrison to discover if any aid was going to Scotland.[67] Such rumours were particularly rife after Pinkie.[68] However, other issues engendered contact.

64 *TA*, viii, 305; *LP*, xix (1), no. 751.
65 *RPC*, i, 77; Christensen, p. 63, says a letter by Arran of 1 January 1545 actually refers to a fleet with 2000 men to be sent to Scotland.
66 *LP*, xix (2), 131.
67 *LP*, xxi (2), nos. 679–80, 707, 758, 775 (fo. 97). His instructions apparently do not survive (*ibid.*, no. 647, no. 50).
68 *Odet de Selve*, 254, 289; *CSP For.*, i, 21, 23; *CSP Scot.*, i, nos. 313, 357 (10); *CSP Domestic*, ed. Lemon and Green (London, 1870), vi, 378, 390.

Denmark remained a place of refuge for Scottish exiles. In the aftermath of Beaton's assassination in May 1546, the Governor, fearful that accessories to that deed had fled to Denmark, wrote to Christian, begging co-operation. George Leslie, 4th Earl of Rothes, was father to Norman, notorious for his participation in the slaughter: his own brother and two of his sons were also directly implicated. George was almost certainly innocent, but he sensibly fled and, like others before him and since, landed in Denmark. Christian put Rothes under 'libera custodia'. But by the New Year the Scottish government altered its view: Rothes was welcomed back home by July 1547. During his time at Copenhagen, he became quite cordial with the King and left a handsome gift. By his own account, he then spent several years praising Christian's liberal humanity and virtues to all who would listen.

A second point of discussion was the little Queen. As early as July 1543 the regent of the Low Countries suggested that Christian desired Mary's hand for one of his sons; Danish reluctance to declare against Scotland in May 1544 was thought to be for the same reason.[69] By August 1544 the word was that the Scots were offering her.[70] The French fed these aspirations. Richer's instructions of 6 November 1546 promised Christian all possible assistance to gain 'the marriage of the little Queen of Scotland for his son'.[71]

Which son is not certain, but a memorandum to the King in May 1547 concerning the Rothes issue may point to his younger one, Magnus. The schemes, if they were more than just rumour, show how many-faceted dynastic puzzling could be. Such a marriage, it was argued, might have resulted in the resolution of the vexed issue of Shetland and Orkney: they would be re-dowered back. Moreover, it might cement the 'triple entente'. Should Magnus succeed his father, a new Scandinavian North Sea empire might emerge of Scotland-Norway-Denmark, dramatically rebuilding a Kalmar union and recasting the mould of Danish policy. No wonder the Swedes were such reluctant partners in Francis' grand league, and no wonder English statesmen viewed Danish-Scottish relations with such apprehension.[72]

There was a further ingredient, one which would long outlive the turmoils of the Rough Wooings: Scottish retention of its North Seas islands. No Danish King could definitively surrender them: indeed each monarch's election oath or charter (*hand-faestning*) pledged him to effect redemption, and Christian would return to this issue in the later stages of the war. When the Scots sent Sir David Lindsay of the Mount as ambassador to Denmark in December 1548 requesting a fleet, he brought back the subsequent Spring an envoy raising the issue.[73] Now it was Arran's turn to repay Christian for his flummery of 1544.

The Governor replied on 5 January 1550, perhaps pointedly, from the siege camp at

69 *LP*, xviii (1), nos. 878, 925; xix (1), 478.
70 *LP*, xix (2), no. 131; the tale was again current in May 1548 (*Odet de Selve*, 338).
71 Christensen, 65, no. 32; *Lettres et Memoires*, i, 600, 606–7.
72 See Somerset sending John Borthwick, another St. Andrews Castilian, to Denmark. Christensen, 68, nos. 52–53.
73 *RPC*, i, 104; *CSP Spain*, ix, 383; NAS, Elphinston MS, ii, 78, 116–20; *Treaties*, III, 4; *TA*, viii, 365, 478; ix, 259; *Mary of Lorraine Corresp.*, 178.

Broughty. The incessant demands of the war and the priority of its victorious conclusion meant he could not find space in which to consult the national archives in Edinburgh Castle. Nor could he gather about him a Council learned in the matter. In any case (the all time cop-out of all minority governments), nothing could possibly be decided until the monarch came of age. The French, also approached by Christian (who indeed had levied a special tax for the necessary funds), smoothly put numbers on that elastic term: 'in three years and four months'.

Then, in February, Arran sent Rothes; he arrived at Itzehoe in April. In a protracted and detailed set of negotiations Rothes did not deny that the Danes had some rights, but rejected a Danish solution that unless the Scots proved the lack of Danish rights during the period, then the sovereignty should automatically revert to the Danish Crown upon Mary's perfect age. In June 1551, Arran virtually terminated further discussion of the matter.[74] The issue would be raised on several occasions during the course of the century: one embassy even turned up with the money for redemption in 1560.[75] Denmark finally accepted the loss of the islands in 1590.

CHARLES V, HOLY ROMAN EMPEROR
AND RULER OF THE LOW COUNTRIES

Christian III may have been cautious in his dealings with Scotland; Charles V, however, was not to be. By the time of the Treaty of Speyer, he had decided to declare the Scots enemies, a move which was to result in six long years of war between the Low Countries and Scotland. How this came about is a complex story.

Scotland had always been on good terms with the Low Countries, the principal contact being trade. This gave rise to the 1427 Treaty of Perpetual Peace which had been renewed for 100 years as recently as 1529–31. Habsburg-Valois antagonism had not hurt the commercial ties but there was a consequent increase of Imperial interest in Scottish politics owing to James V's marital eligibility; for a while a Habsburg bride was seriously considered.[76] Given the fact that the Low Countries were Scotland's major trading area, the monarchy and the Convention of Royal Burghs did everything possible to maintain harmonious relations.[77] This interest was reciprocated, and through the 1520s and 1530s there was a sharp rivalry between Middelburg and Veere in Zealand for the Scottish staple; Veere finally gained it in 1541.[78] Certainly Scottish

---

74 Christensen details the matter nicely, 70–73.

75 It has been suggested that Christian contemplated sending a fleet to join with one of Mary Tudor's which did harry the Northern Seas in 1558 so as forcibly to regain the islands. But authorities differ. See the issue being raised in 1560: L. Laursen, *Danmark-Norges Traktater*, iii, 2–4; *TA*, ix, 377, 385, 387, 428.

76 Both Mary, Queen Dowager of Hungary (who was strongly against the idea, especially after her marriage to Lewes II), and one of the Danish princesses were considered (Donaldson, *Scotland*, 23–24).

77 Rooseboom, *Scottish Staple*, 62–70; J. Davidson and A. Gray, *The Scottish Staple at Veere*, 113–71.

78 *Bronnen tot de Geschiedenis van Middelburgh in den Landsheerlijken Tijd*, ed. W.S. Unger (Rijks Geschiedkundige Publicatien, no. 75, 1931), iii, no. 590.

trade seems to have been vigorous: in the period 10 August 1543–9 to February 1544, fully 115 ships sailed to Scotland.[79]

The war with France during 1542–44, however, did cause considerable damage to the trade. Scottish involvement in the Franco-Imperial war was gradual and arose primarily from Charles's need of English assistance against France. As early as December 1541, overtures for a renewal of the Anglo-Imperial alliance were being made and on 5 May 1542 Charles, obviously concerned about the impending war with France, formally instructed Eustace Chapuys[80] to commence negotiations with Henry.[81] When the war with Francis broke out in July, the matter became urgent.

By January 1543 the ambassador's reports became distinctly pessimistic. He saw Henry's zeal to gain Scotland, 'which the King intends prosecuting to the last at any risk', as giving the English 'very plausible excuses' for procrastination and he gloomily considered that further negotiation was only a sham. In particular he feared French exploitation of the turn of events.[82]

Chapuys did, however, begin to see certain advantages in this sudden turn of events. The French could not afford to allow Scotland to slip out of their orbit. If matters prospered for Henry VIII, Francis would be forced to divert military support to Scotland. That would make Henry increasingly anti-French and thus would cement Anglo-Imperial co-operation.[83] Chapuys did try to influence English policy, and on 2 February he was bold enough to remind his opposite numbers, if somewhat elliptically, of the precedent of Robert the Bruce[84] and Edward II: however disorganised the Scots might appear, they had bested mighty princes in the past. Henry should wait for things to come to him and not press the Scots too hard; that might 'perchance unite all parties against him and compel the Scots to look out for help and assistance elsewhere'.[85]

Imperial apprehension over the Scottish distraction was dispelled by the sudden readiness of the English to negotiate in early February and the alliance Treaty of 11 February 1543.[86] But as early as May, concern returned owing to Henry's threats to

79 *Ibid.*, no. 607; *Handel met Engeland*, i, no. 706.
80 Garrett Mattingly's thesis on Chapuys has never been printed, but much of his work can be seen in his *Catherine of Aragon, Renaissance Diplomacy*, and his article, 'A Humanist Ambassador', *Journal of Modern History*, iv (1932), 175–85.
81 See *LP*, xvii, nos. 63, 293; Scarisbrick, *Henry VIII*, 433–5, 440–1.
82 *LP*, xvii, no. 1241; xviii (1), nos. 44, 63.
83 *LP*, xviii (1), nos. 144, 150, 171, 201, 248.
84 *CSP Spain*, vii, 25 (oddly not mentioned in *LP*, xix (I), no. 84). He elaborated his reminder in a despatch to the Queen Dowager of Hungary on the same day (*LP*, viii (2), appendix 4). One of the intriguing aspects of the 1540s is how much the shadow of Bruce still stretched. The Scottish Act of Parliament renewing the French alliance in December 1543 hallowed its antiquity by recording its continuation 'sence king Robert the bruce', indeed 'past momoury of mann' (*APS*, ii, 154). In 1548, the French ambassador in London, Odet de Selve, similarly exasperated Somerset by pointedly reminding him of Bruce's successful war. The Protector retorted heatedly that 'ne fault poinct en cela alléguer examples du roy Robert' (*Odet de Selve*, 248). Just how much Scottish history did Europeans know during the sixteenth century?
85 *LP*, xviii (2), appendix no. 4.
86 *LP*, xviii (1), nos. 259, 353, 383.

invade Scotland, then vanished with the Greenwich treaties, then returned when the Scottish settlement evaporated in the autumn.[87] Charles remained anxious until English troops actually landed at Calais in June 1544, and this may explain his exaggerated delight at Hertford's burning of Edinburgh the month before.[88] By this time, however, Charles had become a participant in Henry's war with Scotland and not merely an observer.

Here it is necessary to point to four of the clauses of the Treaty of 11 February 1543,[89] as they were to cause considerable friction both in 1544 and subsequently. They were commonplace enough. Two, clauses 3 and 4, created a 'common enemies' stipulation: each prince was enjoined to wage war against an enemy of the other. Two others, clauses 13 and 15, the 'comprehension proviso', stated that no truce or peace could be made by one prince with Francis or with any of his confederates, without the consent of the other. The 'common enemies' stipulation was the first to cause difficulty. As early as 3 May 1542 Charles did not press the matter.[90] Then on 2 February 1543 the English asked for the Scots to be declared enemies of both. Chapuys refused, but later pointed out that the Emperor would insist on a declaration against Denmark; this time it was the English who demurred.[91] As matters proceeded so well in Scotland, Henry dropped his demand for a while and was even willing to admit that the Danes were included in the 'general clause' as common enemies. But Charles could not agree and continued to press for a specific declaration against Christian III. The English simply temporised.[92]

The issue became serious when, with Scottish affairs turning against him, Henry began to press earnestly for an Imperial war against Scotland. On 2 November, the English ambassadors in Brussels were instructed to ask for it: so later was Dr. Nicholas Wotton.[93] Granvelle's smooth reply was that the matter was simplicity itself if only Henry would formally certify that a state of war existed, that actual hostilities were occurring and that Scottish trade had been interdicted. Henry duly informed Charles on 28 January 1544 that 'war was open between us and the Scots'; shortly afterwards Charles did likewise regarding Denmark.[94]

It seems that at first neither Charles nor Mary of Hungary really saw much difficulty over the Scots, but Henry was adamant that he would not declare against Denmark, a determination doubtless strengthened by an assurance of Christian on 31 March 1544 that no aid would be given the Scots.[95] Charles protested that Denmark

---

87 *LP*, xviii (1), no. 566. Chapuys was beginning to feel that Henry deliberately exaggerated his Scottish difficulties so as to force more concessions from Charles (*LP*, xviii (2), no. 254). Philip was also concerned; see his droll comment of January 1544 (*LP*, xix (1), no. 90).

88 Charles sent three special envoys in late 1543 to expedite English aid (*LP*, xviii (2), nos. 464–46, 492). See also *LP*, xix (1), nos. 96, 118, 147, 318, 497, 518, 547, 566, 579.

89 *LP*, xviii (1), nos. 144; xix (1), no. 70.

90 *LP*, xvii, nos. 446, 616, 1008, 1229; appendix B, 17, 21.

91 *LP*, xviii (2), appendix no. 4.

92 *LP*, xviii (1), nos. 120, 383, 397, 612, 632, 732, 925, 954.

93 *LP*, xviii (2), nos. 331, 420.

94 *LP*, xix (1), nos. 4, 5, 20, 32, 54, 70, 81, 183.

95 *Ibid.*, nos. 84, 118, 127, 147, 185, 216, 269, 284.

was a more serious threat to him than Scotland was to England. Moreover, it was necessary to consult the government of the Low Countries, and this uncovered a serious problem for Charles.

By March 1544 Mary had deliberated with her Council and they were firmly against it. Not unnaturally, a strong opponent of the war was Maximilian de Bourgogne, Admiral of Flanders and the Lord of Veere, the new site of the Scottish Staple in the Netherlands.[96] On 9 March she put the case to Chapuys in full:

> The prejudice to her countries of the declaration against Scotland is too notorious to be asked. For, firstly these countries have never been at war which should not be lightly infringed; secondly, if at war with Scotland and Holstein [the King of Denmark], the countries are entirely debarred from the navigation of the East and from fishing, especially this fishing of the herrings which they take towards the North under the coasts of Scotland – a prejudice much greater than all that the English allege to excuse their declaration against Holstein . . . the prejudice is so great that, even though the declaration against Scotland is made, she does not see how it can be observed unless the king also declares against Holstein and the English are debarred from the navigation of the East, like those here. Otherwise it would be impossible to content them.[97]

To these arguments, Charles added some of his own. As the alliance was so old, ought he not to give the Scots a chance to conform before opening war against them? Could he not mediate between Henry and them? Should not Henry beware of too open aggression against them which would give the Pope a plausible excuse to aid the French? Chapuys dutifully laid these points before an increasingly exasperated English Privy Council.[98] Charles may have been sincere in his reluctance to become involved with Scotland, but three factors, which began to emerge in March and April, weakened his resolve.

In the first place, Henry intimated that if there was no war against Scotland, his invasion of France might be delayed. On 2 March Chapuys ominously reported that whilst refusal to declare would not halt the invasion, 'it might cause many things to cool'. Henry made it quite clear in a long interview with Chapuys on 11 April that he could content himself with Scotland alone that year.[99] Moreover, by April arrangements were afoot for Danish ambassadors to come to Speyer to treat with Charles; it did not help the Imperial position that the English knew of this. Though the negotiations were delicate, it was clear that accommodation was possible.[100] If these two developments weakened his resistance to Henry's demand, a third was to make continued opposition seem pointless. This was the fact that by April relations between the government and the Scottish merchants in the Low Countries were distinctly hostile.

---

96 The English especially felt him to be someone 'to have always favoured the Scots' (*ibid.*, no. 147). They were correct to do so (Rooseboom, *Scottish Staple*, 61–65).
97 *LP*, xix (1), no. 183.
98 *Ibid.*, nos. 166, 206, 318.
99 *Ibid.*, nos. 168, 318, 323–4.
100 *LP*, xix (1), no. 437.

During the 1542 war with England, Scots naturally had raided English shipping. Their navy was not formidable: three to five vessels under John Barton, son of the famous Robert. The *Mary Willoughby*, the *Lion of Scotland* and the *Salamander* picked off crayers from Whitby, fishers and other small craft.[101] After James's death, raids off the east coast decreased, but a number of Scottish ships continued to work out of the French Channel ports of Rouen and Dieppe as well as Brest. Their numbers were swelled by Frenchmen masquerading as Scots. Damage to English shipping was much greater here and, on one celebrated occasion, eleven ships containing wine for the King himself were captured. (Upon hearing of the sale of the cargo in Edinburgh, Lord Lisle purchased some of it himself for Henry.)[102] Francis' acquiescence in this piracy formed part of the English complaints in Henry's pre-war defence of June 1543. Francis did halt these raids for a while, and this may explain the arrest of Barton in Dieppe.[103] Such restraint did not last; with Anglo-Scottish relations deteriorating, especially after the seizure of Scottish ships in September, the pirates were soon roving again.[104]

In late December 1543, a Scottish fleet sailing to Veere came across a small English vessel off the Norfolk coast. One of its number seized it, took it to Veere and tried to ransom it there. But the Scot fond himself arrested by the Governor of the town, an event the English tried unsuccessfully to blow out of all proportion. At first it was said that many Englishmen had been taken and that all of the Scots had been arrested, but Layton, the English agent at Brussels, soon divined that there was only one English captain, a 'poor knave' so terrified by the incident that he refused to return to Veere to claim his £30 or £40, and that only one Scottish captain, ship and crew had been arrested. However, other Scots bringing more English prizes were similarly treated and soon many were locked up; by March their number was said to be 150.[105]

The night of 11 March transformed what hitherto had been a minor complication. Many of the imprisoned Scots were, complained Mary, but 'rabblement' with neither baggage nor funds and Layton reckoned they cost her forty guilders a day to feed. The Regent sensibly ordered their release. However, resentment amongst the Scots at Veere ran deep and thirty of them enlisted the aid of other Scots just arrived to protest. In harbour at the time was the *James*, owned by Henry Anderson, a leading merchant of Newcastle. The *James* was a full 100 tons and freshly loaded with cargo worth £2300. In the dark of night, the freed Scots and their comrades stormed the vessel. They slipped the ship out of harbour; the adventurers kindly dropped their English captives off the Yorkshire coast, then apparently made for Aberdeen where they disposed of the goods.

The uproar over this escapade was considerable. The rest of the freed Scots were quickly re-incarcerated, the English pressed for the arrest of all Scots in the Low

---

101 *LP,* xviii (1), nos. 44, 36, 153, 851; (2), nos. 529–30.
102 *LP,* xviii (1), nos. 28, 63, 104, 108, 117, 124, 140, 153.
103 *Ibid.,* nos. 44, 46, 62, 91 (2) (3), 106, 113, 754; Brussels, Etat et Audience, 405a.
104 *LP,* xviii (2), no. 476.
105 *LP,* xix (1), nos. 7, 16, 20, 31, 69, 105, 284.

Countries and the Lord of Veere came in for severe censure; even his resignation as Admiral was suggested. More Scots in the country were arrested and their goods impounded to indemnify the English.[106] It thus began to seem that there was no point in trying to protect the Scottish Staple as most of its members were locked up.

The incident had a profound effect on the common enemies issue. When Charles finally did declare against the Scots, he stated that the fracas at Veere was the major cause. The Scots may have been allied with France and thus with the Turk, but foremost was the fact, inserted by Charles himself, that the Scots,

> coming on colour of trading, have pillaged English ships at sea and brought them prisoners into the Emperor's havens and have there seized English merchandise, contrary both to the treaties with Scotland and to the Treaty of close and perpetual alliance which the Emperor has with the King of England.[107]

As late as 12 April, Chapuys had been trying to avoid the issue of a formal declaration, contending that the arrest of the Scots after the Veere incident was sufficient as Scots would hardly now dare to traffic in the Low Countries. Henry would not be put off; on the 14th he delivered the form of the declaration he wished. Mary found much wrong with the draft and wrote Charles to ask his opinion. The Emperor, however, had finally made up his mind. Although he had resisted a unilateral declaration as late as 5 March, he informed Wotton on 21 April that he would write to Mary to treat all Scots as enemies. On 7 May his proclamation was issued.[108]

The final wording was different from Henry's (despite an earlier agreement to adopt the English form). Scottish invasions of England were ignored and primary emphasis was laid on the seizure of English ships. A marginal note in a draft explained the change: 'This is to guard honesty towards the Scots and demonstrate that the treaties with them are not broken without sufficient cause'. All Scots were 'forbidden to haunt the Emperor's dominions, notably the Low Countries', their goods there were to be confiscated, any Scots captured at sea would be just prizes and all trade with Scotland would cease. The proclamation was hastily sent to England. Mary was concerned about English reaction to the changes, but Chapuys declared Henry 'greatly satisfied' and particularly applauded the speedy despatch, 'as any further delay might have greatly prejudiced affairs'.[109]

Thus Charles resolved the question of war with Scotland. His decision demonstrates his almost desperate desire for English aid and Henry's penchant for skilful bluff. Charles believed he needed massive English assistance in the coming months, was concerned that the English might still back out and no longer had a credible Danish counter. With most of the Scots in the Low Countries arrested and trade effectively at a halt, there was little to restrain him. Yet it is clear the move was a blunder for two reasons. In the first place, the English alliance was to help him for

106 Rooseboom, *Scottish Staple*, 65–7; *LP*, xix (1), nos. 262, 311; 224, 311.
107 *LP*, xix (1), no. 480. Scots were also to see this as the main cause of the war. See the comment of Lesley, the only historian to mention it. Dalrymple, *Historie*, ii, 287.
108 *LP*, xix (1), nos. 166, 318, 330, 381, 392.
109 *LP*, xix (1), nos. 330 (2), 482, 519.

only three and a half months, from Henry's entry into France in force in late June until Charles's peace with Francis on 18 September. In the second place, the declaration resulted in six years of intermittent warfare with Scotland which would cost the Low Countries dearly.

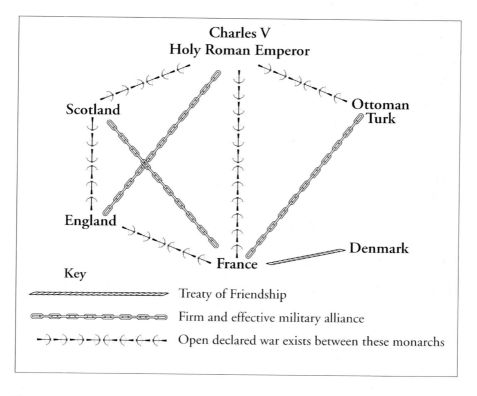

Fig. 7.2. 7 May 1544. Henry VIII finally forced Charles V to declare war on the Scots, and thus all trade between the Low Countries and Scotland ceased. Scottish merchants found themselves incarcerated and their goods confiscated. Export records for 1544-45 show a dramatic decline in goods leaving Scotland. But the war also proved a great opportunity for Scots with ships which could be armed and used to attack Dutch vessels, and this they did with great zeal. Against such maritime guerrilla warfare, the mightiest emperor in Europe was powerless, and hostilities would continue down to 1551.

CHAPTER EIGHT

The Six-Year War with Charles V

THE DUTCH WAR

On 14 April 1559,[1] there was communicated to Queen Elizabeth I's newly installed Privy Council a detailed (seven pages in Latin) memorandum from her ex brother-in-law, Philip II, then in the Low Countries directing the concluding phases of the war against France which had broken out in 1557 and which he had clearly won. When the memorandum was originally drafted, the Treaty of Cateau-Cambrésis still had not been definitively ratified; this happened on 2 April. The mistimings are intriguing, but given sixteenth-century communications, hardly unique.

In the treaty, the English had lost Calais (although initially for only eight years). That Mary Tudor had been devastated by the French capture of England's remaining bulwark and entrepôt on the Continent is widely known. The most spectacular evidence for this was not engravings upon her heart, but money from her Treasury. No sooner had the thunderclap of this disaster been assimilated by her and her advisers than they embarked upon the largest single construction programme in England's sixteenth century: the utter refashioning of the fortifications of Berwick-upon-Tweed. Calais' surrender was concluded on 7 January 1558. On 14 January, Sir Richard Lee was appointed Chief Surveyor for the works at Berwick and advanced the first tranche of payments (initially to buy up property to be demolished) which would ultimately (1570) total £128, 648; 'by a very long way the costliest single work of Queen Elizabeth's reign'.[2]

The reason of course was the threat presented by a French army in Scotland whilst a war was still technically in progress. Elizabeth (very concerned about the new French fortification at Eyemouth) clearly approached Philip earlier, asking that as she was fighting France as part of the Anglo-Habsburg coalition, should not he declare war against the Scots, with whom she also was at war? Philip said no; his father had done that for Henry VIII in 1544 and had lost heavily. Given their 'notorious poverty', although the Scots were 'frequently defeated' during 1544–50, they 'gained upon the whole infinitely more than they lost'. He reminded her in particular that the Dutch 'great fishery' consisted of herring in the North Sea and was critical to the prosperity of Holland, Zealand, Flanders and Friesland. War with Scotland would see that commerce 'annihilated'.

It is an interesting echo from the Rough Wooings of Henry VIII. The Emperor's declaration against the Scots in 1544 may have been something of a surprise to Arran's

---

1 *CSP For.,* 1558–59, no. 528.
2 Colvin, *King's Works,* iv, 664.

government, which had tried to avoid annoying Charles. Perhaps prompted by Sadler's threats on leaving Edinburgh that war with Flanders would ensue, Arran wrote Charles on 9 November 1543 asking for continued protection of Scottish traders despite Scotland's war with England. To Maximilian Bourgogne, Lord of Veere, he stated that because Henry 'boasts that, by a new treaty he has made with the Emperor, the enemy of the one is to be held enemy to the other', Scots were afraid of 'unfriendly' treatment there.[3]

Nonetheless, the government tried to observe sensible restraint. When in March John Barton turned up in Scotland with an English prize taken at Veere (probably one different from that taken on the 11th), the government acted fairly swiftly to prevent the sale of the goods on board, as 'considering thar is pece standard betwuix this realm and the empriours, the taking . . . may be occasion of the rupture of the pece, geif sche be fund na lauchfull prise'.[4] On 22 March, the day after the arrest of Barton's prize, Arran reappointed John Moffat as conservator of the Scottish privileges in Flanders. Moffat had long been in the Low Countries and was active and respected. Arran had replaced him very early in his regency by one of his Protestant supporters, James Henrisoun, and now obviously thought better of it. As late as July 1544, licences to trade in Scotland were being given to merchants resident in the Low Countries.[5]

When sure word came of the seizure of the Scots in Veere, both government and merchants were alarmed; Adam Otterburn, provost of Edinburgh, wrote the Queen Dowager, 'the merchandis of Dunde and this toune hes thocht rycht hevy that thair nychtbouris ar lyand in presoun in flandris and ar abill to peris and de in presoun without help'.[6]

Plans were afoot as early as 5 April to send to Flanders Sir Walter Lindsay, preceptor of Torphichen and chief of the order of St John of Jerusalem (Otterburn protested that the ambassador must be 'the said lord or sum uther grete man' and not just a herald, as 'our errandis will nocht be perfitely endit and sped be ane herald'). The embassy was thus expanded on 30 April to include lord St John and Sir David Lindsay, Lyon King of Arms. Sir Walter was to attempt a settlement of the Veere incident with Mary and the Lord of Veere; Sir David was to return to Charles himself the order of the Golden Fleece which had been bestowed upon James V in 1532.[7]

At the same time as this embassy was readied, so were others to the Papacy and to Denmark, and the government was obviously hoping to approach all interested foreign powers, now that an English invasion was imminent. However, it is clear that the ambassadors to Charles did not depart in May; doubtless the English fleet moving up the east coast and the subsequent attack on Edinburgh caused them to scatter.[8] At first the Scots apparently did little to retaliate against the Emperor, but on 14 November 1544 a merchant of Veere lost all of his goods in Scotland, 'throw oppin

3 *LP*, xviii (2), nos. 368–98; and see *Brosse Missions*, 42.
4 *TA*, viii, 275; *ADCP*, 547–8.
5 *RSS*, iii, nos. 673, 858.
6 *Mary of Lorraine Corresp.*, 92–93.
7 *LP*, xix (1), nos. 294, 434–6; *TA*, viii, 278, 283.
8 *TA*, viii, 285, 319.

proclamation of weris maid betuix the inhabitaris of Flanderis and the liegis of this realme, and taking of Scottismennis gudis in Flanderis'.[9]

Soon 'Duchemen' were complaining of the 'spoiliatioun' of their goods, and letters of marque were issued, such as that to *le Petit Lyon*, 'pour faire nuisance et porter dommaige a lempreur et ses subgeitz lors comme a present notrez enemys [in order to annoy and damage the Emperor and his subjects since they are now our enemies]'.[10] If the Scots were at first reluctant to press the war in which they found themselves, similar aversion was displayed by the government of the Low Countries. Whilst elaborate measures were taken to provide compensation for Englishmen who had their ships taken by Scots in Veere, moves were also afoot for the freeing of the merchants. Through the efforts of Moffat, 95 Scots were allowed to leave on 6 August, but 'ung bon et competent nombre des plus riches merchans' were still held. Moffat and three colleagues arranged with the Council of Veere to become cautioners for the rest and on 19 August 67 more left with safe-conducts from the Governor; by the end of 1544 all the prisoners were released. Their goods, however, stayed. Commercial intercourse between the two countries remained severely ruptured. During the period 10 February to 10 August 1544 only one ship sailed to Scotland, in contrast to the 115 of the previous period when peace prevailed. During the subsequent six months there were none.[11]

There was, however, one hopeful event. On 18 September 1544, Charles and Francis signed the Treaty of Crepi and the peace thereby created was to last for seven years. The Low Countries emerged from two years of grave threat, high taxes and interruption of trade. The Baltic had opened up the year before with the Treaty of Speyer; now the route to Spain was also free. At the time, both the Scots and the Flemish thought that an end to their war would only be a matter of time. However, it would not be until early 1551 that normal trade was fully restored.

THE TREATY OF CREPI, 18 SEPTEMBER 1544

There is a great temptation to see the Anglo-Scottish war as extending without interruption from late 1543 (if not 1542) until April 1550. By May 1544, Scotland was at war not only with the English but with the Emperor, and the war did not end until the Treaty of Boulogne on 24 March 1550 with the one and the Treaty of Binche on 15 December 1550 with the other (ratification of which would not happen until the following January). There was, however, a fairly long lull in serious warfare from the Autumn of 1545 until September 1547. During this period efforts of a sort were made to end the conflict. On the one hand there was an attempt to utilise the Franco-Imperial peace and to end the Scottish exclusion from the Low Countries. On the other hand, the French did what they could to end the Anglo-Scottish war when they ended the Anglo-French one. These moves towards peace do not fall into a neat pattern. The best way to approach them is to take the Imperial moves first, then the English.

---

9 *RSS*, iii, no. 965.
10 *ADCP*, 539; *RPC*, i, 10.
11 Rooseboom, *Scottish Staple*, 66–67. There is also evidence in the Veere Papers relating to the Scottish Staple (in possession of Rijksarchief in Zeeland, Middelburg) that Scots were still suing for return of their goods in the 1550s. *Handel met Engeland*, nos. 723, 725.

The Treaty of Crepi of 18 September 1544 had several consequences, such as the distinct worsening of Anglo-Imperial relations which was to continue virtually until the accession of Mary Tudor.[12] It also gave rise to a series of interviews in October and November 1544 between the French and English over possible comprehension of the King of England.[13] But Henry refused to surrender Boulogne and Francis would not pay high enough compensation. Moreover Francis would not renounce the Scots or conclude peace without their inclusion.

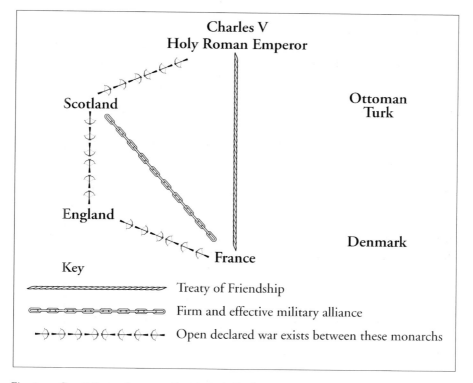

Fig. 8.1.   On 18 September 1544, Francis and Charles came to terms in the Treaty of Crepi (or Crépy-en-Laonnois, as it is now spelt), and the Habsburg-Valois war thus ended until 1552. Suleyman (whose fleet had wintered for eight months in Toulon in 1543-44, thus enabling it to raid up the Italian coast to Nice in 1543 and then back along to Naples in 1544) was furious. He threatened to impale the French ambassador publicly for Francis' sell-out. But he soon ended his Hungarian war. Scotland was not included in this peace, however, and hostilities thus continued between them and Dutch traders in the North Sea, much to the profit of the Scots.

12 See Scarisbrick, *Henry VIII*, 450–56, 458–70 for treatment of this period. Evidence of the strained relations is profuse, but a good idea can be gathered from *LP*, xix (2), nos. 365, 369, 382, 506, 577, 605, 662 and especially 517.
13 *LP*, xix (2), nos. 392, 456, 546, 654 (3).

One further matter not resolved at Crepi was the Low Countries-Scottish war. The French negotiators had obviously pressed for their comprehension in the general peace but Granvelle refused. Imperial stubbornness perhaps has a twofold explanation: while Scottish depredations on Low Countries shipping had been serious enough to make some sort of compensation necessary, Charles was also concerned about Henry's reactions to his sudden exit from the war and felt he had to maintain hostilities with Scotland. Granvelle was to say several months later that Imperial failure to comprehend Henry should be set beside French failure to comprehend the Scots. Certainly Charles knew that in any future Franco-Imperial war, English aid might again be most useful. Thus he was anxious to save as much as possible from the volte face of Crepi. Given the low level of Scottish attacks during the period May to September 1544, this second explanation seems the more plausible.

If Henry was given to understand that the Scots had not been included, the French had a slightly different rendering. This emerged during the Crepi negotiations when Granvelle conceded that whilst no mention of the Scots could be written into the public treaty, he was himself prepared to give them 'verbal comprehension'. What this meant in practice was to occupy French and Scottish diplomats for some time. For their part, the Scots were certainly of the opinion that they had been included, and even Flemish merchants thought that the war had ended. In December 1544 Andrew Mowbray, an Edinburgh burgess, was sent to Antwerp to settle some of the grievances of Scots expelled in March. Whilst there he was a guest of the Lord of Veere, a circumstance which did not prevent commissioners from Middelburg calling upon him to enquire whether the Scots would consider moving the Staple back to their port. Predictably they were put off but not for six months. Bruges also made a bid for the Staple and even sent commissioners to Scotland.[14]

Wrangling over the Staple, although indicative of a return to peacetime habits, was not what the Scottish government looked for from Crepi. As early as 19 November, Arran sent Charles a moderately long introduction to David Paniter, who had been sent to France in April. Before Arran's assumption of the governorship Painter had been a relatively obscure churchman, commendator of the abbey of St Mary's Isle. On 20 January 1543 he was appointed secretary to the Governor and keeper of the Queen's signets and he soon found himself in constant attendance upon Arran, a member of parliament and of the Privy Council.[15] He had arrived in France by 22 April 1544 when he reported, 'We are weill tane with as ony men can be', but then dropped from sight. He had with him 500 francs given him in March and a letter of protection; in December 1544, he received a further 500 francs for 'the tyme of his being in France and Flanders', but there is no record of his going to Flanders in 1544 or of his doing much in France.[16]

The letter which Arran drafted in November introducing Paniter was a model of

---

14 Rooseboom, *Scottish Staple*, 67; *LP*, xviii (1), no. 825; *Handel met Engeland*, i, nos. 731, 759.

15 *RSS*, iii, no. 42; *LP*, xviii (1), nos. 456, 671, 747, 769, 966; (2), nos. 14, 127–28, 132; *APS*, ii, 408, 415, 427.

16 *Mary of Lorraine Corresp.*, 74–75; *RSS*, iii, no. 678; *LP*, xix (2), no. 709 (2); *TA*, viii, 278, 283, 335.

its kind. James V, it reminded Charles, had in 1531 ratified the renewal (1529) of the ancient league with Burgundy not so much for the sake of trade as out of love of the Emperor's virtues; the Scots protested that for their part friendship continued, but 'timid merchants (on account of the injuries of certain private persons) fear that it has been tacitly dropped'. Thus the young Queen was sending Paniter either to renew the 1531 pact or to conclude a new one to enter the 'fellowship in the league' between Charles and Francis. The accompanying letter to Mary of Hungary made similar points and asked that the magistrates of the Low Countries act with expedition to settle the private injuries.[17] On 29 November another letter was penned to Charles concerning the return of James's Golden Fleece (apparently forgotten about shortly before). This would have been returned sooner, but the Scots had not known the Emperor's whereabouts. On 1 January 1545 yet another letter was penned introducing Paniter to Charles.[18]

The Scots had heard of the Treaty of Crepi almost as soon as the ink was dry on it. The captain of the Scottish archers, who later led the French force to Scotland in 1545, wrote to Mary of Guise on 4 October telling her the good news, 'que je pence ouvraige plus de Dieu que des hommes [which work I think was more due to God than to men]', and which he supposed she would have heard already.[19] This doubtless spurred the government to revitalise the embassy to the Low Countries. Certainly there was some pressure to do so from merchants: a tax agreed by the burghs in March to cover the cost of the mission was being collected and forwarded to Arran in December.[20] Meanwhile, Francis had been expounding to Charles the case for Scotland's retrospective inclusion in the treaty. The French ambassadors at Brussels had obviously raised the point with several members of the Council of the Low Countries and had been put off. Hence on 9 December Francis instructed le sieur de Morette and the same Mesnage who had been in Scotland the previous year to remonstrate with the Emperor and with Granvelle. Mesnage was to argue that the Scots had been allies of France for 500 years, that the Emperor had said at the time of Crepi that the matter could be negotiated later, that the Scots were pressing Francis and that Francis could not ignore this just demand

> sans blesser son honneur, rompre son serment et perdre sa reputation devant toutes les nations du monde, et oultre als faire dommaige et perte irreparable a son royaume, chose qu'il ne vouldroit faire pour tous les biens de la terre [without wounding his honour, breaking his solemn pledge and losing his reputation before all the nations of the world and moreover causing damage and

---

17 *LP*, xix (2), nos. 637, 639. But see NAS, SP 1 Caprington Mun., fos. 237–239 which may be the letter referred to in *LP*, xix (2), no. 638; there the ambassador is named as Sir Walter Lindsay.

18 *LP*, xix (2), no. 679. The herald was almost certainly Alexander Guthrie, Snowdon Herald; if so it was a rare break for him from the tedium of his normal duties in Scotland (*TA*, viii, 295, 314, 477–8, 489 and see especially 472). He received £55 to take the 'Empriouris collar to my lord Secretar in France' (*ibid.*, 340). *LP*, xx (1), no. 6.

19 *Balcarres Papers*, i, 107–9.

20 *Abdn. Counc*, i, 204; *ADCP*, 615; *TA*, viii, 335.

irreparable loss to his kingdom, something he would not wish to do for all the goods on earth].[21]

On 21 January 1545 Mesnage addressed a long memorandum to Granvelle arguing for Scottish comprehension. The treaties of Madrid (1526) and Cambrai (1529) had been confirmed in the text of the Treaty of Crepi and were still in effect: Scotland had been included in both, and so should be included in Crepi. The object of the pact was 'la generale pacification de la Republique chrestienne'; why, then, was Scotland excluded, especially when the comprehension had been 'asses expressement et suffisaument' agreed by the negotiators, but not written down 'pour quelque peu de jours'? Moreover, could not Francis nominate any prince to be included, as the treaty allowed, or a servant or subject or ally? Charles had comprehended all 'quilz soient obeyssans a lemperaur'; why could not Francis include his allies? The real issue was Charles's demands for compensation. Mesnage made a subtle distinction here: if a belligerent lost 'immeubles [real property, like land]', then a claim for compensation was in order, but if only 'meubles' had been lost, there was no case. Shipping and their cargoes were 'meubles'.[22] The Emperor's reply a week later was quite placatory. He agreed that 'les subjects d'icelle ne feront aulcunnement la guerre aveques le royaume descosse [the subjects here [of the Low Countries] have no wish to go to war with the kingdom of Scotland]', and for that reason he 'donnera par sa bouche a nous deux sa parolle [he would give his word by his own mouth to us two]'. But he asked Francis not to demand 'aultre escripture et publication pour le present [any written statement or publication for the present]', as the English were closely pressing him not to give aid against the French. The French ambassadors then had an interview with Granvelle on 8 February and insisted on a formal declaration from Charles on the matter. Granvelle protested that they should treat Charles's 'seule parelle comme la plus solennel escripture [sole word as the most solemn writing]' and elaborated the Emperor's difficulties with England: the King of England must not be able 'imputer s'il ayt rompu le contract dentre eulx [to impute that he had broken the treaty between them]'.[23]

Meanwhile Paniter, though in France, apparently had not been informed either of the details of the negotiations in Brussels or of the non-inclusion of the Scots in Crepi. He did deliver to Francis what was to become the standard Scottish declaration to the French: without aid in men and money the kingdom would have no recourse but to come to terms with England. This, he archly reminded them, would strengthen Henry's hold on Boulogne, and it is possible that by the time Paniter left the French court early in February 1545, Francis had decided to send Lorges de Montgomery's force to Scotland in May.[24] Once he left the court, Paniter made for the Imperial frontier with a train of nine servants. On 26 February he wrote to Mesnage and Morette to thank them for preparing his way (they had sent him

21 BN, MS fr., 17,889, fos. 2–3.
22 BN, MS fr., 17,888, fo. 403.
23 BN, MS fr., 17,889, fos. 59, 61; and see Weiss, *Granvelle*, iii, 59.
24 *LP*, xix (1), no. 457.

credence for one of his servants to race ahead to Brussels), and in a strangely reflective mood ('messuers, je pense que considerez bien quelle est la charge dung ambassadeur [Gentlemen, I am thinking hard just what is the duty of an ambassador]') he told them his charge:

> de demander a lempereur lettres ratifficatoires de la comprehension du royaulme descosse faite et accorde en le traicte dernier, ou bein, si tel est le desire de lempereur, de contracter et traicter de nouveau par telles conditions que la derniere paix fut traictee [to demand of the Emperor letters which ratify the comprehension of the kingdom of Scotland made and agreed in the last treaty, or else, if it is the desire of the Emperor, to contract a new on the same conditions as the last treaty].

He could only hope that the Emperor did not wish ill towards his country which had done nothing which 'donne occasion de guerre come jespere, aidant Dieu, luy faire entendtre [gave occasion of war, which I hope, with God's help, to make him understand]'.[25] Four days later he wrote Charles, saying he had come 'jusques aux limites de voz pais' (he was at Peronne) and asking for safe conduct to Brussels to treat of 'le bien publique, tant de voz subjectz comme ceulx descosse [the public wellbeing of your subjects as well as those of Scotland]'.[26] He apparently took this missive as the occasion of sending Alexander Guthrie, Snowdon Herald, to return James's Golden Fleece.

Guthrie's appearance in Brussels did not please the numerous English there.[27] In reply to their remonstrances about the possible arrival of a Scottish ambassador, Granvelle was transparently evasive: first he said that none was needed as the French did all their negotiating, then that if one came Charles would refuse him audience out of respect for Henry. But the English were not fooled. Paniter had entered the country without difficulty, the Emperor was feigning illness and the Queen Dowager had gone hawking suspiciously near Paniter's route. By late February the Privy Council in London was distinctly annoyed, and not without reasons; by early March the Scottish ambassador had taken up residence in Brussels, albeit in not particularly splendid apartments.[28] Close on his heels came detailed, if somewhat exaggerated, reports of the dramatic Scottish success at Ancrum Moor.[29]

The English had cause to be alarmed by the news from Scotland, for it strengthened Paniter's position. The Queen Dowager of Hungary roundly informed them that the Low Countries had no quarrel whatsoever with the Scots and asked what they thought she should do. Paget temporised, saying firstly that he had no instructions to cover this eventuality, then that she tell the Scots to come to peace with the Emperor by coming to peace with Henry. Mary dumbfounded Paget by lighting on his seeming desire for peace and suggested that the negotiations start

25 BN, MS fr. 17,889, fo. 42.
26 Brussels, Etat et Audience, 1673/4/c.
27 *LP*, xx (1), no. 84. Their worry was based on the rumour of a Habsburg marriage for Mary; see *ibid.*, nos. 571, 630, 652, 689, 696, 850.
28 *LP*, xx (1), nos. 229, 231, 237 and of 310.
29 Brussels, Etat et Audience, 1673/4.a; *LP*, xx, nos. 332, 334, 344, 367. Word soon reached Paris and Venice also (*ibid.*, nos. 682, 797, 501).

there and then: the Emperor would be pleased to mediate. Paget could only ask for time to consider. He was in no better mood when a member of the Low Countries Privy Council went to his apartments to suggest that surely just one meeting with this Scottish ambassador would not matter.[30] Paget's reports of these events to the Privy Council were also requests for guidance. The reply, sent on 16 March, was both prosaic and ingenious. Firstly, Paget was to tell the Emperor to send the Scots away unless they undertook to reconcile themselves to Henry. If Charles demurred, Paget was to ask if the Emperor realised that by allowing the Scots to make peace he was aiding the Turk. Paget was to add that English losses at Ancrum Moor 'were very small and less than the Scots'.[31]

THE 'AGREEMENTS' OF ANTWERP AND OF EDINBURGH

Events, however, were outstripping the ingenuity of both the Privy Council and Paget. There can be little doubt that Mary of Hungary was sincere when she told Chapuys, on 9 March 1544, of the 'notorious' damage which would be caused by war between Scotland and the Low Countries. Veere and many other ports had lost considerable trade over the previous nine months, the fishing fleets into the North Sea had been disrupted and sailings were falling off. Henry's refusal to declare against Christian of Denmark had been unpopular, at least with members of Mary's Council who were aware – it was a point made several times in 1544 – that they could not rule their subjects in the arbitrary way that Henry treated his. Thus, as Paget further pressed the Imperialists, he was increasingly put off.[32] Paniter's persistence was rewarded, and probably around 23 March he had his first audience with the Queen Dowager and some members of her Council.

It was then Paniter's turn to be disconcerted by what he was told: Scotland had not been comprehended at Crepi and no new treaty could be considered. The pill was sweetened when he learned that Charles was prepared to agree to an arrangement by which trade might be regulated. On 1 April Granvelle was instructed to encourage him to consider a scheme whereby merchants carrying safe-conducts from the other country's government would be protected from pirates. Mary also urged this solution.[33] As ambassadors do in moments of crisis, Paniter complained of his allies' betrayal and asked for new instructions. His request arrived in Scotland on 22 April and the government rapidly drew up new letters for him on the 29th and 30th.[34] But matters had moved even more swiftly, for on 28 April 'the Agreement of Antwerp' had been concluded. Charles maintained that he could not comprehend the Scots in Crepi or renew the Burgundian alliance of 1529, but he declared he 'entend en aucune maniere envahir ledict Royaulme d'Escosse [intended in no manner to invade the said Kingdom of Scotland]' or harm the subjects thereof.[35] The agreement then

30 LP, xx, nos. 329, 334.
31 Ibid., no. 367.
32 LP, xx, nos. 372, 406, 452, 495, 545.
33 Ibid., nos. 425, 473, 503.
34 Ibid., nos. 611, 617, and of 547, 590; TA, viii, 365–66.
35 Numerous copies were made; see Rijksarchief in Middelburg, Copulaet, ix, fos. 378–80.

detailed that merchants of the Low Countries carrying safe-conducts under the Great Seal of Scotland could trade freely in Scotland whilst Scots with Scottish safe-conducts could trade in Flanders. Possession of such safe-conducts would protect merchants at sea from the men-of-war of either. If ships were taken, fair restitution would be made. The final two conditions (the first one being somewhat odd) stated:

> But the subjects of either side having such letters of attestation shall not enter the ports of the other unless for stress of weather, and even then shall not land anything, without licence from the officer of the port and shall leave with the first favourable wind.

> Subjects who have the safe-conducts above mentioned may sue for things wrongly taken from them before the declaration of the war, save those of Scotland shall not claim what was employed to recompense the English for the ship taken at Veere; but they may take action for the surplus.[36]

The English, smarting from the defeat at Ancrum and worried over the widely publicised French expedition to Scotland, were obviously disturbed at Paniter's activities, although it is doubtful that they knew about the agreement.[37] However, by July 1545 the Scots most certainly did. On his return home, Guthrie was directed to visit all the major ports on the east coast from Leith to Banff and Inverness,

> chargeing that na schippis depart furth of thai porttis towart Flandris without salf conductis and to cum to my lord thesaurar and resave the samyn.[38]

Even before Guthrie's departure, Paniter acted on the agreement. The Scottish goods seized in May 1544 were set against the tally of Scottish depredations; on 12 May he asked for 'le doubles des Inventoires et comptes quilz on faict sur le bien des navires escossious qui furent arrestees lannee passee', in addition to 'La rest des sauf-conduictz' and 40 more of them. Paniter must have felt pleased with his labours. He had reopened trade with the Low Countries, where the Scots were soon to be found in Antwerp, Middelburg, Veere, Ostend, Bruges and elsewhere, and the government was again able to purchase the munitions necessary for war. How long he remained in the Low Countries after May is not clear[39] but he was back in Linlithgow by 19 December 1545 when he delivered to the clerk of the privy Council

---

36 The quote is from *LP*, xx (1), no. 589; Rooseboom, *Scottish Staple*, gives the full version, appendix, no. 58.

37 For evidence of their concern and ignorance, see *LP*, xx (1), nos. 495, 544–5, 590, 652, 801. Paget was to claim no knowledge of it as late as that December, but he may well have been dissembling (*LP*, xx (2), no. 1024). Word of it reached France by late June for certain (*LP*, xx (1), no. 1069).

38 *TA*, viii, 394.

39 Brussels, Etat et Audience, 1673/4/c. Mary informed Granvelle that Paniter was leaving on 12 May (Weiss, *Granvelle*, iii, 143) but on 30 August sent him a memorandum and a letter to Arran of commendation for the secretary's work. These may have been forwarded to him in France (Brussels, Etat et Audience, 1673/4/c). See also *LP*, xxi (1), no. 911. There is an interesting account of his mission in *LP*, xxi (1), no. 1371.

the trete maid betwix the Emperor and the said Maister Dauid as ambassadtour
for the tyme for the realme of Scotland, tuiching the frequenting and hanting of
merchandis to Flandris and sik lik the Emperouris subject is to this realme, to be
kepit in the realme as use is.[40]

Trade between the two countries was regularised, but only within certain limits.
During the year since the start of the war, the Scots had acquired a taste for the fruits
of piracy and the system arranged by Paniter was more easily put on paper than into
practice. To make privateers selective was as difficult in 1545 as it was to prove in
1572.[41] Scots could still attack English shipping, and it is obvious that in the period
after July 1545 they were not over-careful if a ship happened to be from any of the
Low Countries' havens. True, piracy did diminish for a while in 1545. For one thing
Francis barred the Norman ports, though not the Breton ones; hence the Scots
increased their attacks on Iberian traders so much that by April 1546 Charles
instructed all Spanish ships for the Low Countries to sail in convoy.[42]

Low Countries trade in the North Sea and the Channel was only briefly immune.
On 6 and 7 December Mary of Hungary wrote to Paniter and Arran demanding the
return of the goods of an Antwerp merchant.[43] In May 1546 she sent a merchant of
Veere, of Scottish descent, David Magnus, with more safe-conducts to see if he could
arrange better protection. The English, however, captured him and held him in
Newcastle for six months.[44] By 28 June Mary was obviously exasperated and again
wrote to Arran and Paniter demanding an end to 'les grosse fouless, oppresions et
Injures' of the Scottish pirates and recompense to the Flemish fishermen. Officials at
all her ports were also instructed to inspect all incoming Scottish ships to ensure that
none carried goods stolen from her subjects.[45]

Another ground of complaint was that the Scottish courts were not awarding
speedy compensation, as required by the agreement. Suits could last for years.[46]
The complications were manifold: Flemish ships carrying English goods were
considered fair game by the Scots and ships taken before the agreement were also
considered just prizes.[47] Suits for compensation were dealt with initially by the
Admiralty Court at Edinburgh whose nominal head was the earl of Bothwell.
Bothwell, however, not only had a vested interest in the disposition of captured
goods but he also fitted out ships to raid the English and Flemish.[48] Small wonder

40 *RPC*, i, 18 (*LP*, xx (2), no. 1009). He apparently was delighted to be back home (*ibid.*, no.
    986).
41 See B. Dietz, 'Privateering in North West European Waters, 1568–1572' (unpublished Ph.D.
    dissertation, University of London, 1959). Trade between the two did increase after the
    agreement. See W.S. Unger, *Bronnen tot de Gechiedenis van Middelburg in den
    Landsheerlijken Tijd* (Rijks Geschiedkundige Publicatien no. 75, 1931), 498, 502, 531, 533, 538.
42 *LP*, xxi (1), nos. 515, 558, 782.
43 Brussels, Etat et Audience, 1673/4/c.
44 *LP*, xxi (1), nos. 911, 1034; (2), no. 14.
45 Brussels, Etat et Audience, 1673/4/a and b.
46 *ADCP*, 579, 592, 594, 607–10, 620.
47 Vienna, PA, 70, fo. 223.
48 *RPC*, i, 41; *LP*, xxi (2), no. 94; *ADCP*, 539–40, 550–2; *LP*, xx (2), no. 162.

that the Council of the Low Countries considered that most members of the Scottish government shared in the profits of their compatriots' piracy and thus wished to see the continuation of the war. Nonetheless the Queen Regent and the Emperor still preferred to deal with the Scottish authorities; the alternative was open war and this they hoped to avoid. Thus they maintained a lively interest, though one unilluminated by concrete information, in the Anglo-French negotiations which had begun at the end of the summer of 1545.

ANGLO-FRENCH NEGOTIATIONS:
THE TREATY OF CAMP, 7 JUNE 1546

Whilst the Scots and the Netherlanders attempted to resolve their conflict, the French and English did likewise, but only after a period of war. Francis, relieved from his war with Charles, determined to dislodge the English from Boulogne by force. His strategy was grandiose even by sixteenth-century standards. Boulogne would be closely invested and English aid cut off by a massive armada in the Channel. England itself would be invaded along the south coast, along the north-east coast and from Scotland. The attack was met with great resolution by the English. By the end of July the projected Franco-Scottish projected invasion of the North of England had accomplished little except to divert some English forces. By mid-August the duel in the Channel had ended with the French if anything defeated. In September their siege of Boulogne was raised. To all intents the war came to an end. Both princes were financially exhausted and thus turned to negotiations; these were to last until 7 June 1546 when the treaty, known to the French as the peace of Ardres and to the English as that of Camp, established formal peace between the two countries.

For a variety of reasons Charles V was anxious that England and France should come to terms. He thus offered to act as mediator between the combatants in March, in July and in August 1545.[49] By September he was successful and the Imperial diplomatic network was being used as a clearing house for the initial but hostile responses.[50] By November emissaries of the two princes were meeting at Bruges where Gardiner, Thirlby and Carne began discussions with Gilbert Bayard, sieur de Font, a secretary of state to Francis. Granvelle also intervened, but his motives were naturally suspect.[51] The Bruges interviews became less important when Paget, Tunstall and John Tregonwell went to Calais at the end of the month to establish contact with the French through the agency of German Protestants close to the French court. Of particular importance as mediators were Johann Sturm of Strasbourg, and Dr. Hans Bruno of Metz, an ambassador of the Protestant princes resident with Francis. Sturm and Bruno maintained a regular contact between the English commissioners and Claude, seigneur d'Annehaut, admiral of France, Pierre

---

49 *LP*, xx (2), nos. 406, 462, 1203; (2), nos. 149, 178, 180. For a Scottish reaction, see *Mary of Lorraine Corresp.*, 135–36.

50 *LP*, xx (2), nos. 276–7, 331, 376, 561, 632.

51 *Ibid.*, no. 773.

Remon, first president of the parlement of Romon and Guillaume Bochetel, secretary to Francis I.[52]

These negotiations, it is worth remembering, did not move quickly. From November 1545 to January 1546 all major issues were discussed and the participants' positions clearly laid out. Henry, angered by French intransigence, broke off discussions early in the New Year and in the Spring persuaded Charles publicly to renew the alliance in such terms that a French attack on either Calais or England would be cause for Imperial assistance. The fleet was put in readiness; Calais and Boulogne were reinforced. Francis began to come to terms. By 17 April direct but secret negotiations were again in progress at Ardres, just outside the Calais pale, and at Camp, just inside. On 7 June 1546 the final form of the treaty was accepted and formalised. England was to keep Boulogne for eight years after which the French had the right to repurchase if for two million crowns. Henry was to be paid 10,000 crowns whilst he lived; his successors to have pension perpetually.[53] Most of this was straightforward; however, the clause comprehending the Scots, which took up considerable time during the negotiations, was ambiguous. Perhaps the best way in which to expound this move towards an Anglo-Scottish peace is to examine how, and in what terms, the comprehension was agreed.

The Imperial ambassadors mentioned the possibility of Scottish comprehension very early in their preliminary discussions with the English in London. When Francis van der Delft (Charles's replacement for Chapuys)[54] and Cornelious Scepperus, sieur d'Ecke and a member of the Emperor's Council, broached the possibility of a peace they mentioned Francis' concern to include the Scots. Henry then cut them off, but a fortnight later he was at least prepared to enter into some sort of discussion.[55] Simultaneously Imperial ambassadors in France, Jean de St. Mauris (Granvelle's brother-in-law) and the sieur de Noirthoudt, tested the firmness of Francis' resolve. Francis' reply was unequivocal: in no circumstances would he allow the subjection of Scotland by the marriage of Mary to Edward.[56] The point was in turn made to Henry that there could be no peace without the comprehension. Henry retorted that Scotland in no way concerned the French and elaborated English arguments that the Scots had previously agreed to the marriage and that his treaty with them had precedence over the French one.[57]

This set the pattern of discussion for the next seven months. Although prepared to accept that England was concerned about Scotland, Francis was adamant that the Scots must be comprehended for their security and for his honour. If the French

---

52 These negotiations have been treated by Dr. D.L. Potter, 'Diplomacy in mid-sixteenth century: England and France, 1536–50' (unpublished D. Phil. dissertation, University of Cambridge, 1973).

53 *LP*, xxi (1), no. 1014. Scarisbrick, *Henry VIII*, 451–56, 458–64, and R.B. Wernham, *Before the Armada*, 162–63, differ in their renderings of the treaty.

54 Chapuys did not leave until May 1545, but van der Delft came in December 1544 and increasingly did much of the work.

55 *LP*, xx (2), nos. 149, 178, 180.

56 *Ibid.*, nos. 276–7.

57 *Ibid.*, no. 376 and cf no. 632.

position was simplicity itself, the English rejoinder was diffuse. They refused to discuss the matter; Scotland was no concern of the French; it had not been included in previous treaties with England and the Empire, and thus this sudden preoccupation with honour was misplaced. The stance altered: England was bound by its treaty to Charles of 11 February 1543 which stipulated that they could not comprehend the Scots without his consent. As he had refused comprehension at Crepi, he surely would not grant it now. Behind these different attitudes there was a fundamental resolve: the Scots would not be included unless they accepted the treaties of Greenwich.

All of these positions were elaborated during the first phase of serious discussions from 17 November to 3 January. On 27 November Paget simply refused to discuss Scottish inclusion in a proposed truce; he reiterated this veto in early January.[58] Nonetheless the Scots were talked of a great deal. Paget was of course acting under instructions and his brief of 4 December was simple if not naive. If the French made much of their obligations, he was to marvel at their earnestness. Surely what was being discussed was a final and complete resolution of all Anglo-French grievances to ensure perpetual peace, whereas inclusion of the Scots would certainly lead to future variance. He was to remind the French of their lapses in the past; had not the Scots been left out of Crepi? Did not the French ambassadors confide to the English during talks at Boulogne in December 1544 that they only desired good reasons to forget about the Scots? Had they not been satisfied when shown a certified copy of the Treaty of Greenwich which proved that the Scots then had abandoned them? If the French remained unmoved by these arguments, Paget was then to admit the Scots could be comprehended, but only if they agreed to the marriage treaty, allowed some minor alterations to it and delivered the queen.[59]

At first, the French intimated that there was some hope of an understanding. On 11 November Bayard confided to Gardiner at Bruges that while Francis had to have the Scots covered somehow, he was not going to be 'an enemy to England for their sake'. Whatever this vague statement meant, its predictable effect was to harden the English attitude, especially when Granvelle told them that French aid to the Scots after the peace would be grounds for Charles to declare war on Francis.[60] But the English were soon confronted by a much less amenable Bayard. By the end of December, Francis confessed that he had left the Scots out of the formal treaty with Charles, but excused his action with calculated mention of the 'private promise' from Granvelle. It was now the turn of the French to be ingenuous: Francis particularly could not leave them out this time as the more often he did so, the more his honour was touched. Paget helpfully supplied instances of French failures in the past to include the Scots, but such a line of argument was obviously going to be futile and for a while Paget and Henry discussed alternatives.[61] One idea of Henry's, conveyed to his secretary on 11 December, centred on the Emperor. Fastening on Granvelle's

58 *LP*, xx (2), no. 880; *LP*, xxi (2), nos. 12–13, 23.
59 *LP*, xx (2), nos. 798, 826.
60 *LP*, xx (2), nos. 775, 793; cf nos. 798 and 925.
61 *LP*, xx (2), nos. 1957, 1515.

aside to Gardiner, the King asked Paget to press the French to renounce the Scots because any aid given them after the peace would mean war with the Empire. Paget dutifully put the point to Bruno who brought back the French contention that there was a 'privy contract between them and the Emperor'. The English response was that events showed otherwise, 'the Scottes beying enemies to the Emperor and so used by hym and his subgettes and also they so used by the Scottes'. When Paniter had attempted to make peace after Crepi, 'he durst not enter the Emperors domenes without saveconduct' and, even when admitted, was not allowed into Charles's presence. The secretary soon recognised the basic weakness of this gambit: the war with Scotland was very unpopular in Flanders and the Council was known to desire its end; the point had been frequently made to him during his time in Brussels (February–May 1545) that war was continued only for Henry's sake. For the moment, then, this argument was dropped.[62]

During this period, the Protestant envoys, Bruno and Sturm, were quite active trying to arrange the peace, and for various reasons Paget took the two envoys into his confidence. They saw English concern over Scotland as an aggravating side issue and Sturm rebuked Paget for wanting both Boulogne and Scotland. The secretary retorted, 'These be Hanniballs persuasions to Scipio'. The Protestants proposed two possible resolutions of the matter; Henry could have possession of Mary Queen of Scots when she came of age, or she could be placed in an English Border fort commanded by a German of Henry's choice.[63]

All such attempts, however ingenious, fell on stony ground. The French delegates refused to acknowledge the Treaty of Greenwich and its provisions; their mandate was to include the Scots in the peace but not to bind their ally in respect of former pacts. The encounter of 1–3 January is a good illustration. In a last effort to keep the talks going, the Protestants suggested they might bring the French to compose if Henry at least agreed not to make war on the Scots during the truce then under discussion. Paget's public response was to insist upon the marriage; privately he undertook to prevent any invasion. He asked the Protestants to put it in such a way that the French might take his private word to reflect the thinking of his master. The French, however, refused to be drawn by such a ploy and by 6 January Paget had returned to Dover and the negotiations were broken off.[64]

However, the break did not last and negotiations recommenced. On 17 April Sir John Dudley, viscount Lisle, Paget and Hertford were given their commission and on 24 April talks began at Guines.[65] Again Scotland figured. At first the English tried, and failed, to exclude the topic, saying that the Scottish war with Charles prevented its discussion. Jean de Monluc, an experienced French ambassador who joined d'Annebaut, Remon and Bochetel for these new talks, pointed out that the Scots now freely traded in Flanders and that Charles agreed there was no war with them. As

---

62 *Ibid.*, nos. 793, 969, 1024, 1036, 1044, 1060.
63 *LP*, xx (2), nos. 856, 917, 925, 984, 1011, 1024. Scarisbrick, *Henry VIII*, 465–67, briefly discusses the Protestant missions.
64 *LP*, xxi (1), nos. 12–13. Note Paget's initial displeasure at this turn of events.
65 *LP*, xxi (1), nos. 572, 610, 715.

this implied possible Imperial consent to Scottish comprehension in Crepi, the English dropped this argument.[66]

Thus the matter came under direct discussion and within a short time precise proposals were being exchanged. The English line was that the Scots could be comprehended as in the last relevant treaty with France (that of 17 August 1515), i.e., that as long as they did not give any new occasion of war, they could be parties to the peace. They were to make compensation for damages on the Borders and would not invade England with a force of more than 300 horse. These uncontroversial terms were, however, conditional upon Mary's deliverance 'presentlie into our hands' and Scottish acceptance of Greenwich. If Mary's immediate delivery was impossible, then the Scots should deliver hostages for her delivery in 1552: any 'default of performance of convenants, to be taken for no comprehense'. All this was plainly unacceptable and the French refused to entertain any such explicit injunction.[67] They did however suggest two possible ways around the difficulty. One was a promise to induce the Scots to agree to the marriage if Henry still desired it when Mary came of age. The alternative was even vaguer, that the current treaty would not prejudice any capitulation or treaty which either party might claim to have with the Scots. The French saw their suggestions as reasonableness itself, but when Henry heard of these proposals on 9 May, he was enraged.[68]

The French were unmoved, however, and remained 'wilful'. On 15 May they again stated their conditions and apparently remained adamant; the article which the English accepted by 4 June, when the final draft of the treaty was prepared, was that proposed by the French a month before. Scotland was comprehended, 'sine prejudicio Tractatium quos alteruter Princeps habere practendit [without prejudice to any treaties which either prince may have pacted]', with the specification, 'contra quos Scotos serinissimus Angliae Rex Bellum gerere aut movere non poterit, nisi nova occasione data [against the Scots the serene King of England shall not move any war without new occasion]'. 'Nova occasione' was defined as in the Treaty of 15 April 1515 with the single alteration that the French now had thirty days to notify the Scots of the terms of comprehension instead of the previous fifteen.[69] Thus was Scotland brought on 7 June 1546 to peace with England.

Henry had kept a very close eye on the negotiations, and in other areas (such as the precise limits of the pale around Boulogne) had been fastidious. Why, then, did he permit comprehension of the Scots in terms, however ambiguous, which in no way met his original instructions? No explanation emerges from the correspondence between 9 May and 4 June; nor can any precise picture of his plans regarding Scotland be deduced from his actions during the months which remained to him. Henry simply may have become bored with Scotland. Though he was to help the holders of St. Andrews Castle, he mounted no new attacks. Rumours of preparations remained current in the summer and autumn of 1546 and Henry was to rail at

66 *LP*, xxi (1), nos. 723, 733, 749.
67 *Ibid.*, no. 610.
68 *Ibid.*, nos. 763, 775.
69 *LP*, xxi (1), nos. 841, 994, 1014; *Foedera*, xv, 97–98.

Scottish ambassadors in London in December, but he did little else and neither the French nor the Scots seemed worried. The King of course was not well and it may have been that he was once again absorbed by fears of a Catholic attack led by the Emperor. Thus, perhaps, he did not mind how the Scots were comprehended and he may have felt that the ambiguities of the clause were such that he could at any time exploit them.

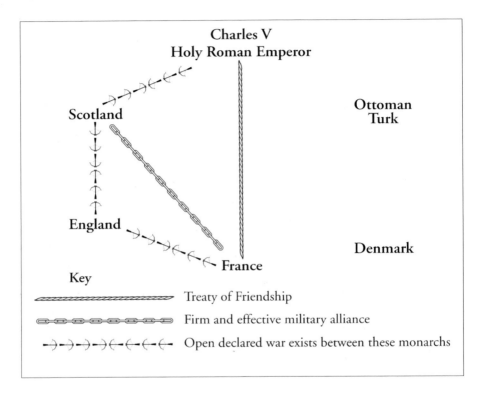

Fig. 8.2.   On 7 June Henry VIII and Francis I agreed the Treaty of Ardres or Camp in which Scotland was 'comprehended' as an ally of Francis. Henry VIII's 'Rough Wooing' was thus ended. Once again, the Scots were not comprehended over their war with Charles V, but Henry VIII did allow them to be included in this general peace amongst the Princes of Christendom. Although neither he nor Edward VI formally ratified the comprehension, it was observed until September 1547.

The ambiguities could also be exploited by the French. The clause may not have been as airtight as either Francis or the Scots would have liked but it was a considerable improvement on Crepi, left it open for France to aid Scotland in the future and was much more than the English had said they would contemplate. During 1543–46, the French had sought to insure that Scottish usefulness against England was not diminished by the unique opportunity of Mary's eligibility. By and large this was achieved. Even if the comprehension did not fully protect the Scots, at least it did not aid the English. This said, Francis then served his allies rather well. The Scots, it must be said, did not think so at first.

SCOTTISH COMPREHENSION

Throughout the long negotiations, the Scots must have maintained some sort of interest. Throughout 1544 and 1545, Arran had made a number of conciliatory gestures towards Henry, but each time he was rebuffed.[70] He must have resolved then to leave the matter in French hands. But there seems to have been very little Scottish impact upon the negotiations. Neither Paniter nor John Hay, who replaced him firstly during his embassy to Brussels and then in February 1546, seems to have influenced events.[71] News did come about the negotiations and the 'obstination grande' which the English displayed against Scotland. One cryptic memorandum warned that the Scots 'pourroient avoir cause juste de se lamenter du Roy [of France] en cest endroict'.[72] But it was not until the end of June that the Scots heard any detailed outline of the treaty, when Henri Cleutin, sieur d'Oysel et de Villeparisis et St. Aignan, made what was probably his first visit to the country which was to preoccupy him for the next fourteen years. He must have brought with him a copy of the treaty and doubtless had some trouble explaining the terms of the comprehension to the government.[73] On 5 August, the admiral d'Annebaut, obviously worried that the Scots might be annoyed at the comprehension, wrote to the Queen Dowager admonishing her to do nothing 'qui contremenne au bien que le Roy faict au royaume d'Escosse en le comprenant a cedict traicté de paix [which undermines the good which the King has done to the Kingdom of Scotland in comprehending it in this said treaty of peace]'. As he was about to depart for London, whence he also wrote to her, for the ratification of the peace, he advised the Scots to move with caution and to accept the treaty for the moment.[74] The government did complain to the Pope, for one, of 'the small help given by France and the feeble comprehension of Scotland', but by 21 August the three estates and the Council accepted it and within a very short time the Scots were also using its ambiguities to advantage.[75]

The French, English and Scots certainly were to exploit the ambiguities in the treaty in their dealings with the fourth most interested party: the government of the Low Countries. Immediately upon the conclusion of the treaty, the government of the Low Countries attempted to discover just how the Scots were affected, but with little success. At Brussels, the Queen Regent was told by the English that the Scots were only conditionally included but by the French that the inclusion was 'simpliciter'.[76] Her

70 For example, see *LP*, xx (1), no. 819.
71 *TA*, viii, 342, 400, 415; *Balcarres Papers*, i, 132–33, 166; *Mary of Lorraine Corresp.*, 136, 150–51, 158, 160–61.
72 *Balcarres Papers*, i, 247–48.
73 *LP*, xxi (1), no. 1124; *TA*, viii, 462.
74 *Balcarres Papers*, i, 137–38, 143–46.
75 *LP*, xxi (2), no. 227; *RPC*, i, 38–39.
76 *LP*, xxi (1), nos. 1047, 1090, 1112, 1144, 1243, 1390, 1429.

ambassadors abroad were equally deceived. At the French court in Melun, St. Maruis never received the same interpretation twice.[77] In London, van der Delft also never received a straight answer. As late as 4 September, all the English would admit was that peace with Scotland was by no means certain and that further negotiations were necessary. The Privy Council took an obvious delight in telling him that Scottish comprehension 'was like the Emperor's comprehension of us in his treaty with France'.[78]

The motives behind these contradictory renderings are fairly clear. Low Countries shipping had been harmed by the Scots; as both Henry and Francis knew, they were anxious to end the war. As an ally of Henry, the Low Countries had a right either to demand comprehension, if he had come to peace with Scotland, or the right to withhold their consent to it. Perhaps Henry was simply exacting a certain revenge for Charles's sell-out at Crepi. On the other hand the English may have been slightly embarrassed by not mentioning the Emperor in the treaty. Certainly they were not anxious for the Low Countries to come to peace with Scotland; that would only weaken their already very tenuous position there. Hence they fudged the comprehension issue and disavowed it when Mary directly taxed them with it. The French could only encourage Anglo-Imperial discord for obvious reasons.

Mary of Hungary resolved to break out of this morass by sending an ambassador to Scotland direct, much to the displeasure of Henry who still held captive her last emissary, David Magnus. The man chosen was Mathias Strick, secretary to the Emperor and member of his Council. Strick's instructions were probably prepared on 16 July; they reflect both Charles's and Mary's annoyance at not knowing the terms of the comprehension, as he was ordered to find out just what the terms were and to see a copy if possible. They also reflect their small hopes for any real end to the Scottish raids: initially he was to insist that compensation be paid or restitution made, and then to suggest he might consider a renewal of the Burgundian treaty; but if the Scots temporised over paying for the deprivations, he should only negotiate an extension to the Antwerp agreement.

Strick probably left the Low Countries around the end of July and arrived at Leith on 6 August; he left after little more than a month on 10 September. He spent a great deal of time in discussion with Paniter and the Privy Council and also met Arran (who always needed to have Paniter present, as 'ledict governeur n'entend le langue Francois [the said Governor does not understand the French language]'), Bothwell, Huntly (the new Chancellor upon Beaton's death) and others such as the French ambassador who arrived the day before he did. Though his letters concentrated on his charge, they also give the most detailed account of affairs in Edinburgh since

77 *Ibid.*, nos. 1083, 1213.
78 *LP*, xxi (2), no. 19. For his earlier attempts to discover the truth, see *LP*, xxi (1), nos. 1047, 1227, 1323, 1481; (2), no. 14. English attempts to mislead Mary may explain the 'Treaty of Camp' calendared in *ibid.*, no. 1015 which includes this extraordinary clause: 'in case the scottes woll not Agre to suche articles as they ones promissed to the kinges highnes, that then the french kinge not to breake leage whiche is now betwixt them, but also to warre appen them' (BL, MS Add. 9835, fo. 18).

Sadler's; all things considered, they show him to have been a shrewd and observant envoy and it is not surprising that he returned later to Scotland.[79]

Strick brought with him a formidable bundle of documents relevant to compensation and restitution: a fifteen-article remonstration which he tendered to Arran and Paniter before a full Privy Council, fourteen different affidavits, many of them translated from Dutch into French, an inventory of all these documents and original safe-conducts granted in Veere and elsewhere.[80] This catalogue, which was to be augmented by three new complaints whilst he was in Edinburgh, is striking testimony to the growth of Scottish piracy and its effect upon the Low Countries. Complaints came from the burgomasters, aldermen and council of almost every major port in the area: Amsterdam led the list followed by Rotterdam, Delft, the Hague, Flushing, Dunkirk, Dordrecht, Ostende and others.

Initially the Scots seemed eager both to end the piracy and to make some sort of settlement. A Scottish merchant who spoke privately with Strick complained bitterly of the loss of trade and against the lord high admiral, Bothwell, who ignored merchant interests. The government also seemed sympathetic; when a Scot inopportunely arrived in Leith with six Flemish ships in tow three days after Strick's arrival, Paniter had him arrested and promised quick restitution. Just before five of Bothwell and Ruthven's ships set sail, the Privy Council bound them not to take any

> Flemyngis and Hollandaris, alsweill haifand salf conductis, attestationis, or testymonyalis of the Quene of Ungarie as utharis of that natioun with quhome thair is commoning, for new renewing of the auld alliance.

The government further instructed all masters of 'schippis upoun the sey' or passing forth in 'weirfair' not to do so without special licence from the Governor. In Aberdeen a merchant who had turned to piracy against the Flemish suddenly found himself ostracised because 'ther is na weir betuix ws and them'.[81]

However, these gestures and Paniter's fair words did not mean much. For one thing Strick could rarely get the same story twice. Arran was reason itself, saying that compensation would be paid if only Charles agreed to a renewal of the alliance. Paniter thought an entirely new treaty would be better. Huntly (whom Strick found rather young and brash) could not see the necessity for any negotiations since Scotland was comprehended in the Treaty of Camp; being at peace with England meant being at peace with the Empire. Others maintained that Scotland now had no need of peace and did not want it since the war was obviously in Scotland's favour.

Negotiations then quickly settled down into a respectable stalemate. Strick insisted that once compensation was paid or restitution made of ships taken, then the Emperor would consider a renewal or new treaty. The Scots insisted that since

---

79 The material for Strick's mission is in Vienna, PA 70, fos. 220–49, which contains his three long reports of 23 August (fos. 220–29), 31 August (fos. 231–8) and 9 September (fos. 239–43). All references, unless otherwise stated, are from these despatches. A summary of his mission is to be found in *LP*, xxi (2), nos. 92, 162 and *CSP Spain*, ix, 215–16.

80 These documents are in NAS, SP 13/51. The remonstrance is printed in *Handel met Engeland*, no. 788 (pp. 651–5) from the copy in Brussels, Etat et Audience, 405b.

81 *RPC*, i, 41–42; *TA*, viii, 476; *Abdn. Counc.*, i, 241–2.

Charles had started the war, first a new treaty must be agreed, then they would consider compensation. The Scots threw out a variety of objections. Nothing could really be done until St. Andrews was retaken and affairs with England settled. They would not compensate any ships taken before the Antwerp agreement nor those taken which did not carry a safe-conduct issued by the Scottish government. Some captains had only carried letters of attestation from the Council of Veere; others had carried English safe-conducts which obviously disqualified them. Some of the pirates were not Scots, but Frenchmen masquerading as Scots (something the French ambassador admitted might be true). Arran did make a four-folio detailed reply, but it in no way met the complaints. He also insisted on a new treaty.[82]

Strick stuck to his charge and went so far as to warn that Charles 'auroit faict de nouveau declarer le guerre aux escossois'; but the Scots were unmoved. Moreover Strick was being hounded by further complaints from Brussels and from Flemish merchants in Edinburgh itself; the Scots put him off every time he passed these on. Strick quickly, and rightly, concluded that no compensation would be forthcoming and that his mission was doomed to inconsequential results.

The result was a statement signed on 5 September 1546 at Edinburgh that the last treaty had broken down because 'aulcune peine fust introduicte contre les delinquans et infracteurs dudict traicte'. Thus it was agreed that if subjects of the one side despoiled those of the other who were carrying proper safe-conducts, then the respective governments would restore the goods and ships to their owners 'incontinent et sans delay [immediately and without delay]'. Moreover the robbers henceforth would be punished 'non seullement comme infracteurs de traictez . . . mays aussy comme pirattes [not only as breakers of the peace, but as pirates]'.[83]

On 10 September Strick took ship bearing the treaty, a letter to Mary from Arran, one to Granvelle from Paniter, and 60 safe-conducts: all that Paniter could prepare in the time. The voyage home was frightful; the day after landing at Veere, Strick wrote Granvelle that he had to rest there as 'Je me suis trouve tellement indispose du traveil et tormente que par lespacae de huyt Jours Jay endure sur la mer [I found myself so indisposed by the travail and torment by the space of the eight days I endured on the seas]'. He forwarded his full report, the 60 safe-conducts and the copy of 'le petit traicte'. He emphasised that he had agreed that it would be published throughout the Low Countries on 1 October and urged that this be put in hand. But he doubted if any good result would ensue, not the end of the attacks nor the restitution of the goods 'malprinses' (wrongfully seized).[84]

Mary praised his hard work and agreed. In the very letter in which she informed Charles of Strick's return, she speculated as to what measures would have to be taken if the agreement did not work out.[85] In November she sent through England 70 safe-

---

82 Vienna, PA 70, fos. 267–70.

83 The full version is in Rooseboom, *Scottish Staple*, appendix, no. 59; *LP*, xxi (2), no. 24. There is also a copy in Vienna, PA 70, fo. 249.

84 Vienna, PA 70, fos. 264, 247.

85 *Ibid.*, fo. 248. She also immediately sent a report of the agreement to Spain (Archivo General, Simancas, Inglaterra, 806 and see Flandes, 502).

conducts to Scotland, 60 for Arran, 10 for Paniter. Van der Delft had to give the messenger a 'passport without search' to prevent English discovery of the agreement.[86] On 1 October the Scots published the treaty in Leith and Edinburgh and a fortnight later they again restricted Bothwell's ships from taking prizes from any subjects of the Emperor.[87]

Nonetheless, either because the Scottish government had not the capacity or because it had not the will, piracy continued. By 23 December 1546, Mary was again writing to Arran complaining of continued attacks. In Edinburgh, Low Countries and Spanish merchants continued to sue in vain for restoration of their ships and goods.[88] Imperial pressure was simultaneously being put on Denmark to refuse Scottish traders, and the situation was such that Francis offered to mediate.[89] But the Scots did not seem concerned. When Odet de Selve taxed their ambassadors in London (one of whom was Paniter) about the problem in January 1547, they maintained they did not fear war with Flanders. When a French ambassador in Flanders spoke with Scepperus on the matter at much the same time, he was told that although the Scots had 'grand tort [great fear]' of a war with the Emperor, Charles intended nothing against them and would not aid England in any war.[90] Moreover, others were not very concerned. When Charles tried first with Francis and then with Henry in early 1547 to resolve the problem, he met with no assistance.[91] In November of that year Paniter, then in Paris reeling from the shock of Pinkie, did plead with the Imperial ambassador that compensation would be paid if only Charles would try again, but nothing came of it.[92] During 1548 when the English seemed on the verge of conquering Scotland, Charles approached Somerset for a solution. When the French then besieged Haddington, he turned to Henry II. Neither gave any help. The only answer which lay within Charles's own hands, outfitting men of war to protect the shipping, was effected in 1548 and special taxes were levied in Holland and Zealand. But the Scottish raids were to continue until finally at the end of 1550 peace was arranged.

86 *LP*, xxi (2), no. 392.
87 *TA*, viii, 483; *LP*, xxi (2), no. 94.
88 Brussels, Etat et Audience, 16763/4/a; *ADCP*, 578, 563, 566.
89 *LP*, xxi (2), nos. 735, 609.
90 *Ibid.*, no. 662, 675; *Lettres et Memoires*, i, 601.
91 *CSP Spain*, ix, 11, 43, 504, 543, 214–16.
92 *Ibid.*, 108, 186, 192–41, 231 (for attempts with Somerset); 314–15, 319, 322, 335 (for attempts with Henry II).

CHAPTER NINE

Peace, Deaths and the Return to War, 1546–47

In retrospect, one can see that the two moves towards peace (Crepi and Camp) were only that: no more than moves. The Emperor's foolish declaration against the Scots in May 1544 unleashed forces which could not easily be brought under control despite the willingness and the strenuous efforts of the government of the Low Countries to undo the results of that declaration. Their efforts might have borne fruit had Camp led to a lasting peace between England and Scotland, but Camp did not extinguish English desires to attain the marriage of Mary to Edward and with it the union with Scotland. It did, however, give the Scots a breathing space of over a year. Before examining those fifteen months of peace it is necessary to review the general impact of foreign concern on the Scottish problem during this period.

In the first place, it must be emphasised that Henry VIII had failed in three years of diplomatic and violent effort to gain the betrothal of Mary to Edward. In large part this was due to the fact that he never concentrated his efforts on Scotland; rather he hoped to gain both Mary and something in France. Had he not fortuitously (for Scotland) captured Boulogne in September 1544, he might have been forced to come to terms with the French then. However, his capture of the port resulted in almost two more years of concentration on continental affairs during which the Scots easily kept him at bay. The lessons to English policy-makers (especially Edward Seymour and William Paget) must have been clear: as long as England was engaged in a costly struggle on the Continent, no genuine success could be gained in Scotland.

Three circumstances were also important in the Scottish success. In the first place, the Scottish government was not prepared to accept the English marriage and had considerable political and military resources with which to support this resolve. In the second place, English non-involvement on the Continent did not mean total freedom to handle Scotland; as long as the French were not involved in conflict with the Emperor, they could give the Scots both military and financial assistance. Thirdly, no French monarch who took a long-range view of his diplomatic needs could allow the Scottish alliance to be lost. None of these circumstances was to be as fully appreciated as it should have been by the English in the time to come.

Failure by the English to appreciate the first circumstance, Scottish capacity to resist, was in part due to ignorance of Scottish affairs, an ignorance which the English shared with most Europeans. Failure to appreciate fully the other two points may have been due to the French not having made their position sufficiently explicit. This in turn raises the question of Francis' motives at this time. It must have been clear in 1546 that the French King was not prepared to leave the Scots to a fate with England, but such resolve was not made as apparent as it might have been. The strong line taken by the French commissioners at Camp on the Scottish question may have been misunderstood owing to the ambiguities in the comprehension clause itself, by the failure to include the Scots in Crepi and by the rumour that such intransigence was largely in an effort to gain better terms for Boulogne. It would be remembered that the French bargaining position in the spring of 1546, although not desperate, was weak; Francis doubtless felt that he had to give in so as to gain a momentary breathing space. Contemporaries were quick to remark that in eight years (1554), when Boulogne was to be restored to France for an indemnity, Mary Queen of Scots would be of age, and not for the last time was it noted that English retention of Boulogne and the resolution of the Scottish marriage were inextricably linked.[1] Moreover, if Francis was thinking of a French marriage for Mary (and rumours to this effect had intensified since 1543, especially when Lorges went to Scotland), he was hardly being given any encouragement either by Arran or by Beaton.

In assessing the major impact of the Treaty of Camp to be the creation of a breathing space, one should not forget its most important result: the loss of Boulogne. Simply put, the loss was to warp French diplomacy for six years; the recovery of the city remained the first priority until March 1550. This had vital consequences for European diplomacy, for as long as France was determined to effect recovery, French policy towards Charles V had to be relatively pacific. The lesson of 1543–44 was all too clear: France could not handle a war with both England and the Emperor; thus Francis I and then Henry II were to do all possible to ensure that such an alliance did not again take place. One of the great successes of French diplomacy in the period 1544–50 was the estrangement of Charles from the English. This enabled Henry II to concentrate on single objectives: firstly to stop English success in Scotland in 1548, then to regain Boulogne in 1549–50, and then to intervene in Germany in 1551. However, this success was by no means inevitable; for the time being the French had to remain on good terms with the Emperor and this was to have a considerable effect on Anglo-Scottish relations during this period.

Another point which must be borne in mind is that the Emperor also needed a period of peace with France during which he could concentrate on German affairs. The attempt by Protestant mediators, Bruno and Strum, to create an anti-Imperial alliance shows their worry about Charles. Protestant desire to reinvolve the French in Germany, particularly after Mulberg, explains the ease with which Henry was able to recruit German mercenaries in the period 1547–48. But for the moment, Charles and the French had little wish to be in conflict with one another. This in part explains why Anglo-Imperial relations were to remain so cool during this period and why in 1549 when the English desperately sought active Imperial assistance, the Emperor, perhaps foolishly, refused it.

The Treaty of Camp is thus part of a period when the English and French were primarily concerned with one another. However, in 1546–47 both were in severe financial difficulties and neither could engage in immediate conflict over Boulogne. During this period of stalemate amongst the larger monarchies changes took place

1 See *LP.*, xxi (1), no. 625.

which were to significantly alter the struggle for the marriage of the Scottish Queen. The most important must be the change of the personnel at the centre of affairs: in May 1546, Beaton was assassinated; in January 1547 Henry VIII died; Francis I followed him in March. Let us now examine the impact of these changes.

<h2 style="text-align:center">THE DEATH OF CARDINAL BEATON:
'THE KING IS RID OF SUCH A CANKERED ENEMY'</h2>

The first of the protagonists to be removed was David Beaton, assassinated in St. Andrews Castle on 29 May 1546.[2] The story is one of the most celebrated in Scottish history. Killing off your enemies before their time is hardly a phenomenon restricted to any particular king or epoch: what else are warfare, rebellion and the laws of treason? Edward II, Richard II, Henry VI, Edward V and Richard III were all thus eliminated as purposeful figures upon a political stage; so too Thomas Cromwell, not to mention

Fig. 9.1.   It is often forgotten how much power was devolved in early modern Europe. Aristocrats were virtual mini-kings within their jurisdictions: they collected money, dispensed justice and granted charters. All 'corporations' in the medieval polity did so: nobles, burghs, abbeys, and priories. As monarchs did, their transactions were validated by a waxed seal affixed to their documents. The Treaty of Greenwich was similarly treated. Some seals lasted for generations, others altered with each individual. Here is Beaton's made after he had become Cardinal (1538), Archbishop of St. Andrews (1539) and Legate *a latere* of the Apostolic See. (1543).

2 Wharton in Carlisle heard on 2 June; by early June the news had reached Newhaven. *LP*, xxi (1), nos. 957–58, 990–979.

Ann Boleyn and Catherine Howard. Normal political life in France is replete with such occurrences and would be even more so come the religious civil wars. On his accession in 1520, Suleyman the Magnificent despatched all possible rivals to his Sultanate; on his death in 1566, except for his designated heir, all his sons were similarly murdered. So, too, his Grand Vizier when an Ottoman expedition to Malta ended in failure in 1565. Scottish history is actually rather tame in comparison, although judicial murders and assassinations did occur. Beaton's was one of the more melodramatic.

Beaton had been conspicuously unpopular within Scottish politics ever since his high favour with James V; in that sense he was remarkably similar to his fellow Cardinal, Thomas Wolsey. One of Arran's most popular measures in early 1543 was his putting Beaton to one side, but it says a great deal both about Arran and about how Scotland operated that he did not eliminate 'this troublesome priest' then and there. Not doing so in truth was one of the smartest things Arran ever did, for Beaton emerged during 1543–46 as an enormously effective ingredient in the Queen's government. By 1542, Henry VIII had something of a psychotic phobia about Cardinals: Wolsey, Pole, Beaton. Scots anxious to gain the King's approbation (and pensions) played on this fixation with telling effect, witness John Elder's diatribe against Beaton in 1542.[3]

On 19 May 1543, Sir William Murray of Tullibardine attacked the Cardinal's convoy of wagons and personal effects which was being moved from Stirling to St. Andrews by an intriguingly indirect route (Doune, Castle Campbell, Kincardine in Menteith and Falkland). At Dunning, Tullibardine struck, hoping perhaps to ambush Beaton himself. Baulked of that prize, he nonetheless carried off £s2800 worth of the Cardinal's silver and many of his symbols of dignity, such as his mitre and processional cross.[4] Tullibardine even spoke of sending these as gifts or trophies to the English king. The message was then quite clear quite early: elimination of Beaton was seen by Henry as praiseworthy, reward-worthy and an acceptable act before God.

Meat then began to be put onto such bones. While he tarried due to contrary winds at Tynemouth in April 1544, the Earl of Hertford received a proposal from the laird of Brunstane (via a 'Scottishman called Wishart') offering either to seize Beaton (obviously to have him sent to England) or to assassinate him. At this point, Henry rather brushed the offer[5] aside, using it instead to get this anti-Beaton grouping to 'assure' and aid the forthcoming invasion. However, a year later, in July 1545, Brunstane again offered to orchestrate the despatch of the Cardinal. This time, it was Sir Ralph Sadler, back on the Borders due to the French threat, who handled the negotiations. Giving what he maintained was purely private advice ('mine own

---

3 M. H. Merriman, 'Home Thoughts from Abroad'.

4 That this was not just a case of highway theft is attested by Tullibandine's contacts with the English before the hijack and his removal of these prizes to Cockpool, near Dumfries, ready to be handed over to the English Warden of the West Marches, Sir Thomas Wharton (Sanderson, *Cardinal of Scotland*, 183).

5 Which was, it must be said, somewhat far-fetched and too far-ranging: Brunston was to carry out an attack upon Arbroath, some 150 miles to the North of his lands (Sanderson, *Cardinal of Scotland*, 184; the letter is calendared in *LP*, xix (1), no. 350 and see no. 404). Note that the redoubtable Robertson was the first to publish this letter in full, although both Keith and Mackenzie had also seen it at Hamilton.

fantasy'), Sadler promised 'liberal reward' for Beaton's removal, 'paid immediately upon the act executed'. Sadler purred that it would be 'a service to God, and His Majesty, and a benefit to the country [Scotland]'.[6]

Fig. 9.2.   George Wishart was a notorious heretic and a formidably articulate preacher who travelled extensively about Scotland in 1545 proselytising. Beaton really had no choice but to have him arrested and examined in what became one of the most celebrated trials of the century. Wishart's defence of his faith became almost a textbook mantra for reformers. He was tied to a stake in his shirt, supposedly with bags of gunpowder attached to his body (not shown in this woodcut from Holinshed), surrounded by bales of hay, and burnt to death in St Andrews on 1 March 1546. Compared with England, Spain, and the Low Countries, Scotland was relatively free of such public *autos da fé*.

If Beaton's high profile on the political stage, along with his declared adamant hostility towards Henry VIII's plans, were not enough to create groupings against him, two further aspects of his career went even further. One was his crusade against heresy; the other – quite different – was his political and social power within the community of Fife landowners. On the one hand, it is incontestable that the highly public show trial in February 1546 and explosive execution of George Wishart on 1 March inflamed an already vibrant anti-clerical hostility towards this particular prelate. Inquisitions always did, wherever they occurred in Europe. It had been in

6 *LP*, xx (1), no. 1178.

Brunstane's house that George Wishart[7] found succour in early 1546. Wishart, who had studied at Cambridge in 1543, had come to Scotland from England the next year and must have been aware of Brunstane's plots. Although evidence as to Wishart's participation in any scheme against Beaton is ambiguous, his activity as a Protestant preacher is well attested, even though Knox and others may well have exaggerated both his impact and his following.[8] The execution of Wishart doubtless caused other Protestants to fear for their lives. Revenge was certainly one of the stated motives. One of the murderers, James Melville of Carnbee, urged Beaton to repent of the martyr's death before running him through.[9]

Beaton knew quite well that he was hated, hence the large mercenary armed guard of some one hundred he had at the trial and around his person and within his property (including seven trained gunners). Even more telling was the major construction work being carried out at his principal residence in St. Andrews Castle itself, which was being recast into an even stronger fortress than it had been before, able to both house and resist artillery.[10] Wolsey may have possessed more splendid palaces (Hampton Court), but few other episcopal figures in the British Isles held such a redoubtable stronghold as did Beaton in 1546.[11]

Beaton's unpopularity amongst a swathe of Fife landowners has long been appreciated and there is no doubt that personal and financial animus against the Cardinal as a lay figure in the area contributed to his slaughter.[12] Beaton was arrogant, pushy and litigious; he was also in serious debt and had too many pots on the boil. Thus he made enemies both on the national stage and on a more parochial one. His relations with Bothwell were never as cordial as the Earl's capture of Wishart might indicate. Lord Ogilvy found himself in court of arrears for tithes [teinds] due for lands of Arbroath. Mary of Guise's household chief, Sir James Campbell of Lundy, owed him £s860. Angus, Cassillis, Lord Ruthven, George Douglas: all professed themselves ill content with him. His most fatal feud, however, lay with Norman Leslie, Master of Rothes, Sheriff of Fife, the eldest son of George 4th Earl Rothes.[13] Although the two were bound by a bond of manrent, they had quarrelled

7 See O. Rogers, 'Memoir of George Wishart, the Scottish Martyr', *Trans. Royal Historical Society*, 1st ser., vi (1876), 260–363.
8 The government certainly appreciated, especially after the Cardinal's death, that heresy had spread and that parts of the Kingdom were 'now infectit with that pestilencious hereseis of Luther'. In March 1547 it ordered the churchmen to 'gif his Grace the names of the heretikis that ar relapsis', but it is not clear if such a list was prepared, *RPC*, i, 61, 63.
9 Donaldson, *Scotland*, 74.
10 See the new Historic Scotland guidebook to the site, although the old Ministry of Works one (as ever is the case) still has much mileage in it.
11 Bishops of Durham possessed Norham Castle, and took refuge there during the Pilgrimage of Grace. But it was hopelessly antiquated and still badly protected even after the rebuild following its capture by James IV in 1513. See my section on it in Colvin, *King's Works*, iv, 679–82.
12 Evidence of Beaton's unpopularity is contradictory. Can the government have been disingenuous when it made proclamation that none molest any 'Castilian' coming to Edinburgh to appear before the Council 'because the said umquhile Cardinale hes mony greit freindis in Fiff, Lowthiane, Angus and utharis pairtes'? *RPC*, i, 32.
13 Sanderson, *Cardinal of Scotland*, 221, 223.

bitterly and publicly. Several of Leslie's friends had been ill treated supposedly by the Cardinal: Sir James Kirkcaldy of Grange lost his post of Treasurer of the realm;[14] Henry Balnavis was supplanted as Secretary to the Crown.

Howsoever, there came together, on the morning of 29 May 1546, a gang of plotters who made their way to the castle gatehouse whilst workmen and servants bustled about. Beaton's 'wife', Marion Ogilvy, mother to his eight children, slipped out the postern gate on her errands just as they arrived.[15] They were a varied bunch. Norman Leslie had arrived in the city the night before where he was joined by Grange's son, William. Leslie's father's brother, John of Parkhill, arrived later, as did James Melville of Carnbee, Peter Carmichael of Balmedie and maybe a dozen more. Once at the gate, they snatched the keys from the porter, Ambrose Stirling, slew him and dumped his body in the ditch. The security at the castle was utterly lacking; Leslie was able to enter, allow the servants and workmen out, then secure the main gate while racing to guard the postern in case Beaton escaped thereby, as apparently he tried to do in his bedclothes. Beaton then secured his bedroom door, but when hot coals were dumped outside, he allowed it to be opened and fell into a chair. Sir James Melville, a close friend of Wishart's, then pronounced a rather longwinded sermon ('a very compendious kind of bringing men to repentance')[16] before running him through. 'Fye, all is gone' were Beaton's last words. When citizens gathered before the castle, the Cardinal's body was shown to them atop the eastern (newly constructed) blockhouse where a man called Guthrie undid his trouser flies and 'pischit' into Beaton's open mouth. The 'Castilians' then dumped his carcass into a salt cast and quickly set to making the castle secure. There they were joined by others, such as two other sons of George Lord Leslie, Grange himself and, in time, John Knox.[17]

Word of Beaton's death (whereof several were 'blythe') reached Edinburgh later that day. One correspondent wrote from St Andrews that Saturday advising a friend to tarry not: 'great dispositioun of benefices at this time' would be made. 'Show yourself a wise man and you may profit.' Thence word filtered to Berwick, London and abroad at much the same time as news of the conclusion of the Anglo-French peace.[18] The English agent in Venice, Edmund Harvel, knew of both by July and exulted how Scotland could now be reduced to Henry's 'vow'.[19] In Paris and Rome shock was tempered with speculation as to the disposal of the Cardinal's offices and Francis immediately impounded what money Beaton had banked in Paris.[20] By the time confirmation reached the French court on 7 July, Jean de Monluc, Bishop of

14 Dalrymple, *Historie*, i, 291.
15 Until Sanderson (1986, 221–34), no authoritative account of the episode existed. Her chapter is entitled, with sharp irony, 'Careful Cardinal': a quote from Knox. Donaldson, *Scotland*, 27–28, 73–77, gives a dispassionate and clear account, but reference should also be made to Herkless and Hannay, *Archbishops of St. Andrews*, iv, and to Dickinson's edition of Knox's *History* which has very useful footnotes. The papers in the Rothes collection (*HMC*, 3, 4th R., 492–511) do not throw too much light on the assassination.
16 A quote (so I have always been told) rediscovered by Donaldson, *Scotland*, 74.
17 Knox, *History*, i, 76–76, 80, 81–86.
18 *Ibid.*, nos. 1030, 1214.
19 *Ibid.*, no. 1310.
20 *Nonces en France, 1544–46*, 434, 440; *CSP Spain*, ix, 14.

Valence, was angling for Mirepoix although he had strong competition from candidates of the Admiral, Claude d'Annebaut, and of Anne de Pisseleu, Madame d'Etampes, Francis I's mistress.[21] Everyone was certain that the death was Henry's doing and anxious that it might give grounds for fresh conflict.[22]

Arran's capacity for decisiveness was tellingly evident in the hectic period after the assassination. His immediate reaction was to advance his family; two days after the Cardinal's death he transferred the temporalities of the Archbishopric to John Hamilton, Bishop of Dunkeld.[23] The Governor thus now controlled both arms of the state. Arran then went to Stirling to confer with the Queen Dowager; the next day a large Council met there followed by one of 5 June at which Huntly was given Beaton's office of Chancellor.[24] Hitherto Arran had not particularly favoured him despite their affinity, as Huntly was a confidant of the Queen Dowager. His appointment must have been made to gain the support of both. After this date they were rarely absent from the Council.[25] The Governor certainly felt he had to widen the base of his support. During the Convention of 9–12 June he agreed that 'certane Lordis remane with my Lord Governor and be off Secret Counsel with him in all materis'. This attendant Council of four lords was to change monthly and mirrored opinion amongst the nobility. Lord Ruthven and George Douglas balanced the Bishop of Orkney and the Earl of Huntly, Catholic and hostile to England. The other rota were also representative. Continuance of the arrangement in March 1547 for another seven months is tribute to the scheme's success.[26] On 11 June, for 'gude concurrance' and 'staunching of divisioun', Arran freed from their pledge all who had agreed to support the marriage of his son to the Queen. He also had to cancel all bonds of manrent with nobles of the realm; Mary of Guise agreed to do likewise.

The Convention then agreed a flurry of measures designed to restore order within the realm: none was to aid the 'Castilians'; men of Fife were ordered to Edinburgh to advise the Council how best to tackle the recovery of the castle of St. Andrews; officers of the Crown were to move against any 'evill disponit personis' bent on destruction of church property. Lord Maxwell, recently returned from England, was put under a £20,000 pledge to repair and keep Lochmaben Castle 'surelie fra Inglismen' upon its being returned to his charge; at the same time Glencairn may well have been put under a similar constraint to ensure his loyalty.[27] Many of the

---

21 *Nonces en France, 1541–46*, 440. The confirmation may have come from Paniter in a letter sent to France on 15 June (*TA*, viii, 462). John Hamilton also wished to have Mirepoix and Beaton's red hat (*CSP Scot.*, i, no. 10).

22 *LP*, xxi (1), nos. 1058, 1214.

23 *RSS*, iii, no. 1696.

24 The evidence is contradictory as to the exact date of the Council (*RSS*, iii, xxxv; *RPC*, i, 23). Note the curious reference to the Great Seal of James V being broken on this occasion. See also *TA*, viii, 455.

25 Note entry from household book dated 8 August that both were with Arran 'in cena' (*RSS*, iii, xxxv); and see *Mary of Lorraine Corresp.*, 177.

26 *RPC*, i, 23–25, 65; *APS*, ii, 598. See also discussion by Beveridge of these events in his introduction to *RSS*, iii, xvi.

27 *CSP Scot.*, i, no. 26. So may Somerville (*CSP Dom. Add. 1547–65*, 337).

Assured Lords of 1543 (Angus, George Douglas, Cassillis and Maxwell) formally renounced the marriage and peace treaties and their contracts with Henry VIII. It was doubtless at this time that Angus's bastard son George was granted Arbroath Abbey, the temporalities of which went to his father.[28] Apparently the religious riots which followed Beaton's death heightened a perhaps related problem, 'the grete convocatioun maid in the realme for putting and laying men furth of thair takkis and stedingis [leases and buildings]'; against this the Convention also found time to legislate.[29] Everywhere, supporters and friends of the 'Castilians' were hounded, so much so that the Earl of Rothes felt compelled to flee to Denmark.[30]

Nor did the government's resolution end there. In the spring of 1546, Henry VIII had decided to let Lennox make one more attempt upon Dumbarton before an Anglo-French peace was agreed. By April, Lennox and his brother Robert were ready to sail from Chester to Ireland and thence to the Clyde.[31] The Captain of Dumbarton since 1 January 1545 was George Stirling of Gloret, brother-in-law to Thomas Bishop, Lennox's secretary. Through this affinity, Lennox hoped to gain possession of the stronghold.[32] But when he arrived in the Clyde in mid-May, Stirling refused to deliver his charge, and the Earl returned to the small fleet which had brought him from Ireland, leaving his brother in the castle.[33] When the Convention dissolved on 12 June, Arran immediately went to Glasgow and thence to Paisley and Irvine. Although he was forced to return to Stirling and Edinburgh on 18 June, it was doubtless during this quick visit that he was informed that Stirling would not deliver the castle to the government either; hence the Governor resolved to secure Dumbarton once and for all. On 27 June John Hamilton and a number of local lairds repaired to Dumbarton; two days later Arran left Edinburgh and arrived before the stronghold with artillery and forces on 1 July, accompanied by Huntly, Argyll (who also brought some artillery) and, later, Glencairn.[34]

Although there was a vigorous siege, the artillery had little effect upon the castle itself, as was to be the case at St. Andrews two months later. As at St. Andrews, the Governor decided to negotiate. On 15 July Stirling surrendered his charge to the government in return for a free pardon for himself and his garrison for all their crimes.[35] Once the bargain was made, Arran honoured it, thus gaining Stirling's support and loyalty.[36] The castle secured, Arran set about its reinforcement and

28 RCP, i, 55, 57; TA, viii, 463; ix, 37; Knox, History, i, 79; Diurnal of Occurrents, 42. Arran also con-cluded a marriage contract between his daughter Jane and Glencairn's heir Gilbert (RPC, i, 42).
29 That some rioting against religious houses occurred is certain (TA, viii, 468–9) but it is not clear if that explains the 'kaill distroytt and dountrod be mennis feit' at the Greyfriars in Stirling (Ibid., 461).
30 Having first demanded exoneration 'by trial or by instruments' (Thorkild Lyby Christensen, 'The Earl of Rothes in Denmark', The Renaissance and Reformation in Scotland, eds. I.B. Cowan and D. Shaw (Edinburgh, 1983), 60–74 at p. 61). He was in Denmark by September 1546.
31 LP, xxi (1), nos. 1246, 1255, 1273.
32 RSS, iii, nos. 1014, 1121.
33 TA, viii, 459; LP, xxi (1), no. 979.
34 RPC, i, 42; TA, viii, 464–5, 467; RSS, iii, xxxv–xxxvi; Dalrymple, Historie, i, 289.
35 TA, ix, 73; RPC, i, 34–35; RSS, iii, nos. 1755, 1756, 1755–6, 1975–6, 2187–8.
36 TA, viii, 442; ix, 80; RPC, i, 66; RSS, iii, no. 2163.

repair; the new Captain was Andrew Hamilton, formerly in charge of Linlithgow.[37]

A further valuable prize of the siege was the defection from his brother of Robert Stewart. When he went to England in 1544, the temporalities of his Bishopric, Caithness, and his other benefice, the provostry of Dumbarton, had been redistributed: Caithness was granted to Alexander Gordon, brother of Huntly; Dumbarton went to a Hamilton.[38] However, during the siege Arran and Stewart entered into discussions as to his possible rehabilitation; on 14 July, the day before the castle's capitulation, Stewart appeared before the Council to ask for a remission for his crimes and for a pension equal to his previous living.[39] This was agreed and on 16 July he received a full pardon.[40] In time Stewart did find himself once more Bishop-elect of Caithness[41] although he did not at this time recover Dumbarton.[42] The whole episode demonstrated Arran's ability to act decisively, and had he been able to reduce St. Andrews as quickly, the reputation of his administration would be much higher.

THE SIEGE OF ST. ANDREWS CASTLE

However much their murder of Beaton may have been driven by spiritual matters, the behaviour of the 'Castilians' was highly secular. Even Knox, who did not join them until April 1547, described many as 'men without god'; Pitscottie, normally favourable to Protestants, vividly describes their activities:

> They wald ryde and wshe out athort the contrie quhair they pleisait and quhillis burnand and raissand fyre in the contrie and slay and shed bloode as they plessit, quhillis wssit thair bodyis in leichorie witht fair wemen, servand thair appeityte as they thecht goode.[43]

Initially the government could not move with any dispatch as on the same day as word came of 'the slachter of the Cardinall', so did news that 'the Inglische shippis arrivat at Dunbertane'.[44] This distraction in June gave the Castilians time to bring into the castle both supplies and men 'that was nocht at the slaughter bot was willing and content thair into'.[45] The castle which they occupied had been consistently strengthened and was 'well fensed'. Moreover it contained James Hamilton, Arran's heir.

Whilst Arran was occupied with the siege of Dumbarton, judicial action proceeded; by 30 July the summons of treason before Parliament contained the names of Norman Leslie and thirty-seven others. The Council on 3 August debated 'giff it be tresoun to sla ane Chancellar of the realme or nocht' and agreed that it was. On 16 August Parliament declared doom of forfeiture against Leslie and his accomplices.[46] Arran agreed that his son should be declared no longer third person

37 *TA*, viii, 567; ix, 74; *RSS*, iii, nos. 1848, 1501, 1873.
38 *RSS*, iii, nos. 751, 863, 915, 1394; *ADCP*, 539; *TA*, viii, 407; *RPC*, i, 42.
39 *ADCP*, 553–4.
40 *RPC*, i, 35; *RSS*, iii, no. 1758; *ADCP*, 554.
41 *Mary of Lorraine Corresp.*, 268; *ADCP*, 553, 574, 576–7.
42 *RPC*, i, 41; *ADCP*, 545–6, 564; *RSS*, iii, no. 2561.
43 Pitscottie, *Historie*, ii, 86–87.
44 *TA*, viii, 459.
45 Pitscottie, *Historie*, ii, 85.
46 *RPC*, i, 33–34.

of the realm in the line of succession.[47] The Governor felt that the only manner in which he could regain his son was to compromise with the Castilians, and as early as 9 August he gained the consent of the clergy in Parliament for a remission for the slayers if the Pope granted an absolution and the boy was released.[48] Nothing, at the time, came of this offer.

Thus stymied, Arran resolved upon military action. On 14 August a tax was granted and on 21 August plans were approved for dividing the realm into quarters, each of which would man a siege of the castle for twenty-one days. Arran and some of the Council then moved to St. Andrews from which most government business was conducted until December.[49] During this period the siege continued with the musters of the quarters operating fairly smoothly.[50] The tax 'grantit be the kirk for covering of the hous' was collected, although some clerics objected to paying.[51] The siege however did not go as well as many would have liked. Some suspected a lack of will on Arran's part, others blamed 'the gounnaris or wther tressonabill men', but obviously Beaton's work over the previous three years had made the position very strong by Scottish standards. A 'vehement' outbreak of the pest must also have hindered the siege.[52]

The castle could easily be supplied by sea, though there was no direct English aid for well over three months. Kirkcaldy of Grange only arrived in London at the end of August, and even then it was not until 18 September that 'speedy relief' was agreed.[53] One possible reason for English delay was the Castilians' refusal to hand over Arran's son. Various articles were drawn up in London in September and November which stipulated support for the marriage and for the 'word of God', but none appears to have been signed then by the Castilians.[54]

Despite English help, the besieged were in serious trouble by December: the castle was badly battered, meat had to be rationed and a 'deadly sickness' infected the garrison.[55] Plague and fatigue also affected the besiegers and winter had set in. Arran's force had hewed expensive and difficult mine through solid rock, but it had been countered;[56] the musters were becoming difficult to maintain.[57] On 19 December the decision was made to raise the siege if certain conditions could be agreed. Huntly made the proposal, arguing that St. Andrews had occupied the Governor for five months,

> quhilks hes bene varay costlie to him and the haill realm, and is unable to be gottin bot be hungir quhilk will nocht be hastelie done; and the King of Ingland preparis all his powar to cum upoun this realme hastellie.[58]

47 *APS*, ii, 474 (*LP*, xxi (1), no. 1456).
48 *APS*, ii, 469 (*LP*, xxi (1) no. 1436).
49 *RPC*, i, 41–57 and especially 44; *TA*, ix, 442. Arran's wife stayed with him during the siege (*Ibid.*, 42).
50 One contingent did have to wait at Cupar on 5 November 'becaus of the multitude of pepill being in Sanct-androis' (*Ibid.*, 38).
51 *RPC*, i, 55–56; *TA*, viii, 481–2.
52 Pitscottie, *Historie*, ii, 86; *Abdn. Counc.*, i, 242.
53 *LP*, xxi (1), no. 990; (2), no. 114; *TA*, viii, 480; *Mary of Lorraine Corresp.*, 170.
54 *LP*, xxi (2), nos. 122, 123 (2), 524 (2).
55 *Ibid.*, nos. 542, 576 gives a very interesting account of the siege, although the originals (*SP Henry VIII*, v, 572, 580) repay reading.
56 Odet de Selve is the only person to have commented on it at the time (*LP*, xxi (2), no. 380).
57 *Abdn. Counc.*, i, 243–5. Lord Grey, shortly to join with the Castilians, also received permission to remain from the siege (BL, MS Add. 28, 747, fo. 1).
58 *RPC*, i, 57–58.

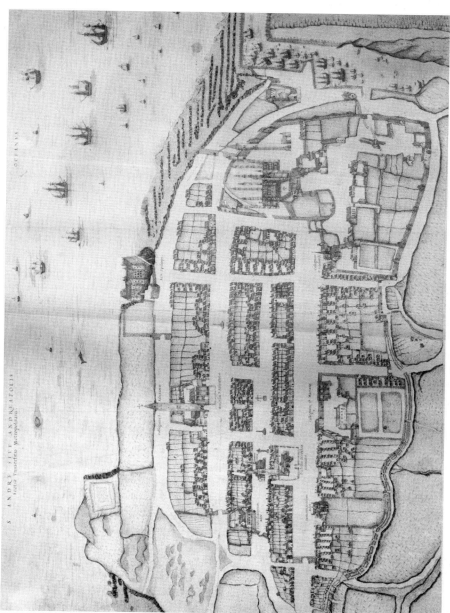

Fig. 9.3. St Andrews was a large and bustling church capital city – a Canterbury with a University – of which Beaton and then John Hamilton was 'king'. The castle here (upper shore line) is actually Archbishop Hamilton's. Note the steeple erected atop St. Salvator's College chapel to prevent future placement there of artillery, as the French did so successfully in July 1547.

Huntly proposed that a papal pardon should be sought so long as the Castilians refused to deliver the castle to England 'and my Lord Govenoris sone nocht to be deliverit in the Inglismennis handis'. Although Arran, perhaps disingenuously, protested his readiness to continue the attack, he was brought to 'appouncт'. The siege was lifted, hostages were exchanged, the Castilians were allowed to move about and to gather supplies (so long as none came from England) and the Governor agreed to give them a Scottish remission once papal absolution came, at which time they were to surrender both the castle and Arran's son.[59]

On 27 December the Governor retired to Linlithgow whilst a large part of the army dispersed, taking the plague with it to the rest of the realm. From Linlithgow Arran doubtless wrote to the Pope calling for the absolution and to Francis I asking him to effect its speedy dispatch. On 20 January 1547, the French King did so by special messenger to Rome; he shrewdly guessed that the Castilians hoped for papal delay in order to gain time for English suppliers to reach them before better weather came.[60] For the moment, the problem was shelved.

Although, as the first reporter of the death of Beaton reported, 'the alteration wilbe grete in this realme', it is difficult to argue that much changed There were no serious defections from the regime. England's aims were not markedly advanced. What the siege did vividly demonstrate was Scottish incapacity to wage modern warfare: one well-defended fortified position could be, in Francis I's words, 'such a thorn in their vitals'. A year later, a thoughtful Scot was to compare the siege with one then in progress at Broughty. At St. Andrews great expense and time had been employed, and 'sobir arttalzerij', but the castle had not been won, thus giving the 'persons wyth haldaris of mair curage to perseveir in tharis hei contentemtioun and was greit comfort to all thair fauvararis and greit dispair till gud trew leigis'.[61] Edward Seymour, kept aware of events in Scotland in 1546, doubtless drew the moral which St. Andrews so amply afforded.[62]

SCOTTISH PEACE WITH ENGLAND, 1546–47

During these events, England, France and Scotland tried to put their relations on a normal peacetime basis. With the conclusion of the Treaty of Camp, England and France had recommenced diplomatic relations and permanent ambassadors were exchanged, Dr. Nicholas Wotton being sent to France and Odet de Selve to England. Both Wotton and de Selve were to remain at their posts until August 1549 when Anglo-French warfare again broke out. Both were relatively competent ambassadors, but Odet de Selve was in many respects the abler and his embassy a

---

59 *LP*, xxi (2), nos. 576, 611 (3), 695.

60 *Nonces en France, 1546–51*, 134–38; and see *LP*, xxi (2) nos. 576, 727.

61 *Mary of Lorraine Corresp.*, 208–09.

62 William Robertson, writing in the 1750s, captured the issue nicely: 'One part of military science, the art of attacking fortified places, was then imperfectly understood in Scotland. The weapons, the discipline, and impetuosity of the Scots, rendered their armies as unfit for sieges as they were active in the field'. *The History of Scotland, during the Reigns of Queen Mary and of King James VI* (1759). I have employed the 1824 edition, p. 107. His comments are too sweeping, but contain an interesting grasp of the issue.

model of how a skilful ambassador should conduct himself. Immediately after the conclusion of the Treaty of Camp, Henri Cleutin, sieur d'Oysel arrived in London, received a safe-conduct and proceeded North a good week before de Selve's arrival on 3 July.[63] The Scots were otherwise occupied at the time and did not react to the news of their inclusion in Camp until 23 July when they requested safe-conducts from the English for ambassadors to go to London to negotiate the finer points of the comprehension. On 10 August Henry issued the passport.[64] On 5 August a French herald arrived in Edinburgh with what must have been Francis' advice that the Scots should make every effort to accept the comprehension, and three days later the Scottish Council determined that the comprehension 'sulde be accepit, without prejudice of hir grace, hir realme and liberties'.

On 14 August Parliament accepted it in the same terms.[65] Parliament also stated Scottish requirements: Francis should ensure that the English fully accepted the inclusion, proclaimed peace in London and on the Borders, agreed to ransom the hostages of 1543, returned Langholm and Edrington, refused to succour Scottish rebels and in particular sent no aid to the Castilians. Letters patent were drawn up to this effect on 17 August; the Council again debated them four days later before they were sent South on 25 August.[66] At much the same time, French envoys in London presented the Scottish acceptance to the English Privy Council. Henry remarked upon the inserted phrase 'absque tamen regni nostri et libertatum ejusdem prejudicio [without prejudice to our queen and liberties]' and insisted on adding a clause to protect the English marriage treaty with Scotland. Before d'Annebaut could protest, Henry adjourned the meeting for dinner and the matter was dropped.[67]

The Scots and English did effect the comprehension. On 17 August George Lord Hume, recently appointed Warden of the East and Middle Marches, was instructed neither to invade England nor to allow others to do so; four days later, shipmasters were commanded not to 'make weir upoun Inglische schippis'.[68] English wardens were instructed on 20 August to cease open warfare, according to the comprehension clause.[69] Although the English continued to protect their collaborators in Scotland and the Scots maintained their spies in England,[70] the general level of hostilities fell off markedly and normal intercourse gradually recommenced.[71]

If the Scots were relatively quick to amend the comprehension, they were sensibly leisurely in getting down to direct negotiations with the English. Rumours of an English invasion were still rife and the government delayed until the campaigning

63 *Odet de Selve*, 39; *LP*, xxi (2), nos. 1124, 1237.
64 *TA*, viii, 469; *LP*, xxi (1), nos. 1445, 1537 (14).
65 *RPC*, i, 35; xiv, 3; *APS*, ii, 473–4 (*LP*, xxi (1), no. 1530); Vienna, PA 70, fo. 220.
66 NAS, SP 7/32; *RPC*, i, 38–39; viii, 476. The dates are not clear (cf *Ibid.*, 475).
67 *LP*, xxi (1), no. 1530 and of nos. 1398, 1518.
68 *HMC*, 26, 12th R., viii, 183; *TA*, viii, 475; *RPC*, i. 39.
69 *LP*, xxi (1), no. 1314.
70 *LP*, xxi (2), nos. 171, 199, 229, 304, 428; *TA*, viii, 479, 483; ix, 34–35, 43, 61.
71 Leading for one thing to a fall in the price of wine (*Edin. Burgh Recs.*, ii, 114–127 *passim*). *LP*, xxi (1), nos. 1501, 1527, (2), 678; *APC*, ii, 495; BL, MSCalig. B. viii, fo. 276. *CPR Edward VI*, vi (1), 247.

season was past.[72] By late September it was decided to send two ambassadors, Adam Otterburn[73] and David Paniter, who were first to go to England, 'and if we agree nocht', then to go to France 'to knaw the kyng of Francis mynd'.[74] Final instructions were drawn up by the Council at St. Andrews on 2 October: the ambassadors were to accept comprehension if it protected Scottish liberties and to press for English acceptance of 'ane pece and abstinance of weir as salbe devisit for ane space lang nor schort'. If Henry 'will nocht accept the comprehension in maner and forme as it is maid', they were to see Francis I to inform him how Scotland 'is dampnagit and skaithit throw the said generall comprehensioun' and to demand aid, as well as a declaration of war, should England invade.[75] On 19 October the Queen Dowager wrote to de Selve asking that he aid the ambassadors in all matters.[76] Still they tarried; Otterburn wrote to the Queen Dowager on 20 October complaining of illness and lack of credentials and remarked bitterly, 'I have gottin na hors and na money that will furnis me to Mussilburght'.

Shortly afterwards both were given money, safe-conducts and protections and set off with a servant of d'Oysel's, arriving in London on 10 November 1546.[77] Relations between the two were not cordial. De Selve remarked that Otterburn continually tried 'derober de son compaignon [get away from his companion]', and van der Delft was able to provoke a violent quarrel between them as to how faithful an ally Francis I had been.[78] Nonetheless both men were highly experienced and they set about their mission with dispatch, immediately contacting de Selve and making plans to see Henry on 11 November.

The King however was not prepared to make them welcome. They cooled their heels for ten days chatting with de Selve until on Sunday the 21st Henry gave them a short and tempestuous interview at Oatlands. He refused the letters patent accepting the comprehension, railed that the Scots had already broken the peace, 'blasmant fort les Escossoys d'estre de peu de foy [strongly condemning the Scots as faithless]' and swore vengeance: all typical Tudor bombast.[79] The Scots yawned. Henry then referred them to the Privy Council. Neither seemed surprised by the King's behaviour; three days later Paniter informed de Selve that he fully expected Henry to resume the war and remarked that it was five times cheaper for France to attack England through Scotland than elsewhere.[80] On 27 November the Scots took dinner

---

72 *LP*, xxi (2), nos. 347, 415, 423, 444. Some reports were that war had recommenced (*Ibid.*, no. 440).

73 See J.A. Inglis, *Sir Adam Otterburn of Redhall, King's Advocate, 1524–38.*

74 *Mary of Lorraine Corresp.*, 171.

75 *RPC*, i, 44.

76 *Odet de Selve*, 71.

77 *Mary of Lorraine Corresp.*, 172; *TA*, viii, 485; *RSS*, iii, no. 1971; *LP*, xxi (2), no. 396.

78 *Odet de Selve*, 54–55, 73; *CSP Spain*, ix, 50.

79 It is not clear just how Henry regarded Scotland in the last months of his life. Paget, reminiscing in 1549, said that the King 'vpon consideracon of his estate and condition at home' decided firmly 'to forbeare the warres with scotland'. Paget argued that this was 'not dishonor to him at all'. Northants Record Office, Ms.

80 *Odet de Selve*, 51, 57–58; *LP*, xxi (2), no. 443.

with the Privy Council; de Selve and van der Delft were also present. It too was 'tres agitee'. The Council argued that Henry was quit of the comprehension owing to new unspecified causes of war and because of his alliance with Charles with whom the Scots were still at war. The meeting broke up with the English convinced that the Scots were 'very cunning' and concerned only to gain time.[81]

On 11 December the two had yet another interview with the King, who took a new line, arguing that if the Scots sincerely desired peace, then they should raise the siege of St. Andrews, a suggestion which had been put to Henry several days previously by one of the Castilians. Paniter and Otterburn, who had noted the arrival of various envoys from St. Andrews with annoyance, maintained that their instructions were insufficient but promised to pass on the request to Arran. On 20 December Henry wrote to Arran directly on the matter; a joint letter from the ambassadors the next day copied the King's wording.[82] Thus December passed with little accomplished, and each side saw the other as merely temporising.[83] On 20 January 1547 there was another fruitless interview with the King.[84] Eight days later, Henry VIII died.[85] The only Scottish reaction was an immediate renewal (13 February) of the letters patent accepting the comprehension and the issuance of new instructions to their ambassadors.[86] The King's death did cause a certain speculation as to the future.[87] Perhaps the peace might become permanent.

EDWARD VI:
'I SEE NA THING BOT AS THE ALD KYNG WER LEVYNG'

However, such restraint apparently was alien to Somerset. As early as 3 February, when the Scottish ambassadors first interviewed him (and Paget), they found, 'as we fand at all tymes', that no peace treaty would be considered which did not include the marriage. Otterburn was convinced that war was in the Protector's mind and advised his government to 'mak provisioun, and spetialie for the strength of Edinburgh and qwenis housis of Lothiane'. Two months later: 'As for tydingis heir, I see na thing bot as the ald kyng wer levyng and ilk day I heir of our infelicite'.[88]

One event did raise Scottish hopes: the death of Francis I. Ever since July 1546, the government had been apprehensive about what seemed to be an Anglo-French rapprochement. Rumours that Francis might swap support of the Scots for a return

81 All four participants reported the interview; *LP*, xxi (2), nos. 459, 455; *Odet de Selve*, 66–67; *Mary of Lorraine Corresp.*, 172–3.
82 *LP*, xxi (2), nos. 542, 532, 580, 591.
83 *Odet de Selve*, 68, 72, 83, 86; *LP*, xxi (2), nos. 444, 533, 602, 605, 675, 679, 684, 713.
84 *LP*, xxi (2), no. 760.
85 For notices sent abroad in February, see *CSP For.*, nos. 2–3. French reaction was initially one of delight (*CSP Spain*, ix, 492–93). Otterburn sent the news North on 4 February and Somerset in his first interview with the Scottish ambassador insisted they receive a new commission owing to the death of Henry (*TA*, viii, 58; *Mary of Lorraine Corresp.*, 174–75).
86 *APS*, xii, 43 is a copy of NAS, SP 7/33. The commission was received in London on 21 February (*Odet de Selve*, 105).
87 *CSP Spain*, ix, 41–42, 492–3. Mary of Hungary had reason to be concerned (*CSP For.*, nos. 14, 22, 46, 47; *CSP Spain*, ix, 49).
88 *Mary of Lorraine Corresp.*, 174, 180.

Fig. 9.4. The coronation of Edward VI on 17 February was actually rather a rushed
        job; its organisers were forced to go back to accounts of Henry VIII's in 1509
        (and earlier). Edward obviously succeeded the moment his father died on 28
        January 1547, but the proclamation was delayed for three days. At one
        fountain, boys sang of him becoming king of four kingdoms.

of Boulogne may well have reached their ears, and Otterburn was particularly
distressed to see that 'The ambassadouris of France ar wele tretit and as freyndis, and
we as inymyis'. On 14 March he perceived 'sik kyndnes betuix France and Yngland
that France with nocht displeis thame'. Paniter at much the same time wrote to the
Scottish Council for instructions

> gif the King of Franch wald nothir caus Ingland to comprehend us nor yit
> ansueir us of support conformand to our desyre bot stand undir the fair wordis
> of Ingland without ony uthir securite.[89]

Somerset played on these apprehensions and pressed the Scots to agree to the
marriage, arguing that Francis would no longer aid them, being more concerned 'de
plus grandes entreprinses du coste d'Italye'.[90] Plainly worried, Arran made ready new
embassies for France.

89 *Ibid.*, 177.
90 *Odet de Selve*, 120

At the start of 1547, then, the Scottish government was confused as to how best to treat with the French. At first it had ordered both Otterburn and Paniter to go to France if their negotiations in England proved fruitless, and even before the death of Henry VIII Paniter had asked for (and was refused by Paget) a safe-conduct.[91] On 24 January a new commission was drawn up for Paniter and John Hay to ask Francis' support since Henry would 'in no wise be induced to embrace the peace and observe the article of the comprehension'.[92]

As the English were refusing to permit Paniter's departure, the government then prepared an entirely independent embassy. Originally it was to consist of John Hamilton, Arran's brother, and Hay, but Hamilton's place was taken by James Stewart, Abbot of Dryburgh, one of James V's bastard sons. They set sail in *The Lion* at the beginning of March.[93] In the meantime the English had allowed Paniter to leave on 5 March, his last official function being attendance at the funeral of Henry.[94] It was well that Paniter did leave, for the ship bearing Hay and Dryburgh 'perrest' in a battle with an English fleet near Dover; both were brought to London under close arrest.[95] Thus Paniter alone was the Scottish ambassador in France.

French coolness towards the Scots may have been exaggerated, although it is clear that from June 1546 until Francis' death in March 1547 Anglo-French relations had been more than cordial. Nonetheless, Odet de Selve and others consistently put the Scottish case for comprehension and frequent embassies were made to Scotland itself.[96] Francis consistently sought to protect Scottish interests with the Emperor, and to bring a settlement of that war.[97] Direct military aid was also sent.[98] Nonetheless, Somerset had been correct as well as shrewd to mention the pre-occupation with Italy. But Francis' death on 31 March dramatically changed matters.

As it was, two issues caused a sharp deterioration in relations: the captivity of Hay and Dryburgh and English retention of Langholm. Increasingly acrimonious correspondence ensued from April to June concerning the two ambassadors,[99] although by July one was allowed home on payment of a ransom.[100] Langholm, on the southwest March, had been a constant worry to the government throughout the peace. The English forces there 'subjewis the cuntres adjacent', forced Scots to assure and resulted in a situation in which 'nobody advertissis nor takkis part with

91 *Ibid.*, 174; *Odet de Selve*, 83, 87, 97–87, 105, 107, 109.
92 *LP*, xxi (2), no. 740; *Mary of Lorraine Corresp.*, 174.
93 *LP*, xxi (2), no. 695; *CSP Scot.*, i, no. 5.
94 *Odet de Selve*, 113; *Mary of Lorraine Corresp.*, 175; *CSP Spain* ix, 46–50; *CPR Edward Vi*, v, 396.
95 Otterburn had warned of the English fleet and felt their capture could have been avoided. *Mary of Lorraine Corresp.*, 176, 180; *Odet de Selve*, 117–19; *TA*, ix, 58, 444.
96 *LP*, xxi (2), nos. 509, 547, 684; *Balcarres Papers*, i, 148–56; *TA*, viii, 335, 361; ix, 52, 58; *APC*, ii, 448; *Mary of Lorraine Corresp.*, 174.
97 *CSP Spain*, ix, 12, 42–43.
98 *TA*, ix, 64; *APC*, ii, 467, 471; *CSP Scot.*, i, no. 10; *CSP Dom.*, *Add.*, 1547–65, 321.
99 *CSP Scot.*, i, nos. 9, 15, 18, 1180. The French were also concerned and exerted some pressure for their release (*Odet de Selve*, 123; *Balcarres Papers*, i, 159–65; *CSP Spain*, ix, 112–13, 147–9; *Mary of Lorraine Corresp.*, 185).
100 *CSP Dom.*, *Add.*, 1547–65, 325, 351; *Odet de Selve*, 292.

scotland' and which the government considered to be 'plane conquest without remand'.[101] The Scots determined that if the French could not effect its surrender, then they would besiege it even though 'the article of comprehension is in danger to be disolved'. A retaliatory Border raid into England in March, the size of which the English deliberately exaggerated, exacerbated relations.[102]

Arran clearly determined to strike, and a Convention at Linlithgow on 8–13 April agreed to reduce Langholm.[103] On 17 May Arran demanded that Somerset release Johnstone and both governments prepared for hostilities.[104] Arran set out for Langholm on 12 June with the Queen Dowager but was forced, probably by the 'ewill wedder' and insufficient numbers, to retire from Dumfries on 23 June.[105] However, on 11 July he returned to Peebles with a much larger army which included upwards of 7,000 of Huntly's 'wild Irish'. By 17 July, Langholm was forced to yield.[106]

'YOUR FREYNDIS AR GRET CONSALORIS AND REULARIS' AND: 'CESTE PETITTE CAMPAIGNE'

Henry II and his father had never been on warm terms. Henry detested many of those, such as d'Annebaut, who had been Francis' closest colleagues. His accession – the news of which reduced the dead King's mistress, Madame d'Etampes, to hysterics – meant an almost clean sweep of the old court and the creation of a new one.[107] As early as 6 April, Wotton reported that the constable Anne de Montmorency was returned to favour: a stunning reversal of his exile since 1541. Moreover, the Guises were in great favour: 'for the authority of these their brethren, it is thought that the Scots shall lack neither help nor favour'.[108] Paniter, in France since early March, similarly reported a change in Scottish fortunes. He had an early interview with the new King and informed Mary of Guise, 'your freyndis ar gret consaloris and reularis'. At the end of May, Arran's information was that the Queen Dowager's 'fader and

101 BL, MS Add. 21, 198, fo. 9. The capture of the laird of Johnstone, the government's only loyal supporter of note, in April was a serious blow; in English eyes, 'sa profitable ane thing for the west Border of ingland sens the solway moss' (PRO, SP 50/1, fo. 32v [*CSP Scot.*, ix, no. 13]; see also *Odet de Selve*, 130, 159; *CSP For.*, 10–11; *Diurnal of Occurrents*, 43). *CSP Dom., Add., 1547–65*, 320–23.
102 *Odet de Selve*, 124; *APC*, ii, 467.
103 *Mary of Lorraine Corresp.*, 117; *CSP Dom., Add., 1547–65*, 323–24.
104 *CSP Scot.*, i, no. 1180; J. Nicolson and R. Burns, *History and Antiquities of the Countries of Westmorland and Cumberland* (1777), i, lvi-lviii; *CSP Dom., Add., 1547–65*, 325; *APC*, ii, 94, 477–8, 485, 493, 497, 501, 511; *Odet de Selve*, 157.
105 *TA*, ix, 77–81, 84; *Diurnal of Occurrents*, 44. Odet de Selve also mentioned 'du maulvais tempts qu'il faict audict pays' (*Odet de Selve*, 159).
106 There is considerable evidence for this raid: *Diurnal of Occurrents*, 43–44; Dalrymple, *Historie*, ii, 294; Pitscottie, *Historie*, ii, 89; Ridpath, *Border History*, 559; *CSP Scot.*, i, nos. 19–23; *CSP Dom., Add., 1547–65*, 326–7; *Odet de Selve*, 159, 160, 173 (he also mentioned 'sept mil saulvaiges').
107 The death of Francis and its ramifications are handsomely captured by R.J. Knecht, *Francis I*; J. Jacquart, *François Ier* and Ivan Cloulas, *Henri II*, 133–44.
108 P.F. Tytler, *England Under the Reigns of Edward VI and Mary* (1839), i, 35–37. See *CSP For.*, 331–2 and also warning to the Council of the North of 12 April (*APC*, ii, 475).

freyndis standis in guyd fawwor wyth this kyng', news, coupled with the suggestion that Henry was interested in a French marriage for the Scottish Queen, that left Arran 'bot sobyrlye content'.[109]

Three full sets of instructions exist. Those received by Paniter in Paris on 23 May 1547 largely incorporated the articles formulated on 14 August 1546 and augmented on 26 November.[110] In the first place, the French King was to ensure that comprehension was confirmed so that Scotland would have 'perfite peax with Ingland siclike as the realme of france hes'. Four further demands were made: English wardens to keep days of truce on the Borders; return of the pledges given after the death of James V; return of Langholm tower; release of Hay and Dryburgh. The French King was to aid the Scots by ensuring that Lennox received no favour and by gaining a new absolution from Rome for the Castilians.[111] Externally he was to help negotiate peace with the Emperor and to gain aid from Denmark. However, the brunt of the Scottish demands was for military assistance against the English. In November 1546, the Scots expected an English attack in February; by May 1547, the date had slipped forward, to midsummer:

> It is actualie weir betwuix scotland and ingland quhilk hes continewit yis vj zeiris bigan. It hes extrymiate yis realme quhilk may not gudlie sustene langar ye saidis weir without yis maist cristin King do for his part conforme to ye aldis ligh and bandis betuix ye realme of france and scotland yat is to say ye said King of france do declare him innemy to ye said King of ingland and mak weir upon him with all his power bayth by sey and land.

The aid considered necessary in May was: enough money to sustain 10,000 soldiers for six months (calculated in November as 200,000 Crowns of the Sun: approximately £s202,500) plus 10,000 pikes with artillery and munitions. One significant request was for twenty-four 'cunning men expert in the weris for the ordering of batles and that can reinforce strengthis'. Henry II was particularly exhorted to make himself 'sa streichen by sey yat he may be maistir'; he should also plan to invade England; he would 'the sonner cum to his intent rather yan to mak the weir upoun bullonze'. All of this was remarkably shrewd and demonstrates a vigorous and accurate strategic sense by Arran's Council. Since they continued to refuse the marriage, England would shortly make war.

Arran may well have wished to celebrate this victory, but he had to hasten North to St. Andrews. There both sides had been holding back since December awaiting the papal absolution. The Castilians, so an English spy reported, would rather 'hayf

109 *Mary of Lorraine Corresp.*, 182–3.
110 The three sets of instructions are to be found respectively in: *APS*, ii, 471 (*LP*, xxi (1), 1456); *RPC*, i, 56 (*LP*, xxi (2), no. 451); BL, Add MS 23, 108, fos. 8–9. This last set was also probably described by Fraser in *HMC*, 4, 5th R., 651, but his notes are not full and he mentions an extra article. It is he who gives the date of the instruction's arrival in Paris. See also *Epistolae Jacobi, Quarti, Jacobi Quinti et Mariae Regum Scotorum*, ed. T. Ruddiman (Edinburgh, 1722–24), i, 376.
111 Oddly enough, the May instructions made no mention of 'My Lord Governouris pensioun and callaris of the ordour as wes desyrit of befor' (*RPC*, i, 56).

ane boll of quhet nor all the papes remessyhones', an assessment with which Odet de Selve agreed.[112] When it finally did arrive in March or April, they refused it, cavilling over the clause 'Remittimus Irremissibile'.[113] The government duly sent the French messenger back for a more acceptable version and on 6 May Arran wrote to the Pope direct for the form of words 'that thai in the Castell desires'.[114] An obvious reason for the Castilians' resistance was the considerable aid they now received from England. One of the first acts of Somerset's regency had been to enter on 6 February into a formal agreement with them. Balnavis received something like £1180 as pensions for the principal conspirators and for wages to a number of soldiers.[115] Later in the month Andrew Dudley sailed North with the supplies and a set of detailed contracts for the Castilians to sign.

In return for aid and money, the Castilians were to hold St. Andrews against the Scottish government 'for the better staye and suryte of themselfes and his Majesties freendis in Scotland and thadvancement and perfection of the said mariage' which was to create 'a perpetualle peax, unite and hardy naturall love between both the Realmes'. In return for English livings [incomes] equal to their own, they would surrender the castle to an English force which they would then aid, and they would finally surrender Arran's sons to Somerset.[116]

These articles were signed on 15 March.[117] Dudley also had discussion with Patrick Lord Gray, and on 11 March he signed articles especially drawn up for him. He was to 'do all thyngs that I can untyll the said mariag to tak Effectuall end', deliver his castle of Broughty Craig to the English and help the English to capture Perth. In return Gray was to receive compensation for his fishing rights at Broughty, release of his brother then held in London and help in 'recovering of the town of Stanct Johnstoun [Perth] In my keepyng and to put my Ennemes furth of the samnyn'.[118]

Once the articles were signed, the English sent substantial aid to the castle and the pensions and wages were promptly renewed in May.[119] When Balnavis arrived in

112 *CSP Scot.*, i, no. 10; *Odet de Selve*, 134; *TA*, ix, 69; *Mary of Lorraine Corresp.*, 175.

113 Knox, *History*, i, 94.

114 BL, MS Add., 32,091, fo. 140. One version of the May 1547 instructions to Paniter contained a request to Henry II that he obtain a more sufficient absolution from the Pope than that obtained by Francis I (*HMC*, 4, 5th R., 651).

115 *APC*, ii, 12–13. *CSP Scot.*, i, no. 8; *Odet de Selve*, 109; *CSP Spain*, ix, 49, 51; *Mary of Lorraine Corresp.*, 175.

116 *CSP Scot.*, i, nos. 2–3. The much amended draft of these articles is in PRO, SP 50/1, fos. 6–9 and 12–14 (a further draft, but not just for Rothes, as stated in the calendar). See also *CSP Spain*, ix, 140 where Somerset complained at their continued refusal to hand over Arran's son.

117 *Foedera*, ix, 145.

118 PRO, SP 50/1, fo. 15v (*CSP Scot.*, i, no. 4); *Mary of Lorraine Corresp.*, 184. Gray's treason was unknown to the government until very late indeed; for but one example, see grant to him of 8 September 1547 (BN, MS fonds anglais, 132, fo. 2). Note also pardon given to Henry Durham who doubtless helped the English to prepare the very specific articles for Gray (*RSS*, iii, no. 2420).

119 *APC*, ii, 89–90; *CSP Scot.*, i, nos. 13, 19; *CSP Spain*, ix, 102.

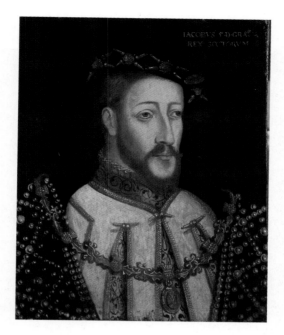

James V, King of Scotland (1513–42), nephew to Henry VIII of England (1512–42), son-in-law of Francis I of France (1537) and father of Mary Queen of Scots (1542).

Mary's birthplace and home for eight months: Linlithgow Palace. From Michel Bouquet, *Scotland. The Tourist's Rambles in the Highlands* (Paris, c.1850).

Francis I, father of Madeleine (b.1521), Queen of Scotland (1537) and Henry II, King of France (1547–59).

Francis' great rival, Karl von Habsburg (b.1500), Charles of Burgundy (1506–55), King of Castile (1506–56), King of Aragon (1516–56), Charles V, Holy Roman Emperor (1519–56), died 1558.

Henry Tudor (1491–1547), King of England (1509–47), father to Queen Mary (b.1516), 1553–58, King Edward VI (b.1537), 1547–53 and Queen Elizabeth (b. 1533), 1558–1603.

Henry's son: Edward Tudor, Prince of Wales (1537–53), King of England (1547–53).

Edward Seymour (b. 1506?), Earl of Hertford (1537), Duke of Somerset (1547), executed in 1552.

Henry II of France (b.1519), Dauphin (1536–47), King of France (1547–59).

Mary Queen of Scots (1542–67), executed in 1587, portrayed in 1552 at the age of ten.

François d'Angoulême-Valois (b. 1544), Dauphin (1547–59), King of Scotland (1558–60), Francis II of France (1559–60).

English warman: Andrew Wyndham, Vice-Admiral of the Fleet, as painted by Hans Eworth in 1550.

English warman: Sir John Luttrell, Captain of Broughty garrison (1548–50), as painted in 1590 from an original by Hans Eworth, executed in 1550.

(Top) medallion struck to commemorate the marriage of Francis and Mary in 1558; (bottom) seal of Francis and Mary as King and Queen of France, Scotland, England and Ireland (1559–60).

London in April, he was given both money and considerable military and building supplies, in particular two tons of 'yron and stele'. Equally useful were 'Archane de Arrain', whom Otterburn reported to be 'the best gunnar in Yngland',[120] and Guillaume di Rossetti, an Italian surveyor who was to advise as to the strengthening of the castle.[121] The danger lay in the Castilians' future utility to the English and as a magnet for disaffected Scots. In April Balnavis supposedly brought the signatures of twenty-three nobles 'oblising thame to this kyng', and a later report mentioned a register in the castle of 200 Scots who had assured to aid the English.[122] The government did make some moves against the castle,[123] but as late as May Arran still seemed to hope that the papal absolution would solve the problem.

The fact that Arran was at Langholm when a French force arrived[124] may indicate that the expedition was readied with speed and secrecy. Certainly the English were caught totally unawares.[125] Henry II of France had been worried by events in Scotland and by Arran's plans to marry the Queen to his son.[126] Odet de Selve had kept him fully informed of the potential threat which the castle represented, and in a remarkably perceptive report to the constable on 24 April he argued:

> Ce seroyt ung tres grand dommaige que ladicte place de Saunct-Andre vint entre les mains des anglogs ausquelz il seroyt tres malaise de lever ce pied de l'Escosse s'ilz luy avoint ugne foiz mictz, car vous scaves, Monseigneur, comme ilz tiennent et fortiffient ce que ilz peuvent prendre, et a ce que j'entendz des ceste heure ladicte place n'est pas foyble et sy a la commodite d'estre rendue merveilleusement fort avec peu de temps et de despence.

> It would be a serious hurt if St. Andrews came into the hands of the English whom it would be very hard to extricate once they had taken possesion of it, because as you know, Monsieur, how they have held and fortified where they can and I understand that even now that [St. Andrews] is not weak, and also it is capable of being rendered marvellously strong in a very short time and without great expense.[127]

As early as 9 May he was sending maps of Scotland to France and later he sent an untranslated 'livre de la navigation'.[128] Throughout the English were ignorant of French intentions, and when the fleet of seventeen sails was sighted in the Channel

---

120 *Mary of Lorraine Corresp.*, 184; *CSP Scot.*, i, no. 14; *CSP Spain*, ix, 102; *APC*, ii, 90. De Selve was informed that the man sent was Henry Benoist, a master artillerist (*Odet de Selve*, 141–4).

121 He made two trips to Scotland at this time, in May and June, and clearly investigated sites in Fife for future English forts (*Mary of Lorraine Corresp.*, 188; *CSP Scot.*, i, no. 27). Pitscottie said that he was in St. Andrews at the time of its capture by the French, but he probably is in error (Pitscottie, *Historie*, ii, 90).

122 *Odet de Selve*, 141; *CSP Scot.*, i, no. 33. Cf. *Mary of Lorraine Corresp.*, 184.

123 *TA*, ix, 76; *RPC*, i, 62, 73.

124 It was during this raid on Langholm that the father of Rothes, John Lesley, Earl of Rothes, was acquitted of complicity in his son's deeds (*HMC*, 2, 3rd R., 504).

125 *CSP Spain*, ix, 35, 112–13; *Odet de Selve*, 126, 129.

126 *Odet de Selve*, 123, 162.

127 *Ibid.*, 134.

128 *Ibid.*, 143, 145–6.

on 3 July Somerset had no idea as to its purpose.[129] Initially he speculated that it was to take Mary to France; Paget thought it brought aid for the siege of Langholm.[130] The papal nuncio in France knew of its purpose as early as 9 July; English agents did not know until 23 July that it aimed for St. Andrews. Somerset was even driven to asking de Selve of its progress.[131]

The fleet probably arrived off St. Andrews on 16 July;[132] by the time Arran and the Queen Dowager returned from Langholm on 25 July, the siege under Leon Strozzi had begun.[133] It succeeded brilliantly and by 30 July the Castilians had surrendered.[134] On 3 August Mary of Guise despatched de Combas, the messenger who had brought the papal absolution several months earlier, with news of the success 'de ceste petite campaigne' and praise for 'les vertueulx gentilz hommes' who had taken the castle.[135] Henry immediately wrote to Brussels and Rome that St. Andrews 'a remis . . . en les mainz de la Royne et governeur'.[136] Having sacked the castle and imprisoned the 'heretiques', Strozzi departed for France on 7 August.[137]

Again Arran could spend little time celebrating for on 3 August he hastened from St. Andrews to prepare for the English invasion which he now knew would shortly descend upon Scotland. Throughout the spring and summer Otterburn had continued his fruitless negotiations in London, aided by de Selve and a special French envoy sent in May. But the list of English grievances against Scotland expanded as the year wore on: Border incursions, piracy, aid to Irish rebels, then the attack on Langholm.[138] On 28 April Otterburn suggested that Somerset 'sall nocht invaid oure realme this yeir' and he remained optimistic as late as 4 June.[139] But by 29 June the die seemed cast:

129 *Ibid.*, 158, 161, 163, 166; *CSP Dom., Add., 1547–65*, 326–8.

130 Somerset immediately put to Otterburn the view that the French were to remove the Queen (*Odet de Selve*, 161; *CSP Dom., Add., 1547–65*, 328). *CSP Spain*, ix, 124.

131 *Nonces en France, 1546–51*, 210; *CSP Scot.*, i, no. 30 and CF nos. 32, 36; *Odet de Selve*, 169, 176, 178; *CSP Spain*, ix, 129.

132 The fleet passed Holy Isle on 13 July (*CSP Dom., Add., 1547–65*, 326–28). The *Diurnal* gives the date as 24 July, but it may be confusing that with date of commencement of the siege (*Diurnal of Occurrents*, 44). None of the other narrative sources gives the arrival date, only that of surrender (Dalrymple, *Historie*, ii, 295; Pitscottie, *Historie*, ii, 88–91) except Knox who states it to have been on 30 June (Knox, *History*, i, 94–97), but he is obviously wrong, as is Jordan to have followed his dating (*Edward VI*, 245).

133 *RSS*, iii, xxxv; *Mary of Lorraine Corresp.*, 191; BN, MS fr. 3152, fo. 85. Artillery from the siege of Langholm accompanied him (*TA*, ix, 96, 102).

134 The terms which Henry II outlined in his letter of 15 August (BN, MS fr. 20,449, p. 76) differ considerably from those given by Knox (Knox, *History*, i, 95).

135 BN, MS fr., 3152, fo. 85; *TA*, ix, 444.

136 BN, MS fr., 2,449, p. 76; *Nonces en France, 1546–51*. The purpose of the letter to Brussels was to assure Charles V that the fleet intended nothing against the Low Countries; the date in this copy, 11 July, must be incorrect as the Imperial ambassador in Paris reported arrival of the news on 15 August, whereupon Henry immediately wrote to Brissac, his ambassador with the Emperor (*CSP Spain*, ix, 123, and see 129, 132, 139–40, 512–15 for French justifications of the act).

137 *Diurnal of Occurrents*, 44.

138 *Mary of Lorraine Corresp.*, 176–88;1 *Odet de Selve*, 124, 141, 147–50, 153; *CSP Spain*, ix, 90, 103, 106–08; *CSP For.*, 10–11; *APC*, ii, 492.

139 But de Selve did not agree (*Odet de Selve*, 141, 144, 181).

Ther is na apperance of motion in this cuntre except aganys ws. Ther folkis proposls to bryng graith [war supplies] and werkmen to sett up fortilis quhar thai think best in Fiff or Lothiane and quhar thai have moniest fawveraris, of the quhilkis I dreid thai have our mony [too many].[140]

It appeared possible that war might be avoided when Somerset made two offers to resolve the matter without 'the effusioun of blude and distructioun of the pure pupill'. On 12 July he offered to Otterburn (who as early as 23 May had asked to return home) 'to depute certaine commissionaris' to settle Border grievances and resolve the comprehension.[141] Elaborate instructions were issued to the English negotiators who were to insist upon the elimination of 'the root of all the stryfe': Scottish refusal to agree to the marriage.[142] However, the Scottish recapture of Langholm so angered Somerset that on 28 July he ordered the meeting be cancelled.[143] On 7 August Otterburn was called to Hampton Court, informed that it was unreasonable 'that I suld remain in tyme of hostilite' and given £75. However, as he packed the next morning Somerset asked him for a last interview on 9 August. The ambassador appeared early in the morning to hear a long protestation from the Duke, in the presence of Edward VI, that 'I am ane man gevin alwayis adressit for the eis of bayth the realmz'. If Arran would commission George Douglas to negotiate at Newcastle on 27 August, war might not be necessary.[144] Otterburn recommended compliance, but Arran raised so many objections that this second approach also misfired.[145] Somerset was not to gain his ends by threat.

The threat by August was very real, as Otterburn's eloquent description testified: 'I saw afoir my eis verray gret preparatioun of weir and actualle the gret hors the harnes the hagbutaris and all gorgious reparrale set forwart towart our realme'.[146] Otterburn's warnings were amply supplemented throughout the summer by de Selve, by the Scottish herald who carried letters to London and by the spy Alan Turner.[147] By May English preparations were well afoot, musters were being held in the shires and considerable activity took place along the Border.[148] By 23 July de Selve's network of spies had given him the numbers, route and target of the English army.[149]

---

140 *Mary of Lorraine Corresp.*, 187–88.

141 *Odet de Selve*, 144; *Mary of Lorraine Corresp.*, 188.

142 The instructions to Bowes and Tunstall are in PRO, SP 50/1, nos. 51–53.

143 *APC*, ii, 515.

144 *Mary of Lorraine Corresp.*, 192–93; *APC*, ii, 112.

145 *CSP Scot.*, i, no. 35. Odet de Selve thought the proposal was an attempt 'a endormir le gouverneur' (*Odet de Selve*, 180).

146 *Mary of Lorraine Corresp.*, 192.

147 *Odet de Selve*, 168–69; *CSP Scot.*, i, no. 13; *TA*, viii, 479–80; ix, 33–35, 56, 58, 61, 63, 113.

148 *APC*, ii, 115, 489, 511; *Hamilton Papers*, ii, 596; *CSP Spain*, ix, 107; *CSP Scot.*, i, nos. 26–34; *CSP Dom., Add., 1547–65*, 322–25; *Miscellany of Maitland Club* (Maitland Club, 1833–47), iv, 21–22; *Illustrations of British History*, ed. E. Lodge (1838), i, 144–45; PRO SP 10/2, fos. 4, 9; BL, MS Harl., 6986, fo. 17.

149 *Odet de Selve*, 169–75. Van der Delft was not informed by Somerset that war was definite until 24 July (*CSP Spain*, ix, 143).

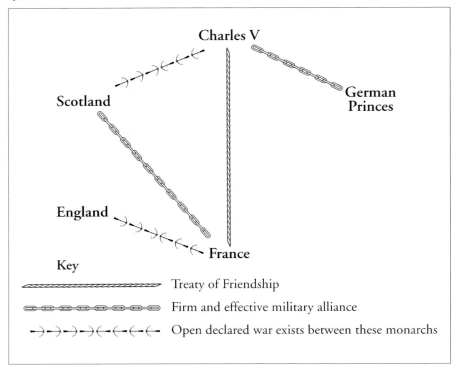

Fig. 9.5.   June 1546–September 1547. During this period, Anglo-French relations remained peaceful, but in variable form. Until Francis I died in March 1547, relations between them were remarkably cordial and little assistance was afforded the Scots by their auld ally. However, with Henry II's accession, Scotland became once more important to French policy-makers as was witnessed by a French naval expedition in June–July 1547 which effected the reconquest of St. Andrews Castle. It immediately departed, taking John Knox and others as prisoners to France.

The Scots took heed of these omens, and as early as 19 March musters were ordered and clear advice of the approaching war was given to all the great nobles of the realm.[150] Troops of horse were stationed along the Marches on 3 May and three weeks later warning beacons were manned throughout the East March and along the coast. On 1 July all Scots were ordered to be ready for war on 1 August and a tax of £35,000 was levied, seeing that the Council was 'surlie informit of the greit preparationis the tyrany divisit and ordanit be our saidis auld ynemeis for the distructioun of the realme this next harvist approchant'.[151]

Edinburgh Castle, Hume, Dunbar and Annan were all strengthened and re-inforced; artillery, some of which had gone first to Langholm, thence to St. Andrews,

150 *RPC*, i, 62–63; *TA*, ix, 665.
151 *RPC*, i, 73–76; *TA*, ix, 71, 76–77.

was gathered for the army; a fleet was prepared to guard the west coast.[152] As the English forces began to gather at Newcastle, Arran issued progressively urgent instructions: on 3 August all men were ordered to be ready on eight hours' notice; on 17 August 'the hale greit men of the North' were called to Edinburgh; on 21 August the rest were summoned and 'al kirkmen to com forward to the army'. Finally, on 23 August, 'being surelie advertisit that the army of Ingland wes at hand', five messengers with 'proclamatioun witht the fire croce' were sent throughout Scotland ordering all to assemble near Edinburgh in eight days' time.[153] Then the Scottish host would move towards Musselburgh. On 27 August, Somerset arrived at Newcastle and then moved North to Berwick-upon-Tweed with the great army with which he was to invade Scotland for the third time in his career.

152 *TA*, ix, 99–104. Even at this late date, ships were sailing from Leith 'conforme to the tyme of peax' (*Edin. Burgh Recs.*, ii, 129).

153 *TA*, ix, 106–11; *CSP Scot.*, i, nos. 34, 37, 40; *RPC*, i, 77–78; *CSP Dom.*, *Add.*, *1547–65*, 329; *HMC*, 2, 3rd R., 422; *Yester Writs* (Scottish Record Soc.), 55.

CHAPTER TEN

The Second Rough Wooing: Somerset's War, 1547–48

Utque Angli, fusque tua gens effera Scota
Dextra, qua nunquam visa est victoria major
Det DEUS imperium per te coeamus in unum
Simus et unanimes per secula cuncta Britanni

The English by your right hand defeated the wild people the Scots
By a victory, greater than which never has been seen
Let GOD comand that through you we shall join in one
And be united as the Britons through all the centuries[1]

SOMERSET AND THE NEW WAR[2]

In 1546, England and Scotland had come to peace. Mary Queen of Scots remained safe in Stirling Castle under the care of her guardians and mother. Despite some anti-clerical rioting in the aftermath of Cardinal Beaton's murder, the kingdom was in fact fairly peaceful, with the exception of the embarrassing, but contained, cancer of the 'Castilians' holed up in Beaton's powerful castle at St. Andrews. Henry VIII growled defiance and menace, but these were the empty bombast of a dying man and meant little.

His death in January 1547 might have meant an end to the war for Mary's betrothal to the ten-year-old boy who was now King Edward VI. But that opportunity was refused when the regime which took over the government of England quickly slid under the dominance of Edward Seymour (Edward's mother's brother), earl of Hertford and now Protector and Duke of Somerset. Somerset was a typical sixteenth-century aristocrat, but a highly intelligent one (in certain limited ways) and he hid his thuggishness at first under the appealing cloak of an idealist. As a politician Somerset suffered from a gambler's instinct, poor judgement, an appalling bad temper and tunnel vision. He seemed totally unable to act on sound advice. Not

---

1 Such was the boastful epigram penned by Armigil Wade in Somerset's honour after hearing the news of the great victory of Pinkie, for which a *Te Deum* was celebrated in St Paul's on his return from the field.

2 No student of Somerset's campaign can ignore Michael Bush's stunning study of the Protector's policy, the centrepiece of both Somerset's career and Bush's book, *The Government Policy of the Protector Somerset* (1974). But now, all such students must also comprehend the massive and highly successful reinterpretation of Somerset's war to be found in Phillips, *The Anglo-Scottish Wars*. Chapter 5, 'The Campaigns of 1547', 178–201, is essential as a starting point.

surprisingly he would fall from power in 1549 and lose his head in 1552. But he did have a certain brilliance, particularly when it came to the waging of war.

Indeed he had made his name through warfare. After a short episode as commander in the North in 1542, he was then in charge of major field armies invading Scotland in 1544 and 1545 and also prominent in France in 1544–46 with the capture and refortification of Boulogne. From these 'schools of war' he had learned much. Even if he adhered to the King's basic strategic mistake, he sagely reversed many of Henry's tactics. The Rough Wooing of 1544–46 had consisted of ineffective pinpricks or hit-and-run raids, neither of which forced the Scots into submission.

His key innovation (which had been growing in his mind since 1542) was to defeat the Scottish government through a permanent conquest of part of the realm. This would be accomplished through stationing fulltime garrisons of troops in strongholds. So far, so good, but it took him time to work this brainstorm (which, of course, Edward I had tried before) out in his head and he made numerous little learning mistakes (such as a classic bungle of proposing a fort at the utterly indefensible Kelso Abbey) as he went along. But he was learning all the time, especially in France. There he had seen on the ground how Italian military engineers working for Francis I could build in several months fortifications to an entirely new design which were remarkably resistant to bombardment by artillery. These quick, cheap forts, called nowadays the *trace italienne*, were characterised by thick earth walls (50 to 60 feet thick as against the 12 feet at stone-built Tantallon) and a diamond-shaped bulwark attached to the wall called an angle-bastion. Built, armed and garrisoned, these structures could both house mini-armies 'in the bowels now of the realm' which were able to raid, pillage and harry the Scottish countryside and withstand any siege, particularly by the Scots, unable even to reduce St. Andrews Castle (a task accomplished in 1547 by a French force).

And so his grand plan unfolded. In the summer of 1547, Somerset gathered together another largeish (15,000), relatively professional army many of whose combatants were foreign mercenaries with wide experience on the Continent. In particular, the army was provided with moveable field artillery and hand-held guns (micro-artillery if you will). Up the coast road from Newcastle it tramped, to Berwick, past Cockburnspath and into the East Lothian plain. Somerset also appreciated the use of sea power (a lesson he applied so well in 1544) and a large fleet shadowed the army, in part as logistical support (carrying food, munitions and supplies), but also as a large cluster of bobbing, movable gun platforms.

But what greeted him when he surmounted the crest at Fawside Brae above Pinkie on 10 September must have proved something of a shock, for Somerset was not the only one able to learn from the experience of war. Arran had done so too. Whereas he had been caught napping at Edinburgh in 1544, now an efficient and accurate spy network gave him full details of what he had to confront. Secondly, long campaigns on the Borders since 1542 meant that the Scots were much more organised and experienced in warfare. They still did not have enough trained gunners for their artillery, and sufficient horsemen were also lacking, since most of the Scottish cavalry were badly mauled on the 9th. Still, the army at Pinkie was a remarkable accomplishment: one of the largest Scottish hosts in history lay mustered on the west bank of the Esk; moreover it stood behind well-prepared trenchworks, including some which faced seawards, further evidence of Arran's preparedness. The army very effectively shielded Edinburgh from any attack, for its left was bounded by the sea and its right by an impenetrable marsh. It looked as if Somerset would either have to make a frontal assault on the formidably defended Scottish position or retire ignominiously home, as had happened to Norfolk in 1542 and to himself in 1545.

Battles invariably are confused affairs and most pre-twentieth-century ones are desperately difficult to reconstruct in retrospect; Pinkie (despite numerous eye witnesses) is no exception. But the broad outlines are fairly certain.[3] Somerset, clearly hoping to employ his superior firepower against the Scots, shifted his right wing to take Eskdale Kirk (just off the old A1) as a gunnery position. For reasons which remain obscure, Arran decided to attempt to assault the English as they seemed to be offering their flank to him. The day began with the Scots moving with remarkable and frightening rapidity, dragging their artillery with them up the slope of Fawside Brae. For a breath-stopping while it seemed as if the Scots pikemen would catch the English on the hop and Somerset was reduced to something of a panic. But the Earl of Warwick, the future Northumberland, kept his cool and a furious, desperate shock charge by the heavy horse was orchestrated against the advancing Scots.. This at least halted the Scottish host. Then gradually English gunfire (the fleet helped here, too) wore the Scots down. Suddenly the army began to disintegrate and it was Arran who panicked. When he fled the field, the Scots, despite Angus's resolve, lost cohesion and ran too.

The killing field in mediaeval battles usually happened when one force broke and fled. Indeed at Pinkie the two sides only confronted each other hand to hand (or pike to horse) for less than an hour. It was in the bombardment, but much more in their flight, that the Scots lost most of the 10,000 who perished on Black Saturday. For as the footmen dashed for the safety of the marsh or of Arthur's Seat, they were ridden down and slaughtered. As Patten graphically described the gory scene:

> Dead corpses lying dispersed abroad. Some with their legs cut off; some but ham-strung and left lying half dead: others, with the arms cut off; divers, their necks half asunder; many, their heads cloven; of sundry, the brains smashed out; some others again, their heads quite off: with a thousand other kinds of killing. . . . And thus, with blood and slaughter of the enemy, this chase was continued.

And so Somerset was master of the field. A great Wembley roar went up from the English force which could be heard in the very streets of Edinburgh, and a Niagara of beer was disbursed to the victors as they celebrated in Leith the next day. Scotland for

---

3 All too many accounts of the battle exist, one example being Sir Charles Oman's in his 1937 *A History of the Art of War in the Sixteenth Century*, 358–67. David Caldwell then revolutionised our understanding of the day with his excellent 1991 monograph, The Battle of Pinkie', in *Scotland and War, AD* 79–1918 (ed. N. Macdougall), 61–94. However, no account has ever really made sense to me until Phillips's in *Anglo-Scots Wars*, 191–200 despite the lack of any diagrams or plans.

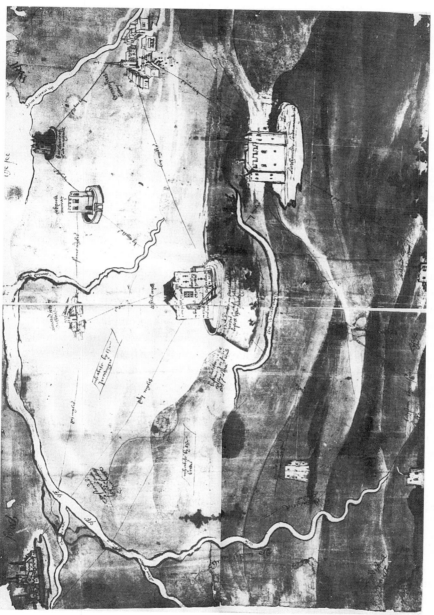

Fig. 10.1. Oman's view of Pinkie. In 1897, whilst researching his famous work, *The Art of War in the Middle Ages*, Charles Oman was working, as ever, in the Bodleian Library, Oxford and had one of those most delicious of moments: when you find something new. It was a magnificent 'battle portrait' of Pinkie. What he had laid his hands on was not the original illustration which had been lost, doubtless in a domestic fire, the great destroyer of historical documents before saturation bombing. Still, it – shown here – was extraordinary: a drawing, doubtless by the famous antiquarian John Ramsay, of the original. As with so many such works, it covers three days all crammed onto one canvas: the Scots cavalry being driven off on 9 September, the high point of the battle on the day, and the English army at its ease in Leith on the 11th.

the moment had ceased to exist as a military power. But Somerset, curiously, then did little. Edinburgh was not assaulted (its castle remained one of the strongest in Europe), or torched. Arran sensibly had Mary spirited to safety into the fastness of the Highlands, but Stirling was in no danger, the English army remaining passive at Leith. Somerset waited, not very expectantly, for Scottish submissions; Arran refused. Then, after a fortnight, the great English host rose and departed southwards, over Soutra and home.

The Battle of Pinkie was the subject of intense interest at the time and since: how did it unfold, why did the Scots lose so and the English win spectacularly and what were its lessons? Modern historians have analysed it over the decades: Sir Charles Oman, David Caldwell, Gervase Phillips. I have little to add to their wisdom. But there are some refinements I should like to suggest. Pinkie has always aroused the same comments: that Arran fled the field, once again, and thus his unfitness was confirmed, the Scottish were incompetent (they were impetuous and immature on the battlefield), and lastly the English were superb fighters (Agincourt come again). Well: yes and no.

Somerset's army was perhaps the finest military machine hitherto put together in English history: a brilliant mixture of foreign mercenaries, domestic levies, excellent artillery, valiant cavalry, potent sea power and effective logistical supply. It marched further and won a more total victory in the field than even Henry VIII's Boulogne expeditionary force of 1544 and with one third the manpower and at much less cost.

But the Scottish host at Musselburgh was also a remarkable accomplishment. Parts of it had been in the field for the entire summer, gathered (as was Huntly's Battle) from the North, widely travelled (Edinburgh to Langholm, then back to St. Andrews again and fianally off to Gladsmuir). On the morn of 19 September it was arrayed before the River Esk in one of the most sophisticated field encampments ever erected in the country. It was possessed of a remarkably manoeuvrable field artillery train which almost won the battle. Arran's extensive spy network in England had given his all the 'Enigma' information any commanding general could ask for and he used its indications superbly. When Somerset crested the hill at Inveresk, the Scots most certainly were waiting for him. The one thing the Scots lacked (grievously, as it transpired, and in some senses surprisingly, for they had one of the best light horse in Europe) was a large enough cavalry unit. And thus they lost.

There are three aspects of the battle which, I think, need to be borne in mind. The first is that Somerset did so little with his Agincourt (just as Surrey did so little with his Flodden). He should have taken Edinburgh (the castle could have been ignored, as was done by Prince Charles Edward in 1745) and the town and Canongate fortified against their occupation and use by the Scots. At least he could have fortified and garrisoned Leith, as the French were to do so well a year later. Instead, the fifteen thousand men rested a while by the seaside and then marched home. Why? I think Somerset had worked his war-winning strategy well in advance and stuck to it rigidly despite this magnificent opportunity. Pinkie in that sense was irrelevant. He wanted to fortify along the fringes of the country (so that the garrisons could be cheaply and easily suppied) and did so. He wanted to win as cheaply as he could and Edinburgh was a site too far. I think it was a massive blunder on his part and cost him the war.

Secondly, Somerset's victory was not just a matter of triumphing on the day: it was the result of four long years of activity. England's armies and raiding parties had humiliated and pinpricked the Scots almost constantly since the summer of 1542. While they lost at Haddon Rigg and Ancrum Moor, elsewhere they were invariably successful. Edinburgh was humiliatingly fired in 1544, the Tweed Valley desecrated in 1545. Numerous tower houses were razed; sheep and cattle had been filched from their Scottish owners. The Scots did little in return and made no retaliatory invasions of England, not even in the summer of 1545, when a professional French mini-army reinforced them. Arran followed a Fabian policy. It actually had been successful: he retired and waited for the English to go away, and go away they did every time. At the end of five years of warfare, a massive Scottish army was still in being and indeed one forged on the anvil of those years of practical experience. But, the Scots had had enough. They were goaded into impetuous defeat not just by the events of the first week in September 1547, but by all the long cruel years of war.

Lastly there is what I would call the temper of the age and the shadow of history. The Scottish host on the morning of 10 September was (as were all European aristocratic societies) a chivalric elite armed for battle. Huntly rode out from the camp richly arrayed in his gorgeous new armour. They wanted, they needed, to prove themselves on a field of glory. Merely forcing the English to turn tail and go back to Newcastle was not enough. This was particularly so for Arran. I have suggested elsewhere that James Hamilton was a patriot and will argue in my conclusion that he was the saviour of his country. Had he won at Pinkie, statues to him would dot the landscape today and his place in the textbooks would be assured. He might just have become king, as had Bruce. And that is the real point. What Arran wanted on that Saturday – indeed what the whole Scottish army wanted – was another Bannock-burn. Somerset's evident indecision as to what to do, the English host's real exposure and confusion as they deployed on Fawside, presented Arran with what he sought: a seemingly golden opportunity to achieve a really decisive victory. He might even have captured the persons of Somerset and Warwick, warded them in Edinburgh Castle for their ransoms, and forced a peace treaty out of them. Now, would that not have been a pretty sight?

But, again, he failed and he lost. But what then? He retired to the safety of Hamilton and, in this winter of Scotland's discontent, brooded on what best to do. In the end, he accepted the inevitable: French intervention. It did not win him the textbook hero worship lavished on Wallace and Bruce. But it did save his country.

Somerset commenced the setting up of permanent garrisons with a will. By the time he had recrossed the Tweed, forces were stationed at a new fort at Eyemouth, the first *trace italienne* fortification built in the whole of the British Isles. Troops were also placed in the first besieged and now repaired Hume Castle, also in a rebuilt Roxburgh. His navy transported some 300 to Inchcolm and a further force to the Tay, at Broughty, while on the West Marches, English troops garrisoned Castlemilk, Dumfries and other strongholds. Somerset returned to London to the praise of his King, the plaudits of the Commons and with the expectation that the Scots would simply not be able to resist these St. Andrews castles dotted all over the richest parts of the kingdom.

Indeed English exactions were grievous: Dundee almost destroyed, Fife harried, Kirkcudbright assaulted and the East Borders virtually an English shire. Edinburgh was crowded with refugees; so were monastic houses in the safe parts of the realm with monks from those many religious houses within the compass of English fury. 'This winter war', as one English commander exulted, 'much grieves the hearts of the Scots.'

An appealing vision of a brotherly Anglo-Scottish union of equals with no superiority was widely circulated in 1547–48 through another of the Protector's innovations: a propaganda campaign aimed at convincing thoughtful (and Luther-an-minded) Scots that Union was the better way. Some Scots did collaborate – or 'assure' – and worked for English victory; many were members of the then underground minority of Protestants, who come the Reformation would emerge in the new regime. Some assured Scots had plotted the death of Cardinal Beaton, and Knox knew various of them personally. How much Somerset really believed in the soothing words of the propaganda issued in his name is not clear, but at least he did deliberately recruit unionist Scots, such as the Edinburgh merchant, James Henrisoun, who then produced tracts (some five were printed and circulated in 1547–48: within the context of the sixteenth century, a veritable flood of leaflets) for a Scottish audience and for an English one as well. However, neither was converted.

The war, in truth, was vastly beyond the capabilities of England. Despite all of Somerset's ingenuity and quite sophisticated tactical flair, the brute facts of Scottish geography and European international relations would conspire, not least with his own arrogance, to defeat his policy. That and the proud tenacity of the Scots, determined not to surrender their independence, would nullify his dreams and delay Union at least until 1603, if not 1707. If then, some might say. The point to appreciate is that Arran, for one, was never seduced by English visions of surrender and peace. His back may have been against the wall, but he definitely had alternative options, something Somerset should have appreciated before he began his disas-trously expensive and politically ruinous war. It is to fine details of that war that we now turn.

DREAMS AND PROPHECIES

On 3 September 1547 Edward Seymour took a promenade about the walls of Berwick whilst the great English army assembled around him after its march from Newcastle. The next day, it would invade Scotland. Seymour was one of the great political stories of sixteenth-century England. A mere knight from 1523, his sister's pretty looks in the meat market which was Henry VIII's matrimonial quest in 1536 brought him advancement. As Jane became a Queen, so he was elevated as Viscount Beauchamp

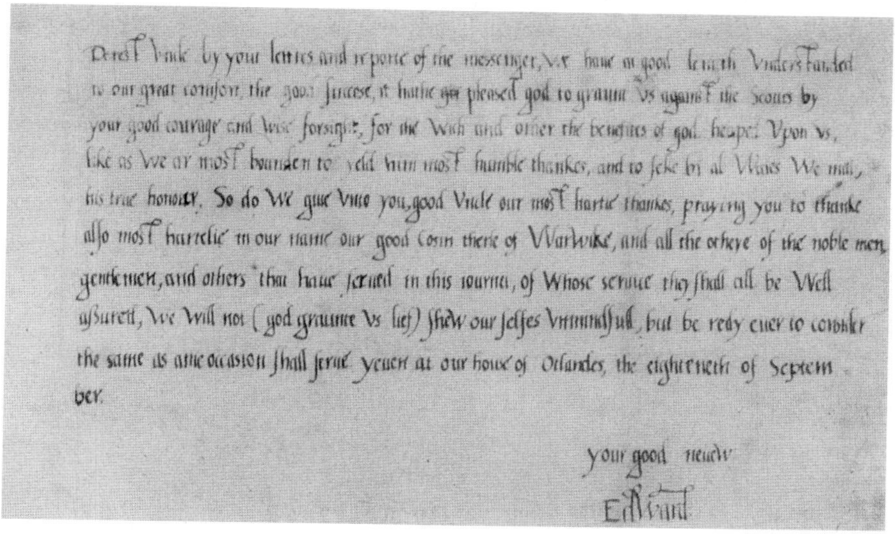

Derest Uncle by your letters and reporte of the messenger, We have in good length Understanded to our great comfort, the good successe it hathe pleased god to graunt us against the Scottes by your good courage and wise forsight, for the wich and other the benefites of god heaped Upon us, like as We are most bounden to yeld him most humble thankes, and to seke bi al Waies We mai, his true honour, So doe We give unto you, good Uncle our most hartie thankes, praying you to thanke also most hartelie in our name our good Cosin therle of Warwike, and all the othere of the noble men, gentlemen, and others that have served in this journei, of Whose service thay shall all be Well assured, We Will not (god graunte Us life) shew our selfes Unmindfull, but be redy ever to consider the same as anie occasion shall serve. Yeven at our house of Otlandes, the eighteneth of September.

Your good neuew
Edward

Fig. 10.2. Somerset returned to London very quickly indeed after the campaign to receive the plaudits of the nation: a *Te Deum*, the handsome poetry which opened this chapter and this holograph letter from his king. It makes charming reading even today, as youthful letters so often do.

of Hache. In 1537, he became Earl of Hertford. With the death of the old King on 29 January 1547, he quickly moved to the centre of the political stage, was appointed Protector to the King and created Duke of Somerset on 17 February.[4] He came in effect from nowhere, but unlike the Boleyns, who returned to obscurity on the death of their sister, Seymour had prospered and would see his son married into the Tudor line. Without question, he was a remarkable man: intelligent and single-minded. He was also the first 'ruler'[5] of England since Henry IV in 1400 – Richard III was only Gloucester in 1482 when he penetrated as deeply as Edinburgh – physically to invade Scotland: not a comforting thought had it occurred to him.[6] As William Patten, author of the most popular contemporary account of the campaign, recounted the episode six months later, the Protector paused on the northern wall facing Scotland and recalled a recent dream:

> he was come back to Court, where the King's Majesty did heartily welcome him home, and every Estate else: but yet him thought he had done nothing at all in this voyage.[7]

Why should Somerset at the time have been so troubled? Perhaps his ambitious brother Thomas confided to him the same forebodings which he told Edward VI, that the army should never get far into Scotland (past the Pease at Cockburnspath), that many Englishmen would die 'and therefore that he spent a great Summ of Money in vayn'.[8] Perhaps he remembered the words of a recent disturbing prophecy.[9] Perhaps he was simply afraid of failure. If so, he had every right to be worried. Scotland could always be invaded, but the only result of two and a half centuries of conflict was English retention of Berwick-upon-Tweed. Somerset knew of these fiascos as well as any man. He obviously hoped to avoid repeating the many mistakes of the recent past, and fear of failure may well have contributed to his troubled sleep. Could Somerset, as he gazed North, also have asked why he found himself there at all?

When examining policy formulation under the early Tudors, one is constantly faced with a lace of material; not until Cecil's detailed memoranda are historians able to speak with any authority as to why men did what they did. This is due to a fundamental lack of data: very few of Somerset's letters concerning Scotland survive;

---

4 *Handbook of British Chronology* says the 16th.
5 See Paget's characterisation of him in 1549, just before his fall, as 'QQQ'.
6 Somerset was a student of history, as many of his conversations demonstrate: see *Odet de Selve*.
7 Patten, *Expedition*, 82.
8 Samuel Haynes and William Nurdin, *Collection of State Papers . . . left by William Cecil, Lord Burghley* (London, 1740–59), i, 74.
9 Richard Laynam (who as far back as 1528 had prophesied seven wives for the King) told an acquaintance in Wiltshire that there would be a great battle in the North in which 'a cock of the North busk himself'. In 1545 he told another man, in London, that Scotland would cause England great trouble when 'poor men shall be oppressed and the commons shall be so handled they will make insurrection'. The Earls of Huntly are known as 'the Cock o' the North'. See *LP*, xxi (1), nos. 1013, 1027, 1424.

those that do shed little direct light on his reasons for going to war.[10] One is thus forced to rely on public declarations, on conversations reported by ambassadors and on the assumptions which appear to lie behind his actions.

'THE VERAY CAUSE' OF THIS CONFLICT

There was a time when Edward Seymour was seen to be a remarkable idealist: a visionary who saw in Anglo-Scottish union the end to war and the creation of a new country composed of equal partners. This view was based on Somerset's numerous public pronouncements explaining his actions. One good example is the proclamation of the Norray Herald to Arran and his government shortly after the battle of Pinkie:

> The veray cause and occasion that moved his grace at this present to enter [replacing original word 'invaid'] this Realme of Skotland with an Armie was only to bring to good effecte the moste godly purpose of the Mariage . . . for the benifite and perpetual uniting of both Realmes together . . . [The government of Scotland] could do her no gretter honour then to make her [Mary] being now but Quene of thone Realme, as Quene of both Realmes, and her issue God willing to be Kinges and Masters over us besides the setting at a paraite concorde and union of two suche realmes as ar England and Skotland with both their honours and reputacions by this meanes preserved to lyve and love togwither as oone nacon of oon towng and oon lande.[11]

These fine words, all too often isolated from their context of a brutal war, have been used to paint the picture of Somerset as gentle and farsighted. It is an appealing vision and neatly complements that of Somerset the social reformer. But Seymour rose to pre-eminence in the 1540s primarily as a military leader, as a 'can-do' man of action and not as one of 'high statesmanship'. Propaganda was, and is, a means to an end. The man who emerges from this Rough Wooing has little appealing idealism about him; he simply wished to win the war. He was, in short, a typical product of his class: an aristocratic thug. The Scots were to be coerced into doing what they were told.

It could be that Somerset simply lacked the imagination to consider reversing Henry VIII's basic policy. Certainly voices were raised advocating an end to the Scottish strategy. The most trenchant was that of the Bishop of Winchester, Stephen Gardiner, an enormously powerful figure under the late King,[12] but now being

---

10 Dr Bush found only six concerning Scotland which he feels were written by Somerset alone although it is obvious that he must have written many more, perhaps as many as 42. (I am grateful to Dr Bush for allowing me see the draft of his article, 'Somerset and Scotland', which confirmed many of my own ideas and suggested some new insights). Paget's Letter Book (Northants. Rec. Office, F (M) C21) is the closest there is to 'memoranda', but none of his letters refer to the decision to go to war against Scotland, only how to win it and then, later, how to get out of it. His 'consultacon' of August 1546 (fos. 21–22) hardly mentions Scotland.

11 PRO, SP 51/1 fos. 111–12 (*CSP Scot.*, i, no. 50).

12 He had been Henry's Principal Secretary as early as 1529 and was rewarded with Winchester in 1531. That he might have replaced Wolsey is one of the intriguing 'ifs' of Henrician politics.

seriously marginalised: he would shortly be imprisoned in the Tower and remain there (except for six months in 1548) until Edward's death in July 1553. During the early months of Somerset's Protectorate, when he still felt he had Seymour's ear,[13] he argued strongly against any new adventures. The kingdom was weary of disruption, dangerously volatile, friendless abroad and bankrupt at home. On 28 February 1547, he mused:

> And if I wer sworn to say what I think of the state of the world, I would for a time let Skots be Skots, with dispair to have them, unlesse it wer by conquest, which shalbe a godly enterprise for our yong master when he cometh of age.[14]

Somerset in 1547 stood virtually *in loco parentis* to King Edward VI, then only nine years of age (he was ten on 17 October). As such, the Protector might have seen it as his duty to effect the match which the father had arranged. When on 19 February 1547 Edward was taken from the Tower to his coronation at Westminster, he stopped by a fountain flowing with wine in Fleet Street to hear a 'Ballet of the King's Majestie', sung by two boys. It contained the couplet, 'when he waxeth wight, and to manhood doth sprynge, he shalbe straight of iiij [four] realmes the kynge'.[15] Perhaps Somerset took his guardian's duty seriously enough not to wait for the King's majority in order to add the fourth realm. By so doing, he would earn the gratitude of the King, not to mention a certain glory, and glory is a potent wellspring.[16]

There was a further consideration in the Spring of 1547, what might be called making the most of bad money. The Scottish war had already cost a lot, but as yet there was little to show for it save two toeholds and a number of supporters. Still, Beaton had been eliminated, Protestantism was more active, and Francis I was anxious for an accommodation with England. To wait until Edward's manhood might well leave it too late, whereas to spend more money now could bring victory and thus justify the earlier war. One of Somerset's first actions was to give substantial aid to the Castilians.

Moreover, the Protector had been annoyed by the Scottish government's recapture of Langholm of 17 July. Otterburn was particularly taxed on this point and was told 'the Kingis honour [is] grevously hurt be Langholme and uther

---

13 He reminded the Protector of a time when they both were in Brussels (1545) 'divising of the world at large'. William Paget would make similar remarks in August 1549, telling Somerset that his duty was to bequeath a 'realme as florishinge and as welthy bothe at home and outwardly as his father lefte yt'. This (and subsequent quotes from Paget's Letter Book, in the care of the Northamptonshire Record Office) were taken from the note slips first written down, but then given to me, by Professor Bindoff, a typical piece of kindness. They have all been printed as 'The Letters of William, Lord Paget of Beaudesert, 1547–1563', ed. B.L. Beer and S.M. Jack, in *Camden Miscellany, xxv* (1974), 11–134. This letter is on p. 78.

14 Gardiner's letter is printed in John Fox, *Actes and Monuments* (1870), vi, 25. See also J.A. Muller, *Letters of Stephen Gardiner*, 364.

15 S. Anglo, *Spectacle, Pageantry and Early Tudor Policy*, 292.

16 On 18 August, Somerset wrote to Shrewsbury inviting him to participate in the invasion, 'to see the order of things which may, God willing, be worthy of memory' (E. Lodge, *Illustrations of British History* (1791), i, 144–5).

injuris'.[17] However, neither desire to shore up an inherited position nor anger over the loss of a small castle, nor the loss of St. Andrews, adequately explains the return to war. The timing does not work. On 8 July, Sadler, soon to be treasurer of the English expedition, was given his first instalment of funds for the forthcoming invasion: £5000 from the Tower. On 25 July he received a further £20,000.[18] On 14 July Somerset ordered Archbishop Cranmer, who had already prepared fifteen horses 'for service in the field', to have them at Newcastle on 24 August.[19] On 18 July Sir Ralph Vane was similarly instructed.[20] This was a week before news of Langholm's fall reached London.[21]

One further explanation has been advanced for Somerset's return to war: he knew that the accession of Henry II would lead to a French endeavour to take over Scotland, thus drastically altering England's European position.[22] It is a nonsense. That the French did triumph in Scotland and did for a time severely restrict English mobility is of course true. But it was English military success alone which forced the Scots to agree to a French marriage. The argument rests largely on a particular interpretation of the St Andrews affair. Firstly the removal of Beaton in May 1546 is seen as greatly strengthening the position of the Queen Dowager and that of a pro-French party. However, on the one hand it is difficult to see that an active pro-French party did exist at this time; on the other, although the Queen was increasingly important, her emergence as a major force in Scottish politics rested primarily on the necessity for French aid in the Battle of Pinkie in September 1547. The English were distressed by the sudden appearance of the French off St Andrews, and Somerset worried that they came to remove Mary.[23] But the French left as abruptly as they came, and in any case the decision to go to war predated French intervention. To suggest that the army which invaded Scotland on 4 September 1547 originally intended to relieve St Andrews is absurd.[24]

Nonetheless, the French intervention, the third in four years, does raise an important question. Why did Somerset underrate the possibility of massive foreign assistance to the Scots, especially with a new monarch in France? As ever, it is difficult to document the Protector's thinking, but in all sixteenth-century warfare there was a certain element of gamble, witness the ill-fated 'enterprise of Paris' in 1544 and the 'enterprise of England' in 1588. In both cases they went forward because the decision-makers felt that something lucky might happen, and if they did not at least try, nothing could happen. Of course, the monarchs did all they could in terms of

---

17 *Mary of Lorraine Corresp.*, 193. See also Norroy Herald's words on this point (PRO, SP 50/1, fo. 111).
18 Sadler, *State Papers* (1809), ii, 358. His appointment as treasurer was made on 26 July (*CPR Edward VI*, i, 139–40).
19 BL, MS Harl. 6986, fo. 17. Cf. *Mary of Lorraine Corresp.*, 184.
20 PRO, SP 10/2, fo. 4.
21 *CSP Spain*, ix, 126; *Odet de Selve*, 167, 175.
22 Wernham, *Before the Armada*, 168–9; Jordan, *Edward VI*, 243–6.
23 His most explicit expression of this worry was to van der Delft on 23 July (*CSP Spain.*, ix, 127–8), but he did not refer to the French again and very little was made of the French threat in the propaganda of 1547, although by February 1548 it became a major theme.
24 As Jordan suggests, *Edward VI*, 245–6.

rational planning to give luck every chance, and this Somerset most certainly also did.

Every aspect of Somerset's strategy demonstrates an attempt to learn from the past, and perhaps because of his innovations Somerset may be forgiven for thinking he had a better chance of success. In the first place he sought to avoid Henry's cardinal mistake of being heavily involved on the Continent. To a certain extent he misread French intentions: French military assistance to the Scots in the past had been limited and relatively short-lived, witness Albany in 1522–1523 and Montgomery in 1545. Moreover, French assistance in the past had been limited because of involvements on the Continent, and the Protector reasonably expected that Henry II would not be able to concentrate on Scotland.

Somerset anticipated that the French would, as he put it to Odet de Selve and to the Scots, engage in 'de plus grandez entreprinses du coste du Italye'.[25] He hoped that the Habsburg-Valois conflict would continue. This explains why English reaction to Charles's great victory over the Protestant princes at Mulburg in April 1547 was so ambiguous. Although it was distressing to see co-religionists brought low, the strengthening of Charles's position could only augur well for the Scottish campaign, with the French distracted by the destruction of their German allies and the possibility of a new war with Charles. Moreover, Henry II was much more concerned to recover Boulogne. Somerset obviously hoped to dissuade the French from giving aid to the Scots by promising to ease the terms for its redemption. On 16 November 1547, a Frenchman[26] told de Selve that Warwick wanted just that sort of settlement.[27] Later, similar proposals appeared to come from Somerset himself and doubtless the Protector hoped that he could prevent help to Scotland by such offers.[28]

A further hope was that the French simply would not be able to afford to give significant support. Somerset warned Odet de Selve in December:

> Vous trouveries en fin que L'Escosse ne vous serviroyt que d'unge esponge pour tirer vostre argent sans nul proufict et qu'il vauldroict beaulcoup mieulx que vous le minssies en aultre lieu dont vous pourries avoyr grand honneur et grand proffict. [You will find that Scotland will only be a sponge to soak up your money without any profit; it would be much better for you to become involved somewhere else where you might find great honour and great profit][29]

Somerset may even have considered that war was a vastly expensive business, and should the French send massive aid to Scotland, the necessary taxation might lead to

---

25 *Odet de Selve*, 120. Certainly the English saw the despatch of Pietro Strozzi to Italy in October as a sure sign that the French and the papacy 'vont entrer en guerre contre l'empereur l'ete prochain [want to wage war against the Emperor next summer]', a deduction confirmed by Charles's instructions that Philip go to Italy (*Ibid.*, 225).

26 Le sieur de Berteville who had an extraordinary career. A French mercenary in the English force at Pinkie, he also kept Odet de Selve constantly informed of what he knew of English actions (Odet de Selve, *ad indices*) and wrote an account of Pinkie, *Recit de L'expedition en ecosse l'an 1546* [sic], *et de la battayle de Muscleburgh*, Bannatyne Club, no. 10 (1825).

27 *Odet de Selve*, 235.

28 *Ibid.*, 238, 251; *CSP Spain*, ix, 225.

29 *Odet de Selve*, 249.

rebellions within France, as had occurred in 1544. However, the Protector knew well that such contingencies were largely beyond his control and he clearly sought by an intelligent and coherent military strategy to ensure success even if the French did assist the Scots. In examining this strategy, one can see a further reason why Somerset went to war for Scotland in the first place.

BLACK SATURDAY: A GREAT VICTORY

On the evening of 11 September 1547, Protestor Somerset found himself and his army at Leith after winning one of the most spectacular victories in the history of Anglo-Scottish warfare. The thrill of the achievement must have been considerable and, as Englishmen tend to do when victorious against superior numbers, they recalled the great upset of Agincourt.[30] Somerset also ordered the distribution of 70 tuns of beer 'for the relyese of the armye at Lethe after the Bataile at Muskelbroughe'.[31] He may also have puzzled, before retiring, over the significance of dreams, for surely he had already done much and he planned to do more. During 1543–46 Henry had failed because he did not concentrate solely on Scotland. His attacks were either major but not sustained, such as the May 1544 assault on Edinburgh, or where they were sustained, along the Marches, they were too weak to affect the Scots in any significant manner. This military ineffectiveness meant that little positive support for the English marriage could be elicited either from the great nobility of Scotland or from the 'assured Scots'. Somerset moreover knew that military victory was useless unless it resulted in political change and negotiations which in turn resulted in a treaty effecting the marriage. It was these considerations which led Somerset to adopt the policy he did after Pinkie, a policy best described as one of creating an English 'pale' in Scotland.

He had long advocated a strategy of holding part of Scotland by permanent garrisons stationed in easily defended fortresses or strongpoints. In 1543, Henry had desired castles such as Edinburgh, Dumbarton, Tantallon, Stirling and Blackness, but he was never prepared to expend the effort necessary to realise such a forward policy.[32] During 1543–45 other places were considered, although not very seriously.[33] Moreover, under Henry, the battle zone remained the Anglo-Scottish Border from Carlisle to Berwick, and the area which could easily be attacked lay far from both the administrative centre and from the richest and most fertile part of Scotland. Moreover, neither Berwick nor Carlisle was a particularly convenient jumping-off point, even for major English invasions: a fact Somerset recognised by the extensive use of sea power in both the May 1544 and September 1547 campaigns.

Distance, however, was only one hindrance. The natural invasion route into Scotland, constantly used during the previous two-and-a-half centuries, lay along the east coast. But there were formidable physical barriers, and these were increasingly

---

30 Patten, *Expedicion*, 58, 105; most accounts of the battle exaggerated the numbers of the Scots, e.g. *CSP Spain.*, ix, 150, where they were said to number 40,000.

31 PRO, E 351/127, memb. 4.

32 *LP*, xix (1), nos. 314, 319.

33 Such as Tantallon, Kelso and Roxburgh (*LP*, xix (1), nos. 589, 594; xx (1), nos. 129, 837; xx (2), nos. 96, 328, 437, 359, 400).

important in an age of heavy artillery. In particular, the Lammermuir Hills spread almost to the coast, and for a distance of approximately fifteen miles there is a narrow funnel between the sea and the hills through which all movement must pass. This is why the pass at the Pease, a mile before Cockburnspath and Dunglass, was so important, and why Somerset and others were surprised that the Scottish army did not oppose him there.[34] Once past this point, an army could move into East Lothian and past Edinburgh to Stirling without encountering any serious physical obstacle, and this in part explains why Somerset did not waste his time or his force in reducing two important Scottish castles along the east coast, Dunbar and Tantallon.

However, the east-coast route was not the only easy way into Scotland. From Berwick, one could move down the fertile Tweed Valley, enter Scotland at Wark and march from there, to Roxburgh or Melrose. At this point the easiest route would be to proceed up the Gala Water to Stow and Borthwick and thence to Dalkeith and Edinburgh; or one could proceed much further westwards, continuing along the Tweed to Peebles, and from there to Penicuik, Roslin and Edinburgh. A slightly more difficult route, but shorter and further east, would be from Roxburgh to Lauder and thence over the Lammermuir Hills, but this would require negotiating land over 1000 feet before reaching the east-coast shelf on which both Edinburgh and Haddington lay. Of course, invasion routes work both ways. Were one to create strongpoints both along the coast and in the Tweed Valley, one could both prevent Scottish attacks on England and effectively advance the jumping-off point for any English invasion of Scotland. Such purely geographic considerations must have been appreciated by Somerset.

These considerations, in addition to an understanding of the debate between Henry and Somerset in 1544 over the policy for winning Scotland, are critical for understanding the strategy of Somerset's war in 1547. This involved the creation by military force of an English pale based on permanent garrisons in strongpoints. This would have three major advantages over the Henrician system. It could advance the Border and thus enable English forces to raid more deeply into Scotland; it would lay the foundation of a system of forts which could be expanded at any time; and it would protect those Scots who assured with England. The creation of the pale might thus, in conjunction with a sustained propaganda campaign stating English goals in moderate language, induce Scots outside the pale to assure. Given the intelligence of his plan, perhaps he had some justification for arrogance when discussing Scotland with Odet de Selve on 5 December 1547. There was no point alluding to Robert the Bruce's victory. English strategy now was entirely different; under Edward I and II

les conquestes et pertes des royaulmes deppendoint de hazard d'unge bataille et ne faisoyt l'on ponct de fortiffications garder ce que l'on avoyt conquis [conquests and the loss of kingdoms depended on the chance of one battle and they did not build fortifications to keep what they had conquered].[35]

34 Patten, *Expedicion*, 85.
35 *Odet de Selve*, 248. Somerset was, of course, quite wrong with his history: the English both occupied and reconstructed numerous castles in the fourteenth century.

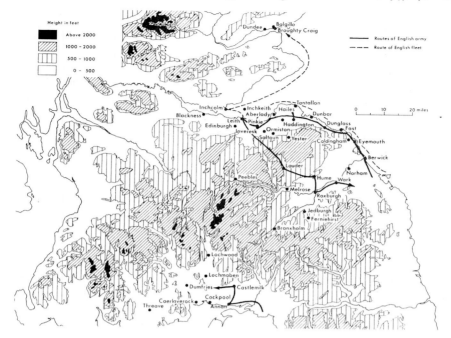

Fig. 10.3. Somerset's entry and exit were both well planned in advance, for he intended from the start to plant garrisons along the Cockburnspath route (what we may call the A1) and the Soutra one (the A68). But what made his campaign so immensely successful was his imaginative employment of the navy. The very large fleet which worked hand-in-hand with him as he invaded carried not only more troops and more artillery, but also a massive amount of army supplies and equipment, not to mention that mainstay of all English forces: beer.

Between September 1547 and October 1548 Somerset's grand strategy evolved and showed itself flexible and sensible. That it ultimately failed should not blind one to the fact that it came very close to success. The details of the collaborating aspect and the use of propaganda are treated fully elsewhere; here it is necessary to show how these two aspects rested on the foundation of military strength.

Before we turn to Somerset's strategy, it should be emphasised that the war must be viewed in four distinct phases: (a) September 1547 to January 1548 when English military measures were directed against the Scots; (b) February 1548 to October 1548 when they were directed against the French; (c) November 1548 to August 1549 when the English simply held on in the hope that something might reverse the effect of the Scottish Queen's removal to France and continued French assistance and; (d) August 1549 to March 1550, when with the popular uprisings in the summer of 1549 and the French attack on Boulogne in August, they held on in order to have something with which to bargain when the peace negotiations inevitably occurred. This chapter deals only with the first phase.

'SKOOLS OF WAR' AND THE MILITARY REVOLUTION

On 1 May 1549, new blood was infused into the most important military post in Scotland with the appointment of Sir Henry Manners, Earl of Rutland, as Warden of the East March.[36] Probably after the fall of Haddington in September 1549, Rutland gathered into his possession plans, or 'plats' as they were termed, of all the important remaining English strongpoints in Scotland: Roxburgh, Lauder, Eyemouth, Dunglass, Fast and one of the forts at Broughty.[37] This important collection of Rutland's, which he kept after the war, demonstrates exactly what the English did with many of the strongpoints they took in 1547–48.

The way Patten told it, it seemed that, after Pinkie, Somerset placed garrisons in strongpoints as the army went, but it is clear that he had a plan before the campaign took place. Only this can explain his seemingly extraordinary failure to make the most of the total defeat of the Scottish army at Pinkie. Certainly the Scots expected him to strike for Stirling, and the government's first action was to send the Queen for safety to Inchmahome Priory, thirty-five miles into the Highlands.[38] Instead Somerset allowed his army to rest for eight days at Leith, and even then he did not endeavour to capture Edinburgh Castle. Nor did he attempt to fortify Leith, his original suggestion of 1544. The army's hangover could hardly have lasted a week; nor could it have been so disorganised by its surprise victory.

The Protector may have been reluctant to move away from the coast and Clinton's fleet, which supplied the army. Moreover, either Edinburgh or Stirling would have been difficult to take and the army, despite a large mercenary element, could not be kept in the field for too long a period. Furthermore, it was an expensive army; Sadler's account (excluding naval costs) was £45,912.13s, much in excess of the original estimate of £24,113.6s.8d.[39] Somerset may have felt that the victory was sufficient for his needs and that there was little point in pressing the Scots too vigorously. But he must have appreciated the critical importance of timing. September was the limit of the campaigning season for 1547; not until the subsequent summer could he hope easily to place such a large force in Scotland, and by then the Scots might have received considerable aid. Certainly he was aware of the possibility of French assistance, as the references to 'forrein succour' in the Norroy Herald's declaration indicate.

The solution to this puzzle may lie in the existence of Somerset's plan. Victory

36 Jordan, *Edward VI*, 296–97.
37 Rutland MS, Letters, vol. ii, fos. 54–65 contains the platts of Roxburgh, Lauder, Eyemouth, Broughty, Fast and one-half of a plan of an unnamed fort (fos. 64–65); the other portion is in Misc. Box No. 34, map no. 121. Map 120 in Misc. Box No. 36 is of Dunglass.
38 Dalrymple, *Historie*, ii, 301. She was certainly there by 12 September when Arran wrote to the Queen Dowager who accompanied her (*TA*, ix, 122). When Grey invaded in February 1548, the government's first fear was that he would strike for Stirling (*CSP Scot.*, i, no. 166).
39 PRO, SP 10/13/22. I am grateful to the late Mr Michael Pickering who brought this document to my attention. It is to be noted that figures exclude victual charges. Somerset had always been worried about cost, as has been shown by Dr Bush in 'The Rise to Power of Edward Seymour, Protector Somerset, 1500–1547' (unpublished D.Phil. dissertation, Cambridge 1964).

would come, not 'de hazard d'unge bataille', but through the easily supplied artillery fortifications 'garder ce que l'on avoyt conquis'. The strategy rapidly unfolded during the month-long campaign during which the English established five areas of control: the east coast, the Tweed Valley, the Forth, the Tay, and the Southwest.

The most important two areas were those through which Somerset's army passed during its advance and retirement. As the opening of the narrow ledge of fairly low land along the east coast lay a small peninsula above the fishing hamlet of Eyemouth. Somerset had viewed the spot, six miles north of Berwick, on 2 September, when work may have begun on a fort there. It was in order to protect Eyemouth that, when Dunglass was captured on 5 September, the tower was destroyed and its foundations weakened by 3000 pioneers under John Brende.[40] Then, when Somerset's army left Leith on 18 September, it deliberately took the inland route home, apparently heading straight for Lauder.[41] On 20 September, the army arrived before Hume and besieged the castle. Upon its surrender two days later, a garrison under Sir Edward Dudley was placed there. On 23 September the army came to Roxburgh, and there Sir Richard Lee was ordered to build a fort. Lee chose a high plot of land situated between the Tweed and the Teviot, which had been the site of a castle now derelict. Construction began immediately, Somerset himself turning a spade two hours every day, and by 28 September the place was considered 'tenable' for a force under Sir Ralph Bulmer. The day after Bulmer's installation, Somerset sped south to receive the congratulations of his King.[42]

The army at Leith had not been entirely inactive. Various strongholds, such as Dalkeith and Blackness, had been either taken and destroyed or at least inspected. But its principal achievement was to provide the garrison, under Sir John Luttrell, which was established on 13 September on the island of Inchcolm in the Forth. The site of an Augustinian abbey, it lay under a mile off the Fife coast and was seen as a base from which the towns along the coast could be raided and as a haven for English vessels either attacking Fife or blockading Leith.[43] Meanwhile, two other campaigns rounded off the five areas.

A commonplace English tactic during this period was to make simultaneous attacks on both the East and West Marches. The West March was seen by Somerset as important although secondary, and considerable activity went on there whilst the more dramatic action took place at Pinkie. On 10 September a force under Wharton and Lennox secured the capitulation of Castlemilk from its tutor, James Stewart.[44]

40 Patten, *Expedicion*, 87.

41 It is not clear what route the army took from Edinburgh to Lauder. *Ibid.*, 143.

42 He also was to receive, 9 October, a grant of land worth £500 for 'perpetuall memorye' of the good service done during the invasion; the phrasing of the grant is revealing as to how the war was viewed (*CPR Edward VI*, ii, 27 and cf. 96). Also see *Literary Remains of Edward VI*, ed. J.G. Nichols (Roxburghe Club, 1867), i, 51. Somerset left so precipitously that he forgot thirteen Scottish standards, a prize of Pinkie; Grey forwarded them on 1 October (*CSP Scot.*, i, no. 52). Somerset's behaviour after Pinkie has been the cause of some puzzlement: see Jordan, 262.

43 Patten, *Expedicion*, 139.

44 *CSP Scot.*, i, no. 42; *RSS*, iv, no. 3267; *TA*, ix, 111; *CSP Dom.*, Add., 1547–65, 320–1.

The next day, the Scottish force in Annan steeple was battered into submission and the structure was cast down in a general destruction of the town. English forces were stationed around Lochmaben and at Moffat. By 17 October the burgesses of Dumfries assured with England, and three days later the Langholm force took up garrison in the town. Lochwood was then captured and garrisoned. On 19 November the tower of Cockpool was delivered into English hands. A pale had been created in the Southwest of Scotland.[45]

The fifth strongpoint was to a certain extent fortuitous. Dundee, Perth and the Tay area in general had long been noted as Protestant. An early collaborator with the English was Dr Michael Durham, who had connections in the area through his brother, a retainer of Lord Grey and captain of Grey's castle of Broughty which stood on the northern side of the mouth of the River Tay. On 18 September, as Somerset's army broke camp at Leith, the fleet under Clinton set sail with a force of footmen and hackbutters under Sir Andrew Dudley to receive Broughty; Dr Michael Durham was also on board.[46] On the morning of 20 September, the castle was formally surrendered and Dudley's force installed.[47]

All strongpoints had a double function of harassment and protection, but before they could begin their task of making the war a continuous process their structures had to be strengthened. The structures which were built in Scotland pointedly illustrate Somerset's growth as a military leader and his break with the policies of Henry VIII.

Some of the strongholds, such as Castlemilk and Cockpool in the Southwest, were not significantly altered in order to take English garrisons. Enough work had already been done at Hume before the English invasion to hold over 80 men and two culverins, one saker, three brass falconets and eight other pieces of ordnance.[48] Some new construction was effected by a hundred pioneers, but the 'new wark' was not very substantial and by the following February had fallen in.[49] Nonetheless the castle was commodious and had a good brewhouse which provided the wants of those at Roxburgh during the autumn of 1547.[50] At Broughty, the English found themselves in charge of a fifteenth-century castle in a very bad state.[51] Dudley complained to Somerset on 8 October that in addition to lacking coal, candles and glass, he had 'scant window to shut, nor door, lock, nor bolt, lach or nail'. Here again repairs were commenced and some modernisation was effected; a platform was built on the roof for cannon, gunloops were inserted into the masonry walls and the curtain was reinforced.

45 CSP Dom., Add., 1547–65, 323–49.
46 Patten, Expedicion, 141; CSP Scot., i, no. 46.
47 CSP Scot., i, nos. 46, 207; Patten says it capitulated on 21 September. See also Mary of Lorraine Corresp., 203.
48 Patten, Expedicion, 142–45.
49 So did the ramparts built by the Scots earlier (CSP Scot., i, nos. 129, 147).
50 CSP Scot., i, nos. 58, 129.
51 I am grateful to H.M. Colvin for first suggesting to me in 1963 that BL, MS Augustus, I, i, 76 might be of Broughty. See also the conjectural restoration of the castle, c. 1700 (I. MacIvor and D.M. Walker, Broughty Castle, ed. F. Mudie).

Fig. 10.4. Seymour was a great tripper on his military campaigns. Whenever he had the time, he would explore the countryside. While the 1544 fleet lay becalmed at Tynemouth, he went in to see Newcastle and immediately appreciated the military potential of the site of Tynemouth Abbey. In 1545, while sojourning at Kelso, he went upstream to view what remained of Edward I's great castle at Roxburgh, captured and levelled by the Scots in 1460. So, too, after Pinkie, he took ship to view the Forth. But he never saw the West Marches and commissioned a special survey team to map the area for him. The result was this 'platte of Castlemilk' (1547) which William Cecil firmly kept in his possession when Somerset fell.

At Roxburgh, the castle had to be reconstructed almost from scratch, although some of the fifteenth-century walls were still standing; Somerset and his army spent their time mending them by inserting turf where gaps had appeared and inserting gun loops where the walls still stood. Still, much new work had to be done, particularly trenches at either end and buildings to house the garrison. Construction did move apace, but even by 6 November the great complaint was the lack of a brewhouse, bakery, kitchen, grain mills and smith's forge. There was a stable for 20 horses, but the storehouse still lacked part of its roof owing to the lack of slates.[52] The winter and the 'rotten grownde' obviously made the provision of necessary materials difficult and there was a proposal to send supplies up the Tweed in 'a greate shallowe and flatt boote'.[53] Ramparts, and what the captain called 'bulwarks', were also constructed and these were quite

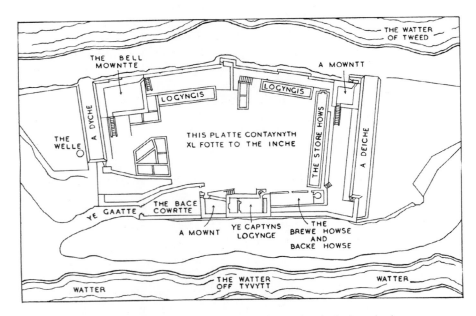

Fig. 10.5. When Somerset returned to the Borders after Pinkie, he had resolved to rebuild Roxburgh Castle. What emerged on this remarkable site was no medieval castle, but the best that Italianate technology could offer, given the geography. Two thick earth walls were erected at either end with deep ditches. Those dry moats were guarded by tiny flankers: gun emplacements at the end of each ditch. The entrance was likewise so guarded. And flankers ('murderers' as they were called earlier in the century) were inserted into the walls whenever they had to change direction. Thus no blind spots existed and the structure was made secure.

52 *CSP Scot.*, i, nos. 58, 62, 72.
53 *CSP Scot.*, i, nos. 58, 66, 131: cf. 72.

important innovations.[54] It is difficult to know exactly what work was done at Inchcolm, but some construction was necessary, even if Luttrell could easily house his men and store his munitions and supplies in the abbey buildings and the island was protected by the sea.[55] At all of these sites, certain modernisations were effected, particularly at Roxburgh, but the surveyors were never able to apply fully the techniques of fortification which had developed on the Continent, particularly in Italy, during the previous forty years.

However, at Eyemouth where there was an ideal site and no existing structure, these new designs were employed. To understand the Eyemouth fort, discussion of the impact of firepower on the art of war is necessary. With the Battle of Pinkie and the construction of the fortress at Eyemouth, modern warfare had come to Scotland. In many ways there was little modern in the Battle of Pinkie. However, the English army had a fair amount of firearms, both handpieces carried by cavalry and foot and mobile field guns. Moreover the fleet which stood off the Esk during the engagement was also well provided with artillery. It was the combination of these two sources of firepower which stopped and then disintegrated the Scottish host with so little loss of English life. Insofar as the battle was determined primarily by the use of firepower, it was a 'modern' one.[56]

The increased and extensive use of field guns and siege artillery had two effects on the art of war. In the first place it led commanders gradually to shun the major engagements involving open combat and to 'garder ce que l'on avoyt conquis' by stationing their forces in castles. However, artillery was no more respectful of masonry than it was of men; even fifteenth-century firepower could reduce what had previously been impregnable castles. The characteristic mediaeval castle had high curtain walls to impede scaling by ladders and higher towers at intervals to protect both the front of the curtain wall and the parapet of the wall should it be scaled. At obvious points of weakness, such as entrances, these towers could be clustered to give further protection. The town walls of Berwick were excellent examples of this sort of fortification which the entrance (through a drawbridge and barbican) could necessitate. Both Berwick and Tantallon were adequate protection against a mediaeval army, but neither could withstand modern siege warfare in which concentrated firepower could breach their high, relatively thin masonry walls.[57] To meet the

---

54 See Fig. 10.6. Note especially the small flankers inserted in various places to protect the curtain by fire from hand-held guns.

55 Luttrell certainly asked for building necessities such as 'tymber, spadys, pike axes, bastkettis, whypsawis and fylys for them, masons, quaryers and some more pioners' in addition to 'Tentis' (*Mary of Lorraine Corresp.*, 206–7); he did receive some of these items (NAS, Treaties with England 49 b. 7). Somerset ordered that a fort be built on Inchcolm as late as January 1548 (*Mary of Lorraine Corresp.*, 216). The site is described in J.W. Paterson, *Inchcolm Abbey*.

56 Sir Charles Oman, 'The Battle of Pinkie, 10 September 1547', *Archaeological Journal* (xc, 1933), 1–25, remains the best description of the engagement; he revised it somewhat for his *A History of the Art of War in the Sixteenth Century*. On the subject of warfare in the sixteenth century the best survey is C.G. Cruickshank, 'The Renaissance', in *A Guide to the Sources of British Military History*, ed. R. Higman, 65–83.

57 I. MacIvor, 'The Elizabethan Fortifications of Berwick-upon-Tweed', *Antiquaries Journal* (xlv, 1965), 65–96. The best description of Tantallon is J.S. Richardson, *Tantallon*.

danger from field guns, drastic changes in the design of strongpoints was necessary. Over the first four decades of the sixteenth century considerable advances were made in the evolution of artillery fortifications; two different examples were at Turin and at Boulogne.

Broadly, what were these new principles of fortification?[58] In place of the high masonry walls which ran from tower to tower in the mediaeval structure, the curtain was now low and squat. But more importantly the curtain, although often faced with masonry, was primarily composed of huge and deep mounds of earth. Although the twelve or more feet thick curtain walls at Tantallon seem massive, those at the artillery fort built at Berwick in 1558–70 were almost 60 feet thick, the masonry being only ten feet, but bound tightly into the counterforts, internal buttresses which supported the back of the masonry curtain and about which the earth was packed. However, it was not necessary to face the earthworks with masonry; earthworks surfaced only with turf could be difficult to maintain and often simply fell down, but they could be erected much more rapidly, and speed of construction during a war was vital.

Secondly, these curtain walls were on the inside edge of a broad ditch or trench, usually created by the removal of the very earth which made the curtain in the first place. The surface of the curtain wall facing the ditch was generally called the scarp. On the other side of the ditch was another earth wall, called the counterscarp, which performed two functions. It created an obstacle which an advancing force had to breach in order to approach the curtain wall and it provided the first line of protection (at least in these early artillery fortifications) against besieging firepower.

The third major development, rounding out the defence of the fort, was the bastion or bulwark. Artillery bastions were massive affairs, again composed primarily of earthwork and usually not much higher in elevation than the curtain walls which they interrupted at regular intervals. They were elongated triangular affairs, linked into, but projecting away from, the curtain walls at a point called the gorge and causing the counterscarp works to curve around them to maintain a certain width of ditch about the entire structure. Somewhat later, these Italianate angle bastions provided platforms on which cannon could be mounted either to impede the advance of attacking footmen or to counter-attack artillery fire directed either at the curtain wall or at themselves. But in the 1540s their major function was to provide protection for what were called the flankers. Flankers were gun-mounts sunk into the earth of the bastions for two or even four guns which provided raking fire over the distance between themselves and their opposite flanker imbedded in the adjacent bastion, thus protecting the curtain. They in turn were protected from artillery fire from the besiegers either by projecting ears, called orillons, which curved away from the wall of the earth-filled bastion and joined the curtain wall at the flanker, or by angled flanks.

Although the English were well aware that fortified sites had to take account of

---

58   I am grateful to I. MacIvor for his permission to reproduce Plate 3 which illustrates many of the principles of artillery fortification discussed here.

artillery, the work at Berwick in the 1530s, along the south coast in 1538–40 and at Guines in 1541–42 was carried out to a quite different design.[59] However, the English experience at Boulogne during the period 1544–46 brought them very much in contact with the mainstream of European thinking.[60] The work at Boulogne was largely that of Sir John Rogers, whose engineering amply demonstrates his determination to build the most modern and powerful protection for the town against any future French attack.[61] Several Englishmen significantly involved in Scotland in 1547–48 saw at first hand the sort of modern work Rogers was completing at Boulogne.

Hertford for one must have come to know of the new techniques when sent by Henry with detailed instructions to accelerate the repair and new construction which had been undertaken immediately upon the town's capture. In April 1546, he headed a commission to inspect the defences of the entire Boulonnais and to make recommendations as to future construction.[62] Somerset thus had a firm idea of the new designs, as did others who were to be deeply engaged in Scotland such as William, Lord Grey of Wilton, who until 1 May 1549 was Governor of Berwick, Warden of the East March and General of the Northern Parts.[63] Grey had been commander at Boulogne from April 1546 until August 1547; his tenure was 'the most productive period' in the history of the English works at Boulogne.[64]

Sir Richard Lee and Sir Thomas Palmer also acquired much knowledge from time spent at Boulogne. By now Lee was probably the most knowledgeable of all English architects or military engineers.[65] He had already been to Scotland before and he was appointed as 'devisor of the fortifications to be made' in the September 1547 invasion force.[66] Sent to Calais as early as 1533, by 1536 Lee was surveyor of the works there and

59 B.H. St. O'Neill, *Castle and Cannon* is the easiest introduction to English adaptations to the impact of firepower. The subject is complex; perhaps the best way to see the change is to compare the plats for Guines (1541) with those for Ambleteuse (1544), Shelby, *Rogers*, plates 2 and 3 with 16 and 17.

60 The source and transmission of this knowledge is difficult to document as printed books outlining the new techniques do not appear until after 1550 (Shelby, *Rogers*, 143n), although the literature may well have been in circulation in manuscript. See *Ibid.*, 138–43 for discussion of works on the south coast of England. Foreign engineers in English service may also have transmitted ideas. See L. White, 'Jacopo Aconcio as an Engineer', *American Historical Review* (lxxii, 2, 1967), 425–44.

61 Shelby, *Rogers*, 57–75, 143–44 is the best introduction to the Boulogne works. See *Ibid*, plate 21 (cf. plan on p. 62).

62 *LP*, xx (1), no. 121. Their report is *LP*, xxi (1), no. 565 (but see Shelby, *Rogers*, 67–68, 84 for clearest exposition of this episode). That Hertford learned from the experience can be seen by his independent recommendations to Henry in June 1546 (*LP*, xxi 91, no. 1159).

63 At which time he may have handed over the platts to Rutland. See Jordan, *Edward VI*, 265, 296.

64 Shelby, *Rogers*, 87 and see 55, 73, 75, 98–90.

65 One must say 'probably' because there is as yet no biography of Lee.

66 Patten, *Expedicion*, 78. His previous trip to Scotland in May 1544 was the occasion of his execution of a famous plan of Edinburgh and Leith (to which he was to return in 1560) and the looting of the brass eagle lectern and the font from Holyrood Abbey, which he then gave to the abbey church of St. Albans (*DNB*).

in 1540–41 was probably the man responsible for the reconstruction of Guines.[67] During 1544–46, he was in Boulogne working with Rogers although he also made trips to Scotland and elsewhere, often in company with Italian engineers.[68] He was to be in the North during the next two and a half years as 'generall Surveyour of the King Majesties workes and fortificacons' on the Marches and in Scotland.[69] Lee actually spent most of his time at Berwick and Wark maintaining oversight of all the forts within his charge; but on one occasion he did supervise the complete construction of a fort.[70]

Sir Thomas Palmer had been treasurer of Guines in 1543–45 and in charge of the construction of an important structure, the Old Man, at Boulogne in 1544–46.[71] Palmer seems to have been quite a man (Paget idolised him).[72] He must also have been on good terms with Grey of Wilton; they once carried out a night raid on a French fort near Boulogne.[73] Palmer was to design the new fort at Broughty in early 1548, and then to work with Grey on the design of the great fortress at Haddington in April-June.

Three other surveyors supervised much of the actual site work: William Ridgeway, Thomas Petit and Guillaume di Rossetti. Ridgeway had previously done work at Berwick, Sandown and HaselNorth.[74] Petit was master mason at Wark in 1543, then was sent in 1544 to view the castle of Ross on Bute.[75] He was then sent back to Wark in 1545 before being appointed surveyor of Calais on 30 January 1546, a post he appears to have held well into the 1550s.[76] He too found himself employed in Scotland in 1547–48 until captured in July 1548.[77] One of Petit's tasks, in June 1548, was to confer about the possibility of building a fort at Burntisland in Fife with Lee and Guillaume di Rossetti.[78] Rossetti, or John de Rosset, or 'Mr John the Ingineer', was in English service by 1541 when he was granted a £40 annuity by Henry VIII, and

---

67 Shelby, *Rogers*, 8–11, 20–21, 138–43.
68 Such as Archary, who may have been sent to St. Andrews in 1547 (*Mary of Lorraine Corresp.*, 184). *LP*, xx 91), nos. 99, 141–42; Shelby, *Rogers*, 60, 76–77, 87.
69 That is his title in PRO, AO1/283/1067.
70 *CSP Scot.*, i, no. 303; *APC*, ii, 156, 163, 214, 234, 268. His duties were often totally unconnected with engineering (*Ibid.*, 144, 396; *CSP Scot.*, i, no. 327; PRO, E. 315/258, fo. 75v).
71 Shelby, *Rogers*, 55, 65, 87. References to him are too numerous to cite; letters from him are *LP* xx (1), no. 423; (2) 582; xxi (2), no. 424.
72 Paget, upon hearing of his capture in July 1548, wrote: 'I loved the man in particular frendshippe, which had beginnings of his aptenesse to serve the Kinges majestie' (Northants. Rec. Off. F (M) C21, fo. 5v).
73 The adventure, typical of Palmer (his capture by the French in July 1548 was in part due to his own impetuosity), landed both men in some trouble (Shelby, *Rogers*, 105). For his capture in July 1548, see *CSP Scot.*, i, nos. 293, 301; *Mary of Lorraine Corresp.*, 266 and n.
74 *LP*, xx 91, no. 1275; xxi (1), no. 154; PRO, E 101/483/13, 14, 15.
75 *LP* xviii (2), no. 382; xix (1), nos. 813, 881; (2), no. 252. See entry for Petit in J. Harvey and A. Oswald, *English Medieval Architects: A Biographical Dictionary down to 1550*.
76 *LP*, xx (1), nos. 53, 190. For his career at Calais, see Shelby, *Rogers*, 126 and BL, MS Stowe 571, fo. 40 and 'the platte of the Lowe Countrey att Calleys' (BL, MS Augustus, I, ii, 57b).
77 *CSP Scot.*, i, no. 301. He must have been released quickly and continued to work in the North until 1550 (*APC*, ii, 322, 371).
78 *CSP Scot.*, i, no. 303.

he too may have seen service in France.[79] Sent twice to Scotland to view St Andrews
Castle in April and May 1547, he returned in the fleet which transported Dudley to
Broughty Craig and was immediately set to work repairing the tower and viewing
possible sites.[80]

THE EXAMPLE OF EYEMOUTH:
'GARDING WHAT ONE HAS CONQUERED'

It is clear, then, that Somerset was determined to hold large parts of Scotland by the
use of the most advanced techniques available,[81] as can be seen at Eyemouth. Lee,
perhaps on 2 September, had drawn up a plan for a fort to be built on the north side
of the river Eye where a pronounced promontory rises and juts into the sea. By 15
October, when Grey viewed the work, much had already been done. The design was
a model response to the site, embodying much that had been learned of Italian angle
bastions.

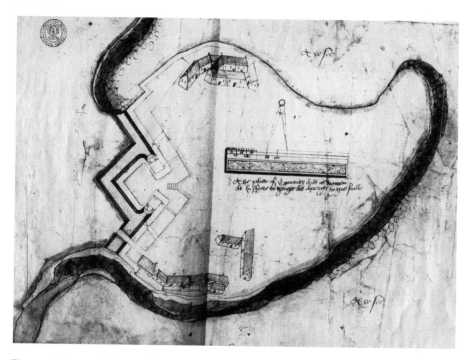

Fig. 10.6. Eyemouth Fort. What is illustrated here is the site plan drawn in 1549 for
the Earl of Rutland on his taking charge in the British Isles.

---

79 The renewal of his pension on 20 January 1549 (*CPR Edward VI*, ii, 354) was the occasion of
its being raised to £100. The name 'Ioven Rosset' is inscribed on a platt of Guines and
Ardes (BL, MS Augustus I, ii, 74); and see *LP*, xxi (2), appendix, no. 33 (20).
80 PRO, E 351/213, E 315/257, AO1/286/1067.
81 For Somerset's strategy unfolding, both in the South-East and at Broughty, see Phillips,
Anglo-Scots Wars, 201–223.

In the centre, equidistant from the sea cliffs on either side, was a full, orillonated bastion. Sunken behind the orillons were two flankers which protected two curtain walls approximately 55 feet thick projecting to the cliff edge. Along the curtain, around the bastion and then along the other curtain wall, in which there was a breach for entrance, ran a ditch of perhaps 20-foot width, bounded by a counterscarp. By October the bastion and curtains had been almost completed, but the north curtain, 'the flank from Coldingham', was not sufficient as yet; so Somerset ordered Ridgeway to be sent from Roxburgh to hasten the work.[82] By January 1548 it was considered fit to withstand any attack.[83] Ridgeway was concerned at the lack of masonry facing on the curtain scarp: 'ther ys neyther stone to make lyme nor yet for to make wale on noe nerer to be had then barwick', and the carriage of the stone he felt would be costly. Still, 'yt wyll be sufficyent ynowghe for thys yere'.[84] The captain, Thomas Gower, had been receiver, marshal, and surveyor at Berwick in 1545–46.[85] His command was small.[86] Supply was never difficult but Gower on occasion was to complain bitterly of lack of money.[87] Despite its smallness and distance from the main theatre of action, Eyemouth was important as the first of a series of strongpoints up the east coast which protected the supply trains to Haddington.

THE KING'S LORDSHIP OF SCOTLAND

The five areas of control created an English 'pale' known as 'the King's Lordship of Scotland'.[88] Central to understanding how the English saw the pale is the realisation that if they wished to build up a body of Scots supporting the marriage, and thus bring pressure to bear on the Regency to accept it, they would have to provide protection for the assured Scots.[89] The converse function of the forts was to act as

82 *CSP Scot.*, i, no. 58, 62. No financial records survive for the work at Eyemouth. For the construction there, our knowledge has been enormously enhanced by D.H. Caldwell and G. Ewart, 'Excavations at Eyemouth, Berwickshire, in a mid 16th-century trace italienne fort', *Post Medieval Archaeology*, xxxi, 1997, 61–119; and see my piece in Colvin, *King's Works*, iv, 702–705, and my 'Eyemouth Forts: Anvils of Union?' Somerset instructed that if Lee's plan was not 'taken', then the earth should be scraped down to the rock and thrown into the sea. Coldingham Priory had held an English garrison in 1544, and in 1547 its roof provided timber for the work at Eyemouth (*CSP Scot.*, i, no. 57).

83 *CSP Scot.*, i, no. 129.

84 PRO, SP 15.2, fo. 403.

85 Gower had an interesting career at Berwick; see *LP*, xx (1), nos. 175, 295, 658, 663, 686. He was on bad terms with Evers, for which he suffered somewhat (*Ibid.*, nos. 678, 822, 986), but he had experience of war in Scotland (*LP*, xxi (1), no. 1279[pp. 626, 628]) and his talents could not be ignored. He was captain at Eyemouth from 2 October 1547 (*Hamilton Papers*, ii, 610) until 14 January 1550 (PRO, AO1/286/1067), at which time Cuthbert Musgrave, a protégé of Wilford's, was put in charge (*APC*, ii, 365).

86 In addition to the normal complement of a drummer, surgeon, ensign, clerk, master gunner, two porters and several lieutenants and their staff, it contained over a period of time ten light horse, 34 hackbutters of different sorts, 30 hackbutters on horse, and 20 footmen (PRO, AO1/286/1067).

87 *Hamilton Papers*, ii, 610, 747–8; *HMC*, 26, 12th R., iv *Rutland*, 34, 46.

88 *CPR Edward VI*, vii, 162.

89 See M.H. Merriman, 'The Assured Scots: Scottish Collaborators with England during the Rough Wooing', *SHR*, xlvii (1968), 10–34.

staging posts for constant raids upon those Scots still loyal to the regime. One example, out of many, of the relationship between the forts, the assured and harassment will demonstrate the point. In mid-January, Grey of Wilton gathered together at Wark several of his captains, 160 hackbutters from Roxburgh and several assured Scots. The party then marched almost 28 miles to the lands of Sir Walter Scott of Buccleuch and Branxholm. The force attacked Buccleuch's house of 'Newewarke', burnt his 'towns' (which must have meant Branxholm and Harden but perhaps not Buccleuch itself) and took much livestock. As the assured Scots in the expedition were 'railed at by those in the house', Grey decided to place upwards of 300 horse near the Kerrs for their protection.[90]

This sort of exercise occurred everywhere in the initial phase of the English occupation. From Inchcolm, Luttrell daily raided the Fife coast, confiscating the ferryboat at North Queensferry and burning the town, destroying part of Aberdour (the nearest port to the island), and firing ships in the harbours. Luttrell's band in the Forth did its best to 'empesche' Scottish communication and to encourage Scots in the Fife ports to assure.[91] The result was a constant flow of Scots to see him at the abbey, many of whom brought provisions: sheep and '18 loves of brede' from 'scots of Kynokorn', 'vytall of the scottes of Bornt Iloonde' and fish 'browght of the men of must-borowghe'.[92] From Broughty the English intimidated Dundee and by 27 October had laid a garrison there.[93] The point of such exercises was clear: to make sure that resisting Scots 'shal feele of the whypp'.[94] The fortresses enabled the English to make the whip felt throughout the year; as Thomas Windham remarked from his ship stationed off Dundee on 12 January 1548, 'Thys Wynter war greves the harts of the Scottes gretely'.[95]

The Newark expedition that month also illustrated another function of the forts. When the attack was conceived, Grey judged that the capture of Newark would extend the area under permanent English control. All the forts were seen as centres from which new strongholds could be captured or which could offer succour and protection to troops stationed in camps. As early as October Eyemouth provided cover for horseman stationed several miles away at Ayton, and on 28 January a force from the fort captured and garrisoned Billie Tower, on the edge of the Lammermuir Hills. Roxburgh performed a similar service, part of its garrison being laid at Jedburgh and at Kelso.[96]

Thus pressure was maintained on the Scots during the autumn and winter of 1547–48. Somerset had learned much from the mistakes of Henry: the pressure was constant and within Scotland itself, not intermittent or on the fringe; the military force which applied it was the most modern which could be devised; it led to active

---

90 *CSP Scot.*, i, no. 129.

91 *Ibid.*, no. 122.

92 NAS, Treaties with England, 49B (now RH 9/6), fos. 16–17.

93 *CSP Scot.*, i, nos. 71, 84, 84; *Mary of Lorraine Corresp.*, 209.

94 *CSP Scot.*, i, no. 140.

95 *Ibid.*, no. 127.

96 *Ibid.*, nos. 58, 98, 117, 143.

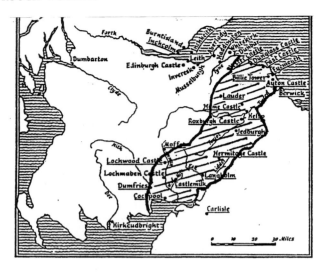

Fig. 10.7. This sketch map captures how radically the war was altered by Somerset's strategy of placing permanent garrisons in Scotland and creating thereby an English pale. Raiding parties by definition are usually fairly small and are dangerously exposed if they camp out at night. They thus need a secure haven for the protection of themselves and their mounts. Given that a party can ride between ten and twelve miles from base before having to return to its security (with slow-moving booty such as sheep or cattle), the outreach of parties jumping off from the frontier line of the Anglo-Scottish Border is quite limited. But when they operate from Lauder, Haddington and Broughty, warfare becomes much more intensive for the Scottish community.

support by many Scots who otherwise could not or would not have aided England. Somerset also went further then Henry in that he tried, during this period of success, to consider what success might mean. Whereas nothing indicates that Henry seriously contemplated what union with Scotland would entail, Somerset did turn his mind to the implications of actually winning the war.

The creation of the pale was more than a means of attacking opposing Scots, aiding assured Scots and weakening the Scottish Regency. It also aimed at the great nobles of the realm, for only they could eventually force Arran to agree to the marriage. Lord Gray did not have to be coerced; allied with the English since March 1547, he worked assiduously with them once they held Broughty. Of all the Scottish nobles, he was the only one (Lennox excepted) to be of any use. Gray was probably a convinced Protestant, but he also had a political grievance against the Regency over the provostship of Perth which doubtless influenced his action. Patrick Earl of Bothwell was like all the great Border magnates, very much a law unto himself. At the time of Pinkie, when Arran had rallied virtually the entire Scottish aristocracy about him, Bothwell lay a prisoner in Edinburgh Castle. Released the day after the battle, he went immediately to the English camp and was taken into protection. He was not a prisoner of war, as was Huntly, but neither was he treated as an open ally, like Lennox.[97] He acquiesced in the capture of some of his castles, such as Hailes, but he never agreed to the surrender of Hermitage.[98] When, in August 1549, he finally signed formal articles, in return for which he was very generously rewarded with £1225 (almost £s5000), his service was of no use.[99]

Somerset had learned to be generous with Scottish nobles, as can be seen with the pensions offered Argyll and Huntly. During negotiations in the first phase of the English war, Argyll was paid 1000 crowns (£s1000) on 5 February 1548, 500 'royals' (£281. 5s or approximately £s1125)[100] two days later, and he even received a gold chain.[101] To Huntly large offers were made, but he never appeared, a sound enough risk for the money to be advanced. Of the other nobles who had practised with the English so notably in 1543, and to a lesser extent in 1544–45, little was heard. Glencairn engaged in a long, almost dutiful correspondence with Wharton before and after Pinkie, but nothing concrete ever came from him.[102] Angus talked with various English captains and with collaborators such as Ormiston and Brunstane, as did his brother, but they were seen as devious and not to be trusted.[103] Of Cassillis, Errol and Somerville, all once prominent dealers with the English, little was heard.[104]

97 *CSP Scot.*, i, nos. 33, 49; Patten, *Expedicion*, 81–82; *Odet de Selve*, 258, 265; *TA*, ix, 80–81.

98 For the negotiations, which were fruitless, see *Odet de Selve*, 253–303, 314–24 *passim*; *CSP Scot.*, i, nos. 57, 69, 168, 211, 217. Also see *TA*, ix, 331, 414 and *Mary of Lorraine Corresp.*, 204–205.

99 *CSP Scot.*, i, nos. 353–55; *APC, ii*, 179, 203, 318; PRO, AO1/283/1067 registers the extraordinarily high sum given him; there are other payments in E315/257 fo. 71.

100 In 1543, an English Crown was valued at 5 shillings; a Ryal was 11s. 3d.

101 PRO, AO1/283/1067; *CSP Scot.*, i, nos. 147, 150, 152.

102 *CSP Scot.*, i, nos. 11–12, 57, 67–68; *CSP Dom., Add., 1547–65*, 334, 344–45, 354.

103 *Ibid.*, 354, 361; *CSP Scot.*, i, nos. 69, 85, 102, 157, 170, 240; *APC*, ii, 535–39.

104 *CSP Scot.*, i, nos. 63, 67; cf. nos. 130, 164.

Maxwell did attempt to be of some help. In late November 1547 he instructed his brother John to render Lochmaben, Caerlaverock and Threave into Wharton's hands. But nothing came of this, and after assuring with the English for a short time, John revolted.[105]

On 17 October 1548, Secretary of State Sir Thomas Smith[106] wrote Somerset with an engaging proposal concerning one Scots future noble. He recommended that an approach be made by Edward himself to the 18-year-old James Stewart (bastard son of James V and later Lord Moray), Prior of St Andrews, making much of their 'proximitie of bludde' and sending 'som rynge, broche or other token which the said poir beyng a young man wold mych esteme'. A letter over Edward's signature was sent arguing:

> The french you may perceyve seke their own purpose and when they have obteyned rule over you, wil not care what becommeth of you, nor when you shal have most nede of them, you shal wel know that either they shal be otherwise occupied or the long passage of the see or any numbther of other impedyments shall conspyre to kepe there ayde at home.

The young man did not reply.[107]

The two Scottish nobles with whom the English had the most protracted negotiations, which resulted in a specific programme of how the marriage of Mary and Edward would be managed, were Huntly and Argyll, two of the most resolute adversaries of the English alliance. Huntly had been sent to London after his capture at Pinkie. From late September 1547 until his escape in December 1548, he was forced to consider terms for his possible release. He remained evasive and only rarely did he respond to English requests that he should write to his friends in Scotland.[108] In so far as these discussions concern the ransom of a great earl they are of little interest, but they also reveal Somerset's views on Scotland; easily the most significant proposals were those made to Huntly in January 1548.

'GRETE BRITAYN WHICH IS NO NEW NAME BUT THOLD NAME TO THEM BOTH'

Two months after Huntly's release, the estates of Scotland should meet and agree to the marriage of Mary to Edward. A month later, Scottish ambassadors with full powers would deliver this resolution to the King of England and Mary would be formally declared betrothed to him. For the next three years Mary would live at Berwick, in the care and instruction of Englishmen chosen by Edward. During this

---

105 *CSP Dom., Add.*, 1547–65, 320–65 *passim*.

106 Author of *An Epitome of the title that the King's Majesty hath to the Sovereignty of Scotland*.

107 BL, MS Calig. B. vii, fos. 462–63; *CSP Scot.*, i, 345–46 and cf. nos. 343–44.

108 The material on these prolonged negotiations is voluminous, especially in *Odet de Selve*, 223–479 *passim*. The Earl clearly was allowed access to almost anyone he wished to see in London and kept the French ambassador well informed of Somerset's interviews with him. See also *CSP Scot.*, i, nos. 56, 73, 119, 194, 218, 308; *Mary of Lorraine Corresp.*, 223, 230, 234; *APC*, ii, 172–233 *passim*; *Miscellany of the Spalding Club*, iv (1844–45), 144–50.

period the King would continue to control the recently established pale. No Scot who had assured with the English should suffer any penalty, nor should any Scot who renounced his obedience to the Pope. However, during this time no Scot would be allowed to serve any foreign prince without the express permission of the King of England; instead they would serve the King of England for the same pay and terms as Englishmen did. Furthermore, the Scottish estates would also agree to the extinction of the names 'Scotland' and 'Scottish' and 'England' and 'English'. The two peoples and the two kingdoms would be united, in the words of Odet de Selve's translation, 'En ung empire quy sera dict et nomme toujours l'empire de la Grande Bretaigne et le prince dominateur d'icelluy empereur de la Grande Bretaigne [in one empire which will always be referred to and entitled the Empire of Great Britain and the ruling prince of which to be the Emperor of Great Britain]'.[109]

For further elaboration of these plans, one must examine the negotiations with Argyll. When Dundee was captured by the English, Argyll made a weak and unsustained assault upon Broughty Castle in November; he returned on 21 January 1548 with a much larger force, but again retired after ten fruitless days. From the beginning of these assaults, the English commanders, Dudley and Windham, had tried to contact the Earl in hopes of bringing him over.[110] By 7 February it seemed that they were having some success. The pension he received on that date for a vague assurance not to attack the garrison at Broughty was quickly followed up by a personal set of proposals from Somerset, put in the care of Sir John Brende who made the trip to the North especially to negotiate directly with Argyll. The Earl did have a long interview with Brende on 6 March,[111] but he quickly came under the suspicion of the Governor and the Queen Dowager; fear of their wrath led to his breaking off contact.[112] By the time French money and troops arrived in June, his loyalty was no longer in doubt, even though as late as March 1549 Somerset thought that he still might be useful.[113]

The articles were firstly an outline of how he was to aid the English cause.[114] For a yearly pension of 2000 crowns, half of which was to be in land in England, and a reward of 10,000 crowns, Argyll was to remain in his country with all his friends, tenants and supporters and to do nothing to aid the Governor to resist the English. He should place himself and his followers under the 'rule' of the Protector who would protect and assure them all. If he could not move the Governor to agree to the marriage, then he was to declare openly for the King of England, and by midsummer 1548 he was to do all he could to put Dunbar and Edinburgh Castle into English hands and if possible deliver the Queen herself. Brende at this point was to say, 'as of yerself . . . that in cace of deposicon of the Governor for not according to tharticles, thene there is no man so mete for that office as the sayd Erle'.

109 *Odet de Selve*, 268–70.
110 *CSP Scot.*, i, nos. 110, 148, 150, 177, 186; *APC*, ii, 170.
111 *CSP Scot.*, i, nos. 188, 192, 194; *APC*, ii, 543, 551.
112 *Mary of Lorraine Corresp.*, 226, 238, 243, 245. See also *CSP Scot.*, i, no. 163.
113 *CSP Scot.*, i, nos. 345–46.
114 PRO, SP 50/3, pp. 181–93 (*CSP Scot.*, i, no. 177).

So far this is familiar material, but the articles also tried to allay Scottish noble fears of how union with England would affect their position. Arran's tenure as Governor was guaranteed until Mary's 'perfect age'; should he die, 'some other nobleman of skotland to be chosen by the Counsail therof without accompt or payment of her treasure or revenue'. Noble Scots appointed by the Council would also be allowed to be resident about Mary. Moreover 'No man person within Scotlande be out from his holdes, Landes, tackes offices or possessions but every man shal enioye the same . . . as they do nowe'. If Edward died before the marriage or without a successor born of their bodies, then Mary would be allowed to freely return to Scotland 'to be there maryed'. After the marriage Edward would appoint Scots for the ordering of the revenue of Scotland, the keeping of castles and the execution of justice; however, customs officers were to be Englishmen, as were the captains of all the forts then held by the King. These limitations aside, Edward promised to protect the liberties of Scotland as Henry had done in the Treaty of Greenwich. During the period before the marriage 'famylyer entrecourse and free traffique without any sauf conducte betwixt Scottes and engleshe both be see and land' would be permitted. It was hoped that 'marriage be made entrechangeably' by nobles and parties of all sorts 'on both sydes', who would also 'perswade their sonnes and daughters for encresaseng of frendship and amities betwixt both nacions'. Once again, reference was made to the name which would bless this union. Scrawled at the bottom of one page, an obvious afterthought, was this clause:

> We shalbe contented and agree that for avoyding confusion [significantly the word which first came to mind was 'inequalitie'] of names bothe the Realmes thus united shal bere the name of grete britayn which is no new name but thold name to them both.

The proposed agreements with Huntly and Argyll are the clearest enunciation to be found of Somerset's war aims. His efforts to create an English pale in Scotland demonstrate his tenacious determination to effect these aims. Directly relevant to both aims and efforts was his encouragement of a remarkable propaganda campaign from July 1547 to May 1548. If one can take propaganda to mean in its broadest sense a public utterance meant to be read or heard by men with a view to affecting their attitude, then during that period no fewer than five pieces concerning the war were printed. These tracts, plus what is known from the agreements and Somerset's efforts to effect a union lend weight to the contention that there were serious plans for the amalgamation of the two kingdoms into one kingdom of 'Great Britain'. Let us now turn to that engaging concept.

CHAPTER ELEVEN

A War of Words

'ZOUR BUIK OF WEIR': BOOKS OF WAR

Concern over the eventual terms of union reflected both Henry VIII's desire for union and Somerset's attempts to avoid the mistakes of his former master. A similar desire to profit by the mistakes of the past can be seen in the production of a considerable amount of propaganda directed primarily at the assured Scots. Somerset sought to improve the method by which Scots were encouraged to collaborate with the English. Firstly, the very creation of a pale meant that Scots who favoured the English could be effectively and continuously protected. Secondly it meant they could be rewarded not only by the rents and lands of Scots who opposed the English, but also by regular payments of wages for their services and by fairly constant raids on the goods of unassured Scots. Thirdly, constant English presence meant that much more comprehensive and binding oaths of allegiance could be demanded of the assured. Many Scots did 'come in' during the period of English superiority (September 1547 to June 1548) and they were immensely useful to the English as planners, troops, spies, victuallers and workmen. They also, of course, acted as magnets for others Scots to assure. For some of the most thoughtful of the Scottish collaborators, such as James Henderson and Robert Lockhart, this period was the time when collaboration emerged as a genuine example of the benefits of eventual union, implying not servitude, but brotherhood. To understand the attitude of such Scots more fully, one must examine the propaganda campaign of Henry, but more particularly, Somerset.

It has been said that three developments of the fifteenth century only matured into their own in the sixteenth: the discovery of the New World, gunpowder artillery, and the printing press. Artillery has already figured in our story. America was represented meaningfully at Rouen. We know so much about that great fête because of the printing press. It was a deliberate policy of Henry II to insure that knowledge of this great triumph was disseminated by printed accounts[1] throughout his kingdom. Governments and Europeans in general were fascinated by this new technology, and with good reason. Without it Martin Luther's impact would have been stupendously reduced. As the celebrated English martyrologist John Foxe stated:

> Hereby tongues are known. Knowledge groweth, judgement increaseth, books are dispersed, the scripture is seen, times compared, truth discerned, falsehood detected. . . . Through printing the world beginneth now to have eyes to see and hearts to judge.

---

1 Also through medallions. The 1550 one celebrating 'pax cum Anglia' had on the reverse a delicate rendering of the King's chariot at Rouen.

At first, printers confined their production to devotional tracts, but they quickly spread their scope to include chronicles, histories and the classics and whatever topics the reading audience was prepared to pay for. Statutes and laws were early favourites, as one would expect. All governments took a keen interest in the new technology both to censure information and to display it. That is why Henry VIII's initial refusal to acknowledge Polidore Vergil's *History* and then his decision to support it are so revealing. Indeed the Reformation brought on a massive upsurge in governmental involvement in publishing in England.

A nice example of this development can be caught in the career of Sir Richard Morison.[2] Morison slipped onto the central stage of public life through the tutelage of Wolsey, time spent in Cardinal Pole's famous household at Padua and then via Cromwell. Literate, engaged and learned, Morison quickly found himself sucked into the vortex of dramatic history when the Pilgrimage of Grace (October 1536 to June 1537) broke about the Tudor regime. While the King fretted and the mighty such as Norfolk parlayed with the insurgents, Morison was set to writing pamphlets against rebellion. It is a beguiling and charming vision, that words could stay men's passions: 'the ragious outcries of souldiours, noyse and brayeng of horses, clutteringe and ienglynge of harneys'. Can one really imagine that Aske and his multitude would cast down their spears on hearing the opening lines of Morison's *A Remedy for Sedition*, which came out in print in October 1536? 'The prynce of Oratores Marius Tullius Cicero, whoose facundious eloquence was dailie exercised in making oration.'

Of course not. But publishing had become a reflex for governments: almost a drug. Men such as Morison were thus worked off their feet. He ruefully narrated that one of his efforts, *A Lamentation*, was pasted together 'in my botes . . . in a after none and a nyght'. Indeed the Pilgrimage rebellion brought forth a flood of tracts from a large number of the humanists who found themselves in essence in the King's employ as his ministry of information. Printers such as Berthelet and Grafton were the other side of the coin, the HMSO. An interesting example of this reflex occurred at the start of our period, in 1542, when war broke out between Henry VIII and James V. As the King sent an army into the field, so he activated his propaganda machine.

As we know from an earlier chapter, on 3 October the Archbishop of York and the Bishop of Durham were instructed to search their 'old registers and ancient places of keeping such writings' to provide proof of the King's lordship of Scotland so that 'the king's title to the realme of Scotland be more fully playnly and clerely set fourth to all the world, that the justness of our quarell and demaunde may appear'.[3] The ultimate fruits of their labours was a book, *A Declaracion, conteynying*

---

2 Additional to the *DNB*, the best concise biography is by Helen Miller in Bindoff, *Parliament*, ii, 633–34.

3 *SP Henry VIII*, v, 212–13; *LP*, xvii, no. 898. Six years later, when Tunstal was sent on a similar errand, he remarked on having seen a copy, probably made at this time, of a book of homage compiled by the Chancellor of England 'in henry vii dayes' (BN, MS Calig, B vii, fo. 336).

the iust cavses and consyderations, of this present warre with the Scottis, wherein alsoo appereth the trewe & right title, that the kings most royall maiesty hath to the soueraynitie of Scotlande.[4]

One tack, never absent, was that Scotland quite simply belonged to the King of England. Though intellectually the crudest argument and, one would have thought, the one with least appeal, the contention that Scotland was the fief of the King of England was made repeatedly in almost all of the English pronouncements, though the stress varied with the circumstances. That is why *A Declaracion* is important, not just for the crisis of 1542. Virtually every single future English pronouncement accepted its case, though in Somerset's *Epistle* it was very lightly touched on and in Henrisoun's *Exhortacion* the author made several corrections and emendations. Bodrugan, or Adams, also felt that there was more to be said on the subject of the past union of the isles. As we shall see, one Scot was so moved by it that he spent 22 folios refuting it point by point. Henry himself was to get a fair amount of mileage out of it also.

With the death of James, leaving a week-old girl as Queen and a pro-English Arran as Regent, Henry had temporarily dropped his public pressing of the claim. Arran, it is true, was occasionally referred to as the 'pretended governor' and the assured lords swore featly to Henry as their lord superior, but these references were muted and unsustained. The Scottish ambassadors sent to negotiate peace and marriage in 1543 refused to even discuss the mater with the Privy Council, and no mention of any superiority is to be found in the treaties of Greenwich. Once war broke out, Henry returned to his former position. His explanation to the Emperor drew heavily on the spurned gentle uncle pose. He was furthermore 'a dere and tendre frende' who, when James died, could have 'brought them lowe to knowledge their bounden duities of allegeaunce and subjeccion towards His Majeste', had he so desired.

Henry also used this posture to gain public acceptance of the war with Scotland in his dealings with parliament. The subsidy act of 1544 (34 & 35 Henry VIII c. 27)[5] was granted mainly to enable the King to fight the Scots, though in fact most of the money went to fight the French. The Commons declared themselves convinced of the King's 'good juste tytle and interest to the Crown and Realme of Scotland', especially after their 'searche sight and examinacion of divers and soondrye old manifestly exhibited and maturely read and debated in this present Parliament'. The preamble referred to James as 'the late pretended King of Scotland being but a usurper of the Crown and Realm of Scotland, by the ayde and succour of the subjects of the same', and some hint of the situation created by Mary's accession to the Scottish throne was given in this revealing passage: 'it hath pleased Allmightie God by his Divine Providence to call to his mercye the late pretensed King of Scotes, by reason wherof the Kings Majestie . . . hath nowe at the present (by the infinite

---

4 *STC*, no. 9179; reprinted in *Complaynt*, ed. Murray, 192–206. The two following extended quotes are from pp. 196–98.
5 *Statutes of the Realm*, ed. A. Luders and others (1810–28), iii, 938.

goodness of God) a time apt and prospryse for the recoverye of his said right and tytle to the saide Crown and Realm of Scotland'.

A different justification of the war was based on the Scottish renunciation of the betrothal of Mary to Edward: the injured suitor argument. The Scots firstly must be made to agree to the marriage and secondly must suffer the chastisement owed to covenant breakers. On 20 December 1543 an English herald had delivered Henry's final ultimatum to the Scots. His declaration made a great deal of the fact that the Scots had ratified the treaty for the marriage of Edward to Mary, 'which the Kinges majestie hath in his possession to shewe', and then had renounced it. 'Ye both forget with whom ye have covenanted, and to whose commotitie and benefite the covenant tendeth.' Henry was a 'Prince of honour, that will not suffre your disloyaltye unpunished and unrevenged'. The agreements were for the 'behalf of your maistres, and the commens lyved in quiet, to there great welth and benefite'; the actions of the Scottish government, characterised as 'foyles and perverse fansies', would result in just the opposite result. Two other threads were also touched on: the unreliability of France and the wickedness of Cardinal Beaton. The Scots set their honour beneath both a 'promesse of gayn out of Fraunce' and the 'mayntenaunce of the cardinalles appetities and affeccions, the glory of the spritualtye there'. Such truculence, as we know, had no effect on the Scottish government's basic stand with regard to the marriage, and war ensued.

The fullest exposition of Henry VIII's case was to be found in the *Proclamation* which accompanied the May 1544 invasion. In March, Hertford, then at Newcastle, wrote to the King enclosing his 'plat of a proclamacion rufli hewen and pennid bi mi dulle wite, withowght the advise of ani other' for the king to correct as he saw fit. The germ of this idea, so Hertford declared, lay in one of Henry's brainstorms, that the captains of English raiding parties were to affix on church doors and prominent places a bill directing the Scots that 'they might thank ther Cardinall' for the destruction wrought. Hertford's *Proclamation* did include a certain railing against the Cardinal, but the case he wished to present was much more comprehensive. 'The just titulle and intrest that his highnis hath unto this realme of Skotland' was mentioned, but not stressed, while much was made of the fact that the Scots had solemnly accepted but now rejected the marriage. The main charge was laid at the feet of the 'most crafti, divillish, and subtull mene of your Cardinalle and his complists'. Hertford came both to demand possession of the young Queen and to see punished those who refused the marriage 'with fiar and sourd that your persicusion shalbe aninsampull for ever'.

But the main aim of this invasion, Hertford declared, was to effect the marriage, 'soo as be that conjuccion both reaulmes might be yunitid perpetually to lyve in pose and quiatnis for evar'. To those who agreed and became assured, Hertford offered exemption from his destruction, protection and 'the libarti and fredum of this reaulme with all ther lands, possecions and goods in as larg and ampull manar as they doth now att this present'. This last clause was particularly important, Hertford felt. The main purpose of the *Proclamation*, as he saw it, was to encourage 'your majstes frinds . . . more willingli to declare them selves for you, and allso to indeuse others to your majestes purpos'. Hertford sent his draft to the King on 21 March, and on the 27th Henry returned it with a minor addition that Scots involved in making the treaties in the first place were especially bound by 'honour and conscience to joyne with me'.[6]

By 24 April, however, the King had second thoughts and he sent a different version.[7] Henry inserted a phrase about the Governor breaking the contract by the 'sinistre intisement and persuasions' of the Cardinal and it condemned the Scots' 'dishonorable behavours and untrue and disloyal procedinges'. Where Hertford wished to offer exemption before the 'fiar and suord' struck, Henry was insistent that Edinburgh and the other towns must first be burnt and only 'afterwarde to take suche to marcye as shall come in to you'. Consequently Hertford declared, 'when I shall have executed such punishment for your sayd desloyaltyes', then would he assure Scots who favoured the King's purpose and preserve them from Henry's 'swoorde, nowe redy to be drawen against them'.[8] Before his invasion of September 1545, there was yet another round of consultations as to how lenient the *Proclamation* should be.[9]

Even after Somerset's rise to power, it seemed as if the old line would continue, the subsidy act of 1547 (1 Edward VI, c. 13) speaking of war solely in terms of its being against the king's 'Rebelles, the Scottes'.[10] However, once he resolved to embark upon a new military campaign to win the war with Scotland, Somerset also initiated a fresh propaganda offensive remarkable for the sixteenth century. The first blast came from James Henrisoun.

'AN EXHORTACION'

The first and only piece of his work to be circulated was printed sometime before the September 1547 invasion, entitled: *An Exhortacion to the Scottes to conforme themselfes to the honorable, Expedient, & godly Union betweene the two realmes of Englande & Scotland.*[11] Henrisoun's case was firstly a massive elaboration of previous points. He not only specifically referred his readers to *A Declaracion* if they wished to see the case for English suzerainty of Scotland, 'exactelie set furthe', he drew up his own version drawing from sources other than those used in *A Declaracion* and made several small but subtle corrections to it. Henrisoun devoted 34 folios to prove that England was 'justly entitled' to the whole isle of Britain, but his main point was that the island had once been united. 'We were britions at the beginning, come of one king and lineage, under one monarchy.' Moreover, in Henrisoun's eyes, the superiority 'enduceth no seruitude, but fredome, libertie, concord and quietnesse, and serueth aswell for Scotland, as Englande, makyng equalitie without superioritie'.

---

6 *Hamilton Papers*, ii, 311–12, 314–15, 349–51.

7 *LP*, xix (1), nos. 231, (2), (3); 389 (3).

8 In the actual invasion, Hertford followed his instruction implicitly, as his conversation with the burgesses of Edinburgh the day before his assault on the city shows (*Ibid.*, nos. 472, 533).

9 *LP*, xx (1), nos. 202, 547, 651; xx (2), no. 216.

10 *Statutes of the Realm*, ed. A Luders and others (1810–28), iv, 22.

11 *STC*, no. 12858; reprinted in *Complaynt*, 208–36.

Fig. 11.1. Henrisoun's tract was probably printed in the summer of 1547 as an invasion
pamphlet or 'buik of veir': it speaks of Somerset's invincible army coming in
the future to crush opponents to the marriage. It was a remarkable argument
by the man who had become Somerset's propaganda officer in matters
Scottish. Henrisoun entered fully into the origins debate then raging within

¶ To the right high and mightie prince, Edward, Duke of Somerset, Erle of Hertford, Viscount Beauchamp, lorde Seymour, Gouernor of the persone of the kynges Maiestie of Englande, and Protector of all his Realmes Dominions and Subiectes, his lieuetenaunt generall of all his armies, bothe by lande and by sea, Tresorer and Erle Marshall of Englande, Gouernor of the Isles of Gernsey and Gersey, and knight of the moste noble ordre of the Garter: James Harryson Scottisheman wissheth healthe, honor, and felicitie.

Allyng to mynde (as I do oft) moste excellent Prince, the ciuill discencion and mortal enemitie, betwene the twoo Realmes of Englande and Scotlande, it bryngeth me in muche marueill, how betwene so nere neighbors, dwellyng within one land, compassed within one sea, allied in bloude, and knitte in

a.ii. Christes

England and Scotland and utterly dismissed the Scottish version in favour of that spelt out in Henry VIII's 1542 tract. But he also argued for contemporary benefits which would flow from union: not just prosperity, but the reformed faith. In it he employed the term 'Briton' or 'Britain' 103 times.

The Treaties of Greenwich had been duly ratified by the Scots, 'not by our auncestors, but by our selfes'. Then they renounced them. Why? 'What madnes or deuill . . . hath so moued, or rather distracte our myndes?' One set of villains leapt to his mind: those men 'issuying from the prince of darknesse', the papist clergy. Everywhere in Europe, in Italy, in Holland, they had brought forth 'an vnhappie babe, called contencion'. Henry, 'a prince no lease Godly then prudent', had seen the light. The other villains were the French, 'whom we cal our auncient frendes, where their are in deede our auncient enemies'. A great deal was made of the disadvantages of the French alliance, Flodden being the prime case in point. Scots had become 'common hirelynes to a forrein naction'. Not only had they no honour, not only had they followed a disastrous path of a false religion and a false ally, they courted harsh retribution from the conqueror. Somerset comes, he warned in the summer of 1547, 'with a puisaunt & invincible army' to punish all those remaining in 'stubborn and wilful disobedience'.

'We bee taught,' he reminded his readers, 'to repute a body as to be monstrous that hath two heads and no less is the realm that hath two kings.' The war between England and Scotland was an 'unnatruall devysion', a 'ciuill warre' between countries 'of one natyve tongue and bredd in one ile compased with the see'. This war was being fought to end these conflicts and the suffering which had plagued the island since its fall from unity. Let us blot out for ever those 'hatefull termes of Scottes and Englishmen' in favour of 'Briton'. Central to Henrisoun's case was a further point, not previously made. 'For howe godly wre it, yat these two Realmes should grow into one, so should thei also agre in the concorde & vnite of one religion, & the same ye pure, syncere & incorrupt religion of christ.'[12]

Henrisoun's long and thoughtful tract was quickly followed by Somerset's invasion. A *Proclamation* dated 4 September 1547 had been printed by Grafton and was widely circulated in Scotland.[13] It too was conciliatory in its language and generous in its offers. It apologised for the foraging of the army, 'quhilk can nocht be avoyded quhair ane army merchis', and offered considerable concessions to those who assured. No mention was made of the claim to superiority:

> We mynd nocht by this conjunctioun of marriage to do ony moir prejudice to this realm of Scotland than to the realme of England, bot with the advice of the noble men and gude men of baith realmes to unite thame togidder in any name by the name of Britounis and in such a freindlie kind of leving and suche a libertie and preservatioun of justice to ilk persone equalie as they sall weill find both the glories of God and his worde advance, this bischop of Romes usurpted jurisdiction abolisheit, the honour of baith weil satisfied and contented.

---

12 *Complaynt*, 225, 227, 228, 231.
13 *STC*, 7811; *Warrender Papers*, ed. A.I. Cameron (SHS, 1931), i, 17. The only copy of the original is in the Society of Antiquaries of London.

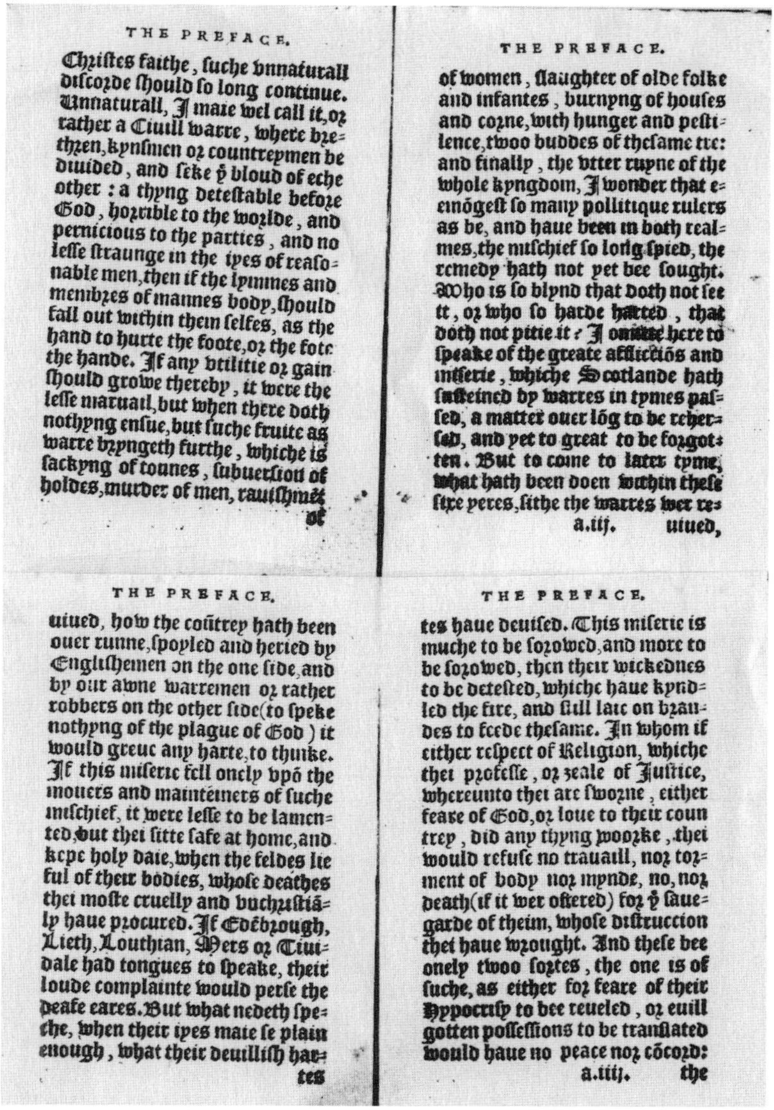

THE PREFACE.

Chziftes faithe, fuche vnnaturall difcozde fhould fo long continue. Vnnaturall, J maie wel call it, oz rather a Ciuill warre, where bze- thzen, kynfmen oz countrepmen be diuided, and feke ý bloud of eche other : a thyng deteftable befoze God, hozrible to the wozlde, and pernicious to the parties, and no leffe ftraunge in the ipes of reafo- nable men, then if the ipinnes and membzes of mannes body, fhould fall out within them felfes, as the hand to hurte the foote, oz the fote the hande. Jf any vtilitie oz gain fhould growe thereby, it were the leffe maruail, but when there doth nothyng enfue, but fuche fruite as warre bzyngeth furthe, whiche is fackyng of tounes, fubuerfion of holdes, murder of men, rauifhmét of

THE PREFACE.

of women, flaughter of olde folke and infantes, burnyng of houfes and cozne, with hunger and peft- lence, twoo buddes of thefame tre: and finally, the vtter ruyne of the whole kyngdom, J wonder that e- einógeft fo many pollitique rulers as be, and haue been in both real- mes, the mifchief fo long fpied, the remedy hath not yet bee fought. Who is fo blynd that doth not fee it, oz who fo harde harted, that doth not pitie it? J omitte here to fpeake of the greate afflictiós and miferie, whiche Scotlande hath fufteined by warres in tymes paf- fed, a matter ouer lóg to be reher- fed, and yet to great to be fozgot- ten. But to come to later tyme, what hath been doen within thefe fixe yeres, fithe the warres wer re-
a.iij.   niued,

THE PREFACE.

niued, how the coûtrey hath been ouer runne, fpoyled and heried by Englifhemen on the one fide, and by our awne warremen oz rather robbers on the other fide (to fpeke nothyng of the plague of God) it would greue any harte, to thinke. Jf this miferie fell onely vpó the mouers and mainteiners of fuche mifchief, it were leffe to be lamen- ted, but thei fitte fafe at home, and kepe holy daie, when the feldes lie ful of their bodies, whofe deathes thei mofte cruelly and buchzzftiá- ly haue pzocured. Jf Edébzough, Lieth, Louthian, Mers oz Ciui- dale had tongues to fpeake, their loude complainte would perfe the peafe eares. But what nedeth fpe- che, when their ipes maie fe plain enough, what their deuillifh har- tes

THE PREFACE.

tes haue deuifed. This miferie is muche to be fozowed, and more to be fozowed, then their wickednes to be detefted, whiche haue kynd- led the fire, and ftill laie on bzan- des to feede thefame. In whom if either refpect of Religion, whiche thei pzofeffe, oz zeale of Juftice, whereunto thei are fwozne, either feare of God, oz loue to their coun trey, did any thyng woozke, thei would refufe no trauaill, noz toz- ment of body noz mynde, no, noz death (if it wer offered) foz ý faue- garde of theim, whofe diftruccion thei haue wzought. And thefe bee onely twoo foztes, the one is of fuche, as either foz feare of their Hypocrify to bee reueled, oz euill gotten poffeffions to be tranflated would haue no peace noz cócozd:
a.iiij.   the

Fig. 11.2. (a) These pages from Henrisoun nicely capture how crude such early publications were, but that should not detract from how this new technology was. Most self-justifications were drafted for a domestic audience: the taxpayers. Henrisoun's was unusual: a propaganda tract aimed directly at the enemy in an attempt to seduce the hearts of the people to Somerset's opinion. Octo books such as this were very portable but read quite differently when taken in by the little bites of words which the small pages allow. When the words are reprinted in modern form, it all feels different. Murray's edition of 1873 got eight pages of Henrisoun's text on to one of his. Thus, as Geoffrey Elton always used to say: 'Go back to the original'.

SOMERSET'S EPISTLE

This was followed, in February 1548, by yet another tract which elaborated the English case in still different terms: *An Epistle or exhortaction, to unite & peace, sent from the Lorde Protector, & others the kynges moste honourable counsaill of England: To the Nobilities, Gentlemen, and Commons, and al others the inhabitauntes of the realme of Scotland.*[14] The timing of *the Epistle* was important. In February 1548 the English were masters of Scotland; two invasions were about to be launched, one up the River Nith to Drumlanrig, another to Haddington. Furthermore, it was becoming apparent that considerable French aid would shortly be sent to Scotland. At this critical juncture Somerset hoped to lay before the Scots the fullest and most moderate case he could, and the *Epistle* was a direct comment on the circumstances at that time. Though short, it was complicated, with three basic elements: the exposition of the justness of the English case, an elaboration of the advantages of the union, and a demonstration of the lack of any alternative course of action.

The Scots had agreed to the marriage; the ratification with the Great Seal of Scotland affixed to it was in English hands for all to see. Only the fear, hope and greed of the Cardinal and Arran had perverted events. This being the case, though battle was an extreme refuge for any Christian man, 'if any man maie rightfully make battaill, for his espouse and wife: the daughter of Scotland, was by the greate seale of Scotland, promised to the sonne and heire of Englands. If it bee lawfull by gods Lawe, to fighte in a good guerre; . . . who hath the better parte?' Once made, the 'just-wooer' argument (which had been made before Pinkie) was slipped over and nothing was made of the claim to superiority. As in Henrisoun's tract, renunciation was marvellous for its myopia. 'What euil & fatal chunce dooth so disseuer your hartes, & maketh them so bline and vnmindull of your profite and to still conciliate and heape to your self mooste extreme mischiefes?'

Fig. 11.3   Somerset, perhaps remembering his experience with war proclamations in 1544 and 1545, was determined that his invasion of 1547 should be fully understood by the Scots. He thus had this broadsheet printed by Richard Grafton during the summer of 1547 (only one copy of which survives to be reproduced here). They were then widely distributed before and during his expedition. Sometimes they were delivered by special couriers; at other times they were nailed up on prominent public buildings throughout Scotland, such as at the Tolbooth in Dumfries and to the door of St. Giles', Edinburgh. He certainly tried to have them given out to the Scottish army encamped at Musselburgh on the morning of the battle, and much was made subsequently of Arran's refusal to permit such a 'fair hearing' of the English case which, when reduced to its simplest form, made the age-old justification for battle: we only make war so as to create peace.

---

14 *STC*, nos. 9181, 22268 (English editions), 9180, 22269 (Latin editions). English edition reprinted in *Complaynt*, 237–46.

Dward, Duke of Somerset, Erle of Hertford, Uiscount Beauchamp, Lorde Seymour, Gouernor of the persone of the kynges Maiestie of Englande, and Protector of all his Realmes, Dominions, and subiectes, his lieutenaunt generall of all his armies, bothe by land and by sea, Tresorer and Erle Marshall of Englande, Gouernor of the Isles of Gernsey and Iersey, and knight of the moste noble ordre of the Garter: To all the nobles and gentlemen of the Realme of Scotlande, and the common people of thesame, gretyng. Whereas the moste victo= rious Prince of famous memorie kyng Henry the . VIII. our late souereigne Lorde now decessed, and the Erle of Arrayn, Gouernor of the Realme of Scotlande, with thaduise and consent of you in Parlia= ment, consideryng what gracious oportunitie and meane, the almightie and liuyng God had then sent (as he yet doth) tappease the wrath, displeasure and enemitie, whiche rather by the prouocacion of others then of our awne inclinacions, beyng bothe of one discent of bloud, and of one language, and by the main seas seperated from all other nacions, had of long tyme continued emonges vs one against the other, thought it moste expedient, aswell to the glorie of God and his holy woorde, honor and suretie of bothe the Princes of Englande and Scotlande, and the weale and benefite of their Realmes and Sub= iectes, that the kynges Maiestie our souereigne Lorde that now is, should take to wife the Quenes grace your Maistres. We vpon the foresaied Godly consideracions, thinkyng theffecte thereof meete to be folowed, and the mariage of bothe Princes, for the weale of bothe the Realmes, the particular commo= ditie of eche persone in euery estate, and for the Godly fulfillyng of Gods pleasure, to his glorie moste expedient and necessarie to be perfaicted and executed, and this goodly occasion that God hath sente, to be of euery honest and true Englishe and Scottishe man, with all his power, harte and will, meete to be embraced, are now vpon greate deliberacion had before hande, with sundery Godly and wisemen, aswell of England as of Scotland, come into this realme: not as an enemie to the Quene or any of the realme, that mynd the perfeccion of this peace and coniunccion in mariage of bothe Princes, but as a frend and a conseruator of them (we take God to iudge) and we are come in this maner, whiche pretendeth a force in apparence (but not in deede) onely to defende and maintein the honor of bothe the Princes and realmes, and by fire and swoorde, to chastice suche as wilbe rebelles to thesame, or go aboute either by practises, assemblyng of armies, or by any other forcible waie or meanes to withstande vs, or to declare themselfes against the perfeccion of the peace, and the mariage of bothe the Princes: Nor wee mynde by this con= iunccion of mariage, to doo any more preiudice to this reamle of Scotlande, then to the Realme of En= glande, but with thaduise of the noble men, and good men of bothe the Realmes, to vnite theim togeders in one name, by the name of Britons, and in one suche a frendly kynde of liuyng, and suche a libertie and preseruacion of the lawes of Scotlande, with an indifferent administracion of Iustice, to eche persone equally, as thei shall well finde, bothe the glory of God and his woorde aduaunced, the bishop of Romes vsurped iurisdiccion abolished, the honor of bothe the Realmes preserued, and the subiectes of thesame well satisfied and contented: Prayng you therefore, and exhortyng you all noble men and good men of this Realme, to ioyne with vs and assist vs in this behalfe: And we assure you of our honor, and before God, that whosoeuer will come into vs, and make vnto vs for their partes, sufficient assurance to theffect aforesaied, we will kyndely and frely accept it, geuyng by vertue hereof, free libertie vnto all suche as will agree to this moste Godly purpose, to entre our Campe: and suche as will bryng vnto vs any kynde of victaill, shall not onely not be endomaged in their persones or goeddes (for we entende to persecute with thextremitie all suche, be thei Englishe or Scottishe, as shal hurte or harme them in body or good, and so we haue notified to all our armie) but also besides their free accesse and conuersacion in our said Campe, thei shalbe by speciall ordre from vs, truely satisfied and contented for thesame. For we entende to passe amicably (if we be not empeched by theim) without diuastacion of any mannes good or cattell, other then of those, who shall declare themselfes repugnauntes, and contrary to the good meanyng aforesaied: and without doyng to the well willers of bothe the Realmes, the least hurte or domage we can, sauyng some= what in forage, whiche cannot be aduoyded where an armie marcheth.

LONDINI, in ædibus Richardi Graftoni Regij impressoris

CVM PRIVILEGIO AD IM=
PRIMENDVM SOLVM.

England only sought the marriage because it would bring peace. 'Ioyne in marriage from high to low, bothe the realmes, to make of one Isle on realme, in loue, amitie, concorde peace and Charitie.' War was a reluctant necessity. History showed how injurious enmity between the two realms had been to Scotland: five times won by the kings of England. Some kings had been taken in war, some slain in battle, some for very sorrow and discomfort upon loss, died. Reflect upon the carnage of Flodden, the misery of this six years' war. Behold how much God's will for the union was so evident. We alone dwell on one island, girded by the sea. 'Of all the naciouns in the worlde, that nacioun only, besides Englande, which speaketh the same language, is Scotland.'

God's will was even more manifest in the most recent events. Think of how this present situation came to pass. First James's two sons die, then he dies leaving a young girl. So perfect a match for England's heir has not been seen, says the *Epistle*, for 800 years. The two monarchs could both have been boys, or girls, or not of 'mete' age. 'If God should speake, what could he speake more then he speaketh in these?' Geography, manners, past experience and God's manifest will demand we join in unity and peace. 'Is it not better to compose and acquitte all this calamitie and trouble by mariage? To end all sorowes and battles by such an honourable peace?'

The *Epistle* next tried to dispel the 'vain fears and phantasies of expulsion of your nacion, changing of your laws, making of conquest, being driven from your holds'. Our antagonists say 'wee seke not equalitie, nor the marriage but a conquest, wee would not be frendes, but lordes'. This was obviously wrong. We come as brothers, as can be seen by our most lenient behaviour. We offer peace when we have overcome in war; we win your strongholds, but only to offer marriage; we conquer Scotland only to give you England. No change of laws was envisioned. England had a tremendous diversity of custom and usage. In France there were great differences, behold Gascony and Normandy. The Emperor's lands had come together through marriage; did they have one kind of law?

The *Epistle* made a strong plea for Scots to collaborate, so as to expedite this godly purpose and to taste its material advantages. They would not be harried, they would live under peace and quietness, they would be treated as Englishmen. They might 'lawfully, and without any trouble and vaxacion, entre into any Porte, Creeke, or Hauen of Englande, and vse their trafique of merchaundise . . . as liberally and as frely . . . then Englishmen'.

The third element in the *Epistle*'s case was lack of alternatives. Mary cannot be left unwed. To marry her in Scotland would unleash 'envy, grydge and malice . . . amongst you'. To marry her abroad would mean the French would 'eat up your victuals, take over your holds, ravish wives and daughters, hold you in subjugation and regard you as slaves. This foreign help was your confusion, that succour was your detriment, the victory so hard, was your servitude'. Furthermore, if you do bring in French help, you will still not be able to dislodge us. In a memorable passage, the *Epistle* trenchantly reminded its readers, 'Be we not in ye bowels now of the realme? Haue we not a great parte therof either in subjeccion, or in amitie and loue?' Resistance now meant a hardening which would destroy benevolence. England had two alternatives: conquest or marriage. 'Ye hate the one, and by refusing the other, you enforce it vpon you.' Even if England was defeated, 'conquest commeth vpon you whether you will or no'.

BOOKS AND READERS

How widely were these tracts circulated? On 24 August 1547, Wharton sent ten copies of the *Proclamation* of 4 September into Scotland; six to Glencairn, who promised to disperse them. One was to be affixed to the castle gate at Stirling, one was for the door of St. Giles in Edinburgh, one likewise for Glasgow Cathedral and one for Dumfries.[15] It was read. Both Leslie and Patten refer to it specifically and give fairly accurate renditions of its contents. On 25 August Arran proclaimed that none read on pain of death 'ane proclamatioun of the Protectour of Inglandis, set furtht in prent in Scotland to seduce the harttis of the pepill to his openyoun'.[16] Knox referred to 'a letter' being sent to the Governor and Council, and said that Archbishop Hamilton suppressed it, though whether or not he was referring to the *Proclamation* is not clear. On 20 December, Dudley and Windham set forth the *Proclamation* in Dundee with certain additions; Wharton doubtless based his *Proclamation* in Dumfries on it.[17] But this was nothing compared with the efforts to insure that the *Epistle* had as wide a readership as possible. To begin with, four different editions were printed: an English version in octavo and quarto executed by Grafton and two Latin editions by Wolf.[18] Every other piece of propaganda had only one edition, each of which has survived.

Moreover, the pamphlet was widely circulated. The declared print date for the *Epistle* was 5 February 1548. When Palmer arrived in Wark on the 11th he had some copies which he gave to Lord Grey of Wilton to distribute during his invasion.[19] Wharton received a consignment on the 15th which he caused to be read to some Scots in Carlisle. On the 18th he received yet another delivery, 260 copies this time, which he ordered to be distributed as far as possible in the West of Scotland.[20] When Grey reached Haddington on the 23rd, he sent a copy to Arran at Edinburgh and proposed to send him a dozen more the next day.[21]

Not only was the *Epistle* seen in Scotland. The Emperor read one of the Latin editions and did not find all of it to his liking. Hooper, in his dedication to Somerset of *A Declaracion of the ten holy commandementes*, printed in Zürich in 1548, made a great deal of Somerset's conquest of Scotland and justified the war very much in the same terms as were used in the *Epistle*.[22] German Protestant concern has no more

15 *CSP Scot.*, i, nos. 34, 37 (1).
16 *TA*, ix, 110; Knox, *History*, i, 98; see also Dalrymple, *Historie*, ii, 195; Patten, *Expedicion*, 76–77.
17 *CSP Scot.*, i, nos. 107, 108; *CSP Dom., Add.*, 1547–65, 360.
18 *STC*, nos. 9180, 9181, 22268, 22269.
19 *CSP Scot.*, no. 156; see Grafton, *History of England*, ed. H. Ellis (1809), ii, 508.
20 *CSP Dom., Add.*, 1547–65, 360–61. He was moved to complain both at the length of time (nine days) it took them to arrive and at the theft of 40 copies.
21 *CSP Scot.*, i, no. 168.
22 *STC*, no. 13746; see fos. Aii^v-Aii^r.

striking piece of evidence than a German translation of Wolf's Latin edition: *Ein schrifftiliche vermanung zum Friede und Einigkeit*, printed in Erfurt in 1549.

The *Epistle* was the high water mark of the English propaganda campaign aimed at the Scots. Events were rapidly outstripping the presses, as they had done in 1542. By June the French were disembarking at Leith, by July Haddington was besieged, and by August Mary had embarked for France, the betrothed of the Dauphin. Scottish collaborators rapidly melted away. Consequently it is not surprising that no subsequent piece of propaganda can be seriously thought to be directed at a Scottish audience. The focus shifted to the English one. All of the booklets doubtless were read by Englishmen. *A Declaracion* was obviously meant for their eyes. Newsletters, such as *The Late expedicon of the Earl of Hertford into Scotland*, printed in 1544, glorified the war and justified it.[23] Scots must be 'condignly punished for their falsehood to the Kinges majestie'.

Another such effort was William Patten's *The expedition into Scotland of the most worthy Prince, Edward Duke of Somerset, etc.*, printed in July 1548.[24] But Patten also spent much of a large introduction justifying the war for English readers. Patten asserted the superiority of the King of England over the Kingdom of Scotland, but did not elaborate it. The Scots were to be pitied for not having the wit to accept the marriage. 'What a marvellous unkind people they are that where we came as wooers for love and quiet, they receive us with hatred and war.' They were implored to cast off the 'feigned friendship of France' but most especially to free themselves from the 'antichrist, from the Pope and his rabble'. Basically it is this point which makes up the core of his case and his long, bitter invective against Roman Catholicism was venomous enough to warm any true reformer's heart. Patten's arguments, however, were hardly meant for Scots and there is nothing to suggest that his book was deliberately circulated amongst them.

The government also used the pulpit. On 18 December 1547, Bishop Boner of London was required by the Archbishop of Canterbury, Thomas Cranmer, to offer prayers in his diocese for the great victory at Pinkie.[25] On 6 May 1548, the Privy Council wrote to Cranmer that since they were surely informed of French preparations for war, he was to command all the curates of his diocese to make devout and hearty intercession to Almighty God, every Sunday and holy day. *A prayer for victorie and peace*, printed by Grafton (dated 10 May 1548) was sent to Cranmer and Winchester[26]

---

23 *STC* no. 22270. Reprinted in *Tudor Tracts*, ed. A.F. Pollard (n.d.), 39–51. See H.S. Bennett, *English Books and Readers, 1475 to 1557*, 142–45. The topic of publishing and literacy in our period has a vast bibliography. Amongst so many others, see Sheila O'Connell, *The Popular Print in England, 1550–1850* (British Museum Press, 1999). I am indebted to Dr. Lindsay Newman for this reference.

24 *STC*, no. 19479. Reprinted in *An English Garner*, ed. E. Arber (1877–96), iii, 51–155 and *Tudor Tracts*, ed. A.F. Pollard (n.d.), 554–154.

25 Lambeth Palace, Cranmer's Register, i, fo. 55ᵛ. I am grateful to Mr. A. Edwards for this reference. Strype, *Memorials*, i, 218–20.

26 *STC*, no. 16503. The only copy of the prayer is in the Pepysian Library, Magdalene College, Cambridge. Manuscript of it in PRO, SP 10/2, fo. 11. Instructions for its use are in Lambeth Palace, Cranmer's Register, i, fo. 55ᵛ; Strype, *Memorials*, i, 253; ii, 26–27, 166.

and 'commaunded wyth all reverent devotion to be sayde in all the Churches of England'. As Grafton remembered, 'by reason therof the campaign 'was the more prosperous'.[27]

God was asked to 'have an eye to this small Isle of Bretaigne' and to complete what He had begun, 'That the Scottish menn and wee might forever and hereafter in love and amitie, knit into one nacion' by the marriage of Edward and Mary. 'Graunt o Lorde that the same might goo forwarde and that our sonnes sonnes and all our posteritie hereafter may fele the benefite and commoditie of thy great gift of unitie graunted in our daies'. Though He was asked to 'putt away frome us all warre and hostilitie', if this was not to be, then He should 'be our sheld and buckle' and 'Lay thy sowrd of punyshement uppoun them' that opposed the marriage. Better still, 'converte their hartes to the better waye'. Despite its effusive phrases, the prayer does show an obvious stiffening of the English position. The very fact that the government felt it had to sell the war in such a direct manner within England indicates dissatisfaction with how events were going. Moreover the prayer came at a time when the government's whole attitude towards propaganda was changing.

The most intriguing question is: what effect did it have on the course of the war? It is very difficult to assess what impact all this had on actual events, on how men thought and acted. But one thing is certain – it most certainly had an effect upon those who thought they had something to add, be it to augment the English case or to refute it. Englishmen most certainly were stimulated by the propaganda. One most interesting case is that of William Thomas, a humanist of some note, and an embezzler.[28] In hopes of paying off his gambling debts, he fled to Italy in 1545 hoping to cash a credit slip there made on the account of his patron, Sir Anthony Browne, a ruse Harvel thwarted. There he languished for four years despite repeated requests to be allowed to return. One of his ploys was a small tract entitled 'The Perygrine' which he submitted to Edward VI.[29] No contempory English publication was made of the tract – an Italian edition, *Il Pellegrino Ingleze*, was printed in 1552 – but it seems to have served his ends: by 1550 he was a clerk of the Privy Council.[30]

In this tract, Thomas related how he had been 'contrained by infortune to . . . walk at the randome of the wide world' and came to Bologna where one evening he dined at a rich merchant's house. It was February 1547 and word had just come of the death of Henry VIII. The locals were quite sympathetic at first and politely pumped him on things English: manners, customs, cosmology – in which, he commented revealingly, 'you must understand Scotland to be comprehended' – and not unnaturally that most noble king, just dead.

27 Grafton, *History of England*, ed. H. Ellis (1809), ii, 501.

28 E.R. Adair, 'William Thomas: a forgotten clerk of the Privy Council', *Tudor Studies*, ed. R. Seton-Watson, 133–60.

29 For manuscript editions, see BL, MS Harl. 353, fos. 8–35; BL, MS Vesp. D. xviii, fos. 46v–63; MS Add. 33, 383. Scotland is discussed on fo. 31v. of BL, MS Harl. 353.

30 The entry for him in the *DNB* differs from Adair's article. Reference to T.F.T. Baker's biography is essential: Bindoff, *Parliament*, iii, 439–43.

Suddenly the other guests laid into him with a 13-point denunciation of the King. Every indictment, of course, was dexterously parried, from Catherine's divorce to the spoliation of Becket's tomb. Point eleven was that Henry 'hath by force subdued the realme of Ireland, whereunto he hath neither right nor tytle; and wasted he hath noe small part of Scotland with intent to subdue the whole whithout cause or reason'. In the case of Ireland, Thomas patiently explained that it was necessary to bring civilisation to the wild, warring barbarians of that land, to give them a 'certain order both of religion and customs'. As for Scotland, the King resolved to marry Mary to Edward, 'either by force or by love', not because he lusted after Scotland's wealth, of which it had none, but solely 'to have made one self divided nation a Realm, one self perpetual united people and peace'.

It is difficult to establish just when Thomas wrote 'The Perygrine' but it was obviously executed before he returned to London in September 1549. The language of his argument about Scotland was quite different from anything he could have read before his flight. He must have read the *Epistle*, which had a wide circulation on the Continent. There is little to suggest he conceived the arguments himself; the whole purport of the tract was simply to gain favour in the sight of the government. His subsequent effort, a history of Italy, was shrewdly dedicated to Warwick.

John Mardeley was another Englishman given to writing, though whether or not it was for favour is difficult to say. Mardeley's most assiduous year was 1548 when three of his tracts hit the stalls: *A Declaracion of the power of Godes worde*, dedicated to Somerset, *Here is a short resytal of certayne holy doctours, collected in myter*, and *Here beginne the necessarie instruction for all couetous ryche men*.[31] Mardeley was too radical. The Privy Council was moved by 13 August 1549 to slap a recognisance on him 'not at any tyme herafter [to] publishe or set foorth in writing or print, any boke, ballet or other work' not previously vetted by Cecil and given a special license by the Privy Council. Mardeley settled back into his previous obscurity as a clerk of the mint at Southwark during its short existence. As Cecil was appointed to keep an eye on his literary productions, it is not surprising to find in his papers at Hatfield one of Mardeley's efforts which did not get into print, 'A symple treates namede an espostolacione complyinge the Ingratytyde of our Countramen the scottes'.[32]

This long work in 'mytre' (dated 6 September 1547) put into verse the messages of both Henrisoun's *Exhortacion* and the *Proclamation*; he dated it 6 September 1547 and probably had read both. Heavily laced with biblical references and long quotes from the psalms and parables, its main purpose was to lay the case why the Scots should

> but come to the fountain and holesome spring
> which is noble Edward our most Royal king
> and fre without boundage with us to remaigne
> As in one hole kingdom collaed great breataigne.

---

31 Mardeley had a brief but spectacular publishing career (*STC*, nos. 17317–17319) which was why a recognisance was slapped on him (*APC*, ii, 311–12).
32 Hatfield, Cecil Papers, vol. 137, fos. 136–43.

Mardeley's near epic was quite a handsome reflection of the propaganda campaign's main themes in the autumn of 1547. The Scots are warned against false friends who 'you tell Beware of Englond, do not with them dwell/Their lawes be onerus to bring you bondage/Therefore take them as Enymies'. England, he declares, is a friend, 'lyke as a moste lovinge father' who only wishes to instruct them 'in knowledge, unitie and quietness'. The Scots broke the treaties even though 'hendry our late kinge with his beningnitie pardoned your offences and put you at lybertie'. Resistance was futile. As in the past, when war with England only resulted in 'The death of your kyng at floghone feld slayne', so shortly if you do not repent,

> As weades ye shalbe gatherede and in the fire throwne
> now this harweste is come, what maye you defende
> for as david by god, had victories agaynst saule
> So shall this noble duke shortely wynne you all.

'Dothe not the Oceane sea inverounde us rounde/both of one language?' Among many other blessings, 'our two Realmes be Joined in one masse'. Scots are enjoined to 'caste Awaye the yocke of Romishe vsaunte'. Mardeley concludes, beseeching God

> To send us grace, of his maynanmytie
> In unitie to be, as brotherne naturall
> All varyaunce to cease, hatred & Enmytie
> So that concorde and peax with love and amytie
> May so encrease emonges us, to the worldes ende
> That we may lyve to gethers as frend and frend.

Though Englishmen might reflect the propaganda, or try to versify it, the Scots had most to say. The first man to present a document was John Elder, an early collaborator. When he arrived in England in 1544, he drafted and presented to Henry VIII a 17- folio tract recommending in violently Protestant terms the union of the two realms. Part of the work was autobiographical, though he was silent on why he fled Scotland, and part of it concerned the fate of 'Redshank Scots', those from the North and the Isles. He railed against the bishops, who now intend 'to drounde all Scotland in bloude'. Reflecting arguments advanced in *A Declaracion*, he castigated the Cardinal and the bishops for alienating James V from Henry and especially for preventing their meeting at York. Union under Henry's superiority would rid Scotland of these proud prelates and their evil superstitions and would pluck the French king out of Scottish hearts.[33] Henry found the work to his liking. Elder was pensioned and lived in England thereafter[34] – but his tract was never printed or used as propaganda.

One man caught up in the business of the tracts was James Henrisoun who took the *Epistle* to be a faithful statement of what the war was about and as a commitment

---

33 *LP*, xviii (2), no. 539. For another tract of his, a Baedeker of his native country, see BL, MS Harl. 289, fos. 4–5.
34 *LP*, xix (1), nos. 278 (71), 1035 (10); xxi (1), nos. 650 (85), 970; *CPR Edward VI*, i, 251; *APC*, ii, 114.

¶An introduction into the history of Fol.i.
Kyng Henry the fourthe.

What mischiefe hath insurged in real=
mes by intestine deuision, what depo=
pulacion hath ensued in countries by
ciuill discencio, what detestable mur=
der hath been cōmitted in citees by se
perate faccions, and what calamitee
hath ensued in famous regiōs by do=
mestical discord & vnnaturall contro=
uersy: Rome hath felt, Italy can testi=
fie, Fraunce can bere witnes, Beame
can tell, Scotlande maie write, Den=
marke can shewe, and especially this
noble realme of Englande can appa=
rantly declare and make demonstracion. For who abhorreth not to ex=
presse the heynous factes comitted in Rome, by the ciuill war betwene
Julius Cesar and hardy Pompey by whose discorde the bright glory of
the triūphant Rome was eclipsed & shadowed? Who can reherce what
mischefes and what plages the pleasant countree of Italy hath tasted
and suffered by the sedicious faccions of the Guelphes and Gebely=
nes? Who can reporte the misery that daiely hath ensued in Fraunce,
by the discorde of the houses of Burgoyne and Orliens: Or in Scot=
land betwene the brother and brother, the vncle and the nephew? Who
can curiously endite the manifolde battailles that were fought in the
realme of Beame, betwene the catholikes and the pestiferus sectes of
the Adamites and others? What damage discencion hath dooen in
Germany and Denmarke, all christians at this daic can well declare.
And the Turke can bere good testimony, whiche by the discord of chri=
sten princes hath amplified greatly his seigniory and dominion. But
what miserie, what murder, and what execrable plagues this famous
region hath suffered by the deuision and discencion of the renoumed
houses of Lancastre and Yorke, my witte cannot comprehende nor my
toung declare nether yet my penne fully set furthe.

Fig. 11.4. In the summer of 1548, probably in July, James Henrisoun prepared a tract,
a 'buik of weir' to accompany Shrewsbury's invasion in August which
relieved Haddington and built Dunglass. Like Morison a decade before, he
was clearly rushed off his feet and, as has happened to many a journalist
since, plagiarised. His source was the newly printed *The union of the two
noble and illustre families of Lancastre and Yorke* which had almost been
completed in 1547 when he died and passed the work over to Richard
Grafton for completion and publication.

by Somerset as to how to govern the pale. In 1549, during the closing stages of the war, he made two long, detailed remonstrances to Somerset, complaining bitterly of the brutality of the soldiers, the ignorance of the English captains and the indiscriminate manner in which all Scots, unassured and assured alike, were harried, burned and robbed. These extremities, he reminded the Protector, were 'contrary to the King's Majesty's epistle' and had lost the English cause 'manie honnest hartes'.

Henrisoun emerges as the one man genuinely concerned about how the union was to be effected and Scotland governed once the war had been won. His 'Littil book' which he submitted in July 1548, 'The godly thinges that James Herrison did wishe the Kinges majestie of england to sett forth in his highenes name for the welth of both the realmes',[35] was an explicit programme for how the war should benefit Scotland.

All of the English tracts were printed to coincide with a specific invasion. In that sense they were what one Scot described as 'war buikis'. This 'godly and golden book' was intended to be leafleted over Scotland during Shrewsbury's invasion in August. It thus had to be executed hastily. Its opening passage began, predictably enough, with a lamentation of the civil war between the two countries and drew parallels from Rome, Bohemia, France, Denmark and Holland, and between 'the Rede Rose and White'. Even worse were the wars between Thistle and Rose. 'What mysery, what morther, what execrable plages, haith this famous regyon of Great Bryttaine suffred by devision our most renowned howses of two kinges, indwellers of the same.' This handsome rhetoric was lifted straight from Halle's *Chronicle* which had just appeared that year. The only way out was union. 'Discord causes decay, so Concord brings renewal and relief.' Union – be it of the Catholic Church and the synagogue, of manhead and godhead, or of man and woman in marriage – was always beneficial. Here too it must come, 'wherby this longe warr pestilence famen and infamyne may take an ende'.

The last article is a plea for people to assure, promising those who take the land of an unassured man that they shall have half of that man's inheritance and goods, those who eject churchmen to have a year's fruits and those who sell victual to English camps to have reasonable prices whilst those nearby who bring none shall be harried. To ensure the bonds of union, it enjoins that there should be extensive intermarriage of Englishmen and Scots, from peers down, and a liberal distribution of the Garter and pensions to Scottish nobles, thus 'discharging them of the blody leage with fraunce'. Younger sons and mere barons would also be liberally helped.

But the rest of the book was highly radical. Once England had won Scotland, it would extend to its undeveloped neighbour a wide range of technological aids. 'A hundrethe fisher shipps with all there apparell' would be given the burghs for their 'florishemente', seeing how much they had already been ravished (by the will of God), along with the wages of a hundred fishermen 'to lerne them to take them and make them and beyld certain havens where shal be nedefull'. Furthermore one hundred English craftsmen of all sorts would have their wages paid for three years

---

35 PRO, SP 50/4, fos. 128–37 (*CSP Scot.*, i, no. 285).

whilst they taught the Scots skills in 'myndes, skynne and hide as myners, cutters of mosses for makinge of mean landes of thos that be but marresse, makers of iron mylls, saw mylls and others, collyerdes, dighter of wull, websters, wallers, tapplishers, makers of wursates and serges, workers in the scole, diers of skynnes and hides, as bowers, fletchers and such other'. There was also large talk of exploiting such resources as gold, copper, iron and lead. Doubtless the most remarkable scheme was to 'draw the weste and easte sees togither so that partable vessles shall goo between'. Henrisoun would also have prohibited the import of foreign wares and would have tightened up the regulations regarding merchant status, especially against those who left the burghs to make and sell goods in the country.

These were not the only economic changes the English were to effect. Tenants and 'poor labourers of the grounde' were to be allowed to have their land in feu or long tacks at the present rent. A free school was to be maintained in every diocese. Universities were to be improved. Almshouses and hospitals were to be rebuilt so that every parish could care both for the aged and the sick. Parish churches had to be

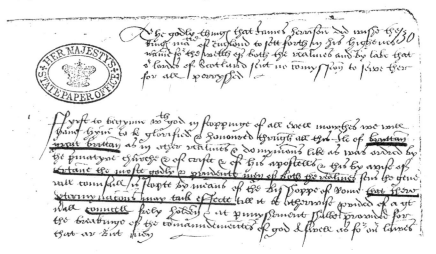

Fig. 11.5. Another telling moment in the history of Somerset's Rough Wooing emerges if you read the following passage from the manuscript of Henrisoun's 'Godlie and Golden Book' (significantly, it was never printed). The new buzz term 'Great Britain' had just formally emerged in 1548 (it was hardly used at all in 1547). In his first proposal for how England's victory should benefit his native country, Henrisoun wrote:

First to begynne with god in stoppinge of all evell mowthes wse will have hyme to be glorified and honoured through all this Ile of bryttain.

But he then immediately realized he had made a serious mistake and thus crossed out 'bryttain' and continued:

Grait bryttain as in other realms and dominions like as was ordred by the primatyve churche and of criste and of his apposstells and this by avise of certaine the moste godly and prudente men of both the realms [etc.]

renovated. The whole structure of the church was to be refurbished. Suffragan bishops were to be disallowed, especially in the Highlands and the Isles where the lack of any church discipline had led to the loss of 'mony sowles'. Parsons would be forced to reside at their parish churches. Churchmen were to be prohibited from engaging in commerce, except under strictly regulated conditions. Consistory courts were to be abolished and the judicial system revamped. Two sessions of 'prudents' were to sit at Edinburgh and Aberdeen. Laws were to be reviewed and brought up to date, and a book of the new code was to be printed 'that none shall perishe through Ignoraunce'. The heart of these proposals was that a general council of learned men of both realms was to meet to determine the form of religion 'thrugh all this Ile of great brittan . . . as was ordered by the primatyve church & of criste & of his apostells'.

Henrisoun was not the only Scot to be compelled to put pen to paper over the great issue of this war and its aims. Another was one William Lamb.[36] At the time he wrote his counterblast to the English propaganda, Lamb, rector of Conveth, stated he was a 'Counsall to our Soverans ladeis College of Justice'. Related to Patrick Liddal, the Scottish procurator at the consistorial court of Rome, he had been in France for some years in the late 1520s and may have been in the household of the cardinal of Ravenna. In 1538 he was appointed as a clerk to the Justice Court.[37] In 1545 he was exempted from paying a tax owing to his position as one of the 'Senators of the College of Justice'.

He was widely read. Some time after 1548 he was prompted, perhaps by the one-sidedness of the press, to refute both *A Declaracion* and the *Epistle* in a work entitled 'Ane Resonyng of ane Scottis and Inglis merchand betwix zekland and lions'.[38] Although he dealt exhaustively with *A Declaracion*, he only began to lay into the *Epistle* when the manuscript abruptly ends on folio 21, just on the other side of Paris. The bulk of what he completed was an extensive point-by-point examination of the case presented in *A Declaracion*. The first half of *A Declaracion* was contradicted by a Scottish account of relations with England leading up to the 1542 war. Mistakes in the calculations of years between each homage are made much of. Scottish authorities such as Beothius and Major (as well as the Italian Polidor Vergil) are called in to confound *A Declaracion* on every homage.

Tedious perhaps, but this is not to say it was not relieved by snatches of quite superb dialogue. We begin with the Scot asking the Englishman who he is, whither he goes and where he is from. In reply, the Englishman inquires solicitously, 'Be zow ane Scott?' 'That I am', responds our friend from across the Border, 'and would have fallowschip be the sam way.' The Englishman ruminates a second, then asks, 'De ze not be eschame to be callit ane scott thir dayis?' Think you 'nocht the inglismen be guid trastie men of warre and victorious peopill that dois baith ruffill zow and the Frenchemen?'[39] Rubbish, retorts the Scot. It is 'owr awin mishaving to God and

36 Lamb's life and career is detailed in R.J. Lyall (ed.), Lamb, *Resonyng*, x–xvii.
37 *ADCP*, 466, 574; *TA*, vii, 383, 384; *RSS*, ii, no. 1131; *RPC*, i, 56.
38 BL, MS Calig, B. vii, fos. 346–67.
39 Lamb, *Resonyng*, 3–5.

misgyding in veirfare'. The English merchant tries another approach: 'Zow do appeir Juge oure weir Inuist'.

Immediately the two tracts are mentioned and a good man of Synon and some other merchants are asked to adjudicate. Only the good man, however, lasts it out. One merchant goes off suddenly, mumbling, 'We merchants make small gain in tyme of weir'; another suspiciously never re-emerges from his lodging house in Rouen. In the long argument, the Englishman seems to lose his temper much more than the supposedly choleric Scot. 'What man be zow, deif or blind', he shouts repeatedly, and at one point glowers, 'Giff I say ye craw is blak than zow will say yat scho is quhytt'. Obviously exasperated, the Scot devastatingly retorts at one juncture, 'Neighbour, quhat wald ze think gife I said to zow yat robert huid had conquerit Italie and maid Romulus kyng of rome'.

In print or not, its intent was quite clear: to demonstrate that English claims to suzereignity over Scotland were quite baseless, the histories quoted false and the failure to mention the Treaty of Northampton dishonest. Acid comments are made regarding the tender carefulness of uncle Henry VIII for his nephew. Contradictions between the *Declaration* and the *Epistle* are pointed out, although Lamb never gets around to the detail lavished on the former piece. As for the *Epistle*, only 'the facil inglis people and the cortiers in the court of lundon' might believe it.

Lamb was not the only Scot to find English reasoning spurious. *The Complaynt of Scotland* also reviled it.[40] *The Complaynt* was the one Scottish publication to be printed at the time concerning the war. It was a masterful piece of patriotic propaganda. It had a fair amount to say about those Scots who assured, as it did about the degenerate state of the country in general. It railed against a covetous nobility, a clergy the clasps on whose bible were shut with rust, and a degenerate commons. It also made a plea for reforms of the body politic: giving tenants securer tenure, insuring fairer and more thorough justice and encouraging trade. The author of *The Complaynt* also agreed with Lamb that English success in the war was due not to their prowess so much as Scottish failings. It was God's punishment of the Scots for their own misdeeds. This admitted no heavenly approval of English actions. Hammering lead benefited the lead not the hammer.

'The oratours of Ingland', *The Complaynt* reminded its readers, 'at there protectors instance, hes set furtht ane buik, quhairbe thai intend to preue that scotland was ane colone of ingland quhen it was fyrst inhabit.' It is difficult to be sure which book is referred to here, *Exhortacion* or *Epistle*. Both mention 'diurse prophane prohesies of merlyne . . . affermit in there rusty tyme, that scotland and ingland sal be vnder ane prince', and both claim that the King of England has 'ane iust titil to make vayr again vs'. *The Complaynt* also refers to:

> ane passage in the said beuk, the quilk the inglishmen hes an ardant desyr to se it cum til effect. The tenor of the pasage sais, that it var verray necessare for the veilfayre of ingland and scotland, that byth the realmis var continuit to be callit the ile of bretan, as it vas in the begynnyng.

40 *STC*, no. 22009. A new edition of this tract is in preparation.

England's real intention is to be 'violent dominatours of oure cuntray'. *The Complaynt* did agree, though, that union was feasible and even desirable so long as the Scots entered it as equals. Prophetically, however, it thought it should not come about by force, nor by a marriage of England's king to Scotland's queen.

THE RETURN TO OVERLORDSHIP

The Imperial ambassador, van der Delft, had kept his government informed of the propaganda campaign. On 6 September 1547 he gave the Emperor a précis of the *Proclamation* and the Emperor also gained possession of the *Epistle*. On 7 May 1548 he wrote that the offers to the assured contravened clause 3 of the 1543 treaty, and two weeks later van der Delft raised this issue. Somerset argued that he had made such offers only to induce 'more division amongst the Scots' and thus bring them to terms. In itself, this remark of Somerset's is not particularly revealing, but during this interview his whole attitude towards the *Epistle* seemed hostile. He was both ignorant of its contents and became angry 'at the foolishness of the draftsman' when some passages were pointed out to him. Perhaps this was simply a ploy, but subsequent events were to show that the Protector's attitude had altered.[41]

On 9 July James Henrisoun approached Sir John Thynne, Seymour's steward, and William Cecil, requesting they 'procur me leif to put in print the littill book' which he submitted, entitled 'The Godlie and Golden Booke to peace and union'.[42] This was a remarkable and radical piece of work. In place of the worthy generalisations about marriage, peace and union, it offered a specific and detailed programme of action. Henrisoun stated twice that Somerset had both 'read and corrected this work'; if so, the Protector no longer felt enthusiastic enough to get it into print. By October, when the collaborators were melting away in the face of French arms and money, Somerset's stance had retrogressed a full six years and the English position was once again that of *A Declaracion*.

In early October Sir John Mason,[43] Sir Thomas Smith and others were spending their time 'serching registres for recordes of mattiers of Scotland'.[44] On the 3rd, Bishop Tunstall received orders once again to research within the archives of the Palatinate of Durham. He replied dutifully, expeditiously (on the 15th) and with some perturbation. In his repository he found the 'renunciation of kinge Edwarde the seconde of the superorytie to the realme of scotlande'. He had 'ofte herde it spoke of by scottes', but had not seen it before. In a staggeringly naïve remark, he warned Somerset that the Scots probably had an original of this in their own records. 'A kinge renouncinge this reight of his crowne cannot reiudice his successours who had at the tyme of there entree the same hole right that theyre predecessours had at there entree'. Civil lawyers would doubtless back him up on this.[45]

41 *CSP Spain*, ix, 147–8, 264, 268–9.
42 *CSP Scot.*, i, no. 285.
43 Henry VIII's French secretary and knighted 22 February 1547 by Somerset. Bindoff, *Parliament*, ii, 582–83.
44 *APC*, ii, 225; *Odet de Selve*, 257–8, 461.
45 BL, MS Calig. B vii, fos. 336–337ᵛ; cf. MS Calig. D. ii, fos, 450ʳ–451ᵛ.

The result was a manuscript book, principally the work of Mason, justifying the King's propriety and superiority of Scotland.[46] The Scots, an incredulous Odet de Selve was told, had rendered homage to the kings of England even down to the time of Henry VII, a claim not even *A Declaracion* was audacious enough to make.[47] Even more far-fetched, as James IV refused to render, Henry VII had prepared to make war, 'but in the end, marrying one of his daughters, prevented the warres for certayne yeares'. Once Henry II was informed of this 'just quarel of his majesty to the sayd sovereignty', Somerset was sure he would refrain from aiding Edward's 'rebelles', as Edward had done with respect to Henry, at the time of the revolt in Guyenne. Odet de Selve suggested it would be best first to see what the Scots found in their registers. Wotton, in Paris, was subsequently sent a copy of Mason's labours with which to confront the French king in person. Reports of the audience do not suggest Henry found the arguments persuasive.[48]

This change of attitude can be seen in the final English tract, *An Epitome of the title that the kynges Maiestie of Englande, hath to the souereignitie of Scotland, continued upon the aucient writers of both nacions, from the beginnyng.*[49] Dated 1548, it would seem to have come out either at the very end of the year, or perhaps early in 1549. The stated authorship was by an MP from West Looe, Nicholas Bodrugan alias Adams,[50] although current scholarship attributes it to Thomas Smith.[51] However, the one letter of Smith's concerning Scotland is only second-hand knowledge which he had been asked to pass on to Somerset by various Scottish exiles in London.

The work was in some respects a hack job, but its contents are revealing. It spent considerable time attempting to dispel Scottish fears of having to live under English laws.[52] It assured its readers that the Scots have horrible laws aplenty, but agreed that 'sondry places must of necessity require sondry laws'. This aside, the tracts dissolved into an odd combination of the claim to overlordship, the rant against the clergy and the folly of the Scots. 'Ah. Scottishmen . . . how long will you remain rebellious children, when shal there be end to your malice?' Though replete with fulsome praises of the benefits of union, it was obviously for domestic English consumption. Much of the game was given away in the Preface with the telling

46 BL, MS Calig. B vii, fos. 296–299, 329ʳ⁻ᵛ; MS Add. 6128; MS Vesp. C. xvi, fos. 80–116, 129–139ᵛ. This list is not exhaustive.
47 *Odet de Selve*, 465; *CSP Scot.*, i, nos. 170–1; BL, MS Calig. B vii, fos. 341–345ᵛ.
48 *CSP Spain*, ix, 305, 330–07.
49 *STC* no. 3196; reprinted (but only in part) in *Complaynt*, 247–56.
50 He later was a member in the session of March and October 1553, and April and November 1554. He sat as a lawyer for Dartmouth, where he resided and where he was noted as a man 'well learned in the law and hath many great friends in these parts'. Though none of this disqualifies him as the author, it must be admitted that it is slender evidence indeed.
51 Dr Dewar, prompted by an eighteenth-century antiquarian's contention that everyone knew the real author to be Sir Thomas Smith, connects it with him, further bolstering this contention with Smith's seemingly extensive knowledge of Scottish affairs. Mary Dewar, *Sir Thomas Smith – A Tudor Intellectual in Office*. BL, MS Calig. B. vii, fo. 443 is his only letter on Scotland.

statement: 'Though the marriage by the iniquitie of some take not effecte, yet to publish to the world sufficient cause, for the mainteynaunce of your maiesties accion against them, wherein the honor of a kyng may not geue place to their wilfull rebellion'.[53]

This, then, is the sum of the English propaganda which was printed and circulated concerning the war with Scotland. Not a truthful insight into the government's actual motives, it does prove to have been a rather sensitive barometer of both its policies and the course of the war. Save in the case of Henrisoun's book, we have very little information indeed on how these books came to pass or who actually composed them. Only one manuscript remains, that for the *Prayer*, and it has no emendations.[54]

'WHAT MURTHER, PLAGUE AND DESOLATIOUN'

What effect, if any, did this propaganda have on the course of the war? Did it change the minds of any Scots who previously had opposed the marriage? Did it convince foreign powers that England's claim to Scotland was reasonable, just or wise? Did it affect the popularity of the war in England and thus enable Somerset to carry on longer than otherwise might have been the case? It is very hard to tell, as G.R. Elton commented when discussing Henrician Protestant propaganda. European Protestants may have snapped up its German translation, but the outcome of war for Scotland was not to be made in Erfurt. Nor did the just title argument cut any ice with Henry II.

As to the domestic impact of the propaganda, little can be said with any certainty. Patten glorified the war, Hooper found it praiseworthy, the *Prayer* invoked God's blessing on it and the *Epitome* defended it when it was obviously lost. Cheeke, in his rebuke of the 1549 rebels, *The Hurt of Sedition*,[55] castigated Kett and his friends for costing England a rich and noble victory, the union of the realms, in terms echoing the propaganda's most purple passages. But it is doubtful that any rebel would have stayed his sword confronted by such a thought. Nonetheless Somerset had considered that domestic utterances such as the *Prayer* and the *Epitome* were worth the money, and people who read Patten's admonishings to the Scots to throw off the papal yoke no doubt approved.

Perhaps the most important impact, domestically, of the propaganda was to introduce the idea of Anglo-Scottish union to Englishmen. Also, it 'introduced' the idea of Great Britain to members of both commonwealths. This is not to say they were convinced of its blessings for quite some time.[56] One man who found it both

---

52 'I have studied a great while the lawes of this realme and . . . have read them all both old and new.'

53 *Complaynt*, 249–50.

54 PRO, SP 10/2, fo. 11.

55 J. Cheke, *The Hurt of Sedicion* (1549); see fos. Gii v-Giiii V (*STC*, no. 5109).

56 S.T. Bindoff, 'The Stuarts and their Style', *EHR*, lx (1945), 192–210; D. Hay, 'The Use of the term "Great Britain" in the middle ages', *Proceedings of the Society of Antiquaries of Scotland*, lxxxix (1955–56), 56–66.

pleasing and significant was William Cecil,[57] even though in some respects he remained an English imperialist. Anyone familiar with his involvement in Scottish affairs, not only in 1559–60 but later, is struck by the unmistakable references in his utterances to the propaganda of this time, especially his references to the 'best worldlie felitictie for Scotland' lying in union or co-operation with England. However, Cecil's stance in 1559–60 could be ambivalent. Certainly his famous memorandum, 'the weighty matter of Scotland' of August 1559, contained as 'imperialist' an interpretation of Anglo-Scottish relations as one could ask for, viz. 'The Crown of England has a just and unfeigned title . . . to the superiority of Scotland'.[58] But such talk was really for the Queen's consumption (not to mention that of his fellow privy counsellors). At that time, Mary Queen of Scots was Queen of France and everywhere proclaimed her entitlement to the throne of England. Her Scottish seal, cast in Paris, gave the style for herself and her joint monarch, Francis, as FRANCISUS ET MARIA REX ET REGINA FRANCOR. SCOT. ANGL. ET HIBER. The over-lordship argument regurgitated by Elizabeth's Principal Secretary was then a counterblast debating point. During the negotiations at Cateau-Cambrésis, the French argued they could not discuss Calais in the treaty with England since it rightfully belonged to Mary Queen of Scots as Queen of England.

Such pretensions ceased in part with the conclusion of that universal peace, and Cecil's stance became much more 'Somersetian'. Rather, one should say, it became much more like Henrisoun's unionist ideological preferences of the 1540s, and John Knox's desire for both the kingdoms to share the same faith. Imperialism was not a policy statement to which William Cecil adhered. Other echoes of the Rough Wooings propaganda also could be heard in the war of words in the Reformation war of religion in Scotland during 1558–60 and especially, at least initially, in the correspondence of both English and Scottish reformers.[59] See the remarkable (indeed, extraordinary) proposals that Elizabeth should marry Chatelherault's son, the Earl of Arran, second person of Scotland should his father die and King should Mary perish as well.

57 Conyers Read, *Mr. Secretary Cecil and Queen Elizabeth* (1955); *Lord Burghley and Queen Elizabeth* (London, 1960). Reference must also be had to a series of articles by J.E.A. Dawson, 'William Cecil and the British Dimension of early Elizabethan foreign policy', *History* (lxxiv, 1989), pp. 196–216; 'Mary Queen of Scots, Lord Darnley, and Anglo-Scottish relations in 1565', *International History Review* (viii, 1986), pp. 1–24; 'Anglo-Scottish protestant culture and integration in sixteenth-century Britain', *Conquest and Union Fashioning a British State, 1485–1725*, ed. S.G. Ellis and Sarah Barber (London, 1995), pp. 87–114. Cecil of course was also the creator of a vast collection of maps of England and Britain: a point nicely captured by Dawson, 'British Dimension', pp. 197–99; and see in particular footnotes 2–7. My first ever article concerned one of his collected maps: M.H. Merriman, 'The Platte of Castlemilk, 1547', *Transactions of the Dumfriesshire and Galloway Natural History and Antiquarian Society*, xliv (1967), 175–81. See also R.A. Skelton, *Saxton's Survey of England and Wales*, Imago Mundi Supplement, No. VI (Amsterdam, 1974). Also J.B. Harley, 'Meaning and ambiguity in Tudor cartography' and W. Ravenhill, 'Christopher Saxton's surveying: an enigma', in S. Tyacke, ed., *English Map-Making, 1500–1650* (London, 1983), pp. 22–45 and 112–19.

58 *CSP Foreign, 1558–59*, 520.

59 See the considerable literature by Dr. J.E.A. Dawson cited in full elsewhere in the body of this book's text and in the Bibliography.

If, then, the propaganda of 1547–48 had an effect on the minds of men a generation later and if in particular it moulded Cecil's ideas regarding Scotland, then its impact was significant indeed and it can stand as one foundation, however minor, of Anglo-Scottish Union. To return to the point: did the propaganda affect the outcome of the war? Certainly some of the diction in the tracts implanted itself in men's minds at the time. Anglo-Scottish correspondence, especially in 1547–49, was heavily laced with such phrases as 'the godly purpose', the 'purpose of the Union', the 'beneficial union and marriage'. Wharton said that when he read parts of the *Epistle* to some Scots who were in Carlisle, they all 'heartilie' received it. He also beamed that no sooner had they done so than Scots who had had the misfortune not to hear his exposition asked to have copies of their very own. He for one figured that all 'charitable' men ought be happy with its contents. In January 1548 Dudley judged that books would do more good about Dundee than men, and he too distributed copies of the *Proclamation* and the *Epistle*. Both commanders soon renounced either books or friendship as effective methods to win the war.

To a certain extent the argument in the tracts did get a good hearing. Brende made much of the case for Union, as did Somerset in a letter to one of James V's bastard sons. Brende said he got a fairly good response from his audience when he emphasised the dangers of the alliance with France. They all mumbled assent. Well, they would, wouldn't they? And he would so report, would he not? Obviously the tracts were read and appreciated by the hard core of collaborators with Protestant leanings. But as one such assured Scot, Robert Lockhart, pointed out in a long triode to Somerset about the course of the war in 1549, the noble sentiments meant little: 'Even inglis menne call vs traitours to our Quene'.

One Scot equally unimpressed was the author of the *Complaynt* who saw the purpose of the tract as 'to persuaid the vulgar ignorans til adhere til inventit fablis contract the iust verite'. He also had the final word when he reminded his readers, 'Realmis ar nocht conquest be buikis, bot rather be bluid'.[60]

60 For examples of the tracts being read to Scots, see *CSP Scot.*, i, nos. 156, 168, 1922, 345–56; *CSP Dom., Add., 1547–65*, 360; *Complaynt*, 82.

CHAPTER TWELVE

French Intervention, 1547–48

Conquest certainly seemed imminent in late 1547. Recalling the fiasco at St. Andrews a year before, Henry Lord Methven lamented 'the asseg of Bruchtie procedit of lycht report'. On 24 November, Arran had appeared before the tower but, lacking artillery, he left after little over a fortnight. Writing at the end of December, Methven charged that the Governor's departure

> has caussit the Inglis be heycht and to get new support and mak of new mair strang fortifeying of Bruchty and do nychtlie greit troublis and skaythis be fyr heirschippis ravising of wemen borning of abbayis and halding of the legis in conte[n] wall lawbouris exspenss and feyr.

His sage and sensible prescription for success, 'Greit arttalzerij puderis bullattis gunnarris and hagbutterris and uther men of weir and peonarris be largelie furnest', did not exist in Scotland:

> Gif this substantious help and provisioun be nocht speid delyentlie heyr . . . bot mn heyr of ennymis daly tryumphe and ma nocht put remeid therto, quhilkis salbe mayr disurag to all the legis than befor, and occasioun to Ingland to perseveyr in that contenwaill supley sending to thaim, and causing the legis in thir partis to dispar the apoynt wyth tham and to delyver tham ma strythis . . . The langer our ennymeis be contenwat the starkar ar thai, and salbe the grettar fors that sall repuss them and put tham away.[1]

The government had but three options. It could simply retreat, keeping the Queen in its control but leaving large parts of the Kingdom either held by English troops (as was Broughty) or under almost constant attack (as was Dundee) or threat (as was Perth, whence Methven sent his despairing analysis). Arran knew that such a course of action could only lead to an extordinarily difficult and protracted war. The second possibility was surrender. Nothing suggests that this was seriously considered. In August 1547, Arran would pay £2 5s. for 'the buke of Wallace'; perhaps something like patriotism simply blinded him to the rationale of capitulation.[2] Certainly nothing suggests that the Scottish government seriously considered acceptance of English terms.[3] This was doubtless due to the fact that a third recourse existed:

---

1 *Mary of Lorriane Corresp.*, 208–11.
2 *TA*, ix, 225.
3 There were rumours that they would capitulate. On 2 December 1547, Henry II was told 'que les escossois estoient prestz de se soubmettre a touts les conditions que voudroit le Roy dangleterre' (BN, MS fo. 16,088, fo. 77), and on 10 June 1548 'advis toutefois incertain' from Rome was that 'les Anglois et escossois estoient en voie daccord' (*Ibid.*, fo. 106v). Such rumours as those in Brussels were probably spread by the English.

betrothal of the Queen to the heir to the French throne in return for French expulsion of the English.[4]

'LA PROTECTION, DEFENSE, ET CONSERVATION DUDIT ROYAUME D'ESCOSSE'

In September 1547 reports of the English preparations for war against Scotland attracted much attention abroad (perhaps simply because most of the rest of Europe was at peace). French opinion was complacent: 'The King of England could not do more than harry the Lowlands and then retire, which was the kind of war usual between the Scots and the English'.[5] In any event Boulogne and the Emperor seemed much more important; so did possibilities 'du coste d'Italye'. The English could easily be forgiven for thinking that the French would not send much aid to the Scots as they 'had already spent large sums of money upon them for which up to the present [they] had not seen any result'. Montmorency's reaction in late July to the news 'grant preparatifz darmes de mer' was that they were only 'soubz couller daller faire la guerre en escosse'; really the English were out to attack French ships. On 9 September the papal nuncio reported that the French suspected 'les mauvis desseins [of Somerset] sur l'Escosse. Mais on dit qu'ils ne feront rien et que les Escossais n'ont rien a craindre [the evil designs on Scotland. But they were not going to do anything and the Scots did not have anything to fear]'.[6]

Such confidence was shattered by the news of Pinkie.[7] By 12 October condolences from France were made to Mary of Guise by Montmorency who declared:

La Nouvelle que le Roy a eue de la fortune advenue au royaume d'Escosse et de la perte que ledict royaume a faicte en ceste bataille que les Anglois ont gaignee a tant enuye ledict Seigneur et toute ceste compaignye que je vous puis asseurer que plus grand deplaisir ne scaurions nous recevoir si ladicte perte se feust adressee en nostre endroict [The news that the King has heard of how fortune has hit Scotland and the loss that the said kingdom has sustained in this battle which the English have won has so saddened the said Seigneur and all of the court here that I can assure you that we would not have felt greater sorow if the defeat had been suffered here].[8]

Word from Scotland itself to Henry II had arrived in Paris as early as 30 September when Sir Walter Ogilvy and d'Oysel hastened news of the disaster. On 21 October yet a further Scottish messenger brought amplification and the warnings of Arran and Mary of Guise that, without French aid, the Scots would have to come to terms with Somerset.[9]

4 *Memoires-journaux de Francois de Lorraine, duc de Guise, 1547–63*, ed. Michaude et Poujoulat (Paris, 1854), 32–36. See also *Balcarres Papers*, ii, 6–13.
5 *CSP Spain*, ix, 517.
6 *Ibid.*, 131, 127; BN, MS fr. 20,449, p. 85; *Nonces en France, 1546–51*.
7 *Odet de Selve*, 199–208; *CSP Spain*, ix, 150–52; *Nonces en France, 1546–51*, 240; *Lettres et memoires*, ii, 70. By 1 October, English agents at Calais sent 'les tresbonnes nouvelles de la bataille' to friends in the Low Countries (BL, MS Harl. 288, fo. 95).
8 *Balcarrees Papers*, i, 172. For other reactions, see *Ibid.*, 176–240. The French at first suspected that the Scots exaggerated their losses in hopes of more money (*Nonces en France, 1546–51*, 240).
9 *CSP Spain*, ix, 189, 217.

Shortly afterwards, Paniter, who had been in France since March 1547, went to see St Mauris, the Imperial ambassador; he was distraught by the news but defiant against the English and vituperative against the French and the little effort they had previously made. Nonetheless he maintained that no agreement would be made with the English, despite the news that they had not just harried the Lowlands, but remained there in permanent garrisons.[10] There was obvious distress within the French court. Montmorency professed to the Imperial resident ambassador that France still wanted good relations with England, but as early as 15 October St Mauris suspected that the French sought 'to mix themselves up with Scottish affairs'. His assessment was that Henry

is extremely anxious to succeed in this latter object, as he sees clearly that otherwise Scotland will be utterly lost and nearly ruined. He has this subject much at heart, and would avoid such a wound at the beginning of his reign.[11]

The reasons for the King's determination (and it is clear that by December massive aid for Scotland had definitely been decided upon) can be deduced. The French believed that they could not allow the Scots to be lost to England. Henry had bitterly resented his father's surrender of Boulogne (of which he was 'count'), going so far as to register his protestation in the acts of the Parlement de Paris. He was deeply anxious to re-annexe Boulogne. That aside, the loss of Scotland would have embarrassed Henry and might have encouraged the Emperor to take action against France.[12] There was also a sudden concern from Rome. As recently as 13 August, the Pope, in discussion with Cardinal Jean du Bellay, had been distressed that the French were not arming against the real enemy, Charles, but were allowing themselves to be distracted by 'cette diversion advenue par la guerre d'Ecosse'. Du Bellay, however, brought Paul III to reciprocate French concern by arguing, 'Je luy reprochair du Royaume d'Ecosse que si Vostre Majestie eust moins faict ce qu'elle a fait, laquelle pert fust, en grand partie retombee sur l'eglise [I reproached him on the subject of Scotland saying that if Your Majesty had done less than you did, that loss would in great measure have fallen upon the Church]'.[13] Then, with the news of Pinkie, the Papacy immediately readied both money and a cardinal for its support.[14]

10 *Ibid.*, 213, 217.

11 *Ibid.*, 176, 233.

12 Fear of the Emperor was to haunt the French throughout this period, as Lucien Romier has demonstrated in his first volume ('Henri II et l'Italie') of *Origines Politiques des guerres de religion*. See also F. Decrue, *Anne Duc de Montmorecy*, ii, 46–70 and P. de Vaissière, *Charles de Marillac, ambassadeur et homme politique, 1510–1560*, 108–23. Recovery of Boulogne was also central to Henry II's policy; see D.L. Potter, 'Diplomacy in the mid-sixteenth century: England and France, 1536–50' (unpublished D.Phil. dissertation, University of Cambridge, 1973), 165–97. See also *Balcarres Papers*, i, 193.

13 *Lettres et Memoires*, ii, 50.

14 J.E. Law and J.M. Manion, 'The Nunciature to Scotland in 1548 of Pietro Lippomano, Bishop of Verona', *Atti e Memorie della Accademia di Agricoltura Scienze e Lettere di Verona*, IV, xxii (1970–71), 403–48.

GUISE POWER AT COURT[15]

An important factor in Henry II's decision must have been the position of the Guises at his Court. It should be remembered that during the first half of the sixteenth century, Valois Kings rarely acted without consulting the circle of confidants and advisers which made up their Court. Henry II did this probably even more than his father.[16] In particular the new King relied on Anne de Montmorency, Grand Master of the King's Household and a Constable of France, a close friend since boyhood. He assumed a role not dissimilar to that played by Wolsey to Henry VIII or Granvelle to Charles V: formulating policy, advising on possible courses of action, receiving envoys and instructing French ambassadors and military commanders.[17] The King could be influenced by others. The principal alternative to Montmorency was Claude de Guise.[18]

The rise of the Guise family is one of the spectacular success stories of sixteenth-century European politics. Arrivistes, they only entered French court life in 1505, but then through shrewd marriages, handsome good looks and remarkable ability on the battlefields of Italy, they rose inexorably. Throughout the reign of Francis I, the Guises had been marginally responsible for the execution of policy towards Scotland: de la Brosse, one of the ambassadors in 1543,[19] Lorges, commander of the 1545 expedition, and d'Oysel, ambassador in 1546, were all part of the Guise affinity. Duke Claude's eldest child, Mary, was still fondly remembered within Francis' Court – at which she had been noted for her beauty and charm – after her departure in 1538 to marry James V. Throughout 1542–47 almost everyone at Court kept in touch with her, even enemies of her family.[20] Henry's accession brought the Guises very much to the front as 'gret consaloris and revlaris [regulars or familiars]'.[21] The fact that a reliable member of the family was there in Scotland in a position of some power

15 This topic has begun to be revolutionised with studies of the Guises. In addition to David Potter's works (see Bibliography), reference should be made to S. Carroll, *Noble Power during the French Wars of Religion – The Guise Affinity and the Catholic Cause in Normandy*, 13–15, 46–48, 93–100.

16 As Dr. Potter makes clear. Professor G. Dickinson made much the same assessment in her unfinished biography of Henry II. See also B.C. Weber, *Personalities and Politics at the Court of Henry II of France, 1547–1559*.

17 This can be clearly seen by the number of letters which de Selve sent to Montmorency (*Odet de Selve, passim*) and by Montmorency's frequent dispatches to Mary of Guise (*Balcarres Papers*, i, 41, 146, 171, 196, 198, 202, 219, 220, 222, 226, 240–43). In particular, see Decrue, *Anne Duc de Montmorency*, ii, 1–94, and G. Ganier, *La politique de Connetable Anne de Montmorency, 1547–59*.

18 The rise of the Guises before 1559 has evoked considerable study. In addition to the sources already cited, see H. Forneron, *Les Ducs de Guise et leur epoque*; J.J. Guillemin, *Le Cardinal de Lorraine, son influence politique et reigieuse au XVIe siècle*; H.O. Evennett, *The Cardinal of Lorraine*.

19 As is made clear in J. de la Brosse, *Histoire d'un Capitaine Bourbonnais au XVIe siècle: Jacques de la Brosse, 1485–1562: ses Missions en Ecosse*, 19–31.

20 *Balcarres Papers*, i, xxxv; *Maitland Misc.*, i, 210–18.

21 Lorges went out of his way in June 1547 to assure Mary of Henry's goodwill towards Scotland. *Mary of Lorraine Corresp.*, 180, 183; *Balcarres Papers*, i, no. 124.

doubtless encouraged Henry to see real possibilities for a return on any investment there.

The prime reason, of course, was that Mary's daughter, the only surviving heir of James V, was one of the most desirable dynastic partners in Europe. Henry II (no less than Henry VIII five years earlier) must have perceived the attractiveness of the match for his eldest son. The example of Charles V's empire must have been clearly before him. Scotland may well have been a small and distant piece of territory, but it was a Kingdom. Strategically, it was located at the back of one of the Emperor's most constant allies. Dynastic union between the two houses could make Scotland a much more effective force against the Tudors and the Habsburgs. It had to be saved, and during the winter, as the expedition for its salvation was readied, the French Court was engulfed by that rare excitement and sense of enthusiasm which accompanies any return to war. Nowhere perhaps is this heightened expectation captured so evocatively as in this letter from the eleven-year-old Duke of Longueville to the five-year-old Queen of Scots:

> Madame,
> I received your letter which you were so kind to send me by Mons. Oysel and it pleased me to hear your news and since I wish that I could come to aid you, I am practising every day to wear military armour and tilt [on horseback] at the ring so that I may save you and give such service as I can against those [English] who want to harm you. With the aid of God, Madame, I promise to do this for you all the days of my life. I pray to God, Madame, to give you a very good and long life, asking humbly for your good grace to me.
> Your most humble and very obedient brother. FRANÇOYS dORLEANS

The following statements explain how the King's thinking had evolved. He had turned to Scotland so early in his reign firstly to prevent 'ce pauvre royaume d'Escosse [poor Scotland]' from falling under the sway of England, secondly to make Scotland 'his' and thirdly to unite the three Kingdoms of France, Scotland and England into one self-same monarchy: the Imperial song sung so flamboyantly at Rouen. Writing to his ambassador in Constantinople on 3 August 1548, after he knew that the Scots had agreed in Parliament to betrothe Mary to his son Francis, but before her arrival in France, he was somewhat low-key and reserved:

> Sans mon aide et secours, ce pauvre royaume d'Escosse demeureroit en proie et a la discretion desdicts Anglois, qui le vouloient usurper sous ombre d'un mariage qu'ils vouloient faire de la petite reyne pupille avec leur roy [Without my aid and help, this poor Kingdom of Scotland would be under the power and at the disposition of the English who want to usurp it under the colour of a marriage which they wanted to make between the little child Queen with their King].[24]

22 For Francis' life, see Marshall, *Mary of Guise*, 35–40, 44–45, 48–49. He died in 1551 in his mother's arms (*ibid.*, 191–92).
23 His frustration can be seen in *Balcarres Papers* i, 169–70, 196–97, 204–206. This letter is published at pp. 176–77.
24 *Négotiations de la France dans le Levant*, ed. E. Charrière (1848–60), ii, 71.

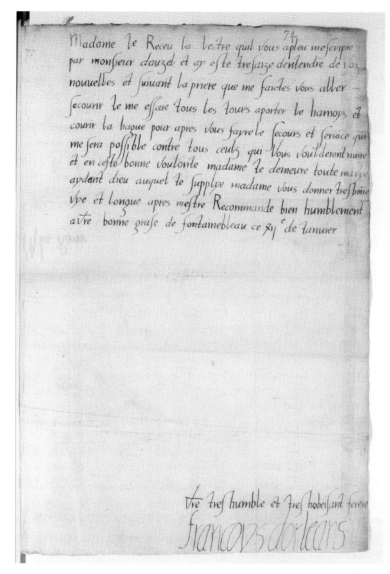

Fig. 12.1. Francis, Duke of Longueville, had been born on 30 October 1536; he was thus eleven years old in January 1548 when he penned the above letter to his half sister Mary. Francis, an orphan (his father died 9 June 1537) and 'unique' (his only brother, Louis, born on 4 August 1537, died at four months), was a charming child; constantly writing to his mother (once sending her a piece of string to show how tall he had grown). Mary clearly had written to him at the end of 1547 with news of the defeat at Pinkie. Was this her first letter? On 12 January, Francis, bitterly disappointed not to be allowed to go with the expedition to save Scotland, wrote directly from Fontainebleau this delightful piece of brotherly bravado.

At much the same time, however, he gave to Odet de Selve rather fuller insight into his thinking on the possibilities gained by his intervention in Scotland. The Scots had accepted that

> mondit Fils, lequel a este en ce faisant reconnu pour Roy d'Escosse. A cette cause vous irez trouver le Protecteur d'Angleterre auquel vous direz et ferez entendre de ma part, que por estre les choses reduites es termes que ie vous ecris, ie suis tenu pour mon deuoir et part obligation, a la protection, defense, et conservation dudit Royaume d'Escosse, comme du mien propre, n'estant a resent tous deux qu'une mesme chose l'un auec l'autre [my son has been by this [the Treaty of Haddington] become known as King of Scotland. For this reason you should go find the Protector of England whom you should tell and make understand that for my part . . . I hold as my duty and obligation: the protection, defence and conservation of the said Kingdom of Scotland as if it were my very own, both of them having now become one same thing, the one with the other].[25]

In September 1550, again to his envoy at the Porte, but now with victory his and from the heady atmosphere of Rouen, Henry laid before the Grand Sultan his most grandiloquent vision of what the Scottish adventure was all about. The English expelled from Scotland, Boulogne reconquered and peace concluded, the King summed up the first three years of his reign by saying he had now made the three Kingdoms 'une mesme monarchie'. 'J'ay pacifie le royaume d'Escosse, que je teins et possede avec tel commandement et obeissance que j'ay en France [I have brought peace to Scotland which I hold and possess with the same order and obedience that I have in France]'.[26] Potent, stunning, Imperial: it was good propaganda and struck a distinctive clarion note at the opening of his rule. Equally revealing is Henry's statement of his war aims when in late 1548 he was forced by the rising costs of the war to ask for an *aide* from his subjects.

'A NOTRE TRESGRAND REGRET, ENNUY ET DESPLAYSIR'

The view commonly held about the Renaissance French monarchy – one strongly influenced by the vision of Louis XIV's 'absolutism', not to mention by the rhetoric of Francis and Henry themselves – is that French Kings taxed at will. But the facts (such as the great revolts of 1544 and 1548) certainly do not bear out the vision of a supine tax-rendering populace. Nor does the rhetoric and manner in which the King solicited his *aides,* the unrepayable loans which he requested from his subjects. What concerns us here are the reasons Henry put forward to his public which necessitated his asking for yet more money. They are contained in a remarkable document, the formal request by the King's *conseil prive,* signed by the King and all his close Council: Montmorency, Guise, d'Aumale, St. Andre, Vendome, the Cardinals of Guise, of Lorraine and Chastillon, then sealed with his Great Seal. It was sent to all of

25 *Lettres et Memoires,* ii, 152.
26 *Lettres et Memoires,* ii, 288–90; and see *Négotiations de la France dans le Levant,* ed. E. Charrière (1846–60), ii, 121.

the *pays d'élection* such as Dauphiné, Provence, Languedoc and all the great *ancien provences*.

The argument contained in the *demande* was reasonableness itself and presented almost pleadingly. Henry reminded his audience, the taxpayers, that he had only come to the throne the year before and since then he had but one goal: to give peace and justice, for which 'les Roys sont principallement establiez'. Such was his concern for 'notre pauvres peuples' that he had reduced by half the tax granted to his father.

He had heavy expenses providing for the security of the realm: repairing and building new fortifications throughout 'noz villes, chasteaulx et places fortes', particularly 'a la point du pays de boullenoys pour la seurete et couverture de notre frontiere de ce coste la [for the surety of our frontier around the Boulognais]'. Additionally there were galleys, round boats, *gens d'armes*, artillery, powder, bullets, his guards, pensioners and a special reserve fund established for 'le Recouvirement de notre ville de Boulougne'. Also, there was the ordinary household 'de notre trescher et tresaimee compaigne La Royne de noz treschers et tresaimez enffans et soeur unique, Marguerite de france Et de notredite petite fille la Royne dudit escosse [of our most beloved companion the Queen, our beloved children and our only sister, Margaret of France and our said little daughter, the Queen of Scotland]'.

Scotland indeed was the main reason for the demand. It began by reminding its readers that the King was forced to provide the money required by

notre tresschere et tresaimee soeur et cousine La Royne douairiere descosse et notre trescher et tresaime cousin le conte dharn guverneur dudit pays Et aultres seigneurs et estatz decelluy de secourir ledit pays en son extreme necessite [our very dear and beloved sister and cousin the Queen Dowager of Scotland and our very dear and beloved cousin the Count of Arran, Governor of that country. And other gentlemen and estates there for the security of that country in its extreme necesssity].

The demand then went on to remind its audience that Scotland and France had been allies ever since 'le Roy Charlemaigne' and indeed that France had insured that Scotland was comprehended in the last peace with England. Despite that peace, however, Scotland now found itself

assailly et Infeste par les angloix qui La avoyent gaigne une bataille sur les escossoys, prins leurs navres et vaisseaulx Et fortiffie quelquez villes, places et chateaux dedans ledit pays, tellement que pour ne abandonner lesdits escossoys, anciens et perpetuelz amys et alliez de la couroune de france en ung si emminent peril et dangier [assailed and infested by the English who have won there a battle against the Scots, stolen their ships and vessels and fortified several cities, places and castles within that country such that there is an imminent danger to the Scots, ancient friends and allies of the crown of France].

The King had already sent two large forces ('ung bon numbre de gens de cheval et de pied, Artillerie, pouldres, boulletz et munition pour le secours de terre') as well as a large number of ships to guard the sea. Additionally he had sent 'grandes sommes' so that Mary of Guise and Arran could pay Scottish soldiers. But the King now knew that the English, persisting in their 'ambitieulx desir quilz ont de Reduyre ledit Royaulme descosse en la subiection de leur Roy', planned a new offensive for the next year. The King had resolved that the Scots must be aided further 'cest hiver'. Remembering, of course, that all of the Scots had agreed to send to France 'Notre petite fille La jeune Royne dudit escosse et accorde le mariage delle avec notre trescher et tresaime filz Le daulphin'.

If this substantial aid was not urgently given, the insatiable ambitions of the English ('si odeuse nation') would lead to 'une grande Ruyne et confusion' and the King would not be able to attend to all of the measures for the defence of France. So far the war in Scotland had resulted in 'une extreme et Incroiable despence', and the King had already spent all of his money, including that raised by an extraordinary tax paid by the prelates, benefices and *villes closes* of France. Despite his 'premiere intention' and 'A notre tresgrand Regret, ennuy et desplaysir', he had to demand this aid: 4,000,000 livres as an ordinary one for this year and 600,000 extra. To the taxpayers of France at least, the King's intentions in Scotland were modest, in comparison to the high-flown rhetoric lavished on the Sultan. Scotland simply had to be saved from the English. The aid demanded for the next year (1550) would make much of English retention of Boulogne and England's self-evident desire violently to possess 'toute la France'.

THE MAKING OF THE TREATY OF HADDINGTON[27]

Serious negotiations for the betrothal must have begun almost immediately upon d'Oysel's return to France in late September. He then returned to Scotland in October. From 22 October to 23 December, with the exception of two short trips, Arran spent his time at Stirling where he, the Queen Dowager and the French ambassador conferred further.[28] On 23 November d'Oysel left Scotland with John Hamilton of Milnburn and a score of other Scots.[29] He took with him a letter from Arran of 16 November asking d'Aumale to remind Henry of 'la grande fidelete et bonne diligence ou il sest tousjours employe pour la service dudict seigneur en tout ce qui luy a este possible'.[30] D'Oysel returned to a Court 'grandement troublees' by news of continued English success, and he was immediately closeted for three days with the King and his small Privy Council.[31] The ambassador was not to return to Scotland until March, but aid for the Scots was despatched in December.

On 27 January 1548 Arran pledged that in return for the Duchy of Chatelherault, worth £12,000 per annum, and the marriage of his son to an illustrious French bride, he would gain the consent of the Scottish Estates to the betrothal, to Mary's removal to France (where she would be raised in the King's household) and to the rendering

27 E.A. Bonner. 'The "Auld Alliance" and the Betrothal of Mary Queen of Scots: Fact and Fable', *Journal of the Sydney Society for Scottish History*, iv (1996), 3–22.
28 *TA*, ix, 115; *CSP Scot.*, i, nos. 88, 92.
29 *CSP Scot.*, i, no. 92; *TA*, ix, 127, 15.4.
30 BN, MS fr. 20,457, p. 7.
31 *CSP Spain*, ix, 217.

Fig. 12.2. Arran's seal as Chatelherault. Gordon Donaldson once characterised this seal as the most opulent and grandiose for any member of the Scottish aristocracy that he had seen. In it one can detect both the statement that he was a Duke (the only one then in Scotland) and his entitlement to wear the great chain of the Order of St. Michael: see the cockleshells (it was often called by Scots the 'order of the cockle')

of important Scottish castles into French hands.[32] In February Arran and the Queen Dowager put to a Convention of most of the Scottish nobility at Stirling the case for acceptance of French terms in return for their military assistance in the expulsion of the English.[33] The terms accepted, on 28 February, Lords Erskine and Livingstone, two of the Queen's guardians, moved her to Dumbarton Castle, now in the control of Mary of Guise, in readiness for the trip to France.[34] News of the successful conclusion of the Convention resulted in a further guarantee to Arran from Henry on 28 April 1548 that his Governorship would be protected as it had been in the Treaty of Greenwich (he would not be held accountable for Crown revenues on Mary's coming of age) and that his eldest son's bride would be the daughter of the

32 The contract is reprinted in J.A.B. Teulet, *Memoire justificatif du Droit qui appartient a M. le duc d'Hamilton de Porter le titre de Duc de Chaterlherault*. The gift of Chatelherault to Arran is detailed in *Actes de Henri II*, nos. 2091, 2856, 2857, 3388, 3908, 4370, 4421, 4895. But see also no. 6698.

33 The date of this meeting is not clear; 8 February 1548 is usually cited, but Arran was only in Stirling 16–20 February. The evidence for this convention is very slight, but see Dalrymple, *Historie*, ii, 304–05; *CSP Scot.*, i, nos. 125, 128; *Mary of Lorraine Corresp.*, 224.

34 *APS*, ii, 453; *TA*, ix, 117, 177. In April, de la Brosse coyly spoke of 'estat pour ceste petite personne en France' and asked that two of his family be placed in Mary's establishment (*Balcarres Papers*, i, 193).

Duke of Montpensier. By this time he had also received the rank of 'Chevalier de nostre ordre'.[35]

Mary of Guise was by all accounts delighted by these events and she now set about binding Scottish nobles to her and to what became the French interest. Lord Methven, as ever, gave her the shrewd advice:

> The Lordis that is greit and utheris lordis and barronis to be cherisit favorable wyth your graic and wyth all the prynsipall men of gud quhay that cummis out of France heyr, for the nater of this pepill is of this realm; first to be gentillie don to, and that tha persaif luf and all gudnes in the Kingis graice of France. And als this realm is pwyr and the greit men cn na way beyr greit exspens of thar awn leving.[36]

This Mary was to do, not only in 1548, but for the next six years, in an effort first to expel the English and then to secure the Regency. As early as 14 April 1548 she entered into an obligation with Alexander Gordon, Huntly's brother, to secure for him a pension of £t400 plus a one-off of £t1000 from Henry II in compensation for his loss of the Bishopric of Caithness.[37] It was the first of many such pensions and resulting bonds of manrent.[38]

Pensions, however, would not bring down the walls of the English fortresses. As Lord Methven had remarked back in December 1547, Scotland's critical need was for

> cappidennis . . . out of France quhilkis has intelligens of ordour of men on the feildis; also is to be had of the cappidens that has best intelligens to asseg and ordouring arttalzerij and that can mak the samyn to be weill an perfitlie ussit.[39]

February's Convention had stipulated that the Queen would not be allowed to leave Scotland until agreement to the marriage had been made by a full meeting of the whole Estates of the Realm. That consent was strictly contingent on the arrival of a full French army which would engage the English in the field. On 22 December 1547 an advance contingent of some seven ships arrived at Dumbarton with 50 French captains under Jacques de la Carbonieres de la Chapelle-Biron. With him also came an Irish refugee (Garet of Kildare), powder, munitions, artillery and, so it was rumoured, enough money to pay 10,000 Scots for a year.[40]

---

35 *Balcarres Papers*, i, 197–98; ii, xxxvii; *APS*, ii, 508–10; BN, MS fr. 6612, fos. 2–3. This was confirmed on 17 June 1549 (BL, MS Add. 10,012, fo 1).

36 *Mary of Lorraine Corresp.*, 242.

37 Teulet, *Relations*, i, 162–63; *Mary of Lorraine Corresp.*, 231, 234–45.

38 On 26 June, she gave Angus 2500 francs 'in name and behalve of the maist cristen King of france for payment of our pension of the first terme'. He also received 'the maist honorable ordour of the Coquillie' (NAS, E34/14/5). George Douglas received 1000 crowns (NAS, E34/14/6) and Sir Walter Scott of Buccleuch 400 crowns (NAS, E34/14/12). She had even been able to arrange a bond of manrent with Huntly, who had been seen at Newcastle by Alexander Gordon in April (NAS, SP 13/58). See also bonds with Alexander Gordon, Lord Gray and Robert Carnegy of Kynnarde (NAS, E 13/55, 56, 59).

39 *Mary of Lorraine Corresp.*, 210.

40 *CSP Dom., Add., 1547–46*, 352–54; *CSP Scot.*, i, nos. 117, 120; *TA*, ix, 139; PRO, SP/10/3, fo. 11.

Chapelle, as he was called, immediately saw the Queen at Stirling, inspected Dundee and Broughty (causing some concern to the English there) and set some of his men to work to 'seik salpeter and necessaris to make it with in the west cundtre'.[41] Chapelle then reported to Aumale, on 22 March 1548, on how he found things:

> Les gens de ce pays se ressenttent tant de la perte de la batille [Pinkie] et de la crainte qu'ilz ont des fortz que les ennemys tiennent, qu'ilz ne peuvent reprendre sans l'ayde du Roy, au moyen de ce qu'ilz ont peu d'artillerie et munition, que, sans l'assurance que l'on leur donne du secours du Roy, ilz seroient en dangier de bientost prandre l'autre party, et eussent plustost actendu le secours quatre annees, avant la dicte batille qu'ilz ne feront a present quatre moys. Qui doit estre cause qu'il ne leur fault faillir dudict secours. [These people enormously resent their defeat at Pinkie and fear the fortifications which the enemy hold, which they cannot repossess without the aid of the King. Since they lack artillery and munitions, without the assurance of the King's support, there is a great danger of them going over to the other party. Even before the battle, they had been waiting four years for help; now it is barely four months. We must not fail to help them.][42]

However, the Scots were already helping themselves well before the arrival of massive French assistance. Arran as ever had opprobrium heaped upon him for Pinkie. Walking through Edinburgh for a christening, he was forced to seek shelter in St. Giles: 'the wyffes war lyke to have stoned hym to death'.[43] But he was doing what he could, burying the dead[44] and giving pensions to their survivors.[45] Taxes were raised,[46] spies retained,[47] troops were hired[48] and musters held.[49] New artillery was being cast.[50] Anyone expert in firearms was prized.[51] A small Scottish navy harassed the English on Inchcolm. Scots who found themselves under severe pressure from

---

41 *CSP Scot.*, i, no. 134; *Balcarres Papers*, i, 187; *TA*, ix, 143. He quickly reported to d'Aumale what he saw at Dundee (BN, MS fr. 20,457, p. 13).

42 Teulet, *Relations*, i, 160–61.

43 *CSP Scot.*, I, no. 73. See *TA*, ix, 148.

44 *TA*, ix, 121, 123, 133, 141, 160.

45 Spalding Club, ii, 33.

46 *RPC*, I, 79–80; *TA*, ix, 120–21, 130, 133–34; *Ayr Burgh Accounts*, 87–119.

47 *TA*, ix, 113, 166, 169, 173, 176. Warning systems within the country were also maintained (*Ibid.*, 131, 167, 182, 186, 197).

48 Many examples exist, especially James Dog whose career went back as far as 1544. By 1548, he commanded a company of 700 men. *Mary of Lorraine Corresp.*, 273–74; *CPS Scot.*, i, nos. 56, 73, 76; *TA*, ix, 85, 138, 151, 178.

49 *TA*, ix, 123, 139–40, 168–69, 181–82.

50 Jacques Rowane worked feverishly in Edinburgh Castle manufacturing new pieces. Some artillery also arrived from France during the winter and the Scots were helped by the desertion of John Seill, 'Inglischeman, gunnar, cannoner'. *TA*, ix, 124, 133–34, 176, 183, 192, 199–206.

51 None were to depart Edinburgh 'that can handill and schute ony maner of artailyery' (*Edin. Burgh Recs.*, I, 133).

the English were treated with understanding.[52] Although his attacks on Dundee came to nought, two campaigns, what we may call the Drumlanrig one and the Hailes one, bore fruit. Both demonstrate vividly that in war, as Wellington commented, 'time is everything'. To which he should have added, so is distance.[53]

Somerset knew by the New Year that his war against the Scots was about to be become one against the French as well. No fleet could confidently expect to sail to Scotland until the summer; thus there was some time. He thus resolved to mount pre-emptive strikes by invasions and new constructions. With the Scottish army effectively destroyed (so he thought) at Pinkie, he calculated that he would encounter scant resistance. In this he was only partially correct. Although enhanced fortifications were successfully commenced in the pale, invasions could be countered.

One area seemed particularly promising: the Southwest. In some senses, this was a sideshow and had been since the fourteenth century: most major Anglo-Scottish warfare took place in the East, and this was even more so now that artillery had to accompany armies. The 'cockpit' of Scottish warfare was there. Only Northern Italy and (more so) the 'Benelux triangle' have had more battles fought over such a small area, as 1870, 1914, 1940 and the German Ardennes Offensive of 1944 (the Battle of the Bulge) demonstrate.

As far as Carlisle was concerned as a command post, the self-same geography which split England split Scotland, and English armies in the West Marches were virtually in a cul de sac. But the Southwest was never totally neglected, as Solway Moss (1542) demonstrates, and it should perhaps not be forgotten that Edward I, en route to attack Robert the Bruce, died in 1307 at Burgh-by-Sands, Cumberland, not far from that battlesite. During the fourteenth century, Liddesdale had been virtually part of England, as the work at the Hermitage shows. During 1544–45 English troops were garrisoned at various Maxwell strongholds in the area and in Langholm as recently as July 1547. At the time of Pinkie, Thomas Lord Wharton, in company with Lennox, had effected a major incursion. Annan was taken and garrisoned; so was Castlemilk. English raiding parties roamed at will; in October one reached as far north as Covington, only six miles from Arran's palace at Hamilton. To the west he took Dumfries, attacked Kirkcudbright and terrorised the countryside so that lairds from quite far away came to be assured.

But his prime target was John Maxwell, eldest brother to Robert 6th Lord Maxwell, then held in London. During the five years of his captivity John as Master of Maxwell managed the family's affairs. Easily the most important Scottish noble in the Southwest, he nonetheless faced an uncertain future, as second brothers tended to do. For some time he had sought the marriage of Elizabeth Herreis of Terregles, the richest ward in Arran's quiver of under-aged heirs and heiresses. The Governor, however, kept her in reserve for his eldest son.

---

52 Buccleuch being allowed to 'intercommune with the Protector' as he thought 'expedient' and as he pleased, 'for the saiftie of him, his kin, friendis and servandis, fra heirship and distriction'. All of this was for 'the commun weill of oure realme'. W. Fraser, *Scotts of Buccleuch*, ii, 110–111.

53 J. Keegan, *World War I* (1998), p. 151.

At first, John resisted Wharton's blandishments and was sourly raided. Finally he assured on 12 November 1547; Wharton's weekly tally of assured Scots lept to over 7000, much to Somerset's approval.[54] Very quickly, John, much to his perturbation, came under English pressure to allow Caerlaverock and Lochmaben to be garrisoned. Initially he argued he could do no such thing without express permission from his brother; Wharton duly supplied a letter, the signature of which Maxwell suspected to be a forgery. Nonetheless, when commanded to join his forces with those invading Scotland, Maxwell agreed. The intention was to ravage the lands of John Douglas of Drumlanrig, consistently loyal to Arran's regime.

Maxwell clearly gave warning to his neighbour who prepared to resist. In a remarkable military feat, especially in the dead of winter, Angus arrived with a large contingent as well. Arran, 'fynding how the game lay', agreed to grant Lady Herries' hand should Maxwell revolt.[55] Moving up the Nith towards Drumlanrig, Wharton foolishly split his forces, sending the horse on ahead. Angus and the laird first routed the horse, then assaulted the infantry, whereupon Maxwell's men tore off their red crosses and attacked the English as well. Only by great exertions was Wharton able to retire to Dumfries, but even there he did not feel safe and fled to Carlisle. Maxwell quickly retook Dumfries and began to harry the assured Scots.[56] For his revolt, he immediately received not only the grant but a blanket pardon for all treasons with the English committed in the Southwest.[57] Dumfries was similarly absolved.[58] At first Wharton hoped to recover, but by 6 June he had to confess:

> Thar power also shewed in Scotland draweth those untrewe people more and more from thar ooth and servys to the Kinges majestie whiche with feare was brought to obedience and after the same with rewards and entretaignement servyd notablie agaynst thar own nacione.[59]

By July, the Southwest had ended as a theatre of war and the Scottish government increasingly maintained control.[60]

A second victory occured in the East. Wharton's February attack had been part of a typical two-pronged invasion of Scotland, the other being a force under Grey of Wilton which had taken Haddington and had captured and garrisoned Hailes, Nunraw, Yester, Herdmanston, Waughton, and in three small strongholds belonging to two Scottish collaborators: Saltoun, Ormiston and Brunstane.[61] But no sooner had this late-winter invasion force started establishing a permanent garrison at Haddington than came the news by the Berwick post of Wharton's débâcle. Clearly

54 *CSP Dom., Add., 1547–65*, 331–35, 339, 341, 358. Armstrong, *History*, I, appendix 39.
55 Herries, *Memoirs*, 25–26.
56 *CSP Dom., Add., 1547–65*, 361–64, 374–76, 381–82; *CSP Scot.*, i, no. 174.
57 *RSS*, iii, nos. 2674, 2699, 2830. See also *CSP Dom., Add., 1547–65*, 364–65.
58 It can be seen on display at the Dumfries Burgh Museum; no copy survives in *RSS*.
59 PRO, SP 52/2, fo. 174v (*CSP Dom., Add., 1547–65*, 384).
60 *TA*, ix, 241; *RPC*, xiv, 6.
61 *CSP Scot.*, i, nos. 179–80.

panicked, Grey ignominiously retired to Berwick, 'with banners and outward show' as he put it in a memorable line, 'but al doleful inward'. No sooner did the English retreat than Arran moved the Scottish force which had mustered to meet Grey to besiege the three smaller strongholds. They quickly fell and were dismantled.[62] Hailes was then taken and its famous iron gates were removed to Edinburgh.[63] Such bold action disturbed Grey, who mused platitudinously that the country will 'bende allwayes to the master of the felde'.[64] To crown this month of Scottish triumphs, Somerset was forced to abandon Inchcolm which had been mercilessly harried by Scottish ships. By 1 March Luttrell had razed the fortress and removed his men to Broughty.[65]

The effect of these victories was a distinct increase in the vigour and authority of the Scottish government. In the Southwest Maxwell was soon strong enough not only to contain Wharton, but also to send men to help in the East.[66] The collaborators there, about whom commanders such as Grey and Dudley had been so effusive during the winter, began to melt away and the English became increasingly apprehensive.[67] As early as the end of April the Scottish government was confident enough to offer 'ane frie remission for byganes' to all the assured.[68] By then the government was also besieging the English garrison at Yester, strengthening Dunbar and Fastcastle and preparing to prevent an English working party from constructing a fort at Lauder.[69]

Throughout this time (December until March) constant contact was maintained with France.[70] D'Oysel returned via Brest in March and letters were even sent through England.[71] News of the Scottish victories quickly got abroad and the French made much throughout Italy of the defeat of Wharton.[72] By 18 March, when exaggerated reports of Lennox's capture were being put about, France was in something like a state of euphoria over the Scots venture. Mary of Guise's brother, d'Aumale, who had been given general oversight of the military preparations, was

---

62 They were completely dismantled and the timber (and crops on the land) were removed to Edinburgh Castle (*TA*, ix, 148–52, 161–63, 166, 172; *RPC*, i, 82). Saltoun was given to a Scottish force (SPO, SP 13/57).

63 *RPC*, i, 81.

64 *CSP Scot.*, i, nos. 195, 220.

65 *Ibid.*, no. 184.

66 *RPC*, xiv, 6.

67 *CSP Scot.*, i, nos. 56, 107, 221 (for positive reports); 73, 88, 94, 114, 119, 183, 186, 192, 195 (for increasing apprehension).

68 *RPC*, xvi, 3–4; *TA*, ix, 181, 189.

69 *RPC*, i, 81; *TA*, ix, 176, 179, 184.

70 Teulet does not print much of the material available for January–June 1548 (BN, MS fr. 20,457, pp. 9–38). See also *Balcarres Papers*, i, 176–95.

71 He was at Brest from 14 February until 7 March (BN, MS fr. 20,457, pp. 27, 29, 25), doubtless waiting for a good wind; the sea was very rough at the time (*Balcarres Papers*, i, 195–96). See also *CSP For.*, no. 74; *CSP Scot.*, i, no. 162.

72 *CSP For.*, no. 73; *Balcarres Papers*, i, 188–90. A news-sheet sent to Wotton made much of it (Florence, Archivo di Stato, MS Medici, F. 4592, fos. 544–45. I am grateful to Dr. Potter who supplied me with a transcript of this).

swamped by various captains requesting to be sent on the expedition.[73] Paris apparently granted a loan of 400,000 francs for the expedition and contributions came even from the French possessions in Italy.[74]

The troops came from wherever the French could raise them: Brittany and Gascony provided a large number under the command of various notables such as François de Coligny, sieur d'Andelot; the cavalry (a thousand strong), again mostly French, were under François d'Anglure d'Etoges; Italian mercenaries under the famous Pietro Strozzi; Germans under Jean Philip de Salm, Count Rheingrave. The army which was slowly mustered during the early months of 1548 contained some of the most illustrious and experienced of French captains, most of whom had seen considerable service in the Italian campaign of 1542–44.[75] At its head was André de Montalembert, sieur d'Essé, then 65 years of age, a man with considerable experience of war and rightly regarded with apprehension by the English. Considerable artillery was also gathered. Meanwhile, the armada (including numerous vessels from the Mediterranean fleet) which was to carry the force to Scotland assembled in Brittany and Normandy under Charles de la Meilleraye, the Vice-Admiral of France.[76]

These immense preparations caused much comment throughout Europe, papal, Imperial and English observers being particularly anxious to know the size and disposition of the army.[77] On 20 March three English spies – 'A, B and C' – were sent from Calais to Brest; their report on 27 April described a France echoing to the anvil of Mars. Ships of every description were being provisioned, particularly a large number of galleys. Pikemen, hackbutters, light and heavy horse crowded the roads heading to their embarkation. At St Malo, for example, they saw ten ships all in various states of readiness and the bakers hard at work preparing biscuit. At Morlaix five crayers were ready and a Dutch ship which arrived with wheat found its cargo immediately bought for the fleet. At Brest fully 25 great ships were in the haven and eight had already sailed. There the spies also met a nervous Englishman and his wife, about to be evicted to prevent him sending 'tydings to his natyve countrye'; his estimate was that the armada would comprise 120 sail carrying 12,000 men.[78]

---

73 One of whom was Claude d'Anglure, sieur d'Estauges, who had participated in the 1538 campaign in Piedmont (BN, MS fr. 20,457, p. 23). There were many others (BN, MS 20,542, fo. 130v; BL, MS Add. 30,033, fos. 169–71).

74 *CSP For.*, no. 73; BN, MS fr. 20,548, fo. 75.

75 Much more work needs to be done on the organisation and provisioning of this force sent to Scotland. For an introduction to the French army in the sixteenth century, see F. Lot, *Recherches sur les Effectifs des Armées Françaises des Guerres d'Italie aux Guerres de Religion: 1494–1562*. All of these men were highly regarded, d'Esse particularly. See Brantôme, *Oeuvres Complètes*, ed. Lalanne, iii, 383–95. See also F. de Fourquevaux, *Les vies de Grands Plusieurs Capitaines François*, 320–28.

76 For naval preparations, see C.G.B. de la Roncière, *Historie de la Marine Française*, iii, 432–37; A. Heulard, *Villegagnon, Roi d'Amérique: un Homme de Mer au XVIe Siècle: 1510–1572*, 36–41. Strozzi complained of considerable difficulties (BN, MS fr. 20,537, fo. 20).

77 *CSP For.*, nos. 73, 77, 80, 84, 87; *CSP Spain*, ix, 550, 555, 563, 564–67; *Nonces en France, 1546–51*, 283, 294, 325. See also the interest in Augsburg (J. Strype, *Ecclesiastical Memoirs* (1820–40), ii, 248).

78 BL, MS Harl. 383, fos. 41–43. Estimates of the numbers varied wildly.

The actual numbers are not certain, but the account of the Treasurer, Benoist le Grand, for the army 'pour descendre au royaume d'Escosse', gives the figure of 5440 'hommes de guerre a pied', and the cavalry must have been in addition.[79] The armada consisted of 18 galleys, under command of the famous Leon Strozzi, Prior of Capua; one brigantine, 26 ships-of-war, eight of which were over 200 tons, and 86 transports of approximately 50 tons.[80] It sailed at the end of May and moved up the Channel and into the North Sea, arriving at Leith Roads on 17 June 1548.[81]

The Scots made extensive preparations for the French arrival. Once the fleet was sighted, the populace from as far away as Dumbarton began to 'thresche corne and bring vituellis' to Edinburgh. Oxen and horses from Fife and Linlithgow also came 'to carie the artillerie'. Cannon were removed from the siege of Broughty and brought by ship to Leith; ships from Fife also gathered there to transport supplies to Aberlady so as to supply the French army which gradually drew itself about Haddington in the last week of June.[82] The Scots were delighted at the arrival of the army. Both Arran and Mary of Guise gave its commanders a splendid reception.[83] Early attendants upon the scene were Angus and George Douglas. On the 26th the Earl was given 2500 Crowns of the Sun payment for the 'first terme' of his pension and he was also given by Mary 'of his Maistie of the maist honorable ordour of the Coquille [the Order of St. Michel]'; his brother received 1000 crowns. Both were 'wele Content'. The castle of Dunbar was handed over to the French; Blackness was promised to them (though, significantly, neither Edinburgh nor Dumbarton would be transferred).[84] Meanwhile the lieges of Scotland were mustered at Roslin so that a native army could join the French.[85] By 1 July trenches were being dug about the English fort at Haddington and the next day artillery was planted and began to 'beate at the flankes and into the towne'.[86]

79 BN, MS 5085, fos. 184v–85v. His expenses came to 2,411,554 livres. Benoist's account would seem to be the only one to survive for 1548.

80 C.G.B. de la Roncière, *Historie de la Marine Française*, iii, 436. The figure of 120 sail was widely reported.

81 *Mary of Lorraine Corresp.*, 119–21; Teulet, *Relations*, i, 164–70; BN, MS fr. 20,457, pp. 43–56, 69.

82 *RPC*, xvi, 4–5; *Edin. Burgh Recs.*, ii, 134–35; *TA*, 188–204, 208. Methven complained bitterly about the removal of the artillery from Broughty which put Perth 'in dispar'; he felt some of the French troops should have been brought to Fife (*Mary of Lorraine Corr.*, 243).

83 Teulet, *Relations*, i, 165–76; Beagué, *Histoire*, 9–11; *TA*, ix, 208. Arran received 'the King of Frances hors' (*ibid.*, 197).

84 Teulet, *Relations*, i, 165, 170, 174; *CSP Scot.*, i, nos. 125–26, 146–47; *TA*, ix, 225. The French were to remain at Dunbar, which they had held from 1514–37 until 1560 (E. Forestie, *Un Capitaine Gascon du XVIe siècle: Corbevran de Cardaillac-Sarlabons, Mestre de Camp, Governeur de Dunbar*), but they never gained Edinburgh or Dumbarton.

85 *PRC*, xiv, 6; *TA*, ix, 188–206 *passim*. Some Scots were obviously reluctant to come to the musters (*Ibid.*, 218). Already there was some difficulty between the allies; the French promised to pay for pioneers brought to the siege, 'and nevit payit and thair of (*Ibid.*, 201).

86 *Hamilton Papers*, ii, 597; *CSP Scot.*, i, nos. 270–75.

THE BETROTHAL OF MARY QUEEN OF SCOTS
TO THE DAUPHIN OF FRANCE

Once the French set about besieging Haddington, the Scots agreed to hold the necessary Parliament. Precepts for it had been issued sometime in June and tents were erected near the Abbey of Haddington, in which the Parliament was to be held.[87] To the Estates which assembled on 7 July, d'Essé read his commission. Henry II pledged to employ all necessary 'men of weir munitionn and money' to recover all Scottish 'strenthis castles and fotalices' then held by the English and in effect to 'mantene & defence this realm . . . as he dois the Realme of France'. He flourished 'in face of Parliament' the Great Seal attached to his commission. Arran rose and agreed to the marriage of the Queen to the Dauphin,

> provyding alwayis that the King of France, the said Dolphinnis derrest fader, keip and defend the realme, lawis and liberteis thairof . . . as hes bene kepit in all Kingis tymes of Scotland bypast and to mary hir upone na uther persoun bot upone the said Dolphin allanderlie.[88]

Once Henry had in his hands Scottish ratification of what became known as the Treaty of Haddington, he immediately replied, expressing his confidence in Arran, enjoining unity, praising Scottish wisdom and promising future benefits from union. In particular he swore to regard the Scottish Queen's

> Royaume, ses affaires & subjects estre auec les nostres vne mesme chose . . . desirant de tout nostre coeur auoir l'oeil & pouruoir a ce qui est vtile & necessaire pour vostre bien, repos & conservation [Kingdom, its affairs and subjects along with ours as the same thing. Desiring with all our heart and power to do whatever is necessary for your good, respose and conservation].[89]

The formal treaty concluded, preparations were quickly made to transport Mary to France. In a remarkable voyage, Nicolas Durand, sieur de Villegaignon, sailed north round to Dumbarton, where Mary embarked.[90] With her may have gone Arran's son,[91] Arran's daughter, many ladies-in-waiting and some 'houndes and halkes' from

---

87 *TA*, ix, 183, 108, 197, 207, 214–15, 219–20. The abbey was already being used by the French to attack Haddington and the English had previously weakened it (*CSP Scot.*, i, nos. 135, 137). Hardly anything remains of it today, but note 'Abbey Mains', not to mention 'Abbey Mill'.

88 *APS*, ii, 481–82. A Latin copy, prepared by James Magill, was sent to France (Pierpont Morgan Library, New York, MS MA 279, fos. 17–20).

89 *Lettres et Memoires*, ii, 150–51. Mary of Guise wrote to her brother the day after the Parliament that each estate 'consentit d'estre subject dudit Seigneur [Henry II], par le moyen de l'honneur qu'il faict a ma file de la vouloir bailler a monsieur son fils'. *Memoires-journaux de Francois de Lorraine, duc de Guise, 1547–63*, ed. Michaud et Poujoulat (Paris, 1854), 3.

90 See Heulard, *Villegagnon, Roi d'Amerique*, 41–42; de la Roncière, *Historie de la Marine Française*, iii, 438–39. Some Scottish ships also went (*TA*, ix, 219).

91 Arran's son is not mentioned in the copious correspondence about the Queen's voyage. But preparations for his departure went on throughout May (when he received £600) to July (*TA*, ix, 183, 187, 212, 218, 221). See also *Balcarres Papers*, i, 206.

the North of Scotland.[92] From 31 July to 7 August, Villegaignon and his precious cargo lay in the Clyde awaiting a fair wind; he then sailed to Brittany, reaching Roscoff by the 18th.[93] Mary was sent across country, reaching St Denis in easy stages by 14 October.[94] The French were clearly delighted.[95] D'Aumale exulted to Montmorency: 'Dieu continue a estre bon Francoys'.[96] Initial word from Scotland told of a rigorous siege and of the English badly mauled in the encounter known as 'Tuesday's Chase' (17 July) in which many were killed and captured. Henry bragged to his ambassadors in Switzerland that his army held most of the important castles so that 'Adinton demeure assiege et sans esperance de pouvoir longuement demeurer en mains des Angloys [Haddington remains besieged and without hope of remaining long in the hands of the English]'.[97]

Unfortunately this was not correct. No sooner had the French army arrived than Mary of Guise complained that it was too small and poorly provisioned, and she warned that both the army and the fleet would have to stay all winter. D'Essé agreed. As early as 6 July, after his inspection of Haddington, he confided to d'Aumale: 'Vous assure que l'avons trove beaucoup plus forte que l'on ne nous avoyt faict entendre [I assure you that we are going to find it much more strongly fortified than ever we have been given to understand]'.[98] To appreciate his disquiet, it is necessary to examine the resilient English reactions to the French intervention.

SOMERSET'S SECOND OFFENSIVE

The situation which confronted the French in Scotland was radically different to that of December 1547. Somerset had been kept fully informed of their direct response to Pinkie. Wotton, English ambassador with the Court, had emphasised the power of

---

92 The hawks may have been sent later (*TA*, ix, 231). See also Beaugué, *Histoire*, 26–28; Stevenson, *Selections*, 26; The voyage was celebrated by du Bellay, *Entreprise du Roy Dauphin* (Paris, 1558).

93 There has been a certain controversy concerning exactly where Mary disembarked; see W.M. Bryce, 'Mary Stuart's Voyage to France', *EHR*, xxii (1907), 43–50. Breze wrote to Aumale on 18 August (BN, MS fr. 20,457, pp. 121).

94 *Lettres Inédites de Diane de Poytiers*, ed. G.-M. Guiffrey (Paris, 1866), 35; *Balcarres Papers*, ii, 6–10. See also the useful note by M.-N Baudouin-Matuszek, 'Mary Stewart's Arrival in France in 1548', *SHR*, lxix (1990), 90–5.

95 *Mémoires-Journaux de François de Lorraine, duc de Guise, 1547–63*, ed. Michaud et Poujoulat (1854), 2; *Négotiations de la France dans le Levant*, ed. Charrière (Paris, 1848–60), 71. To Humières, the master of his household, Henry wrote on 24 August from Turin, 'Jay en certaines nouvelles de larrivee en bonne sante de ma fille la Royna descosse . . . qui ma ete tel plaisir' (BN, MS nou. acq. 7699, fo. 146). See other letters from the King to Humières stressing Mary's royal position at court: BN, MS fr. 3134, fo. 12 *et seq*. Marillac at Brussels received the news from the King on 18 September (BN, MS fr. 3098, p. 3). Henry wrote to Switzerland on 27 September (Sotheby Sale Catalogue, *André de Coppet* (1955), part 2, no. 104). Henry finally saw Mary in early November and found her 'le plus parfaict enfant que je vys jamais' (BN, MS Clair. 341, fo. 8883). See also *Lettres Inédites de Diane de Poytiers*, ed. C-M. Guiffrey (Paris, 1866), 44–47.

96 BN, MS Clair, 342, fo. 9213.

97 Sotheby Sale Catalogue, *André de Coppet* (1955), part 2, no. 104; BN MS. fr. 3098, p. 3.

98 Teulet, *Relations*, i, 174–76, 182.

the Guises and that the new King was not prepared to countenance English victory.[99] Chapelle's arrival in Scotland at the end of 1547 must have made it clear that French assistance would be more than token. By January 1548 the whole nature of the war was changing.[100] Somerset quickly and resolutely determined to build more and better forts and to place much larger garrisons within them. As early as 19 December, de Selve was sending warnings to Paris, repeated in more detail on 14 January. Nine days later, Claude de l'Aubespine, first secretary of state to Henry II, informed

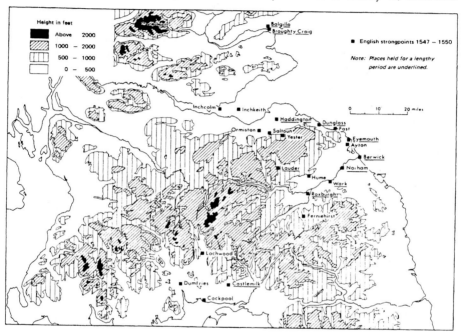

Fig. 12.3. English strongpoints in Scotland, 1547–50. As ever, such maps can actually make the issue more obscure. What is mapped here is all of the points held by the English during this period. But it should be remembered that there were losses (Dumfries, then Saltoun, Haddington and Hailes in February 1548, Inchcolm im March 1548) and new acquisitions (Broughty in March 1548; likewise Lauder, Haddington in April–June; Dunglass by September 1548 and Inchkeith in June 1549). Inchkeith was immediately recaptured by the French.

99 P.F. Tytler, *England under the Reigns of Edward VI and Mary* (1839), i, 87–89. For English concern, see also BL, MS Harl. 299, fo. 102; PRO, SP 10/4, fo. 34; PRO, SP 46/5, fos. 255–56; Brussels, Etat et Audience, 1673/4 (a). Notice also English concern to prevent aid from Bremen or Hamburg (*CSP For.*, nos. 44, 64, 119, 127) and from Denmark (*CSP Spain*, ix, 264).

100 Paget's 'Remembraunce to the Duke of Somerset at Candlemas 1547' (Northants Record Office, MS F(M) C21, fo. 5) gives some indication of the discussions of the dangers facing England since 'the frenche men sends no small ayde' to Scotland and the season for building new forts 'ys farre onwarde'. Paget was against any 'new fortificacons'.

d'Aumale of de Selve's news 'que les anglois se preparent le plus qu'il peust pour ses entreprise en escosse [the English are preparing the largest enterprise they can for Scotland]' and that matters there would soon be much more difficult.[101] The war was moving into its second phase.

The numbers of troops stationed within Scotland and along the Border on any day is difficult to determine, but two sets of figures will illustrate the dramatic difference between the first and second phases. On 20 October 1547, when the pattern of the initial phase had taken shape, Grey of Wilton asked for money to pay garrisons totalling 1528 men. When, after the war, Gregory Railton presented his declared account for the costs of the war in Scotland during his period as Treasurer of the North (from 26 September 1548 to 31 October 1550), he accounted for 17,315 different soldiers stationed in Scotland and on the Borders.[102] When one realises that this figure excluded the troops in the Pinkie campaign or any of the relief armies for Haddington in 1548–49, the 'escalation' becomes apparent.

There is also the evidence of English construction in Scotland during January-July 1548. Even before Somerset had certain knowledge of Henry II's intentions, tentative efforts had been made to expand the English pale. In the Southwest, the Protector began to consider pushing further west from Dumfries, captured on 17 October 1547, so as to take Kirkcudbright.[103] Ridgeway was sent to view the town in November; Thomas Petit was also sent from London on 9 November to map the pale. A feeble attempt was made to capture Kirkcudbright, but they could not get around a well-entrenched garrison.[104] With winter settling in, the plan was shelved.

Ridgeway meanwhile returned to London where he may have conferred with Sir Thomas Palmer who, with news of French preparations confirmed, had been hastily summoned from Boulogne.[105] Palmer's first task was to go to Broughty. The place was structurally weak, lacked sufficient storage and was dank.[106] It was also overlooked by a hill (Balgillo) some 2000 feet to the north.[107] Rossetti had already made plans for a new Italianate fortress, to be built in two easy stages and surrounded by a 'freshwater' ('aqua dolce del mare grand') moat. Fortifying the town of Dundee had been considered: it was further up the river and had ample accommodation for a garrison. Dudley had long advocated a force there and John Luttrell was promised the captaincy.

---

101 BN, MS fr. 20, 542, fo. 123v. He may have been referring to de Selve's depatch of 19 December or that of 14 January (*Odet de Selve*, 257, 267).

102 PRO, A01/286/1067. Although Railton paid for some of Uvedale's debts, he did not take over his predecessor's account and it would appear that Uvedale's accounts were never audited.

103 Somerset must have been relatively ignorant of the south-west of Scotland and this may explain the execution and survival of a large map of the area.

104 *CSP Dom., Add., 1547–65*, 336.

105 *CSP Scot.*, i, nos. 123, 131. It is not clear if he and Palmer both went to Broughty. Ridgeway is mentioned in PRO, E. 351/213 and it is clear he at least forwarded materials (PRO, SP 15/2, fo. 80).

106 *Mary of Lorraine Corr.*, 212; *CSP Scot.*, i, no. 132.

107 Indeed when the French captains who arrived with Chapelle went there in January, one pranced mockingly along the hill, finely armoured, on a white charger.

Palmer made a whirlwind tour of all the possible sites before departing for Berwick after only six days. Dundee he immediately rejected as impractical. The town was too sprawling, had been badly mauled by repeated English attacks and Scottish recaptures and was overlooked by the hill known as Dundee Law. Palmer also vetoed Rossetti's 'aqua dolce' fort, since it too would be commanded by Balgillo. Broughty could not be strengthened any further. He thus chose to checkmate the French by building on Balgillo before they did.[108] Grey of Wilton was so impressed by Palmer's plan that he went ahead without waiting for Somerset's approval.[109] By the time Palmer returned in February, work on the new fortress was well advanced, the pioneers protected by reinforcements sent earlier by Grey.[110] He also made a detailed survey of Dundee.[111] Work at Balgillo apparently proceeded fairly rapidly, English pioneers being aided by local Scots.[112] As early as 27 February the surveyor judged it ready to be 'crystened' even though the work was still to proceed for some time.[113] By 6 March, the ditch had been greatly extended: 20 feet broad about the bastions and 54 feet at the curtain; stubborn rock limited the depth to eight feet.[114] The need for more building material remained acute and on 15 March Rideway sent

> 20 wallers, ten breakers of stone with all such tools as was nessessary for them on ship laden with lime and another ship beyng frawgheed with 40 tone of timbor and plankes of all sortes.[115]

When Luttrell arrived from Inchcolm on 2 March, the place was considered strong enough for his garrison, and when he wrote to Somerset on 19 March, he did so proudly from 'The new fort besyde Broughty'. Palmer departed two days later with the praises of both Luttrell and Dudley.[116]

Palmer returned on 6 April to find Berwick feverish with activity. Ridgeway was busy strengthening the strongholds at Eyemouth, Hume and Roxburgh whilst Grey of Wilton was preparing for the new invasion of Scotland. The weather was still awful – it was hailing – and it was a symptom of English determination to make their position in Scotland impregnable before the French arrived in force that such work was being advanced at this worst time of the year.[117] Somerset's intention had been to expand the pale by another two-pronged invasion with Wharton (and Lennox) capturing Drumlanrig and Grey of Wilton Haddington.[118] Grey's campaign at first

108 Rossetti also viewed and prepared a plan for a fort on another site, apparently along the coast but very near to Broughty (Hatfield, Cecil Papers, 205/78).

109 *CSP Scot.*, i, nos. 136, 138, 145–6.

110 Palmer may have gone to London in between his two visits to Broughty (*Ibid.*, nos. 154, 156). Grey sent some 160 troops to augment the 150 already in the castle (*Ibid.*, no. 147).

111 *Ibid.*, nos. 154, 160, 186, 196.

112 PRO, E 351/213. See also *CSP Scot.*, i, no. 160.

113 *CSP Scot.*, i, no. 176.

114 *Ibid.*, nos. 183, 188.

115 PRO, SP 15/2. fo. 80.

116 *CSP Scot.*, i, nos. 196, 199, 200.

117 *Ibid.*, no. 193; PRO, SP 15/2, fo. 403 (*CSP Dom., Add., 1547–651*, 363–67).

118 *CSP Scot.*, i, no. 135 may well be the first order (19 January) for the invasion, which was definitely decided upon by 17 February (*Ibid.*, no. 149). For preparations, see *Ibid.*, nos. 138, 140, 143, 166.

was quite successful: Haddington was easily garrisoned on 21 February 1548 and his outriders quickly gained Hailes, Saltoun, Nunraw (on the 23rd), and Yester, Herdmanston and Waughton (on the 24th). However, these easy and promising successes quickly turned to dust when word came by the Berwick post of Wharton's débâcle. Most of Grey's prizes were abandoned and the others were quickly recaptured by the Scots.

These reverses only stiffened Somerset's resolve. Grey and Sir Robert Bowes, Warden of the Middle March, were convinced both by him and by the advice of the assured Scots that it would 'much establish the country' if a major new fort was built.[119] Dunbar and Haddington were the alternatives and the February expedition had been in part to gain sufficient information so as to decide between them. Grey had long been asking to see Somerset personally, in particular about the Protector's constant badgering. Money was, and would remain, a problem, as distraught letters from the Treasurer, Uvedale, demonstrated only too well; indeed the strain drove him to his grave. Grey addressed his letters with a gallows.[120] Grey was becoming increasingly exasperated by Somerset's inability to comprehend how expensive the war was and as early as 7 February asked to be relieved, in part prompted by pique over the lavish praise of Wharton's efforts in the Southwest.

In the middle of March he sped South to confer with the Protector as to future plans.[121] Dunbar was easily the best site; it was already fortified and had a commodious harbour. Both in terms of expense and ease of supply it would have been ideal. But the place was strongly held and was strong in itself, as the plan sent to Somerset on 6 March doubtless showed.[122] Once again, Arran's preparations in 1547 were bearing fruit and Dunbar would resist several attacks in 1548. Haddington was thus chosen instead and Grey quickly returned North, reaching Tynemouth on 5 April and Wark two days later.[123]

During his absence, Bowes had set out to expand the English position in the Tweed Valley.[124] Petit had already stated (17 February) that Lauder was the best place for a new fort[125] and Bowes, as instructed by Grey, departed for the place on 23 March with 300 pioneers and began building on 5 April.[126] By 19 June a garrison was settled in.[127] It was modern and remarkably complex. A trench encircled three sides

119 *Ibid.*, no. 175.
120 *Hamilton Papers*, ii, 605–08, 612–13. By 21 June, shortly before his death, he was obviously under considerable strain (*CSP Dom., Add., 1547–65*, 383). Indeed everyone was (*CSP Scot.*, i, nos. 80, 149, 182).
121 *CSP Scot.*, i, no. 193. Odet de Selve knew of the conference (*Odet de Selve*, 307, 313–17), whilst van der Delft got it all wrong (*CSP Spain.*, ix, 260).
122 *CSP Scot.*, i, nos. 86, 147, 174, 175, 180.
123 *Ibid.*, nos. 214–15, 218–19.
124 *APC*, 148, 163, 173.
125 The alternative site was Soutra Hill, on the western ridge of the Lammermuir Hills, eight miles north of Lauder (*CSP Scot.*, i, 159). Both sites posed difficulties and Petit was correct in predicting that Lauder would be tedious to construct (*Ibid.*, no. 216).
126 *Ibid.*, no. 220. Bowes only moved during the day as the way was 'deep and dangerous' (*Ibid.*, no. 204). For arrival date, see *Hamilton Papers*, ii, 610.
127 *CSP Dom., Add., 1547–65*, 383.

of the fortress which sat on the edge of a cliff; two demi-bastions with orillonated flankers protected the most exposed curtain wall whilst smaller bastions guarded the shorter, less vulnerable curtains.[128] It protected the English positions in the Tweed Valley by controlling Lauderdale and gave Grey a second route into East Lothian.

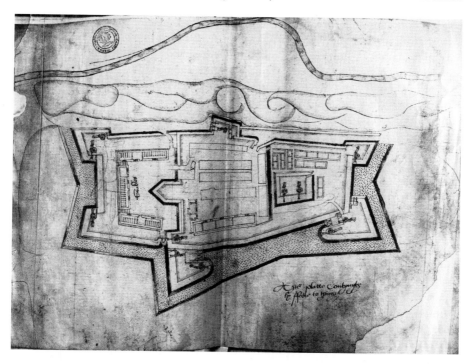

Fig. 12.4. Lauder was actually quite a complex site and may well have benefited from quite separate design and construction programmes. After Haddington and the encampments about Broughty, it was the largest and most redoubtable stronghold in English possession. Indeed, it was here that the war ended, the French and Scots having settled down to besiege it after taking Broughty in February 1550 and subjecting it to some bombardment when word came of the peace concluded at Boulogne.

The war was not to be won either at Broughty or at Lauder. Neither of these forts was designed to take more than 300 men and they were not particularly well armed.[129] In the next two hectic months Palmer in concert with Grey was to design a massive major fortress able to withstand whatever the French could throw against

128 The fort was near enough to the town for Petit to find materials from the parish church for the brewhouse roof (*CSP Dom., Add., 1547–65*, 383). It is nearly impossible to survey Lauder as a very large part of it has been overbuilt: only two bastions remain and part of the mount. Overbuilding is a problem which also affects discussion of Balgillo and Haddington.

129 *Hamilton Papers*, ii, 628–31.

it.[130] On 23 April he and Grey left Berwick with a large force of labourers and troops to protect them. They arrived at Haddington the next evening. At first light the two surveyed the site whilst a trench for a temporary encampment was dug. Grey judged that it would be the 'fairest' town ever fortified in the area and the 'daunter' of Scotland.[131]

Two contemporary French accounts give some idea of the strength of the fortress which was built there during the next two months.[132] Odet de Selve was naturally anxious to know all he could and very quickly sent a spy North. In May Somerset 'm'en voulloyt monstrer le dessaing en plateforme [desired to show me a plan of its design]', and his description tallies with that given by Jean de Beaugué, a member of the French army of 1548–50.[133] The overall plan was quadrilateral, 'ung peu longue que large', and bordered the River Tyne, by which the town sits. Each corner was protected by a large bastion whose flankers covered a turf wall. Somerset stated that the ditch was 30 feet wide and 12 feet deep. It was a massive affair able to hold as many as 2500 men. Bertville warned de Selve it was 'une des plus belles et fortes places apres Thurin [One of the finest and strongest after Turin]'.[134]

Palmer and Grey were certainly pleased with their handiwork. To give some idea of the relative size of the structure, one need only examine the costs which Railton presented after the war for the garrisons stationed in Scotland and for such items as running repairs, cartage, munitions (but excluding victuals) during the period September 1548 to the end of the war: for Eyemouth, the costs were £3,598 9s. 1d; for Roxburgh, £5,303.9s.10d; for Lauder, £6,656.15s.3d; and for Haddington (which had been evacuated well before the others, in September 1549) the figure was £31,640.12s.4d.[135] The size of garrisons also gives an indication: Eyemouth had, over the period as a whole, 399 men; Roxburgh 441 men; Lauder 671 men; Haddington 4,529 men. It is hardly surprising that Grey exulted to Somerset on 28 June that the keeping of Haddington would be the winning of Scotland; as the French began to appear before him, he complacently remarked that despite their expertise in the wars, 'they shall fynde enough to truble ther heddes withall'.[136]

---

130 He appears to have kept in touch with Rogers, sending him a platt of his design for Haddington in May (*Odet de Selve*, 341).

131 *CSP Scot.*, i, no. 228.

132 Many platts, none of which have come to light, were made; in addition to those by the English, Odet de Selve saw or had others made (*Odet de Selve*, 256, 330, 341, 344, 478).

133 *Ibid.*, 366, 376. Jean de Beaugué, *L'histoire de la Guerre d'Escosse*, 22–23.

134 *Odet de Selve*, 360.

135 PRO AO1/287/1067. Odet de Selve thus spoke with some insight when he admonished Somerset in June: 'Ceste fortresse luy avoyt coste bon a faire et cousteroyt encore plus a garder estant sy grande de circuyt'. Somerset retorted that it would actually save money (*Odet de Selve*, 366).

136 *CSP Scot.*, i, nos. 265, 273. See also *Literary Remains of Edward VI*, ed. J.G. Nicholas (Roxburghe Club, 1857), 61; *Hamilton Papers*, ii, 599; Stevenson, *Selections*, 24–25.

THE WAR FOR HADDINGTON

There is no point in detailing the daily encounters or the form and nature of the French siege,[137] but the character of the war completely changed in the period January to July 1548 as the English extended their pale from a ring of garrisons in obsolete structures to one larger in area and in the most modern fortresses that could have been built in the time. The previous pale had been to daunt the Scots; the purpose of the extended pale was to nullify French assistance, hence its size and modernity.

Despite the impact of French aid, the English were, and had reason to be, confident. Since Haddington absorbed virtually all of the French army, the other fortresses remained secure and did not need large garrisons. Although beaten in some of the engagements with the French,[138] the English held their own and supplies were forced into Haddington.[139] Somerset's preparations for resisting the French had gone further than merely strengthening and building forts; he intended that as soon as they landed, an English army would engage them.[140]

As early as May 1548, Clinton had been issued detailed instructions to prepare for a late-summer massive naval assault on Scotland to be made in conjunction with a main field army.[141] On 27 June, Francis Talbot, 5th Earl of Shrewsbury, was instructed to drive his way into Haddington for its relief.[142] His force was almost as large as that at Pinkie: 11,412 footmen, of whom 1200 were hackbutters, 1800 cavalry and 1300 troops sent in the fleet. They left Berwick around 18 August, and by 23 August the army was placed along the coast from Aberlady to Longniddry, to the north and east of Haddington. The French, outflanked, raised their siege and retired to Leith and Edinburgh where they were forced to remain until October.[143] The fresh

---

137 It and its relief are fully covered in Phillips, *Anglo-Scottish Wars*, 224–39. See also Teulet, *Relations*, i, 164–84; *CSP Scot.*, i, nos. 275–312; *Mary of Lorraine Corr.*, 237–39; 243–44, 248–51; *Balcarres Papers*, ii, 3–4; Spanish reports are to be found in Teulet, *Relations*, i, 218–34 (and in translation in CSP Spain, ix). See also *Odet de Selve, ad indices*. There is also much material in manuscripts, e.g. BN, MS fr. 20,457, pp 51, 65–75, 99–102, 179; MS. fr. 3035, fos. 96v, 98; MS fr. 16,088, fo. 121; see also Beagué, *Histoire*, 20–58; J-A de Thou, *Histoire Universelle*; J.H. Jamieson, *A Short History of Haddington*, 10–21.

138 *CSP Scot.*, i, nos. 293, 299, 301, 303.

139 *Ibid.*, no. 284; *Hamilton Papers*, ii, 598–99; *Mary of Lorraine Corr.*, 243.

140 This was the brunt of Paget's 'remembraunce' of early 1548: 'Whot dishonour besides daunger should ensue yf any the peces which youe now have or shall take a freshe in hand enowe to fortefie in Scotland shuld be loste agayne'. This was why he implored that no more forts be taken but instead Somerset 'appoynte such a number of horsemen and footmen to serve for the Northe, as may be hable to defend your owne and helpe to kepe that youe have taken' (Northants. Rec. Office, MS F (m) C21, fo. 5).

141 By the time the instructions were issued, it was too late for Clinton to fulfil his first task: preventing the French fleet from reaching Scotland. He was also to land Palmer and Rossetti at a suitable island in the Forth (doubtless Inchkeith) or at Burntisland where another fort was to be built. PRO, SP 10/4, fos. 14–24.

142 *CSP Scot.*, i, nos. 262, 267, 288, 309. Clinton's orders were altered somewhat after Shrewsbury had a conference with Grey (*Ibid.*, nos. 292, 309, 313).

143 *Ibid.*, nos. 314–21.

men and provisions which Shrewsbury's force put into the fortress did much to lift English morale, especially after some severe reverses in the field during July and August.[144] As Shrewsbury's force retired back along the coast, it paused at the head of the Pease at Cockburnspath and protected a force of 500 pioneers under the direction of Sir Richard Lee who entrenched the village of Dunglass and constructed yet another artillery fortress on the bluff overlooking the hamlet. Thus the English effectively annexed Berwickshire.[145] Shrewsbury appears to have considered keeping the whole army there, but Somerset's outrage at the cost compelled him to retire, leaving 1096 men 'for the more spedye Dispatche of the said ffortfycacons'.[146] The work was rapid, even given the smallness of the place, and was put under the command of Christopher Asheton with over 120 hackbutters, gunners and light horse.[147]

The removal of the Queen to France in August 1548 should have caused a fundamental rethinking of English policy, but de Selve reported Somerset not the least concerned. The Protector doubtless felt that should the French be defeated in Scotland, they would have to hand her over. Moreover as England still held Boulogne, he held a powerful card should France's Scottish adventure overstretch them.[148] This seemed to be happening in the summer of 1548. The raising of the siege of Haddington, infusion of new troops into Broughty and the building of Dunglass considerably embarrassed the French and emboldened the English.[149] Even better news was to come. On 7 September word was sent to Somerset's brother that in France 'the countrye ar risen agaynst ther kyng for the demand that he made of the gabelle of salt, and among them in muche busines'.[150] By 19 September de Selve was keeping a close watch on English ports in case any of the rebels arrived in England asking for support. Within a fortnight rumours were rife that an English fleet would shortly sail with aid to Bordeaux.[151] On 15 October Somerset pointedly reminded de Selve that the Scots were rebels in English eyes and that he considered

144 Tuesday's chase, 16 July, in which Palmer and others were taken, was especially upsetting. Somerset called it an 'evill chance' in a letter to his brother in which he discussed ways in which to minimise the defeat (PRO, SP 10/4, fo. 72). Paget particularly blamed Somerset for having 'provoked him [Palmer] to muche forward with letters accusing his stillnes, slacknes and slepinge' (Northants Rec. Office, MS F (M) C21, fo. 5v). See also *CSP Spain*, ix, 290; *Hamilton Papers*, ii, 614–19.

145 Dunglass Water marks the northern boundary of the county.

146 *CSP Scot.*, i, no. 325.

147 There is little correspondence on the construction at Dunglass, although, as ever, Odet de Selve knew of it (*Odet de Selve*, 444, 446, 478). Lee's account for the construction is in PRO, E 351/3540 (3541 is a duplicate). PRO, AO1/287/1067 gives the numbers of troops and the dates for the commanders: Ashton was resident until 5 November 1549 and his place was filled by Francis Aslaby on 9 January 1550.

148 *Odet de Selve*, 443.

149 Note Somerset's threats (31 August 1548) to go to war directly with France: *Odet de Selve*, 437, 441, 443.

150 John 'Graynsyed' sent the news to the admiral on 7 September 1548 (PRO, SP 10/5, fos. 4–5).

151 *Odet de Selve*, 447–8, 455–8; *CSP Spain*, ix, 305, 547, 576, 578.

de favoriser et soustenir les rebelles vos subjects comme vous faictes les siens, et qu'encores aura il plus de raison d'aultant que ceulx de Guyenne ont este aultres fois ses subjects de temps que les roys d'Angleterre tenoint le duche de Guyenne [you are favouring and sustaining our rebels which is thus more reason for us to do likewise in Guyenne since there was another time when its people were subjects of kings of England who then possessed the Duchy of Guyenne].[152]

With hindsight, it is clear that the events of July 1548 should have given the English pause for thought. Massive French aid of men (though not enough) and the funds injected into Scotland, the signing of the Treaty of Haddington, the betrothal of Mary Queen of Scots to the Dauphin, her imminent removal to France and Henry II's obvious determination to make the most of the Scottish situation completely reversed the events of September 1547. August and September 1548 brought, so it seemed, another dramatic shift of fortunes. The English garrisons were secure and in France serious rebellion spread. The Emperor, moreover, had suddenly disappeared from Augsburg and returned to the Low Countries. Might he not see this as the moment to strike? As the summer of 1548 drew to its end, Somerset remained robustly buoyant. To the worries of the Captain at Haddington that French bribes would erode Scottish support, the Protector scoffed that the French would have plenty to spend their money on in Brittany and Gascony. He boasted, 'And so hath God provyded bettre for us then we could wishe, to kepe them from to be hable to spare money to their neighbours'.[153]

152 *Odet de Selve*, 458.
153 *CSP Scot.*, i, no. 328.

CHAPTER THIRTEEN

The Auld Alliance Triumphant

With the introduction of mercenary troops, gunpowder, artillery and massive fortifications across Europe, it became a commonplace of warfare during the period 1550–1650 that, as the Spaniard Aytona remarked, 'he who has the most money wins'.[1] Certainly Somerset recognised the brute necessity of finance when he hoped that French commitments would leave them little spare money for Scotland. Although France was by far the wealthier monarchy, grounds for English optimism did exist and in September 1548 Somerset's chimera still shimmered tantalisingly.

FRENCH PANIC: THE AUTUMN OF 1548

Charles V's reaction to French involvement in Scotland was critical. Fear of the Emperor's returning to Flanders in preparation for a strike against France was constant throughout the period 1547–48, but in April 1548 de la Brosse reported to Mary of Guise that all was well on that point.[2] But on 12 September 1548, Henry heard of Charles's 'inoppine partement d'Allemagne avecques la dilligence dont il a use ne peult estre sans occasion inopportune [sudden departure from Germany which he never does without good reason]'.[3] For fully a month, the King remained convinced that a new war with Charles was imminent, but the Emperor had returned to Flanders largely because he was short of money.[4] Border disputes in the Boulonnais were another worry. Although French nervousness was never to be wholly allayed, there were no real threats.[5]

The Emperor's 'sudden departure' was disturbing enough, but it came at a time when Henry was faced with the serious rebellion in Guyenne which consumed the efforts of both Montmorency and d'Aumale and diverted men and money from the Scottish enterprise.[6] In October Wotton laid before Henry several ominous threats

---

1 Quoted in G. Parker, *The Spanish Road*. Pages 1–21 contain an excellent brief introduction to the topic which refines much of the wisdom to be found in M. Roberts, *The Military Revolution*. But for a thorough examination of this now richly explored topic, see first Parker's *The Military Revolution*.

2 See Charles's advice to Philip of 18 January 1548 (Weiss, *Granvelle*, iii, 286–87) which shows they had reason to be apprehensive. *Odet de Selve*, 52, 391, 451: *Balcarres Papers*, i, 194.

3 BN, MS fr. 3124, fo. 17. See also worries of a new Anglo-Habsburg 'amytie' (*Odet de Selve*, 455, 461, 463, 465, 473).

4 *Lettres et Memoires*, ii, 173.

5 As Dr. Potter has shown: 'Diplomacy in the mid sixteenth century: England and France, 1536–50' (unpublished Ph.D. thesis, Cambridge, 1973), pp. 183–90.

6 S.C. Gigon, *La Révolté de la Gabelle en Guyenne, 1548–49*, is the best account. Troops 'allant dernierement en Escosse,' from Piedmont were diverted to Guyenne on 3 September (*Ibid.*, 259) and the navy was recalled from Scotland (Pierpont Morgan Library, MS MA 22; BN, MS Clair, 344, fo. 226). See also BN, MS fr. 20,555, fos. 44, 77; BL, MS Add. 38,029, fos 411–12; *CSP Spain*, ix, 576.

of war. Although it might be 'a pernycious example and daungerous to all pryncis', the English spoke of aiding 'the gascons and bretons in ther rebellions agaynst ther kyng'. 'So long . . . as the king . . . doth thus mayntene the Scottes beyng the kinges majesties vassals and rebelles agaynst the kyng ther soveraigne lorde, yt wer the greatest dyshonour in the world if we will suffre it'.[7]

There was also distressing news from Scotland. The unsuccessful siege of Haddington culminating in its relief by Shrewsbury had been a severe reverse. The French army had retired to Leith and Edinburgh[8] where the German and French troops quickly became particularly unpopular. Arguments soon broke out; one in September led to an open affray in which the Captain of Edinburgh Castle and other townsmen were killed. D'Essé determined to restore French popularity by a surprise night attack on Haddington which just failed.[9] While the army was absent, vengeful townspeople slaughtered wounded Frenchmen in their very beds. The English were naturally delighted and made much of these strained relations.

However, strenuous efforts were being made to render Scotland more secure, despite the failure to retake Haddington either by frontal siege or by stealth. This is very much the story of an Italian 'famous captain' who was sent to recast Scotland's most important fortified sites, Migiliorino Ubaldini. When the French first took up the Scottish war, they clearly thought that they would only have to carry out a number of minor St. Andrews-type sieges to expel the English, none of them lasting much longer than a couple of weeks. They would be home by Christmas. Instead, they had to fight a prolonged war of fortifications, firstly to ring and cut off the English strongholds, and secondly to have redoubts for their own security should English armies counter-attack in force, as they did. The war had become in effect a war for Haddington, in the keeping of which, one field commander told Somerset, 'ye win Scotland'.

'INGEGNERI MILITARI ITALIANI'

But from the start of this adventure, the French did know that however brief the war might be, they would have to upgrade and modernise Scotland's defences. This is clear from a remarkable document in the Archivo Generales at Simancas, Estado 804: Letters Patent over the Great Seal of Scotland, issued by the Governor of the realm on 2 February 1548. Translated by Armand Baschet during the 19th century, it reads as follows:

> Henry II, king of France, the constant friend and ally of Scotland against the English, had sent to Scotland the famous Italian soldier Captain Ubaldino to perfect the Scots in the knowledge of arms and to organise the defence of the realm. He is hereby appointed to the supreme command for this purpose of all

7 BL, MS Harl. 249, fos. 18–24; BL, MS Calig. B. vii, fos. 341–44v.
8 Teulet, *Relations*, i, 185–91.
9 There is much evidence for these difficulties: Stevenson, *Selections*, 30–33; Knox, *History*, i, 104–06; Dalrymple, *Historie*, ii, 279; Pitscottie, *Historie*, ii, 108; Beaugué, *Histoire*, 76–81; see also *Balcarres Papers*, ii, 1–2.

the Scottish forces by land and sea, and to have access to all the fortresses, munitions, etc.

For this document to make sense, some more background material is necessary, this time a discussion of the French campaigns in Scotland from 1548 to 1550. Once they had determined to send aid to Scotland in late 1547, the French requested that the Scots hand over to their control a number of already existing strongholds: Edinburgh was denied them, but they did gain Blackness on the Forth, just to the west of Leith, which became their main storehouse of munitions; Dunbar, which guarded the coastal invasion route into the country; and Inchgarvie, an island in the Forth where their fleet could shelter. It would also seem they garrisoned Inchcolm, captured by the English in September 1547, but abandoned in March 1548.

They then proceeded to build new strongholds of their own about Haddington: at Luffness, Aberlady and Inveresk. When a main English army of over 12,000 relieved Haddington in August-September and as it became clear the war would continue into the next year, they fortified Leith. Moreover, gradually, English-held castles were recaptured and garrisoned by the French, Hume in December 1548 being but one example. It was into this eventful year that Migiliorino Ubaldini found himself thrust.

Although the Scots knew full well the necessity of adapting their castles to house artillery and rebuilding them to resist artillery, it is clear from the extensive works done in the 1530s (such as the rebuilding of Tantallon) and during 1544–47 at Edinburgh, Dunbar and Blackness that they employed their own conception of what might be termed stone-casemented blockhouses, similar to the sort of works which Henry VIII had erected about the coast and within England during his massive re-fortification programme of 1538–42. At Dunbar, they benefited from inheriting (in 1536) one of the first structures built in the whole of the British isles to house artillery, the duke of Albany's great ravelin which he must have built in front of the late medieval castle by the early 1520s. But the Scots were largely ignorant of the new practices of fortification perfected in Italy during the early decades of the century and which the English were erecting in such profusion against them (and the French) in 1547–48.

Unable even to reduce one of their own home-built stone castles, St. Andrews, in 1546, they were obviously at a severe disadvantage against the modern English post-Pinkie structures. When they laid siege to Broughty in the winter of 1547, their efforts were woefully in vain, as Henry Lord Methven lamented. He demanded that 'Greit arttalzerij puderis bullattis gunnarris and hagbutterris and uther men of weir and peonarris be largelie furnest', and went on to specify the utter necessity for

> cappidennis that is cum out of France quhilkis has intelligens of ordour of men
> on the feildis; alsua is to be had of the cappidens that has best intelligens to
> asseg and ordouring arttalzerij.[10]

That is where Ubaldini so forcefully enters the story of this war, for he clearly was a man of 'intelligens to asseg' in its widest sense.[11] Our problem is that little appears to have survived concerning him: date of birth, training, previous experience. Nor have I been able to discover what happened to him after he left Scotland. His Letters Patent deemed him a 'famous capitain'. But it has to be said that his sixteenth-century fame never reached the printed sources I have been able to consult in the twentieth. That is a pity, but really does not affect our interest in his Scottish career.

Well before Ubaldini's presence at Dumbarton on 2 February 1548, the Scots were planning massive alterations to their two principal castles, Edinburgh and Stirling, despite considerable work having already been done at both during 1542–46.[12] On 2 April 1547, a spy for the English urged immediate haste for their invasion:

> yf Ingland mak not thair armis with all gudly hayst in dew tyme, thai shall never pereshance hayf the castell of Edinburgh nor Sterleng, be reason thai ar cuttand the holl before the castle yait of Edinburgh, and intendis to mak ane blokhous quhar on cofedes all the takin of the said castell, and siklyk in the castel of Sterling.

Dumbarton, on the west coast of Scotland, was a major stronghold in its own right situated on the north shore of the river Clyde, some sixteen miles from Glasgow. It was well known to French naval personnel and mariners who frequently landed supplies and troops there, as in April and November 1543, July 1545 and December 1547. This last landing was an advance party of captains, some soldiers and considerable munitions. The captains had immediately gone to Stirling to be presented to the Governor of Scotland and the Queen Dowager, Mary of Guise. Amongst them may have been Ubaldini, for his correspondence shows him to have been on relatively easy terms with the Queen.

His task was clearly confined to the modernisation of Scotland's principal strongholds to secure them not just for the current campaigning season, but for a longer-term future. His first assignment was Edinburgh, and in March 1548 he, the 'Italiane devisar of the forte of the castle hill', is to be found lodged with Patrick Barron's wife. She was paid £11 for his expenses.[13] At the time, Patrick Barron of Spittlefield was a clerk to the Court of Session, but even then he was clearly a burgess of some means, for his house stood at the top of the town's principal thoroughfare, the High Street, on the south side. To the west stood the lands of Patrick Edzear, also a burgess, but next door to Edzear's slice of land, which ran down to the Cowgate (one assumes Barron's did as well), lay 'the castell hill of Edinburgh one the west parte'. So, Ubaldini was living one door down from his office of works.[14]

Just what did he accomplish whilst resident in Scotland's capital? Again, we suffer from a dearth of hard financial records or correspondence, but enough tantalising

11 By that later phrase, 'in the widest sense' I mean able to conduct sieges but also being besieged. *Ingegneri militari* had to be polymaths, as the discussion of the English Italians demonstrates vividly: master gunners, experts at the employment of ordnance, mathematicians, draftsmen, designers of siege works and fortifications.

12 *CSP Scot.*, i, no. 10.

13 For documentation for this passage on French construction, see my article, 'Ubaldini' cited in the Bibliography.

14 *RSS,*. no. 3239.

items have come down to us to enable us to speak with some confidence. For one thing, quite a lot of money was spent on the Castle during this period of war. In 1550, when the 'maister of wark' finally submitted his register to the Crown's treasurer, the accounts for Edinburgh, which covered the period January 1548 to 19 July 1550, totalled £6387 2s. 10d. Thus we are looking at 12,774 *livres tournois*, quite a considerable sum of money spent over two years.

Secondly, there were reports at the time of work being done at the Castle. In October 1548 an English prisoner of war, held in Edinburgh for over three months, finally raised his ransom and returned to Berwick, then, as now, part of England. The man in question, Thomas Carlisle, had been captured during a confused sortie made with others from Haddington. Much of Carlisle's report on his arrival at Berwick to Thomas Fisher actually concerned Leith, which Pietro Strozzi was then in the process of transforming into one of the most modern *trace italienne* fortifications in Europe so as to counter Haddington. Strozzi had himself been badly wounded in the skirmish in which Carlisle had been captured and had to be carried about Leith in a chair.

Fig. 13.1. Ubaldini's spur in action. It is actually quite rare to see any drawing of a Scottish place of strength under attack, which is one of the reasons this sketch of the siege of Edinburgh Castle by the English in 1573 has been so widely reproduced. One can see that the bastion built in 1548 was formidable, giving soldiers a secure spot to shoot from and the gunners a broad platform on which to load and fire their cannon.

But Carlisle also reported that the French had at their first coming to Scotland 'devised a traves walle betwene the towne of Edenbrugh and the castell'. This wall 'with a poynted bulwerk in the myddes' was being constructed in the summer of 1548 when Carlisle was brought to the town; by October the wall was already up to a man's height. What Carlisle described to Fisher – and he drew a 'grocely pricked out' line drawing of the wall – must be the 'fort of the castle hill', also called 'the spur', which was to cause the English such trouble when they besieged Edinburgh Castle in 1573. The 'engener' (Carlisle's term) must be Ubaldini.

Thirdly, we have clear graphic evidence for a massive alteration to the forefront of Edinburgh Castle at some point before 1560, and this must be Ubaldini's Spur of 1548. Plate N clearly shows Edinburgh Castle as drawn in 1544: nothing stands before its characteristic medieval east-facing wall. However, additional to Carlisle's 1548 sketch, we also have an intimately detailed overall portrait of the fortifications of Leith as they stood on 7 July 1560. Close examination of the Castle clearly reveals a bulwark of some sort now in front of it. This is without doubt the famous Spur which appears so dramatically in Hollinshed's picture of the siege of 1573.

Moreover, there survives a description of the Castle, penned on 26 January 1573 by Rowland Johnson, then Surveyor of Works at Berwick-upon-Tweed, an engineer intimately knowledgeable and utterly reliable about *trace italienne* fortification. Johnson's description is infuriatingly imprecise on certain points (such as the lengths of the spur's walls), but he does definitely describe Ubaldini's work: 'we fynd upon the said este syde a spurre lyke a bulwarke standing befor the foot of the rocke',

which sp[urre] enclosethe that syde flanked out one bothe sydes; on the sowthe syde is the gaite wher they enter into the castle. Which spur is like 22 foote high vamured with turfe and basketes set and furnished with ordinance.

But the siege of the Castle has left us one further magnificent piece of evidence for Ubaldini's Spur. Sometime afterwards, when the Castle was being rebuilt and gained its now characteristic, almost totemic, Half-Moon Battery, various proposals for fortifying the outworks of the site were being discussed. We are not certain of their date, but two such plans were discovered by John Dunbar of the Royal Commission on the Ancient and Historical Monuments of Scotland and published in 1969. One of them has to be what Ubaldini designed in 1548. The overall impression of the site can be seen from a modern reconstruction.

By June, Ubaldini had clearly quit Edinburgh, for he then wrote to Mary of Guise from a place he identifies as Calder which may be the Calder in Lanarkshire or Cadder, part of Glasgow. He thus did not supervise the completion of the Spur. This often happened all over Europe with military engineers. Such was the press of work for them during periods of warfare that they would arrive at a site, survey it, draw up plans, see the ground being staked out with marker pegs and then leave for another job. In early 1545, Sir Richard Lee, then emerging as England's foremost expert on modern fortifications, was at Tynemouth. However, he left almost immediately, being back in London as early as 14 March so as to hasten himself to Portsmouth for its strengthening against a French attack which came that summer. A similar sort of work pattern may well have been Ubaldini's lot.

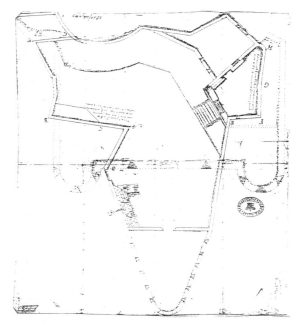

Fig. 13.2. Edinburgh spur. This drawing, printed upside down here for clarity's sake),
was probably done after the Great Siege when plans were being considered
for what became the castle's Half-Moon Battery.

Fig. 13.3. This handsome representation of the Spur before the walls of Edinburgh
Castle, 1548-73 (how did fortifications actually look then to a person standing
in the ditch?) was executed by the staff of Historic Scotland.

On 23 June, his intention was to depart the next day 'ver li selvagi', that is to say to head into the Highlands of Scotland, so perhaps he also had a holiday. Cadder, interestingly enough, has a prominent portion of the Antonine Wall still standing which Ubaldini may have wished to see. Since his next letter is dated 3 September 1548, we have what might be three missing months for his Scottish career. My strong inclination is that he was sent to survey Stirling Castle and to set in motion the building of the Spur there. But I cannot prove it. We have no financial records detailing expenditure of any magnitude at Stirling for 1548. No contemporary reference to works exists and no sixteenth-century illustrations. But the Stirling Spur is so strikingly similar to the Edinburgh one (compare figs. 13.4 and 13.2) as to suggest very strongly that Ubaldini did it, and thus it was done in 1548.

Stirling Castle is one of the most impressive fortified sites in the British Isles and is a veritable jewel for architectural historians.[15] It is also strikingly similar to Edinburgh. If both were 'spurred' by our Italian, then something of an interesting dialogue can now take place between the two bastions, as indeed has always been the case for the two castles in their medieval robes. Their locations are near identical; thus one should not be surprised that similar solutions were erected at each.

This is highly relevant, for it is clear that at Dunbar, Ubaldini designed yet another single-bastion upgrading of the site's defence. But, one critical point to appreciate about the *trace italienne* is that to create 'dead land', there must be interlocking fire-power so that no blind spots exist: a plan from Scala's memoirs aptly illustrates this point. Single-bastion fortifications can find the face of their bastion accessible, as the English discovered at Eyemouth. French engineers tended to prefer two interlocking bastions, as one can see from their re-fortified Eyemouth in 1557.

What lends a certain urgency to this is what little we know of what was built at Dunbar in 1548. The first point to appreciate about the site is how it differs from Edinburgh and Stirling. They are what might be termed 'hill fortifications', thus needing massive construction only on one face. Dunbar, however, does not lie at the top of a hill, although it likewise requires only one face because it is a peninsular fortification. Mounted on a rocky outcrop of land which juts into the sea, it is

15 Although there is a reference for de Termes being there in July 1549 'to put things in strengthe'; he then went to Dunbar on a similar errand (Stevenson, *Selections*, 37). There are three main easily accessible studies: the Official HMSO Guide by J.S. Richardson and Margaret Root, first published in 1936; the survey executed by the Royal Commission on the Ancient and Historical Monuments of Scotland (RCAHMS), published in 1963, pp. 179–223; and *Stirling Castle* by Richard Fawcett (Batsford/Historic Scotland, 1995). Fawcett's text reads as follows: 'Edinburgh and Stirling were also eventually provided with new outworks which would allow the approaches to those castles to be defended by and from artillery, and it is now realized that substantial parts of what was built at Stirling still survive in modified form. There is a tradition that the outer defences pre-dating those now seen were built by the French troops of Mary of Guise, who had become regent of the kings . . . in 1554. The date sometimes given is 1559, though work could have started some years before'. As late as 1680 the out-works were still being called 'the French Spurre' (pp. 65–66). RCAHMS gives a not dissimilar account: 'In 1559 the castle was occupied for a time by French troops; there is a tradition that the Queen Dowager, Mary of Lorraine, caused them to build the Spur battery to command the bridge'. See p. 184, no. 22.

surrounded on three sides by water. It is very much like numerous other Scottish peninsular castles: Fast, Tantallon, St. Andrews are but three of a host of similar strongholds. When the English built their first *trace italienne* fortification in Britain, at Eyemouth, they too chose a peninsula where only one side needed to be fortified in any strength.

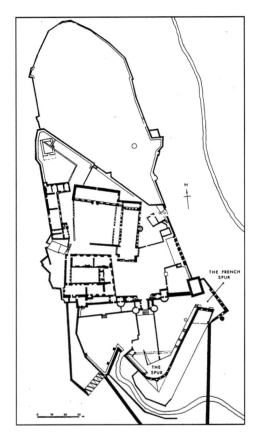

Fig. 13.4. Stirling Castle before 1708 from a plan by Captain Theodore Dury.
Conventional wisdom about 'The French Spur' at Stirling has always placed its date as during the Regency of Mary of Guise, probably 1558. That, in truth, is when Leith was being made truly formidable and may be correct. No evidence exists conclusively to prove that Ubaldini worked there, as definitely is the case for his designs at Edinburgh and Dunbar. But so similar is the Stirling Spur (shown here just before the castle was radically recast in the reign of Queen Anne) to Edinburgh's and what we know about Dunbar that it may well be by Ubaldini, executed during his missing three months between his being at Edinburgh and then at Dunbar. The burgh council also set about protecting the urban area of the burgh by construction in 1547-48 of its version of Edinburgh's 'Flodden Wall' which was still to be laboured on in 1560.

By 3 September Ubaldini had certainly arrived there, whence he wrote a letter to Mary of Guise but in which he gives precious few clues as to what the fortification looked like. He complained about lack of small denomination coins with which to pay his not always industrious workforce. Pietro Strozzi, recently designing Leith, clearly had begun some sort of work and he continued to help Ubaldini for a while after the latter's arrival until he departed precipitously. Ubaldini was now in sole charge and set to making the castle 'very redoubtable'. He also hoped to fortify the town, 'which would be the finest thing in the world', but he appears to have abandoned such an ambitious endeavour.

Dunbar, as Ubaldini saw it in 1548, was the result of three major building campaigns. First a medieval castle had been rebuilt there for James IV in 1496–1501. Then in c. 1520, Jean duc d'Albany, then regent to the infant James V, had constructed a formidable artillery blockhouse, perhaps the earliest such structure in the British Isles. Intriguingly, the broad brushstroke conception may have been the brainstorm of none other than Antonio da Sangallo the younger.[16] Regardless of the inspiration, the result was formidable strength.[17] As Lord Dacre, a field commander with considerable experience, reported to Cardinal Wolsey in 1523, the 'new bulwark and sett with ordinance' made the place 'a thing in maner unprenable'.[18]

Nonetheless, when the flames of war once again scorched Scotland during the Rough Wooings, the Earl of Arran insured that it was yet further strengthened, as expenses during the period 1544–47 amply testify. It is strongly arguable that Arran's successful enhancement of Dunbar's defensive capabilities and its garrisoning by Scots in 1547–48 is what won the war for Scotland (perhaps one should say for the Auld Alliance). Had Somerset been able to station his massive garrison there in June 1548 instead of at Haddington, England might have won, but Arran's efforts denied Somerset that advantage.

However, as was the case at Edinburgh in 1544–46, it must still have been a defence by masonry and artillery, but not by Italianate bastions. What Ubaldini designed as his Dunbar was demolished in 1567 and fortunately we have details of that deconstruction (although the accompanying plan would seem to have been lost). One set of three groups of construction workers took down a long curtain wall stretching west to east from 'the castle gate' some 86 paces. If we take a normal pace to be approximately a yard/metre, we are looking at a curtain wall 252 feet long on the west side of a large bastion, what is termed 'the great platfourme' in the 1567 survey. Its dimensions and shape are not detailed, however, except that on one face it would appear that the matching counterscarp was 40 paces long. It would also seem that the

16 See *The Architectural Drawing of Antonio da Sangallo the Younger and his circle*, ed. Nicholas Adams, Architectural History Foundation of New York (MIT Press, Cambridge, Massachusetts, 1994), vol. I, entry U 1051A *recto* which was inscribed 'Fortezza opinione del Duca dalbana'.

17 Iain MacIvor, 'Artillery and Major Places of Strength in the Lothians, 1513–1542', in *Scottish Weapons and Fortifications, 1100–1800*, ed. David H. Caldwell (Edinburgh, 1981), pp. 94–124. Plate is from his Figure 42 on p. 96.

18 *LP*, iii (2), no. 1976. as quoted by MacIvor, p. 111.

platform was surmounted by a great 'blockhowse', making it look tantalisingly like one of the strongholds illustrated by Scala (plate N), although this may well have been constructed after Ubaldini's time.

To the west of the bastion a curtain wall of undefined length ran until it met a flanker which guarded an entrance into the complex: interestingly at the same location as built at Edinburgh and Stirling. But it is difficult to match these dimensions with what we know is on the ground today with any precision, especially as the spur's two wings end at the old castle gate on the one hand and at 'the castle ditch' on the other. But it is clear that this work at Dunbar is strikingly similar to Edinburgh/Stirling, despite being a very different piece of geography: a massive single bastion with curtain wall and flankers.

Ubaldini's Dunbar (again, perhaps one should say the Albany/Arran/Ubaldini fort) did its job magnificently. Although annoyed by English attacks in 1548, it was never taken by assault. Its garrison during the Rough Wooings constantly harassed English supply trains attempting to revictual Haddington and it played no small part in the abandonment of the fortress by the English in September 1549. For the French, keeping Dunbar meant winning the war.

FRANCO-SCOTTISH RECOVERY: 'LE COUP DE SECCOURS'

Nonetheless, matters looked extraordinarily difficult for the French at the end of 1548. It must have been at this time that d'Andelot was sent to France with details from the Queen of just how bad the situation was. Her letter does not survive, but in a later one she complained bitterly of the demands made upon her ('jamais femme ne fut plus mal traictee [never has a woman been so badly treated]') and outlined the difficulties facing her in the job of reconciling the Scots to French control:

> le commun bruit esoit part tout qu'il ne falloit que jamais Escossois esperast bien de France . . . un royaume qui a accoustume de n'estre subjet nouveau seigneur, le commencement en estant fort difficil. Mais c'est sur moy que toute la peyne tombe: car il fault que je fasse deux choses, l'un contre les enmemis, et l'autre a ranger ces gens la a nouvelle subjection.

> [Popular gossip is that Scots can never hope of any good from France. For a kingdom which has been accustomed to be subject to no master, the beginning is highly difficult. But it is all on me that the trouble falls because I have to do two duties: fight against our enemies and on the other hand reconcile these people to their new subjugation.][19]

Both these tasks were being made impossible by the King's attempts to do the job on the cheap (as Mary of Guise remonstrated, 'quant il est question de la perte d'un royaume, il n'y fault rien espargner car on n'en gaigne pas d'autres aysement') and by mismanagement. She was particularly scathing about d'Essé: 'ce que il a faict du passe

---

19   *Mémoires-journaux de François de Lorraine, duc de Guise, 1547–63*, ed. Michaude et Poujoulat (Paris, 1854), 32–36. See also *Balcarres Papers*, ii, 6–13.

a este par ignorance [Everything he's done in the past has been through stupidity]'.[20] There was 'bien du desordre parmy les officers [much disorder amongst the officers]' and money was being wasted and stolen. Whilst she appreciated the apprehension 'a cause que l'Empereur est en Flandres', the King must concentrate more troops and more money on Scotland.

D'Andelot had arrived in France by 27 September, when he was sent to Montmorency, then suppressing the revolt at Bordeaux.[21] The King was obviously distressed to learn that his affairs in Scotland suffered from 'quelque desordre par faulte que les payemens n'ont este envoyez de meilleure heure' and 'mon argent y ait este et soit bien mal administre [disorder because money has not been sent earlier and that my money has been and is being badly administered]'. Throughout September there had been considerable dissatisfaction at the King's Court because of Scotland's cost. The wife of Louis de Bourbon-Vendôme, Prince Condé, was particularly vituperative about the venture and accused Guise of pushing it 'for his private ends'. When word came that the Haddington siege had been raised because Scottish troops had not arrived in time, the King 'remained in a rage a long time'. St Mauris reported that the populace lamented the cost and the shame Scotland was bringing on France.[22]

Nonetheless the King was determined. If he did not defeat the English in Scotland, he would lose his one chance 'reconquerir ce qu'ils [the English] ont occupe en mon royaume'. In a long letter of 19 October to Montmorency, he suggested sending 'quelque honneste personnaige experimente en faict des finances [some honest person experienced with money]' and to manage affairs 'sans laisser choses en la confusion qu'elles sont [without losing things in the confusion they are in]'. Already he had despatched enough funds to last until 11 February 1549, but more was essential.[23] Meanwhile Henry wrote to Mary promising more aid[24] and instructed Montmorency and d'Aumale to send as much as they could spare. By 9 November the rebellion had been sufficiently crushed for Montmorency to scrape together 15,000 ecus[25] (£Sc15,000) which he sent with 1200 'Provencealx' troops under the command of Becarrie de Pavie, sieur de Fourquevaux and Scipione de Fieschi, sieur de Visque.[26] They no sooner sailed from Bordeaux than 'par fortune de temps, este contrainct relascher en Betaigne [were forced to ride out the storm in Brittany because the weather turned against them]'.[27] But by January 1549 they

---

20 He was an old man, suffered from gout, and was ignorant of the country. But at sixty-five, he still had a mistress with him and would die valiantly at the siege of Thérouanne in 1553.
21 BN, MS fr. 6620, fo. 2.
22 *CSP Spain*, ix, 576, 580; and see *Ibid*, 361 for similar later complaints.
23 BN. MS fr. 6620, fos. 7–9.
24 *Maitland Misc.*, I, ii, 214–15; *Balcarres Papers*, ii, 16, 25, 29; Fourquevaux, *Mission*, 9, 13.
25 *Balcarres Papers*, ii, 16–17; Fourquevaux, *Mission*, 14. See also BN, MS fr. 6620, fo. 15.
26 Fourquevaux, *Mission*, 8; P.F. Tytler, *England under the Reigns of Edward VI and Mary*, i, 157.
27 *Maitland Misc.*, I, ii, 219. The same letter told Mary of his delight at the marriage of her brother D'Aumale to Anne d'Este (see also *Balcarres Papers* ii, 18, 20) at which 'dancer mon filz le Daulphin avecques ma fille la Royne descosse'.

landed at Dumbarton.[28] The task of the two envoys was to inspect the French garrisons in Scotland: numbers of troops, state of the artillery, condition of the food and wine. They were to praise Arran, Mary of Guise, d'Essé and others for their arduous labours of the past year (although d'Oysel was criticised for not writing more frequently), to apologise for the tardy despatch of the wages and to promise reinforcements. As far as the King was concerned, they were to say that there 'ne fet point de difference de ce Roiaume et Celui d'Escosse [there is no difference between France and Scotland]' and that he regarded Mary Queen of Scots 'sa fille comme la sienne propre [his daughter as if his very own]'.[29]

The situation which confronted Fourquevaux in Scotland was serious. The Scots were certainly war-weary and stretched. Over the last year and a half, they had mounted seven armies and held numerous musters.[30] Scottish morale had reason to be low: the weather was foul, the Queen, who had expended considerable sums to pay the troops,[31] was bedridden 'suspect of the pest' and food was scarce.[32]

Nevertheless, the French and Scots allies did what they could.[33] In November they pushed the English out of Dundee and bottled Luttrell up in his two forts at Broughty.[34] Whilst the army was there, Arran captured Lord Grey's house of Huntly and Grey himself.[35] Then in December, by a stratagem by which Arran claimed to be 'Inventeur de la surprise', Hume was recaptured from the English.[36] As a final boost to Scottish morale, the earl of Huntly climbed through a window in the toilet at Wark and escaped from his English captors. He made Christmas at Court where 'he was ressauit with blythnes'.[37]

28 TA, ix, 275–76; Hamilton Papers, ii, 624.
29 Fourquevaux, Mission, 9–14.
30 Hosts were held in July, August and November 1547 and February, June, July, August and September 1548. For representative examples of men charged with being absent, see RSS, iii, nos. 2460, 2549, 2892, 2848, 2863, 2864; iv, no. 90; TA, ix, 205–06. Many more musters were to be held; in 1549 there were nine (TA, ix, 273, 293, 311–12, 318, 333, 341, 361); see also RPC, xiv, 7.
31 On 8 December 1548 she wrote to France for more plate, 'ayant faict foundre et convertyr la vostre au payement de la soulde des gents a cheval' [having had yours melted down and converted into the pay for the horsemen] (Balcarres Papers, ii, 29–30).
32 Evidence for the dearth is profuse, but see CSP Scot., i, no. 337; Stevenson, Selections, 36; Teulet, Relations, i, 188; Mary of Lorraine Corresp., 295. For Mary's illness, when she was nursed by lady Barbara, Arran's daughter, see TA, ix, 250–51, 254–55; the pest continued well into the summer (BL, MS Add. 15,937, fo. 8). Arran apparently had use for another copy of 'the buke of Wallace', perhaps to keep his spirits up (TA, ix, 225).
33 And with some considerable success: see Phillips, Anglo-Scots Wars, 239–49.
34 For a full account of the war at Dundee, see A. Maxwell, The History of Old Dundee, 97–133. He by no means consulted all the evidence; see CSP Scot., i, nos. 322, 329, 336; Mary of Lorraine Corresp., 274–77, 282–83; CSP Scot., i, no. 342; Teulet, Relations, i, 187; Beaugué, Histoire, 80–83; TA, ix, 237, 252–53, 264, 277; BN, MS fr. 20, 457, p. 159.
35 TA, ix, 261, 264, 266; Mary of Lorraine Corresp., 280; CSP Scot., i, no. 355. The French insisted he be executed, but Arran saved him (CSP Dom., Add., 1547–65, 390; TA ix, 15).
36 Fourquevaux, Mission, 29; Beaugué, Histoire, 85–93; TA ix, 264; Diurnal of Occurrents, 47 (where the date is given as 16 December but in 1549).
37 Diurnal of Occurrents, 47; Mary of Lorraine Corresp., 280, 283. The English were clearly upset by his escape (CSP Spain, ix, 345, 350). He made it home for the marriage of his son to Arran's daughter lady Barbara (TA, ix, 250, 262, 264, 269, 281); the newlyweds were given a French tutor to 'lerne and instruct thame' (TA, ix, 249, 291), but see Diurnal of Occurrents, 50.

Meanwhile a French force was stationed at Jedburgh throughout the winter, giving the English some concern and the loyal Scots much encouragement.[38] The Scots were given more than just encouragement, for it became an accepted part of French plans that they should be welded into a coherent permanent fighting force. In October Cassillis had been appointed Lieutenant-General of the Scottish army,[39] and under him there emerged a standing force of some 800 light horse who constantly harassed the English.[40] Another such force was also formed under the Master of Hume.[41] By mid-February 1549 either these Scots or the French under d'Essé captured Ferniehirst Tower.[42]

As the French dispensed honours and pensions,[43] the Scots rewarded those who had suffered for their loyalty.[44] Meanwhile, Arran's government set about raising money. Henry had been angered by Scottish reluctance to defray some of the costs of the war,[45] but by 1549 the Scots were making considerable efforts. Margaret Seton, countess of Eglinton, paid to John Hamilton 2000 marks (one mark was worth 6s. 8d.; thus the figure was £s667) on 14 September 1548 and it would appear that a Convention that month agreed to a tax for the war.[46] On 6 May 1549 the Council imposed a tax of £12,000 upon the burghs;[47] on 3 July a Convention ordered the raising of £35,000.[48] Taxation of the clergy was not neglected. For some time Henry had been attempting to gain from the Pope the power to raise funds in Scotland. In January 1549, Jean de Monluc, Bishop of Valence, was sent to Scotland to initiate construction of forts,[49] but there obviously had been some difficulty over the matter and de Termes was

---

38 Beaugué, *Histoire*, 99–114; Stevenson, *Selections*, 29, 48–51 (the dating should be 1548); *Mary of Lorraine Corresp.*, 288–91; *Hamilton Papers* ii, 629–30; *TA*, ix, 239, 281, 283, 285, 306; Fourquevaux, *Mission*, 21–26. Huntly joined the force, as a letter of d'Aumale of 21 February testifies (BN, MS fr. 20,457, p. 161) and a Scottish army mustered there at this time (*RSS*, iv, no. 155).

39 *RPC*, i, 98; Fourquevaux, *Mission*, 16, 28. See payment made to him for 'chevaux legers escossais' in 1550 (BN, MS fr. 3124, fo. 19).

40 They suffered considerably at certain times (Fourquevaux, *Mission*, 26) but were an obvious threat (*Hamilton Papers*, ii, 624–25).

41 BN, MS fr. 3124, fo. 19; MS fr. 18,153, fos. 17, 19; NLS, MS Adv. 29.2.5, fo. 71.

42 *RSS*, iv, 710n and no. 464; *TA*, ix, 389; *Mary of Lorraine Corresp.*, 289; *Diurnal of Occurrents*, 47; *Hamilton Papers*, ii, 624.

43 NLS, MS Adv. 29.2.5, fos. 68–69, 71, 123–25; NAS E34/14/15–19. Note Arran's incorporation into his heraldic arms of 'the collar that day that my Lord of Angus and Argyle ressavit the Ordoure' (*TA, ix,* 233).

44 *TA*, ix, 261, 330, 428, 440; NLS, MS Adv, 29.2.5, fo. 121.

45 *CSP Spain*, ix, 361.

46 *HMC* 10, 27; *TA*, ix, 241, 275, 277–78, 295; some were exempt (*RPC*, xiv, 7); those who had not paid were ordered to muster at Melrose in May to resist an English force (*TA*, ix, 311).

47 *RPC*, xiv, 7, 9. The Northern burghs were to pay for 'the garysoun luyand at Brouchtye' (*TA*, ix, 332).

48 *APS*, ii, 600; *RPC*, xiv, 8; *ADCP*, 573–75, 583, 586, 591–92, 597, 599.

49 *Nonces en France, 1546–51*, 289, 409; *Balcarres Papers* ii, 29. He had arrived by 2 February (BN, MS fr. 20,457, p. 155).

instructed to put the matter right.[50] By April 1549, the clergy agreed to raise £s30,000.[51]

All of these moves had a daunting impact upon the English. In sharp contrast to the lively and boastful activity of the previous winter, commanders were told 'for this thyme lie there as you were ded for the while'.[52] Somerset warned Luttrell, on 2 January 1549, not to trust any Scot; it was indicative of the position everywhere regarding the assured. Although some efforts were still made to protect them, there were very few left to befriend. Two incidents illustrate the situation.

On 17 October, Sir John Mason had a long interview with James Hamilton of Stenhouse, ex-Captain of Dunbar and father to the Captain of Edinburgh Castle just slain in the September riot. He had no reason to love the French, but refused to write to his kinsman Arran of the 'manifest ruyne and miserye' which they brought Scotland. Stenhouse was adamant that 'no fruyte at all cowlde coom thereof' and he would only be 'mocked and skorned'.[53] On the same day, Sir Thomas Smith drafted a letter to James V's natural son James Stewart making many similar points. No fruit came of that either. But Somerset was reconciled to the failure of the collaborators and was clearly determined to continue. The war was now in its third phase: the English would simply hold on until such time as 'any numbther of other inpedyments shal conspyre' to force the French to retire.

How did the monarchy with the more money counter-attack against an established system of interlocking and self-protecting forts? The first priority was to over-extend the adversary so as militarily and financially to exhaust him: pick off his extended and weak points, then isolate the important garrisons and reduce them by either siege or starvation. Central to this policy was the need for new forts which would protect one's own troops as well as constraining the enemy. It was to this aspect that d'Essé addressed himself during the autumn and winter of 1548–49.

From the start, it must be recognised that Haddington was a poor site for the principal English stronghold in Scotland. It could only be supplied by overland pack trains. Had Grey of Wilton's original suggestion of Dunbar been adopted, supply would have been easy by sea where the English still held superiority.[54] But Dunbar Castle was remarkably strong and recently modernised by Arran.[55] Grey and Palmer had thought to fortify so as to 'inrynge the castle, and some parte mate it'. That was simply not possible and although the English attacked frequently, they were

---

50 The King had already sent by Montluc 'les bulles de nostre saincte pere le pappe' to raise two clerical tenths 'pour employer au faict des fortiffications'. Baudouin-Matuszek, 'Expéditions françaises', 377, 380.

51 *RPC*, xiv, 7. The figure was £35,000 by 13 July (*Ibid.*, 10); £4000 more was granted in March 1550 (*RPC*, i, 83). Agreement had been sought as early as 22 January 1549 (*TA*, ix, 275).

52 *Mary of Lorraine Corresp.*, 282, 295, 300; *CSP Scot.*, i, no. 337; *Hamilton Papers*, ii, 627–32. Note, however, French concern that 'les Anglois ont delibere envoyer fere une bruslerie des ditz pais le plus avant qu'ils pourront' (Fourquevaux, *Mission*, 13).

53 BL, MS Calig. B. vii, fo. 443

54 See Fourquevaux, *Mission*, 17. French supplies to Scotland were often 'brusle par les angloys' (BN, MS fr. 20, 537, fo. 8).

55 I am grateful to Mr I. MacIvor for allowing me sight of his unpublished survey of the castle.

consistently beaten off.[56] From the start, the French recognised the importance of the place; it was handed over to Chapelle on 18 June 1548.[57] By 1 September they had determined to strengthen the castle, fortify the town and build a new Italianate bastion. Work continued throughout the autumn and winter.[58] It was an ideal location both to harass English supplies to Haddington and to give warning of English moves.[59] Keeping it, they won the war.

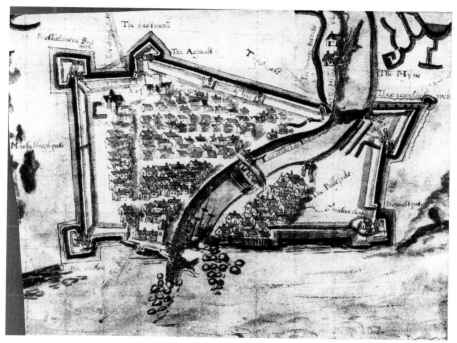

Fig. 13.5. Plan of Leith, 1560. That work was commenced by the French at Leith in 1548 is certain from both correspondence and financial records. But just when the port became a fully fortified town is not clear. To make such a large site secure by such massive bastions and thick walls takes years, as we know from the examples of Turin, Antwerp and Berwick-upon-Tweed. It also involves quite sizeable construction crews. But the broad outlines of the French fortification must have been staked out (literally with wooden stakes hammered into the ground) during our period. The walls were still viewable when Cromwell built his citadel next door to the port in 1652 and exist on a 1708 map in France. When urbanisation gobbled them up (as happened at Haddington), they became the basis of the principal streets in modern Leith: Constitution Street, Great Junction Street and Commercial Street (as happened in Vienna: the famous Ringstrasse).

56 *CSP Scot.*, i, nos. 86, 174–75, 241; Teulet, *Relations*, i, 188.
57 *TA*, ix, 445; *CPS Scot.*, i, nos. 147, 228, 257, 265. Note French payments of £1,370.12s.6d for victuals there (*TA*, ix, 21).
58 Teulet, *Relations*, i, 185, 188–89; *Hamilton Papers*, i, 623.
59 *CSP Scot.*, i, no. 332; *Balcarres Papers*, ii, 28, 50; *TA*, ix, 295, 446; *Mary of Lorraine Corresp.*, 295.

The French set to strengthening both Edinburgh and Stirling Castles. They also fortified Leith. As early as 20 June, d'Andelot had determined that the place had to be protected if only to create a secure citadel for French troops. During August much preliminary work was done and plans were drawn up by Pietro Strozzi.[60] By September the entire town was surrounded by a 'trench' and two bastions were well advanced: one on the sea side and one facing Edinburgh.[61] Much of the general outline of the fortification as it appeared in 1559–60 must have been laid out in 1548.[62] They also took over a small stronghold at the harbour of Milhaven, near Leith[63] and Blackness Castle further along the Forth.[64] Leith, however, was a defensive position and most French energy went into the fort 'appointet to be biggit at Innerest' (Inveresk), beside Musselburgh church. The decision was taken on 10 January 1549 and over 500 men laboured well into March.[65]

By the end of February, de Fourquevaux and de Visque were ready to return to report on the current situation, and they carried with them letters from d'Essé, d'Oysel, Mary of Guise, Arran, Argyll and Huntly. Although everyone pleaded for more money, more soldiers, more pioneers, more munitions and more victuals, they all breathed with confidence. D'Essé bragged of the forts he had begun at Dundee, Dunbar and Inveresk and called Leith 'une forte belle ville de guerre'. He also hoped by the capture of Ferniehirst 'tenir en garde seurete toute ceste frontiere'. Arran suggested a fort at Jedburgh and maintained that he had not lost hope of taking Lauder. He would have attacked Wark earlier, 'mais que la neige et tres maulvais temps nouz en garderent [snow and really bad weather prevented us]'. Argyll spelt out an ambitious scheme for an assault upon Ireland making use of his long boats and his connections in that country. If the King could supply 2500 trained mercenaries, he would raise a further 2500 Islesmen to descend on Carrickfergus and make for Dublin which was 'simple et vieille muraille [rudimentary and with just an old wall]'.[66] Huntly had an equally extravagant scheme to capture the Isle of Thanet at the mouth of the Thames. (Had he toured there whilst a prisoner in London?) The harbour was commodious and on the route to Scotland. It 'nourrist Londres de bledz [fed London

---

60 Teulet, *Relations*, i, 169; *CSP Scot.*, i, no. 158.
61 *TA*, ix, 217; Stevenson, *Selections*, 35; Teulet, *Relations*, i, 185. Edinburgh Castle was also strengthened (*CSP Scot.*, i, no. 265) at a cost of £4070 (*TA*, ix, 21).
62 See Plate 8.
63 *Maitland Misc.*, I, ii, 234–35.
64 It is not clear just when Blackness was garrisoned and captained by the French. (*Diurnal of Occurents*, 46). Considerable artillery and munitions were stored there by the autumn of 1548, but Mathew Hamilton of Milnburn was still Captain as late as March 1549 (*RSS*, iv, nos. 144, 147). Mary of Guise advised Henry on 25 February 1549 to appoint 'quelque sage et advise gentilhomme' (Fourquevaux, *Mission*, 19), which he did (Baudouin-Matuszek, 'Expéditions françaises', 379). *RPC*, i, 119.
65 *RPC*, xiv, 6–7; *Hamilton Papers*, ii, 623; *TA*, ix, 274–76, 281, 286, 292–95, 318; Fourquevaux, *Mission*, 26, 34.
66 It certainly was; see N. Burke, 'Dublin's North-Eastern City Wall', pp. 113–32.

with wheat]' and its possession could 'empecher ladite Riviere [blockade the Thames].'[67]

The major demand was for money. As de Fourquevaux trenchantly remarked, it would bind the Scots to Mary of Guise and 'ce faisant tout le Royaulme marchera arme a sa [Henry II's] faveur et la devotion desdits seigneurs sera tout plus encline au service et bien de Roy [this would make the entire kingdom march under arms for Henry's favour and the devotion of these noblemen would incline everyone towards the service of the king]'.[68] Mary recommended 'les trois chevaliers de lordre' (Arran, Argyll and Angus) but also Huntly (mentioned by everyone with approbation), Cassillis, George Douglas, Hume, Errol and Marischal. In addition there were a host of minor requests: d'Oysel wanted 'une petite abbay' for himself; Arran asked Henry 'envoyer deux enfants siens au college a Paris [send his two boys to college at Paris]'; Mary of Guise asked for provision to the abbey of Cambuskenneth for a son of Lord Erskine's.[69] Mary also asked for a hackney and mules as hers were being used for the wounded. She also specifically requested 'mineurs bien experimentez aux mines dor et dargent [miners experienced in searching for gold and silver]'. French miners were also extracting saltpetre (potassium nitrate, an essential component for black gunpowder).

The two envoys had returned to France by 30 March and their letters were quickly acted upon. Henry replied on 15 April that 'tout prendre une finale resolution suivant mon intention laquelle ne tend a aultre chose, que au bien, grandeur et repoz de vostre Royaume [everything will be put in hand for the final determination of this war, following my intention to concentrate on nothing else except the grandeur and contentment of your kingdom]'.[70] On 18 January 1549 the papal nuncio had reported the arrival at St Germain of Paul de la Barthe, sieur de Termes. De Termes was a major military commander, widely experienced, whose valour was praised by all, not least by Gargantua. By the end of February Wotton knew that he was to be sent to Scotland to replace d'Essé.[71] Preparations for further reinforcements to Scotland had

67 Fourquevaux, *Mission*, 23–35, 29, 33–34. Scottish optimism was reflected in Paris where plans were discussed for a siege of Berwick, 'the which is reckoned easy to win' (P.F. Tytler, *England under the Reigns of Edward VI and Mary* (1839), i, 157. An attack was planned for April, although not on Berwick (Teulet, *Relations*, i, 193).

68 Mary made the same point: Henry must give the Scots 'des penssions pour les attirer de plus en plus a luy faire service' (Fourquevaux, *Mission*, 18), a point made more plainly by two Scots in Teviotdale who stated that if she could find them 'sum lywing for ws in Scotland', they would 'rather or we lewit the lyf that we lewe in this contrie pas in ane uther realme to bege owr meit' (*Mary of Lorraine Corresp.*, 299).

69 Fourquevaux, *Mission*, 17, 35, 29, 20, 36. Erskine was quickly satisfied, as his letter of 30 March 1549 testifies (NAS, SP 2/4 fo. 321). See also *TA*, ix, 324; BN, MS fr. 20,457, p. 153.

70 *Maitland Misc.*, I. ii, 215–16; *Balcarres Papers*, ii, 33. See also *CSP Spain*, ix, 361; HMC 58, *Bath*, iv, 107.

71 *Nonces en France, 1546–51*, 285; P.F. Tytler, *England under the Reigns of Edward and Mary* (1839), i, 157. Wotton also reported that Jean de Monluc was to become President of the Scottish Council; such rumours were rife at the time, as Paniter informed Arran (Fourquevaux, *Mission*, 27; *TA*, ix, 302). See Angus's report at the end of the war.

progressed throughout the winter, particularly at Brest.[72] Henry had promised that the aid would sail by 20 April, but de Termes' draft instructions were not completed until 23 April.[73] Doubtless 'la Rigueur de temps' constrained the fleet until late May or so.[74] It arrived at Dumbarton on 23 June with 1143 foot soldiers, 320 cavalry, 300 pioneers and numerous clerks, treasurers, and surgeons.[75] Considerable supplies had already been sent 'par couste de normandye'.[76]

De Termes' instructions clearly mirror the information from de Fourquevaux in March. Highly detailed provisions were made for accurate musters, control of payments, good order in the army and the payment of debts accumulated by Arran, d'Oysel and the Queen. The Scottish light horse were to be regularly paid. Pensions were to be distributed: 10,000 francs for the Queen Dowager for the half year, 6,000 francs for Arran, 6,000 for Huntly and lesser sums for others.[77] John Hume of Coldenknowes received 500 écus from the Queen; so did Patrick Hume of Broomhouse. She also entered into a number of bonds of manrent with men such as George Meldrum of Fyvie and Sir William Scott of Kirkhope, Buccleuch's heir. Of particular importance was her bond with John Erskine of Dun on 30 September 1549, made the same day as he received 500 Crowns of the Sun and 'ane ruby greit and ane hart of diamond' as part-payment of a further 1000 crowns in return for which he handed over the castle of Montrose for her troops.[78]

But most importantly, de Termes was instructed to continue

en dilligence les fortz commencez et aussi en faire dautres tant en la frontiere de Tevidel, que en plusieures autres endroictz qui sont congneuz plus domageables a l'ennemy et de plus grant service et consequence au pays, affin que, venant ledit ennemy a marcher en pays il soit empesché de prendre pied en lieu d'importance.

[as diligently as possible the forts begun and also those made as much at the frontier of Teviotdale as many other places which are known to be the most damaging to the enemy and greatest service and consequence to the country in

---

72 BN, MS fr. 18,153, fo. 52; MS fr. 20,510, fos. 20, 23; MS fr. 20,532, fos. 9–10; *HMC* 58, *Bath*, iv, 107; *CSP Spain*, ix, 371.

73 *HMC* 26, *Hume*, 94–95; *Mary of Lorraine Corresp.*, 295–97; *ADCP*, 589–91; *Maitland Misc.*, I, ii, 215–17; *Maggs Sale Catalogue*, 64 (1937), no. 1000; Teulet, *Relations*, i, 192. The delay can also be seen in that Fourquevaux' commission as Captain of Hume Castle was not signed until 12 April. Hume had been formally handed over to the French on 15 March for a pension to lady Hume.

74 BN, MS fr. 20,457, pp. 169, 171; *CSP Spain*, ix, 387; *Balcarres Papers*, ii, 45; *TA*, ix, 291.

75 BN, MS fr. 18, 153, fos. 66v–72; *TA*, xi, 318, 320. They were conducted by Villegagnon (*Maitland Misc.*, I, ii, 220–22). It is not absolutely certain when de Termes arrived in June; Tytler (*History of Scotland*, vi, 49) gives the date of 23 June, but Rabelais (*Oeuvres de Rabelais*, ed. L. Moland (Paris, 1937) says that both d'Essé and de Termes shared in the glory of the attack on Inchkeith on 20 June. Beaugué also says that de Termes arrived before the attack (Beaugué, *Histoire*, 128).

76 Baudouin-Matuszek, 'Expéditions françaises', 378.

77 For the management of the army, see Baudouin-Matuszek, 'Expéditions françaises', 374–77.

78 NLS. MS Adv. 29.2.5, fos. 123–25; NAS, SP/13/65–66, 68; NAS, E/34/15/5.

order that should the enemy march into the country, he will be prevented by having to take an important location].

for which £20,000 was especially set aside.[79] As the surveyor already there was sick, Henry sent another. Dunbar, Hume and Blackness were all to be reinforced and the men and captains regularly paid.[80]

The aim of this 'coup de secours' was 'la seurtte et conservation' of Scotland. It was also prompted by news that the English prepared 'une plus grande entreprise'. Indeed it seemed that the English were going to carry out the new invasion about which the French and Scots had been concerned all winter.[81] In February 1549 the English had fortuitously gained Fast Castle, thus protecting Dunglass and the coastal route. Haddington was resupplied, as were all the forts, and plans were apparently discussed for the enlargement of Lauder.

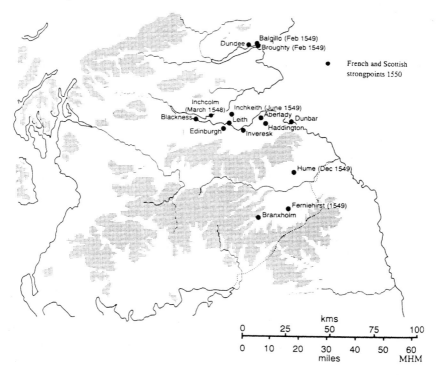

Fig. 13.6. This map shows the French garrisons at the height of the conflict, 1549-50, and many of them were either returned to the Scottish government or simply abandoned after the war was over. They had two functions within the context of the Rough Wooings: first to contain and then expel the English, and then to make Scotland secure against any future English invasion. Thus new strongholds were either built or rebuilt in 1557-58.

79 Baudouin-Matuszek, 'Expéditions Françaises', 375–76.
80 Baudouin-Matuszek, 'Expéditions françaises', 379.

THE LAST THROW OF SOMERSET'S DICE

On 1 May Grey of Wilton, obviously exhausted, was replaced by Henry Manners, the Duke of Rutland.[82] He moved a sizeable force to Stichill, near Hume, in June and forced the French to retire from Jedburgh, recaptured Ferniehirst Tower and devastated the land of loyal Scots.[83] Plans were also afoot for a major army (rather like Shrewsbury's in August 1548) to move up the coast in conjunction with the navy to relieve Haddington and to build yet another new fort, possibly at Aberlady or Musselburgh.[84] As early as March, Warwick was rumoured to be its commander and throughout the spring and early summer German and Italian mercenaries were recruited.[85] On 13 June, an English fleet landed some 600 mercenaries and English troops on Inchkeith in the Forth and began to construct a fort there.[86] Somerset boasted to van der Delft on 8 June that by so cutting off French supplies he would have them out of the country by Candlemas.[87]

One highly engaging aspect of Somerset's last push for victory concerns Berwickshire. The war was clearly nearing its concluding phase and the Protector was ever conscious of the need to get value for money expended. It would appear that he thus considered annexing Scotland's most south-eastern shire. This would enormously enlarge the buffer zone as 'the Bounds of Berwick' and thus protect that obviously and increasingly inadequate fortification. This could be accomplished if the Anglo-Scottish boundary was extended by one acquired county, a lasting fruit of war. The proposal, clearly rendered for Rutland when he had prepared for him 'plates' of all his command posts within Scotland after the loss of Haddington in September 1549, can be seen from his map collection which he retained after the war was over.

Since mediaeval Scottish shires were established, the county of Berwick had as its boundary line with the county of Haddington (East Lothian) the water flow known as the Dunglass Water. Here in September 1548, Shrewsbury's relief army had halted and re-edified the tower, trenched the hamlet and built on the hill that overlooked it a massive artillery battery. Sometime in 1549, plans were made massively to expand this site by the building of a remarkable new Italian fortification on the field just to the north of the Dunglass Water, on the seacliff edge. In Sir John Hale's assessment in 1982,

81 Baudouin-Matuszek, 'Expéditions françaises', 375; Fourquevaux, *Mission*, 13, 16–17, 23, 26; *Nonces en France, 1546–51*, 285.

82 *CSP Scot.*, i, no. 265; *Mary of Lorraine Corresp.*, 309; *APC*, ii, 265; *CSP Dom., Add., 1547–65*, 937–98; HMC 24, *Rutland*, i, 35–37.

83 *Hamilton Papers*, ii, 622, 628–29; Teulet, *Relations* i, 194; HMC 24, *Rutland*, i, 39–41; *Collection of State Papers . . . left by William Cecil Lord Burghley*, ed. S. Haynes (1740–59), i, 109; *Diurnal of Occurrents*, 48; Beaugué, *Histoire*, 117–23; BM, MS Calig. B. vii, fo. 382.

84 *CSP Spain*, ix, 393; *TA*, ix, 321, 325. See also PRO, SP 46/2, fos.

85 Warwick was not keen on the idea (*CSP Spain*, ix 345). For the gathering of troops, see *CSP For.*, 33; PRO, SP 46/2, fos. 30–33.

86 *TA*, ix, 319; *Diurnal of Occurrents*, 48; Beaugué, *Histoire*, 124–27; *CSP For.*, 42; BL, MS Titus B. v, fo. 33.

87 *CSP Spain*, ix, 393. The Protector was not alone in his optimism; a correspondent of Cardinal Pole's bragged on 4 June, 'it is no newes to England to have warre with bothe those nacions and not to lose' (PRO, SP 10/7, fo. 75v).

It represents a symmetrical angle-bastioned citadel encompassed by a square bastioned enceinte containing regularly arranged blocks of barracks or service buildings intersected by diagonal pathways leading from the citadel to the external bastions.

At the time, he considered such a sophisticated work 'the ideal fortified town plan of Italian inspiration and Imperial practice', incapable of being erected in Britain.[88]

The Protector's illusions did not last beyond Corpus Christi, 20 June 1549. The previous day d'Essé assembled a small fleet at Leith. Waved off by the Queen who reputedly made one of those great antique rhetorical speeches of which the French were so fond, it quickly made for Inchkeith where it caught the English garrison by surprise and in a sharp fight forced them to yield.[89] The seven captured English banners or ensigns were proudly displayed by d'Essé in Paris on his return the next month, an occasion remembered by Rabelais. Two days later, for the 'ease and proffeitt' which would result from 'the biging of ane fort upon Incheith', the Scottish Council resolved that all of the Fife and Forth coast ports should supply pioneers. Inchgarvie was also fortified. On the same day it was resolved to commence the building of a fort at Luffness (or Aberlady); by August work was well advanced.[90]

Although the Scots and French were now stronger, the main ingredient in their eventual success was to lie outside Scotland. As early as January, Arran had urged Henry that 'the warre may breake on that parte, wherby thei doubte to recover all'.[91] On his arrival in June, de Termes informed the Governor, 'C'est qu'il pleust au roy declarer la guerre a l' Angloys de ce cousté de deça [It pleases the King to declare war on the English on this side here]:

Le roy se comporte tellement avec leditz angloys quilz sont tous les Jours en guerre autre desorte quil ne se trouve Riens a mal faire sur eulx [The King will then so work on them that the English will find their days so full of war that they will not be able to do anything bad against the Scots].[92]

Henry had to leave his attack until very late in the campaigning season, for there was a delicate period during the summer when Paget negotiated with the Emperor to

88 Colvin, *King's Works*, iv, 401. Rutland's 'plate' for this enormous site had to be drawn on four sheets of normal paper which then were glued or pasted together. The adhesive then perished and the four sheets separated; I have found three of them. I am grateful to Dr. I. Whyte of the Department of Geography at Lancaster University for his redrawing of this 'plate'.

89 *Diurnal of Occurrents*, 48: Beaugué, *Histoire*, 127–40; Pitscottie, *Historie* ii, 110; *TA*, ix, 320, 323, 325–36. The English Council knew of the loss by 4 July (*CSP For.*, 42). D'Essé captured seven ensigns which he displayed at Paris in July 'with great glory and triumphe' (BL, MS Calig. E. iv, fo. 228v; *CSP Spain*, ix, 440).

90 *RSS*, iv, 717n; *Diurnal of Occurrents*, 48; HMC 24, *Rutland*, i, 42; *RPC*, xvi, 8; NLS, MS Adv. 29.2.5, fos. 40–41. Work continued at Inveresk during this time (*TA*, ix, 302, 311), and Inchgarvie, also in the Forth, was fortified (*RPC*, i, 90).

91 *Hamilton Papers*, ii, 623.

92 Baudouin-Matuszek, 'Expéditions françaises', 381.

have the Boulonnais included as part of the territory covered by the 1543 alliance which pledged Charles to aid England if attacked. His mission was unsuccessful.[93]

Somerset's great hopes for victory in Scotland began to collapse the day after his confident chat with van der Delft; on 9 June the western rebellion began. By 10 July, Grey of Wilton was sent west with over 1500 foreign mercenaries who otherwise would have found themselves in the North. Then on 11 July, word reached London of the rising at Norwich. For the moment the government kept its nerve and the next day issued Warwick's commission to invade Scotland. But on the very day of his departure, 3 August, news arrived in London of the débâcle at Norwich; early in the morning of 11 August Warwick received orders at Kenilworth to make for Cambridge and thence to Norfolk.[94] But on 8 August Odet de Selve informed Somerset that Henry II 'hath declared open warre agenst the kinges majestie'.[95] There were initial French successes. On 25 August, one of the key out forts near Ambleteuse fell after only four hours' bombardment. The town was quickly occupied and the next evening the garrison of 1200 in the new (1546) fortress capitulated. Blackness (the fort just up the coast at Cap Griz Nez) quickly fell. Henry II then made ready to assault Boulemberg: it was deserted. Boulogne was now closely besieged.

By high summer, the English position in Scotland, after the flush of activity in June, had also deteriorated. Luttrell's men were 'nakyd and barefote, neyther havinge fyar to keape them warme nor wherwithall to dresse ther meate'.[96] Along the Border, the plague was rampant and the foreign mercenaries now refused to serve in Scotland. By August the garrison of Haddington, that 'evell taken town', was debilitated by plague, death and desertion.[97] News in July of even more French reinforcements and the total collapse of the assurance system[98] must have distressed the stoutest heart.[99]

93   *CSP Spain*, ix, 369, 391–94, 405, 421; *CSP For.*, 36–45. See P. de Vaissière, *Charles de Marillac, ambassadeur et homme politique, 1510–1560*, 121–24; Jordan, *Edward VI.*, 301; R.B. Wernham, *Before the Armada*, 176–77; D.L. Potter, 'Diplomacy in the mid-sixteenth century: England and France, 1536–50' (unpublished Ph.D. dissertation, University of Cambridge, 1973), 194–203. See also S.R. Gammon, *Statesman and Schemer: William, First Lord Paget: Tudor Minister*, 154–56.

94   The juddering of Somerset's regime to its collapse is an oft-told story. For Phillips's account, see *Anglo-Scots Wars*, 250–55. I am indebted to Mrs M. Power who kindly allowed me sight of two relevant chapters in her work on the rebellions of 1549. See Jordan, *Edward VI*, 453–93. The French were naturally delighted to hear of 'ces emotions et seditions populaires' (BN, MS fr. 3099, pp. 30, 85, 88, 94).

95   BL, MS Add. 27, 457, fo. 28; *CSP For.*, 47; Jordan, *Edward VI: The Threshold of Power*, 116–19. Villegagnon, who had gone back to Scotland after transporting the Queen to France (Baudouin-Matuszek, 'Expéditions françaises', 381), was recalled as early as 23 June for the attack on Boulogne (Heulhard, *Villegagnon, Roi d'Amérique*, 45–46).

96   *Mary of Lorraine Corresp.*, 309–11.

97   *CSP Scot.*, i, no. 356; *CSP Dom., Add., 1547–65*, 399–401; HMC 24, *Rutland*, i, 43–44; *Harleian Miscellany* (*1808–13*), ix, 371–73; PRO, SP 46/2, fos. 40–41.

98   See Henrisoun's bitter complaints in August (*CSP Scot.*, i, no. 357; BL, MS Calig. B. vii, fos. 467–69v).

99   Wotton reported 4,000 on their way (BL, MS Calig. E. iv, fo. 224v). They were doubtless for Boulogne.

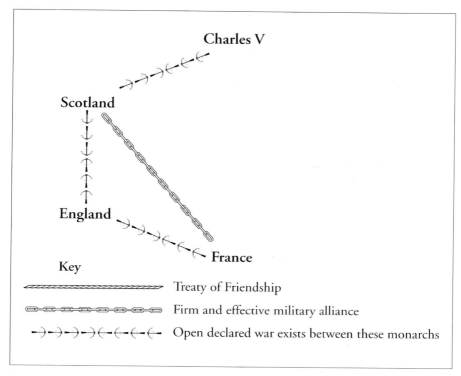

Fig. 13.7 9 August 1549. Henry II declared war against England and mounted a
massive attack upon the English positions at Boulogne. Most of the outer
fortifications fell, but the Boulogne garrison put up a splendid defence and
the city never fell to the French siege. The conjunction of this new war with
Ket's Rebellion and the Western Rising effectively terminated Somerset's
regency.

Haddington had been a worry for some time and as early as March members of the
Court were saying it could not be held. The war was rapidly becoming unpopular
and Bishop Hooper, John Hales, Paget and others lamented England's exposed
position.[100] Paget, apparently, had made his reservations plain enough on 17 April:

> We haue bene in warre with the Scottes these viij yeres, and yet contynewe still
> entendinge conquest of the realme . . . They haue good willes to kepe them
> selfes in libertie out of thraldome of England. They want not money, what their
> owne at home, what from frendes abroad.[101]

By 28 August, his renunciation of the Scottish adventure was complete. In 1545–46,
Francis I had argued 'he wolde rather lose his realme then leave them', and now

100 *CSP Spain*, ix, 345; *Original Letters*, i, 52; Strype, *Ecclesiastical Memorials*, ii, 383–85, 432; BL,
     MS Lansd. 238, fos. 292–304.
101 *Paget Letters*, 76. For Paget's role as 'Cassandra' to Somerset, see S.R. Gammon, *Statesman
     and Schemer: William, First Lord Paget: Tudor Minister*, 130–59.

'warre with Scotlande bringe warre with Fraunce'. It was in this frame of mind and at this time that Paget argued for the abandonment of Haddington, thus releasing troops which could be sent to Boulogne, as 'a wisdome and so reputed through the world' unless 'youe shalbe able to kepe yt all the wynter and by som practise in the meane tyme to falle to some agrement'.[102]

On 22 June, Sir Thomas Smith had informed Somerset that until October there was virtually no income with which to pay for the costs of the war.[103] The only immediate expedient, foreign borrowing, quickly appeared impractical. William Dansel, the English agent at Antwerp, reported to the Protector on 24 July that news of the rebellions 'doth wonderously discourage' the bankers; the interest rate proposed for a loan of £100,000 was a steep 13%.[104] Two days before the French declaration of war, Paget spelt out to Somerset the harsh realities of war economics:

> You have to maintayne contynally duringe the warres great nombers of men against Scotland, great garrison against fraunce both by land and sea and no small power thorough your Realme for the reducynge of the same to the kinges obedience. Al which can not be furnished without great sommes of money.[105]

Now that the war with France was open, Somerset had little resource but to evacuate Haddington. A relief force was gathered which on 19 September escorted the garrison back to Berwick and thence to Newcastle where many of the mercenaries took ship for Calais and Boulogne.[106] 'Youe do consider I am sure', Paget wrote Somerset on 28 August, 'how great a prince the French kinge is.' Indeed, Henry's attack on Boulogne had given the Scots the success they had sought for over a year, although Montmorency was surely being disingenuous when he wrote Mary of Guise the same day, 'cest entrepreise a este faicte plustost pour divertir plustost leurs dessaings d'Escosse que pour autres utilite [our attack on Boulogne has been carried out mostly to divert England's designs on Scotland]'.[107]

With the loss of Haddington, as Rutland recognised, the war was now a frontier one, and the new English Council which took over after Somerset's fall in October did reinforce the North. But on the East March soldiers were 'in suche miserie they do not onlie continually fall sick but also ronne way daily'; both weather and French troops made resupply most dangerous.[108] Along the West March, the situation was worse. Counter-attacks were contemplated, but none of the plans was practicable.[109] The initiative now lay firmly with the allies. The entry of de Termes and Arran into Haddington greatly heartened Mary of Guise, who wrote to the Rheingrave exulting

102 *Paget Letters*, 78.
103 PRO, SP 10/7/38.
104 *CSP For.*, 45, 47.
105 *Paget Letters*, 76–8.
106 *Harleian Miscellany* (1808–13), ix, 372–73; Teulet, *Relations*, i, 196; *Chronicle of Elis Gruffudd*, ed. M.B. Davies (Cairo, 1944–50), 73.
107 *Balcarres Papers*, ii, 55; *Maitland Misc.*, I, ii, 225.
108 HMC 24, *Rutland*, i, 50–51; APC, ii, 345–46 *et seq.*
109 J. Nicolson and R. Burns, *History and Antiquities of the Counties of Wetmorland and Cumberland* (1777), i, lxi–lxix; BL, MS Calig. B, vii, fo. 422.

that she could match his good news of Ambleteuse with 'notre de Haddington: Les ennemys ny ont laisse que la peste derriere eulx [the enemy have left nothing behind them but the plague]'.[110] With the major strongpoint in Scotland now theirs, the French quickly turned their attention to other areas.

Difficulties remained. Although regular accounts were now kept,[111] Mary continued to complain of finances 'sy mal mene' and of the atrocious management of the victuals. By November she was refusing to countersign de Termes' accounts.[112] French troops had become uncontrollable, pillaging the Scots and refusing to pay for their supplies. The disorders were 'ynseuprotable' to a people who had borne war for eight years, and many Scots, Mary declared, had been driven to suicide. Matters were such that she was forced to remain in the middle of the army, 'de peur que nos gens se teuase les otres [for fear our people are going to kill each other]'.[113]

Nonetheless the allies were on the offensive. In early November an attack was attempted upon the English frontier; only the flooding of the Tweed stopped the army.[114] Plans were discussed to besiege both Lauder and Dunglass. Fast was recaptured. By 29 November Mary was reporting the English prepared to negotiate peace with the Scots.[115] Such was the enthusiasm of the time that even Argyll's schemes were entertained. In December 'ane gentillman of Ireland' was at Stirling and 'le faict dirlande' became a serious proposition.[116] Monluc and de Fourquevaux were sent there in January 1550 to investigate the possibilities of a rising. Little came of the scheme (save Monluc's embarrassment with a chambermaid), but it worried the English government and a Scottish force temporarily captured a castle there.[117]

More positive results soon came. In early February 1550 a large Franco-Scottish force besieged Balgillo fort and the garrison was isolated from Broughty castle. The fort was quickly 'dung down with great ordnance' and then 'courageously and stoutly assailyeit'. Luttrell's men surrendered at midnight on 12 February, 'blyth in hart that thai escapit with their lives'.[118] On 24 March a Council at Edinburgh determined 'to

110 Pierpont Morgan Library, MS RE 1598. See also BN, MS Moreau 774, fo. 167; *Lettres et Memoires*, i, 244–46. The Rheingrave had left Scotland to raise troops in Denmark (*CSP Spain*, ix, 364, 369, 481).

111 NLS, MS Adv. 29.2.5, fo. 71; BN, MS fr. 153, fos. 66v–72, 91; MS fr. 3124, fos. 17–19v.

112 Teulet, *Relations*, i, 202, 209; *Balcarres Papers*, ii, 73, 79.

113 Evidence is profuse but see Teulet, *Relations*, i, 197–210; *RPC*, i, 105–06; Lord Herries, *Historical Memoirs of the Reign of Mary Queen of Scots and a Portion of the Reign of King James the Sixth*, ed. R. Pitcairn (Abbotsford Club, 1836), 25.

114 J. Nicolson and R. Burns, *History and Antiquities of the Counties of Westmorland and Cumberland* (1777), i, ixiv, ixviii, ixx; Teulet, *Relations*, 208.

115 Teulet, *Relations*, 212; *HMC 24, Rutland*, i, 46–48, 51; BN, MS fr. 20,457, p. 231.

116 *TA*, ix, 361; BL, MS Calig. B, vii, fo. 345; BN, MS fr. 20,457, p. 239.

117 Teulet, *Relations*, i, 214; *Calendar of State Papers, Ireland, 1509–1563*, ed. H.C. Hamilton (1860), nos. 92, 103, 106–07; Sir James Melville, *Memories of His Own Life, 1549–93*, ed. G. Scott (Bannatyne Club, 1829), 9–12; G. Dickinson, 'Instructions to the French Ambassador, 30 March 1550', *SHR*, xxvi (1947), 167; P.F. Tytler, *England under the Reigns of Edward VI and Mary* (1839), i, 269.

118 *Diurnal of Occurrents*, 49; Dalrymple, *Historie*, iii, 319; *Mary of Lorraine Corresp.*, 332n; *TA*, ix, 375. The English were clearly caught off balance by the sudden attack (*APC*, ii, 393). Mary wrote on 26 February of 'lassault et prisse des fortz pres dondy'; both Balgillo and Broughty must have fallen (BN, MS fr. 20,457, p. 237).

pas and saige Lauder': by 31 March the siege had begun and the captain quickly announced his decision to surrender. Apparently, Dunglass was also under attack. However on 6 April word arrived from France that the war was over.[119]

THE TREATY OF BOULOGNE

The abandonment of Haddington in September and the fall of Somerset the next month clearly meant that the war had entered its fourth phase. Positions were maintained in Scotland only to have something with which to bargain.[120] Serious peace feelers had been put out by the English to the French as early as November and by January they were wrangling over the arrangements for the conference. Genuine bargaining began on 18 February. As to Scotland, the English commissioners were given four negotiating positions, ranging from insisting that the Treaty of Greenwich be enforced to a surrender of their claim to the marriage. They hoped to comprehend the Scots in no more firm a manner than they had done in 1546. The French would only entertain complete comprehension of Scotland. English demands for the marriage were quickly dropped.[121]

The discussion came down to the eventual dispossession of the English forts in Scotland. Even in their earliest instructions the English negotiators were allowed to surrender Balgillo, Broughty, Lauder and Dunglass. But retention of Roxburgh and Eyemouth was to be obtained. The English position was obviously weakened by news of the loss of the Tay forts, and they must have known that Franco-Scottish attacks would be mounted on the others. The English negotiators thus could never be sure just what cards they held in their hand. Initially the French demanded the surrender of all the forts. By 6 March they agreed to a sliding-scale compromise which tried to meet the confused situation. If the English still held Lauder and Dunglass, then they could retain Roxburgh and Eyemouth; if they had lost the first two, however, then they had to demolish the last two. However, stipulation was made for a middle position. If the Scots agreed to demolish and never to refortify Lauder and Dunglass, then the English would agree to demolish Eyemouth and Roxburgh. Such was Scotland's comprehension in the Treaty of Boulogne of 24 March 1550.[122]

---

119 *Diurnal of Occurrents*, 50; *TA*, ix, 383; *APC*, ii, 406, 409–10.
120 Virtually all of the evidence for the negotiations is in manuscript form only, but my own research at the BL, BN, Archives Nationales and Ministère des Affaires Etrangères has been largely superseded by that of Dr M.L. Potter, 'Diplomacy in the mid-sixteenth century: England and France, 1536–50' (unpublished D.Phil. dissertation, University of Cambridge, 1973). His last chapter (pp. 211–71), based upon more extensive archival search, particularly at Villebon and in Italy, covers the subject much more comprehensively than I could. I have drawn on his study (especially pp. 255–66) for these two paragraphs. My own work on the topic contradicts his only in terms of emphasis.
121 Archives du Ministère des Affaires Etrangères, Corr. Politique, Angleterre, 8, fos. 99–104.
122 Archives du Ministère des Affaires Etrangères, Corr. Politique, Angleterre, 2, fos. 292–9Av; *Foedera*, xv, 212–15. The articles concerning Scotland (9–14) were to cause some controversy in 1559–60 and both governments were to look at them again regarding Eyemouth (*CSP Scot.*, i, nos. 436, 472, 487); note 'Extrait des deux articles faisant mencion des fortz descosse' contained in a volume of material for the period 1557–61 (BN, MS fr. 3155, fo. 45r–v). See also Ministère des Affaires Etrangères, Corr. Politique, Angleterre, 7, 247v–56. The Scottish copy of the treaty is NAS, SP 7/34.

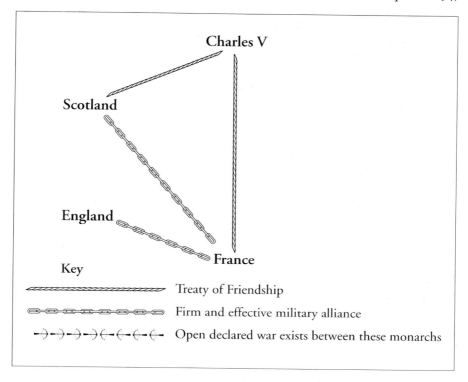

Fig. 13.8. Treaty of Boulogne, 24 March 1550; Treaty of Binns/Binche, 15 December
  1550; Treaty of Norham, 10 June 1551; Treaty of Northampton and Angers, 19
  July 1551. By the Boulogne pact, war ceased between the Kings of England and
  France; the Queen of Scots was 'comprehended' in this general pacification as
  the ally of Henry II. At Norham, Scotland and England resolved a series of
  outstanding problems over the frontier between the two. By the third treaty,
  England became an ally of France and Edward VI was betrothed to Henry II's
  eldest daughter, Elizabeth (Isabella) de Valois. Norham also resulted a year
  later in the Border commission which divided the Debatable Lands
  permanently. When Mary Tudor became Queen of England in July 1553, the
  alliance with France was voided and she recreated the Habsburg pact through
  her marriage to Prince Philip who thus became King of England.

It was a messy solution and the instructions of the French envoy sent to Scotland
on 30 March, François de Seguenville-Fumel, sieur de Thors, reflect this.[123] He
arrived in Scotland by 13 April and on 22 April his articles were debated at some
length by a large meeting of the Scottish Council. The Scots quickly ratified their

123 G. Dickinson, 'Instructions to the French Ambassador, 30 March 1550', *SHR*, xxvi (1947),
   154–67; *Balcarres Papers*, ii, 62. Another ambassador followed him on 25 April, but his
   instructions concerned the return of the French army (BN, MS fr. nou. acq. 23, 147, fos. 1–
   17; NAS, SP/13/69).

comprehension,[124] but the government was anxious about the dispositions of the forts and decided 'it is thocht expedient' that all four 'be all cassin doun'.[125] By the end of the month a herald went to Dunglass 'to resave the fort' and on 14 June Scottish forces arrived before it and Lauder 'with pikis, spadis and schulis to caste doun' the two. The artillery remaining in Dunglass was taken to Dunbar, that of Lauder to Hume.[126] The English, however, still kept Eyemouth and Roxburgh;[127] not until the Anglo-Scottish Treaty of Norham of 10 June 1551 were they finally surrendered and dismantled.[128]

The Treaty of Norham also resulted in the resolution of most of the Border disputes between the two countries; it had been largely negotiated by the French and was seen as an ending of all grounds for future Anglo-Scottish hostility.[129] The French were also to be forward in protecting their client's interests with the Emperor. Fumel's instructions advised the Scots 'de faire cesse telz molestes' of Low Countries shipping. At first they reluctantly agreed, but by 6 July new letters were issued for 'weire schippis of this realme' to attack those of 'Holand, Flussing, and uthiris and Lawlandis of Flandaris'.[130] The Scots wanted peace with Charles and even hoped he would protect Mary Queen of Scots against the English 'becaus he, of his Imperiall dewite, is oblist to defend pubillis'.[131] But they would not be bullied, and not until 15 December 1550 did they, again with considerable help and direction from the French, conclude the Treaty of Binche which restored normal relations with the Low Countries.[132]

124 Thomas Erskine was sent South on 24 April (TA, ix, 393–94, 397) and the ratification was formalised on 15 May (NAS, SP/6/49; cf BL, MS Calig. CSP Spain, x, 91, 98, 168). The gradual resumption of peaceful Anglo-Scottish relations – the ending of piracy, exchange of prisoners and resolution of outstanding grievances – is a complex topic and cannot be treated here, but see RPC, i, 87, 97, 102; CSP For., 58; ADCP, 601–03.

125 So Erskine was to inform the French after he finished in London (RPC, i, Journaux de Francois de Lorraine, duc de Guise, 1547–63, ed. Micharde et Poujolat (Paris, 1854), 8, 31).

126 TA, ix, 396, 421, 423–24; Diurnal of Occurrents, 50. The English agreed to Lauder's surrender on 14 April (APC, ii, 429).

127 Archives du Ministère des Affaires Etrangères, Corr. Politique, Angleterre, 2, 368v.

128 RPC, i, 99; APC, iii, 47, 97, 171, 222; CSP For., 48, 50; Foedera, xv, 265–66.

129 W.M. Mackenzie, 'The Debatable Land', SHR, xxx (1951), 109–25.

130 G. Dickinson, 'Instructions to the French Ambassador, 30 March 1550', SHR, xxvi (1947), 162–63; RPC, i, 87, 104.

131 RPC, i, 89–93.

132 The most accessible account of the negotiation is in Rooseboom, Scottish Staple, 69–71, appendix 59. See also Weiss, Granvelle, iii, 433–49; CSP Spain, x, 157, 167, 174, 193–94, 197–201.

CHAPTER FOURTEEN

The Wooings' Long Shadow:
'A generall rehersall of warres'

'DA PACEM DOMINE': GIVE PEACE O LORD[1]

After 'thys crewl weire of ix yeris', it was Scottish comprehension in the treaty with England that the Scots most desired and 'acceptis maist thankfully'. 'Blythe' to have peace at last, 'every man', in Lesley's words, 'addrest himself to policie and to big, plant and plenish what had been wastit, brint, spulyeit or destroyet'.[2] The reconstruction would take some time, particularly for burghs such as Dundee and Haddington.[3] Some of the religious houses and churches in the Tweed valley and along the Borders would never be rebuilt.[4] Many nobles and lairds took years to recover from the devastation of their land and Scotsmen of all ranks must have suffered members of their families killed, maimed and imprisoned.[5] In 1553, the government issued its first silver coinage since the reign of James V. The testoon and half testoon bore the simple and unique legend, 'DA PACEM DOMINE': Give peace o Lord. It was a heartfelt supplication.[6]

We have spoken here of war and the glory and the pity of war. What were the results and costs? It can easily be argued that nothing of consequence ensued. It did cost a great deal of money as well as killing a lot of people (mostly Scots) and it did leave a trail of material destruction in its wake. But its poetic resonance is extraordinarily muted. Lewis II perished at Mohacs: his slaughter (and the con-

---

1 J.K.R. Murray, 'The Scottish Coinage of 1553', *British Numismatic Journal* (xxxvii, 1968), 98–109.

2 *RPC*, 86; Dalrymple, *Historie*, ii, 243. The day the news arrived, 'fyvve Franche trumpettis . . . playit at his graces [Arran's] lugeing in the mornying' (*TA*, ix, 393).

3 The destruction caused by the war is a topic which cannot be treated here; Haddington and Dundee were only two of the burghs severely damaged (see A. Maxwell, *History of Old Dundee*, 114–31; *Charters, Writs and Public Documents of the Royal Burgh of Dundee*, ed. W. Hay (Dundee, 1880), 39; W.F. Grey and J.H. Jamieson, *A Short History of Haddington*, 22–25; P.H. Brown, *Scotland in the Time of Queen Mary*, 54).

4 The topic of church destruction remains controversial despite a flurry of recent serious work on it. Hay Fleming argues one view (*The Reformation in Scotland*), D. MacRoberts ('Material Destruction Caused by the Scottish Reformation' another, in his *Essays on the Scottish Reformation*, 415–62. But both have axes to grind.

5 Just how much noble and common Scotsmen suffered is particularly difficult to estimate. Throughout the 1550s, grants were made to those who had suffered especially (see *RPC*, i, 248; *The Exchequer Rolls of Scotland*, ed. J. Stewart and others (Edinburgh, 1878–1908), xviii, 123, 155, 173, 218–19, 227). *The Complaynt of Scotlande* is most eloquent about the ravages of the war.

6 P.F. Purvey, *Coins and Tokens of Scotland* 9, 60, but for the coins mentioned see also the more authoritative I.H. Stewart, *The Scottish Coinage*.

current annihilation of the Hungarian army) would have the Turks at the gates of Vienna in under three years and significantly contribute to the balkanisation of the Balkans and a series of self-feeding and destructive wars which would stretch down not just to 1918, but to 2000. Richard III's death at Bosworth led not just to the transient Tudors, but to one of Shakespeare's most enduring dramas. The romance of James IV's death at Flodden fuelled Scottish poetry deep into the nineteenth century and lies at the heart of the most haunting of all piper's laments, 'The Flowers of the Forest', by tradition performed only upon the death of a British monarch (although the Black Watch did play it for John F. Kennedy in 1963 in Washington). What, if anything, have the Rough Wooings left?

WINNERS

I have argued elsewhere that the Rough Wooings promoted the Reformation in Scotland, a perhaps far-fetched view. But they certainly helped 'make' John Knox. They gave him his first real opportunity to bear witness to his faith by his ministrations to the Castilians at St. Andrews, instead of being a mere schoolmaster to 'bairns'. Thereby, he found himself chained to an oar in a galley. Neither was the castle his Gethsemane nor the galley his Golgotha: both, however, were powerful moments in the Knoxian myth. Remember that he was released through international pressure early (1549) from the galley, became a Chaplain to a King and almost became a Bishop. Unlike others of his Protestant-exile colleagues in England, he was not burnt at the stake by Mary Tudor. But her accession sent him on his epoch-making travels to Geneva, his years in the Wilderness. Of all the characters in our story (monarchs apart), only Knox has had statues erected to him, even though the one that was in Parliament Square in Edinburgh resides today under cover in St. Giles and not outside where it belongs. Knox never lived in the John Knox House, but his association with it meant it was not demolished during Edinburgh High Street's great reconstruction in the nineteenth century.[7]

There were, of course, other 'winners'. One was James Hamilton, Duke of Châtelherault; another was Mary of Guise. Châtelherault never became King of Scotland, but the war cemented his being second person of the realm; it gave him an income vastly superior to those of his peers and, for twelve years at least, a remarkably lavish lifestyle. Arriviste politicians all did that then, witness Wolsey and Somerset, but Somerset enjoyed his similar building and enrichment mania for just over thirty months. And whereas Somerset would lose his head in 1552, Châtelherault merely lost his Governorship in 1554, but took full revenge in 1560. In the meantime, he basked in the profits of peace (from April 1550 to April 1554). On his retirement as Governor before Parliament on 12 April 1554, he was declared to be 'ane noble and mychtie prince' and honeyed tributes to his valour were made:

> Having fund and ressauit this our said soueranis realme and domynionis vnder cruell weris Regnand betuix the samyn and lieges thairof and the realme of

7 Mawbray House next door is actually older.

Ingland . . . The said noble prince not onlie expendit and debursit the [Crown's revenues and treasure] . . . Bot alswa hes expendit the haill proffittis males [rent-taxes] rentis and revennewis of his awin proper patrimony In the defence of this our souerane ladijs realme lieges and liberteis thairof And hes be his grit laubouris vihement expenssis and daylie danger of him self his kyn and freyndis Relevit our souveranis maist noble persoun fra the cruell enristfull persute of the king and counsell of Ingland And hes left free the haill realme and domynionis of oure said souerane ladie without ony part thairof withaldin be hir hienes auld Innemeis of Ingland.[8]

Arran-Châtelherault's wartime accomplishment had in truth been quite considerable.[9] He also skilfully implemented critical enhancements of the country's defence system, such as the further adaptations to house artillery at Edinburgh Castle, 1544–46, and the refortification of Dunbar in 1547.[10] Never once did he seriously consider surrender. When his political survival meant accepting coalitions with Cardinal Beaton and then with Mary of Guise, he wisely acquiesced. That saved not only his position, but also his country. Somerset was never possessed of such political nous and paid for it with his head, as he deserved to. Arran knew full well that by accepting Henry II's rescue in 1548, he was involved in a most dangerous gamble. But he considered it a risk worth taking and it worked, both in 1548–50 and, let us not forget, during 1559–60.

Of course, he sought to capitalise on his nearness to the Scottish throne and he became a Duke (a title rare in Scottish aristocratic society, normally awarded only to members of the royal family). That is what all aristocratic politicians of this period did, witness not just Edward IV, Richard III and Henry VII, but the Duke (in 1551) of Northumberland (Lady Jane Grey)[11] and the Dukes of Guise (Mary Queen of Scots to François de Valois). Charles V married his eldest son to the Queen of England (a failure) but his dynastic strategy would see that son attain the crown of Portugal in 1580.

Châtelherault never sold his country short to save his skin or enhance his position. But he could not have defeated Henry VIII and Somerset had he not been backed by the widest of political spectrums within the kingdom. Despite all the factional infighting which was (and is) the meat and bones of politics, he was backed. Scotsmen of all ranks did literally fight and die for their country's independence. They exhibited, as did Arran-Châtelherault, what can only be termed patriotism. In a remarkable letter written as the wars raged about him in 1544, George Lord Hume gently informed Mary of Guise that he was no more a Frenchman than she was Spanish:

8 *APS*, ii, 603–604.
9 Note Phillips' favourable assessments of Scottish warmaking and how Arran almost did win at Pinkie: *Anglo-Scots Wars*, 193–94, 199–200, 257–59.
10 A process dramatically continued by the French, it is true.
11 And note the marriage in 1560 of Somerset's eldest son Edward to Lady Catherine Grey, sister to Queen Jane.

lat ws nocht think to tyne [lose] sa noble ane realme to our ennymeis that our foirbearis hes sa lang kepit and defendit. Lat ws tak ane cumfortable curage heirin and put our haill confidence in God considerand it is in our defence and our ennymeis sa crewellie persecuting ws; for better it is to ws to de with honour than leif with perpetuall schame of all cristin regionis, and to our powaris we salbe trew Scottis men and never consent to the desyre of our ennymeis sa lang as we may be ony party [opponent] to thame or keip our self out of thair handis or leif in ony part of this realme.[12]

Another winner was Archibald Douglas, Earl of Angus. In November 1542, he was little more that a mere pensioner of a notoriously headstrong and unreliable king, little more than a political mercenary. He had been virtual ruler of Scotland during 1523–28 and brother-in-law to a reigning European monarch. In 1542, his career seemed dead. He had become a hireling. But as early as 1545, he was grandfather to a future 'king' of Scotland. Had he lived to 1566, he would have found himself great-grandfather to the only Prince of Scotland, the man who would unite the kingdoms.[13]

The saviour of the artillery train during the near-débâcle at Coldingham in the winter of 1544, the handsome victor of Ancrum Moor in February 1545, the only Scottish commander to emerge with any credit from Pinkie, and the agent of the war-winning engagement at Drumlanrig in February 1548, Angus survived the cauldron of the wars[14] restored to his patrimony, having augmented his family's income and having deliciously thumbed his nose at Henry VIII in public, something few did (Cardinal Pole excepted). As the battle of Ancrum Moor began, Angus was suitably nonchalant yet characteristically aristocratic. Seeing a heron flap its way across the field, he jested that he wished he had his goshawk on his wrist so as to make two meals in the victory. Afterwards, supposedly, he was reproached by Henry himself. Angus, typically, snorted:

> What! Is our brother-in-law offended because I am a good Scottish man, because I have revenged the defacing of the limbs of my ancestors at Melrose upon Ralph Evers? Little knows King Henry the shirts of Kirnstable [a peak near to his castle of Douglas]. I can keep myself there from all his English host.

His post-war retirement was pleasant indeed. Striding across the courtyard of his castle at Douglas in 1550, now into his sixties, he encountered a messenger from England with letters from his daughter Margaret. He clearly missed her, his exiled son-in-law and 'that young boy there' (Darnley) who were so far from him, 'which brekes my hart'. He passed over the news that:

> There is a great man to come forth of Fraunce this yere to take the rule and authority of the realme upoun him. Yt is suspect he will be strait to great men here and we will abhorree franche Lawes and thei be scharpe.[15]

12 *Mary of Lorraine Corresp.*, 79–80.
13 Of course, George I was the first King of Great Britain, but James VI was styled as King of Great Britain in Scotland from 1603.
14 See favourable assessments of his abilities as a military commander in Phillips, *Anglo-Scots Wars*, 169–70, 145–48, 170, 173, 193–98, 214–16.
15 BM, MS Calig. fo. 423.

Have patience, he counselled. 'The worlde ys very strange and I have sene mony chenges'. Sharp laws never troubled his final years, and indeed in the first proper full Scottish Parliament after the war (February 1552), both he and his brother had their previous treasons once again voided and they were pardoned for all their crimes against any Scotsman during 1528–42. As he lay, clearly on his deathbed, one of his folk said he was surprised Angus should expire not under a battle standard. The mighty Earl, so the tale goes, kissed a crucifix: 'Lo, here is the standard under which I shall die'. When he did so in 1557 at Tantallon, it was in the faith of the Douglases. A great career, then, and a good death.

His was, indeed, a remarkable life[16] but he was not the only exile eventually to flourish. Matthew Stewart may well have been outlawed from Scotland in 1544, but he married into the Tudor line. Eventually he returned home in 1564 and his son married the Queen of that kingdom. In 1570, he found himself in Arran's shoes as Regent to that kingdom.

Another winner, albeit short-term, was John Dudley, Viscount Lisle, who became Duke of Northumberland in 1551.[17] In 1538 he was the Deputy Governor of Calais. His tenure of that post may have left to posterity one of the richest collections of domestic (and national) correspondence since the Paston Letters, but it was hardly a rich political plum. War made his bones: Lord High Admiral in 1542, a participant in the Edinburgh raid of 1544, he then captured Boulogne that September. One of the key architects of the English victory at Pinkie, he washed clean the taint of his father's execution for treason in 1510. After Pinkie, he was given numerous rewards for his valiant action there. These continued after the war. The most notable was his being created Duke of Northumberland (along with which he was granted £40 p.a. from the customs of Newcastle-upon-Tyne). On 11 October 1551, the patent declared his elevation to be in grateful thanks not only for being Admiral under Henry VIII, but:

> Also at the Musselburgh fight, being captain general of the van and all the cavalry, repulsed with slaughter and shame the Scots who were threatening the realm's destruction, and moreover in the late detestable conflagration of intestine war, as the king's lieutenant in Norfolk he repressed the rebels so that popular madness which had pervaded the realm was extinguished.[18]

Dudley was a creature of fortune, but then were not they all? Thanks to Somerset's arrogance and incompetence, he rose as his erstwhile colleague fell. Once in power, he began a process of reform and recovery which Queen Mary Tudor would continue and from which Elizabeth would benefit. I for one no longer believe his Protestantism to have been a devious mask, but a genuine expression of his

---

16 Although his marriage to James IV's widow did help.

17 For his career see B.L. Beer, *Northumberland: The Political Career of John Dudley, Earl of Warwick and Duke of Northumberland* (Kent State, 1973) and his article 'Northumberland: the Myth of the Wicked Duke and the Historical John Dudley', *Albion* (xi, 1979), 1–14. For his role in the fall of Somerset, see *Northumberland*, 72–91.

18 *Calendar of Patent Rolls, Edward VI*, iv, 115. And see also 117–19.

religiosity. Echoes of the 1552 Prayer Book are with us today. By marrying his eldest son to Lady Jane Grey, he hoped to save his Reformation. Naturally, as well, he wished to bed his family into the royal race, something Hamilton had tried to do in Scotland and the Guises were doing with Mary Queen of Scots in France. By seeking to place Queen Jane on the throne, by force, he was doing nothing more than Edward IV had done, or Henry VII. Yes, he failed. Yes, he followed Somerset to the block. But all that lies outwith the Rough Wooings.

Who else 'won'? Henry II of France clearly did. So did Mary of Guise and her brother Francis, now Duke of Guise (their father Claude died in April 1550). And so did the seven-year-old Mary Queen of Scots. Their emergence on a European-wide stage of political vitality and importance is so obvious that it need not be further elaborated here, except to say this. The Rouen fête with which we began our story was a grandiloquent declaration of the stunningly successful start to the reign of 'Henri Second'. It breathed an imperial splendour that not even his father ever enjoyed. As the 1550s unfolded, Henry would do everything to capitalise on the rich opportunity Mary provided for his dynasty. Even in a document as mundane as a tax request, the King gloried in this accomplishment. Writing from St. Germain en Laye on 2 August 1550, the Secretary of the Council addressed collectors of aides and tailles for La Rochelle in glowing terms, telling how the king had reconquered everything 'usurped' by the English in Scotland:

> The which kingdom we esteem as our own as well on account of having taken it into our protection as on account of the marriage negotiated and agreed on by the estates of the said kingdom between our very dear and very beloved son the Dauphin and our very dear and very beloved daughter the young Queen of Scotland.[19]

By the time of their marriage, the royal vision stretched almost to the limits of dynastic aspiration. In his wedding anthem in April 1558 for Francis and Mary, Michel de l'Hospital rhapsodised about how all of Henry's 'gallant boys' would shortly establish dominion over Europe's empires: Gaul, Lombardy, Britannia. But it was Mary Queen of Scots who provided the essential keystone for this imperial archway. Through her would 'one house the world's vast empire share'.[20]

The war had many other legacies, but the most important one was the establishment of French power in Scotland. Even when hostilities ceased, the Scots still asked for 1000 French troops to garrison the forts of Dunbar, Blackness, Broughty and Inchkeith.[21] By December 1550, d'Oysel commanded 1100 men scattered about the

---

19 Maggs Brothers' Sale Catalogue 606 (1935), 43–44. I wish to record my appreciation of the kindness of Ms Polly Beauwin of Maggs Bros. for supplying me with a Xerox copy of this in 1999. Interestingly, the next document was a household account of 1552 for 'Monseigneur le dauphin, messieurs les ducs d'Orleans et d'Angouleme, la reine d'Ecosse et mesdames filles du roi'.

20 Merriman, 'Queen of France', 44

21 Scottish troops in Hume were to be paid by the French. Luffness, Inveresk, Inchgarvie, Balgillo and Montrose were all to be demolished (*RPC*, i, 90, 119).

country.[22] For the time, the Scots clearly wanted French protection. As Sir David Lindsay of the Mount put it:

Quhat cummer [trouble] haue ye had, in Scotland, Be our auld enemies of Ingland? Had nocht bene the support of France We had been brocht to great mischanse.[23]

In that sense, Scotland was a winner. It emerged from the Rough Wooings with its sovereignty intact and the English repulsed. Numerous factors extraneous to the country contributed. After Henry VIII's invasion of France in June 1544, Scotland simply did not exist as a serious item on his agenda, especially with his disastrous capture of Boulogne. The sustained intervention by Henry II of France was another stroke of good luck. Britain's geography was important. So, as ever, was the weather. But the Scots were never supine, as Somerset found when he mounted the most sustained and intelligent attempt to gain the country since that of Edward I and before Oliver Cromwell. The political nation (and at Pinkie that amounted to almost every able-bodied man in the country) resisted handsomely. They could be, and were, mustered: over 25,000 of them. Unlike the English army, largely mercenary and composed of a considerable number of foreigners, a Scottish host really was the 'nation in arms'. The gathering at one place of such a large number of men says a great deal. Scotland's population in 1547 could not have been much more than 750,000, half of whom were women and half of whom were under the age of sixteen. For such a host to stand at the River Esk, each one of them privately armed (and many with their own tents) and having brought with them their own food, is a real statement about national consciousness. Many came with Argyll from almost the other end of the kingdom (Aberdeen to Edinburgh is 125 miles and that is with ferries across both the Tay and the Forth: much longer if you go via Perth and Stirling, as most did). Moreover, Arran and Angus between them still could and did win significant minor victories: Ancrum Moor in February 1545 and Drumlanrig in February 1548. Note also the military careers of Huntly, Argyll, Hume, Methven and even Cassillis. That list could be tripled.

How else did Scotland benefit? Two aspects are particularly striking: one experiential, the other material. Scots and the Scottish government found their country on almost a permanent war footing for six years out of the eight between the summer of 1542 and the spring of 1550. Semi-permanent Border patrols were created, mercenaries ('wageouris' as the language felicitously named them) were hired, armed and trained. Permanent garrisons were placed in strongholds, many of these men well trained in the exercise of artillery. The catastrophic losses of ordnance pieces at Flodden had been made good by 1542, and those at Pinkie were quickly replaced by French imports and domestic fabrication at Scotland's major industrial plant, the foundry in Edinburgh Castle. The navy and Scotland's merchant marine were marginally enhanced. Although royal ships were lost to the English, privateers

---

22 BN, MS fr. 18,153, fos. 170–71; MS fr. 4552, fos. 31, 48r-v, 50r-v; MS, fr. 3140, fos. 76–77.
23 *The Collected Works of Sir David Lindsay*, ed. J. Small (Early English Text Society, 1865–71), lines 4560–64. Lindsay also drew certain inspiration from the war, as his *Tragedie of the Cardinall* (1547?) testifies.

expanded considerably, as Dutch fishing fleets venturing into the North Sea found to their cost. Scottish pirates would remain a menace down to the 1580s. Scottish armed bands found employment on the Continent in 1552, 1558–59 and in Sweden later in the century.

True, the emergence of a properly trained Scottish military competence would have to wait until the outbreak, first of Swedish involvement in the Thirty Years' War, and then the Bishops' Wars with Charles I in 1638–40. It also has to be admitted that the rebel army raised by the Lords of the Congregation in 1559 had very mixed fortunes. Moreover, such was its lack of military clout that the government of James VI had to bring in an Elizabethan task force to reduce Edinburgh Castle in 1573, just as Arran had to do with a similar French expedition in 1547 to regain St. Andrews Castle. But Scots could now fight better than they did before, as Gervase Phillips argues so persuasively in his recent study.

A most illustrative example can be found in the staid pages of *The Register of the Privy Council of Scotland* two years after the Rough Wooings. In 1552, Henry II finally went to war with Charles V, a conflict dominated by the great siege of Metz. In this return to the ways of his father, Henry called upon all of his allies to help, not least Scotland. In November 1552, the King requested that 'ane certane number of fitmen be resit and upliffit of this realme, to be send in France for the support of the maist Christeinet Kyng'. The organisation of this expeditionary force (even Highlanders were to be sent) became quite a sophisticated piece of bureaucratic business, and even though it never got to France (the war ended in 1553), the three hundred from the burghs ('all thai to be hagbutteris, weill furnist with pulder flask, morsing horne, and all uthair geir') and the methods for tax collection demonstrated how much had been learned during the years 1544–50.[24] Come the 1557–58 fighting between Henry II and Philip II, Scots would arrive and serve valiantly in the fields of Flanders.

The reason Edinburgh Castle proved so formidable during 1571–73 lay in the good work accomplished by the French during their time in Scotland. Edinburgh, Stirling and Dunbar were all dramatically strengthened, especially during 1548. Shortly afterwards, Inchkeith received a jewel of a *trace italienne* fort which proved entirely too hard a nut for Winter's fleet to crack in the winter of 1559–60. Eyemouth was rebuilt in 1557–58 to counter Berwick-upon-Tweed, and whilst Mary Tudor's fleet swept far to the North, English armies during the 'Calais War' of 1557–59 never ventured beyond Eyemouth. During the 1550s, another modern place of strength was erected at Langholm on the previously unfortified (Hermitage excepted)[25] West Marches. None of this would have happened had it not been for the Rough Wooings.

Such was the official 'maist humyl thankis' for Henry's purchase of 'our unestimable wele' that on 23 April 1550 Arran and all the Council proclaimed to Henry II how much they looked forward to the marriage of Mary and Francis, so that one day

---

24 *RPC*, I, 129, 132, 136–37.
25 I still think the great V-shaped bastion built to the west of it was most likely erected during this period.

his Hienes to be callit the gudschir [Grandfather] of ane of the maist victorious princes in the warld and kyng to ryng lang prosperouslie abufe baith the realmes.[26]

Within eight years Scottish coins would celebrate the marriage with a biblical text: JAM NON SUNT DUO SED UNA CARO: They are no more twain, but one flesh (Matthew, xix, 6).[27]

LOSERS

The most immediate loser was Edward Seymour. How the world had changed since his glorious return to London in September 1547: his political career was wrecked, in no small part due to his Scottish adventure, and in time he would lose his head.

It is easy sometimes to forget just how central war making can be to politics and political careers. Had Alexander the Great merely stuck to city planning or Alcibiades stayed friends with Socrates or Scipio simply ranted in the Senate, or Hannibal just trained elephants, none of them would have been so vividly alive to readers in the sixteenth century. What worked for Early Modern History also worked in Modern History. How would Napoleon become Emperor had it not been for Marengo? Or Wellington become Prime Minister had it not been for Waterloo? George Washington without Yorktown? Who ever would have thought that Hyram Ulysses Grant or Dwight Eisenhower would become Presidents of the United States?[28] Both did so through supreme military commands crowned with victories at Appomattox and Lüneburg Heath.[29] Somerset was just that sort of politician and his rise to near kingly power was firmly based on military success, just as his fall was in no small measure due to the failure of his Scottish war. What would have happened to Margaret Thatcher had the Argentineans primed their bombs correctly or sunk either of the British carriers during the Falklands War? As with so many politicians, he both 'lived by the sword and died by the sword'.[30]

What lessons might he have learned from the experience of the previous seven years? The clearest one must have been that war is a vastly expensive business and that when it came to fighting 'how great a prince' as the French king, England would probably lose. It was true that Henry VIII had been able to defeat Francis I in 1544–46, but the victory was to insure French hostility when England invaded Scotland. Even against Scotland, England could not rely on its relatively superior finances to win, for the Scots could simply retreat and wait for the English to weary of the cost and duration of their efforts. On top of this, there is Scotland's geography. Edinburgh is 405 miles from London. Kirnstable and its sisters make Douglas (even today) a very difficult place to go to. The self-same Highlands which gave

---

26 *RPC*, i, 88.

27 An alternative legend was 'FECIT UTRAQUE UNUM': He has made them one; see P.F. Purvey, *Coins and Tokens of Scotland*, 62, 66.

28 Grant was 40 in 1862; Eisenhower in 1930. John Kennedy was 45 when elected President.

29 Montgomery took the German surrender at Luneburg on 4 May 1945; Eisenhower at Reims shortly thereafter. Indeed, Appomattox did not actually end the American War Between the States. As ever, one can 'bandy with the dates'.

30 The quote comes from James Callaghan speaking of Mrs Thatcher's downfall in 1991.

Bruce security still existed for Mary Queen of Scots, hence those idyllic three weeks on Lake of Menteith in September 1547.

Perhaps the clearest lesson which could have been learned from this episode, and one which William Cecil seems to have appreciated, was that Anglo-Scottish union could not be forced. As John Hales reflected during his time as a member of Somerset's circle, making 'Scotland a parcel of this kingdom' could never come about except through force 'as long as the world doth stand'.[31] Force clearly failed. Only by an 'amytie' between the two regimes, an Anglo-Scottish coalition, could England hope to influence the Northern Kingdom. Such a neo-alliance did gradually emerge and when English soldiers once again found themselves on Scottish soil (1560, 1570, 1571, 1573), they came at the invitation of Scottish politicians and governments, not as conquerors.[32]

SCOTLAND

The wars visited upon Scots and their country many miseries. Some were not dire. When Alexander, 4th Earl of Glencairn disembarked at Dieppe in the autumn of 1550, he immediately sought out John Mason, the English ambassador, to 'complain bitterly' about the treatment of his two sons. They had been laid at the start of our story as hostages for the good behaviour of their grandfather, William, who had died in 1548. For the previous two years, they had been lodged with 'the Archbishop' (presumably Cranmer). Glencairn protested that his lads were kept solely to work in the kitchen 'without increase of their learning or virtue'.[33] He wanted it seen to, now that peace existed. Most of the war's incidents were not so funny.

It must never be forgotten that parts of Scotland suffered most grievously from this, its most protracted war since the fourteenth century, in particular, the East Marches, the Church and certain burghs. Everywhere along the Anglo-Scottish Border, of course, suffered from property losses and the burnings of residences, whatever form they took. Dumfries, which was under direct attack for only a brief period of time, still took something of a battering. Kirkcudbright suffered much less, in no small part due to the robust defence the townsmen made in 1547. Langholm Tower was battered down and up. But many of the towers survived quite well, such as Castlemilk. In part, this was because the English captured them and kept them for periods of time, like Lochwood. Threave, Caerlaverock and Lochmaben likewise do not appear to have suffered grievously. Hermitage was hardly touched, even though the English held it in 1549. Drumlanrig was as formidable in 1550 as it had been in 1542, in no small measure thanks to its remarkable defence in February 1548, not only by its proprietor Sir James Douglas but also by the remarkable campaign by Angus in its salvation. Raiding parties did penetrate as deeply North as Lamington, but their effects were largely superficial. In 1563, William Cecil commissioned a remarkable survey of the strengths of the Scottish West Marches. This lavishly illustrated report described a redoubtable clutch of hardy and well-maintained strongholds.

31 BL, MS Lansdowne 238, fos. 292–304.
32 James was also to proclaim, 'FACIAM BOS IN GENTEM UNAM': I WILL MAKE THEM ONE NATION; see P.F. Purvey, *Coins and tokens of Scotland*, 7, 70–71.
33 *CSP For.*, 58 (no. 247).

In the East, however, the story was wholly different, for here was Scotland's most devastated cockpit of war.[34] The devastation was the work of warmen, but there were so many of them and in such various forms during 1542–50. The Merse and Teviotdale were hammered firstly by a series of massive main field armies: Norfolk's incursion of November 1542, Hertford's army returning home from Edinburgh in May 1544, the September 1545 assault from Kelso eastwards, the march northwards by Somerset along what may be deemed the A1[35] to Pinkie and then that army's retirement over Soutra to Hume and Roxburgh after its rest at Leith, Grey's first attempt to take Haddington in February 1548 and its return in April, Shrewsbury's relief force to Haddington in August-September 1548, and lastly Rutland's September 1549 march to uplift the garrison at Haddington.

But there came also a series of what might be called not so much armies, as mega raiding parties. The battle of Ancrum Moor is rightly celebrated as a famous Scottish victory. But before Sir Ralph Evers and Sir Brian Layton were brought to a clash of arms by Angus and Arran at that field, their force was really quite large: 1500 Borderers, 700 assured Scots (including 300 Highlanders) and 3000 'strangers', mostly Spanish: over five thousand men. This was no ordinary raiding party, but a mini army on the march, and it ravaged its way as far north as Melrose on which it wreaked much violence before beginning to retire when it was brought to its decisive defeat, with both Evers and Layton slain along with 800 others. Over a thousand were taken prisoner.[36] Destroyed themselves, they had already harried, burned and slain before being brought to their ends. Battle groups of such magnitude were rare (especially in winter), but other examples could be cited.

The normal-sized parties operated from their Border boundary starting points: out at night, back for the morning, on a regular basis.[37] But such England-based instruments of warfare could only operate northwards, into Scotland. In addition to this limitation, the parties were tethered to England: they had to get back home to enjoy security. The Merse and Teviotdale thus became something of a wasteland, but beyond them men were relatively secure, except for the armies mentioned above, and they were rare and short-lived phenomena. The *Complaynt of Scotland* contains an eloquent passage in which the poor 'laberaris of the grond' describe how the war affected them:

> [We] could nocht resist the Inglish men; for ve that hed our vyuis and barnis, our cattel and corne, and our gudis in the bounds [who refused to assure] mony vs hareyt furtht of house and herberye, quhilk is occasion that mony of vs ar beggand our meit althrourt the cuntre.[38]

34 Few other triangles of territory in Europe are so pockmarked with crossed-swords, with the very substantial exception of what may be termed the wider Benelux pocket: Waterloo (1815) to the Battle of the Bulge (1944). Northeastern Virginia suffered similarly during the American Civil War (1861–65). Northern Italy is another good example.
35 Actually, his troops deviated from that route at various points, but not that much.
36 Alternative spellings: Eure and Larton. Bindoff, *History of Parliament*, gives both for Sir Ralph.
37 R. Robson, *The English Highland Clans: Tudor Responses to a Medieval Problem* (Edinburgh, 1989), 78–110, 179–93.
38 Murray, *Complaynt of Scotlande*, 135.

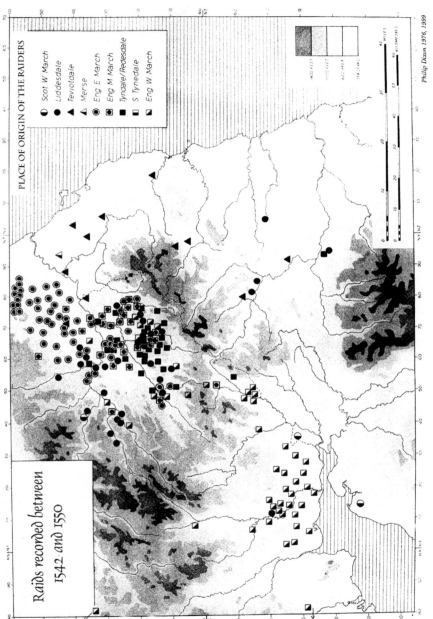

Fig. 14.1. The destruction in the Borders for the period 1542-50, in a map from Philip Dixon's PhD thesis, shows how intensive such primitive warfare still could be. It looks almost like a photograph of any of the European cities subjected to saturation bombing in World War II. Certainly Dundee was levelled almost as comprehensively as Dresden.

This situation was of course radically altered in 1547–48 by Somerset's expanding web of fortress-based permanent garrisons. From Lauder, Hume and Roxburgh the troops could deploy in any direction: 360-degree devastation if you will. It did cause great disruption as can be seen by Maitland's case:

> Albeit the Englisch did possess Hadington and Lauder qwhair besydis al his leving and landis ly except a littil in the Mers in tua myls and les to Ingland, and thairfoir did leiue al that tyme with verye great difficulties having a wyffe, manie children, and a great familie.[39]

However, even here two considerations must be borne in mind. One is that the garrisons depended on the agrarian produce and livestock resources of the countryside in which they found themselves planted. Moreover, there emerged (particularly when the English were masters of what they surveyed) archipelagos of no-go zones: the lands of Scots who had assured. Surrounding Roxburgh, for example, were over forty-seven 'townes and persones' in East and West Teviotdale exempt from attack because they 'have promest for there payments to bring and cary Graine Victuelles Beives and Muttons' to the fort. A further thirty-six were similarly exempt from harassment 'bicawse they be not able' to pay what were in effect their local taxes.[40]

Indeed when the assuring system was working most effectively, the fortress captains paid compensation when supplies were plundered from Scots whose names were 'inscribed in the book' as, effectively, subjects of the King of England. Whilst there is no doubt that the garrison policy brought the war to the doorsteps of Edinburgh and Perth and enormously expanded the practical effects of having soldiers in the field every day in any year, the impact was mixed in terms of physical destruction and loss of possessions.

Edinburgh was mauled in May 1544, but not much thereafter. Haddington was hammered. Indeed more damage was done to it by the French than by the English, who may have left it a wreck, but not materially levelled. When the English abandoned Haddington, St Mary's Kirk was left roofless and remained so for centuries. Dundee on the other hand was virtually 'Dresden-ed' with not only its clock stolen, but virtually all its public buildings (in particular the Kirk) and private tenements roofless shells. For the moment, it would be exempt from military services and from taxation (and rightly so). A particularly poignant story concerns Robert Wedderburn, the author of *The Complaynt of Scotland*: his house would take years to rebuild. Another bookman to suffer was Henry Scrimgeour. When he returned to his native Dundee in February 1547 armed with a letter from Henry II's Secretary Bochetel, Mary of Guise was asked especially to keep an eye on his house there, something she was utterly unable to do after September 1547. Indeed he held the benefice of the chapel there and the rectory of Glassary. Neither provided him (or his

---

39 *Maitland's Narrative of the Principal Acts of the Regency, During the Minority; and Other Papers Relating to the History of Mary, Queen of Scotland*, ed. W.S. Fitch (Ipswich, 1842), fo. 1.
40 Rutland Ms (Belvoir Castle), Misc. Papers.

Fig. 14.2. St Mary's, Haddington, after re-roofing in 1978.

mother) with any income, given the war.[41] So much for being a renowned European lecturer and teacher of the sons of the great.

Who else lost? Perhaps the most significant was the Scottish Catholic Church. It is debatable just how grievous a loss was David Beaton's assassination in 1546. He was actually getting on in years then and was deeply unpopular. But he was a man of powerful energy when roused and might have wrought a Scottish Counter Reformation. However, one should never forget that his successor, John Hamilton, was a powerful reformer in his own right (witness not just his formidable reconstruction of St. Andrews Castle and his new college, but also his three Church Councils of 1549, 1552 and 1558). That he failed should not blind us to just how popular the Catholic Church remained in the 1550s and how deeply tainted Protestantism was by its association with the English during the 1540s.

The Rough Wooings were a grievous assault on the resources of the Church. Much of its land (how much we simply cannot quantify with precision) was mortgaged, if not sold (the process known as alienation) by the taxation demands of Scotland's resistance. Moreover, many of its physical workplaces were ruined by English destruction, theft and iconoclasm. Many of its rockface workforce fled, never to return. Some indeed perished in battle. The kirks, chapels and religious houses of

41 John Durkan, 'Henry Scrimgeour, Renaissance Bookman', *Edinburgh Bibliographical Society Transactions* (v, 1971–87), 4–5, 10.

the Merse and Teviotdale never recovered until well after the Reformation, if then.[42]

There was also a quite long criminal/judical tail stretching from the war into the 1550s. Well into the regency of Mary of Guise (April 1554), men and women were being prosecuted for crimes they committed (or were alleged to have committed) during the Rough Wooings. Many of these offences (theft, murder, fire-raising, heresy) happened all the time, in war and peace. But the wars clearly were a time when justice in general broke down all over large parts of the kingdom, as anyone can see from the most casual inspection of Pitcairn's *Criminal Trials*, or the manuscript records of the judicial courts, or from pardons issued under the Secret Seal. Other crimes were sharply war-specific and can be broken down into four sorts: the treason of assurance taken with the English; complicity in the murder of Beaton; raiding at the behest of the English (very much a Highland and Isles offence); and remaining away from properly assembled military hosts. A fifth, rather wider, category also emerges from the records: coming in armed rebellion (usually with a banner unfurled) against the authority of the Governor. But this could be simply a symptom of the normal political process, and Arran often used it to attack people who had opposed his father in 1527 at Linlithgow.

To take the case of assuring, sixty Scots found themselves suffering loss of their possessions or being put to the horn (outlawed) during the period 1550–54 for this crime. On 31 October 1552, Margaret Jelly of Lauder lost all of her father's lands in the burgh which should have passed to her on his death (they went to their neighbour). During the war, Margaret had obviously become overly familiar with the English garrison: 'thair accumpanyng with thame'. When the troops marched back to England, she went with them 'and thare yit remandand amangis the saidis auld inimeis be the space of thre yeris'.[43]

The government normally pardoned most crimes, but these pardons were seldom free: a composition (in effect, a fine) was necessary for the exemption to be issued. During 1550–55, 547 such pardons were issued. That 326 of these occurred in the last year of Châtelherault's Governorship (and only five in 1555) is just one indication of how partial 'justice' could be.[44] These fines could be severe. Years after the event, one commentator remarked how Patrick Lord Grey's treasonable assurance at Broughty had cost him (and his family) over £Sc1000 and thus 'permanently' impoverished the

---

42 Reference should be had first to Sanderson, *Cardinal of Scotland*, whose appendix 3 (pp. 270–84) treats of the spread of reformers in the 1540s. See her even more felicitous *Ayrshire and the Reformation: People and Change, 1490–1600* (East Linton, 1997) and Frank Bardgett's *Scotland Reformed: The Reformation in Angus and the Mearns* (Edinburgh, 1989). The Durham dissertation of Dr. Susan M. Keeling, 'The Church and religion in the Anglo-Scottish border counties, 1534–72' (PhD, Durham, 1975) is a goldmine on how much religious life was disrupted by the wars.

43 *RSS*, iv, 1735.

44 Certainly at the time the comment was made (amongst others by Mathias Strick, back in Scotland for the Emperor) that it was the wealth of the accused, not his guilt, which determined the sentence. Justice ayres, it should be noted, were often highly intimidatory. Lennox's secretary, Thomas Bishop, wrote Wharton in November 1552 that Châtelherault arrived for an ayre at Jedburgh 'with the number of fower thousande horsemen' and he had with him 'fower faulcones, field peeces' (Stevenson, *Selections*, 57)

family. Moreover, Acts were passed allowing 'faithful' Scots to raise legal actions against 'assured' Scots who had harmed them during the wars.[45] The most notorious case was that of Sir Walter Scott of Buccleuch and Branxholme against most of his neighbours: the Kerrs of Cessford and Ferniehirst, Brunstane, Ormiston, Traboun, Colston and Longniddry.[46] So acrimonious did the court case in Edinburgh become that Kerrs finally murdered Scott in the very streets of the capital in 1552.

This is a rich and vital topic on which more research is necessary. Assurance clearly occurred mostly where the war actually happened: along the Borders. Out of a national total of 955 found guilty of this crime, only fifteen came from Perthshire, and thirty-three from the North-East. On the other hand, for the Lothians and Berwickshire, 229 assured Scots can be placed. In the records 171 appear from the South-West. But these figures need to be treated critically. Many of the grants tacked on numbers: 'and 57 utheris'. Can this be taken as accurate? Some were tried locally and thus do not appear in national records, as in the case of 192 Dundee residents indicted in the Tolbooth before the Earl of Argyll on 8 March 1553.[47] There is also one pardon (that for everyone in Dumfries) which does not appear in the register.[48] And in one celebrated pardon (the one to John Maxwell which flowed from his revolt against Wharton at Drumlanrig), everyone else was forgiven 'infra bondas Vallis Annandie, de Nethisdale et Galwidie ab aqua de Cre'.[49] That is some blanket. But the obvious point holds true: assurance was largely a phenomenon of the war zones.

As for other war crimes, we should probably put to one side the Highlanders' and Islesmen's treasons and those connected with Beaton's murder (both of them special cases, as it were). However, remaining away from armies was a nationwide experience. It was also the most numerous crime, with fully 1311 found guilty of it for the period 1543–1555. These need much closer analysis before any significant deductions can be made, but whereas only thirty-three from Perthshire collaborated with the English, fifty-one refused to turn up fully arrayed at a muster. On the other hand, 113 lived in burghs. One interesting set of numbers concerns the Borders, loosely defined. Only thirty-six came from that area. Various explanations can be offered, not least the fact that these people were under almost daily muster in any case, given English raiding parties. Another is that most collaborators by definition were already guilty of this crime as well. And here another pattern recurs: most of these names appear in records made during 1550–54.

---

45 *APS*, ii, 484; *ADCP*, 628.

46 Scott claimed that Ormiston and Brunstane alone had destroyed more than £Sc8000 of his property during Somerset's wars (*RPC*, xiv, 295) for which he 'hes gottin na recompensatione'.

47 See both of A. Maxwell's books, *The History of Old Dundee* (Edinburgh, 1884) and *Old Dundee . . . prior to the Reformation* (Edinburgh, 1891). This list appears as an appendix at 393–395. They were all acquitted. In my national count of 1955, I found only ten from Dundee, an absurdly low figure.

48 The date on the one displayed at the Dumfries Burgh Museum seems to be different to the one mentioned for *RSS*, iii, no. 2830.

49 *RSS*, iii, no. 2698.

ENGLAND

Somerset's failure went even deeper than losing his job and then his head. As ever, the central blame for this aspect (one of so many) of the mid-Tudor crisis lies at the door of Henry VIII, but Somerset did seriously aggravate the impoverishment of the Crown so spectacularly begun by his mentor. During the period 1538–50, something like £3,491,468 was spent on warfare. Some of this massive outpouring of funds (£290,663) came before 1544: the fortifications along the coasts during 1538–42; Calais during the same period; £26,500 for a relief army to aid Charles V in 1543; and perhaps one should take out the 1549 rebellions: £17,330. That still leaves a staggering sum: £3,146,975. Most of that global figure (£2,134,783) was spent by Henry, and most of his charges related to the conquests in France (£1,440,028). That leaves £350,262, which was expended in Scotland. If we take Henry VIII's war as lasting effectively from April 1544 to June 1546, that works out at a monthly average of £12,972 16s 6d. For Somerset, the Scottish costs were both a higher percentage (78%) of his total war-related costs, but at £603,871 for a war lasting effectively from August 1547 to March 1550, a monthly average of £18,870 19s. Still, one must bear in mind that Scotland's burden was only about a third of the grand total.

Some have argued that this crass profligacy destroyed any chance of the English Crown gaining the fiscal independence to impose either a Tudor or a Stuart despotism. In Dietz's wonderful argument (albeit very American and very 1920s), 'the people' achieved democratic life and Englishmen were spared autocratic tyranny. Charles I did lose his head and the monarchy was abolished in 1649, and not really until the reign of William III was England ever a major participant in military terms on the Continent again. All of that can be laid at the door of mid-Tudor warmaking and one-third of that still rests with Scotland.

The financial cost of the wars in terms of minted coinage to England and France was high, but many faceted. One of Henry's VII's minor war triumphs had been the restoration of a pension paid by Louis XI to Edward IV over the English King's claim to the title of France. It is not easy always to know just how much this came to, but down to 1509 something like £160,000 probably had been received. That pension, renewed on Henry VIII's accession, naturally lapsed whenever the King fought France. The peace, however, resulted in an increase in those annual payments, as did French desire to recover Tournai. War again (1522–25) intervened.

But when Francis was desperate for an English alliance after his humiliation at Pavia in 1525 and again in 1527, he upped the payments (both good examples of Wolsey's diplomatic skills). 'Make merry', the cardinal bragged, now that Henry was 'the richest prince of the world . . . [with] more treasure out of France yearly than all his revenues and customs amount to'. That was a typical piece of Wolsey's bombastic rhetoric, but payments did amount to varying sums between £20,000 and £50,000 over the next several years. However, Henry then found himself making necessary counter-bribes to Francis to keep his friendship during the divorce (£112,437 in 1527–29 alone). By the end of 1534, French pensions again ceased, so pressing was Henry's need for French non-hostility. Francis might have reconsidered, however, in

1543, but Henry was adamant for war; thus was lost a not inconsiderable source of regular income. Also, it should not be forgotten how close the Anglo-French rapprochement in 1546–47 appeared, especially to the outside world, not least to the Scots.

One might regard the compensation for Boulogne (over £100,000) as a restoration of the 'French pension' for a brief while. But then, in 1552, that money ran out. Northumberland's Council ordered a retrospective analysis of royal expenditure since 1538, when the Crown had appeared solvent, if not wealthy. The result was an extraordinary document, 'the greate and notable chardges of warre which the victorious Prince of famouse memorye [and Edward VI] lately hadd'. It was awesome, detailing the daunting expenditure of just under £3.5 million. Boulogne (1544–50) was nothing less than a treasure-consuming monster: the most expensive single item in Tudor history. Total costs for the three-month siege campaign came to a staggering £586,719, and that figure excludes shipping and naval costs (impossible to ignore). To that must be added the modest expenses of refortifying the prize and its surrounding pale: £47,167 during the remaining twenty-eight months of the king's life (but Edward would have to spend 50% more in the three years he held it).

But the 'kepyng of the towne' was formidably dear when it came to wages of the garrisons, their food and drink, munitions, horses and victuals 'lost, stolen and decayed'. Fully £379,140 was spent after 13 September 1544. Thus, for Henry's reign, this single conquest cost a staggering £1,013,025, making it a 'greate and notable chardge' indeed. Some 'invisible costs' should be reckoned as well. Those for the king's diplomatic service consequent upon the business (ambassadors, postage, prisoners' ransoms) were minuscule: £7996. But how much did Henry 'lose' by forfeiting any chance of the restoration of his French pension? And how much of the £276,766 spent remodelling Calais and garrisoning it during 1538–47 should also be laid at the door of the Boulogne enterprise? Moreover, the war's shadow stained deep into Edward's reign: £329,527 more for Boulogne and £94,664 for Calais. The French possessions as a whole for the period 1538–50 came to a monumental £1,713,981. In a sense, France thus saved Scotland twice over and bankrupted England.

Northumberland's decision to cut England's losses in 1549–50 was an act of desperate necessity. It also demonstrated commonsense and statesmanship. But it came at a high price. For England in 1550 found itself thus a client of France, as soundly bested as it had been a century before. Edward VI was betrothed to Elizabeth de Valois, and whilst Henry II was being bombastic in claiming to unite all three monarchies, it might have worked out that way. Edward's tuberculosis was a salvation, but that only meant that Mary Tudor had little choice but to make England a Habsburg client. Elizabeth was thus faced in 1559 with continuing the enormously complex refortification of Berwick, the most single expensive work in the entirety of her reign. She also had to accept the loss of Calais and a highly costly, if diplomatically successful, intervention in Scotland in 1559–60.

But even that triumph was nearly a fiasco. Leith never fell to her arms in 1560; indeed Norfolk's expeditionary force was a very near disaster. The ladders, for example, were too short for the walls when dramatically assaulted one night: a classic Tudor fiasco. Had the French relief force assembled so carefully by Mary of Guise's brother at Le Havre in the winter of 1559 not been blown off course by a tempest in which most of the ships were driven ashore in Denmark and many of the troops drowned, matters might have been quite different. But not only did this Protestant wind abort the French armada, it enabled Winter's fleet to break loose from a weather stranglehold which had made it impossible for him to get up the east coast. He only attained Leith Roads after more than a month of painstaking endeavour. Thus was aid finally sent to the Lords of the Congregation. Distance, weather, luck and timing thus emerged as English advantages. The tumult of Amboise in March 1560 comprehensively deflected Guise and French commitment to the retention of Scotland, as did Mary of Guise's death at age 45. England thus escaped from its mid-Tudor crisis by the merest of threads. Suppose Elizabeth had succumbed to smallpox early in her reign, as she almost did.

Add to that the costs of Scotland, the debasement of the currency, the continued rape of the religious houses, and inflation: all of which can be attributed entirely or in large part to this great adventure. In one estimate drawn up later, English charges for the wars against Scotland during the period 1 January 1544 to 1 May 1550 were put at £954,135. 18s. 7 1/4d. Of this figure, almost £603,900 was incurred during 1547–50,[50] and it would take decades for English finances to recover from the vast expenses of the wars of the 1540s.[51]

How much the French spent for Scotland is difficult to estimate. Henry II made it a round 'million of gold' in 1558, but that figure must have been fanciful. In December 1549 an 'impot' of £t400,000 was levied for 'la deffense et conservation' of Scotland, but it was only collected in the 'villes closes'. Some idea of the enormous cost of the war in Scotland can be seen in one set of precise figures: £t211,503 were provided for the month of August 1549.[52] Averaged out over a year, that would come to over £t2,500,000.

---

50 PRO, SP 10/15/11; see also F.C. Dietz, *English Government Finance*, i, 144–58, 178–87. These figures are suspect. The account was probably prepared in 1558–59, is not added up accurately and is contradicted by totals which can be made from the financial records cited above. Again, much more investigation is necessary.

51 See R.B. Cuthwaite, 'The Trials of Foreign Borrowing: The English Crown and the Antwerp Money Market in the mid-sixteenth century', *Economic History Review*, xix (1966), 209–35 and 'Royal Borrowing in the Reign of Queen Elizabeth I: The Aftermath of Antwerp', *EHR*, xxxvi (1971), 251–63.

52 *A Source Book of Scottish History*, ed. W.C. Dickinson and others (Edinburgh, 1958), ii, 158–60; Teulet, *Relations*, i, 235; BN, MS fr. 18,153, fo. 91. An abstract of receipts and expenses for 1549 has the notation: 'payemens pour les gens de pied et autres affaires descosse: 800,000 livres', but the light horse (19,205 livres) was in addition to this (BN, MS fr. 3127, fos. 91–93).

ROMANCING THE WAR

In 1575, Ulpian Fulwell[53] (d.?1586) published his *The Flovver*[54] *of Fame*. The focus of his eye was 'the bright renowne, & most fortunate raigne of King Henry the viii', but his overview stretched back to Bosworth and ranged as wide as James IV's 'sonne who was but a chylde' in 1513 and who 'tooke his death after the overthrowe of his menne at Solomos'.[55] His duties as rector of Naunton Church in Gloucestershire allowed him the leisure to compose a 'treatise' on Henry VIII, but before he got it to the publisher in London, he 'chaunced into the company of certaine Capitanies that had serued in king Henries warres, and in King Edwards'. Conversing at length with these veterans, Fulwell found himself, a literary man, much taxed by them. 'They seemed greatly to lament that so noble a piece of servyce as was done at Hadington, shoulde be so streyghtlye passed thorough the handes of Cronographers.' He thus determined ('being by them earnestly requested') to recount their heroic adventures and expanded his work.

What emerged was an addendum purely about this critical episode of the Rough Wooings. Many of the stories which made their way on to his pages exist nowhere else and they make for gripping reading.[56] But what most sharply emerged for Fulwell from these interviews was the high regard in which all of the old soldiers held their commander, Sir James Wilford:

> He was so noble a capitaine, that he wonne the hartes of all
> Souldiers. He was in the towne among his Souldiers and
> friends, a gentle lamme. In the field among his enemies, a Lyon.

The devotion of this highly professional officer (he was Provost Marshal of the 1547 army) to that 'furious dame, Bellona' was such he 'was able to make of a cowardly beaste, a couragious man'. Clearly Wilford's service at Haddington was the central point of his life's work and it figures prominently among the four portraits of him which were executed during the sixteenth century. What is remarkable, however, is that Wilford commanded at Haddington for little over half a year. At Lauder in April 1548, he only took up post at Haddington in June and became commander on the departure of William Lord Grey of Wilton at the end of the month. Captured early in 1549 during a bungled attack on Dunbar, he then languished a prisoner of war

53 Roberta Buchanan, 'Ulpian Fulwell' (unpublished PhD dissertation, Birmingham University, 1980), 80–94.

54 *STC* 2, no. 11475. The printer did not have any more W's in his tray that day and thus employed two 'V's. The work was printed by William Hoskins in Fleet Street and was first reprinted in the *Harleian Miscellany* (1808–13), ed. Thomas Park, iv, 337–75. Fulwell was a Somerset man originally who had little actual experience of the wars (Oxford BA in 1573). Much of his material was lifted straight from Hall, but a close colleague, Edmund Haskins, who had fought at Boulogne, gave him considerable information.

55 'This conflict stroke him to the hart, wherof he dyed incontinently. Whereby we may be sure that God stroke the stroake.' *Flower of Fame*, 26.

56 See Phillips, *Anglo-Scots Wars* for the miseries suffered by the troops and the garrisons.

Fig. 14.3. Portraits of Sir James Wilford painted during the sixteenth century: note how in each one his shirt collar is different and often his armour. A fanciful Haddington under siege is depicted top right in three of the portraits.

until eventually exchanged, probably that November.[57] Still suffering from his wounds, he arrived at York 'very weak' on the 21st. A year later, he died; the sermon at Little St. Bartholomew's, Otford, Kent was delivered by none other than Miles Coverdale.[58] His, then, was a short life (he was 34, at the outside, on his death), but a gallant one. In Fulwell's verse, Dame Bellona prepared garlands for all 'those lustie Capitaines' who served in Scotland:

> And then shee calles by name
> the rest to take their hyre:
> Whiche was, that they shoulde to the toppe
> of mounting Fame aspyre
> Sir Wilforde come thou first,
> Receive thy iust rewarde
> Thy hautie harte, of furious foe
> Had never yet regarde.

What gives this publication especial interest is that Fulwell was not the only man to recall Wilford's heroism almost three decades after the siege. Another veteran of Haddington was Petruccio Ubaldini.[59] Once back in London, he gave a full account of his time in Scotland to the Venetian ambassador who incorporated much of that material in his account of 1551. Ubaldini then settled permanently in England during the reign of Elizabeth and had a remarkable artistic and literary career. In 1588, he not only brought out a vivid account of the Spanish Armada, but also a *Descrittione del Regno di Scotia et delve Isole sue Adjacenti* (printed in Antwerp) and dedicated it to one of the Queen's closet councillors, Sir Christopher Hatton.[60] But the manuscript had been prepared as early as 1576,[61] and much of that clearly had been put together in 1550. He, too, found space to praise Wilford, arguing that it was he who made the town 'una roccaforte assai munita e ben difesa [an excellently appointed and well defended stronghold]'.[62]

Another essayist to dedicate one of his works to Hatton was Thomas Churchyard (d. 1604).[63] Churchyard was actually more of a lively journalist, almost a hack. He

---

57 On 24 July 1549, Somerset was informed that Wilford was being 'so straightly kept' that he could have 'no kind of lib[erty]' and that his surety had been placed as high as £10,000 (Stevenson, *Selections*, 38).

58 His wife Joyce was buried beside him in 1580.

59 As far as I can determine, he was not related to Migiliorino Ubaldini who did such sterling work at Edinburgh, Dunbar and probably Stirling in 1548 as a military engineer, but I discuss Petruccio's career briefly in Merriman, 'Ubaldini', 233–34 and 'Italian Engineers'.

60 The earlier manuscript edition was dedicated to Henry Fitzalan, Earl of Arundel. Interestingly, Fulwell's *Flower of Fame* was dedicated to William Cecil, by then Lord Burghley. Fulwell's most famous work, *The Art of Flattery* (1576), was dedicated to Burghley's wife Mildred.

61 BL, MS Royal, 14.A.16.

62 G. Pellegrini, *Petruccio Ubaldini* (Milan, 1967), 13–18. I am grateful to Dr. Maurice Slawinski for translating this for me.

63 See the PhD theses of R.A. Geimer, 'The Life and Works of Thomas Churchyard' (North Western University, 1965), and Henry O. St. Orge, 'Thomas Churchyard: A Study of his Prose and Poetry' (Ohio State University, 1966).

wrote on almost anything: the infamous Mistress Shore, an earthquake at London, Queen Elizabeth's progress to Bristol, an epitaph upon the 'Death of kyng Edward', James I's triumphant progress through London from the Tower to Westminster in 1603, and his utterly charming *The Worthiness of Wales* (1587). He, too, cast his dedicatory net wide: Cecil, Essex, Raleigh. Sir Julius Caesar would become his patron. Churchyard sought (and received) patronage at Court, as did our other litterateurs. But his early career was firmly military with thirty years of active service in Ireland, France, with Charles V, at Calais, Leith and Antwerp. That war odyssey began, again, at Haddington in 1548 and, like Wilford, he was captured at Dunbar. His two most popular pieces of military literature were *Churchyard's Chippes* (1575, 1578)[64] and his equally celebrated *A Generall Rehersall of Warres* which came out in 1579. His was a blatant romancing of military chivalry. War was a supreme moment when 'every simple subiecte, was given to the aduaunsement of his Country'. For him, the apogee for these fields of valour was during the reign of Henry VIII:

> Whose famous memorie shall laste whiles this worlde standeth. All cheualrie was cherished, Soldiours made of, and manhoode so muche esteemed that he was thought happie and moste valiaunt that sought credite by the exercises of Armes, an dissipline of warre. Whiche did so animate the noble mindes of men, that in a maner he was counted no bodie, that had not been knowen to bee at some valiaunte enterprise.

Again, 'the greate mynde and manly courage' of Wilford shine through the luxuriant prose. Nothing daunted him:

> The more was the miserie, the grater grewe his harte, and hope to have good fortune for the whiche assured fortitude and determinate purpose, he purchased everlasting renowne. And lives at this daie in as freshe memorie as he were seen presently before all the eyes of the people.

There is much Shakespearean rhetoric here and Holinshed acknowledged use of these sources as well as doing primary oral history research on his own, interviewing men who had been in the wars for their first-hand accounts. From his goldmine of great tales, Shakespeare was to reap a rich harvest.

'Romance' takes many forms, of course. One manifestation was the plethora of medallions struck all over Europe to celebrate monarchs' high moments. Another was portraiture. Mention has already been made of Wilford's. These rather dreary pieces are massively overshadowed as paintings by two other captains whose romancings should be examined: Vice Admiral Thomas Wyndham and Sir John Luttrell. Both of their portraits were executed in the summer of 1550 by Hans Eworth in Southwark.[65]

Wyndham's is conventional to the point of being almost iconic. He stands, manly

---

64 *STC*, no. 5243.

65 Eworth probably came to England from Antwerp because of his Protestant conversion and painted for both the Tudor queens. *The Courtauld Gallery at Somerset House* (1998), 38–39.

as Henry VIII, regarding the viewer straight on, his hands arrogantly at his waist belt. A highly elaborate helmet is perched beside his right ear, a 'war portrait' (his sack of Balmerino Abbey) by his left. His garb is profoundly martial: chain mail, jerkin, powder box; and he shoulders a highly sophisticated arquebus of the most modern design. Four centuries later, he stands before the viewer, the ultimate proactive warman. It could be Nelson or Patten. Wyndham's career in Scotland had been highly eventful and in particular he used his navy, based first at Inchcolm and then off Broughty, as a highly effective engine of destruction and defence. But he was a remarkable all-rounder, designing one of the bastions at Haddington and participating in many of the actions there. After the war, he bankrolled his maritime expertise into a remarkable set of exotic adventures, trading with Morocco and dying after passing Cape Verde (a remarkable feat for the time) and venturing into the Bight of Benin to trade up the Niger. The French admiral who transported Mary to France in August 1548, Villegaignon, would perish in Brazil. That's romance.

Sir John Luttrell's portrait has a different moral. Somerset-born (Dunster Castle) and bred, he trained early for an army career and was also celebrated in the romance literature. Churchyard listed him as one who 'did serve valliaunteley a longe tyme'.[66] As happened so often,[67] the war made him but its fearsome physical demands then killed him: like Wilford, he died within a year of its end. Whilst he spent his treasure at Broughty, his family's affairs in Somerset deteriorated sharply, his sister for example, being unable to raise her dowry. His wife's behaviour whilst he was in the field was so notorious that he immediately sought to divorce her on his return home. When finally extricated from Scotland,[68] he set about trying to recoup his losses, but to little avail.[69]

He and Wyndham (although Norfolk-born, Wyndham had moved to Somerset in the 1540s), who had collaborated as fellow officers at Inchcolm and Broughty, met up in London perhaps to embark upon a commercial enterprise. Luttrell also used this trip to the metropolis to have his portrait executed for his family (and for posterity). It is one of the most remarkable works of art of the entire sixteenth century. He stands naked in a foaming sea. About him men drown and a ship burns, its main mast sundered and belching forth fire. The ship's company dive headlong to their deaths. A green-skinned body floats past him in the awful waters. But his right arm is raised in defiance (a salute?) to be gently embraced by Dame Anglia. On a rock before his navel are inscribed words composed by Luttrell himself: 'More then the

---

66 Churchyard, *Rehearsall of warres*, Hi v. Note how frequently he is mentioned in Phillips, *Anglo-Scots Wars*, 197, 202, 207, 212–14, 223, 242–44, 253–54.

67 One example of so many: John Hogeson, merchant, alderman, once mayor of York and an MP, was captured at Ancrum Moor and then held a prisoner of war in Scotland for three years. By the time he returned home, such was the state of his affairs (awful) that he just died. Bindoff, *History of Parliament*.

68 He had found himself not only a POW after the capture of Broughty in February 1550, but arrested for a debt of £519. 11s which he owed a Dundee merchant (*TA*, ix, 443). Arran, with typical kindness, paid it for him.

69 *APC*, ii, 406; *TA*, ix, 443. His ransom was set at £1000; the English Council gave him land worth 100 marks yearly (*Mary of Lorraine Corr.*, 322n).

rock amyddys ye raging seas The constant heart no deanger dreaddys nor fearys'. The Dame in turn is surrounded by an allegory of peace. Horses are being bridled; helmets put away; money for Boulogne is passed between two dames.[70] War brings the ship of state to its fiery destruction with thunder and lightning; peace brings an olive branch and a rainbow. Within a year, at probably little more than 31 years of age, he was dead.[71] 'Long crwell weris' indeed.

War thus made men and destroyed them. Lord Grey of Wilton, having resigned his command in disgust in 1549, no sooner reached home to take up a quiet aristocratic agrarian and shire life than his obvious talents made him indispensable to governments to come. He served in Ireland, and almost everywhere England had military jobs to be done, and when he died, he did so highly celebrated as one of the generals of the age.[72] Henry Manners, the Earl of Rutland, may have been a mere 23 years of age[73] when he took over from Grey, but emerged from his baptism of fire with high credit, and rightly so. On the other hand, Thomas Lord Wharton, whose stock had risen so high by his actions in the field from 1542 to 1548, never fully recovered politically from his blunderings at Drumlanrig in February 1548. But the shadow of the 'romance' stretched long and deep. In 1591, Luttrell's brother's son George had a copy made of the 1550 Eworth portrait. On it he inscribed (translation by Frances Yates):

Effigiem renouare tuam fortissime miles Ingensme meritum fecit amorq tui.

Nam nisi curasse Haeedam scribere fratrem Hei tua contingerant praedia nulla mihi. 1591 G.L.

Your great merit and my love for you, brave soldier, cause me to renew your portrait. For had you not taken care to make your brother your heir, none of your possessions would have become mine. 1591 G.L.

THE MAKING OF A FORT AND A DIKE

On 27 May 1550, Sir John Dudley, Viscount Lisle (1542) and Earl of Warwick (1547), appointed himself Lieutenant General of the North Parts, Governor of North-

70 Yates's 'orthodoxy' on the money bags (see note 71) has been challenged in the exhibition of the Luttrell painting held at the Courtauld Institute in 1999.

71 F.A. Yates, 'The Allegorical Portraits of Sir John Luttrell', *Essays on the History of Art presented to Rudolph Wittkower*, ed. D. Fraser and others (1967), 149–59. I am grateful to Stephen Gritt and Lorne Campbell for their invaluable assistance over the Luttrell portrait, especially to Dr. Campbell who allowed me sight of her forthcoming contribution to an article on it. I am also indebted to Melanie Blake, also of the Courtauld Institute, for assistance over Wyndham.

72 See the appendix to *A commentary of the services and charges of William Lord Grey of Wilton, K.G.*, ed. P. de Malpas Grey Egerton (Camden Society, 1847), which describes a magnificent funeral. Churchyard, as ever, 'was there': see his *Dollfull Discourse*.

73 'He is yet but of young years and not so expert now exercised in the wars as we would have wished'.

umberland and Warden of the East Marches against Scotland. Warwick operated a Cabinet-like government (most letters from the Privy Council were signed by all its members attending that day), in deliberate contrast to the autocratic regime of his predecessor.[74] But he clearly was the man in charge and it was he who had made the critical decision to wind down and then end the Rough Wooings, and to give up trying to keep Boulogne. He was, therefore, a very smart man and a realist.

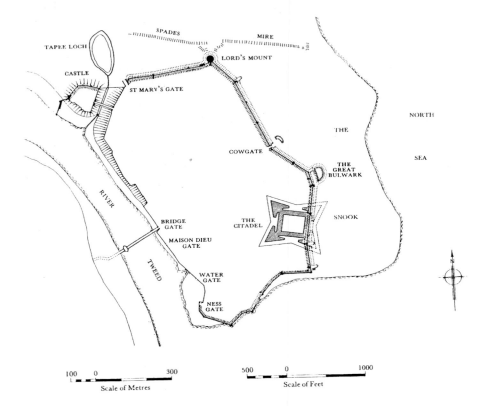

Fig. 14.4. Reconstruction drawing of Berwick's fortifications as they appeared in 1558. The new Citadel was sited on the east side of the medieval walls, on top of the highest rise of land on the peninsula, next to a 1520s attempt to protect that side, 'The Great Bulwark in the Snook'. The Citadel embodied what Lee and Palmer had learned from military engineers on the Continent and from their own work on the ground in Scotland. Lee's next major assignment would be the pinnacle of his career: a completely new fortification for the entire town, one of the most handsome *trace italienne* sites from 1558-70 in Europe, and the single most expensive construction in the whole of Elizabeth's reign.

74 Dale E. Hoak, *The King's Council in the Reign of Edward VI* (1976); see especially 191 *et seq.*, 261, 266–67.

Both these characteristics are evident in his taking over command of the North.[75] He knew full well that the price England had to pay for peace with France was a major French military presence in Scotland, as well as the likelihood of the Scottish Queen becoming a French Queen. As the Privy Council commented on making this decision, 'the Frenchemen arr much encreased in aucthoritrie and power with the Scots'.[76] He thus was determined to make as secure as possible England's northern Calais. The *fin de guerre* brainstorm of retaining Berwickshire by the construction of a massive Italianate fortification just before the Dunglass burn, hamlet and tower which marked the boundary between Berwickshire and East Lothian (and thereby protect the enfeebled and exposed Berwick-upon-Tweed by a massive new 'Bounds') had had to be abandoned in the realities of the negotiation of the Treaty of Boulogne. Interestingly, he had meanwhile refused to surrender either Eyemouth or Roxburgh. 'Refused' is perhaps too firm a term, but somehow the commanders in the North never quite got around to their abandonment and demolition until the next year. Something similar happened at Castlemilk on the West March.

What did these outposts shield? Effectively, Warwick simply took the military engineering establishment already in existence from the war and set it immediately to work. On 22 July 1550, Lee and Sir Thomas Palmer were commissioned to survey all the Border strengths, but especially to decide how so to enhance Berwick that a new citadel would 'both master the towne [the medieval castle was lower than the town] and kepe the haven'. Warwick's regime was actually quite wealthy for the moment, thanks to the massive injection of 400,000 French crowns (worth perhaps £100,000 at 1550 price levels, but given England's debased currency of the time, it is hard to give a precise equivalent) into its coffers. Boulogne's loss, then, would be Berwick's gain.

Lee and Palmer (joined almost immediately by Thomas Gower and William Ridgeway) represented the most adroit practitioners of the art of fortification then in the British Isles, and all four had just emerged from a formidably instructive practical school of war, massively – even arrogantly – competent in the business of military construction. The Privy Council insisted that they get cracking so that the work be completed before that winter and then 'in order of defence'.[77] The site they eventually picked was a high rise of land on the east side of the town which could easily provide raking fire over the town to the Tweed as well as to the castle.

There they staked out a textbook jewel of a *trace italienne*. Over the next two building seasons well over £13,500 was spent and 1220 workmen laboured. It was the largest building site in the island.[78] Design mistakes were made (they dropped their new citadel right across the existing walls which would have meant a serious weakening of the site's overall defence during the building).[79] As ever, the building

---

75 See Beer, *Northumberland*, 133–37.

76 *APC*, iii, 5–6, 10. See Colvin, *King's Works*, iv, 642–44.

77 *Ibid.*, iii, 90–92.

78 We can plot the weekly crews and their wages thanks to the happy survival of the complete account book of the programme's Treasurer, Sir Richard Bonny. I record my gratitude to Major P.I.C. Payne who kindly allowed me access to this manuscript.

79 Almost exactly the same issue arose in 1559 with the building of the Elizabethan Brass Bastion.

of one thing destroyed an existing thing: a section of the medieval wall collapsed, its foundation 'shaken by the working of a bulwark' (which got to the ears of the King).[80] So serious were the resulting problems that by the summer of 1552 nothing but the 'wysdome and ripe experience' of the Duke of Northumberland (as he now was) could resolve the crisis.[81] By July he was there in person.

There are three telling moments about this 1552 episode which are highly relevant to the story of the Rough Wooings. Two will be detailed here; the third I will leave for nearer the end. The first is obvious: England's northern frontier was now dangerously exposed; hence the massive works commenced there almost the moment the war ended. However, the money ran out that summer, and by 13 October 1552 work virtually ceased. The citadel was in truth never completed. Nonetheless, its shadowy outline (parts of it can be seen even today) is an evocative statement about the cost of war. The ending of one conflict means preparing for the next, taking into account both the lessons of the most recent war and its political, military and international consequences.

The second concerns treaties and their executions. Northumberland's inspection tour of the Borders in the summer of 1552 was not only connected to the issues of its protection. One aspect to bear in mind about international treaties is that whilst a prolonged and painstaking summit conference (such as the long discussions at 'Camp' in 1545–46 and the much more important ones at Cateau-Cambrésis during 1558–59) concluded wars, loose ends always remained. These had to be sorted out by follow-on negotiations.[82] In the case of Cateau-Cambrésis (the 'official' date for which is usually rendered as 29 April 1559), it had to be supplemented by Scots and Englishmen meeting face to face to make yet a further contract, the Treaty of Upsettlington of 31 May 1559.[83] That is what Otterburn and Paniter were doing in London at the end of 1546: 'tidying up' Henry VIII's Rough Wooing. Somerset's was finally concluded by the Treaty of Norham of 10 June 1551.[84]

Most of this contract makes, as do they all, tedious reading. The tower of Edrington, just outside the Bounds of Berwick, was restored to Scottish ownership. Fishing rights in the Tweed were regularised, although even in the 1990s they would be the cause of one of the longest civil disputes in English legal history involving, amongst others, the ex-Prime Minister, Lord Hume of the Hirsel; it was resolved not long before he died. What concerns students of the Rough Wooings, however, is the making of what may be deemed the modern Ordnance Survey map of Great Britain. The Debatable Land (or lands, as there were several other patches of non-sovereignty along the Border) had long been a cause of trouble to both governments. The French, used to defined and strictly delineated frontiers, found Scottish insouciance over this matter infuriating and resolved to have it settled definitively.

---

80 *The Literary Remains of Edward VI* (Roxburghe Club, 1857), ii, 344.

81 Moreover, massive peculation was going on, unknown to Northumberland, whose signature would be forged by the Treasurer Richard Bonny in 1553.

82 See how long it actually took to end World War I: Versailles was but one of a series of treaties. The Korean War has still not ended.

83 *Foedera*, xv, 520; *CSP Scot.*, i, nos. 456, 462.

84 *Foedera*, xv, 295; *CSP Scot.*, i, nos. 374–75.

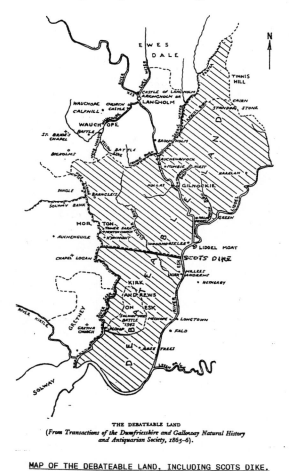

THE DEBATEABLE LAND
*(From Transactions of the Dumfriesshire and Galloway Natural History
and Antiquarian Society, 1865-6).*

MAP OF THE DEBATEABLE LAND, INCLUDING SCOTS DIKE.

Fig. 14.5. A nineteenth-century map of the Debatable Land to show its division in
1551-52, which appeared in that classic testimony to the century's delight in
all things historical, *The Transactions of the Dumfriesshire and Galloway
Natural History and Antiquarian Society,* 1865-6.

The Treaty of Norham, concluded on 10 June 1551, agreed that the land should be
divided between the two countries by means of a special boundary commission, one
of the first in European history. It held 'frequent meetings' in Southampton. William
Paulet, Marquis of Winchester (Edward VI's Lord Treasurer), headed the English
side; Claude de Laval-Boisdauphin, then Henry II's ambassador to the English
Court, signed for the Scots.[85] The arbitration, finally concluded on 16 August 1552,
had been a protracted and obviously vexatious business with much wrangling over
Scottish and English proposals. In the end, a French solution was agreed and duly
marked on a map by two figures of the cross.

85 For Scottish preparations for these negotiations, see *RPC,* i, 119–125.

Fig. 14.6. The line of the Scots Dike. Marker stones can still be found if one walks the full length of the dike today. It would have been much higher in the sixteenth century: both natural erosion and the World War I railway line have flattened it considerably.

Fig. 14.7. This dramatic aerial photograph shows what a broad swathe the Scots Dike makes through the landscape even today with its plantation of pine trees. As one can see, it is not quite as straight a line as it was meant to be.

On 24 September, Henry Bullock, a practised land surveyor, executed 'The platt of the Debatable' which was then the site map for the actual erection of a boundary wall, with ditches on either side and with distinct marker stones emplaced along it.[86]

By the spring of 1553, the Scottish government set to the business of gathering a work crew 'to caus the dikkes and fowseis of the Debatable lande be biggit'. Apparently John Maxwell, Lord Herries of Terregles, was given the charge of overseeing this construction, he being paid £Sc700 the following September.[87] The result was a (relatively) straight-line boundary, which exists today on every O/S map of the United Kingdom. During World War I, a narrow-gauge railway line was built on top of it to harvest timber for the trenches in France, and this continued until 1920 when an article in *The Scotsman* caused the Dike to be taken into the supervision of the then Ancient Monuments Board of Scotland.[88]

EDINBURGH'S NEWEST HOSPITAL

On 14 July, 1551, Edward Seymour, Duke of Somerset, now released from his confinement and restored to membership of the English Privy Council, was detailed to meet Jacques d'Albon, sieur de Saint-André, and Marshal of France, at the gates to Hampton Court and then to conduct him to the presence of King Edward VI. During the next fortnight and more the King and Marshal were to meet on at least eight separate occasions, and by all accounts Edward was charmed by the Marshall's grace and wit. How much Somerset was charmed by the occasion is less clear, but he cannot have viewed the events of the summer of 1551 with equanimity. Saint-André's visit was a ceremonial, but nonetheless important, part of the Anglo-French rapprochement which was initiated with the Treaty of Boulogne of 24 March 1550 and culminated in a series of treaties (Northampton and Norham) in 1551. By the first England surrendered Boulogne, Henry VIII's prize from the war of 1544–46, and began to withdraw from Scotland. By the second the English were forced to renounce their claims to the marriage of Mary Queen of Scots, and to accept the betrothal of Edward and Elizabeth de Valois, Henry II's eldest daughter. The third has just been discussed. As part of this new friendship between two such old enemies, Henry II had already been invested with the Order of the Garter, and on 16 July Saint-André conferred the Order of Saint-Michel on Edward VI, in an elaborate and impressive ceremony at Hampton Court.

The investiture was not Somerset's only reminder of how much things had changed since that heady Saturday when his magnificent victory at Pinkie had seemed to lay Scotland at his feet. Saint-André, either in his discussions with Edward or with members of the Privy Council, went out of his way strongly to request the

---

86 The story is fully detailed in Mackenzie, W.M., 'The debatable land' *SHR*, xxx (1951), 109– 25. Armstrong, *Liddesdale*, reproduced the map as an appendix. See *TA*, x, 41, 43–4, 78–9, 84, 98, 111.

87 *Ibid.*, 170.

88 *The Scotsman* (article by J. Logan Mack), 11 and 21 December 1920. It has since figured very occasionally in other journalistic pieces. See especially Tom Nairn's essay, 'A judgement in stones' in *The Scotsman*'s weekend section of December 10, 1989, pp. i–ii.

release of 'James Harryson, Scottisheman nowe prisoner in one of the Counters [jails] of London'. On 28 July, the Council wrote to the sheriffs of London to see to the matter. Somerset was present at that very meeting (six months before his second fall and subsequent execution); one wonders what his emotions were. Henrisoun was finally released in early August, but only after the government had paid the Lord Mayor of London £20 10s 2d to cover the costs of his confinement.

Henrisoun's incarceration had arisen because of his central participation in a remarkable tale of rich melodrama and the highest of stakes. With the end of the war, he had found himself an exile and without a patron. He complained bitterly about his treatment (they all do[89]) and even threatened Warwick's government with going to the newspapers ('in prent') to publicise his case. His salvation came by the most unlikely of routes. During April 1551, a probable ex-Castilian, who had gone over to the French after his capture, turned up in London with an extraordinary scheme to poison Mary Queen of Scots. Related (how intimately is not clear) to Mary's cook, he planned to insert poison in the Queen's frittered pears. He was also in service to the French Stuarts: indeed to the Comte d'Aubigny, brother to the Earl of Lennox. He outlined his plot to Henrisoun who immediately had him arrested and thus saved his Queen's life. Stuart was transported back to France and executed.[90] Hence the French and Scottish requests for Henrisoun's (his name in French translates as 'hedgehog', not inappropriately) release.

Once home, Henrisoun harvested numerous benefits and preferments. Arran granted him £Sc100 in 1552. By 26 January 1553, he was a pensioner of Mary of Guise, and on 21 May 1554, within a month of her becoming Regent (yet another fruit of the Rough Wooings), Henrisoun would be appointed Conservator in the Low Countries. This was rehabilitation indeed; the grant even went so far as to say that he had held the post twice before (a matter of some contention) and that it had been given to another only 'in absence of the said James' when in truth he had assured with Hertford at Edinburgh in 1544. He continued his active interest in affairs, writing with some audacity to Middelburg in 1552 to ask for payment for his work for the town in 1541 and to encourage them to think again about gaining the Staple. In 1555 he proposed to Mary of Guise a painless way by which the Crown's revenues could be augmented by £Sc30,000. However, by then he clearly was ageing; on 19 February 1555 he had been forced to appoint a deputy to handle his duties in the Low Countries, since he could 'nicht gudlie pas in thai partis'. In October, as a consolation, he was granted a post which seems to have been created especially for him: Overseer-General of the Crown's 'mynis, fischeingis . . . and als of hir hienes cunye [coinage]'.

Still, he did not change his religious persuasion nor his zest for the welfare of his country. Nowhere is this concern more evident than in his remarkable 'articlis and

---

89 Patrick Earl Bothwell, so handsomely rewarded when he passed over Hermitage to the English in 1549, found himself marooned in Newcastle in November 1552. He remonstrated with the Privy Council, 'I am behynd a yeare and ane half unpayit of my pencioun, being now at no lytill charges' (Stevenson, *Selections*, 55–56).

90 Stuart's history forms the heart of Dorothy Dunnett's novel, *Queen's Play* (1964).

ordinances concernyng the commoun weill of this burgh' which he presented to the Edinburgh town council on 7 October 1552. Deploring the fact that residents could not purchase their corn or fish without being rained on, he asked for permission to build proper markets so that all 'that cumis thairto sall stand dry', the revenues from which would sustain him. He also sought to profit by the establishment of a 'pastyme ground for the induellaris' and further proposed the construction of 'an clerkis chalmer to wryte your actis in'. He also suggested how 'ane fair scule to mak pepill cum to the toun' might be financed. Whilst working as a propagandist for Somerset, one of his most extraordinary ideas was the construction of a Forth-Clyde canal. Now he proposed the diversion of the Water of Leith to create 'four fontanis our all pairtis of your toune'.

The central proposal of his list of 1552 was a hospital. Edinburgh, he argued, had a large number of sick and 'nychtbouris dekeit be the weris', but none of them could find medical treatment owing to the degeneration of the hospitals within the town. As remedy he proposed 'ane fair hospital suld be maid . . . intertenyit with ane priest, ane surrigiane, ane medicinar, and xl beddis at vj d the day'. It could be built, he claimed, within seven years and, ever numerate, he made recommendations for its funding. In the end, he did at least act as one of the collectors for a special tax raised after the Reformation for what Michael Lynch has called 'the acceptable face of Protestantism'.[91] Thus one unlikely fruit of the Rough Wooings was Edinburgh's first modern medical centre, even though it took almost two decades to start functioning.

'LES MIEULX VENUS AVEC NOUS': MOST WELCOME AMONG US

There is a third story about Norham and Northumberland. On 29 March 1557, as the final Habsburg-Valois war erupted (and the last Anglo-Scottish war was about to), Henri Cleutin, sieur d'Oysel, wrote from Stirling to an old colleague of his, François de Noailles, Bishop of Dax (in the South of France, not far from Beaton's see of Mirepoix), who had been appointed from Venice to be ambassador in London (replacing his famous brother Jean who had previously held the post during Mary Tudor's reign).[92] Much of the letter does not concern our topic at all: Philip II's return to England to visit his Queen, news from Italy and Flanders, a Scottish embassy to England. But interspersed within this quite chatty missive was d'Oysel's reflection that the English never liked ('les Anglois ne trouvent jamais bonne') to see the French and Scots co-operating. And he said he often recalled a meeting he attended at which the late John Dudley, Duke of Northumberland, suddenly barked at the Scottish representatives when Scots Dike was being discussed:

---

91 M. Lynch, 'The 'faithful brethren' of Edinburgh: the acceptable face of Protestantism', *Bulletin of the Institute of Historical Research* (li, 1978), 194–99.
92 E.H. Harbison, *Rival ambassadors at the Court of Queen Tudor* (1940), *ad indices*. Interestingly, Odet de Selve had been posted to Venice after his embassy at London, 1546–49.

Ne sçavez vous faire vos affaires sans l'ayde des ambassadeurs de France? Vous vous faictes grand tort de vous mettre icy soubs leur tutèle et n'en serez pas les mieulx venus avec nous. [Don't you know how to run your affairs without having to use French ambassadors? You're making a great mistake here by putting yourselves under their tutelage. You will not be the most welcome of people with us].[93]

It might seem fatuous for a victor of Pinkie so to pontificate about 'good avenues' for harmonious relations between England and Scotland. But as a comment on the Rough Wooings, Northumberland's outburst seems most apt.

MARY QUEEN OF SCOTS, 1542–87
AND BONNIE PRINCE CHARLIE, 1745–46

In 1994, arising from a paper I delivered to the colloquia on the social and political identities in European communities at Copenhagen on 26 April 1990, I published two articles, the second of which was entitled 'Stewarts and Tudors in the mid-sixteenth century'. In it I played around with some counter-factual musings, called a clutch of 'What ifs'.[94] After all, while historians must deal with what actually happened, at the time statesmen constantly engaged in contingency planning. So, when considering the dynastic union (or 'accident' as Donaldson called it) of 1603, we should never lose sight of how things might have worked out differently.

I began this book with the question: what if James V had lived to sire a son? After that, the most monumental 'What if' is how would we view the events just detailed if Mary Queen of Scots had died during the period 1542–51? The Duke of Châtelherault would have become James VI of Scotland, and since he was richly endowed with sons (one of whom admittedly went mad), Hamiltons might be Kings of Scotland today. James Stewart, that is to say the James VI of the textbooks, would never have been born: thus no Anglo-Scottish union in 1603.

What if Francis II of France had lived long enough to enjoy a sexually active adulthood and had sired sons on his wife, Mary Queen of Scots? She would have remained in France. Who would have ruled Scotland: a Catholic French viceroy, or (as actually happened in 1560–1) a Council of Scottish Lords? Would civil war have broken out, much as in the Netherlands – with Moray emerging, like William the Silent, to head a Republic? Or might James Hamilton, Duke of Châtelherault (head of the legitimate Scottish cadet line), have been 'elected' King?

What if Queen Mary had married Don Carlos of Spain after the death of her first husband, as was once proposed? She would have lived with Carlos, wherever Philip II sent him. If they had had sons, the eldest would eventually have been King of Scotland as well as of the Spanish dominions. Again, a Dutch Republic scenario, or a Hamilton 'election', does not seem far-fetched.

---

93 Teulet, *Relations politiques*, i, 293.
94 Consider the illuminating insights produced by Geoffrey Parker's counterfactual essay, 'What if the Spanish Armada had landed?', reprinted in his *Spain and the Netherlands, 1559–1659: Ten Studies* (London, 1979).

What if Mary Tudor's marriage to Prince Philip of Spain had resulted in a family which lived to adulthood, all of them raised in the Catholic faith? What if Elizabeth of England had married, and had borne sons of her own? In either case, we surely would not have had Anglo-Scottish union in the early seventeenth century.

On the other hand, that might have happened earlier, if Elizabeth had died of her serious illness in 1562. At that time, Mary seems to have been trying not to offend moderate Protestants, and English religious persuasions were mostly Anglican-Catholic (judging by the *Book of Common Prayer*). Or civil war might have erupted: not the Thistle against the Rose, or one between a red rose and and a white one, but an English war of religion, which would probably have prevented Anglo-Scottish union.

What if Mary had died childless, in, say, 1557 or 1564? Again, Châtelherault would presumably have succeeded, as King James VI. But since the Hamiltons had no family links with the Tudors, there would have been no dynastic union. Yet, if Mary had died, Henry, Lord Darnley would have been Elizabeth's closest relative.[95] Henry, Lord Darnley, as Henry IX, successor to Elizabeth: the mind reels.

Or, finally: what if Darnley had turned out to be an acceptable consort? Surely, then, Mary would have managed to remove Moray and his Anglophile supporters from her Council, as she almost did in 1565. And her son, Charles James, would presumably have been raised a Catholic.[96] What would that have done to his chances for the English throne? By 1603, Protestantism appears to have been established firmly in the English national psyche (especially after the Armada – but would there have been an Armada in these hypothetical circumstances?[97]), and a Catholic succession in England seems, to me at least, impossible. Admittedly, whoever was ruling Scotland towards the end of the century would probably have tailored his or her religious policies to be acceptable to the English ruling elite, or 'electorate'. Nevertheless, the chances of a union of the Crowns would have been much slimmer than they were with the real James VI in 1603.

One final 'What if', if you will: Bonnie Prince Charlie and the A69 trunk road. In November 1745, Prince Charles Edward, in Edinburgh on his quest to restore Great Britain and Ireland to his father, held a 'cabinet meeting' in Holyrood House, the last time that complex acted as a seat of government. He won the debate over his plans for a winter campaign by one vote. He wished to invade England so that all three of his father's rightful inheritances were reconquered. As a result, the Prince had to accept a compromise. Instead of going down the A1, he was forced to invade via Carlisle: a remarkable strategic manoeuvre. He thus accomplished an adroit battle march, utterly wrongfooting Lord Cope, whose enormous army of 15,000 found itself trapped on the wrong side of the Pennines and unable, because of snow, to

---

95 Darnley was the son of Matthew Stewart, Earl of Lennox, and Margaret Douglas, daughter of the earl of Angus and Margaret Tudor (James IV's widow). His son, of course, did succeed Elizabeth. See J.E.A. Dawson, 'Mary Queen of Scots, Lord Darnley, and Anglo-Scottish Relations in 1565', *International History Review*, 8 (1986), pp. 1–24.

96 For the prince's name, see Michael Lynch, 'Queen Mary's Triumph: the Baptismal Celebrations at Stirling in December 1566', *SHR* lxix (1990), pp. 1–21, at p. 6.

97 A point first suggested to me by Sandy Grant.

outflank Charles whilst he quickly captured Carlisle and moved on via Lancaster to Derby and the pages of legend, David Niven and fame.

After Culloden, the Hanoverian regime resolved that never again should Carlisle be cut off from Newcastle-upon-Tyne or the Highlands open to invasion. Thus were built two of the most remarkable structures erected in Great Britain during the eighteenth century: Fort George just outside Inverness, and the route of what is now the A69 trunk road, known then as 'The Military Road'. It was the first such point-to-point road built by parliamentary grant in British history. General Wade, who did so much to open up the Highlands by his roads there, was given charge of the project which he accomplished during the next decade. His task was arduous, as he frequently complained, but not initially. For the first fifteen miles out of Newcastle, he simply built upon the foundations of Hadrian's Wall. Thus were military monuments recycled. Had the Rough Wooings not happened, there would probably never, in my mind, have been a Stuart succession to England, and no Stuarts would probably have meant no Glorious Revolution of 1688 and no Hanoverian succession in 1714. Thus, no role for David Niven to play in 1938 for Alexander Korda's British Lion-London Film, *Bonnie Prince Charlie*. Let that be the main conclusion to be drawn from all this counterfactual musing.

We know now what happened then. They did not at the time. We know that Scotland and England were united by James VI's succession in 1603 as James I. That union did not happen earlier, by the marriage of Mary and Edward, is the core of this book. Thus Scotland and England remained utterly separate, sovereign monarchies within the European power network from 1542 until 1603. They could have gone to war again. Certainly William Cecil made enormous contingency plans for such a possibility and did everything he could to avoid it.[98]

One of the most remarkable testimonies to Cecil's efforts and to the failure of the English Rough Wooings can be seen today on the shelf of any reputable history research library. On the one hand, the *Calendar of State Papers relating to Scotland*, which goes down to 1603, has only one volume of correspondence for the period March 1547 to March 1563 (when Scotland and England were at open war on two occasions and an English army and navy were there in 1560). Fully twelve volumes were published between 1898 and 1952 and it is still in progress. They are very heavy on the wrists. See also the massive two-volume *The Border Papers: Calendar of Letters and Papers relating to the affairs of the Borders of England and Scotland preserved in Her Majesty's Public Record Office (1560–1603)*, edited by the redoubtable Joseph Bain and published in 1894 and 1895. All of these pages concern a time of utter non-belligerency between the two kingdoms.

A NEW HADRIAN'S WALL?

Two final delicious incidents richly illustrate this long shadow of the Rough Wooings and Mary's betrothal to the Dauphin. In November 1542, one of the

---

98 J.E.A. Dawson's handsome clutch of articles richly illustrates Cecil's fixation with Scotland during his lifetime, which stretched down to 1598.

heroes of the 'Battle' of Solway Moss was Sir Thomas Dacre.[99] Dacre was a West-Borderer whose father, Thomas 2nd Lord Dacre of Gilsland, had commanded the English right wing at the Battle of Flodden and thereby had earned lasting renown. Sir Thomas, however, was a bastard and could not succeed to his father's title and lands. But so valiant was his performance at Solway Moss that Henry VIII almost immediately bestowed upon him all of the dwellings and lands of Lanercost Priory, which had come into royal hands with the Reformation. Lanercost was a considerable estate. It ran from the River Irwell up to the stone marker borderline of Hadrian's Wall, then as now standing, if attenuated, and visible.

When Sir Thomas died in 1565, his lands went to his eldest son, Christopher, who led an active frontier life from 1560 when he served in Norfolk's army at the siege of Leith until his death in 1593. Every morning of his life there he gazed upon Hadrian's great edifice, known in contemporary parlance as 'Picts Wall' or 'Picts Dike'. Even with Anglo-Scottish peace, the Borders remained troubled. Dacre complained that he dwelt at the outermost part of England, 'at all tymes cruelly broiken up and spoiled' and always 'in more danger than anye' other Borderer.

Moreover, by the commencement of the 1580s, it was clear to most English statesmen that war with Spain was a real possibility. They thus again looked to England's defences. As Elizabeth always did, she revived one of her sister's Acts of Parliament. Mary and Philip's of 1555 for the defence of the North was thus passed again in 1581. A commission was established to survey faults and propose remedies. Christopher Dacre served on it during 1583–84.

His first proposal was that a series of hedges and ditches be constructed from Bowness on the Solway to Wark on the Tweed, 'towne to towne throughout the said Border', which would be both a safeguard against raiders and 'a defence'. He then prepared and sent a map of this 'hoodge and mane ditch' and a series of new fortifications to the Privy Council for their approval. Back home, he then took to studying the Roman Empire and hit upon the idea of a brand-new Hadrian's Wall. His ideas were then carefully penned onto a manuscript booklet entitled 'The Epystle to the Queen's Majestie'. He argued that what the Romans had done in Britain between AD 122 and 138 could be done now. Caesar moreover had done something similar (a 19 mile wall along the River Rhône) in 58 BC, and Dacre reckoned (using his estimates of how many legions worked on Hadrian's Wall) it would cost only £30,000.

This wall, however, had to be to the most modern standards and he proposed it be 60 feet thick, with fortlets or what he termed 'Insconces' every mile. These would be self-contained fortified villages in which the garrisons would dwell and make their livings during peacetime. At 1d rent per acre, gentlemen gunners and soldiers would account the community (each man was to have a thousand acres for his farming) a 'perrfermente and a good bargaine'. The 'Forteficacions Royall', or what he liked to call 'the Loyall Worke', would thus make England utterly secure along its northern frontier. The Scots certainly, 'in theyr accostomed manner', could never capture any of the sconces:

99 M.H. Merriman, 'The Epystle to the Queen's Majestie and its "Platte".

Neyther the Frenche Kinge wyll have greate lyste to cherdge his crowne any longer with the mayntaynaunce of that kingdome to be a brydell for this estate, neyther wyll the Kinge of Spayne be any thinge hastye to enter into newe Leage that waye. The commondyte whearof yt self is suffycyente to countervayle the resedue of the chardge your Majesty is to be at hearin.

Whatever Cecil thought of this magnificent proposal or its 'commondyte', the costs were obviously prohibitive. Nothing, to Dacre's bitter regret, came of his scheme. It would have been a remarkable construction: a sixteenth-century Maginot Line. The point to appreciate is that none of this would have come down to us today had Mary been married to Edward VI and they had produced offspring.

Now for some more concluding stories. James VI loved the hunt: all Stewart monarchs did. In 1598, he was out chasing the inedibles of the Merse, not far from

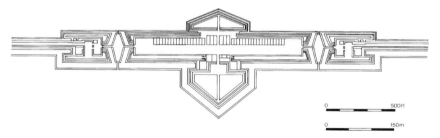

Fig. 14.8 Christopher Dacre first became intimately familiar with all of the frontier line when he helped draw up a map in 1585. He then penned a presentation copy of his proposal for a New Hadrian's Wall, probably in 1587. But his 'platte' of the wall was so large, he had to paste together three sheets of paper. Subsequently, they separated. The left-hand portion remained in his book and was archived in Border Papers. The middle portion and the right-hand one ended up in State Papers, Domestic and State Papers Scotland. Not until the mid-twentieth century were they reunited, thanks to the knowledgeable eye of Howard Colvin. The lower figure is a redrawing of Dacre's proposal, executed for clarity.

the Bounds of Berwick. All Captains of the massive (but woefully incomplete[100]) works there had strict instructions to allow no Scot entrance to, or sight of, the fortifications: England's shield against Scottish invasion. The then Governor, Peregrine Bertie, 9th Lord Willoughby de Eresby, a man with enormous rockface war experience both in the Low Countries and with the future Henry IV of France, rode out to request that James venture no further. James, ever witty, assured him that he would in no way view the walls. He jested, 'Think you I would hazard the Tower of London for the town of Berwick?'

Berwick actually would become a favourite spot on the map for James when he became King of England. Not only did he handsomely pension off its garrison in 1604, but he also made a special visit, on his famous 1603 progress south, to the pugnacious and renowned Captain of the castle on Holy Island, Sir William Read, whose career on the Borders went back to 1558. The artillery by then was so riddled with rust and pockmarked by decay that one piece exploded when fired off in salute to England's new king, killing the gunner.

James then set about one of his most remarkable constructions (if one sets to one side his famous New River to supply London with water): an all-weather, permanent, stone bridge across the Tweed: what one might call a Channel Tunnel for the sixteenth century. Thus were the two kingdoms to be linked indissolubly.[101] The old bridge collapsed in 1605 and 1611. Work started on the new edifice in June 1611 and it was finally completed and opened for traffic, which it still carries today, in July 1627. It cost £12,522 1s. 9d.[102] There are now many more magnificent bridges across the Tweed, the last one being the Berwick A1 bypass. To my mind, the most awesome, worthy of the Roman Empire at its height, is the railway viaduct: the (oddly misnamed) Royal Border Bridge, designed by Robert Stephenson. This stupendous structure (it then cost £250,000 to build) stretches almost half a mile on 28 great arches so as to attain the town's station, built from the very masonry of the old castle where so much Anglo-Scottish history had occurred. When it was formally opened by Queen Victoria on 29 August 1850, Stephenson trumpeted that it and its station represented 'the final act of union'. James VI & I[103] would surely have agreed.

---

100 The Captain in 1598, Lord Willoughby, called it 'a meere showe and opinion of a stronge thinge' and that its garrison, if attacked, would 'be in more danger within than without'. Colvin, *King's Works*, iv, 66.

101 Similar grandiose rhetoric flowed when the brick railway bridge across the Tweed was opened in 1850.

102 The figure actually covers the period 1611–34 and may even then be too low. Colvin, *King's Works*, iv, 769–78.

103 Can anyone give me the factual details as to why Victoria's son was not styled Edward I & VII (or VII & I)? There was an Order in Council at the time of his accession, but I have never been able to trace it. When the United Kingdom of Great Britain was established in 1707, someone should have inserted an iron rule that no future monarch of that kingdom should bear the name of any previous monarch of either England or Scotland.

THE MAKING OF BRITS OR BRITONS

Let us now conclude. During our period, much intellectual cogitation and literary research was expended by scholars and antiquarians trying to trace whence and when Britons first marched onto the stage of history. John Mair (Major) asserted that all men born in the island were British. James Henrisoun argued fiercely that all dwellers there shared what one modern scholar has termed 'a common ethnic blood'. He wrote, 'We were britons at the beginning and come of one kind of lineage under one monarchy'. On the other hand, Gathelus came from Scythia, somewhere 'out there', on the steppes of Asia, to which Jason travelled in search of the Golden Fleece. And from the land of Philadelphia and the Pyramids, he made his way to Scotland.

Fig. 14.9. Wartime is a period of legalised theft. Scotland suffered enormous losses of possessions ranging from royal galleys to German-made working town clocks to humble church silver. This famous bible-holding piece of furniture from the pulpit in Holyrood Abbey kirk was picked up by Sir Richard Lee in 1544 and taken back home[104]. In 1984, this phoenix was re-stolen from its Hertfordshire home and hidden for fifteen years by persons unknown. In 1999, however, the magnificent Dunkeld Lectern (a gift it is said by Pope Alexander VI in 1498) was returned, improbably, to the John Knox House in the Netherbow, Edinburgh. The Rough Wooings were over.

104 For discussion of the losses from Holyrood in 1544, see John Harrison, *The History of the Monastery of the Holy-Rood and of the Palace of Holyrood House* (Edinburgh, 1919), 74–77, 79–80..

Both Matthew Stewart, Earl of Lennox and John Knox were 'kailyard Scots' who had kin and friends 'at home' and knew intimately the gossip of their Scottish neighbours. But they both lived in England for considerable periods. However, when their time on this firmament came to a close, they died in their native country: Lennox by a brawler's bullet at Stirling on 4 September 1571; Knox gently in his bed surrounded by his second wife and young children: a good death in 1572. Both men were in a real sense dual citizens. Lennox was the first Scottish aristocrat I know of since the Wars of Independence who (and whose family) owned landed estates in both Yorkshire and Dunbartonshire (from his restoration in December 1564 until the death of his son Charles in 1576).

Was he not thus the first British citizen, even if he was not the subject of a Britannic Majesty? Knox was another Briton: his last words were to the faithful 'of both the realms'. He married firstly an English girl, and could speak[105] (and write, as Jane Dawson has proved so convincingly) English as well as Scots. He was not only chaplain to an English King, he was almost made bishop of an English diocese. He even sent his sons to Cambridge, surely a remarkable statement about the mental culture in which he dwelt. Had it not been for the Rough Wooings, neither of these men would have become dual citizens, or, as I would prefer to have it, the first Britons of modern history. I invite my readers, and Linda Colley, to think on such things as they conclude this book, for their reading of which I most heartily thank them.

Dynasticism is curious, even bizarre. The rules governing inheritance vary and varied enormously over Europe as a whole and many political societies make it up as they go along. Poles elected their kings: so did and do the Danes, the Swedes, the Bohemians, and the Hungarians. Ever since 1516, Henry VIII had a perfectly legitimate heir, Princess Mary, who indeed did succeed and ruled: there was no real need for the Divorce and (thus?) the Reformation. England might be Catholic today. The Russians certainly made it up as they went along, witness the Romanoff line. How else did a German princess end up as Catherine the Great, ruler of the largest empire (China apart) in the world? Had Victoria been male, monarchs of Great Britain might still be Kings of Hanover. Had Edward VIII not gone off with a Baltimore belle, but made instead a suitable marriage, his descendants (had there been any) would be Britannic Majesties today. Since World War II, the Italians, then the Greeks, voted their monarchs out and dissolved the system entirely. So did the Chinese. On the other hand, Japan still has an Emperor.

Mary Queen of Scots is a classic case study of the system at work. From the moment of her birth she wielded enormous power and did important things. Queen in a week, she performed two vastly important services for her subjects. In the first place, she created peace, at least for a year. Given the enormous potentialities of her marriage, by January 1543 Henry VIII's 1542 war became a series of truces and then,

---

105 Indeed, the Catholic polemicist, Ninian Winzet, used to mock Knox for his English accent, alleging that he had forgotten the good Old Scots he had learned at his mother's knee.

in July, a peace. Secondly, she saved Scotland from what might have been a ghastly and bloody sucession crisis potentially worse than the Bruce/Balliol civil war of the early fourteenth century which almost destroyed the country. Because she lived, neither the Hamilton Arran family nor the Stewart Lennoxes could battle for the succession. There was no possibility or need, thanks to her infant vitality. That is power. She was thus nothing less than the saviour of her country. Not bad for a babe. There is nothing original in this interpretation: Gordon Donaldson made the same point even more trenchantly in 1965. Commentators did so in 1543 and since. It is nonetheless a point worth making again. Mary was in truth a dynastic enormity: Stewart, Tudor, Guise and related to so many other people. Her life was to cause many wars and much political and religous turmoil. But at her birth, she was a child of peace and a joy as well.

Bibliography

AN means the manuscript [not indicated by MS] is to be found in the Archives Nationales in Paris.

BL means the manuscript [indicated by MS] is to be found in what used to be called the BM or British Museum, but now is the British Library in London.

BN means the manuscript [indicated by MS] is to be found in the Bibliothèque Nationale in Paris.

Brussels means the manuscript [not indicated by MS] is to be found at the Archives Générales du Royaume in Brussels.

EHR always refers to the *English Historical Review.*

NAS now means means the manuscript [not indicated by MS] is to be found in the National Archives of Scotland H.M. General Register House, Edinburgh.

NLS means an original source [indicated by MS] consulted at the National Library of Scotland in Edinburgh.

SHR always refers to the *Scottish Historical Review.*

PRO means the manuscript [not indicated by MS] is to be found in the Public Record Office, then in Chancery Lane, London; now at Kew.

SHS refers to a source publication printed by the Scottish History Society.

SRO Scottish Record Office, now National Archives of Scotland.

TRHS always refers to *Transactions of the Royal Historical Society.*

Vienna means the manuscript [not indicated by MS] is to be found at the Osterreichisches Staatsarchiv: Haus-, Hof. und Staatsarchive at Vienna.

LIST OF SOURCES CITED

For abbreviations, I have attempted to employ the suggestions made by the *Scottish Historical Review* in 1968, but there are some exceptions

All books in English, unless otherwise noted, were printed in London.

All books in French, unless otherwise noted, were printed in Paris.

[*Abdn. Counc.*]
Extracts from the Council Register of the Burgh of Aberdeen, 1398–1570, ed. J. Stuart (Spalding Club, 1844–48).

[*Aberdeen*]
Extracts from the Council Register of the Burgh of Aberdeen, 1398–1570, ed. J. Stuart, 2 vols. (Aberdeen, 1844–48).

Accounts of the Master of Works, ed. H.M. Paton (Edinburgh, 1957).

Ackermann, S. (ed.), *Humphrey Cole: mint, measurement and maps in Elizabethan England* (British Museum, 1998).

[*Actes de Henri II*]
Les Actes de Henri II: Ordonnances des rois de France, ed. Marie-Noelle Baudouin-Matuszek and others (ongoing).

Adair, E.R., 'William Thomas: A forgotten clerk of the Privy Council', *Tudor Studies*, ed. R. Seton-Watson (1924), 133–60.

Adams, N., alias Bodrugan, *An Epitome of the title that the kynges Maiestie of Englande, hath to the souereigntie of Scotlande, continued upon the auncient writers of both nacions, from the beginnyng* (1548), reprinted (in part) in the *Complaynt*, 247–56.

[*ADCP*]
Acts of the Lords of Council in Public Affairs, 1501–1554: Selections from the Acta Dominorum Concilii introductory to the Register of the Privy Council of Scotland, ed. R.K. Hannay (Edinburgh, 1932).

Alford, S., *The early Elizabethan polity: William Cecil and the British succession crisis, 1558–1569* (Cambridge, 1998).

Anderson, M.S., *The origins of the modern European state system, 1494–1618* (Longman, 1998).

Anglo, S., *Spectacle, Pageantry and Early Tudor Policy* (1969).

[*APC*]
Acts of the Privy Council of England, ed. J.R. Dasent, 32 vols. (1890–1907).

[*APS*]
The Acts of the Parliaments of Scotland, 1124–1707, ed. T. Thomson and C. Innes (Edinburgh, 1814–75).

Archbold, W.A.J. (ed.), 'A Diary of the Expedition of 1544', *English Historical Review*, vol. 16 (1901), 503–507.

[Armstrong, *History*]
Armstrong, R.B., *The History of Liddesdale, Eskdale, Wauchopdale and the Debatable Land* (Edinburgh, 1883).

[Armstrong, MS]
'The History of Liddesdale, Eskdale, Ewesdale, Wauchopedale and the Debatable Land', vol. ii (unpublished manuscript in the National Library of Scotland, MS 6111).

Ascoli, G., *La Grande Bretaigne devant l'opinion française* (1927).

[*Atlas I*]
An Historical Atlas of Scotland, c. 400–c.1600, ed. P. McNeill and R. Nicholson (St. Andrews, 1975).

[*Atlas II*]
Atlas of Scottish History to 1707, ed. P.G.B. McNeill and H.L. MacQueen (Edinburgh, 1996).

Ayr Burgh Records, 1534–1624, ed. G. Pryde (SHS, 1937).

[*Balcarres Papers*]
Foreign Correspondence with Marie de Lorraine, Queen of Scotland, from the Originals in the Balcarres Papers, ed. M. Wood (SHS, 1923–5).

Bannerman, E., *Les influences françaises en Ecosse au temps de Marie Stuart* (Besançon, 1929).

Bapst, E., *Les mariages de Jacques V* (1889).

Bardgett, F.D., 'Faith, families and factions: the Scottish Reformation in Angus and the Mearns' (unpublished Ph.D. thesis, University of Edinbiurgh, 1987).

Bardgett, F.D., *Scotland Reformed: The Reformation in Angus and the Mearns* (Edinburgh, 1989).

Baudouin-Matuszek, M-N., 'Henri II et les expéditions françaises en Écosse', *Bibliothèque de l'ecole des Chartes* (no. 145, 1987), 339–82.

Baudouin-Matuszek, M-N., 'Un ambassadeur en Ecosse au XVIe siècle: Henri Clutin d'Oisel', *Revue historique* (lxii, 1990), 77–131.

Baudouin-Matuszek, M-N., 'Mary Stuart's Arrival in France in 1548', *SHR*

Baumgartner, F.J., *Henry II, King of France, 1547–1559* (Duke University Press, 1988), [Beaugé, *Histoire*]

L'Histoire de la Guerre d'Escosse: pendant les campagnes 1548 et 1549 par Jean de Beaugé, ed. J. Bain (Maitland Club, 1830) (originally Paris, 1556).

Beer, Barrett L., *Northumberland: The Political Career of John Dudley, Earl of Warwick and Duke of Northumberland* (Kent State University Press, 1973).

Beer, Barrett L., 'Northumberland: the Myth of the Wicked Duke and the Historical John Dudley', *Albion* (xi, 1979), 1–14.

Beer, Barrett, L., *Rebellion and Riot: Popular Disorder in England during the Reign of Edward VI* (Kent State University Press, 1982).

du Bellay, G., *Entreprise du Roy Dauphin* (1558).

Bennett, H.S., *English Books and Readers, 1457 to 1557* (Cambridge, 1952).

Bernard, G.W., *The Power of the Early Tudor Nobility* (Brighton, 1985).

de Berteville, Sieur, *Recit de l'Expedition en Ecosse, l'an 1546; et de la Battayle de Muscleburgh*, ed. D. Constable (Bannatyne Club, 1825).

Bindoff, S.T., 'The Stuarts and their Style', *EHR*, lx (1945), 197–210.

Bindoff, S.T., *The History of Parliament. The House of Commons, 1509–1558*, 3 vols. (1982)

Bjorn, C., Grant, A. & Stringer, K.J. (eds.), *Social and Political Identities in Western History* (Copenhagen, 1994).

Black, Jeremy (ed.), *The Origins of War in Early Modern Europe* (Edinburgh, 1987).

Bonner, E., 'Continuing the "Auld Alliance" in the Sixteenth Century: Scots in France and French in Scotland', *The Scottish Soldier Abroad*, ed. G. Simpson (Edinburgh, 1992), 31–46.

Bonner, E., 'The "Auld Alliance" and the Betrothal of Mary Queen of Scots: Fact and Fable', *Journal of the Sydney Society for Scottish History*, iv (1996), 3–22.

Bonner, E., 'The Recovery of St. Andrews Castle in 1547: French Naval Policy and Diplomacy in the British Isles', *EHR*, cxi (1996), 578–98.

Bonner, E., 'French Naturalization of the Scots in the Fifteenth and Sixteenth Centuries', *The Historical Journal* (1997).

Bonner, E., 'The Genesis of Henry VIII's "Rough Wooing" of the Scots', *Northern History*, xxxiii (1997), 16–51.

Bonner, E., 'The French Reactions to the Rough Wooing of Mary Queen of Scots', *The Journal of the Sydney Society for Scottish History*, vi (1998), 1–161.

Bonner, E., 'Scotland's "Auld Alliance" with France, 1295–1560' *History* (lxxxiv, 1999), 5–30.

Borland, R., *Border Raids and Reivers* (Dalbeattie, 1899).

Boulind, R., 'Ships of Private Origin in the mid-Tudor Navy: The Lartique, the Salmander, the Mary Willoughby, the Bark Aucher and the Galley Banchard', *The Mariner's Mirror*, lix (1973), 385–408.

Braddick, M.J., 'An English Military Revolution?', *The Historical Journal* (xxxvi, 1993), 965–975.

Bradshaw, B. and Morrill, J., *The British Problem, c. 1534–1707* (Basingstoke, 1996).

Bradshaw, B. and Roberts, P. (eds.), *British Consciousness and Identity: the Making of Britain, 1533–1707* (Cambridge, 1998).

Brandi, K., *The Emperor Charles V* (1939).

[Brantley, Thesis]

Brantley, H.W., 'The Foundatiorn of French Influence during the Pre-regency of Mary of Guise-Lorraine, 1547–1554' (unpublished M.A. dissertation, University of Alabama, 1962).

de Brantôme, P. de Bourdeilles, *Oeuvres Complètes*, ed. L. Lalanne, 11 vols (1864).

Brennan, G.E., 'Patriotism, language and politics in England, 1529–1603' (unpublished M.A. thesis, University of Manchester, 1982).

de la Brosse, J., *Histoire d'une capitaine bourbonnais au XVIe siècle: Jacques de la Brosse, 1485–1562: ses missions en Ecosse* (1929).

[*Brosse Missions*]

Two Missions of Jacques de la Brosse, ed. G. Dickinson (SHS, 1942).

Brown, J.B. (ed.), 'The French Troops in the Borders in 1548', *Transactions of Hawick Archaeological Society* (1905), 35–45.

Brown, K.M., *Bloodfeud in Scotland, 1573–1625: Violence, Justice and Politics in an Early Modern Society* (Edinburgh, 1986).

Brown, P.H., *Early Travellers in Scotland* (Edinburgh, 1891).

Brown, P.H., *Scotland before 1700 from contemporary documents* (Edinburgh, 1893).

Brown, P.H., *Scotland in the Time of Mary Stuart* (1904).

Brown, P.H., *The History of Scotland*, 3 vols. (Cambridge, 1908–1909).

Brown, R.R. and Smith, R.D., *Guns from the Sea: Ships' Armaments in the Age of Discovery* (Royal Armouries, 1988).

Bryce, W.M., 'Mary Stuart's Voyage to France,' *EHR* (xxii, 1907), 43–50.

Bryce, W.M.A., 'A French Mission to Scotland in 1543', *Proceedings of the Society of Antiquaries of Scotland* (xlii, 1908), 243–52.

[Buchanan]

The History of Scotland, by George Buchanan, ed. J. Aikman, 4 vols. (Glasgow, 1827).

Buchanan, G., *The History of Scotland*, 3 vols. (Edinburgh, 1821).

Bull, S.B., 'The furie of the ordnance' (unpublished Ph.D. thesis, University of Wales, Swansea, 1989).

Burke, N., 'Dublin's North-Eastern City Wall: Early Reclamation and Development at the Poddle-Liffey Confluence', *Proceedings of the Irish Academy* (74, 1974), 113–132.

Burley, G.H.C., 'The French Ascendancy in Scotland, 1554–60' (unpublished M.A. thesis, University of Birmingham, 1929).

Burn, Michael, *The Debatable Land: A Study of the Motives of Spies in Two Ages* (1970).

Burton, J.H., *The History of Scotland*, 7 vols. (Edinburgh, 1853).

Bury, J., 'Early Writings on Fortifications and Siegecraft: 1502–1554', *Fort*, vol. 13 (1985), 5–48.

[Bush, Thesis]

Bush, M.L., 'The Rise to Power of Edward Seymour, Protector Somerset, 1500–1547' (unpublished Ph.D. dissertation, University of Cambridge, 1964).

Bush, M.L., 'The Problem of the Far North: A Study of the Crisis of 1537 and its consequences', *Northern History* (vi, 1971), 40–63.

Bush, M.L., *The Government Policy of Protector Somerset* (1975).

[Calderwood]

History of the Kirk of Scotland by Mr. David Calderwood, ed. T. Thomson and D. Laing, 8 vols. (Wodrow Society, 1842–49).

Caldwell, D., 'A Sixteenth-Century Group of Gun Towers in Scotland', *Fort*, vol. 12 (1984), 15–24.

Caldwell, D., 'The Battle of Pinkie', in *Scotland and War AD 79–1918*, ed. N. Macdougall (Edinburgh, 1991), 61–94.

Caldwell, D., 'Royal Patronage of Arms and Armour Making in Fifteenth- and Sixteenth-Century Scotland', in Caldwell (ed.), *Scottish Weapons and Fortifications* (Edinburgh, 1981), 73–93.

Caldwell, D.H. and Ewart, G., 'Excavations at Eyemouth, Berwickshire, in a mid-16th-century *trace italienne* fort', *Post-Medieval Archaeology*, 31 (1997), 61–119.

Calendar of Patent Rolls preserved in the Public Record Office, Edward VI, 1547–53, ed. R.H. Brodie, 5 vols. (1924–29).

Calendar of Writs preserved at Yester House, 1166–1625, ed. C.C.H. Harvey & J. Macleod (Scottish Record Society, no. 55, 1930).

[*CSP Dom. Add., 1547–65*]

Calendar of State Papers Domestic for the Reign of Elizabeth, 1601–1603 and *Addenda, 1547–65*, ed. R. Lemon (1868).

[*CSP For.*]

Calendar of State Papers, Foreign to the Reign of Edward VI, 1547–1553, ed. W.B. Turnbull (1863).

[*CSP Scot.*]

Calendar of the State Papers relating to Scotland and Mary Queen of Scots, 1547–1603, ed. J. Bain and others, 14 vols. (Edinburgh, 1898-).

[*CSP Spain*]

Calendar of State Papers, Spanish, ed. G.A. Bergenroth and others, 13 vols. and 2 supplements (1862–1954).

Calendar of State Papers, Venetian, ed. R. Brown and others, 9 vols. (1864–98).

Camden Miscellany vol. XXV (1974).

Camden Miscellany vol. XXXI (1992).

Cameron, J., *James V: The Personal Rule, 1528–1542* (East Linton, 1998).

Campbell, D.S., 'English foreign policy, 1509–21' (unpublished D.Phil. thesis, University of Cambridge, 1980).

Carroll, S., *Noble Power during the French Wars of Religion: The Guise Affinity and the Catholic Cause in Normandy* (Cambridge, 1998).

Carter, C.H., *The Western European Powers, 1500–1700* (1971).

Charrière, E., ed., *Négotiations de la France dans le Levant, ou correspondences, mémoires et actes diplomatiques des ambassadeurs à Constantinople*, 4 vols. (1848–60).

Chauvire, R., *Le Secret de Marie Stuart* (1937).

Cheke, Sir John, *The hurt of Sedicion howe grevous it is to a communewelth* (1549).

Christensen, T.L., 'Scots in Denmark in the sixteenth century', *SHR*, xlix (1970), 125–45.

Christensen, T.L., 'Scoto-Danish relations in the sixteenth century: the historiography and some questions', *SHR*, xlviii (1969), 54–63.

Chronicle of Perth: A register of remarkable occurrences, chiefly connected with that city, from the year 1210 to 1668, ed. J. Maidment (Maitland Club, 1831).

Churchyard, T., *A General Rehearsall of Warres, Wherein is five hundred severall services of land and sea* (1579).

Churchyard, T., *Churchyard's Chippes* (1575)

Clard, S., 'English Naval Strategy during the Anglo-Scottish wars of the 1540s' (unpublished M.Phil. thesis, University of Strathclyde, 1992).

Cloulas, Ivan, *Henri II* (Fayard, 1985).

Colley, L., *Britons: Forging the Nation, 1707–1837* (1992).

[Colvin, *King's Works*]

Colvin, H.M., *The History of the King's Works*, iv [1485–1660: Part ii], HMSO (1982).

[*Complaynt Scotlande*]

The Complaynt of Scotlande vyth ane Exhortatione to the Thre Esstaits to be vigilante in the Deffens of their Public veil (Paris, 1549?), reprinted in *The Complaynt*, ed. J.A.H. Murray (Early English Text Society, 1872–73).

[*Complaynt Scotland*]

The Complaynt of Scotland vyth ane Exhortatione to the Thre Esstaits to be vigilante in the Deffens of their Public veil (Paris, 1549?), ed. Alasdair Stewart (Aberdeen, 1983).

Constable, A. (ed.), *John Major's History of Greater Britain* (SHS, 1892).

Cornish, P. and McBride, A., *Henry VIII's Army* (Oxford, 1987).

Corvisier, André, *Armies and Societies in Europe, 1494–1798* (Indiana University Press, 1979).

Cowan, I.B., *The Enigma of Mary Stuart* (1972).

Cowan, I.B. and Shaw, D. (eds.), *The Renaissance and Reformation in Scotland* (Edinburgh, 1983).

Coward, B., 'The Lieutenancy of Lancashire and Cheshire in the Sixteenth and Early Seventeenth Centuries', *Transactions of the Historical Society of Lancashire and Cheshire*, vol. 119 (1967), 39–64.

[*CPR Edward VI*]

Calendar of Patent Rolls, Edward VI, ed. R.H. Brodie (1924–29).

Crawford, B.E., 'The Pawning of Orkney and Shetland: A reconsideration of the events of 1460–9', *SHR*, xlviii (1969), 18–34.

Crawford, G., *The Lives and Characters of the Crown Officers of Scotland* (Edinburgh, 1726).

Cruden, S., *The Scottish Castle* (Edinburgh, 1960).

Cruickshank, C.G., 'The Renaissance', in *A Guide to the Sources of British Military History*, ed. R. Higman (1972).

Cuisiat, D., *Lettres du Cardinal Charles de Lorraine (1525–1574)* (Geneva, 1998).

Cunningham, A., *The Loyal Clans* (Cambridge, 1932).

Cunningham, S., 'The establishment of the Tudor regime' (unpublished Ph.D. thesis, University of London, 1985).

Dalrymple, *Historie*
  The Historie of Scotland, wrytten first in Latin by the most reverend and worthy Jhone Leslie, Bishop of Rosse, and translated in Scottish by Father James Dalrymple 1598, edited by E.G. Cody and W. Murison, 2 vols, Scottish Text Society (1888, 1895).

Danmark-Norges Traktater, ed. L. Laursen, 6 vols. (Copenhagen, 1916).

Davidson, J., and Gray, A., *The Scottish Staple at Veere* (1909).

[Davies, Thesis]

Davies, C.S.L., 'Supply Services of English Armed Services, 1509–1550' (unpublished D.Phil. thesis, University of Oxford, 1963).

Davies, C.S.L., 'Provisions for Armies, 1509–1550: A Study in the Effectiveness of early Tudor Government', *Economic History Review*, xvii (1964–65), 234–48.

Davies, C.S.L., 'Administration of the Royal Navy Under Henry VIII: the Origins of the Navy Board', *EHR*, lxxix (1965), 268–86.

Davies, M.B. (ed.), 'The "Enterprise" of Paris and Boulogne', Fouad 1 University, Bulletin of the Faculty of Arts, vol. 11 (1949), 37–95.

Davies, M.B. (ed.), 'Boulogne and Calais from 1545 to 1550', Fouad 1 University, Bulletin of the Faculty of Arts, vol. 12 (1950), 1–90.

Davis, H., 'John Brende: Soldier and Translator', *The Huntington Library Quarterly* (i, 1937–38), 421–426.

Dawson, J.E.A., 'The Fifth Earl of Argyle, Gaelic Lordship and Political Power in Sixteenth-century Scotland', *SHR* (lxvii, 1988), 1–27.

Dawson, J.E.A., 'Mary Queen of Scots, Lord Darnley, and Anglo-Scottish Relations in 1565', *International History Review* (viii, 1986), 1–24

Dawson, J.E.A., 'William Cecil and the British Dimension of Early Elizabethan Foreign Policy', *History* (lxxiv, 1989), 196–216.

Dawson, J.E.A., 'The Two John Knoxes: England, Scotland the 1558 Tracts', *Journal of Ecclesiastical History* (xlii, 1991), 555–76.

Dawson, J.E.A., 'Anglo-Scottish protestant culture and integration in sixteenth-century Britain', *Conquest and Union: Fashioning a British State, 1485–1725*, ed. S.G. Ellis and Sarah Barber (1995), 87–114.

[*Declaracion*]

A Declaracion, Conteynng the iust cavses and consyderations, of this present warre with the Scottis, wherin also appere the trewe & right title, that the kinges most royall maiesty hath to the souerayntie of Scotland (1542), reprinted in *The Complaynt*, 191–206.

Decrue de Stoutz, F., *Anne, duc de Montmorency, connétable et pair de France sous les rois Henri II, François II, et Charles IX*, 2 vols. (Paris, 1889).

La Deffaicte des Anglois par les écossois faicte le jour de jeudi sainct dernier et la grande Bataille entre barbe Rousse et des gallères et carraques de Lempereur qui veniont pour avitailler Nice (? Rouen, 1544/45).

Delbrück, H., *The Dawn of Modern Warfare: History of the Art of War*, vol. iv. (1985).

Desjardins, A. (ed.), *Négotiations Diplomatiques de la France avec la Toscane*, 6 vols. (1859–86).

Desmonstiers, P., *Des estats et maisons Plus Illustres de la Chrestienté* (1549).

Dewar, M., *Sir Thomas Smith: A Tudor Intellectual in Office* (1964).

Dickinson, G., *Two Missions of Jacques De La Brose* (SHS, 1942).

Dickinson, G., 'Some notes on the Scottish Army in the first half of the sixteenth century', *SHR*, xxviii (1949), 133–45.

Dickinson, G. (ed.), 'Instructions to the French Ambassador, 30 March 1550', *SHR*, xxvi (1947), 154–67.

Dickinson, G. (ed.), *Mission de Beccarie de Pavie, Baron de Fourquevaux, en Ecosse, 1549. Documents originaux de fond Fourquevaux* (Oxford, 1948).

[Dickinson, *de la Brosse*]

Dickinson, G., (ed.), 'Two missions of Jacques de la Brosse: An Account of the Affairs of Scotland in the year 1543 and the Journal of the Siege of Leith, 1560', SHS (1942).

Dickinson, W.C., *Scotland from the earliest times to 1603* (Edinburgh, 1961).

Dickson, W.K., 'The Scots Law of Treason', *Juridical Review*, x, (1898), 245–55.

[Dietz, Thesis]

Dietz, B., 'Privateering in North West European Waters, 1568–1572' (unpublished Ph.D. dissertation, University of London, 1959).

Dietz, F.C., *English Government Finance, 1485–1558* (1920).

Dietz, F.C., *English Public Finance, 1558–1641* (1932)

[*Diurnal*]

A Diurnal of Remarkable Occurrents that have passed within the country of Scotland, since the death of King James the fourth, till the year 1575 (Bannatyne and Maitland Clubs, 1833).

Dixon, P.W., 'Fortified Houses on the Anglo-Scottish Border: a study of the domestic architecture of the upland area in its social and economic context, 1485–1625' (unpublished D.Phil. dissertation, Oxford, 1977).

[*DNB*]

Dictionary of National Biography, ed. L. Stephens and S. Lee (1885–1900).

Donaldson, G., *The Scottish Reformation* (Cambridge, 1960).

Donaldson, G., 'Foundations of Anglo-Scottish Union', in *Essays Presented to Sir John Neale*, ed. S.T. Bindoff and others (1961).

[Donaldson, *Scotland*]

Donaldson, G., *Scotland: James V to James VII* (Edinburgh, 1965).

Donaldson, G., *Reformed by Bishops: Galloway, Orkney and Caithness* (Edinburgh, 1987).

Douais, C., *Une importante correspondance du XVIe siècle, le baron de Fourquevaux: Ecosse, Italie, Espagne, Languedoc, 1548–1574* (1891).

Dow, J., 'Skotter in sixteenth-century Scania', *SHR*, xliv (1965), 34–51.

Dow, J., 'Scottish Trade with Sweden, 1512–80', *SHR*, xlviii (1969), 64–79.

Dowden, J., *The Bishops of Scotland . . . prior to the Reformation*, ed. J.M. Thomas (Glasgow, 1912).

Downing, B.M., *The Military Revolution and Political Change: Origins of Democracy and Autocracy in Early Modern Europe* (Princeton, 1992).

Duffy, C., *Siege Warfare* (1979).

Dunbar, A.H., *Scottish Kings: A Revised Chronology of Scottish History, 1005–1625*, 2nd ed. (Edinburgh, 1906).

[*Dundee*]

Charters, Writs and Public Documents of the Royal Burgh of Dundee, 1292–1880, ed. W Hay (Dundee, 1880).

Duns, Professor John, 'Notes on a Helmet found at Ancrum Moor', *Proceedings of the Society of Antiquaries of Scotland*, 3rd ser., vi, (1895–96), 317–322.

Durkan, J. and Ross, A., *Early Scottish Libraries* (Glasgow, 1958).

Dwyer, John, Mason R. and Murdoch, A. (eds.), *New Perspectives on the Politics and Culture of Early Modern Scotland* (Edinburgh, 1982).

Easson, D.E., *Gavin Dunbar, Chancellor of Scotland, Archbishop of Glasgow* (Edinburgh, 1947).

Eaves, R.G., *Henry VIII's Scottish Diplomacy, 1513–1524* (New York, 1971).

[*Edin. Burgh Recs.*]

Extracts from the Records of the Burgh of Edinburgh, ed. J.D. Marwick, 4 vols. (Scottish Burgh Record Society, 1869–92).

Edgar, M.G., *Stories from Scottish History* (1906).

Edington, C., 'Sir David Lindsay of the Mount: political and religious culture in Renaissance Scotland' (unpublished Ph.D. thesis, University of St. Andrews, 1992).

Edington, C., *Court and Culture in Renaissance Scotland: Sir David Lindsay of the Mount (1486–1555)* (East Linton, 1994).

[*Edward VI*]

The Literary Remains of Edward VI, ed. J.G. Nichols, 2 vols. (Roxburghe Club, 1857).

Ellis, D.A., 'English military theory and the military revolution of the sixteenth century' (unpublished D.Phil. thesis, University of Oxford, 1992).

Ellis, H., *Original letters, illustrative of English history: including numerous royal letters from autographs in the British Museum*, 4 vols. (1846).

Ellis, S.G., 'A Border Baron and the Tudor State: The Rise and Fall of Lord Dacre of the North', *The Historical Journal*, vol. 35 (1992), 253–277.

Ellis, S.G. and Barber, S. (eds.), *Conquest & Union: Fashioning A British State, 1485–1725* (1995).

Eltis, D., *The Military Revolution in Sixteenth-Century Europe* (1995).

Elton, G.R., *England Under the Tudors* (1955).

Elton, G.R., *Henry VIII: An Essay in Revision* (Historical Association, 1962).

Elton, G.R., *Policy and Police* (1984)

Emmison, F.G., *Tudor Secretary: Sir William Petre at Court and Home* (1930).

[*Epistle*]

An Epistle or exhortacion, to unitie & peace, sent from the Lorde Protector, & others the kynges moste honorable counsaill of England: To the Nobilitie, Gentlemen, and Commons, and al others the inhabitauntes of the Realme of Scotlande (1548), reprinted in the *Complaynt Scotlande*, 237–46. German edition entitled: *Ein Schrifftiliche vermanung zum friede und Einigkeith des obersen Guberhnators vnd aunderer der Furnemsten Regenten und Rethe des Konigreichs Engllendt An den Adell und Gemeine Stende Auch alle andere Einwohner des Reichs Schottenlands* (Erfurt, 1549).

Epistolae Jacobi Quarti, Jacobi Quinti et Mariae Regum Scotorum, ed. T. Ruddiman, 2 vols. (Edinburgh, 1722–24).

Evennett, H.O., *The Cardinal of Lorraine and the Council of Trent* (1930).

[*Exchequer Rolls*]

Rotuli Scaccarii Regum Scotorum: The Exchequer Rolls of Scotland, ed. J. Stewart and others, 23 vols. (Edinburgh, 1878–1908).

[*Exhortacion*]

Henderson, J., *An Exhortacion to the Scottes to conforme themselfes to the honorable, Expedient & godly Union betweene the two Realmes of Englande & Scotland* (1547), reprinted in the *Complaynt* (1873), 208–36.

[*Expedicion*]

The late expedicion in Scotland . . . of . . . the erle of Hertforde (1544), reprinted in *Tudor Tracts*, ed. A.F. Pollard (n.d.), 39–51.

[*Fasti*]

Fasti Ecclesiae Scoticanae Medii Aevi ad annum 1638 (Scottish Record Society, 1969).

Fergusson, J., '1547: The Rough Wooing', *Blackwood's Magazine,* cclxii (1947), 183–94.

Fergusson, Sir James, *The White hind and Other Discoveries* (1963).

Finnie, E., 'The House of Hamilton: Patronage, Politics and the Church in the Reformation Period', *Innes Review,* xxxvi, (1985), 3–28.

Fleming, D.H., *Mary Queen of Scots* (Edinburgh, 1897).

Fleming, D.H., 'Mr. Andrew Lang and the murder of Cardinal Beaton', *Contemporary Review,* lxxiv, (1898), 375–389.

Fleming, D.H., *The Reformation in Scotland: Causes, Characteristics, Consequences* (Edinburgh, 1910).

Fleury-Vindry, *Dictionaire de l'état-major français au XVIe siècle* (Bergerac, 1901).

Fleury-Vindry, *Les Ambassadeurs français permanents au XVIe siècle* (1903).

[*Foedera*]

Foedera, Conventiones, Litterae et Cuiuscunque Generis Acta Publica, ed. T. Rymer (Record Commission, 1816–69).

Forbes-Leith, W., *The Scots Men-at-Arms and Life Guards in France, 1418–1830* (Edinburgh, 1882).

Forestie, E., *Un Capitaine Gascon du XVIe Siècle: Corbeyran de Cardaillac-Sarlabons, Mestre de Camp, Gouverneur de Dunbar* (1897).

Forneron, H., *Les Ducs de Guise et leur époque: Etude historique sur le seizième siècle* (1877).

de Fourquevaux, Baron, M.F., de Pavie, *Les Vies de Plusieurs Grands Capitaines François* (1642).

[Fourquevaux, *Mission*]

Mission de Beccarie de Pavie, Baron de Fourquevaux Ecosse 1549, ed. G. Dickinson (Oxford, 1948).

Fox, John, *Actes and Monuments*, ed. J. Pratt (1870).

Franklin, D., *The Scottish Regency of the Earl of Arran. A Study in the Failure of Anglo-Scottish Relations* (Lampeter, 1995).

Fraser, A., *Mary Queen of Scots* (1969).

Fraser, J., *Chronicles of the Frasers, 916–1674*, ed. W. MacKay (*SHS*, 1905).

Fraser, W., *The Scotts of Buccleuch*, 2 vols. (Edinburgh, 1885).

Fraser, W., *The Douglas Book*, 4 vols. (Edinburgh, 1885).

Fraser, W., *The Melvilles, Earls of Melville and the Leslies, Earls of Leslie*, 3 vols. (Edinburgh, 1890).

Froude, J.A., *The History of England from the Fall of Wolsey to the Defeat of the Spanish Armada*, 12 vols. (1856–70).

Fulwell, U., *The Flower of Fame* (1575), reprinted in *The Harleian Miscellany*, ix, 368–74, ed. T. Park (1808–13).

Gail, J.B. (ed.), *Lettres inédites de Henri II, Diane de Poitiers, Marie Stuart, François, Roi Dauphin addressées au connétable Anne de Montmorency* (1818).

Gammon, S.R., *Statesman and Schemer: William, First Lord Paget: Tudor Minister* (1973).

[Gardiner]

Letters of Stephen Gardiner, ed. J.A. Miller (Cambridge, 1933).

Garrisson, Janine, *A History of Sixteenth-Century France, 1483–1598: Renaissance, Reformation and Rebellion* (1995).

Geimer, R.A., 'The Life and Works of Thomas Churchyard' (unpublished Ph.D. thesis, Northwestern University, 1965).

Gigon, C.M.M.S., *Contribution a l'histoire de l'impot sous l'ancien regime: La Révolte de la Gabelle en Guyenne, 1548–1549* (1906).

Glasgow, T., 'List of Ships in the Royal Navy from 1539 to 1588', *The Mariner's Mirror* lvi, (1970), 299–308.

Glover, J., *The Story of Scotland* (1960).

Goodacre, J., 'Parliamentary Taxation in Scotland, 1560–1603, *SHR*, lxviii (1989), 23–52.

Gordon, W., *The History of the Ancient, Noble and Illustrious Family of Gordon*, 2 vols. (Edinburgh, 1726).

Goring, J., 'The Military Obligations of the English People, 1511–1558' (unpublished Ph.D. dissertation, University of London, 1955).

Goring, J., 'Social Change and Military Decline in Mid-Tudor England', *History*, vol. 60 (1975), 185–197.

Grafton's Chronicle: or the History of England, ed. H. Ellis (1809).

Grainger, J.D., *Cromwell Against the Scots. The Last Anglo-Scottish War, 1650–1652* (East Linton, 1997).

Grant, A. and Stringer K.J. (eds.), *Uniting the Kingdom? The Making of British History* (1995).

[Granvelle, *Papiers*]

Papiers d'état du Cardinal de Granvelle d'après les manuscrits de la Bibliothèque de Besançon, ed. C. Weiss, 9 vols. (1841–52).

Greengrass, Mark (ed.), *Conquest and Coalescence: The Shaping of the State in Early Modern Europe* (1991).

Gregory, D., *History of the Western Highlands and Isles of Scotland from . . . 1493 to . . . 1625* (Edinburgh, 1726 and 1836).

[Grey of Wilton]

A commentary of the services and charges of William Lord Grey of Wilton, K.G., ed. P. de Malpas Grey Egerton (Camden Society, 1847).

Grey, W.F. and Jamieson, J.H., *A Short History of Haddington* (Edinburgh, 1944).

Gruffudd, Elis, *Chronicle*, ed. M.B. Davies (Cairo, 1944–50).

Guilmartin, J.F., 'The Military Revolution: Origins and First Tests Abroad', in Rogers (ed.), *The Military Revolution Debate*, 299–336.

Guillemin, J.J., *Le Cardinal de Lorraine, son influence politique et religieuse au XVIe siècle* (1847).

[Guise, *Mèmoires*]

Mèmoires-Journaux de François de Lorraine, duc de Guise, 1547–61, ed. J.F. Michaud and J.F. Poujoulat (1854).

Gunn, S., 'The French Wars of Henry VIII', in J. Black (ed.), *The Origins of War in Early Modern Europe*, 28–51.

Gunn, S., *Charles Brandon, Duke of Suffolk, 1484–1545* (Oxford, 1988).

Gush, G., *Renaissance Armies, 1480–1650* (Cambridge, 1975).

Guy, I. 'The Scottish export trade, 1460–1599, from the Exchequer Rolls' (unpublished M.Phil. thesis, University of St. Andrews, 1982)

Guy, I., 'The Scottish export trade, 1460–1599, in T.C. Smout (ed.), *Scotland and Europe* (Edinburgh, 1986).

Guy, J., *Tudor England* (Oxford, 1990).

Guy, J. (ed.), *The Tudor Monarchy* (1997).

Haddington: Royal Burgh: A History and a Guide (East Linton, 1997).

Hale, J.R., *Renaissance War Studies* (Hambledon, 1983).

Hall, B.S., *Weapons & Warfare in Renaissance Europe* (1997).

[Hall, *Union*]

Hall, E., *The Union of the two Noble and Illustre Famelies of York and Lancaster . . .* ed. H. Ellis (1809).

Hall, E., *The Triumphant Reigne of Kyng Henry the VIII*, 2 vols. (1904).

[*Hamilton Papers*]

The Hamilton Papers, ed. J. Bain, 2 vols. (Edinburgh, 1890–92).

[*Handel met Engeland*]

Bronnen tot de Geschiedenis van den Handel met Engeland, Schotland en Ierland, 1485–1558, ed. H.J. Smit (Rijks Geschiedkkundige Publication no. 81, 1942).

Hannay, R.K., 'Parliament' and General Council', *SHR*, xviii (1921), 157–70.

Hannay, R.K., 'General Council and Council of Estates', *SHR*, xx (1923), 98–115.

Hannay, R.K., 'General Council of Estates', *SHR*, xx (1923), 263–84.

Hannay, R.K., 'Some Papal Bulls among the Hamilton Papers, *SHR*, xxii (1924), 23–42.

Hannay, R.K., 'The Earl of Arran and Queen Mary', *SHR*, xviii (1921), 258–76.

Hannay, R.K, (ed.), 'Letters of the Papal Legate in Scotland, 1543', *SHR*, xi (1911), 1–26.

Harbison, E.H., *Rival Ambassadors at the Court of Queen Mary* (1940)

The Harleian Miscellany: a collection of scarce, curious, and entertaining pamphlets and tracts found in the late earl of Oxford's library, edited by J. Malham (1808–1811)

Harvey, J. and Oswald, A., *English Medieval Architects: A Bibliographical Dictionary down to 1550* (1954).

Hattaway, H.H., 'Some Aspects of Tudor Military History', *The Army Quarterly*, vol. 98 (1969), 53–63.

Hay, D., *The Anglia Historia of Polydore Vergil* (Camden Society, 1950).

Hay, D., 'The use of the term 'Great Britain' in the Middle Ages', *Proceedings of the Society of Antiquaries of Scotland*, lxxxix (1955–56), 55–66.

[Haynes, *State Papers*]

Haynes, S., ed., *A Collection of State Papers relating to affairs in the reigns of Henry VIII, Edward VI, Mary, and Elizabeth, from 1542–1570. Transcribed from original letters . . . left by W. Cecil Lord Burghley, and now remaining at Hatfield House* (1740).

Head, David M., 'Henry VIII's Scottish Policy: A Reassessment', *SHR*, LXI, 1: No. 171 (April 1982), 1–24.

Henderson, T.F., *Mary Queen of Scots: Her Environment and Tragedy*, Vol. 1 (1905).

Heritage, S. (ed.), *England in the Reign of King Henry VIII, Part 1, Starley's Life and Letters* (Early English Text Society, 1878).

Herkless, J. and Hannay, R.K., *The Archbishops of St. Andrews*, 5 vols. (Edinburgh, 1907–15).

[Herries, *Memoirs*]

Historical memoirs of the reign of Mary, Queen of Scots, and a portion of the reign of King James the Sixth, ed. R. Pitcairn (Edinburgh, 1836).

Heulhard, A., *Villegagnon, Roi d'Amérique: un Homme de Mer au XVIe Siècle: 1510–1527* (1897).

Hill, G., *An Historical Account of the Macdonnels of Antrim* (Edinburgh, 1873).

[*HMC*]

Reports of the Royal Commission on Historical Manuscripts (1870–).

Hoak, Dale E., *The King's Council in the Reign of Edward VI* (1976).

Hodgkin, T., *The Wardens of the Northern Marches* (1908).

Holinshed, R., *The Historie of Scotland* (1805).

Holinshed, R., *The Chronicles of England, Scotland and Ireland*, ed. H. Ellis, 6 vols. (1807–08).

Holinshed, R., *English Chronicles*, Vol. 3 (1808).

Holt, M.P., *The French Wars of Religion, 1562–1629* (Cambridge, 1995).

Holte, C.P., 'Tradition, reform and diplomacy: Anglo-Scottish Relations, c. 1525–42' (unpublished D.Phil. thesis, University of Cambridge, 1992).

Hooper J., *A declaration of the ten holy commandementes* (Zürich, 1548).

Horby, K., 'Christian I and the pawning of Orkney: some reflections on Scandinavian foreign policy, 1460–8', *SHR*, xlviii (1969), 35–53.

Houston, R.A., 'Aspects of Society in Scotland and N.E. England, c. 1550–1750: social structure, literacy and geographical mobility' (unpublished D.Phil. thesis, University of Cambridge, 1981).

Howard, T., 'The Early Career of the 3rd Duke of Norfolk' (University of West Virginia Ph.D., 1984).

Hughes, P.L. and Larkin, J.F. (eds.), *Tudor Royal Proclamations*, Vol. 1 (New Haven, 1964).

Inglis, H.R.G., and others, *The Early Maps of Scotland, 1524–1548* (Edinburgh, 1936).

Inglis, J.A., *Sir Adam Otterburn of Redhall, King's Advocate,* (Glasgow, 1935).

Jacquart, J., *François Ier* (1981).

James, M.E., *Change and Continuity in the Tudor North: The rise of Thomas First Lord Wharton* (York, 1965).

James, S.E., *Kateryn Parr: The Making of a Queen* (Aldershot, 1999).

Jones, T., 'A Welsh Chronicler in Tudor England', *The Welsh History Review*, Vol. 1 (1960–63), 1–17.

Jones, W., *The Mid-Tudor Crisis, 1539–1563* (1973).

Jordan, W.K. (ed.), *The Chronicle and Political Papers of King Edward VI* (1966). [Jordan, *Edward VI*]

W.K. Jordan, *Edward VI: The Young King: The Protectorship of the Duke of Somerset* (1968).

Jordan, W.K., *Edward VI: The Threshold of Power: The Dominance of the Duke of Northumberland* (1970).

Keegan, J., *The Face of Battle* (Penguin, 1991).

Keeling, Susan M., 'The Church and religion in the Anglo-Scottish border counties, 1534–72' (unpublished Ph.D. thesis, University of Durham, 1975).

Keith, R., *The History of the Affairs of the Church and State in Scotland from the beginning of the Reformation . . . to 1568*, 3 vols. (Edinburgh, Spottiswoode Society, 1844).

Kelley, Donald R., 'Jean du Tillet, Archivist and Antiquary', 337–354.

Kendrick, T.D., *Son of Prophecy* (1985).

Kenyon, J.R., 'Early Artillery Fortifications in England and Wales', *Fort*, 1, (1976), 33–36.

Kenyon, J.R. (ed.), 'Ordnance and the King's Fortifications in 1547–48: Society of Antiquaries MS 129. Folios 250–374', *Archaeologia*, cvii, (1982), 165–213.

Kermack, W.R., *The Scottish Highlands* (Edinburgh, 1957).

Kirkpatrick, J. (ed.), 'The Scottish Nation in the University of Orleans, 1339–1538', *SHR Miscellany, ii* (1904), 44–70.

Knecht, R.J., *Renaissance Wrarior and Patron: The Reign of Francis I* (Cambridge, 1994).

Knecht, R.J., *The Rise and Fall of Renaissance France* (1996).

[Knox, *History*]

John Knox's History of the Reformation in Scotland, ed. W.C. Dickinson 2 vols. (Edinburgh, 1949).

[Knox, *Works*]

The Works of John Knox, ed. D. Laing, 6 vols. (Edinburgh, 1846–64).

[Lamb, *Resonyng*],

William Lamb, Ane Resonyng of ane Scottis and Inglis Merchand Betuix Rowand and Lionis, ed. R.J. Lyall (Aberdeen, 1985).

Lamberini, Daniela, 'Practice and Theory in Sixteenth-Century Fortifications', *Fort*, 15, (1987), 5–20.

Lang, A., *A History of Scotland*, 3 vols. (Cambridge, 1900–1907).

Lang, A., 'The truth about the Cardinal's murder', *Blackwood's Magaziine*, clxiii (1898), 344–55.

Lang, A., 'The Cardinal and the King's will', *SHR*, iii, (1906), 410–22.

Lapsley, Gaillard T., 'The Problem of the North', *American Historical Review*, 5 (1900), 440–466.

Lavisse, E., *Histoire de la France depuis les origines jusqu'à la Révolution*, 11 vols. (1900–11).

Law, J.E. and Manion, J.M., 'The Nunciature to Scotland in 1548 of Pietro Lippomano, Bishop of Verona', *Atti e Memorie della Accademia di Agricoltura, Scienze e Lettere di Verona*, IV (xxii, 1970–71), 403–48.

[Lesley, *Historie*]

The Historie of Scotland, wrytten first in Latin by the most reverend and worthy Jhone Leslie, Bishop of Rosse, and translated in Scottish by Father James Dalrymple (1596), ed. E.G. Cody and W. Murison, 2 vols. (Scottish Text Society, 1888–95).

Lestocquoy, J. (ed.), *Correspondance des nonces en France, Capodiferro, Dandino et Guidiccione, 1541–51, avec des documents relatifs a la rupture des relations diplomatiques, 1551–52* (Acta Nuntiaturae Gallicae, 6, 1967).

[*Letters of James V*]

Levy, F.J., *Tudor Historical Thought* (San Marino, 1967).

Lewis, J.E., *Mary Queen of Scots: Romance and Nation* (1998).

[Lindsay, *Works*]

The Collected Works of Sir David Lindsay, ed. J. Small, 5 vols. (Early English Text Society, 1888–71).

Lindsay of Pitscottie, R., *The Historie and Cronicles of Scotland*, 2 vols,. ed. A.J.G. Mackay (Edinburgh, 1899).

Little, P.M., 'The origins of the political ideologies of John Knox and the Marian exiles' (unpublished Ph.D. thesis, New College, University of Edinburgh, 1972).

Loach, J., *Edward VI* (1999).

Loades, D., *The Tudor Navy* (Aldershot, 1992).

Loades, D., *Essays on the Reign of Edward VI* (Headstart Lecture Series, Bangor, 1994).

Loades, D., *Power in Tudor England* (1997).

[Lodge, *Illustrations*]

Eward Lodge (ed.), *Illustrations of British history, biography and manners in the reigns of Henry VIII, Edward VI, Mary, Elizabeth, and James I exhibited in a series of original papers, selected from the manuscripts of the . . . families of Howard, Talbot, and Cecil* (1791).

[*Lettres et mémoires*]

Ribier, G., *Lettres et memoires d'estat des roys, princes, ambassadeurs, et autres ministres sous les règnes de François Premier, Henry II, et François II*, ed. M. Belot, 2 vols. (1666).

Lomas, R., 'The Impact of Border Warfare: The Scots and South Tweedside, *c.* 1290–*c.* 1520, *SHR*, lxxv (1996), 143–167.

Loughlin, M., 'The career of Maitland of Lethington, *c.* 1526–1573', (unpublished Ph.D. thesis, University of Edinburgh, 1991).

Lot, F., *Recherches sur les Effectifs des Armées Françaises des Guerres d'Italie aux Guerres de Religion, 1494–1562* (1962).

[*LP*]

Letters and Papers, Foreign and Domestic of the reign of Henry VIII, ed. J.S. Brewer and others, 21 vols. and 3 supplements (1862–1910, 1920, 1929–32).

Lynch, M., *Edinburgh and the Reformation* (Edinburgh, 1981).

Lynch, M. (ed.), 'Mary Stewart: Queen in Three Kingdoms' Innes Review, Vol. XXXVIII (Scottish Catholic Historical Association, 1988).

Lynch, M., *A New History of Scotland* (1992).

Lynch, M., 'Response: Old Games and New', *SHR*, lxxiii (1994), 47–63.

Lynn, J.A. (ed.), *Feeding Mars: Logistics in Western Warfare from the Middle Ages to the Present* (Oxford, 1993).

Lythe, S.G.E., *The Economy of Scotland in its European Setting, 1550–1625* (Edinburgh, 1960).

MacColl, Alan, 'King Arthur and the Making of an English Britain', *History Today* (March 1999), 7–13.

MacCulloch, Diarmaid (ed.), *The Reign of Henry VIII: Politics, Policy and Piety* (1995).

Macdougall, N., *James IV* (Edinburgh, 1989).

Macdougall, N. (ed.), *Scotland and War, AD* 79–1918 (Edinburgh, 1991).

MacInnes, Allan I., 'Early Modern Scotland: the Current State of Play', *SHR* (lxxiii, 1: No. 195: April 1994), 30–46.

MacIvor, I., 'The Elizabethan Fortifications of Berwick-upon-Tweed', *Antiquaries Journal*, li (1965), 65–96.

MacIvor, I., *The Fortifications of Berwick-upon-Tweed* (1967).

MacIvor, I., 'Survey of Dunbar Castle', Ministry of the Environment, Department of Ancient Monuments (unpublished survey of East Lothian).

MacIvor, I., 'Artillery and Major Places of Strength in the Lothians and the East Border, 1513–1542', in Caldwell (ed.), *Scottish Weapons and Fortifications*, 94–152.

Mackenzie, A., *The History of the Macdonalds and Lords of the Isles* (Edinburgh, 1881).

Mackenzie, W.C., *The Highlands and Isles of Scotland* (Edinburgh, 1949).

Mackenzie, W.M., 'The debatable land', *SHR*, xxx (1951), 109–25.

Mackie, J.D., 'Henry VIII and Scotland', *TRHS*, 4th ser., (xxix, 1947), 93–114.

Mackie, J.D., *The Earlier Tudors, 1485–1558* (Oxford, 1952).

Mackie, R.L., *A Short History of Scotland* (Oxford, 1929–30; revised 1962).

Mackie, R.L., *King James IV of Scotland* (Edinburgh, 1954).

MacMahon, L.M.C., 'The English campaign in France, 1543–45' (unpublished MA thesis, University of Warwick, 1993).

McRoberts, D. (ed.), *Essays on the Scottish Reformation, 1513–1625* (Glasgow, 1962).

Maggs' Sale Catalogue 64 (1937).

Main, A., 'The origins of John Knox's doctrine of just rebellion' (unpublished Ph.D. thesis, University of Aberdeen, 1963).

Maitland, J., *Maitland's Narrative of the Principal Acts of the Regency, During the Minority; and Other Papers Relating to the History of Mary, Queen of Scotland*, ed. W.S. Fitch (Ipswich, 1842).

[*Maitland Misc.*]

Miscellany of the Maitland Club, ed. A. Macdonald and others, 4 vols. (Maitland Club, 1833–47).

Mapstone, S. and Wood, J., *The Rose and the Thistle – Essay on the Culture of Late Medieval and Renaissance Scotland* (East Linton, 1998).

Marshall, H.E., *Scotland's Story: A History of Scotland for Boys and Girls* (Edinburgh, 1906).

Marshall, R.K., *Mary of Guise* (1977).

Martin, C.J.M., 'Ancrum Moor: A Day of Reckoning', *The Scots Magazine*, vol. 83 (1965), 146–52.

Mason, R. (ed.), *Scotland and England, 1286–1815* (Edinburgh, 1987).

Mason, R., *Kingship and the Commonweal – Political Thought in Renaissance and Reformation Scotland* (East Linton, 1998).

Mason, R., 'Scotching the Brut: Politics, History and National Myth in Sixteenth-Century Britain', in Mason (ed.), *Scotland and England*, 60–84.

Mason, R., 'Usable Pasts: History and Identity in Reformation Scotland', *SHR* (Vol. lxxvi, 1: No. 201: April 1997), 54–68.

[*Mary of Lorraine Corresp.*]

The Scottish Correspondence of Mary of Lorraine, ed. A.I. Cameron (SHS, 1927).

Mattingly, G., 'A Humanist Ambassador', *Journal of Modern History*, iv (1932), 175–85.

Mattingly, G., *Catherine of Aragon* (Boston, 1941).

Mattingly, G., *Renaissance Diplomacy* (1955).

Maxwell, A., *The History of Old Dundee* (Edinburgh, 1884).

Maxwell, A., *Old Dundee . . . prior to the Reformation* (Edinburgh, 1891).

Maxwell-Irving, A.M.T., 'Early Firearms and their influence on the Military and Domestic Architecture of the Borders', *Proceedings of the Society of Antiquaries of Scotland*, vol. 103 (1970–1), 192–224.

McKee, A., 'Henry VIII as Military Commander', *History Today*, vol. 41 (1991), 22–29.

McKerlie, E.M.H., *Mary of Guise-Lorraine, Queen of Scotland* (1931).

McKerral, A., 'West Highland Mercenaries in Ireland', *SHR*, (xxx, 1951), 1–14.

[McNeill, Thesis]

McNeill, P.G.B. 'The Jurisdiction of the Scottish Privy Council, 1532–1708' (unpublished Ph.D. dissertation, University of Glasgow, 1962).

McRoberts, D. (ed.), *Essays on the Scottish Reformation, 1513–1625* (Glasgow, 1962).

Meikle, M.M., 'Lairds and Gentlemen: a study of the landed families of the Eastern Anglo-Scottish Borders, c. 1540–1603', (unpublished Ph.D. thesis, University of Edinburgh, 1989).

Melville, Sir James of Halhill, *Memoires of his own life, 1549–93*, ed. J. Fullarton (Bannatyne and Maitland Clubs, 1829).

Merriman, M.H., 'The Platte of Castlemilk, 1547', *Transactions of the Dumfriesshire and Galloway Natural History and Antiquarian Society*, xliv (1967), 175–81.

[Merriman, Assured Scots]

Merriman, M.H., 'The Assured Scots: Scottish Collaborators with England during the Rough Wooing, 1543–50', *SHR* xlvii (1968), 10–35.

Merriman, M.H., 'War and Propaganda during the "Rough Wooing"', *Scottish Tradition* (9/10, 1979–80), 20–30.

Merriman, M.H., *The History of the King's Works*, Vol. IV (1982), ed. H.M. Colvin: Part IV, 'The Scottish Border', pp. 607–726.

Merriman, M.H., 'Italian Military Engineers in Britain in the 1540s', in *English Map Making*, ed. S. Tyacke (British Library, 1983), pp. 57–67, plates 17–30.

Merriman, M.H., 'The Epistle to the Queen's Majestie' and its 'Platte', *Architectural History*, 27 (1984), pp. 25–32.

[Merriman, Henrisoun]

Merriman, M.H., 'James Henrisoun and "Great Britain": British Union and the Scottish Commonweal', in *Scotland and England, 1286–1815*, ed. Roger A. Mason (Edinburgh, 1987), pp. 85–112.

Merriman, M.H., 'Mary, Queen of France', in *Mary Stewart – Queen in Three Kingdoms*, ed. M.J. Lynch Oxford, 1988) and *Innes Review* special issue (xxxviii, 1987 [1988]), pp. 30–52.

[Merriman, Eyemouth]

Merriman, M.H., 'The Eyemouth Forts: Anvils of Union?', *SHR* lxvii (1988). 142–55.

Merriman, M.H., 'Henry VIII as a European Builder', *History Today*. June 1991.

[Merriman, Home Thoughts]

Merriman, M.H., 'Home thoughts from Abroad: Scottish Exiles in the mid-16th Century', in *Social and Political Identities in Western History*, ed. K. Stringer (Copenhagen, 1994), 90–117.

Merriman, M.H., 'The High Road from Scotland: British Unionism in the 16th Century', in *Uniting the Kingdoms? The Making of British History*, ed. A. Grant and K. Stringer (1996), 111–22.

[Merriman, Ubaldini]

Merriman, M.H., 'Intelligens to asseg – Migiliorino Ubaldini and the Fortification of Scotland in 1548', *Architetti e ingegneri militari italiani all'estero dal XV al XVII Secolo*, ii, ed. Marino Viganò (Rome, 1999), 233–55.

Michel, F., *Les Ecossais en France: Les Français en Ecosse*, 2 vols. (1862).

Mignet, F., *Histoire de Marie Stuart* (1851).

Miller, A.H., 'Scotland Described for Queen Magdelene', *SHR*, i (1904), 27–38.

Miller, G.J., *Tudor Mercenaries and Auxiliaries, 1485–1547* (Charlottesville, 1980).

Miller, J., *The Lamp of Lothian; or the history of Haddington, connection with the public affairs of East Lothian and of Scotland* (Haddington, 1844).

Mitchell, K.L., *Fast Castle: A History from 1602* (Edinburgh, 1988).

Mitchison, R., *A History of Scotland* (1970).

Morgan, P., 'Elis Gruffudd of Gronant – Tudor Chronicler Extraordinary', *Journal of the Flintshire Historical Society*, x (1974), 11–20.

Morris, T.A., *Europe and England in the sixteenth century* (1998).

Mowat, S., *The Port of Leith – Its History and Its People* (Edinburgh, nd? 1996).

Mudie, F. and others, *Broughty Castle* (Abertay Historical Society, 1970).

Muirhead, I.A., 'M. Robert Lochart', *Innes Review*, xx (1971), 85–100.

Mulgan, C., *The Renaissance Monarchies, 1469–1558* (Cambridge, 1998).

Muller, J.A., *Stephen Gardiner* (1926).

Murray, A.L., 'The Exchequer and Crown Revenues of Scotland, 1437–1542' (unpublished Ph.D. thesis, University of Edinburgh, 1961).

Murray, J.K.R., 'The Scottish Coinage of 1553', *British Numismatic Journal*, xxxvii (1968), 98–109.

Murray, P.J., 'The Lay Administrators of Church Lands in the Fifteenth and Sixteenth Centuries', *SHR*, lxxxiv (1995), 26–44.

Nicholls, M., *A History of the Modern British Isles, 1529–1603: The Two Kingdoms* (Oxford, 1999).

Nicholson, G.D., 'The nature and function of historical argument in the Henrician Reformation' (unpublished D.Phil. thesis, Cambridge, 1977).

Nicholson, J. and Burns, R., *History and Antiquities of the Counties of Westmorland and Cumberland*, 2 vols. (1777).

Nicholson, R., *Scotland: The Later Middle Ages* (Edinburgh, 1974).

[*Nonces en France*, i]

La Correspondance des Nonces en France; Dandino, Della Torre et Trivultio, 1541–46, ed. J. Lestocquoy (*Acta Nuntiaturae Gallicae*, iii, 1963).

[*Nonces en France*, ii]

La Correspondance des Nonces en France: Dandino, Della Torre et Trivultio, 1546–51, ed. J. Lestocquoy (*Acta Nuntiaturae Gallicae*, vi, 1967).

Oathwaite, R.B., 'The Trials of Foreign Borrowing: The English Crown and the Antwerp Money Market in the mid-sixteenth century', *Economic History Review*, xix (1966), 289–305.

Oathwaite, R.B., 'Royal Borrowing in the Reign of Elizabeth I: The Aftermath of Antwerp', *EHR*, lxxxvi (1971), 251–63.

[*Odet de Selve*]

Correspondence politique de Odet de Selve, ambassadeur de France en Angleterre, 1548–49, ed. G. Lefèvre–Pontalis (1888).

Oman, C.W.C., 'The Battle of Pinkie, 10 September 1547', *Archaeological Journal*, xc (1934), 1–25.

Oman, C.W.C., *A History of the Art of War in the Sixteenth Century* (1937).

Oman, C., 'The Art of War', in H.D. Triall (ed), *Social England*, vol. 3 (1897), 70–202.

O'Neill, B.H. St. J., 'Stefan Von Haschenperg: An Engineer to King Henry VIII, and his Work', *Archaeologia*, xci (1945), 137–55.

O'Neill, B.H. St. J., *Castle and Cannon* (Oxford, 1960)

Ordonnances des rois de France, (1902–).

[*Original Letters*]

Original Letters Relative to the English Reformation, ed. H. Robinson (Parker Society, 1846–47).

[*Paget Letters*]

The Letters of William, Lord Paget of Beaudesert, 1547–1563, Camden Society Miscellany, xxv (1974), 1–142.

Parker, G., *The Army of Flanders and the Spanish Road, 1567–1659* (Cambridge, 1972).

Parker, G., *The Spanish Road* (1973).

Parker, G., *The Military Revolution* (Cambridge, 1988).

Parker, G., 'In Defence of the Military Revolution', in Rogers (ed.), *The Military Revolution Debate*, 337–366.

Paterson, J.W., *Inchcolm Abbey* (HMSO, 1950).

Paterson, R.C., *My Wound is Deep: A History of the Later Anglo-Scottish Wars, 1380–1560* (Edinburgh, 1997).

[Patten, *Expedicion*]

Patten, William, *The Expedicion into Scotlande* (1548), reprinted in *Tudor Tracts*, ed. A.F. Pollard (1903), 54–154.

Paul, J.B. (ed.), *The Scots Peerage*, 9 vols. (Edinburgh, 1904–14).

Paul, J.B., 'Edinburgh in 1544 and Hertford's Invasions', *SHR*, viii (1910), 113–31.

Pepper, S. and Adams, N., *Firearms and Fortifications: Military Architecture and Siege Warfare in Sixteenth-Century Siena* (Chicago 1986).

Percival, S.M., 'Some Sixteenth-Century French Artists having Connections with Scotland: the Quesnel Family and Jehan Decourt' (unpublished Ph.D. dissertation, University of Edinburgh, 1962).

Percy, E.S.C., *John Knox* (1937).

Perlin, E., *Description des Royaulmes d'Angleterre et d'Escosse* (1551).

Phillips, J.E., *Images of a Queen* (Berkeley, 1964).

Phillips, Gervase, 'The Army of Henry VIII: A Reassessment,' *Journal of the Society for Army Historical Research*, lxxv (1997), 8–22.

Phillips, Gervase, 'In the Shadow of Flodden: Tactics, Technology and Scottish Military Effectiveness, 1513–1550', *SHR*, lxxvii (1998), 162–82.

[Phillips, *Wars*]

Phillips, Gervase, *The Anglo-Scots Wars, 1513–1550* (Woodbridge, 1999).

[Pitcairn, *Trials*]
Criminal Trials in Scotland from 1488 to 1624, ed. R. Pitcairn, 3 vols. (Edinburgh, 1833).

[Pitscottie, *Historie*]
R. Lindsay of Pitscottie, *The Historie and Cronicles of Scotland*, ed. J.G. Mackay, 3 vols. (Scottish Text Society, 1899–1911).

Plattard, J., 'Scottish masters and students at Poitiers in the second half of the sixteenth century', *SHR*, xxi (1923), 82–86, 168.

[de Poitiers]
Lettres inédites de Dianne de Poytiers, ed. G-M. Guiffrey (1866).

Pollard, A.F., 'Somerset and Scotland', *EHR*, xiii (1898), 464–72.

Pollard, A.F., *England under Protector Somerset* (1900).

Pollard, A.F., *Henry VIII* (1902).

Pollard, A.F., *The history of England from the accession of Edward VI to the death of Elizabeth, 1547–1603* (1913).

Pollard, A.F., 'The Late Expedition in Scotland', in Pollard (ed.), *Tudor Tracts* (n.d.), 39–51.

[Potter, Thesis]
Potter, D.L., 'Diplomacy in the mid-sixteenth century: England and France, 1536–50' (unpublished D.Phil. thesis, University of Cambridge, 1973).

Potter, D.L., *War and Government in the French Provinces: Picardy, 1470–1560* (Cambridge, 1993).

Potter, D.L., *A History of France, 1460–1560: The Emergence of a Nation State* (1995).

Potter, D.L., 'Foreign Policy in the Age of the Reformation: French Involvement in the Schmalkaldic War, 1544–47', *Historical Journal*, xx (1977), 525–44.

Potter, D.L., 'French Intrigue in Ireland during the Reign of Henri II, 1547–1559', *International History Review*, v (1983), 159–180.

Potter, D.L., 'Foreign Policy', in *The Reign of Henry VIII: Politics and Piety*, ed. D. MacCulloch (1995), 101–34.

A prayer for victorie and peace (1548).

A Proclamation [on entry of English army into Scotland, 4 September 1547].

Purvey, P.F., *Coins and Tokens of Scotland* (1972).

Rabelais, Oeuvres, ed. L. Moland, 2 vols. (1937).

Rae, T.I., 'The Administration of the Scottish Border in the Sixteenth Century' (unpublished Ph.D. dissertation, University of St. Andrews, 1961).

Rae, T.I., *The Administration of the Scottish Border in the Sixteenth Century* (Edinburgh, 1964).

Rait, R.S., *Mary Queen of Scots* (1899).

Rait, R.S., 'Scottish Parliaments before the Union of Crowns', *EHR*, xv (1900), 209–37, 417–44.

Rait, R.S., *The Making of Scotland* (1911).

Rait, R.S., *The Parliaments of Scotland* (Edinburgh, 1924).

Redworth, G., 'The political and diplomatic career of Stephen Gardiner, 1538–51' (unpublished D.Phil. thesis, University of Oxford, 1985).

Reid, W.S., 'Clerical Taxation: The Scottish alternative to dissolution of the monasteries, 1530–1560', *Catholic History Review*, xxxiv (1948), 129–53.

Reid, W.S., *Skipper from Leith: The History of Robert Barton of Over Barnton* (Philadelphia, 1962).

Reid, W.S., 'The Place of Denmark in Scottish Foreign Policy, 1470–1540', *Juridical Review*, lviii (1966), 183–200.

Rentale Sancti Andree, ed. R.K. Hannay (SHS, 1913).

Richards, J.M., ' "To Promote a Woman to Beare Rule": Talkng of Queens in Mid-Tudor England', *Sixteenth Century Journal*, xxviii (1997), 101–122.

Richardson, J.S., *Tantallon* (1960).

Richer, C., *Mémoires de Sieur Richer, ambassadeur pour les roys François Ier et Henry II en Suede et en Dannermarch* (Troyes, 1652).

Ridley, J., *John Knox* (Oxford, 1968).

Ridley, J., *Henry VIII* (1984).

Ridpath, G., *The Border History of England and Scotland . . . to the Union of the two Crowns*, revised by P. Ridpath (1776).

Riss, T., *Should Auld Acquaintance Be Forgot: Scottish-Danish Relations, c. 1450–1707*, 2. vols., (Odense, 1988).

Roberts, M., *The Military Revolution* (Belfast, 1956).

Robertson, W., *History of Scotland during the reigns of Queen Mary and King James*, 2 vols. (Edinburgh, 1761).

Robson, R., *The English Highland Clans – Tudor Responses to a Mediaeval Problem* (Edinburgh, 1989).

Rogers, C.J. (ed.), *The Military Revolution Debate* (Boulder, 1995).

Rogers, C.J., 'The Military Revolution in History and Historiography', in Rogers (ed.), *The Military Revolution Debate*, 55–94.

Rogers, O., 'Memoir of Goerge Wishart, the Scottish Martyr', *TRHS*, 1st ser. (vi, 1876), 260–363.

Romier, L., *Les origines politiques des guerres de religion*, 2 vols. (1913–14).

de la Roncière, C.G.B., *Histoire de la Marine Française* (1899).

[Rooseboom]

M.P. Rooseboom, *The Scottish Staple in the Netherlands: An Account of the Trade Relations between Scotland and the Low Countries from 1292 till 1676*, (The Hague, 1910).

Ross, C., *Edward IV* (1974).

[*RPCS*]

The Register of the Privy Council of Scotland, 1545–1625, ed. J. Hill Burton and D. Masson, 14 vols. (Edinburgh, 1877–98).

[*Royal Burghs*]

Records of the Convention of the Royal Burghs of Scotland and Extracts from other records relating to the affairs of the Burghs of Scotland, 1295–1738, ed. J.D. Marwick, 6 vols. (Edinburgh, 1866–99).

[*RPCS*]

The Register of the Privy Council of Scotland, ed. J.H. Burton and others (Edinburgh, 1877–).

[*RSS*]

Registrum Secreti Sigilli Regum Scotorum: The Register of the Privy Seal of Scotland, ed. M. Livingstone and others, 8 vols. (Edinburgh, 1908–).

de Ruble, A., *La première jeunesse de Marie Stuart* (1891).

Russell, J.G., *The Field of the Cloth of Gold: Men and Manners in 1520* (1969).

St. Onge, H.O., 'Thomas Churchyard: A study of his Prose and Poetry' (unpublished Ph.D. thesis, Ohio State University, 1966).

[Sadler, *State Papers*]

The State Papers and Letters of Sir Ralph Sadler, ed. A. Chifford, 2 vols. (Edinburgh, 1809).

[Sanderson, *Beaton*]

Sanderson, M.H.B., *Cardinal of Scotland: David Beaton, c. 1494–1546* (Edinburgh, 1986).

Sanderson, M.H.B., *Ayrshire and the Reformation: People and Change, 1490–1600* (East Linton, 1997).

Saunders, A., *Norham Castle* (English Heritage, 1998).

Scarisbrick, J.J., *Henry VIII* (1968).

[*Scots Peerage*]

The Scots Peerage, ed. Sir J. Balfour Paul (Edinburgh, 1904–14).

Scott, W., *Tales of a Grandfather*, 3 vols. (Edinburgh, 1827).

Seguin, J-P., *L'Information en France de Louis XII à Henri II* (Geneva, 1961).

[Shelby, *Rogers*]

Shelby, L.R., *John Rogers: Tudor Military Engineer* (Oxford, 1976).

Shirley, T.F., *Thomas Thirlby: Tudor Bishop* (1964).

Showalter, D.E., 'Caste, Skill, and Training: The Evolution of Cohesion in European Armies from the Middle Ages to the Sixteenth Century', *The Journal of Military History*, 57 (1993), 407–30.

Simpson, G.G. (ed.), *Scotland and the Low Countries, 1124–1994* (East Linton, 1996).

Sinclair, G.A., 'The Scots at Solway Moss', *SHR* ii (1904), 372–77.

Slavin, A.J., *Politics and Profit: A Study of Sir Ralph Sadler, 1507–1547* (Cambridge, 1966).

Smit, H.J. (ed.), *Bronnen tot de Geschiedenis van den Handel met Engeland, Schotland en Ireland, 1548–1558* (Rijks Geschiedkundige Publicatien, no. 81, 1942).

Smout, T.C., *A History of the Scottish People, 1560–1830* (1969).

Sotheby Sale Catalogue, André de Coppet, part 2 (1955).

A Source Book of Scottish History, ed. W.C. Dickinson and others, 3 vols. (Edinburgh, 1953–54).

[Spalding Club]

Miscellany of the Spalding Club, ed. J. Stewart, 4 vols. (Spalding Club, 1844–45).

[*SP Henry VIII*]

State Papers Published under Authority of His Majesty's Commission. King Henry VIII, 11 vols. (1830–52).

[Spottiswoode]

History of the Church of Scotland, by John Spottiswoode, ed. M. Russell and M. Napier, 3 vols. (Spottiswoode Society, 1851).

Stair Society, *An Introductory Survey of the Sources and Literature of Scots Law*, ed. H. McKenzie (Edinburgh, 1936).

Stair Society, *An Introduction to Scottish Legal History* (Edinburgh, 1958).

Starkey, D.R., *The Reign of Henry VIII: Personalities and Politics* (1985).

Statutes of the Realme, ed. A. Luders and others, 11 vols. (1810–28).

[*STC1*]

A Short-Title Catalogue of Books Printed in England, Scotland and Ireland and of English Books Printed Abroad, 1475–1640, ed. A.W. Pollard and R.R. Redgrave (1926).

[*STC2*]

A Short-Title Catalogue of Books Printed in England, Scotland and Ireland and of English Books Printed Abroad, 1475–1640, (1986–97).

Steele, R.R., (ed.), *Tudor and Stuart Proclamations, 1485–1714* (Oxford, 1910).

Steer, F.W., 'A Map Illustrating the Siege of Leith, 1560', *Proceedings of the Society of Antiquaries of Scotland*, xcv (1961–62), 280–83.

Stephen, L. and Lee, S. (eds.), *Dictionary of National Biography*, 63 vols. (1885–1900).

[Stevenson, *Selections*]

Selections from Unpublished Manuscripts in the College of Arms and the British Museum, illustrating the reign of Mary Queen of Scotland, 1543–68, ed. J. Stevenson (Maitland Club, 1837).

Stewart, I.H., *The Scottish Coinage* (1955).

Strong, R., *Art and Power: Renaissance Festivals, 1450–1650* (Woodbridge, 1984).

Strype, J. (ed.), *Ecclesiastical Memorials, relating chiefly to religion and the reformation of it, and the emergencies of the church of England under King Henry VIII, King Edward VI, and Queen Mary*, 3 vols. (Oxford, 1820–40).

Stuart, M.W., *The Scot who was a Frenchman: Being the Life of John Stewart, Duke of Albany, in Scotland, France and Italy* (Edinburgh, 1940).

Sturge, C., *Cuthbert Tunstal: Churchman, Scholar, Statesman* (1938).

Sutherland, C.H.V., *Art in Coinage* (1955).

Symms, P.S.M., 'Social control in a 16th-century burgh: a study of the burgh court book of Selkirk, 1503–45' (unpublished Ph.D. thesis, University of Edinburgh, 1989).

Sypher, S., 'Henry VIII's Foreign Policy, 1538–1547' (unpublished Ph.D. dissertation, University of Wisconsin, 1971).

[*TA*]

Accounts of the Lord High Treasurer of Scotland, ed. T. Dickson and others, 12 vols. (Edinburgh, 1877–).

Tabraham, C.J. and Good, G.L., 'The Artillery Fortification at Threave Castle, Galloway', in Caldwell (ed.), *Scottish Weapons and Fortifications*, 55–72.

Tallett, F., *War and Society in Early-Modern Europe, 1495–1715* (1992).

Taylor, S.E., 'The crown and the north of England, 1559–70: a study of the rebellion of the Northern Earls, 1569–70, and its causes' (unpublished Ph.D. thesis, University of Manchester, 1981).

Terry, C.S., *A History of Scotland* (Cambridge, 1920).

Teulet, J.A.B., *Inventaire chronologique des documents relatifs a l'Histoire d'Ecosse* (Abbotsford Club, 1855).

Teulet, J.A.B., *Mémoire justicatif du Droit qui appartient à M. le duc d'Hamilton de Porter le titre de duc de Chatelherault* (1864).

Teulet, J.A.B., (ed.), *Papiers d'état, pièces et documents inédits, ou peu connus relatifs à l'histoire de l'Ecosse au XVIe siecle*, 3 vols. (1851–60).

[Teulet, *Relations politiques*]

Relations politiques de la France et de L'Espagne avec l'Ecosse au XVIe siècle, ed. J.A.B. Teulet, 5 vols. (1862).

Theiner, A. (ed.), *Vetera Monumenta Hibernorum et Scotorum historiam illustrantia quae ex Vaticani, Neapolis ac Florentia tabulariis deprompsit et ordine chronologico disposuit A. Theiner* (Rome, 1864).

Thornton, Tim, 'Scotland and the Ise of Man, *c.*1400–1625: Noble Power and royal Presumption in the Northern Irish Sea Province', *SHR*, lxxvii (1998), 1–30.

[Thou, *Histoire*]

Histoire Universelle de Jacques-Auguste de Thou, 1543–1607 (1609–14), ed. P. du Ryer, 3 vols. (1659).

Todd, J.R., 'The reformation in the diocese of Dunblane' (unpublished Ph.D. thesis, University of Edinburgh, 1973).

Tuck, J.A., 'Richard II and the Border Magnates', *Northern History*, iii (1968), 27–52.

Tuck, J.A., 'War and Society in the Medieval North', *Journal of Northern History*, 21 (1985), 33–52.

Tyler, Royall, *Charles V* (1956).

Tytler, P.F., *The History of Scotland*, 9 vols. (Edinburgh, 1828–43).

Tytler, P.F., *England under the Reigns of Edward VI and Mary*, 2 vols. (1839).

Unger, W.S. (ed.), *Bronnen tot de Geschiedkundige van Middelburg in den Land-sheerlijken Tijd* (Rijks Geschiedkungidge Publicatien, no. 75, 1931).

Vaissière, P. de, *Charles de Marillac, ambassaduer et homme politique . . . 1510–1560* (1896).

Vershuur, M.B., 'Perth and the Reformation: society and reform, 1540–60' (unpublished Ph.D. thesis, University of Glasgow, 1985).

Viollet-le-Duc, E.E., *Military Architecture* (1990).

Warner, J.C., *Henry VIII's divorce: literature and the politics of the printing press* (Woodbridge, 1998).

The Warrender Papers, ed. A.I. Cameron (SHS, 1931).

Watson, Godfrey, *The Border Reivers* (Sandhill Press, 1974).

Watt, D.E.R., *Fasti Ecclesiae Scoticanae Medii Aevi ad annum 1638* (2nd draft), (Scottish Record Society, 1969).

Weber, B.C., *The Youth of Mary Queen of Scots* (1941).

Wever, B.C., *Personalities and Politics at the Court of Henry II of France, 1647–1559* (New York, 1955).

[Weiss, *Granvelle*]

Papiers d'état du cardinal de Granvelle, ed. C. Weiss (1841–52).

Wernham, R.B., *Before the Armada: The Growth of English Foreign Policy, 1485–1588* (1966).

Whisker, R.F., 'John, duke of Albany, 1481–1536: servant of Scotland and France', (unpublished M.A. thesis, University of Liverpool, 1939).

White, A.J., 'Religion, politics, and society in Aberdeen, 1543–93' (unpublished Ph.D. thesis, New College, University of Edinburgh, 1986).

White, D.G., 'Henry VIII's Irish Kerne in France and Scotland, 1544–45', *Irish Sword* (iii, 1957–58), 213–25.

White, L. Jr, 'Jacopo Aconcio as an engineer', *American Historical Review*, lxxii (1967), 425–44.

Williams, J.H. (ed.), *Stewart Style, 1513–1542: Essays on the Court of James V* (East Linton, 1996).

Williams, H.N., *Henri II: His Court and Times* (1910).

Williamson, A.H., 'Scotland, Antichrist and the Invention of Great Britain', in Dwyer, Mason and Murdoch (eds.), *New Perspectives on the Politics and Culture of Early Modern Scotland* (Edinburgh, 1985), 34–58.

Williamson, A.H., 'George Buchanan, Civic Virtue and Commerce: European Imperialism and its Sixteenth-Century Critics', *SHR*, lxxv (1996), 20–37.

Wintroub, A.M., *To Triumph in Paradise: The New World and the New Learning in the Royal Entry Festival of Henri II (Rouen, 1550)* (D.Phil. dissertation, University of California, 1995).

Wood, M. (ed.), *The Flodden Papers* (SHS, 1933).

Wormald, J., *Lords and Men in Scotland: Bonds of Manrent, 1442–1603* (Edinburgh, 1985).

Wormald, J., *Mary Queen of Scots: A Study in Failure* (1988).

Wriothesley, C., *A Chronicle of England during the reign of the Tudors*, ed. W.D. Hamilton, 2 vols. (Camden Society, 1875–77).

Yates, F.A., 'The Allegorical Portraits of Sir John Luttrell', in *Essays on the History of Art presented to Rudolph Wittower*, ed. D. Fraser and others (1967), 149–59.

Yellowless, M.J., 'Dunkeld and the Reformation' (unpublished Ph.D. thesis, New College, University of Edinburgh, 1990).

Index